IRISH TAX REPORTS

1999-2000 Cases,
Cumulative Tables
and Index (1922-2000),
and
Determinations of
the Appeal Commissioners

Butterworths

IRISH TAX REPORTS

1999-2000 Cases, Cumulative Tables and Index (1922-2000), and Determinations of the Appeal Commissioners

Edited by

B H Giblin BA BL

and

Susan Keegan AITI

Butterworths

Ireland	Butterworth (Ireland) Ltd, 26 Upper Ormond Quay, DUBLIN 7
United Kingdom	Butterworths a Division of Reed Elsevier (UK) Ltd, Halsbury House, 35 Chancery Lane, LONDON WC2A 1EL and 4 Hill Street, EDINBURGH EH2 3JZ
Australia	Butterworths, a Division of Reed International Books Australia Pty Ltd, Chatswood, NEW SOUTH WALES
Canada	Butterworths Canada Ltd, Markham, ONTARIO
Hong Kong	Butterworths Asia (Hong Kong), HONG KONG
India	Butterworths India, NEW DELHI
Malaysia	Malayan Law Journal Sdn Bhd, KUALA LUMPUR
New Zealand	Butterworths of New Zealand Ltd, WELLINGTON
Singapore	Butterworths Asia, SINGAPORE
South Africa	Butterworths Legal Publishers (Pty) Ltd, DURBAN

A CIP Catalogue record for this book is available from the British Library.

These reports should be cited thus:

[Year] (Volume) ITR (Page)

ISBN for complete set: 1 85475 7008

ISBN for this book: 1 85475 7458

ISBN 1-85475-745-8

9 781854 757456

Printed by Antony Rowe Ltd, Chippenham, Wiltshire

Visit us at our website: http//www.butterworthsireland.com.

Introduction

This book contains the tax cases in 1999-2000. It also contains the Determinations of the Appeal Commissioners which have been released for publication for the first time this year. As with previous editions of this book it also serves as a cumulative tables and index volume for the five volumes of Irish tax reports and the 1998 cases volume. These tables and index should ensure that the required cases are easily and quickly recovered. If you have any comments or suggestions for improvements please contact the editor.

1 **Contents 1999-2000**

This outlines cases and determinations contained in the 1999-2000 volume.

2. **Contents 1922-2000** **1**

This is a complete *chronological* list of all the cases reported in the entire set which also shows key words relating to each case and references indicating where the case was previously reported.

3. **Determinations of Appeal Commissioners 2000** **55**

Included here are all determinations reported to date.

4. **Cases 1999-2000** **65**

These are all the relevant cases heard since the 1998 publication.

5. **Cases reported** **245**

This is an *alphabetical* list of the cases reported.

6. **Cases reported and considered** **255**

This is an *alphabetical* list of the cases reported, however, this table is extended to include cases referred to in judgments or cases cited in the cases reported in full. The cases reported in full are shown in italics.

6. **Statutes considered** **299**

This table lists in *alphabetical and numerical* sequence the statutory provisions considered by the courts.

7. **Destination table (Taxes Consolidation Act 1997)** **321**

This table enables the reader to trace the present *location* of legislation between 1967 and 1997.

8. **Index** **415**

This is an *alphabetical* subject index which sets out the subject matter of each case in the five volumes.

Susan Keegan
Editor
May 2000

Contents 1999-2000

Determinations of the Appeal Commissioners

Capital Gains Tax - Re TCA 1997 s 552, 1 AC 2000 .... 1999-2000 p 55
Capital Gains Tax - Re TCA 1997 s 573, 2 AC 2000 .... 1999-2000 p 55
Vehicle Registration Tax - Re FA 1989 s 92, 3 AC 2000 .... 1999-2000 p 55
Vehicle Registration Tax - Re FA 1989 s 92, 4 AC 2000 .... 1999-2000 p 55
Vehicle Registration Tax - Re SI 59/ 1993, 5 AC 2000 .... 1999-2000 p 55
Income Tax - Re ITA 1967 s 61, 6 AC 2000 .... 1999-2000 p 56
Income Tax - Re ITA 1967 s 61, 7 AC 2000 .... 1999-2000 p 56
Income Tax - Re ITA 1967 s 255, 8 AC 2000 .... 1999-2000 p 56
Income Tax - Re TCA 1997 s 112, 9 AC 2000 .... 1999-2000 p 57
Income Tax - Re ITA 1967 s 255, 10 AC 2000 .... 1999-2000 p 57
Income Tax - Re TCA 1997 s 669, 11 AC 2000 .... 1999-2000 p 57
Income Tax - Re TCA 1997 s 271, 12 AC 2000 .... 1999-2000 p 57
Income Tax - Re TCA 1997 s 669, 13 AC 2000 .... 1999-2000 p 57
Income Tax - Re TCA 1997 s 1017, 14 AC 2000 .... 1999-2000 p 58
BES Relief - Re FA 1984 s 12, 15 AC 2000 .... 1999-2000 p 58
VAT - Re VATA1972 First Schedule, 16 AC 2000 .... 1999-2000 p 58
VAT - Re VATA1972 Sixth Schedule, 17 AC 2000 .... 1999-2000 p 58
VAT - Re VATA 1972 s 4, 18 AC 2000 .... 1999-2000 p 58
VAT - Re VATA1972 Second Schedule, 19 AC 2000 .... 1999-2000 p 59
VAT - Re VATA 1972 Second Schedule, 20 AC 2000 .... 1999-2000 p 59
VAT - Re VATA 1972 s 4, 21 AC 2000 .... 1999-2000 p 59
Excise Duty (Hydrocarbon Oil) - Re FA 1976 s 41, 22 AC 2000 .... 1999-2000 p 59
Excise Duty (Hydrocarbon Oil) - Re FA 1995 s 105, 23 AC 2000 .... 1999-2000 p 60
Income Tax - Re TCA 1997 s 997, 24 AC 2000 .... 1999-2000 p 61
Capital Acquisitions Tax - Re CATA 1976 s 39, 25 AC 2000 .... 1999-2000 p 62

1999-2000 Cases

Criminal Assets Bureau v Gerard Hutch .... 1999-2000 p 65
Patrick J O'Connell (Inspector of Taxes) v Fyffes Banana Processing Ltd 1999-2000 p 71
Sean MacAonghusa (Inspector of Taxes) v Ringmahon Company .... 1999-2000 p 81
Hibernian Insurance Co Ltd v MacUimis (Inspector of Taxes) .... 1999-2000 p 113
Patrick J O'Connell (Inspector of Taxes) v Thomas Keleghan .... 1999-2000 p 143

Determinations of Appeal Commissioners are reproduced courtesy of the Office of the Appeal Commmissioners and Institute of Taxation in Ireland.

Contents

Arthur Guinness Son & Co Ltd v Commissioners of Inland Revenue
1 ITC 1, [1923] 2 IR 186 .... Vol I p 1

Income tax and excess profits duty - liability in respect of transactions under DORA requisition orders - trade or business - ITA Sch D - FA 1915 (No 2) s 38.

McCall (Deceased) v Commissioners of Inland Revenue
1 ITC 31 .... Vol I p 28

Excess profits duty - purchase of whiskey in bond by a publican - whiskey in bond could be sold to best advantage - whether sale at cost plus interest constituted a trade - whether an investment with capital gains - whether a trade is carried on as a question of law and fact - whether facts found by Special Commissioners can be reopened.

Boland's Ltd v Commissioners of Inland Revenue
1 ITC 42 .... Vol I p 34

Excess profits duty - whether profits to be ascertained by actual profits or a percentage standard - percentage standard based on 6 per cent of company's net capital - whether proper deduction for wear and tear and capital expenditure on replacements of capital items - whether assessment can be reopened - doctrines of res judicata and equitable estoppel - whether inspector entitled to recompute percentage basis - whether appellants precluded from introducing new grounds of appeal.

Evans & Co v Phillips (Inspector of Taxes)
1 ITC 38 .... Vol I p 43

Income tax - Schedule D - obsolescence of assets - ITA 1918 Sch D Cases I & II rule 7.

Irish Provident Assurance Co Ltd (In Liquidation) v Kavanagh (Inspector of Taxes)
1 ITC 52, [1930] IR 231 .... Vol I p 45

Income tax - Schedule D - interest on money - ITA 1918 Sch D Case III.

The King (Harris Stein) v The Special Commissioners
1 ITC 71 .... Vol I p 62

Confirmation of assessment - request for case stated by taxpayer - allowance of expenses where assessment has been confirmed

Phillips (Inspector of Taxes) v Keane
I ITC 69, [1925] 2 IR 48 .... Vol I p 64

Income tax - Schedule E - deduction - travelling expenses - ITA 1918 (8 & (Geo V, Ch 40)), Sch E, rule 9.

Phillips (Inspector of Taxes) v Limerick County Council
1 ITC 96, [1925] 2 IR 139 .... Vol I p 66

Income tax - Sch D Case III - interest - deduction.

Commissioners of Inland Revenue v The Governor & Company of The Bank of Ireland
1 ITC 74, [1925] 2 IR 90 .... Vol I p 70

Corporation profits tax - the Governor and Company of the Bank of Ireland incorporated by letter patent - Act of Irish Parliament 1783 - whether a company within the meaning of FA 1920 s 52(3) - unpaid debts of bank - whether personal liability of members unlimited.

Boland's Ltd v Davis (Inspector of Taxes)
1 ITC 91, [1925] ILTR 73 .... Vol I p 86

Income tax - Schedule D - discontinuance - distance trades - set-off for losses - ITA 1918 Sch D Cases I and II and miscellaneous rules.

Fitzgerald v Commissioners of Inland Revenue
1 ITC 100, [1926] IR 182, 585 .... Vol I p 91

Excess profits duty - deductions - expenditure on temporary premises - restoration of destroyed premises under covenant to repair.

The Alliance & Dublin Consumers' Gas Co v Davis (Inspector of Taxes)
1 ITC 114, [1926] IR 372 .... Vol I p 104

Income tax - Schedule D - profits of trade - deduction - capital loss - ITA 1918 Sch D, Cases I & II, rule 3.

The City of Dublin Steampacket Co v The Revenue Commissioners
1 ITC 118, [1926] IR 436 .... Vol I p 108

Corporation profits tax - company formed mainly for purpose of trading by use of steam vessels - cargo business and carriage of mails between Dun Laoghaire and Liverpool and Holyhead - cargo business ceased 1919 - mails contract terminated 1920 - whether running down of business constituted a trade or business - whether collection of debts a business undertaking - periodic payments on foot of an earlier debt and acquisition of profits - whether carrying on a business.

Donovan (Inspector of Taxes) v Crofts
1 ITC 214, [1926] IR 477 .... Vol I p 115

Income tax - husband and wife living apart - "married woman living with her husband" - ITA 1918 rule 16 of general rules.

Commissioners of Inland Revenue v The Dublin and Kingstown Railway Co
1 ITC 285, [1930] IR 317 .... Vol I p 119

Corporation profits tax - The Dublin and Kingston Railway Co was incorporated in 1831 to make and maintain a railway between Dublin and Kingston - railway lines leased to another company at an annual rent - all the property of owning company (except offices) passed to lessee company - whether collection of rents and dividends and distribution of profits thereout to shareholders constituted a trade or business - whether company has a corporate existence.

Green & Co (Cork) Ltd v The Revenue Commissioners
1 ITC 142, [1927] IR 240 .... Vol I p 130

Excess profits duty - stock relief claim - "trading stock in hand" - FA 1921, Sch 2 Pt II, rule 1.

Wing v O'Connell (Inspector of Taxes)
1 ITC 170, [1927] IR 84 .... Vol I p 155

Income tax - Schedule E - vocation - professional jockey - whether present from employer taxable emolument or gift.

The Executors and Trustees of A C Ferguson (Deceased) v Donovan (Inspector of Taxes)
1 ITC 214, [1927] ILTR 49, [1929] IR 489 .... Vol I p 183

Income tax - Sch D Case 1 - business carried on abroad - control by trustees.

Hayes (Inspector of Taxes) v Duggan
1 ITC 269, [1929] IR 406 .... Vol I p 195

Income tax - Schedule D - profits on sweepstakes - illegal trades not assessable to tax - ITA 1918 Sch D Cases II & VI.

The Alliance and Dublin Consumers' Gas Co v McWilliams (Inspector of Taxes)
1 ITC 199, [1928] IR 1 .... Vol I p 207

Income tax - profits of trade - compulsory detention of ships by government - compensation payment - capital or trading receipt - ITA 1918.

MacKeown (Inspector of Taxes) v Roe
1 ITC 206, [1928] IR 195 .... Vol I p 214

Income tax - public office or employment of profit - solicitor to local authority - ITA 1918 Sch E, rules 1 & 5 - profits not received in the year of assessment.

The King (Evelyn Spain) v The Special Commissioners
1 ITC 227, [1934] IR 27 .... Vol I p 221

Mandamus - finality of Special Commissioners' decision on claim for relief -income tax - income accumulated for minor - benefit taken by way of capital - ITA 1918 ss 25 & 202.

Conyngham v The Revenue Commissioners
1 ITC 259, [1928] ILTR 57, 136 .... Vol I p 231

Super tax - total income - trust deed - trust for expenditure of moneys upon property beneficially occupied by life tenant - ITA 1918 s 5.

The Revenue Commissioners v Latchford & Sons Ltd
1 ITC 238 .... Vol I p 240

Excess profits duty - loss in trade - forward purchase contracts - fall in market value of goods before delivery - FA 1915 (No 2) Fourth Schedule Pt I rule I.

Prior-Wandesforde v The Revenue Commissioners
1 ITC 248 .... Vol I p 249

Income tax - Schedule D - domicile and ordinary residence - foreign possessions - ITA 1918 Case V rule 3, FA 1925 Sch D (No 28) s 12.

Earl of Iveagh v The Revenue Commissioners
1 ITC 316, [1930] IR 386, 431 .... Vol I p 259

Income tax - Schedule D - super tax - domicile and ordinary residence, foreign securities and possessions - ITA 1918 Sch D Case IV rule 2(a) & Case V rule 3(a) - FA 1925 (No 28) s 12.

Kennedy (Inspector of Taxes) v The Rattoo Co-operative Dairy Society Ltd
1 ITC 282 .... Vol I p 315

Corporation profits tax - The Rattoo Co-operative Dairy Society Ltd - registered under the Industrial and Provident Societies Act 1893 - milk supplied by members and non-members - whether monthly surpluses retained by the society arose from trading - whether surpluses arose from trading with its own members - whether exemption under FA 1921 s 53 applied.

The City of Dublin Steampacket Co (In Liquidation) v The Revenue Commissioners
1 ITC 285, [1930] IR 217 .... Vol I p 318

Corporation profits tax - company's contract to carry mails between Ireland and England terminated in 1920 - petition to wind up the company filed on 11 August 1924 - income from company's investments continued after winding up application - business - whether during a period of winding up a company may earn income - whether winding up order prevents carrying on business for tax purposes.

The Cunard Steam Ship Co Ltd v Herlihy (Inspector of Taxes), and
The Cunard Steam Ship Co Ltd v Revenue Commissioners
1 ITC 373, [1931] IR 287, 307 .... Vol I p 330

Income tax - Schedule D - non-resident company - exercise of trade within Saorstat Eireann - ITA 1918 Sch D, rule 1(a)(iii).

The Great Southern Railways Co v The Revenue Commissioners
1 ITC 298, [1930] IR 299 .... Vol I p 359

Corporation profits tax - The Great Southern Railways Co - Railways Act 1924 - absorbed the Dublin and Kingston Railway Co - lessor of railway line - whether a railway undertaking - whether precluded from charging any higher price or distributing any higher rate of dividend - whether lessor company carries on a railway undertaking - whether prices under control of lessee company.

McGarry (Inspector of Taxes) v Limerick Gas Committee
1 ITC 405, [1932] IR 125 .... Vol I p 375

Income tax - deduction - expenses of promoting bill in Parliament - ITA 1918 (8 & 9 Geo V, Ch 40), Sch D, Cases I & II, rule 3.

Beirne (Inspector of Taxes) v St Vincent De Paul Society (Wexford Conference)
1 ITC 413 .... Vol I p 383

Income tax - exemption - trading by charity - work done by beneficiaries - FA 1921 (11 & 12 Geo V, Ch 32) s 30(1)(c).

Davis (Inspector of Taxes) v The Superioress, Mater Misericordiae Hospital, Dublin
2 ITC 1, [1933] IR 480, 503 .... Vol I p 387

Income tax - Schedule D - Hospital - whether carrying on a trade - profits derived from associated private nursing home - ITA 1918 Sch D.

Hughes (Inspector of Taxes) v Smyth and Others
1 ITC 418, [1933] IR 253 .... Vol I p 411

Income tax - disposition of income - deed of trust in favour of charitable objects with provision for re-vesting of income in settlor in certain contingencies - FA 1922 (12 & 13 Geo V c 17) s 20(1)(c).

Robinson T/A James Pim & Son v Dolan (Inspector of Taxes)
2 ITC 25, [1935] IR 509 .... Vol I p 427

Income tax - Sch D Case 1 - ex gratia payment by British government - recommendation by Irish Grants Committee - whether income of appellant assessable to income tax.

Howth Estate Co v Davis (Inspector of Taxes)
2 ITC 74, [1936] ILTR 79 .... Vol I p 447

Income tax - family estate company - claim for relief in respect of expenses of management - "company whose business consists mainly in the making of investments, and the principal part of whose income is derived therefrom" - ITA 1918 s 33(1).

The Agricultural Credit Corporation Ltd v Vale (Inspector of Taxes)
2 ITC 46, [1935] IR 681 .... Vol I p 474

Income tax - Schedule D - profits on realisation of investments - whether trading profits.

Estate of Teresa Downing (Owner)
2 ITC 103, [1936] IR 164 .... Vol I p 487

Income tax - Land Purchase Acts - arrears of jointure - ITA 1918 rule 21 of general rules.

Cloghran Stud Farm v A G Birch (Inspector of Taxes)
2 ITC 65, [1936] IR 1 .... Vol I p 496

Income tax - Schedule D - profits from stallion fees.

Davis (Inspector of Taxes) v Hibernian Bank Ltd
2 ITC 111 .... Vol I p 503

Income tax - Schedule D - banking company - change effected by Railways Act 1933, in company's holdings of railway stock - whether equivalent to sale or realisation.

Birch (Inspector of Taxes) v Delaney
2 ITC 127, [1936] IR 517, 531 .... Vol I p 515

Income tax - Schedule D - builder's profits - whether fines and capitalised value of ground rents are assessable to tax.

The Trustees of The Ward Union Hunt Races v Hughes (Inspector of Taxes)
2 ITC 152 .... Vol I p 538

Income tax - exemption - Agricultural Society - FA 1925 s 4.

The Pharmaceutical Society of Ireland v The Revenue Commissioners
2 ITC 157, [1938] IR 202 .... Vol I p 542

Income tax - exemption - charitable purposes - ITA 1918 s 37(1)(b) - FA 1921 s 30(1)(a) - trade - ITA 1918 s 237.

Mulvey (Inspector of Taxes) v Kieran
2 ITC 179, [1938] IR 87 .... Vol I p 563

Income tax - husband and wife living together - husband's income from securities - additional assessment on husband in respect of first year of wife's income from securities etc - ITA 1918 General Rule 16 - FA 1929 ss 10 & 11 and Sch 1 Pt.

The State (at the prosecution of Patrick J Whelan) v Smidic (Special Commissioners of Income Tax)
2 ITC 188, [1938] IR 626 .... Vol I p 571

Income tax - Schedule D - assessment of builder's profits - ruling of Special Commissioner on question of discontinuance - variation of ruling before figures agreed upon or fixed - determination of an appeal - ITA 1918 (8 & 9 Geo 5, c 40) ss 133, 137 & 149, FA 1929 (No 32 of 1929) s 5.

Connolly v Birch (Inspector of Taxes)
2 ITC 201, [1939] IR 534 .... Vol I p 583

Income tax, FA 1935 Sch D s 6 - assessment of builders profits - inclusion in 1935-36 assessment of amounts received in respect of fines and capitalised value of surplus ground rents created prior to the coming into operation of the section.

O'Reilly v Casey (Inspector of Taxes)
2 ITC 220, [1942] IR 378 .... Vol I p 601

Income tax - provisions in codicil to a will charging the rents of the testator's real and leasehold property with the payment of 10 per cent, thereof to a named son so long as that son continued to manage the property - whether such payment was remuneration chargeable upon the recipient under ITA 1918 Sch E - ITA 1918 Sch E - Charging Rule: FA 1922 s 18.

Mulvey (Inspector of Taxes) v Coffey
2 ITC 239, [1942] IR 277 .... Vol I p 618

Income tax - Schedule E - emolument of office - grant to a President of a college on retirement - whether chargeable to income tax - ITA 1918 Sch E rule 1 - FA 1929 s 17.

O'Dwyer (Inspector of Taxes) and The Revenue Commissioners v Irish Exporters and Importers Ltd (In Liquidation)
2 ITC 251, [1943] IR 176 .... Vol I p 629

Income tax and corporation profits tax - whether or not a sum of money payable and paid to a limited liability company under a prior agreement by the Minister for Agriculture in the event of his having terminated, within a prescribed period, a supply of the raw material of the trade of another company, (promoted by the first company at the request of said Minister), is or is not a receipt of the first company's trade - ITA 1918 Sch D Case 1 - FA 1920 s 53.

Kealy (Inspector of Taxes) v O'Mara (Limerick) Ltd
2 ITC 265, [1942] IR 616 .... Vol I p 642

Income tax - deductions - whether expenses preliminary to, and in connection with, the formation of a "holding company" were admissible as part of trading expenses of a bacon manufacturing company - ITA 1918 ss 100(2), 209 and Sch D, rule applicable to Case I, and rules 1(1) & 3 of Cases I & II.

Dolan (Inspector of Taxes) v "K" National School Teacher
2 ITC 280, [1944] IR 470 .... Vol I p 656

Income tax - Schedule E - professed nun employed as national school teacher but bound by constitutions of her order to hand over all her earnings to the order - whether or not assessable Schedule E as having earned or exercising an office or employment, as national school teacher - ITA 1918 Sch E rule 1.

McGarry (Inspector of Taxes) v Spencer
2 ITC 297, [1946] IR 11 .... Vol II p 1

Nurseries and market gardens - ITA 1918 Sch B rule 8 ss 186 & 187 - whether rule 8 applies in Eire, that is, whether the income is chargeable with reference to annual value or upon profits estimated according to the rules of Schedule D.

Gilbert Hewson v Kealy (Inspector of Taxes)
2 ITC 286 .... Vol II p 15

Income tax - Sch D Case III - interest and income from securities and possessions - execution of document under seal in the Isle of Man - contention that beneficial interest in the said securities and possessions had been transferred - original document not produced - secondary evidence of its terms not admissible.

The Revenue Commissioners v Switzer Ltd
2 ITC 290, [1945] IR 378 .... Vol II p 19

Excess corporation profits tax - company on "substituted standard" - portion of issue of debenture stock bought back by company - whether in computing substituted standard such portion of the issue should be taken into account - FA 1941 s 39 as amended by FA 1942 s 16.

Property Loan & Investment Co Ltd v The Revenue Commissioners
2 ITC 312, [1946] IR 159 .... Vol II p 25

Corporation profits tax - company incorporated under the Companies Acts 1908 to 1917 - business consisting of the advancement of moneys to persons not members of the company for the purpose of enabling them to acquire dwelling-houses - whether company carries on "the business of a building society" - FA 1929 s 33(1)(d), as amended.

Vale (Inspector of Taxes) v Martin Mahony & Brothers Ltd
2 ITC 331, [1947] IR 30, 41 .... Vol II p 32

Income tax - Schedule D - deduction - expenditure upon mill sanitation.

Davis (Inspector of Taxes) v X Ltd
2 ITC 320, [1946] ILTR 57, [1947] ILTR 157 .... Vol II p 45

Income tax - Schedule D - profits of trade - deductions - new factory in course of erection - interference with rights as regards light and air claimed by tenants of adjoining houses - settlement of action - sums paid to tenants as compensation and for legal costs.

AB v Mulvey (Inspector of Taxes)
2 ITC 345, [1947] IR 121 .... Vol II p 55

Income tax - Schedule D - business carried on by sole trader - partner admitted at beginning of year - business sold later in year to private company - whether assessment on sole trader for the previous year can be reviewed - ITA 1918 Sch D Cases I & II rule 11 - FA 1929 s 12.

A and B v Davis (Inspector of Taxes) 2 ITC 350 .... Vol II p 60

Income tax, Schedule D - appeal to High Court by way of case stated from decision of Circuit Judge - failure of appellants to send to respondent, at or before the required date, notice in writing of fact that case had been stated etc - ITA 1918 s 149(1)(e).

O'Sullivan (Inspector of Taxes) v O'Connor, as Administratrix of O'Brien, (Deceased)
2 ITC 352, [1947] IR 416 .... Vol II p 61

Income tax - Schedule D - compulsory sale to Minister for Finance, in return for sterling equivalents, of dollar balances consisting of income from securities, etc, in the USA - whether moneys so received assessable - FA 1929 Sch 1 Pt II.

Tipping (Inspector of Taxes) v Jeancard
2 ITC 360, [1948] IR 233 .... Vol II p 68

Income tax - Schedule E - office of profit within the State - director, resident abroad, of a company incorporated in the State but managed and controlled abroad.

Ua Clothasaigh (Inspector of Taxes) v McCartan
2 ITC 367, [1948] IR 219 .... Vol II p 75

Income tax - husband and wife- "married woman living with her husband" - ITA 1918 general rule 16.

O'Dwyer (Inspector of Taxes) v Cafolla & Co
2 ITC 374, [1949] IR 210 ....Vol II p 82

Income tax - dispositions of income - father taking his elder children and his mother-in-law into partnership - subsequent assignment of mother-in-law's interest to his younger children - whether income of children to be deemed to be income of father - FA 1922 s 20 - FA 1937 s 2.

The Attorney-General v Irish Steel Ltd and Crowley
2 ITC 402 ....Vol II p 108

Income tax and corporation profits tax - company in hands of a receiver - preferential claim - Companies (Consolidation) Act 1908 ss 107 and 209.

O'Dwyer (Inspector of Taxes) v The Dublin United Transport Co Ltd
2 ITC 437, [1949] IR 295 ....Vol II p 115

Income tax - Schedule D - cessation - deduction of corporation profits tax and excess corporation profits tax in computing profits for income tax purposes - ITA 1918 Sch D, Cases I & II, rule 4 - FA 1929 s 12.

The Revenue Commissioners v R Hilliard & Sons Ltd
2 ITC 410 ....Vol II p 130

Corporation profits tax (including excess corporation profits tax) - accounting period - accounts made up half-yearly - yearly account for general meeting prepared from half-yearly accounts - whether Revenue Commissioners required to determine the accounting period - FA 1920 s 54(1).

CD v O'Sullivan (Inspector of Taxes)
2 ITC 422, [1949] IR 264 ....Vol II p 140

Income tax - Schedule D - bad debts - executor carrying on trade - recovery by executor of debts allowed as bad debts in lifetime of deceased - whether a trading receipt.

O'Loan (Inspector of Taxes) v Noone & Co
2 ITC 430, [1949] IR 171 ....Vol II p 146

Income tax - Schedule D - fuel merchants - whether a new trade of coal mining set up or commenced - FA 1929 ss 8(1) & 9(2).

Moville District Board of Conservators v Ua Clothasaigh (Inspector of Taxes)
3 ITC 1, [1950] IR 301 ....Vol II p 154

Income tax - Schedule D - surplus revenue of Board of Conservators - whether annual profits or gains - ITA 1918 Case VI.

Corr (Inspector of Taxes) v Larkin
3 ITC 13, [1949] IR 399 ....Vol II p 164

Income tax - Schedule D - sum recovered under loss of profits policy - whether a profit or gain arising from the trade - year in which assessable.

Associated Properties Ltd v The Revenue Commissioners
3 ITC 25, [1951] IR 140 .... Vol II p 175

Corporation profits tax -"the shareholders" - whether a "post-appointed day company" was a subsidiary of the appellant company - whether appellant company director-controlled and, if so, whether its managing director was the beneficial owner of, or able to control more than 5 per cent of its ordinary shares - FA 1944 s 14 - FA 1941 s 36(4).

The Revenue Commissioners v Y Ltd
3 ITC 49 .... Vol II p 195

Corporation profits tax (including excess corporation profit tax) - Industrial and Provident Societies - society trading with its own members and with non-members - investments and property purchased out of trading profits - whether the dividends and rents form part of the profits or surplus arising from the trade - additional assessments - FA 1920 s 53(2)(h) - FA 1921 s 53 - FA 1946 s 24.

The Veterinary Council v Corr (Inspector of Taxes)
3 ITC 59, [1953] IR 12 .... Vol II p 204

Income tax - body corporate performing statutory functions - surplus of receipts over expenditure - whether annual profits or gains - ITA 1918 Sch D Case VI.

The Exported Live Stock (Insurance) Board v Carroll (Inspector of Taxes)
3 ITC 67, [1951] IR 286 .... Vol II p 211

Income tax - Sch D Case 1 - statutory body set up to carry into effect a compulsory insurance scheme - whether statutory body was carrying on a trade within the meaning of Sch D Case I and whether the surpluses arising from the carrying on of its statutory activities were taxable as profits of such a trade - ITA 1918 Sch D Case I.

Flynn (Inspector of Taxes) v John Noone Ltd, and
Flynn (Inspector of Taxes) v Blackwood & Co (Sligo) Ltd
3 ITC 79 .... Vol II p 222

Income tax, Schedule D - capital or revenue - lump sum paid on execution of lease - whether capital payment and receipt or rent paid in advance - ITA 1918 Sch D Case III rule 5 and Cases I & II, rule 3(a).

L v McGarry (Inspector of Taxes)
3 ITC 111 .... Vol II p 241

Income tax - Schedule B - whether rule 8 applicable where the lands occupied as gardens for the sale of produce comprise part only of a unit of valuation - power to apportion valuation and land purchase annuity - ITA 1918 ss 186 & 187 and Sch B rule 8.

McGarry (Inspector of Taxes) v E F
3 ITC 103, [1954] IR 64 .... Vol II p 261

Income tax - general manager of company "Y" - professional services rendered to company "X" without agreement as regards remuneration - payment made by company "X" on termination of services - whether chargeable as income - ITA 1918 Sch E rule 7 and Sch D Case VI.

Hodgins (Inspector of Taxes) v Plunder & Pollak (Ireland) Ltd
3 ITC 135, [1957] IR 58 .... Vol II p 267

Income tax - Schedule D - deduction in computing profits - cost of replacement of weighbridge house - ITA 1918 Sch D Cases I & II, rule 3(d) and (g).

The Revenue Commissioners v L & Co
3 ITC 205 .... Vol II p 281

Corporation profits tax - foreign company trading in this country - expenditure attributable to Irish trading not transferred from company's Irish resources to head office in the USA - devaluation of sterling - deduction from profits.

Collins and Byrne and Power v Mulvey (Inspector of Taxes)
3 ITC 151, [1956] IR 233 .... Vol II p 291

Income tax - Schedule D - profits from illegal trade - admissibility of evidence of illegality - ITA 1918 Sch D Case I.

O'Conaill (Inspector of Taxes) v R
3 ITC 167, [1956] IR 97 .... Vol II p 304

Income tax - Schedule D - trade carried on wholly in England - basis of assessment under Case III - "single source" - ITA 1918 Sch D Case III rule 2 (FA 1922 s 17) - FA 1926 Sch 1 Pt II s 2(2) & 1(3) - FA 1929 ss 10, 11 & 18 and Sch 2 para 3.

Mac Giolla Riogh (Inspector of Taxes) v G Ltd
3 ITC 181, [1957] IR 90 .... Vol II p 315

Income tax - Schedule D - company trading in bloodstock - animal bought in course of trade, sent to stud after successful racing career and subsequently sold to a syndicate - whether amount realised on syndication a trading receipt - ITA 1918 Sch D Case I and FA 1939 Sch B s 7.

The Revenue Commissioners v Orwell Ltd
3 ITC 193 .... Vol II p 326

Corporation profits tax and excess corporation profits tax - whether excess corporation profits tax is exigible for accounting periods in respect of which no corporation profits tax (other than excess corporation profits tax) is payable - FA 1941 s 37.

Colclough v Colclough
[1965] IR 668 .... Vol II p 332

Income tax-funds in court - (a) whether rules 19 and 21 of the general rules applicable to ITA 1918 Sch A, B, C, D and E apply to the court when paying interest on debts out of funds in court and - (b) whether tax deductible from income accrued to funds in court for years prior to 1922/23.

EG v Mac Shamhrain (Inspector of Taxes)
3 ITC 217, [1958] IR 288 .... Vol II p 352

Income tax - Sch D Case III - Settlement of income - deed of appointment by parent in favour of child - power of revocation - FA 1922 s 20(1), FA 1937 s 2(1) - rule 16, general rules applicable to all Schedules.

Curtin (Inspector of Taxes) v M Ltd
3 ITC 227, [1960] IR 59 .... Vol II p 360

Income tax - Schedule D - profits of trade - deduction - expenditure on rebuilding of business premises - whether portion thereof deductible in computing profits.

O'Broin (Inspector of Taxes) v Mac Giolla Meidhre
O'Broin (Inspector of Taxes) v Pigott
3 ITC 235, [1959] IR 98 .... Vol II p 366

Income tax - Schedule E - deductions - expenses - ITA 1918 Sch E rule 9.

Bourke (Inspector of Taxes) v Lyster & Sons Ltd
3 ITC 247 .... Vol II p 374

Income tax - Schedule D - profits of a trade - sum received in part payment of a debt previously treated as bad-res judicata - jurisdiction of Circuit Court Judge when hearing on appeal against an assessment.

Milverton Quarries Ltd v The Revenue Commissioners
3 ITC 279, [1960] IR 224 .... Vol II p 382

Corporation profits tax - deduction from profits - expenses of removing top soil from surface of quarry - whether capital or revenue expenditure - ITA 1918 Sch D Cases I & II rule 2 - FA 1920 s 53.

McHugh (Inspector of Taxes) v A
3 ITC 257, [1958] IR 142, [1959] ILTR 125 .... Vol II p 393

Income tax - Schedule D - pension, annuity or other annual payment - payments made by a British company to a person resident in the State - whether income from a foreign possession - ITA 1918 Sch D Case III, FA 1922 s 18, FA 1929 s 11, FA 1932 s 4.

The Revenue Commissioners v Associated Properties Ltd
3 ITC 293 .... Vol II p 412

Corporation profits tax - Interest paid to a person having controlling interest - FA 1920 s 53(2)(b).

AB Ltd v Mac Giolla Riogh (Inspector of Taxes)
3 ITC 301 .... Vol II p 419

Income tax - Schedule D - finance company dealing in stocks and shares - whether investments should be valued at cost or market value.

Casey (Inspector of Taxes) v The Monteagle Estate Co
3 ITC 313, [1962] IR 106 .... Vol II p 429

Income tax - estate company - claim for relief in respect of expenses of management - "company whose business consists mainly in the making of investments and the principal part of whose income is derived therefrom" - ITA 1918 s 33(1).

Connolly (Inspector of Taxes) v McNamara
3 ITC 341 .... Vol II p 452

Income tax - Schedule E - emolument of employment - rent paid by employing company for house occupied voluntarily by employee - ITA 1918 Sch E, FA 1922 s 18.

Kelly (Inspector of Taxes) v H
3 ITC 351, [1964] IR 488 .... Vol II p 460

Income tax - Schedule E - deductions - expenses - ITA 1918 Sch E rule 9.

O'Sullivan (Inspector of Taxes) v P Ltd
3 ITC 355 .... Vol II p 464

Income tax - Schedule D - payment in advance on the signing of a lease - whether a capital receipt (ie a fine or premium) or rent paid in advance assessable to income tax - ITA 1918 Sch D Case III, FA 1929 s 11 and Sch 1 Pt II.

Swaine (Inspector of Taxes) v VE
3 ITC 387, [1964] IR 423, 100 ILTR 21 .... Vol II p 472

Income tax - Schedule D - builder's profits - whether fines and capitalised value of ground rents are assessable to tax.

Molmac Ltd v MacGiolla Riogh (Inspector of Taxes)
3 ITC 376, [1965] IR 201, 101 ILTR 114 .... Vol II p 482

Income tax Schedule D - carry forward of losses - managing of "six following years of assessment" - FA 1929 s 14.

Forbes (Inspector of Taxes) v GHD
3 ITC 365, [1964] IR 447 .... Vol II p 491

Income tax - Schedule D - pensions payable under the British National Insurance Act 1946, as amended or extended, to persons resident in the State - whether income from foreign possessions - ITA 1918 Sch D Case III, FA 1926 Sch 1 Pt II, FA 1929 s 11.

Casey (Inspector of Taxes) v AB Ltd
[1965] IR 575 .... Vol II p 500

Income tax - Schedule D - legal costs in defending action in High Court for balance alleged to be due to a building contractor in respect of the construction of cinema - whether the costs were incurred in earning the profits assessed, and whether they were capital or revenue expenditure - ITA 1918 Sch D Case I.

Dolan (Inspector of Taxes) v AB Co Ltd
[1969] IR 282, 104 ILTR 101 .... Vol II p 515

Income tax - Schedule D - petrol marketing company-whether expenditure incurred under exclusivity agreements with retailers deductible - ITA 1918 s 209 and Sch D Cases I & II rule 3 - FA 1929 s 9.

Bedford (Collector-General) v H
[1968] IR 320 .... Vol II p 588

Aggregate of monthly payments made in year on account of remunerations less than tax-free allowances-no tax deducted under PAYE - balance of remuneration for year voted and paid in following year - tax deducted under PAYE - assessment made in respect of full remuneration for earlier year - whether tax so deducted under PAYE from balance of remuneration in following year should be treated as covering tax charged in assessment - FA (No 2) 1959 s 13(1) (ITA 1967 s 133(1)), IT(E)R 1960 clause 45(1) (SI 28/1960).

Cronin (Inspector of Taxes) v C
TL 106 .... Vol II p 592

Income tax - Schedule D - personal pension and other assets assigned to company - pension continued to be paid to pensioner - whether pensioner ceased to receive pension as a source of income for himself beneficially - ITA 1918 Sch D, Case III of miscellaneous rules applicable to Schedule D and FA 1929 s 10

Pairceir (Inspector of Taxes) v EM
[Not previously reported] .... Vol II p 596

Income tax - Schedule D - income from the leasing of premises - whether such activity constitutes a "trade" the income from which would qualify for earned income relief - FA 1920 s 16 - replaced by FA(No 2) 1959 s16 - amended by FA 1961 s 3.

S Ltd v O'Sullivan
[Not previously reported] .... Vol II p 602

Income tax - Schedule D - payments made under an agreement for the supply of technical information.

HH v Forbes (Inspector of Taxes)
[Not previously reported] .... Vol II p 614

Income tax - whether profits of a bookmaker from certain transactions in Irish Hospital Sweepstakes tickets should be included as receipts for purposes of assessment to tax under Schedule D.

W Ltd v Wilson (Inspector of Taxes)
[Not previously reported] .... Vol II p 627

Income tax - Schedule D and corporation profits tax, FA 1920 - whether the inspector of taxes had made a "discovery" on finding that inadmissible deductions had been allowed in the computation of the company's tax liability for certain years and whether he was entitled to raise additional assessments for those years - ITA 1967 s 186.

O Conaill (Inspector of Taxes) v Z Ltd
[Not previously reported] .... Vol II p 636

Income tax - whether the appellant company was in occupation of lands, forming part of a military establishment, for the purposes of ITA 1918 Sch B or ITA 1967.

S W Ltd v McDermott (Inspector of Taxes)
[Not previously reported] .... Vol II p 661

Income tax - whether the capital allowances to be apportioned in accordance with the provisions of ITA 1967 s 220(5), in computing the appellant's liability under Sch D Case I were to be confined to the allowances outlined in Part XVI of that Act.

Mara (Inspector of Taxes) v GG (Hummingbird) Ltd
[1982] ILRM 421 .... Vol II p 667

Income tax - Sch D Case I - whether the surplus arising to the company from the sale of certain property was profit of a trade of dealing in or developing land, or the profit of a business which was deemed by F(MP)A 1968 s 17, to be such a trade.

MacDaibheid (Inspector of Taxes) v SD
[Not previously reported] .... Vol III p 1

Income tax - whether a deduction should be allowed under ITA 1967 Sch 2(3) in respect of incidental expenses.

O hArgain (Inspector of Taxes) v B Ltd
[1979] ILRM 56 .... Vol III p 9

Property company - income tax - trade - trading stock - farm land - company letting land to partners on conacre - area zoned for development - land transferred to new company - whether land trading stock of company - F(MP)A 1968 (No 7) s 17.

De Brun (Inspector of Taxes) v Kiernan
[1981] IR 117, [1982] ILRM 13 .... Vol III p 19

Income tax - whether the taxpayer was a "dealer in cattle" within the meaning of ITA 1918 Sch D Case III rule 4 and ITA 1967 s 78.

Revenue v ORMG
[1984] ILRM 406 .... Vol III p 28

Club to promote athletics or amateur games or sports - whether legitimate avoidance of payment of tax - funds provided by one person - total control in two trustees - whether bona fide club - whether established for sole purpose of "promoting sport" - whether two persons can constitute a "body of person" - ITA 1967 ss (1), 349.

MacDermott (Inspector of Taxes) v BC
[Not previously reported] .... Vol III p 43

Income tax - Schedule E - whether the taxpayer was engaged under a contract of service or a contract for services - ITA 1967 s 110.

O'Laoghaire (Inspector of Taxes) v CD Ltd
[Not previously reported] .... Vol III p 51

Corporation profits tax - company engaged in manufacture and erection of prefabricated buildings - deposit of 15 per cent of total cost paid on execution of contract - whether a payment on account in respect of trading stock - whether security for contracts - whether value of stock for stock relief be reduced - FA 1975 s 31.

K Co v Hogan (Inspector of Taxes)
[1985] ILRM 200 .... Vol III p 56

Appellant unlimited investment company - whether dividends arising from sales of capital assets liable to corporation profits tax - whether profits shall be profits and gains determined on the same principles as those on which the profits and gains of a trade are determined - whether company carrying on a trade - whether similar distributions previously charged to corporation profits tax - whether statutory provision can become obsolete on the basis of past practice - whether FA 1920 s 53(2) ambiguous in meaning - whether words of a taxing statute must be clear and unambiguous - whether s (2) is purely for purpose of determining profits for income tax purposes - whether question of distinguishing capital and income arises - whether proceeds of sale of capital assets may be capital in hands of companies selling the assets and income in the hands of the shareholders to whom paid in the form of dividends.

O'Conaill (Inspector of Taxes) v JJ Ltd
[Not previously reported] .... Vol III p 65

Income tax - whether a building which housed offices, a showroom, a canteen, computer department and utilities qualified for industrial building allowance under ITA 1967 s 255.

Doyle & Others v An Taoiseach & Others
[1986] ILRM 522 .... Vol III p 73

Excise duty - levy of 2 per cent of value of bovine animals imposed on the farmer producer - whether ultra vires the enabling provisions of FA 1986 - imposed on proprietors of slaughter houses and exporters of live animals - whether levy operated arbitrarily and unreasonably - whether levy passed on to the prime producer - whether end result untargeted indiscriminate and unfair - FA 1966 - SI 152/1970 and 160/1979 - Treaty of Rome Article 177 - FA 1980 s 79.

GH (Stephen Court) Ltd v Browne (Inspector of Taxes)
[1984] ILRM 231 .... Vol III p 95

Income tax - whether letting fees and legal expenses incurred by the company in respect of first lettings of property qualified as deductions under ITA 1967 s 81(5)(d).

BKJ v The Revenue Commissioners
[Not previously reported] .... Vol III p 104

Family settlement dated 22 December 1955 - discretionary trust - income to beneficiary on attaining thirty years of age until 31 December 1985 and thereafter to the beneficiary absolutely - whether beneficiary took an absolute interest on attaining thirty years of age - whether vested interest subject to contingency of favour of children and remoter issue -

appointment dated 4 April 1978 in favour of beneficiary - whether gift of a contingent interest - whether liable to gift tax - CATA 1976 ss 2, 4, 5, 6.

Breathnach (Inspector of Taxes) v McCann
[1984] IR 340 .... Vol III p 113

Income tax - Sch D Case 11 - profession - capital allowances - whether barrister's books are plant.

In Re HT Ltd (In Liquidation) and Others
[1984] ILRM 583 .... Vol III p 120

Income tax - corporation profits tax - corporation tax - court liquidation - whether deposit interest earned on monies held by the official liquidator liable to tax - whether tax payable a "necessary disbursement" under court winding-up rules - whether tax payable ranks as a preferential payment or an unsecured debt - Companies Act 1963 ss 244, 285 - FA 1983 s 56, Winding Up Rules 1966 r 129.

The State (FIC Ltd) v O'Ceallaigh
[Not previously reported] .... Vol III p 124

Capital gains tax clearance certificate on sale of bonds - whether statutory requirements satisfied - whether applicant is the person making the disposal - whether applicant is the owner of the property and ordinarily resident in the state - whether statutory provision mandatory - whether inspector of taxes is entitled to investigate applicant's title to the property - whether applicant as owner and ordinarily resident in the state is entitled to a clearance certificate.

Madigan v The Attorney General, The Revenue Commissioners and Others
[1986] ILRM 136 .... Vol III p 127

Residential property tax - whether unconstitutional - whether unjust attack on property and family rights - whether invidious discrimination - whether unreasonable or arbitrary - whether taxation statutes presumed to be unconstitutional - locus standi - FA 1983 - Constitution of Ireland 1937 Articles 40(1), 40(3), 41, 43.

JB O'C v PCD and A Bank
[1985] IR 265 .... Vol III p 153

Income tax - particulars of taxpayers bank accounts - bond of confidentiality between banks and customers - strict compliance with statutory provisions - whether reasonable grounds for court application - discretion of court - particulars of accounts - dealings in accounts - name(s), nature of account and dates of opening and closing - whether costs of bank to be borne by Revenue - FA 1983 s 18.

The State (Multiprint Label Systems Ltd) v Neylon
[1984] ILRM 545 .... Vol III p 159

Practice - Revenue case - statutory provision requiring person to express dissatisfaction with the determination of a point of law "immediately after the determination" - whether "immediately" to be interpreted strictly - whether provision directory or mandatory - ITA(No 6) 1967 ss 428, 430.

O'Cleirigh (Inspector of Taxes) v Jacobs International Ltd Incorporated
[1985] ILRM 651 .... Vol III p 165

Corporation tax - whether a training grant paid to the company was a capital or revenue receipt.

McElligott & Sons Ltd v Duigenan (Inspector of Taxes)
[1985] ILRM 210 .... Vol III p 178

Stock relief - whether the company was carrying on a single trade, or several different trades, for the purposes of a claim under FA 1975 s 31 (as amended by FA 1977 s 43).

Muckley v Ireland, The Attorney General and The Revenue Commissioners
[1985] IR 472, [1986] ILRM 364 .... Vol III p 188

Constitution validity of taxing statute - personal rights of citizens - unauthorised exactions - married persons - statute with retrospective effect - enacted in consequence of decision that portion of income tax legislation unconstitutional - whether lawful for the State to collect arrears of tax due under the unconstitutional provisions - FA 1980 s 21 - Constitution of Ireland 1937, Articles 40.1, 40.3, 41

Cronin (Inspector of Taxes) v Cork & County Property Co Ltd
[1986] IR 559 .... Vol III p 198

Corporation tax - property company dealing in land - interest in land acquired and disposed of within one accounting period - whether ordinary principles of commercial accounting apply - whether artificial method of valuation pursuant to F(MP)A 1968 s 18(2) prevails.

Mac Giolla Mhaith (Inspector of Taxes) v Cronin & Associates Ltd
[Not previously reported] .... Vol III p 211

Corporation tax - advertising agency - whether its business consisted of or included the carrying on of a profession or the provision of professional services for the purposes of the corporation tax surcharge provided for in CTA 1976 s 162

O'Srianain (Inspector of Taxes) v Lakeview Ltd
[Not previously reported] .... Vol III p 219

Capital allowances - machinery and plant - whether applicable to the provision of a deep pit poultry house.

Cronin (Inspector of Taxes) v Youghal Carpets (Yarns) Ltd
[1985] IR 312, [1985] ILRM 666 .... Vol III p 229

Corporation tax - whether the expression "total income brought into charge to corporation tax" for the purposes of CTA 1976 s 58(3) meant income before or after the deduction of group relief.

The Revenue Commissioners v HI
[Not previously reported] .... Vol III p 242

Income tax - whether an individual was entitled to repayment of tax deducted from payments made under an indenture of covenant pursuant to ITA 1967 s 439(1)(iv).

Murphy (Inspector of Taxes) v Asahi Synthetic Fibres (Ireland) Ltd
[1985] IR 509, [1986] IR 777 .... Vol III p 246

Irish subsidiary company and Japanese parent company - interest on loan by parent company - whether tax chargeable under Schedule D or Schedule F - Double Taxation Relief (Taxes on Income)(Japan) Order 1974 SI 259/1974, CTA 1976 ss 83/84.

MacCarthaigh (Inspector of Taxes) v Daly
[1985] IR 73, [1986] ILRM 24, 116 .... Vol III p 253

Income tax - whether the taxpayer was entitled to claim a share of capital allowances on the basis of a leasing transaction, involving a purported limited partnership, against his personal income tax liability.

The Attorney General v Sun Alliance and London Insurance Ltd
[1985] ILRM 522 .... Vol III p 265

Excise duty - deed of bond - principal and surety - payment of excise duty deferred - whether creditor to resort to securities received by creditor from principal before proceeding against surety - Excise Collection and Management Act 1841 (4 & 5 Vict c 20) s 24.

O'Connlain (Inspector of Taxes) v Belvedere Estates Ltd
[1985] IR 22 .... Vol III p 271

Trading company dealing in and developing - tax avoidance scheme - series of transactions with associated companies - aggregate of costs of stock in trade - artificial method of valuation under F(MP)A 1968 s 18 - legal consequences of transaction - whether s 18 can be construed to alter legal consequences.

The State (Melbarian Enterprises Ltd) v The Revenue Commissioners
[1985] IR 706 .... Vol III p 290

State side - mandamus - requirement of tax clearance certificate with tenders for Government contracts - refusal to issue by Collector General - whether Revenue Commissioners can have regard to tax default of previous "connected" company - whether Collector General's decision amenable to judicial review - duty to act judicially - requirement not based on statutory provisions.

Heron and Others v The Minister For Communications
[1985] IR 623 .... Vol III p 298

Liability for capital gains tax - compulsory acquisition - tax arising on disposal - compensation determined without regard to the liability of landowner for tax on chargeable gain - Acquisition of Land (Assessment of Compensation) Act 1919 s 2.

McCann Ltd v O'Culachain (Inspector of Taxes)
[1985] IR 298, [1986] IR 196 .... Vol III p 304

Corporation tax - exports sales relief - whether process of ripening bananas constituted manufacturing - no statutory definition of word manufacture - interpretation of taxation statute - ordinary meaning or strict construction - scheme and purpose of statute - test to be applied - matter of degree - CTA 1976 s 54 and Pt IV.

Knockhall Piggeries v Kerrane (Inspector of Taxes)
[1985] ILRM 655 .... Vol III p 319

Income tax - whether the activity of intensive pig rearing constituted farming for the purposes of FA 1974 s 13(1).

Maye v The Revenue Commissioners
[1986] ILRM 377 .... Vol III p 332

Value added tax - installation of fixtures subject to low rate of value added tax - whether or not television aerials attached to roof of a house are fixtures - test based on mode and object of annexation - VATA 1972 s 10(8).

Belville Holdings Ltd (In Receivership and Liquidation) v Cronin (Inspector of Taxes)
[1985] IR 465 .... Vol III p 340

Corporation tax - case stated on question of losses incurred by a holding company, whether notional management fees deductible - whether evidence required to determine the amount of such fees - whether Appeal Commissioner in error - whether a High Court order can be subsequently amended by a further High Court order - whether High Court has jurisdiction to amend order - whether jurisdiction limited to Order 28 rule 11 of Superior Court rules and judgments incorrectly drawn up - whether certainty of administration of law can be breached - whether discretion under ITA 1967 s 428 applied by judge - whether discretion "implicit" in judgment - whether application of s 428(b) an additional remedy - whether amending order be set aside.

Warnock and Others practising as Stokes Kennedy Crowley & Co v The Revenue Commissioners
[1985] IR 663, [1986] ILRM 37 .... Vol III p 356

Income tax - tax avoidance - transfer of assets to offshore tax havens - statutory notice requesting information - whether from of accountants could be requested to furnish relevant particulars in respect of all their clients - ten named territories over a six year period - whether a limit to extent of particulars sought - whether cost of compliance excessive - whether notice ultra vires *the section - FA 1974 s 59.*

Cronin (Inspector of Taxes) v Lunham Brothers Ltd
[1986] ILRM 415 .... Vol III p 363

Corporation tax - relief - losses forward - cessation of company's trade - major change in nature of conduct of trade - change of ownership - CTA 1976 ss 16(1), 27(1), 182 184.

Guinness & Mahon Ltd v Browne (Inspector of Taxes)
[Not previously reported] .... Vol III p 373

Corporation tax - whether a sum which arose to the company on the liquidation of a wholly owned subsidiary was part of its trading profits.

McLoughlin and Tuite v The Revenue Commissioners and The Attorney General
[1986] IR 235, [1986] ILRM 304, [1990] IR 83 .... Vol III p 387

Income tax returns - whether penalties for failure to make returns are punitive - whether proceedings for recovery of penalties are criminal trials - whether unconstitutional - ITA 1967 s 500 - Constitution of Ireland Act 1937 s 34.

Navan Carpets Ltd v O'Culachain (Inspector of Taxes)
[1988] IR 164 .... Vol III p 403

Corporation tax - interest on repayment of tax - no provision for interest in Taxes Act - whether or not award on interest applicable under Courts Act 1981.

Curtis and Geough v The Attorney General and The Revenue Commissioners
[1986] ILRM 428 .... Vol III p 419

Customs duties - locus standi evasion of customs duties on specified goods - whether District Court authorised to determine value of goods - criminal case - whether disputed issue of fact a matter for jury - whether statutory provisions unconstitutional - whether unappealable finding unjust - FA 1963 ss 34(4)(d)(i), 34(4)(d)(iii) - Constitution of Ireland 1937, Articles 34.3.4, 38.1, 38.2, 38.

Williams Group Tullamore Ltd v Companies Act 1963 - 1983
[Not previously reported] .... Vol III p 423

Petition under Companies Act 1963 s 205 - oppression of ordinary minority shareholders - voting and non voting shares - whether preference shareholders entitled to receive a portion of issue of new ordinary shares - whether preference shareholders entitled to participate in capital distribution - whether proposal burdensome harsh and wrongful - whether isolated transaction can give rise to relief - whether for benefit of company as a whole - whether in disregard of interests of ordinary shareholders.

Bairead (Inspector of Taxes) v Maxwells of Donegal Ltd
[1986] ILRM 508 .... Vol III p 430

Corporation tax - whether a company, resident and trading in Northern Ireland was an associated company of a company resident and trading in the State for the purposes of CTA 1976 s 28.

Kinghan v The Minister for Social Welfare
[Not previously reported] .... Vol III p 436

Social welfare - benefits - whether entitled to old age contributory pension - whether issue open to appeal - true construction of statute - jurisdiction of High Court - meaning of entry into insurance - definition of contribution year - Social Welfare (Consolidation Act 1951 s 299).

Cronin (Inspector of Taxes) v Strand Dairy Ltd
[Not previously reported] .... Vol III p 441

Corporation tax - whether the processing of and sale of milk in plastic bottles produced by the company constituted the manufacture of goods for the purposes of the reduction in corporation tax provided for in FA 1980 Pt I Ch VI.

Cronin (Inspector of Taxes) v IMP Midleton Ltd
[Not previously reported] .... Vol III p 452

Corporation profits tax - export sales relief - sale of meat into intervention within the EEC - conditional contracts - when does property in goods pass - sold in course of trade - exporter need not be owner at time of export - F(MP)A 1956 s 13(3).

Director of Public Prosecutions v McLoughlin
[1986] IR 355, [1986] ILRM 493 .... Vol III p 467

Income tax (PAYE) and Social Welfare (PRSI) regulations - whether contract for services between skipper of fishing vessel and crew members - whether a partnership existed - no wages - rights to share of profits and to decide on division of profits but not to share in losses.

Moloney (Inspector of Taxes) v Allied Irish Banks Ltd as Executors of the Estate of Doherty, Deceased
[1986] IR 67 .... Vol III p 477

Income tax - liability of personal representatives - income on estate in course of administration - trustees under Succession Act 1965 - ITA 1967 s 105.

O'Coindealbhain (Inspector of Taxes) v Gannon
[1986] IR 154 .... Vol III p 484

Income tax - fees due to a barrister prior to his appointment to the bench - fees refused but could be paid to a family company if solicitors so wished - whether or not received within the meaning of FA 1970 s 20 - interpretation of taxing act.

Healy v Breathnach (Inspector of Taxes)
[1986] IR 105 .... Vol III p 496

Income tax - exemption of earnings from original and creative works of artistic or cultural merit - whether newspaper articles and journalism qualify - tests for exemption - grounds for setting aside a Circuit Court decision on a Revenue case stated - FA 1969 s 2.

The Minister for Labour v PMPA Insurance Co Ltd (Under Administration)
[1990] IR 284 .... Vol III p 505

Contract of service or contract for services - temporary employee engaged through employment agency - agreement between employee and agency - agreement between agency and defendant hirer - whether defendant liable for employee's holiday pay - nature of contractual relationship between employee and defendant - whether a contract of service between employee and agency - Holidays (Employees) Act 1973.

The Companies Act 1963-1983 v Castlemahon Poultry Products Ltd
[1986] IR 750, [1987] ILRM 222 .... Vol III p 509

Social Welfare Acts - employer's contribution in respect of "reckonable earnings" of employees - when payable - liability of liquidator - preferential status under Companies Act 1963 s 285.

Rahinstown Estates Co v Hughes (Inspector of Taxes)
[1987] ILRM 599 .... Vol III p 517

Corporation tax - surcharge on undistributed income of close company - extension of period for making distribution of dividends - shorter period allowed for making distributions of share capital in a winding up - whether distinction absurd or unjust. CTA 1976 ss 84(1), 100 & 101.

Noyek & Sons Ltd (In Voluntary Liquidation) v Hearne (Inspector of Taxes)
[1988] IR 772 .... Vol III p 523

Voluntary liquidator - interest earned on deposit interest after date of liquidation - whether corporation tax on such interest is a charge within the meaning of Companies Act 1963 s 281 - whether liability of voluntary liquidator is different to that of court liquidator.

Orr (Kilternan) Ltd v The Companies Act 1963-1983, and
Thornberry Construction (Irl) Ltd v The Companies Act 1963-1983
[1986] IR 273 .... Vol III p 530

Liquidation - High Court fees on funds realised by liquidator in course of liquidation - whether applicable to monies payable to secured creditors or to proceeds of sale of property subject to a fixed charge - Supreme Court and High Court (Fees) Order 1984 (SI 19/1984 as amended by SI 36/1985).

Deighan v Hearne (Inspector of Taxes), Fitzgerald, Murphy, Ireland, The Attorney General and The Minister for Finance
[1986] IR 603, [1990] IR 499 .... Vol III p 533

Income Tax Acts - constitutionality -estimated assessments - incorrect description of taxpayer - material enactments and statutory instruments not available - invalid seizure of goods - exercise of judicial function - Courts bypassed - personal rights of citizen violated - constitutional right to have recourse to High Court denied - ITA 1967 as amended.

Masser Ltd (In Receivership) and Others v The Revenue Commissioners
[Not previously reported] .... Vol III p 548

Charge on book debts by deed of mortgage - whether a fixed or floating charge - essential distinction - when is charge effected - test is whether unrestricted use of property is permitted - conflict in terms of deed - determining restriction in prevention of charging, assigning or otherwise disposing of book debts and other debts.

Wayte (Holdings) Ltd (In Receivership) v Hearne (Inspector of Taxes)
[1986] IR 448 .... Vol III p 553

Liability of receiver appointed by a debenture holder to corporation tax provisions of CTA 1976 - company is chargeable and tax assessed on company - whether provisions of ITA 1967 are adopted into corporation tax code - role of company secretary - adoption heavily qualified - whether permissible to adopt paying provision while ignoring charging provisions.

Murphy (Inspector of Taxes) v The Borden Co Ltd
[Not previously reported] .... Vol III p 559

Case stated - whether a dividend declared on 11 December 1980 was received by related company not later than 12 December 1980 - whether payment of cheque required - whether payment through inter-company account was sufficient evidence of actual payment - whether making of journal entries after 23 December 1980 material evidence - whether making of accounting entry a mere record of underlying transaction.

Cronin (Inspector of Taxes) v C
[1968] IR 148 .... Vol III p 568

Income tax - Schedule D - Personal Pension and other assets assigned to company - pension continued to be paid to pensioner - whether pensioner ceased to receive pension as a source of income for himself beneficially - ITA 1918 Sch D Case III, rule of miscellaneous rules applicable to Schedule D and FA 1929 s 10.

Rowan, (Deceased) v Rowan and Others
[1988] ILRM 65 .... Vol III p 572

Domicile - Irish domicile of origin - tests for acquisition of domicile of choice - whether determined by Irish law - whether domicile of origin restored - whether intention without residence sufficient.

The State (Calcul International Ltd and Solatrex International Ltd) v The Appeal Commissioners and The Revenue Commissioners
[Not previously reported] .... Vol III p 577

Corporation/income/value added tax - concurrent determination of tax liability by High Court and Appeal Commissioners - whether mutually exclusive - conditional order of prohibition against Appeal Commissioners - application to make order absolute - tax code only permissible procedure - Appeal Commissioners powers and functions unconstitutional - nature of powers - limited or unlimited - ITA 1967 Pt XXVI and s 488. Articles 34 and 37 of the constitution.

Kennedy v Hearne, The Attorney General and Others
[1987] IR 120, [1988] IR 481, [1988] ILRM 53, 531 .... Vol III p 590

PAYE regulations - whether procedures unfair and unconstitutional - whether Revenue Commissioners involved in administration of justice - enforcement order issue to city sheriff after payment of tax - whether defamatory of plaintiff - question of damages.

Irish Agricultural Machinery Ltd v O'Culachain (Inspector of Taxes)
[1987] IR 458, [1990] IR 535 .... Vol III p 611

Stock relief under FA 1975 s 31 - trade consisting of the manufacturing of goods or sale of machinery or plant to farmers - whether assembly of agricultural machinery constitutes manufacturing - raw materials manufactured goods - changes in appearance but assembly not understood as manufacturing by well informed laymen - whether sales operations constitute a trade under s 31 - sales must be direct to farmers.

Kerrane (Inspector of Taxes) v Hanlon (Ireland) Ltd
[1987] IR 259 .... Vol III p 633

Export sales relief - ambulances manufactured in the State and exported - payments in advance lodged in deposit account - income not "immediately derived" from a trade of business - income received on foot of an obligation with bank - CTA 1976 ss 58 and 59.

Director of Public Prosecutions v Downes
[1987] IR 139, [1987] ILRM 665 .... Vol III p 641

Prosecution for payment of a Revenue penalty - whether criminal or civil proceedings applicable - no indicia of a criminal offence - ITA 1967 ss 17, 127, 128 & 500.

Browne (Inspector of Taxes) v Bank of Ireland Finance Ltd
[1987] IR 346, [1991] 1 IR 431 .... Vol III p 644

Business of banking - government stocks purchased to comply with Central Bank requirements - whether carrying on trade of dealing in securities - whether liable as profits under Schedule D or exempt capital gains on Government stocks - tests to be applied in a case stated by High Court - whether true and only reasonable conclusion to be drawn - Corporation Tax Act.

Patrick Monahan (Drogheda) Ltd v O'Connell (Inspector of Taxes)
[Not previously reported] .... Vol III p 661

Capital allowances - industrial building or structure for the purposes of a dock undertaking - whether bonded transit sheds qualify - nature of business -sheds used as clearing house and not for storage - meaning of undertaking - ancillary to business of dock undertaking - ITA 1967 s 255.

Pandion Haliaetus Ltd, Ospreycare Ltd, Osprey Systems Design Ltd v The Revenue Commissioners
[1987] IR 309, [1988] ILRM 419 .... Vol III p 670

Corporation income tax - hot car wash invention - whether income from patent rights disregarded for income tax purposes - where payable to a non-resident - effect of interpretation of FA 1973 s 34 as given by Revenue Commissioners - whether particular scheme disclosed - whether interpretation binding on Inspector of Taxes - tax avoidance scheme within Furniss v Dawson *principle - declaration by way of application for judicial review.*

The Diners Club Ltd v The Revenue Commissioners and The Minister for Finance
[1988] IR 158 .... Vol III p 680

Value added tax - interpretation of statutory instrument - charge card scheme - method of conducting business - purpose of a charge or credit cards - to facilitate sales by retailer to a purchaser - retailer paid by credit card or charge card company - described in statutory instrument as reimbursement - accepted as meaning paid for - whether debt due to retailer purchased - whether part of overall agreement between credit card company, retailer and purchaser - whether an individual transaction to be looked at in isolation.

McGrath and Others v McDermott (Inspector of Taxes)
[1988] IR 258, [1988] ILRM 181, 647 .... Vol III p 683

Capital gains tax - tax avoidance scheme - scheme technically valid - allowable loss - s 33 of Act plain and unambiguous meaning - whether provision to be disregarded unless a real loss - no equity in taxation - separation of powers - functions of courts and legislature - Superior Courts alone review court decisions - no general anti-avoidance legislation.

Kill Inn Motel Ltd (In Liquidation) v The Companies Acts 1963-1983
[Not previously reported] .... Vol III p 706

Disposal of assets at an undervalue by a company - granting of a preferential mortgage - creditors prejudiced - application by liquidator - gifts made by a company - Fraudulent Conveyances Act 1634 (10 Charles 1).

O'Coindealbhain (Inspector of Taxes) v Price
[1988] IR 14 .... Vol IV p 1

Capital gain on sale of lands - absent landowner - proceeds of sale reinvested in acquisition of further lands - absent owner returns to take on active farming - whether rollover relief on transfer of a trade applies - FA 1974 ss 13, 15, 17 & 21, FA 1975 s 12 and CGTA 1975 s 28.

Murphy (Inspector of Taxes) v Dataproducts (Dublin) Ltd
[1988] IR 10 .... Vol IV p 12

Non resident company - carries on a manufacturing business through a branch in the State - tax free profits from Irish branch paid into a Swiss bank account - whether interest earned on Swiss bank account is chargeable to corporation tax on the Irish branch.

McNally v O'Maoldhomhniagh
[Not previously reported] .... Vol IV p 22

Income tax - capital allowance - plant and machinery used in a designated area - whether used exclusively in designated area - whether allowance extends to plant and machinery used under a hire contract - FA 1971 s 22.

O'Culachain (Inspector of Taxes) v Hunter Advertising Ltd
[Not previously reported] .... Vol IV p 35

Corporation tax - manufacturing relief - advertising company - production for sale of advertising materials such as TV videos - word manufacture not defined - creative concept formed into a film - printing and processing in UK - tangible physical product -whether manufacturing process applied by respondent - nature and complexity of process - view of ordinary man - test of change brought about by process - characteristics and value - chemical reaction - matter of degree - purpose of legislation - promotion of manufacturing industry.

O'Coindealbhain (Inspector of Taxes) v Mooney
[1990] IR 422 .... Vol IV p 45

Income tax - a contract of employment - whether a contract of service or a contract for services - branch manager of local employment office of Dept of Social Welfare - income tax assessed on PAYE basis - whether respondent a self employed independent contractor - whether Court should look beyond terms of written contract - tests to be applied, essential conditions of a contract of service.

Mooney v O'Coindealbhain and The Revenue Commissioners
[Not previously reported] .... Vol IV p 62

Income tax - whether interest recoverable on foot of overpaid income tax - whether basis of assessment under Schedule E or Schedule D - whether branch manager of employment exchange to be taxed as an employee or as a self employed person - whether interest recoverable under FA 1976 s 30 - whether appeal to nil assessments to tax rules out interest on overpayments on tax - whether appeal of assessments under wrong Schedule rules out interest on overpayments of tax - whether implied agreement applies between the parties in regard to years of assessment not appealed.

Dunnes Stores (Oakville) Ltd v Cronin (Inspector of Taxes)
[Not previously reported] .... Vol IV p 68

Capital allowance against corporation tax - plant - expenditure on installation of suspended ceiling in supermarket - whether suspended ceiling constitutes plant - nature of trade - functional test - question of degree - goods distinguished from services.

The Racing Board v O'Culachain
[Not previously reported] .... Vol IV p 73

Levies on course betting by bookmakers - whether an activity analogous to a trade - whether income taxable as profits - scheme of Act - development of horse breeding and racing, statutory body whether to Racing Board and Racecourse - Act 1945 ss 4, 15, 27(1) - ITA 1967 s 537.

The Companies Act 1963-1983 v M F N Construction Co Ltd (In Liquidation) on the application of Patrick Tuffy (Liquidator)
[Not previously reported] .... Vol IV p 82

PAYE/PRSI - company insolvent - Bank of Ireland a secured creditor and revenue debts due to collector general - winding up deferred by reason of scheme of arrangement approved by High Court - collector general agreed to deferral of revenue debt pending completion of contracts by company - unsecured creditors promised 40p in £1 and voted to accept scheme - a third party paid off the unsecured creditors by way of subrogation agreements - whether third party bound by terms of scheme of arrangement.

Cusack v O'Reilly and The Collector General
[Not previously reported] .... Vol IV p 86

This interpleader summons arose out of the seizure by the applicant in his role as Revenue sheriff of goods and chattels claimed to be the property of the claimant in the action. The sheriff on being challenged, issued the interpleader summons to have his claim determined by the court whether or not the chattels in question are:

Texaco Ireland Ltd v Murphy (Inspector of Taxes)
[1989] IR 496, [1991] 2 IR 449 .... Vol IV p 91

Corporation tax -whether petroleum exploration constitutes scientific research - whether such scientific research qualifies for tax relief by way of an allowance under ITA 1967 s 244 - whether proximate sections are relevant to the interpretation of the particular section - whether Act as a whole should be construed - whether proviso to s 244(3) applies - the principles of construction of taxing statutes - whether there is any equity about taxation, whether in imposition, exemption or manner of application - whether capital expenditure herein comes within the application of the proviso - whether the claim for relief comes within the express wording of the proviso.

United Bars Ltd (In Receivership), Walkinstown Inn Ltd (In Receivership) and Jackson v The Revenue Commissioners
[1991] IR 396 .... Vol IV p 107

Company - debentures creating fixed and floating charges - receiver appointed by debenture holder - fixed charges paid off leaving surplus - preferential creditors - priority -

whether surplus to be paid to preferential creditors or to company - Companies Act 1963 (No 33) s 98.

Hearne (Inspector of Taxes) v O'Cionna and Others T/A J A Kenny & Partners
[Not previously reported] .... Vol IV p 113

Employer's liability to deduct PAYE and PRSI from employee's emoluments - deductions to be paid to the collector general - loan arrangement between partnership and limited company - whether partnership liable for PAYE and PRSI of employees of company - special meaning of word employer under Income Tax Acts - no similar meaning under social welfare legislation - whether employer's liability different in respect of PRSI.

Bourke (Inspector of Taxes) v Bradley & Sons
[1990] IR 379 .... Vol IV p 117

Value added tax - service supplied by solicitor on instructions of Insurance underwriter - in relation to insured litigant - whether supplied to underwriter or to the defendant - services to a non-resident in the State but resident within EEC - no establishment in the state - where services are deemed to be supplied.

McMahon (Inspector of Taxes) v Murphy
[Not previously reported] .... Vol IV p 125

Capital gains tax - market value on 6 April 1974 of holding of 73 acres of land - agricultural land situate outside town of Macroom - appeal on value of land as determined in Circuit Court - whether subsequent planning permission for milk processing plant relevant - whether development potential attached to the lands on 6 April 1974 - whether agricultural value the sole determining factor.

Carroll Industries Plc v S O'Culachain (Inspector of Taxes)
[1988] IR 705 .... Vol IV p 135

Appellant company's accounts, based on current cost accounting convention (ie replacement cost) - whether acceptable for tax purposes as a basis for accountancy - whether historical cost accounting convention is the only method of commercial accountancy for tax purposes - Whimster *decision and its two "fundamental commonplaces" - true profits for tax purposes based on difference between receipts and expenditure laid out to earn those receipts and the accounts framed consistently with ordinary principles of commercial accounting - profits and gains for tax purposes not defined in Tax Acts - no particular basis of accountancy stipulated by statute - appropriate accounting method may not give "true profits" - whether provision for inflation applicable - stock relief allowed by Finance Acts - different methods of costing stock - basic premise that profits is the difference between receipts and expenditure laid out to earn those receipts.*

McDaid v Sheehy, The Director of Public Prosecutions and Others
[1991] IR 1 .... Vol IV p 162

Whether applicant validly convicted of an offence and fined for keeping in the fuel tank of his motor vehicle hydrocarbon oil on which custom or excise duty had not been paid - whether Imposition of Duties Act 1957 Constitutional - whether order empowering the government to impose, terminate or vary duties invalid - where delegation of powers is permissible - whether test of coming within principles and policies of Act applies - whether subsequent statutory provision validates order - whether reasonable interpretation to be applied.

Wiley v The Revenue Commissioners
[1989] IR 351 .... Vol IV p 170

Excise duty - what persons may be authorised by order of the Minister for Finance to import goods such as motor vehicles free of excise duties - to what extent must such persons be suffering from disability - whether such persons must be wholly without the use of each of his legs - doctrine of legitimate expectation - whether refunds of excise duty on two previous occasions constitutes a practice - whether expectation is a legitimate one - whether a regular practice can be discontinued or altered without notice.

Waterford Glass (Group Services) Ltd v The Revenue Commissioners
[1990] IR 334 .... Vol IV p 187

Stamp duty - agreement for sale granting immediate possession on payment of deposit followed by agreement for sale of residual interest - whether the transfer of the residual interest stampable on the value of the residual interest or on the value of the entire property - what constitutes a conveyance for sale under Stamp Act of 1891 - whether courts will look at legal effect and legal rights of a transaction - whether FA 1986 s 96(1) applies - whether a contract for sale of legal estate is a contract for sale of property - whether contract conferred a benefit within the meaning of F(1909-10)A 1910 s 74(5).

The Hammond Lane Metal Co Ltd v O'Culachain (Inspector of Taxes)
[1990] IR 560

Corporation tax - whether an agreement between the taxpayer and the inspector of taxes in relation to an assessment of tax under appeal is binding and conclusive - whether full disclosure - whether "discovery" applies - whether unappealed assessment and compromised appeal are subject to the same interpretation - whether discovery constitutes unfair procedure - whether tax avoidance scheme under ITA 1967 Ch VI tax effective - whether premium under lease allowable under ITA 1967 s 91 - whether election under s 83(6) alters lessee's entitlement to deduction for entire premium - whether lessee to be treated as paying an amount according to a formula - whether s 83 is dealing with actualities - whether general rules on deductions overruled.

Bank of Ireland Finance Ltd v The Revenue Commissioners
[Not previously reported] .... Vol IV p 217

Disposal of property by mortgagee - disposal as nominee for mortgagor - whether payment of capital gains tax by purchaser was in accordance with CGTA 1975 - whether absence of a clearance certificate entitled Revenue Commissioners to return the payment - whether mortgagee entitled to a refund of tax paid.

O'Coindealbhain (Inspector of Taxes) v O'Carroll
[1989] IR 229 .... Vol IV p 221

Garda Siochana Pensions Order 1981 - widows contributory pension and children'' contributory pensions granted - whether children's pension income of the widow or income of the children for income tax purposes - widow's pension payable to the widow whereas children's pension payable to widow for children - children's pension not mandatory when widow's pension not payable - rate of tax related to tax status of payee - whether children's pension the beneficial property of children in all circumstances.

Purcell v Attorney General
[Not previously reported] .... Vol IV p 229

Whether implementation of Farm Tax Act constituted unfair procedures - effect of repeal in budget statement in March 1987 - consequences of absence of amending legislation - locus standi of applicant - legislation based on will of Oireachtas - if legislation interfered unlawfully then what remains cannot be enforceable in the future or past.

O Cahill (Inspector of Taxes) v Harding and Others
[Not previously reported] .... Vol IV p 233

Income tax - whether lump sum payments to disabled employees exempt from income tax - closure of assembly works made most of work force redundant - compensation package agreed but no distinction between disabled and other employees - whether disabled employees whose jobs were lost because of redundancy were entitled to claim relief from income tax - whether a distinction to be made between disabled employees whose jobs continued and disabled employees whose jobs ceased.

Frederick Inns Ltd, The Rendezvous Ltd, The Graduate Ltd, Motels Ltd (In Liquidation) v The Companies Acts 1963-1983
[Not previously reported] .... Vol IV p 247

Recovery of outstanding taxes from a group of companies - whether Revenue Commissioners may appropriate payments between separate companies within the group - company law in regard to gratuitous alienation of assets by a company - whether insolvency of a company is relevant to gratuitous alienation of assets - whether Revenue disregarded rights of creditors of individual companies within the group.

O'Grady v Laragan Quarries Ltd
[1991] 1 IR 237 .... Vol IV p 269

Whether lorry owners carrying sand and gravel were engaged in the haulage for hire of materials within the meaning of FA 1970 s 17 - whether the payments to the lorry owners were for subcontracting under a construction contract - whether the lorry owners became the proprietors of the quarry materials - whether any ambiguity attached to the agreements - whether parties are free to enter into form of contract which is tax effective.

Murphy v District Justice Brendan Wallace and Others
[Not previously reported] .... Vol IV p 278

Excise duty - bookmaker convicted and fined in the District Court of offences under the Betting Acts - arising out of non-payment of fines distress warrants issued to Garda Superintendent to distrain against defaulter's goods - return of no goods - penal warrants for imprisonment of defaulter sought by Revenue Authorities under provisions of Excise Management Act 1827 s 90 (as amended) - discretion to Revenue under s 90 to release or retain defaulter in prison for six months - whether such power constitutional and whether s 90 invalid.

O'Culachain v McMullan Brothers
[1991] 1 IR 363 .... Vol IV p 284

Whether forecourt canopies at petrol filling stations constitute plant for tax purposes - competition between petrol companies has led to major changes in the design and facilities at petrol stations - whether a canopy is essential to provide advertising, brand image and attractive setting - whether canopies provide no more than shelter from rain and wind or play a part in carrying on the trade of selling petrol - market research has proven the sales effectiveness of canopies - principles upon which the court approaches a case stated in relation to findings of primary fact, conclusions or inferences and interpretation of the law - test to be applied in deciding whether disputed object is apparatus or not - whether canopy creates an ambience and has a function in the carrying on of the business.

Irish Nationwide Building Society v The Revenue Commissioners
[Not previously reported] .... Vol IV p 296

Whether a conveyance to a building society was exempt from stamp duty by virtue of the Building Societies Act of 1976 - certain categories of instruments relating to the internal affairs of a society were specifically exempted by the Act of 1976 - whether the general provision of the exempting provision contained in s 91 of the Act extended to a conveyance or transfer of a premises to a society for the purpose of conducting its business - ejusdem generis rule - intention of legislature - whether the internal affairs of a society are distinguishable from its commercial dealings.

Murnaghan Brothers Ltd v O'Maoldhomhnaigh
[1991] 1 IR 455 .... Vol IV p 304

Whether lands the subject matter of a contract for sale entered into during an accounting period constitute trading stock for the year ending in that accounting period - trading stock and trade as defined in the Finance Acts - appellant company carrying on trade of building contractors - whether absence of possession, conveyance of legal estate and planning permission fatal to taxpayer's claim for relief - whether inclusion of the lands in the accounts by accountant in accordance with good accounting procedure was the best evidence of the commercial reality of the transaction.

Phonographic Performance (Ireland) Ltd v Somers (Inspector of Taxes)
[1992] ILRM 657 .... Vol IV p 314

Value added tax - whether corporate body exploiting copyrights supplying service within meaning of the Value Added Tax Act - Copyright Act 1963 (No 10), ss 7(1), 7(3) & 17(4) - VATA 1972 (No 22) ss 2(1), 5.

Browne and Others v The Revenue Commissioners and Others
[1991] 2 IR 58 .... Vol IV p 323

Sales representative - motor car "a tool of his trade" - whether in position of tax on benefit accruing from private use of employer's motor car is constitutional - whether legislation impinges on individuals' right to earn a livelihood - whether an unjust attack on property rights in breach of Article 40 of the Constitution - whether legislation impinges on individuals' rights to be held equal before the law - whether any constitutional right infringed - whether tax limited to availability of car for private use - whether tax avoidable

- Constitution of Ireland Art 40 - ITA 1967 ss 117, 118, 119, 120 - FA 1958 ss 23, 24, 25, 26 - FA 1982 s 4.

Quigley (Inspector of Taxes) v Burke
[1991] 2 IR 169 .... Vol IV p 332

Whether the inspector of taxes is entitled to call for production of a taxpayer's nominal ledger - whether the inspector required the nominal ledger to satisfy himself on the adjustments made in the accounts and the reasons for such adjustments made in the accounts - whether the accountant was acting as agent to the taxpayer or as a professional person and client - whether the nominal ledger formed part of the accountant's working papers - whether the nominal ledger was "within the power or possession" of the taxpayer - whether a reasonable person could be satisfied on the income tax computation in the absence of the nominal ledger.

Crowe Engineering Ltd v Lynch and Others
In the Matter of The Trustee Act 1893 s 36
[Not previously reported] .... Vol IV p 340

Superannuation scheme - whether trustees have absolute discretion on the distribution of the fund following the death of a member - whether trustees are bound by a direction in the member's will - whether a separated wife, a common law wife and children are entitled as defendants or relatives to be considered as beneficiaries - whether renunciation under a separation deed rules out entitlement under the superannuation scheme - whether discretion of trustees is absolute - whether court can be called on for guidance.

Forde Decision by Appeal Commissioners
[Not previously reported] .... Vol IV p 348

This appeal was brought by Michael Forde against the refusal of the inspector of taxes to grant him exemption under FA 1969 s 2 in respect of the books written by him on the Constitutional law in Ireland, Company law in Ireland and Extradition law in Ireland. Section 2 grants an exemption from income tax in respect of original and creative works which are generally recognised as having cultural or artistic merit. Subsection 5(b) provides a right of appeal as if it were a right of appeal against an assessment subject to all the appeal provisions of ITA 1967.

Brosnan (Inspector of Taxes) v Cork Communications Ltd
[Not previously reported] .... Vol IV p 349

Cork Communications Ltd providing a cable television system - whether company supplying electricity - whether company transmitting TV and radio signals - whether liable to vat on sales to customers - whether company's system consists of immovable goods and exempt from value added tax.

O'Leary v The Revenue Commissioners
[Not previously reported] .... Vol IV p 357

This application for judicial review was made on the grounds that the interest and penalty provisions for stamp duties which were introduced by FA 1991 s 100 did not take effect until 1 November 1991 and that the previous provision for interest and penalties under Stamp Act 1891 s 15 was repealed on 29 May 1991, the date of the passing of FA 1991.

O'Laochdha (Inspector of Taxes) v Johnson & Johnson (Ireland) Ltd
[1991] 2 IR 287 .... Vol IV p 361

Corporation tax - case stated as to whether the production of J Cloths and nappy liners from bales of fabric is a manufacturing process - whether manufacturing relief under FA 1980 s 42 applies - whether use of a sophisticated and expensive machine constitutes manufacturing - whether absence of change in raw material is relevant - whether product is a commercially different product - what is manufacturing - whether appearance, utility, qualities and value are the characteristics of manufacturing - whether question is one of degree - whether use of expensive and sophisticated machinery is relevant - how product is perceived by an ordinary adequately informed person - whether quality of and product is commercially enhanced by process.

VIEK Investments Ltd v The Revenue Commissioners
[1991] 2 IR 520 .... Vol IV p 367

Stamp duty - proper amount of stamp duty chargeable on a deed of transfer - contracts and consideration structured to minimise stamp duty - substance of transactions - Stamp Act 1891 s 13.

The Minister for Social Welfare v Griffiths
[Not previously reported] .... Vol IV p 378

Whether a member of the crew of a fishing vessel can be an "employee" - whether Social Welfare (Consolidation) Act 1981 applies to self employed persons - whether Act is limited in its application to the traditional relationship of employer/employee - whether there can be an "employee" without there being a corresponding employer - whether scheme of Act and regulations is limited to employer/employee circumstances - whether Minister has unlimited power to make regulations enabling any person to be treated as an employee.

McCrystal Oil Co Ltd v The Revenue Commissioners and Others
[Not previously reported] .... Vol IV p 386

Customs duties - action for damages for retinue and conversion arising out of the seizure by the Revenue Commissioners of an oil tanker - marked gas oil found in one of the tanker's compartments - outlet from the compartment not indelibly marked as required by statutory regulations - tanker seized and gas oil sold - whether there was a breach of the statutory regulation - what constitutes a conveyance under the legislation - whether outlet distinguished from container - whether defendants' case confined to breach in respect of the outlet - whether regulations must be construed strictly - whether court restricted to consideration of the breach of the regulations as pleaded - issue of damages.

Louth & Others v Minister for Social Welfare
[Not previously reported] .... Vol IV p 391

Appeal on a point of law under the social welfare code - whether deepsea dockers working under a pooling arrangement have a right to sign on for social welfare benefit as being unemployed when they are not occupied in unloading ships - whether dockers had a contract of employment with their association - whether level of earnings material to question of employment - whether a contract of service or a contract for services - whether separate contracts with dockers on each occasion of their employment.

The Director of Public Prosecutions v Boyle
[Not previously reported] .... Vol IV p 395

Excise duty - case stated - complaints of non-payment of excise duty payable on bets entered into by the defendant as a registered bookmaker - whether recovery of an excise penalty a criminal matter - whether use of words guilty of an offence and summary conviction indicate a criminal matter - whether amount of penalty is relevant - what is a crime - whether a crime can be defined - whether the act is prohibited with legal consequences - what are the indicia of a crime - whether any words of prohibition - whether option of making a payment as alternative to compliance - whether words such as fine, offence, summary conviction disigrate a criminal offence.

The Revenue Commissioners v Arida Ltd
[Not previously reported] .... Vol IV p 401

Income tax - case stated by Circuit Court Judge pursuant to ITA 1967 ss 428 and 430 - whether or not a Circuit Court Judge hearing an appeal pursuant to ITA 1967 s 429 has jurisdiction to award costs -whether a tax appeal constitutes proceedings under the Circuit Court rules - whether the Circuit Court Judge's jurisdiction is limited to the powers and duties of the Appeal Commissioners - whether the principle "expressio unius exclusio alterius" applies - whether s 428(b) granting power to High Court to award costs is superfluous - whether exception to Circuit Court rule expressly or impliedly stated - extensive jurisdiction of Circuit Court - normal practice on costs.

O'Siochain (Inspector of Taxes) v Morrissey
[Not previously reported] .... Vol IV p 407

Eleanor Morrissey commenced employment with the Bank of Ireland 27 March 1972 - she married respondent 14 May 1977 and resigned employment 10 May 1985 - whether "marriage gratuity" received on resignation was a retirement payment under ITA 1967 s 114 or was a perquisite of her office under ITA 1967 s 110 - whether a conflict between agreement of March 1974 with bank officials and bank superannuation scheme - whether real issue of liability under s 100 considered by Circuit Court Judge.

In the matter of Stamp (Deceased) v Noel Redmond and Others
[Not previously reported] .... Vol IV p 415

Succession - construction of will - whether "issue" included adopted children - whether Adoption Acts changed scope and meaning of family to include adopted as well as legitimate children - whether court bound by words used in will - intention of testator - whether issue restricted to children of marriage - Adoption Act 1952 ss 4, 26(2).

Connolly v The Collector of Customs and Excise
[Not previously reported] .... Vol IV p 419

Excise duty - judicial review - publican's licence - whether new licence obtainable - whether application within six year period - meaning of year immediately preceding.

O'Grady (Inspector of Taxes) v Roscommon Race Committee
[Not previously reported] .... Vol IV p 425

Expenditure on racecourse stand - whether deductible repairs or non deductible capital expenditure or expenditure qualifying as plant - trade of promoting and organising horse races - long established stand used for viewing races - what is function of stand - provides shelter and creates atmosphere of excitement - categories of work carried out - whether works on retained part of stand constitutes repairs - whether new bar and extension to old bar non-deductible capital improvements - whether stand or racecourse is the entirety - whether expenditure on roof a repair - whether word done to walls a repair - whether re-design or lower terracing an improvement - whether stand as renewed and repaired is plant - agreed test - whether stand is part of the means by which trade is carried on or merely part of the place where at which trade is carried on.

JW v JW
[Not previously reported] .... Vol IV p 437

Domicile - constitutional rights - whether common law rule of dependent domicile of a wife constitutional - recognition of foreign divorces - wife's separate domicile.

McGurrin (Inspector of Taxes) v The Champion Publications Ltd
[Not previously reported] .... Vol IV p 466

Respondent is a newspaper publisher - newspapers are "goods" for the purpose of manufacturing relief from corporation tax - whether income from advertising qualifies for such relief - whether indirect income from advertising can be treated equally with direct income from newsagents - whether advertising income is receivable in respect of the sale in the course of the trade of goods - whether advertising income is from a separate trade or providing a service - whether the matter to be considered from aspect of commercial reality - whether proper construction of words of s 41 brought advertisements within definition of goods - whether advertising revenue is received in respect of the sale of newspapers.

Bairead v McDonald
[Not previously reported] .... Vol IV p 475

Appeal against judgment for income tax and interest - what constitutes a proper return of income for the assessment of income tax - whether a return of income equalling income tax exemption limits a valid return - whether lack of records justifies such a return - whether taxpayer treated unfairly by the Revenue - whether practice of allowing late returns amounts to promissory estoppel - whether taxpayer has availed of opportunity to make later returns after assessments had become final - whether treated unfairly by the Revenue - whether adjournment be granted to allow taxpayer to make proper returns - whether counterclaim for damages for harassment untenable.

O'Callaghan v Clifford and Others
[Not previously reported] .... Vol IV p 478

Income tax - appeal against a decision of the High Court to refuse on a judicial review application to quash three convictions with six months imprisonment for each offence imposed in the District Court on the appellant for failure to make income tax returns - inspector of taxes empowered to require of an individual by notice a return of income - civil offence rendered a criminal offence by FA 1983 s 94(2) - whether a certificate by the inspector of non compliance is sufficient proof - whether in absence of accused in court the certificate contains the necessary mens rea - whether refusal in District Court to grant an adjournment denied the appellant the opportunity to defend himself - whether such refusal was unconstitutional - whether limits to District Judge's discretion to refuse an adjournment - whether extra degree of caution called for a criminal matter - whether appellant's right to instruct his counsel denied - whether audi alteram partem *rule and fair administration of justice applies - whether absence of due process on foot of certificate.*

Manning v Shackleton and Cork County Council
[Not previously reported] .... Vol IV p 485

Capital gains tax compulsory acquisition of land - whether property arbitrator obliged to give details of his findings of facts and law and a breakdown of his award - whether applicant is unable to formulate an appeal without being given the reasons for the award - whether breakdown required for capital gains tax purposes - whether award could be justified on the evidence - whether any obligation imposed on arbitrator by the Acquisition of Land (Assessment of Compensation) Act 1919 - whether the giving of reasons necessary for the proper exercise of a judicial or administrative function - whether failure by applicant at the hearing to request an apportionment of the award under the several heads of claim or to request a case stated rules out any further relief - whether failure to advance further arguments of unfairness amounted to acceptance of the normal practice - whether undertakings affected the amount of the arbitrator's award.

Carbery Milk Products Ltd v The Minister for Agriculture and Others
[Not previously reported] .... Vol IV p 492

Classification of milk products - EC regulations - milk protein powder - whether a whey or skimmed milk product - whether export refunds on consignments from EC countries to non EC countries - whether Revenue Commissioners responsible for classification - whether Revenue Commissioners and state chemist negligent and in breach of duty - whether re-classification renders products liable for repayment of export refunds - whether principle of legitimate expectation applies - whether Minister for Agriculture agent for European Commission - whether Minister entitled to counterclaim against plaintiff - whether plaintiff entitled to indemnity against Revenue Commissioners - EEC Regulations 804/68 and 2682/72.

Bairead v Carr
[Not previously reported] .... Vol IV p 505

Summary summonses served on the defendant in respect of tax liabilities the subject matter of earlier appeals - whether dissatisfaction expressed at the Circuit Court appeal hearings - whether dissatisfaction must be expressed immediately after determination by the Circuit Court Judge - whether notice to county registrar must be lodged within 21 days together with the £20 fee - whether requirements are directory or mandatory - whether tax must be paid before the case stated is determined - whether time lapse after expression of dissatisfaction is fatal - whether payment of tax denies access to the courts - whether Circuit Court judge has discretion to accept late filing of notice and fee.

Keller v The Revenue Commissioners and Others
[Not previously reported] .... Vol IV p 512

Importation of used motor vehicles from a Member State - interpretation of excise duties payable under SI 422/1983 - applicant a German citizen residing with his family in Ireland for upwards of twenty years - a collector of vintage Mercedes Benz motor cars - whether his normal residence in Germany - whether requirements for normal residence in Germany satisfied - whether importation for temporary purpose and for transport for private use - interpretation of the expression "a new motor vehicle of a similar or corresponding type" - whether regulations provide guidance on the retail price as may be determined by the Revenue Commissioners - whether regulations contrary to Article 95 of Treaty of Rome - whether excise duties fall more unfairly on imported used cars than on used cars sold on the Irish market - whether credit of German value added tax allowable - whether onus of proof discharged - whether value added tax charged on value added tax contrary to Sixth Council Directive - whether penalty of seizure and forfeiture disproportionate to offence - whether legitimate expectation infringed.

Kelly (Inspector of Taxes) v Cobb Straffan Ireland Ltd
[Not previously reported] .... Vol IV p 526

Case stated on question of manufacturing relief - respondent company carries on business of producing day old chicks - whether day old chicks are goods within the meaning of FA 1980 - whether use of extensive plant machinery and skilled workers constitute a process of manufacturing - whether goods are required to be inanimate - whether question is one of degree - whether raw material in process was not the egg but twenty years of research - whether process is similar to fish farming which required a specific statutory exemption - whether respondent was producing as opposed to manufacturing day old chicks - whether chick is a product that could not be produced by a natural process - whether process constitutes manufacturing.

Hussey (Inspector of Taxes) v Gleeson & Co Ltd
[Not previously reported] .... Vol IV p 533

Case stated on question of manufacturing relief - respondent company a wholesaler of beers and stouts as part of its trade conditions bottled Guinness stout - whether conditioning of bottled Guinness constitutes manufacturing process - chemical change in contents, carbon dioxide added and alcohol level increased - whether plant and equipment sufficiently sophisticated - whether process no more than keeping the stout in an even temperature for fourteen days - whether process of such a degree as to be classified as manufacturing.

Pine Valley Developments Ltd, Healy & Others v The Revenue Commissioners
[Not previously reported] .... Vol IV p 543

Award by European Court of Human Rights for pecuniary and non-pecuniary damages and costs lodged in High Court on foot of a claim by the plaintiffs - part of the award amounting to £273,000 held pending determination of the tax liabilities of the third plaintiff - conceded that £209,250 out of the £273,000 was in respect of income tax on interest accruing in the year 1993/94 - income tax liability would not arise prior to January 1995 - consequently £209,250 released on consent - balance of £63,750 relates to capital gains tax - third plaintiff is resident in the State and entitled to tax clearance certificate from capital gains tax - whether the sum of £63,750 should be withheld.

Dilleen (Inspector of Taxes) v Kearns
[Not previously reported] .... Vol IV p 547

Abandonment of an option within the meaning of CGTA 1975 s 47(3) - tax avoidance scheme - respondent and his wife grant each other options over their separate shareholdings in a private company - series of transactions through a chain of companies including the abandonment by the respondent and his wife of their respective options for sums totalling £2,532,500 - whether abandonment of options for a cash consideration constitutes an abandonment of the option or a chargeable disposal of assets - what is true meaning of term abandonment of an option - whether it means non-exercise - whether ordinary meaning applies - whether the entire and the substance of the transaction to be considered - whether tax avoidance exercise relevant - whether substantial payment for non-exercise can be said to be an abandonment within the meaning of the Act.

Allied Irish Banks plc v Bolger
[Not previously reported] .... Vol V p 1

Stamp duty - mortgage deeds - whether property stamped - whether admissible in evidence - whether admissible on foot of undertaking - whether possession of a premises can be obtained by way of special summons or summary procedure - whether ejectment proceedings required - whether procedure question raised in course of hearing

Airspace Investments Ltd v Moore (Inspector of Taxes)
[Not previously reported] .... Vol V p 3

Corporation tax - whether company carrying on a trade - whether capital expenditure - series of agreements - whether a tax avoidance scheme - whether agreements to be viewed as a composite transaction - whether loan repayable - whether transactions can be considered with the benefit of hindsight.

Brosnan (Inspector of Taxes) v Leeside Nurseries Ltd
[Not previously reported] .... Vol V p 21

Corporation tax - case stated - manufacturing relief - dwarfed potted chrysanthemum plants - whether McCann v O'Culachain properly decided - whether sophisticated process of cultivation constitutes manufacturing - whether a question of change in appearance, quality and value - whether a question of degree - whether "goods" capable of being manufactured - whether goods are inanimate - whether growing plants can be manufactured - whether manufactured or cultivated

In the Matter of Davoren, (Deceased); O'Byrne v Davoren and Coughlan
[Not previously reported] .... Vol V p 36

Trust - Discretionary - interpretation of residuary bequest - whether a valid charitable gift trust for education of children at discretion of trustees - class consisting of children, grandchildren and descendants of specified persons - meaning of the term "descendants" - whether capital of fund to be preserved - whether rule against perpetuities - whether bequest failed for uncertainty.

The Governor & Co of the Bank of Ireland v Meeneghan & Others
[Not previously reported] .... Vol V p 44

Value added tax - UK liability - UK court order restraining the taxpayer from disposing of his assets - whether bank account in Ireland subject to court order - whether foreign revenue debt recoverable in Ireland - whether effect of UK court order prevents the taxpayer from withdrawing the monies - whether principle of international law relating to revenue debts applies - whether value added tax subject to laws of European Union

Travers v O'Siochain (Inspector of Taxes)
[Not previously reported] .... Vol V p 54

Income tax - case stated - appellant's wife employed as a nurse by a Health Board in Northern Ireland - wife's remuneration taxed in Northern Ireland - whether appellant entitled to double taxation relief in Ireland - whether Article 18(2) of Double Taxation Relief (Taxes on Income and Capital Gains) [UK] Order 1976 grants relief.

WLD Worldwide Leather Diffusion Ltd v The Revenue Commissioners
[Not previously reported] .... Vol V p 61

Value added tax - judicial review - non resident company registered in the State - single trading transaction - whether entitled to be registered for value added tax - whether Revenue Commissioners have discretion to refuse registration - whether applicant a taxable person - fiscal advantage - whether application bona fide - whether transaction a trading transaction.

Orange v The Revenue Commissioners
[Not previously reported] .... Vol V p 70

Judicial Review application - applicant dependent upon criminal legal aid work - all legal aid fees due by Minister for Justice attached by respondents pursuant to FA 1988 s 73 whether procedure constitutional - whether court order required -whether constitutional right to earn a livelihood infringed - whether an unfair attack on applicant' s property rights - whether attachment of value added tax element of legal aid fees unconstitutional applicant offered reasonable terms of payment by respondents - whether attack on property rights to be viewed in the light of surrounding circumstances - whether legislation requires amendment.

Erin Executor and Trustee Co Ltd v The Revenue Commissioners
[Not previously reported] .... Vol V p 76

Value added tax - properties leased for ten or more years - VAT incurred on expenditure on leasehold properties - whether credits for VAT allowable - whether reversionary interest outside VAT net.

McAuliffe v The Minister for Social Welfare
[Not previously reported] .... Vol V p 94

Social welfare appeal - appeal as to whether a contract of services or a contract for services - wholesale distributor of newspapers - deliveries of newspapers subcontracted to two individuals - individuals own delivery vehicles and pay all overheads - provide relief drivers - accept liability for losses or delays - time and reliability essence of contracts - whether contracts contain distinctive features of contracts for services - whether differences with contracts of service.

The Revenue Commissioners v O'Loinsigh
[Not previously reported] .... Vol V p 98

Income tax - case stated - series of books known as "Pathways to History" whether original and creative - whether within the meaning of FA 1969 s 2

McCabe (Inspector of Taxes) v South City & County Investment Co Ltd
[Not previously reported] .... Vol V p 107

Corporation Tax - whether periodic payments subject to Corporation Tax - annuity contract - annual payments off £500 plus share of profits in return for capital sum - whether correctly described as annuities - whether income receipts - whether return of capital - whether case law overturns logic of transactions - interpretation of tax statutes and documents - whether content of agreement conforms with its purpose
Additional judgment 1998 p 183

Fennessy (Inspector of Taxes) v McConnellogue
[Not previously reported] .... Vol V p 129

Income tax - respondent resides with his wife in Northern Ireland - respondent employed in Co Donegal and chargeable to Irish tax in his salary - respondent's wife employed in Northern Ireland and because of her residence there her salary not chargeable to Irish tax - whether respondent entitled to a full married allowance and double rate income tax bands - whether allowances restricted to a single person's allowance and single rate bands.

O'Shea (Inspector of Taxes) v Mulqueen
[Not previously reported] .... Vol V p 134

Income tax - lump sum payment on retirement - whether liable to income tax - whether received on account of illness - whether a redundancy payment - whether payment made on grounds of retirement - whether payment made on grounds of ill health.

Brosnan (Inspector of Taxes) v Mutual Enterprises Ltd
[Not previously reported] .... Vol V p 138

Case Stated - Corporation Tax - purchase of trading premises financed by foreign borrowings - losses incurred annually by reason of fluctuations in currency rates - whether allowable against trading profits - whether losses a revenue or capital item - whether a means of fluctuating and temporary accommodation - whether conflicting views of UK courts to be distinguished - whether monies borrowed to be used for purchase of a capital asset - whether monies so used - whether repayable on demand - whether a question of fact or law - whether grounds for setting aside findings of primary facts.

Mooney (Inspector Of Taxes) v McSweeney
[Not previously reported] .... Vol V p 163

Capital Gains Tax - loan to company - loan agreement with right to convert loan into shares - whether a mere debt - whether a debt on a security - whether an allowable loss for Capital Gains Tax purposes - whether characteristics of a debt on a security exist - whether synonymous with secured debt - whether marketable - whether loan had potential to be released at a profit - whether difficulty in finding a purchaser relevant - whether right to repayment and right to convert can co-exist -whether right to convert distinguishing factor - whether proviso to s 46 of Capital Tax Act 1975 applies.

In re Cherry Court v The Revenue Commissioners
[Not previously reported] .... Vol V p 180

Stamp duty - deed of release - whether or not a sale - whether liable to ad valorem stamp duty - series of transactions - whether release of option constituted a sale - meaning of sale - reality of transaction - whether phrases used imply a transfer of property.

In re Private Motorists Provident Society Ltd (In Liquidation) and Horgan v Minister for Justice
[Not previously reported] .... Vol V p 186

Court fees payable by official liquidator - court liquidation fees prescribed by statutory instrument - whether monies received in realisation of assets of a company - meaning of assets - meaning of realisation - whether assets can be realised more than once - whether accrual of interest a realisation - whether assets vested in liquidator - whether monies received from associated companies in liquidation constitute a realisation - whether interpretation of realisations a matter of debate.

In re Hibernian Transport Companies Ltd
[Not previously reported] .... Vol V p 194

Court liquidation - fees payable by official liquidator - fees prescribed by statutory instrument - monies received in realisation of assets of a company - interest earned from monies on deposit - capital gains from disposals of exchequer bills - whether a realisation - whether an investment - rate of court duty - yearly accounts - whether rate in force for accounting period applicable - whether rate at date of certification applies.

O'Culachain (Inspector of Taxes) v McMullan Brothers Ltd
[Not previously reported] .... Vol V p 200

Corporation tax - principles to be applied in a case stated - whether canopies in forecourts of petrol filling stations constitute plant - whether part of the premises - whether part of setting in which business carried on - whether function is to provide shelter and light - whether function is to attract customers - whether view of law correct - whether correct tests applied - whether "setting" and "plant" mutually exclusive - whether conclusion is one which a reasonable judge could not have arrived at.

Irwin v Grimes
[Not previously reported] .... Vol V p 209

Income tax - summary summons issued on 4 October 1989 - whether certificates under Waiver of Certain Tax, Interest and Penalties Act 1993 apply - whether proceedings initiated prior to 1993 Act - whether defendant non resident in the State up to 1992 - whether defendant liable for any taxes.

Daly v The Revenue Commissioners & Ors
[Not previously reported] .... Vol V p 213

Income tax - judicial review - fees paid by Health Board - applicant a medical doctor - payments subject to withholding tax - scheme of withholding tax amended by FA 1990 - self employed taxed on profits and gains of actual year of assessment - windfall gain to established taxpayers - amendment to eliminate gain - effect on new entrants to system -

effect of interim refunds - financial hardship - property rights infringed - proportionality test - whether unconstitutional.

Revenue Commissioners v Arida Ltd
[Not previously reported] .... Vol V p 221

Circuit Court rehearing of tax appeal - whether Circuit Court judge has jurisdiction to award costs - whether a tax appeal constitutes "proceedings" - whether statutory authority required - whether court has inherent jurisdiction to award costs - whether award of costs ultra vires the rules of the Circuit Court - whether jurisdiction of Circuit Court to award costs extends to cases vested in the Circuit Court since the passing of the Courts of Justice Act 1961.

In re Sugar Distributors Ltd
[Not previously reported] .... Vol V p 225

High Court application - whether share issue invalid - whether meetings took place or resolutions passed - whether backdating of transactions invalid - whether acts of company binds company - whether consent of corporators sufficient - whether s 89 be given a liberal "just and equitable" meaning - whether discretion of court under s 89 restricted - whether underlying policy of s 89 to be considered - whether remedy limited to defective title to shares - whether any proprietary interest in shares acquired by "innocent" persons - whether remedy available without court assistance - whether court can accede to a fiction.

Henry Denny & Sons (Ireland) Ltd T/A Kerry Foods v Minister for Social Welfare
[Not previously reported] .... Vol V p 238

Social Welfare appeal - PRSI - whether demonstrator engaged under a contract of service or contract for service - whether on insurable person as an employee or insurable as a self-employed person - whether written contract the determining factor - whether facts and realities govern the relationship - whether Circuit Court decision relevant - whether decision of Appeals Officer incorrect in law - whether control the deciding factor - whether in business on one's own account decisive - whether written agreement the sole source of the relationship - whether agreement fully considered by Appeals Officer - whether each case to be considered on its particular facts - whether Appeals Officer was entitled to conclude that there was a contract of service.

Quigley (Inspector of Taxes) v Maurice Burke
[Not previously reported] .... Vol V p 265

Income tax - whether an accountant acting in the preparation of accounts and computations of taxable income on behalf of a taxpayer is acting as an agent of the taxpayer - whether the relationship is that of a professional person and client - whether nominal ledger drawn up by the accountant is a document within the possession or power of the taxpayer - whether nominal ledger is part of accountant's working papers - whether accountant acting as auditor or agent.

Lynch v Burke & AIB Banks plc
[Not previously reported] .... Vol V p 271

Succession - joint bank deposit account - whether survivor entitled - whether presumption of resulting trust - whether immediate gift to joint holder - whether true joint tenancy -

whether provider retained a life interest - whether intention in favour of survivor - whether trust on death in favour of survivor - whether a testamentary disposition - whether in contravention of Wills Act 1837.

Purcell v The Attorney General Ireland & The Minister for the Environment
[Not previously reported] .... Vol V p 288

Farm tax - Farm Tax Act 1985 repealed in March 1987 - whether legislation lawfully amended - whether application of Act resulted in prejudicial discrimination - whether Act validly imposed - whether tax imposed in disregard of the intention of the Oireachtas - whether classification of farms had first to be completed - whether Act intended to discriminate between farmers according to the acreage of their farms - whether provisions of Act open to more than one construction - whether constitutional construction to be upheld - whether Minister obliged to bring farm tax into operation in the year 1986 - whether statutory instrument made under powers conferred and for purposes authorised by the Oireachtas - whether statutory instrument ultra vires.

The Revenue Commissioners v Young
[Not previously reported] .... Vol V p 294

Case Stated - Capital acquisitions tax - valuation of shares in a private non trading investment company - whether method of valuation of shares governed by CATA 1976 s 17 - whether s 17 subject to the market value rules comprised in s 15 - whether artificial method governed by commercial reality - whether voting rights held by Ordinary Shares could be used to redeem the Preference Shares - whether the application of s 17 mandatory.

O'Grady (Inspector of Taxes) v Roscommon Race Committee
[Not previously reported] .... Vol V p 317

Case stated - whether a stand at Roscommon Racecourse was plant-trade of promoting and organising horse races at the racecourse for viewing by the public - raised stand gives better views and generates an atmosphere of excitement for patrons - provides shelter and a meeting place - work undertaken provides a new and enlarged stand giving shelter, additional viewing space and bars - test is whether the stand is part of the means whereby the trade is carried on or whether it is merely part of the place where the trade is carried on.

O'Rourke v The Revenue Commissioners
[Not previously reported] .... Vol V p 321

Income tax - repayment of overpaid PAYE tax - whether taxpayer entitled to interest - whether FA 1976 s 30 applied - whether requirements for assessments and appeals satisfied - whether implied agreement - whether constructive trust - whether statutory possession required - whether common law right to interest - appropriate rate of interest - Woolwich doctrine of common law rights - whether repayment of tax as a matter of right whether defendants unjustly enriched at expense of plaintiff - whether plaintiff acquiesced without protest in payment of tax - recovery of money paid in mistake of law - development of law of restitution - money paid without consideration - Murphy's case - whether fiscal problem for State - whether present case can be distinguished - small number of affected taxpayers and minimal fiscal consequences - whether taxpayer entitled as of right to interest - whether rate of interest under Courts Acts applicable.

In the Matter of G O'C & A O'C (Application of Liston (Inspector Taxes))
[Not previously reported] .... Vol V p 346

Income tax - appeal to Supreme Court - application by inspector of taxes for High Court order - order to bank to furnish particulars of accounts of taxpayers and their children - whether discrepancy between returns of income and assets owned by taxpayers - whether discovery of illegal export of £500,000 by taxpayers a matter for further investigation - whether inspector had reasonable grounds for application - whether pre-condition of a request to deliver a return of income satisfied - whether findings of High Court erroneous in point of law - whether taxpayers deemed to have made returns of income - whether deeming provision confined to ITA 1967 s 172(4) - whether unjust, anomalous or absurd result would follow.

McMahon and Others v Rt Hon Lord Mayor Alderman & Burgess of Dublin
[Not previously reported] .... Vol V p 357

Residential development - tax benefits for holiday cottages - planning permission for private residential purposes - whether holiday homes a change of use - whether use specified - purpose for which the homes designated - whether exempted development - complaints by permanent residents - appeal against the decision of An Bord Pleanala.

Kenny v The Revenue Commissioners, Goodman & Gemon Ltd (Notice Parties)
[Not previously reported] .... Vol V p 363

Stamp duty - judicial review - instruments incorrectly stamped - whether instrument a promissory note - whether an assignment of a debt fully stamped - whether Revenue adjudication correct - whether taxpayer is entitled to challenge administrative decisions relating to another taxpayer's affairs - defendant is entitled to question the stamping of documents in the course of court proceedings - whether judicial review is an appropriate remedy - whether court has jurisdiction to make declaratory orders against notice parties - whether court has jurisdiction to issue declaratory orders relating to admissibility of documents in proceedings in which the admissibility has been raised.

In Re Estates of Cummins: O'Dwyer & Charleton v Keegan & Ors
[Not previously reported] .... Vol V p 367

Capital Acquisitions Tax - Succession Act 1965 - legal right share - husband survived by wife twelve hours - no children - wife in a coma and unaware of husband's death - whether widow's estate acquired a half share in husband's estate - whether legal right share vests on death - whether legal right share has the same meaning as a share under a will or intestacy - whether intentions of deceased husband and surviving spouse frustrated - law should be certain

Saatchi & Saatchi Advertising Ltd v McGarry (Inspector of Taxes)
[Not previously reported] .... Vol V p 376

Corporation tax - case stated - manufacturing relief for film production - proper construction of FA 1990 s 41 - relief deemed to apply prior to FA 1990 where relief was sought - whether application for relief a pre-requisite - whether scheme and purpose of a statutory enactment relevant - whether procedure irrelevant to taxing statutes - whether equitable principles operate - whether principles of construction of taxing statutes must be applied.

In the Matter of Williams (Tallaght) (In Receivership) and Companies Act 1963-1990
[Not previously reported] .... Vol V p 388

Revenue debts - company in receivership - property subject to floating charge - Revenue as preferential creditors for PAYE and PRSI - company in liquidation - whether Revenue a preferential creditor for corporation tax liability of company - whether double preference claims precluded - no statutory authority to deny double preference claims - whether Revenue debt statute barred - six months limitation period - whether notified - whether known to liquidator - whether actual knowledge required - whether extended to include constructive knowledge - whether statutory time limit can be extended by court.

Action Aid Ltd v The Revenue Commissioners
[Not previously reported] .... Vol V p 392

Income tax - payments under deeds of covenant in favour of named children in Third World countries - whether entitled to exemption limits under FA 1980 s 1 - appellant a registered corporate charity in Ireland and a trustee for the named children - whether withdrawal of relief from 1984 onwards justified - whether payments applied for benefit of covenantees - whether payments made into fund for a group - whether payment must be made direct to covenantee - whether exemption restricted to persons aged over 65 years - whether exemption applies to non residents.

Taxback Limited v The Revenue Commissioners
[Not previously reported] .... Vol V p 412

Value Added Tax - judicial review - goods transported to a destination outside EC member states exempt from VAT - whether foreign tourists to Ireland can claim VAT refunds on goods purchased in Ireland - whether refunds obtainable through refunding agencies - whether accounts of refunding agency in order - whether Revenue justified in withholding refunds

Burke & Sons Ltd v The Revenue Commissioners, Ireland and the Attorney General
[Not previously reported] .... Vol V p 418

Value Added Tax - Judicial review - VAT scheme for retailers - interpretation of scheme - whether scheme based on sales or purchases - alcoholic liquors purchased out of bonded warehouse - whether payment of excise duty to be treated as zero rated - whether applicant's interpretation correct - whether scheme retrospectively altered - whether Revenue acted in breach of natural justice - whether Revenue bound by accepted applicant's interpretation over a period of years

Gilligan v Criminal Assets Bureau, Galvin, Lanigan and The Revenue Commissioners
[Not previously reported] .... Vol V p 424

Income Tax - husband and wife - joint assessment - whether husband is liable for tax on wife's income - whether wife is separately liable on her income - whether both living together for chargeable period - whether wife is obliged to make a return in respect of her own income - whether "Special Provisions" in relation to married couples prevail in all circumstances.

O'Siochain (Inspector of Taxes) v Neenan
[Not previously reported] .... Vol V p 472

Case Stated - Income Tax - increase in Widows Social Welfare Contributory Pension granted in respect of dependent children - whether the income of the widow or the child - whether beneficiary distinguished from qualified child - whether additions to pension for benefit of children - whether a residence relationship applies - whether rate of pension or entitlement attracts chargeability to tax - whether trust in favour of children read into Act - whether purposeful construction to be applied - whether additional payment 'travels' with child - whether payments to qualified children exempt from income tax

Proes v The Revenue Commissioners
[Not previously reported] .... Vol V p 481

Case Stated - Income Tax - domicile of appellant - Irish domicile of origin - English domicile of choice - holiday house in Ireland - death of appellant's husband - whether new domicile of choice acquired - whether existing domicile of choice abandoned - whether wrong test applied - when was domicile of choice abandoned - whether appellant's intention in regard to her permanent home retained.

Hibernian Insurance Company Limited v MacUimis (Inspector of Taxes)
[Not previously reported] .... Vol V p 495

Corporation tax - case stated - investment company - whether expenses of management tax deductible - interpretation of expenses of management - whether management implies regular expenditure - whether expenses of acquisition are capital expenditure - whether expenses of management and expenses by management can be distinguished - whether expenses an integral part of costs of purchaser - whether phrase expenses of management has a technical or special meaning.

Kearns v Dilleen (Inspector of Taxes)
[Not previously reported] .... Vol V p 514

Capital Gains Tax - tax avoidance scheme - options to purchase shares in the same company granted by husband to wife and by wife to husband - 98% of the purchase price paid for the option and 2% payable on the exercise of the option - commercial reality of transactions - meaning of word abandonment - substance of transactions - principles of construction of taxing statutes - whether rights and obligations of parties to the transaction to be considered - whether an abandonment when consideration is received - whether receipt of capital sum a separate taxable disposal

The Attorney General v Power and Others
[Not previously reported] .... Vol V p 525

Estate duty - FA 1894 (57 & 58 Vict c 30), s 5(3) - interest in possession - whether conveyancing form determines liability.

Smyth v The Revenue Commissioners
[Not previously reported] .... Vol V p 532

Estate duty - valuation of private company shares - restriction on transfer of shares - whether dividends paid represented profit earning capacity of the company - whether profit earning capacity is proper test of value of shares - whether remuneration of directors exceeded commercial level - return on monies invested by purchasers - whether a sale of entire shareholding.

The Revenue Commissioners v Doorley
[Not previously reported]... Vol V p 539

Legacy duty - charitable bequest - whether to be expended in Ireland - construction of will - interpretation of taxing statute - exemption from legacy duty - whether charitable bequest had to be expended in Ireland.

Byrne v The Revenue Commissioners
[Not previously reported]... Vol V p 560

Revenue - stamp duty - deed of conveyance - exemption from stamp duty - deed executed by grantors and delivered as escrow - subsequent execution by grantees - inadvertent stamping - repayment of duty - date of execution of deed - whether claim for repayment within two years of date of execution - Poor Relief (Ireland) Act 1838 (1 & 2 Vict c 56) s 96 - Stamp Duties Management Act 1891 (54 & 55 Vict c 38) s 10 - Revenue Act 1898 (61 & 62 Vict c 46) s 13.

In re Swan, (Deceased); Hibernian Bank Ltd v Frances Stewart Munro and Others
[Not previously reported]... Vol V p 565

Will - construction - annuity "free of income tax" - annuitant entitled to refunds in respect of tax borne by testator's estate - whether annuitant entitled to retain such refunds or bound to account for them to testator's estate - ITA 1918 (8 & 9 Geo, 5, c 40) ss 16 and 29, All Schedules Rules, r 19.

O'Sullivan v The Revenue Commissioners
[Not previously reported]... Vol V p 570

Stamp duty - case stated - whether a lease assessable as a conveyance or transfer on sale - money consideration in addition to rent - whether words and scheme of FA 1947 s 13 are appropriate to leases - whether doubt in a Stamp Act construed in favour of the taxpayer - whether a tax upon the citizen must be stated in clear language.

In re Estate of McNamee and Others v The Revenue Commissioners
[Not previously reported]... Vol V p 577

Estate duty - valuation of private company shares - minority shareholding - principles of valuation - profit earning capacity - preservation of assets - dividend policy - past sales - actual sale - imaginary open market.

The Revenue Commissioners v Moroney and Others
[Not previously reported]... Vol V p 589

Estate duty - whether receipt clause in a deed binding - whether stated consideration recoverable - whether extrinsic evidence admissible to contradict statement of consideration - whether doctrine of promissory estoppel applies - whether a question of mistake or rectification.

In Re the Estate of Urquhart, (Deceased) and The Revenue Commissioners v AIB Ltd
[Not previously reported] .... Vol V p 600

Revenue - Estate duty - legal right - whether surviving spouse competent to dispose of statutory share in estate - election - FA 1894 (57 & 58 Vict c 30) ss 2, 22 - Succession Act 1965 (No 27) ss 111, 115.

Murphy v The Attorney General
[Not previously reported] .... Vol V p 613

Income tax -incomes of husband and wife aggregated - tax payable by a married couple in excess of the amounts payable by a husband and wife if taxed as separate persons - whether in breach of constitutional rights - ITA 1967 ss 138, 192-198 - income tax - recovery of tax overpaid - tax improved by statute deceased to be invalid - whether money paid under mistake of law can be recovered.

Stephen Court Ltd v Browne (Inspector of Taxes)
[3 ITR 95] .... Vol V p 680

Corporation tax - auctioneer's commission and solicitor's costs - whether expenses of a revenue or capital nature - ITA 1967 ss 81(5)(d), 81(6)(a)(i) - FA 1969 s 22 - CTA 1976 s 15

AE v The Revenue Commissioners
[Not previously reported] .... Vol V p 686

Revenue - capital acquisitions tax - gift of farm to niece - whether niece worked substantially full-time on the farm - whether herding of cattle under a letting agreement constituted a business - meaning of business - CATA 1976 (No 8) 2nd Schedule, Pt 1, para 9.

Director of Public Prosecutions v Cunningham
[Not previously reported] .... Vol V p 691

Betting duty - whether Inland Revenue Regulation Act 1890 complied with - whether court proceedings preceded by order of the Revenue Commissioners - whether onus on prosecution to prove existence of order of the Commissioners.

McDaid v Sheehy and Others
[Not previously reported] .... Vol V p 696

Excise duties - judicial review - whether applicant entitled to an order of certiorari - whether order validated by confirmation and re-enactment in subsequent legislation - whether court should rule on constitutional validity of legislation when pronouncement of no benefit to applicant.

Re Coombe Importers Ltd (In Liq) and Re the Companies Acts 1963-1990
[Not previously reported] .... 1998 p 59

PAYE/PRSI – payments to employees without deduction of PAYE/PRSI – Company in examinership – estimated assessments by Inspector of Taxes – Company in liquidation – Revenue debt – whether super-preferential status – interpretation of s 120(2) Social Welfare Consolidation Act 1981 – whether Court obliged to look at things done or failing to be done s 301 Social Welfare (Consolidation) Act 1993.

The Revenue Commissioners v Sisters of Charity of the Incarnate Word
[Not previously reported]..1998 p 65

Income Tax – Case stated – foreign charity with a branch in Ireland – whether Irish branch entitled to exemption from income tax on its profits – whether "established" in Ireland – interpretation of ss 333/334 Income Tax Act 1967 – whether geographical limitation contained in the statute – charitable activities in Ireland – whether facts distinguished from Camille case in UK – meaning of word established – whether a sufficient Irish establishment to justify exemption.

Byrne (John Oliver) v Noel Conroy
[Not previously reported]..1998 p 75

Extradition Order - appeal on grounds of a revenue offence - Monetary Compensation Amounts - agricultural levies under EEC regulations - fraudulent charges - whether agricultural levies constitute a tax - question to be determined by Irish law - whether a tax in normal concept of taxes - whether part of revenue of any particular country.

Saatchi & Saatchi Advertising Limited v Kevin McGarry (Inspector of Taxes)
[Not previously reported]..1998 p 99

Corporation Tax - case stated - manufacturing relief for film production - whether relief applies to short advertising films produced for use on television - retrospective application of s 41 Finance Act 1990 - whether claim for relief prior to assessment a pre-requisite - whether strict interpretation of a taxing statute prevails - whether scheme and purpose of a statute relevant.

Sean O'Siochain (Inspector of Taxes) v Bridget Neenan
[Not previously reported]..1998 p 111

Income Tax – Case stated – social welfare benefits – increases in widow's contributory pension by reason of dependent children - whether liable to income tax – whether increases the property of the children or the widow – whether widow liable for income tax on the benefits for dependent children – proper interpretation Chapter II of Social Welfare (Consolidation) Act 1981.

Haughey and Others v Attorney General and Others
[Not previously reported]..1998 p 119

Tribunal of Inquiry - jurisdiction of Oireachtas and Taoiseach - whether Tribunal of Inquiry Evidence Act 1921 applies - whether Tribunal constitutionally valid - whether powers of Tribunal unlimited - grounds of appeal - whether personal rights infringed - right to equality of treatment, privacy and fair procedures - whether powers of Tribunal exceeded

Parkes (Roberta) v David Parkes
[Not previously reported]..1998 p 169

Stamp Duty – Husband purchasing property in wife's name – Presumption of advancement rebutted – whether resulting trust – Husband procuring wife to make false declaration in conveyance – Husband subsequently seeking court's aid to enforce trust – Whether husband entitled to relief in equity

In the matter of The Sunday Tribune Limited (in Liquidation)
[Not previously reported] .... 1998 p 177

Company - Winding up - Creditors - Preferential payments - Test applicable - Unpaid wages of employees or contractual payments Whether employee engaged under a contract of service or a contract for services journalists - Claimants entitled to be paid as creditors preferential - Companies Act 1963 s 285.

B McCabe (Inspector of Taxes) v South City & County Investment Co Ltd
[Vol V p 107] .... 1998 p 183

Corporation Tax - whether periodic payments subject to Corporation Tax - annuity contract - annual payments of £500 plus share of profits in return for capital sum - whether correctly described as annuities - whether income receipts - whether return of capital - whether case law overturns logic of transactions - interpretation of tax statutes and documents - whether content of agreement conforms with its purpose

Criminal Assets Bureau v Gerard Hutch
[Not previously reported] .... 1999-2000 p 65

Income tax - appeal against judgment - assessment made in absence of income tax returns - tax appeal procedures - late appeal - assessment becoming final and conclusive - Collector General's certificate as proof of amount due

Patrick J O'Connell (Inspector of Taxes) v Fyffes Banana Processing Limited
[Not previously reported] .... 1999-2000 p 71

Corporation Tax - Case Stated - company providing banana ripening services - process of maturation of foodstuffs - whether goods manufactured within the State - strict interpretation of taxing statutes - whether any doubt or ambiguity in the statutory provisions - services rendered deemed to be the manufacture of goods - goods manufactured within the State to be distinguished from services rendered in a process of manufacture of goods

Sean MacAonghusa (Inspector of Taxes) v Ringmahon Company
[Not previously reported] .... 1999-2000 p 81

Corporation tax - case stated - whether loan interest was money wholly and exclusively expended for the purpose of trade of the company - company redeemed £6 million Redeemable Preference shares - company raised a loan of £6 million - whether loan for purpose of restricting share capital and paying off shareholders - whether loan a temporary and fluctuating borrowing - purposes of trade is to serve purposes of the trade - object in making the payment is based on the intentions of the taxpayer - whether incidental consequences - question of degree - whether Inspector can direct company on how to finance its business - whether loan needed to continue trade - whether company entitled to a deduction for annual loan interest - whether judge's determination properly within the evidence adduced before him

Hibernian Insurance Company Limited v MacUimis (Inspector of Taxes)
[5 ITR 495] .... 1999-2000 p 113

Corporation Tax - Case stated - investment company - expenses of management deductible - interpretation of expenses of management for corporation tax purposes - expenses incurred in respect of investment appraisals and advices with a view to acquisitions of investments - whether expenses incurred prior to the date on which a decision was made to acquire the particular investment - whether character of expenditure alters depending upon whether the investment was purchased or not - whether expenses were of a revenue or capital nature - Corporation Tax Act 1976, s 15

Patrick J O'Connell (Inspector of Taxes) v Thomas Keleghan
[Not previously reported].. 1999-2000 p 143

Capital gains tax/income tax - case stated - sale of shares - sale price in the form of loan notes - loan notes not transferable or assignable - "paper for paper" transaction - whether capital gains tax deferred pending redemption of loan notes - whether loan notes a simple debt or a debt on a security - whether CGT 1975 Sch 2 para 2 is based on "two fictions" - whether fictions are no more than rules of computing tax - "no disposal fiction" and "composite simple asset fiction" - whether marketability is the essence of a loan note - inducement payment to enter into service contract - whether payment liable to income tax - whether taxpayer ever took up employment on foot of the service contract

Determinations of the Appeal Commissioners

Capital Gains Tax - Re TCA 1997 s 552, 1 AC 2000 .... 1999-2000 p 55
Capital Gains Tax - Re TCA 1997 s 573, 2 AC 2000 .... 1999-2000 p 55
Vehicle Registration Tax - Re FA 1989 s 92, 3 AC 2000 .... 1999-2000 p 55
Vehicle Registration Tax - Re FA 1989 s 92, 4 AC 2000 .... 1999-2000 p 55
Vehicle Registration Tax - Re SI 59/ 1993, 5 AC 2000 .... 1999-2000 p 55
Income Tax - Re ITA 1967 s 61, 6 AC 2000... 1999-2000 p 56
Income Tax - Re ITA 1967 s 61, 7 AC 2000... 1999-2000 p 56
Income Tax - Re ITA 1967 s 255, 8 AC 2000... 1999-2000 p 56
Income Tax - Re TCA 1997 s 112, 9 AC 2000 .... 1999-2000 p 57
Income Tax - Re ITA 1967 s 255, 10 AC 2000... 1999-2000 p 57
Income Tax - Re TCA 1997 s 669, 11 AC 2000 .... 1999-2000 p 57
Income Tax - Re TCA 1997 s 271, 12 AC 2000 .... 1999-2000 p 57
Income Tax - Re TCA 1997 s 669, 13 AC 2000 .... 1999-2000 p 57
Income Tax - Re TCA 1997 s 1017, 14 AC 2000 .... 1999-2000 p 58
BES Relief - Re FA 1984 s 12, 15 AC 2000 .... 1999-2000 p 58
VAT - Re VATA1972 First Schedule, 16 AC 2000.................................... 1999-2000 p 58
VAT - Re VATA1972 Sixth Schedule, 17 AC 2000................................... 1999-2000 p 58
VAT - Re VATA 1972 s 4, 18 AC 2000 .... 1999-2000 p 58
VAT - Re VATA1972 Second Schedule, 19 AC 2000 .... 1999-2000 p 59
VAT - Re VATA 1972 Second Schedule, 20 AC 2000 .... 1999-2000 p 59
VAT - Re VATA 1972 s 4, 21 AC 2000 .... 1999-2000 p 59
Excise Duty (Hydrocarbon Oil) - Re FA 1976 s 41, 22 AC 2000............. 1999-2000 p 59
Excise Duty (Hydrocarbon Oil) - Re FA 1995 s 105, 23 AC 2000........... 1999-2000 p 60
Income Tax - Re TCA 1997 s 997, 24 AC 2000 .... 1999-2000 p 61
Capital Acquisitions Tax - Re CATA 1976 s 39, 25 AC 2000.................. 1999-2000 p 62

1999-2000 Cases

Criminal Assets Bureau v Gerard Hutch .... 1999-2000 p 65
Patrick J O'Connell (Inspector of Taxes) v Fyffes Banana Processing Ltd 1999-2000 p 71
Sean MacAonghusa (Inspector of Taxes) v Ringmahon Company .... 1999-2000 p 81
Hibernian Insurance Co Ltd v MacUimis (Inspector of Taxes) .... 1999-2000 p 113
Patrick J O'Connell (Inspector of Taxes) v Thomas Keleghan .... 1999-2000 p 143

Determinations of Appeal Commissioners are reproduced courtesy of the Office of the Appeal Commmissioners and Institute of Taxation in Ireland.

Determinations of the Appeal Commissioners

Capital Gains Tax - Re TCA 1997 s 552, 1 AC 2000

Whether Probate tax paid allowable as acquisition cost of asset under TCA 1997 s 552(1). The Probate tax was paid by the personal representatives and the deductions were under s 552(1)(a).

Decision: Allow appeal.

Capital Gains Tax - Re TCA 1997 s 573, 2 AC 2000

Sale by executors of land being part of assets of residuary estate. Contract for sale stated that the sale was subject to "... the production by the vendors of a map suitable for registration in the Land Registry showing the property coloured in red."

1. Whether assessable on executors (Revenue) or beneficiaries (Taxpayer)?
2. Whether contract conditional? (Taxpayer)

Decision: Appeal fails on both counts.

Vehicle Registration Tax - Re FA 1989 s 92, 3 AC 2000

Disabled Drivers and Disabled Passengers (Tax Concessions) Regulations 1994 (SI 353/1994)

Taxpayer sole provider of transportation for disabled father. Taxpayer living with wife and family but spending most nights in his fathers house (located close to taxpayers family home) to care for him. Whether taxpayer "residing with" father?

Decision: Allow appeal.

Vehicle Registration Tax - Regarding FA 1989 s 92, 4 AC 2000

Regulation 10(1) Disabled Drivers and Disabled Passengers (Tax Concessions) Regulations 1994 (SI 353/1994)

Taxpayer, male, mid-forties living with elderly female friend for many years. Not living together as man and wife but as long term friends and companions. Revenue agreed that taxpayer was "responsible for the transportation of disabled passenger". Whether "a family member" of such disabled passenger as claimed by taxpayer?

Decision: Appeal allowed.

Vehicle Registration Tax - Re SI 59/ 1993, 5 AC 2000

Transfer of Residence-Regulation 4(1)(b) VRT (Permanent Reliefs) Regulations 1993 (SI 59/1993).

Taxpayer acquired vehicle in Cyprus under scheme applicable to full-time employees of off-shore enterprises and claimed exemption from VRT on its importation into Ireland. Whether the vehicle was acquired under the "General conditions of taxation" in force in the country of acquisition?

Decision: Appeal fails.

Income Tax - Re ITA 1967 s 61, 6 AC 2000

PAYE/PRSI not operated by taxpayer re bonuses to staff. Settlement liability agreed with Revenue based on treating the payments made by the employer as gross from which tax/PRSI ought to have been deducted. Whether payment of the settlement amount (excluding interest and penalties) an allowable deduction?

Decision: Appeal fails.

Income Tax - Re ITA 1967 s 61, 7 AC 2000

Professional firm conducted by three partners. Partnership carrying on its business in premises owned by the partners. Percentage profit shares in partnership not identical to percentages of rental ownership of the property. Whether rent charged in the partnership accounts an allowable deduction in computing the profits of the firm?

Decision: Allow appeal

Income Tax - Re ITA 1967 s 255, 8 AC 2000

Industrial Buildings Allowance - "aparthotel"

ITA 1967 ss 81, 254, 255, 307 and 318; FA 1986 s 42.

Partnership constructing block of apartments in "designated area". Various services provided within complex; shop, cleaning apartments, laundry, security etc. Significant advertising expenditure and comprehensive marketing plan put into operation. Lettings of various terms entered into, many short-term, some longer-term to students etc.
Detailed evidence. Lengthy submissions re case law on all issues.

1. Was the building a hotel within the meaning of s 255? (If so it would fail the requirement under FA 1986 s 42 that it "apart from this section is not an industrial building or structure within the meaning of ITA 1967 s 255)?
2. Was it in use for the purposes of a trade or profession as contended by taxpayer? (With the consequence of the capital allowance claim creating an allowable loss for offset under s 307 against other income for year of assessment)
   Or, as argued by Revenue, should most of the income be assessable as rents - given that s80 states "rent includes ... any payment in the nature of rent..."
3. Was it let on bona fide commercial terms?
   (In the alternative to 2.)
4. Was it a building or structure in use as, or as part of, a dwelling house?

Decision: 1. No.

2. The appellants contention that the partnership was in the business of letting rooms was accepted so that its income was assessable under Case I of Schedule D and not under Case V.

3. Yes

4. No

NB. Another case concerning a similar building, was heard at a later time. Exactly the same legal issues were argued but the facts differed. (eg there were different letting arrangements and fewer services provided to the occupiers.) The Commissioner, having regard to the facts and to the length of the lettings, held that the income SHOULD be assessable under Case V. Otherwise the decision in that later case followed the above at points 1, 2 and 4.

Income Tax - Re TCA 1997 s 112, 9 AC 2000

TCA 1997 ss 112(2)(a), 510(4) and Schedule 3 Part 1. Whether the value of shares issued to an employee under an approved profit sharing scheme should be included as "emoluments" in calculating the Standard Capital Superannuation Benefit (SCSB)?

Revenue argued that TCA 1997 s 112(2) defined "emoluments" in a manner which did not include the value of such shares. Taxpayer argued that that definition was for the purposes of subs (2) of s 112 and should not be applied elsewhere unless specifically so stated in the legislation.

Decision: The definition in Section 112 was not relevant. Giving the word "emoluments" its ordinary meaning, the value of the shares should be included for the purpose of calculating the SCSB.

Income Tax - Re ITA 1967 s 255, 10 AC 2000

Whether hostel is "hotel" and therefore "industrial building or structure"?

Decision: Appeal fails. A hostel providing basic accommodation largely in dormitory style rooms is not a hotel within the ordinary meaning of the word.

Income Tax - Re TCA 1997 s 669, 11 AC 2000

Farmer takes over stock from his father when father ceased to carry on the trade of farming immediately prior to the sons commencement to trade.

Certain trading liabilities and loans incurred by the father assumed by the son.

Significant element of gift re valuation of stock transferred.

Decision: Section 669(1) applies - stock not acquired in "normal conduct of the trade of farming"

Income Tax - Re TCA 1997 s 271, 12 AC 2000

TCA 1997 ss 268, 270 and 271 Industrial Buildings Allowance

Whether the cost of constructing tees and greens on a golf course owned by a hotel company qualifies as expenditure on an industrial building or structure? Alternatively - whether cost of construction of the entire course qualifies?

Decision: Appeal fails on both grounds.

Income Tax - Re TCA 1997 s 669, 13 AC 2000

TCA 1997 s 669(1). Stock relief.

Farmers herd of cattle contracting brucellosis and majority of herd slaughtered. Carcasses sold and grant received from Department of Agriculture. Whether cattle disposed of "... otherwise than in the normal conduct of the trade of farming..." as contended by Revenue?

Decision: Appeal fails.

Income Tax - Re TCA 1997 s 1017, 14 AC 2000

TCA 1997 ss 1017 and 1018.

Legally separated couple. Terms of High Court order made husband liable to pay wifes tax bill. No election to be taxed as a married couple under s 1017. Husband claimed he should be assessed as a single person. Revenue asserted that the terms of the order of the High Court being the law, obliged them to refuse the husbands application so as to ensure that the husband did account for the wifes tax.

Decision: Allow appeal. Whatever the terms of the court order it could not operate to amend a specific section of the Taxes Acts. If the husband did not comply with the terms of the order that would not be a matter for a tax appeal.

BES Relief - Re FA 1984 s 12, 15 AC 2000

Finance Act 1984 s 12(1)(c)(i) (as amended).
Two companies with different shareholders set up to develop and operate adjacent hostels, All shareholders claiming BES relief. Both BES issues having same promoters. Possibility that after five years the properties would be converted to apartments. No shareholders agreements or prearranged exit mechanism (such as put options etc). During the first few months of the operation of the hostels there was little differentiation in the trading activities of the hostels. Subsequently operated as separate entities.

1. Whether both companies "act in pursuit of a common purpose"?
2. Whether both companies are "under the control of any person or group of persons or groups of persons having a reasonable commonality of identity"

Decision: 1. No; 2. Yes.

VAT - Re VATA72 First Schedule, 16 AC 2000

VAT Act 1972. First Schedule paragraph (xix)

6th Directive Annex F paragraph 6

Self-employed gravedigger.

Whether supplying the service of a "funeral undertaking"

Decision: No. Subject to VAT at the standard rate.

VAT - Re VATA72 Sixth Schedule, 17 AC 2000

VAT Act 1972, Sixth Schedule paragraph (xia); Sixth Directive Article 28.2(1)

Whether the supply of Christmas trees from which the "root-ball" had been removed is subject to VAT from 1 September 1997 at 12.5% or at the standard rate?

Decision: Standard rate. The supplies in question cannot be said to relate to either "live trees" or "ornamental foliage".

VAT - Re VATA 1972 s 4, 18 AC 2000

VAT Act 1972 s 4(1)

Builder purchased undeveloped farmland. He developed most of the land and sold it, charging VAT, but certain small portions were unaffected by his development activities. He then sold those remaining portions.

Whether VAT chargeable on the "undeveloped land"?

Decision: No

VAT - Re VATA72 Second Schedule, 19 AC 2000

VAT Act 1972. Second Schedule

Whether sale of ferry zero-rated. Ferry operating across river close to or part of estuary. Whether "sea-going". Expert evidence re flora and fauna, salinity of water etc.

Decision: On basis of expert evidence - appeal allowed.

VAT - Re VATA 1972 Second Schedule, 20 AC 2000

VAT Act 1972. Second Schedule

Whether bottled mineral water chargeable to VAT at 21 % or is zero rated.

Decision: Appeal fails

VAT - Re VATA 1972 s 4, 21 AC 2000

VAT Act 1972 s 4(3); Regulation 19 of 1979.
Taxpayer company developed a number of apartments and leased them to a hotel operating company for use in its hotel business. The agreements contained two option clauses.

(a) After two years and nine months the tenant could exercise an option to extend the lease for a further twelve months, and
(b) After the expiration of the additional twelve months the lessee could exercise a further option to extend the lease for a period of years which would bring the total letting up to twenty years.

The lettings were treated, in accordance with Revenue practice, as being long term and there was a disagreement between the taxpayer and the Revenue as to whether and, if so, how Regulation 19(2)(b) of the Value Added Tax Regulations 1979 applied in relation to valuing the reversionary interests under the leases.

Decision: By virtue of s 4(3) the original leases should be treated as "self-supplies" by the taxpayer. The lessees option to extend the term did not affect this conclusion. The standard Revenue practice was not in accordance with the legislation. Accordingly, the difference of opinion between the Taxpayer and the Revenue in relation to the regulations was not a matter on which the Appeal Commissioners needed to express an opinion.

Excise Duty (Hydrocarbon Oil) - Re FA 1976 s 41, 22 AC 2000

EU Directive 92/81; FA 1976 s 41(1); SI 394/1992; SI 307/1975.

Appellant carrying on dredging operations in harbour area. Claimed refund of excise duty on the basis that they were involved in "navigation by sea." Revenue disagreed.

Decision: Allow appeal.

Excise Duty (Hydrocarbon Oil) - Re FA 1995 s 105, 23 AC 2000

Appeal under FA 1995 s 105 Finance Act, 1995 (No 8 of 1995)

Issues

Whether the Appellant is entitled to a repayment of duty on hydrocarbon oil claimed under Paragraph 12(11) of SI 307/1975 (Imposition of Duties (No 221) (Excise Duties) Order 1975).

Whether an Appeal Commissioner can exercise a statutory discretion granted to the Revenue Commissioners by Paragraph 12(11) of SI 307/1975 (Imposition of Duties (No 221) (Excise Duties) Order 1975).

Facts

The Appellant operated a school bus service under a contract with Bus Eireann. The remuneration of the Appellant was calculated in accordance with the contract on a per diem basis, Claims for repayment of duty paid on hydrocarbon oil used in the supply of the school bus service were made by the Appellant for the period 1986 to 1998. The Revenue Commissioners disallowed all claims relating to periods prior to 1st January 1997 on the grounds that the claims were not made within a four month period from the date on which the oil was used. The Revenue Commissioners declined to operate the discretion available to them under the legislation.

Legislation

Paragraph 12 (11) of SI 307/1975 (Imposition of Duties (No 221) (Excise Duties) Order 1975):

> "Where a person who carries on a passenger road service, within the meaning of Section 2 of the Road Traffic Act, 1932 (No. 2 of 1932), and who either is the licensee under a passenger license granted under Section 11 of that Act in respect of the passenger road service or is exempted from the application of Section 7 of that Act shows to the satisfaction of the Revenue Commissioners that hydrocarbon oil on which the duty of excise imposed by this Paragraph has been paid has been used by him for combustion in the engine of a mechanically propelled vehicle used in the passenger road service, the Revenue Commissioners may, subject to compliance with such conditions as they may think fit to impose, repay to him duty at the rate of £11.41 per hectolitre on hydrocarbon oil so used on receipt of a claim therefor made by him in such form as they may direct, subject to the proviso that no repayment may be made unless the claim is made within 4 months from the date on which the oil was used, or within such longer period as the Revenue Commissioners may in any particular case allow."

Section 2 of the Road Traffic Act 1932 (No 2 of 1932), as amended:

> "the expression "passenger road service" means a service of one or more mechanically propelled vehicles travelling wholly or mainly on public roads and carrying passengers (whether passengers luggage, merchandise, and mails, or any of them are or are not also carried) between specified terminal points or along a specified route or otherwise for separate charges in respect of each passenger"

Arguments: Appellant

The Appellant argued that the Revenue Commissioners had acted unreasonably in refusing to exercise their discretion in respect of claims for periods prior to 1st January 1997. The

Appellant asserted that the Appeal Commissioners had the same discretion as the Revenue Commissioners and that the Appeal Commissioners should operate it in favour of the appellant.

Arguments: Respondent

The respondent conceded that the service provided is not a "passenger road service as defined in s 2 of the Road Traffic Act, 1932 (No 2 of 1932), as amended. That definition requires, inter alia, that there must be a "... separate charge ... in respect of each passenger ..." The appellants contract with Bus Eireann is on a per diem basis; the amount paid by Bus Eireann for the journeys does not vary even if some of the children do not travel,

The respondent, while accepting that the service supplied by the Appellant was not a "passenger road service", noted that an administrative decision had been taken by the Respondent to concessionally treat the service supplied as a "passenger road service".

The respondent allowed the Appellants claims in respect of periods from 1st January 1997 but not in respect of any earlier period.

Decision, The service supplied by the Appellant is not a "passenger road service" as defined in Section 2, Road Traffic Act, 1932 (No. 2 of 1932), as amended, because there is not a separate charge by the Appellant in respect of each passenger.

The appellant is therefore not entitled to succeed with a claim under Paragraph 12(11) of SI 307/1975 (Imposition of Duties (No 221) (Excise Duties) Order 1975) which is only available to a person who carries on a "passenger road service" within the meaning of s 2 of the Road Traffic Act 1932.

The appellants application for a repayment of duty on hydrocarbon oil claimed under Paragraph 12(11) of SI 307/1975 (Imposition of Duties (No 221) (Excise Duties) Order 1975) is therefore refused.

The appellants application having been refused on the above grounds it was unnecessary to consider any further arguments.

Dissatisfaction was expressed by the appellant.

Income Tax - Re TCA 1997 s 997, 24 AC 2000

Facts

PAYE was operated by the Appellants employer using a certificate of tax free allowances which overstated the amount of allowances properly due for the year 1997/98. The Inspector of Taxes raised an assessment for the year showing a credit for the tax actually deducted by the employer.

Arguments

The appellant argued that the amount of the assessment was equivalent to the amount of tax "... estimated to be deductible ..." and that he was entitled to a credit of that amount in accordance with s 997 with the result that his liability was reduced to nil.

The Revenue Commissioners argued that the taxpayer was entitled to a credit in the amount of tax deducted and that he was not entitled to a credit of any other amount.

Decision, The meaning of the Section is clear in that it requires some credit to be given for either the tax actually deducted from emoluments (where the amount is known) or an estimate of the tax which might be deductible or have been deducted (where the amount is not known). It is obvious that failure to give credit for tax which would normally be deducted from emoluments would give rise to many overpayments and result in administrative inefficiencies.

Whether credit for tax deducted or estimated as being deductible from emoluments has been given or, indeed, even if the inspector had ignored the requirements of the Section completely there does not seem to be anything in the Section which prevents an inspector from using the actual amount of tax which was deducted from the emoluments in computing the balance of tax payable by the taxpayer for the year.

Even on the basis of the construction of the section argued for by the taxpayer it is difficult to conclude that the section requires an inspector of taxes to give credit for tax which should have been deducted from emoluments. The taxpayer appears to be arguing that the inspector has no option but to insert the higher of the tax actually deducted or the tax which would have been deducted had the correct tax free allowance certificate been in the hands of the person paying the emoluments. The section does not impose such an obligation on the inspector but gives him the option of using the tax actually deducted or an amount which he estimates to be deductible.

For the reasons set out above, the appeal fails.

Capital Acquisitions Tax - Re CATA 1976 s 39, 25 AC 2000

Background

The Revenue Commissioners raised Gift Tax assessments under s 39 of the Capital Acquisitions Tax Act 1976 ("the Act") in respect of funds which they identified as having been provided to an individual ("the Taxpayer") from the resources of one or more companies (the "payer companies"). The payer companies were not incorporated in the State and the bank accounts from which the funds were made available were situated outside this jurisdiction.

Revenue Commissioners Arguments Legislation

Section 8(1) of the Companies Act, 1963 ("the Companies Act") - "Any act or thing done by a company which if the company had been empowered to do the same would have been lawfully and effectively done, shall, notwithstanding that the company had no power to do such act or thing, be effective in favour of any person relying on such act or thing, who is not shown to have been actually aware, at the time when he so relied thereon, that such act or thing was not within the powers of the company, but any director or officer of the company who was responsible for the doing by the company of such act or thing shall be liable to the company for any loss or damage suffered by the company in consequence thereof."

The Revenue Commissioners argued that:

- the payments to the Taxpayer of funds which were identified in the report of a tribunal as being as the property of one or more companies in a group of companies ("the Group"), were gifts;
- the payments referred to above were:

- made by an individual who was identified in the report of the tribunal and that that individual was the disponer as defined in s 2 of the Act;
- effectively made by a company or companies based in the State;
- in accordance with s 8(1) of the Companies Act the payments to the taxpayer;
- were not within the powers of a company or companies;
- would have been lawfully and effectively made if the company or companies were empowered to make them;
- were effective in favour of the taxpayer who was not shown to have been actually aware, at the time such payments were made, that such acts were not within the powers of the company or companies;
- were valid gifts and constituted dispositions by a director (who was the "disponer" in accordance with s 2 of the Act) to the taxpayer;
- the disponer was domiciled in the State at the times of the dispositions;
- the onus rested with the Taxpayer to establish that the assessments were in fact incorrect.

Taxpayers Arguments Legislation

Section 34 of the Act - ".. a disposition made by a company shall be deemed to be a ... disposition...paid or made ... by the beneficial owners of the shares in the company...".
The Taxpayer argued that:

- the burden of proof of taxability is on the State (*AG v Seccombe* [1990] 2 KB 688 and *McGrath v MacDermott* 3 ITR 683 refers) notwithstanding that the burden of proof in relation to the assessments rests with the taxpayer,
- the Revenue Commissioners had erred in identifying the disponer. The report of the tribunal referred to payments made by a named individual but the tribunal was not concerned with taxation and did not make any findings in relation to the tax consequences of the issues which it addressed.
- the tribunal report found that the funds used for the payments were the property of one or more companies in the Group. None of the payer companies were incorporated in the State. The Companies Act applies only to companies incorporated in the State. Consequently s 8(1) of the Companies Act could not be applied to the payer companies;
- the funds used for the payments were provided by companies and therefore the provisions of s 34 of the Act applied. Thus it was necessary to identify the companies and their beneficial shareholders. The taxpayer was unable to identify the shareholders in the payer companies and asserted that the Revenue should do so;
- in order to determine whether a taxable gift, as defined in s 6(1) and referred to in s 4 of the Act, arises the identity and domicile of the disponer must be determined.
- the identity of a disponer determined the applicable threshold amount in accordance with Part 1 of the Second Schedule to the Act;
- it was necessary to identify the disponer in order to establish whether a person who was beneficially entitled in possession to a benefit under a disposition was deemed to take a gift in accordance with s 5(1) of the Act or deemed to take an inheritance in accordance with s 11(1) of the Act;
- it is necessary to know the number of disponers to establish the donees entitlement to small gifts exemption described in s 53 of the Act.

Arguments were also made concerning, inter alia, constructive trusts, the Statue of Limitations 1957, "valuation date" (s 21 of the Act) and "beneficially entitled in possession" (s 5 and 11 of the Act).

Decision, The Appeal Commissioner:

- noted that a charge to gift tax required, inter alia, a taxable gift as defined in Section 6 of the Act;
- accepted the submission by the Taxpayer that it was necessary to determine the identity and the domicile of disponers in order to establish whether a taxable gift had been made;
- accepted the submissions by the Taxpayer that it was necessary to establish the identity of disponers in order to establish:
- the class threshold amount to which a donee was entitled in accordance with the Second Schedule to the Act; and
- whether a person who was beneficially entitled in possession to a benefit under a disposition was deemed to take a gift in accordance with s 5(1) of the Act or deemed to take an inheritance in accordance with s 11(1) of the Act;
- accepted the submission by the taxpayer that it was necessary to determine the number of disponers in order to establish the donees entitlement to the exemption described in s 53;
- rejected the argument advanced by Revenue that the report of the tribunal identified the disponer for the purposes of the Act and accepted the argument by the Taxpayer that while the report of the tribunal referred to payments made by a named individual the tribunal was not concerned with taxation and did not make any findings in relation to the tax consequences of the issues which it addressed;
- rejected the argument advanced by Revenue that the disponer was identifiable through operation of s 8(1) of the Companies Act. The payer companies identified in the report were not incorporated in the State. The Companies Act applied only to companies incorporated in the State. Consequently s 8(1) of the Companies Act could not be applied to the payer companies;
- noted that as the payments were identified in the report of the tribunal as having been made from the funds of one or more companies it was necessary to identify the beneficial owners of shares in the payer companies in accordance with s 34 of the Act;
- noted that no disponer or disponers were identifiable from the information made available
- determined that, in the absence of a reliably identified disponer or disponers, the assessments under appeal should be reduced to nil.
- considered that it was not necessary for him to advert to the other issues raised by the Taxpayer given his determination above.

Dissatisfaction was expressed by the Revenue Commissioners.

Criminal Assets Bureau v Gerard Hutch

High Court - 14 May 1999 - Morris J

Income tax - appeal against judgment - assessment made in absence of income tax returns - tax appeal procedures - late appeal - assessment becoming final and conclusive - Collector General's certificate as proof of amount due

The Criminal Assets Bureau Act 1996 authorised the Bureau to take all necessary actions under the Taxes Acts to ensure that the proceeds of criminal activity or suspected criminal activity are subjected to tax and that the Revenue Acts are fully applied for the recovery of such tax. Pursuant to the said Act the Bureau made estimated assessments in respect of the income of Gerard Hutch ("the defendant") for the years ending 5 April 1988 to 1997. Four grounds of appeal were submitted on behalf of the defendant as follows:

(i) The Inspector of Taxes in making the assessments and determining the tax exercised a judicial function;
(ii) The defendant had availed of the provisions of the Tax Amnesty Act 1993;
(iii) The obligation to make returns with statements did not apply to periods prior to 6 April 1997;
(iv) The defendant was protected by s 955(2)(a) of the Taxes Consolidation Act 1997 ("TCA 1997") against any claim dating back six years from the date of the claim.

Held by Morris J in giving judgment in the amount claimed by the Bureau that:

(i) The Inspector in making the assessments was computing the amount of tax to be paid and his function was purely administrative;
(ii) The defendant failed to produce the appropriate certificate of clearance in accordance with the provisions of the Tax Amnesty Act;
(iii) The defendant failed to comply with the obligation to make tax returns and furnish statements for either period before or after 6 April 1997;
(iv) TCA 1997 s 955(2)(a) is subject to TCA 1997 s 924 and there were ample grounds under s 924 to justify the making of assessments by the Inspector of Taxes.

Legislation: Criminal Assets Bureau 1996 s 8; TCA 1997 ss 933, 955(2)(a), 966(5)(a), 1097; Waiver of Certain Tax, Interest and Penalties Act 1993 ss 2(2), 3(6); ITA 1967 ss 184, 416, 485; Constitution of Ireland, Arts 34, 37, 40

Cases referred to in judgment: Deighan v Hearne 3 ITR 533, [1986] IR 603
First National Commercial Bank plc v Angland [1996] IR 75

High Court - 14 May 1999

Morris J, This matter comes before the Court as an application for leave to enter final judgment against the defendant on foot of a claim in the sum of £1,984,626.44 together with interest thereon as endorsed in the Special Endorsement of Claim on the Summons herein. The matter came before the Master by way of notice of motion dated the 16 February 1999 and was sent forward for hearing by the Court.

The claim is made pursuant to s 8 of the Criminal Assets Bureau Act 1996 by the plaintiff who is an officer of the Revenue Commissioners nominated by the Revenue Commissioners to exercise the powers and functions of the Collector-General.

The claim is in respect of income tax alleged to be due by the defendant in respect of the years ending the 5 April 1988, 5 April 1989, 5 April 1990, 5 April 1991, 5 April 1992, 5 April 1993, 5 April 1994. 5 April 1996, 5 April 1997.

The defendant was ably represented by Ms Gabrielle M Wolfe, Solicitor who confined the defence to four grounds submitting that on these grounds judgment should not be entered and that the matter should be sent for plenary hearing. Specifically no point was raised concerning the right of the plaintiff to maintain these proceedings nor was any challenge raised to the formal proofs which have been submitted to the Court on behalf of the plaintiff. I have considered these proofs and I am of the view that they are satisfactory to maintain the present claim subject to the consideration of the four points raised by way of defence.

I now proceed to consider these four points.

The first point

The first point raised by way of defence is that it is submitted on behalf of the defendant that the provisions of TCA 1997 s 966(5)(a) constitute the purported vesting in an Inspector of Taxes, who is an Officer of the Revenue Commissioners, the Judicial function of making a determination of the tax due by a taxpayer which function, since the certificate of this officer is to be taken as proof of the amount of the tax due, is one properly reserved for a judge appointed within the terms of the Constitution and accordingly the section is unconstitutional.

Were it not for the fact that in my view, this point has already been considered and rejected by the Supreme Court, I should have adjourned further consideration of this point and invited a representative of the Attorney General to attend at the hearings.

However, I am in no doubt that the determination by the Supreme Court of the issues in *Deighan v Hearne and others* [1986] IR 603 enables me to reject this point.

While it is true that in *Deighan's* case the section under consideration was ITA 1967 s 184 the reasoning in the Supreme Court in that case applies to the present legislation.

When *Deighan*'s case was under consideration the following was the position. ITA 1967 s 184 empowered the Inspector of Taxes to raise an estimated assessment to income tax on a person who had failed to make a return of income when required to do so. Section 416 provided that in default of a notice of appeal against the assessment it became final and conclusive. The Collector-General was empowered by s 485 to issue a certificate setting out that a taxpayer had made default in paying income tax and the County Registrar or Sheriff required to levy the sums certified to be in default.

Mr Deighan commenced proceedings in the High Court seeking a declaration that the actions of the Collector-General and County Sheriff together with certain provisions of the ITA 1967 were in breach of Articles 34, 37 and 40 of the Constitution.

If was held by Murphy J dismissing the claim that the task of the Inspector of Taxes in making assessments was to compute the amount of tax to be paid having regard to the information provided by the taxpayer. So described, his function was purely administrative and the fact that the taxpayer was precluded from disputing an assessment arose by virtue of something akin to statutory estoppel resulting from the inaction of the taxpayer. With this reasoning Finlay CJ, Walsh, Griffin, Hederman and McCarthy JJ in the Supreme Court agreed and the taxpayer's appeal was dismissed.

Under the provisions of ITA 1967 s 416(1) a right of appeal is given to the taxpayer which did not exist at the time the *Deighan* case was decided. That section provides that a person aggrieved by an assessment made upon him by an Inspector is entitled to appeal by giving within 30 days after the date of the issue of the assessment, notice in writing to the Inspector and FA 1995 provides that an Inspector of Taxes may refuse an application for an appeal if he feels a taxpayer is not entitled to make such an appeal. The Inspector is required to notify the appellant in writing of his reasons for the refusal. The taxpayer then is entitled to appeal the Inspector's decision directly to the Appeal Commissioners within 15 days of the date of the issue of the refusal.

Accordingly I am in no doubt that the reasoning of the Supreme Court in the case of *Deighan v Hearne* remains valid notwithstanding the changes in legislation since it was heard.

The second point

The second submission made on behalf of the Defendant relates to the Waiver of Certain Tax, Interest and Penalties Act 1993 ("The Tax Amnesty Act").

It is submitted that the defendant in this case availed of the provisions of that Act and that the plaintiffs are accordingly estopped from pursuing this claim.

The evidence advanced by the defendant in support of this claim is contained in paragraph 8 of the Affidavit of his Tax Consultant, Mr John McGrattan sworn on the 9 March 1999. In this he says:

> I say and believe that the defendant has the benefit of the statutory amnesty under the terms of the Waiver of Certain Tax, Interest, and Penalties Act 1993 which statutory amnesty affords him a defence to all attempts to reassess the defendant for taxes prior to the year 1994.
>
> I say and believe that to my knowledge from an inspection of the defendant's papers for the purpose of this affidavit that no approach has ever been made against the defendant under the appropriate provisions of the Waiver of Certain Tax, Interest and Penalties Act 1993 disputing his entitlement to such amnesty.

Section 6 of the Waiver of Certain Tax, Interest and Penalties Act 1993 provides as follows:

> 6. Demands or other requests for payment
>
> Where in relation to an individual:
>
> (a) The Revenue Commissioners, the Collector-General or any of their or his Officers authorised in that behalf have demanded or otherwise requested the payment of any tax;
>
> (i) In respect of which a settlement amount has been remitted to the Chief Special Collector or
>
> (ii) Which is Value Added Tax in respect of which a remittance has been made to the Chief Special Collector in accordance with s 3(6)(a) and sub-para B the individual has been given a certificate as is referred to in s 2(2) or 3(6)(c) in respect of such tax.
>
> The individual shall produce to the Revenue Commissioners, the Collector-General or the Authorised Officers as the case may be within 30 days of (i) the date of making the demand or request or (ii) if later the date he received the certificate.
>
> The evidence referred to in s 2(4)(b) or s 3(6)(c) as the case may be and the demand or request shall be withdrawn and the amount of tax specified in the demand or request shall be discharged.

In my view it is clear that if the defendant sets up, by way of defence, the 1993 Act it is incumbent upon him to produce to the Court the Certificate therein referred to. Until that is done no defence has been established. No Certificate is produced to the Court. Accordingly I reject this submission.

The third point

The issue that arises in this submission extends to a consideration of whether the appropriate procedure for the defendant to adopt for an appeal from the assessment was the appeal procedure provided for by TCA 1997 s 933 or alternatively ITA 1967 s 416. This issue centred around a consideration of whether TCA 1997 s 1097 which provided that in certain circumstances the obligation to make returns and furnish statements are deemed to come into force on the 6 April 1997 or whether the procedure provided for by s 416 of the 1967 Act remained intact.

In the circumstances of the case I find it unnecessary to determine this issue because I am satisfied from the evidence before me that there has been a failure on the part of the defendant to comply with either of these sections.

Section 416, as has been referred to earlier in this judgment enables a person aggrieved by an assessment to lodge an appeal with the Appeal Commissioners. There is no evidence before the Court that the defendant took this step. Accordingly even if it be correct that the procedure provided for at s 416 is the correct procedure, in my view, the defendant has not complied with that procedure.

The fourth point

It is submitted on behalf of the Defendant that the provisions of TCA 1997 s 955(2)(a) constituted a defence in this case.

This subsection provides:

> Where a chargeable person has delivered a return for a chargeable period and has made in the return a full and true disclosure of all material facts necessary for the making of an assessment for the chargeable period, an assessment for that period or an amendment of such an assessment shall not be made on the chargeable person after the end of the period of 6 years commencing at the end of the chargeable period in which the return is delivered and no additional tax shall be payable by the chargeable person and no tax shall be repaid to the chargeable person after the end of the period of 6 years by reason of any matter contained in the return.

Accordingly, it is claimed that the defendant in this case is protected in respect of any claim dating back prior to 6 years from the date of the claim.

I am satisfied that this section must be read as subject to TCA 1997 s 924 which provides:

> (1)(a) Where the inspector discovers that:
>
> (i) any properties or profits chargeable to income tax have been omitted from the first assessments,
>
> (ii) a person chargeable -
>
> (I) has not delivered any statement
>
> (II) has not delivered a full and proper statement
>
> (III) has not been assessed to income tax or
>
> (IV) has been undercharged in the first assessments.
>
> (iii) a person chargeable has been allowed or has obtained from and in the first assessments any allowance, deduction, exemption abatement or relief not authorised by the Income Tax Acts,
>
> then, where the tax is chargeable under Schedule D, E, or F, the inspector shall make an additional first assessment.

I am satisfied that the circumstances envisaged by s 924 exist in this case and accordingly the defendant is not protected by the provisions of this section.

I am accordingly satisfied that in approaching this case in a manner approved by the Supreme Court in *First National Commercial Bank plc v Angland* [1996] IR 75 the defendant has not established to my satisfaction that he has any real or bona fide defence to be tried by the Court and accordingly I give judgment for the plaintiff in the amount of the claim.

Patrick J O'Connell (Inspector of Taxes) v Fyffes Banana Processing Limited

High Court - 19 May 1999 - Geoghegan J

Corporation Tax - Case Stated - company providing banana ripening services - process of maturation of foodstuffs - whether goods manufactured within the State - strict interpretation of taxing statutes - whether any doubt or ambiguity in the statutory provisions - services rendered deemed to be the manufacture of goods - goods manufactured within the State to be distinguished from services rendered in a process of manufacture of goods

This appeal by the Inspector of Taxes by way of case stated from a determination by the Appeal Commissioners raised a net issue on the interpretation of FA 1980 s 39 relating to manufacturing relief. Fyffes Banana Processing Limited ("the respondent") is a subsidiary company within the Fyffes Group and carries out the ripening process or maturation of imported bananas which are sold on by other group companies. This process of ripening bananas is undoubtedly a process of applying maturation to a foodstuff.

The net issue is whether or not the respondent is denied manufacturing relief by reason of the provision contained in s 39(5) which provides that:

> goods shall not for the purposes of the definition of "goods" in subsection (1) be regarded as manufactured if they are goods which result from a process which consists primarily of ... applying methods of ... maturation or other similar treatment to any foodstuffs.

The net point turns on whether or not the services rendered by the respondent constitute goods as referred to in subsection (5) and as defined in subsection (1) as follows:

> (1) In this Chapter "goods" means goods manufactured within the State in the course of a trade by the company which, in relation to the relevant accounting period is the company claiming relief under this chapter in relation to the trade ...

As regards the services carried out by the respondent subsection (2) reads as follows:

> (2) Where a company carries on a trade which consists of and includes the rendering to another person of services by way of subjecting commodities or materials belonging to that person to any process of manufacturing the following provisions shall apply for the purposes of relief under this chapter -
>
> (a) The rendering within the State of such services shall be regarded as the manufacture within the State of goods.
>
> (b) Any amount receivable in payment for services so rendered shall be regarded as an amount receivable from the sale of the goods.

There are strict rules of interpretation of taxing statutes. Unless there is doubt or ambiguity the courts have not got a function to add to or delete from express statutory provisions to achieve objectives which might appear desirable. The services rendered by the respondent are artificially deemed to be "the manufacture within the State of goods". This is not the equivalent of "goods". The deeming relates to an entire phrase and not to the single word "goods".

Held by Geoghegan J in dismissing the appeal that there is no principle of statutory interpretation to justify a departure from the unambiguous meaning of subsection (2) since the entire activity is deemed to be "the manufacture of goods" and not "goods" as such.

Legislation: ITA 1967 s 428; CTA 1976 s 145; FA 1980 s 39(1), (2) and (5); FA 1990 s 41(5)
Cases referred to in judgment: Inspector of Taxes v Kiernan 3 ITR 19
Charles McCann v O'Culachain 3 ITR 304
McGrath v McDermott 3 ITR 683

Case Stated

Case Stated under ITA 1967, s 428 (as applied to corporation tax by CTA 1976, s 145), by Appeal Commissioners for the opinion of the High Court.

1. At an appeal hearing at No 14 St Stephen's Green, Dublin 2, held on the 21 January 1994, Fyffes Banana Processing Limited, hereinafter called "the company", appealed against the assessment raised for the accounting period ended 31 October 1991, which had the effect of refusing the company's claim to manufacturing relief.

2. The sole matter for determination was the company's entitlement to relief under FA 1980 Pt 1 Ch VI.

3. We found the following facts as admitted or proved:

3.1 The company was incorporated in Ireland on the 22 January 1991, and the first set of accounts covered the period from incorporation to 31 October 1991. Its business is the provision of banana ripening services to other companies within the Fyffes Group. The company is a wholly owned subsidiary of Fyffes plc. Other companies in the Fyffes Group which are wholly owned subsidiaries of Fyffes pie are Banana Importers of Ireland Limited which imports bananas for sale within the Group and to third parties and Fyffes Group Ireland Limited which purchases bananas and sells them ripened (by the company) to third parties.

3.2 The issued share capital of the company is two ordinary shares of IR£2.00 each. One share is held by Fyffes plc and the second share is held by Fyffes Secretarial Services Limited in trust for Fyffes plc.

3.3 The Directors of the company for the period ended 31st October 1991, were Neil McCann, Patrick McNamee, Carl McCann and Richard Kiernan.

3.4 The company carries on the trade of banana ripening in the State which was held in the case of *Charles McCann and Sons Limited v O'Culachain* (3 ITC 304) to be the manufacture of goods. The trade of the company can be distinguished from that of Charles McCann and Sons Limited in that the company does not own the bananas which it ripens. The bananas are owned by other Fyffe companies on whose behalf the company carries out the ripening process.

3.5 It was agreed by both parties that if the company did not come within the provisions of FA 1980 s 39(5) (as inserted by FA 1990 s 41(1)(c)), then the company was entitled to manufacturing relief for the period in question.

4. It was contended by the company as follows:

(a) The provisions of FA 1980 s 39(1), provide that the word "goods" means -

> goods manufactured in the State in the course of a trade by a company which, in relation to the relevant accounting period, is the company claiming relief under this Chapter in relation to the trade .....

(b) The provisions of FA 1980 s 41(2), provide that -

> Where a company which carries on a trade which consists of or includes the manufacture of goods claims ... that, during that [relevant accounting] period, any amount was receivable in respect of the sale, in the course of the trade, of goods, corporation tax payable by the company for that period ... shall be reduced.....

(c) To come within the foregoing provisions, it is essential that the company claiming manufacturing relief should be the company which manufactures the goods and sells the goods in the course of the trade. Therefore, if s 39(1) stood alone, it would only be companies which manufactured goods and sold those goods in the course of their trade which would be entitled to claim manufacturing relief.

(d) However, FA 1980 s 39(1), does not stand alone. The provisions of FA 1980 s 39(2), provide that:

> Where a company carries on a trade which consists of or includes the rendering to another person of services by way of subjecting commodities or materials belonging to that person to any process of manufacturing ... the rendering within the State of such services shall be regarded as the manufacture within the State of goods [and] any amount receivable in payment for services so rendered shall be regarded as an amount receivable from the sale of goods ...

It was submitted that FA 1980 s 39(2), covers a case that does not come within sub-s (1) despite the fact that sub-s (1) commences with the words "In this Chapter 'goods' means ...". Subsection (2) applies in a case in which a company does not manufacture goods - all that is required is that it should subject a commodity "to any process of manufacturing". It applies to the rendering to another person of services and it is expressly provided that "the rendering ... of such services" is to be regarded as the manufacture of goods. The rendering of such services could not be the manufacture of goods as defined in FA 1980 s 39(1).

(e) It was further submitted that the provisions of FA 1980 s 39, had been amended by several Finance Acts in extending the definition of manufacturing to activities which would not normally be considered to be one of manufacturing. All these amendments brought within the relief afforded by FA 1980 s 41(2), activities which would not have constituted the manufacture of goods within the meaning of FA 1980 s 39(1). Therefore, the provisions of s 39(1) cannot provide a comprehensive definition of what constitutes the manufacture of goods.

(f) Finally, it was argued that the provisions of FA 1980 s 39(5) (as inserted by FA 1990 s 41(1)(c)), limited the definition of manufacturing but provided specifically that "goods shall not, for the purposes of the definition of 'goods' in sub-s (1), be regarded as manufactured" if they fall within the provisions of the new subsection; it did not impinge on sub-s (2).

5. It was contended by the Inspector of Taxes as follows:

(a) The provisions of FA 1980 s 39(5), were inserted by FA 1990 s 41(1)(c), and apply to accounting periods beginning on or after 1 April 1990. These provisions state that -

> Without prejudice to the generality of subsection (1) ... goods shall not, for the purposes of the definition of 'goods' in subsection (1), be regarded as manufactured if

> they are goods which result from a process which consists primarily of... applying methods of ... maturation or other similar treatment to any foodstuffs ...

(b) The company is engaged in a process of ripening bananas which is a process of applying methods of maturation to a foodstuff.

(c) The provisions of FA 1980 s 39(2), provide that -

> Where a company carries on a trade which ... includes the rendering to another person of services by way of subjecting commodities or materials belonging to that person to any process of manufacturing ... the rendering ... of such services shall be regarded as the manufacture ... of goods ...

(d) The provisions of FA 1980 s 39(1), state that "In this Chapter 'goods' means goods manufactured within the State ...". Therefore, the amendment introduced by the 1990 Act applies to all references to goods found within FA 1980 Pt I Ch IV, which includes the reference to goods found within FA 1980 s 39(2).

(e) The 1990 amendment (ie s 39(5)) is stated to be subject to a number of subsections, eg (1A), (1B), (1C), etc, but the amendment was not stated to be subject to sub-s (2).

(f) It would not be reasonable to conclude that the Oireachtas, in introducing the 1990 amendment, would seek to restrict claims to relief for certain processes under FA 1980 s 39(1), but that similar processes would continue to enjoy entitlement to relief under FA 1980 s 39(2).

6. The following cases were cited by the parties:

Charles McCann Limited v S. O'Culachain 3 ITC 304;
Patrick McGrath v J.E. McDermott 3 ITR 683;
Inspector of Taxes v Kiernan 3 ITR 19.

7. Having adjourned the case to consider the matter, we gave our reserved Judgment on the 14 April 1994. In interpreting the legislation, the Tribunal was bound by the decisions of the Supreme Court in the cases of *Inspector of Taxes v Kiernan*, and *McGrath v McDermott*. A Court or Tribunal should adopt a literal meaning to legislation and only if this produces a grossly unreasonable result would the Court or Tribunal adopt a schematic approach to interpreting the legislation.

7.1 In the present case the meaning of the legislation is clear and we do not accept that we should enquire whether the Oireachtas was being unreasonable. In fact, we believe that we are precluded from doing so.

7.2 Without prejudice to the point in 7.1 above, we do not consider it unreasonable to suggest that the Oireachtas sought to limit certain claims to manufacturing relief by reference only to claims made under FA 1980 s 39(1). Nor is it unreasonable to suggest that the test required under sub-s (2), ie that commodities or materials be subjected to "any process of manufacturing", is a less onerous test than that imposed under sub-s (1).

Accordingly, we would allow the Appeal.

8. Immediately after we had given our decision, the Inspector expressed dissatisfaction with our decision as being erroneous in law and requested us to state a case for the opinion of the High Court, which we have stated and signed accordingly.

9. The question of law for the opinion of the High Court is whether we were entitled on the foregoing evidence to hold that the company qualified for relief under FA 1980 Pt I Ch, for the accounting period ended 31 October 1991.

10.The document - Description of Manufacturing Process - at Appendix 1, forms part of this Case Stated.

Appendix - Fyffes Banana Processing Limited Description of Manufacturing Process

(a) The appellant is a member of a group of companies, other members of which purchase raw bananas in Ecuador, Columbia, the Dominican Republic, Honduras, Guatemala, Surinam, Belize and Costa Rica. The Appellant does not purchase any bananas but provides a ripening service to other group companies for a fee.

(b) The ripening service is provided by means of ripening rooms which are owned by the appellant. Each ripening room is custom-built with prefabricated four-inch-thick polystyrene insulated panels with air-tight insulated doors. Each room is equipped with compressors, condensers, heaters, coolers and fans located on top of the room. To the side are the controls for the introduction of ethylon liquid. The rooms are capable of maintaining the environment to 0.5 degrees celsius.

(c) The bananas are harvested in a green state and kept in a controlled state at a temperature of 14 degrees celsius during their transport from the growing area to this country. The bananas are unloaded at Cork and transported by temperature-controlled truck to the ripening rooms. During transport, the temperature is maintained at 14 degrees celsius. There is limited change in the unripened fruit during its transportation. The bananas arrive as bunches, contained in polythene bags which, in turn, are contained in boxes or cartons. The cartons are designed to minimise tissue damage to the fruit while allowing ventilation of the contents to avoid a heat build-up.

(d) Bananas ripen either on or off the plant. If they are allowed to ripen naturally off the plant without rigorous control, the result would be the production of a fruit too variable in quality and the process would be too haphazard in its results to yield any sort of orderly marketing so that economic losses would be enormous. The market demands a bright yellow lustrous shiny blemish-free fruit which is produced in the controlled environment. Without rigorous control, the bananas ripen at different rates and some never ripen at all. Bananas which ripen in their own environment do not have the same degree of flavour as those which are ripened artificially. They are more bland in taste than those consumed in Ireland. The ripening process involves the careful monitoring of temperature and humidity in the ripening rooms, the controlled introduction of ethylene gas and the constant testing of the fruit to ensure that the ripening process results in a product acceptable to the market.

(e) On arrival at Dublin, Dundalk and Galway, the bananas, still in their hard and green state, are transferred to the appellant's ripening rooms. If bananas are stored without the temperature being maintained at 14 degrees celsius, some would ripen, some would blacken and rot and the product would be unsaleable.

(f) The ripening process is under the control of a highly-skilled manager at each location. There are about twenty people in the country who have expertise in supervising the ripening process. Of these, only two or three would have a sufficiently high level of expertise to manage the appellant's ripening rooms as no two cargoes of fruit are the same and mistakes could lead to the loss of a whole consignment. The present manager of the appellant's ripening rooms is paid approximately £35,000.00 per annum.

(g) In the ripening rooms, the process on which the appellant bases its claim takes place normally over a period ranging from four or five days to seven to nine days and, in some cases, up to as much as twelve days. The duration of the process is deliberately planned in advance and the factors to be taken into account in predetermining the duration of the process include:

(i) Maturity of the fruit on arrival;

(ii) Its health and physical condition;

(iii) Its required time of delivery to customers. Once placed in the ripening rooms, the fruit requires regular monitoring and the process is controlled by reference to the temperature and humidity within the chamber and the timing of the introduction of ethylene gas.

(h) The ripening process falls into two stages. The initial stage is to bring the fruit to a uniform temperature throughout the ripening room by the controlled introduction of warm air to stabilise the cargo at 14 degrees celsius. To facilitate consistent air circulation, the boxes of bananas are palletised and powerful fans force the air to circulate though the ventilation holes in the boxes in sufficient volume to maintain the pulp temperature at the desired level and to remove the carbon dioxide build-up. When the initial warming-up phase is completed, the ripening process actually begins. This is marked by a considerable increase in the breathing of the fruit releasing heat, vapour and carbon dioxide. This stage of the process peaks at what is called the "climacteric" when up to 100 mg of carbon dioxide per kilogramme is released by the fruit. Due to this breathing, the chamber's oxygen is used up and enriched with carbon dioxide. If, at this period, the temperature of the fruit is not reduced in time, it is possible that heat emitted could cause the fruit to self-heat. With the aid of sensitive temperature control, it is possible to manipulate this critical phase of the ripening process in such a way that overheating is avoided. Apart from normal temperature controls in the ripening rooms, the pulp temperature of the fruit is tested manually. For this purpose, the appellant's personnel use a sterilised probe which is inserted into individual pieces of fruit and which registers the temperature.

(i) At the end of the "climacteric" stage, the intensity of the breathing declines and the colour of the skin continues to turn from green to yellow because the influence of the green chlorophyll on the colour is reduced in the course of the process. This is the commencement of the second stage of the ripening process. It is at this stage that the fruit develops its taste and, to avoid the fruit becoming too soft, it is necessary that the air in the ripening room be renewed through ventilation channels. A mobile catalytic ethylene generator is introduced into the ripening chamber and converts the ethylon liquid to ethylene gas. The ethylene gas is blown though the chamber and penetrates the cells of the fruit. The gas does not accelerate the ripening process but causes the process to commence earlier than it would nominally do. It also enables the synchronisation of ripening so that all the boxes ripen together. During this phase, the temperature is raised to 17 degrees celsius for the ethylene to work. Once the ripening process sets in, the temperature is reduced to 14 degrees celsius.

(j) Ethylene is combustible at high concentrations and there are strict rules regarding its use, including:

(i) Introduction into the ripening room only when the fruit has reached the required temperature;

(ii) Control of the quantum of gas introduced so that the proportion of gas to the content of the ripening room does not exceed the ratio of one to a thousand;

(iii) Air-proof conditions within the ripening room so as to ensure maintenance of the concentration of ethylene;

(iv) Precautions in relation to electrical fittings so as to avoid danger of explosion;

(v) After the introduction of ethylene, the ripening room must remain closed for a period, the length of which is dependent on the planned duration of the ripening process;

(vi) After the ethylene stage, the air in the chamber must be replaced to admit sufficient oxygen, otherwise the fruit will acquire a greyish yellow appearance.

(k) The banana, in its hard and green state, consists almost entirely of water and starch and, in that state, is inedible. The ripening process to which the fruit is subjected produces a chemical change in the fruit which is substantial in nature and which has the effect of turning the unedible into the edible.

High Court - 19 May 1999

Geoghegan J, This is a Case Stated under ITA 1967 s 428 (as applied to corporation tax by CTA 1976 s 145) by the Appeal Commissioners for the opinion of the High Court. The issue involved is whether the respondent is entitled to claim manufacturing relief in relation to the accounting period ended 1 October 1991 having regard to FA 1980 s 39(2). The claim to entitlement is dependent on whether the respondent company comes within the provisions of FA 1980 s 39(5) (as inserted by FA 1990 s 41(1)(c)) or not. The appellant contends that the respondent comes within the subsection, the respondent contends that it does not. It is common case that if s 39(5) of the 1980 Act as amended does not apply, the respondent is entitled to the relief. For the purposes of this case Chapter VI of the Finance Act 1980 as amended contained within it all the relevant provisions relating to relief from corporation tax in relation to certain income of manufacturing companies The relevant part of s 39(1) of the 1980 Act as amended reads as follows:

> (1) In this Chapter 'goods' means goods manufactured within the State in the course of a trade by the company which, in relation to the relevant accounting period is the company claiming relief under this chapter in relation to the trade ...

Several new sub-sections were inserted by amendment into s 39 at this point but although they are of some small relevance I do not find it necessary to cite them. I move now to sub-section (2) which reads as follows:

> (2) Where a company carries on a trade which consists of or includes the rendering to another person of services by way of subjecting commodities or materials belonging to that person to any process of manufacturing, the following provisions shall apply for the purposes of relief under this chapter -
>
> (a) The rendering within the State of such services shall be regarded as the manufacture within the State of goods.
>
> (b) Any amount receivable in payment for services so rendered shall be regarded as an amount receivable from the sale of the goods.
>
> (c) The inspector may by notice in writing require a company claiming relief from tax by virtue of this subsection to furnish him with such information or particulars as may be necessary for the purpose of giving effect to this sub-section and section 41(2) shall have effect as if the matters of which proof is required thereby included the information or particulars specified in a notice under this sub-section.

Although I have not cited the intermediate sub-sections which are (1A); (1B), (1C), (1CC), (1CC1), (1CC2), (1CC3), (1CC4), (1CC5), (1CC6) and (1CC7), I think it relevant to explain that each of these added sub-sections was for the purposes of bringing within the scheme of relief, activities which in the ordinary way would not be regarded as being the manufacture of goods.

The relevant part of FA 1980 s 39(5) as inserted by FA 1990 reads as follows:

> (5) Without prejudice to the generality of sub-section (1) and subject to sub-sections (1A); (1B), (1C), (1CC), (1CC1), (1CC2), (1CC3), (1CC4), (1CC5), (1CC6) and (1CC7), goods shall not, for the purposes of the definition of 'goods' in sub-section (1), be regarded as

> manufactured if they are goods which result from a process which consists primarily of ... applying methods of ... maturation or other similar treatment to any foodstuffs ...

The Case Stated sets out that it was admitted or proved that the respondent company engaged in the business of providing banana ripening services to other companies within the Fyffes group. The respondent is a wholly owned subsidiary of Fyffes Plc. Other companies in the Fyffes group which are wholly owned subsidiaries of Fyffes Plc are Banana Importers of Ireland Limited which imports bananas for sale within the group and to third parties and Fyffes Group Ireland Limited which purchases bananas and sells them ripened (by the company) to third parties. The process of ripening bananas is undoubtedly a process of applying methods of maturation to a foodstuff. The claim for relief is entirely dependent on s 39(2) and on the assumption that that sub-section remains unaffected by s 39(5).

The Appeal Commissioners held that that was in fact the case and I am in agreement with their decision.

A number of cases have been cited to this Court concerning the interpretation of tax statutes. The relevant jurisprudence is to be found in *Inspector of Taxes v Kiernan* [1981] IR 117, *Charles McCann Limited v O'Cualachain* [1988] IR 196 and above all *McGrath v McDermott* [1988] IR 258. In the judgment of Finlay CJ in that last mentioned case at p 276 the following passage is to be found:

> The function of the Courts in interpreting a statute of the Oireachtas is, however, strictly confined to ascertaining the true meaning of each statutory provision, resorting in cases of doubt or ambiguity to a consideration of the purpose and intention of the legislature to be inferred from other provisions of the statute involved, or even of other statutes expressed to be construed with it. The Courts have not got a function to add to or delete from express statutory provision so as to achieve objectives which to the Courts appear desirable. In rare and limited circumstances words or phrases may be implied into provisions solely for the purpose of making them effective to achieve their expressly avowed objectives.

I think it quite likely that it may not have been intended that a company such as the respondent company would be entitled to claim manufacturing relief by virtue of s 39(2) after s 39(5) had been enacted. But it would be neither appropriate nor relevant for me to make any finding to that effect because the question of the intention only comes into play if there is doubt or ambiguity. In this case I cannot see that there is any doubt or ambiguity. Sub-section (5) becomes relevant if for the purposes of considering whether there is a claim for relief or not the word "goods" on its own has to be interpreted. That of course is the case where a company is relying on sub-section (1) rather than sub-section (2) of s 39. If the respondent was selling the bananas it was ripening it could not claim relief having regard to subsection (5) of s 39. But the service which the respondent company renders is artificially deemed by sub-section (5) to be "the manufacture within the State of goods". The deeming relates to the entire phrase and not to the single word "goods". I know of no principle of statutory interpretation which requires that an unambiguous sub-section related in subject-matter to the immediately preceding sub-section must be given a meaning other than the original unambiguous meaning because of some alteration in either the preceding sub-section itself or as in this case in the application of that sub-section.

I do not think that the position is altered in any way by the reference in sub-section (5) to the various sub-sections which were inserted between sub-section (1) and sub-section (2). The fact that the definition of "goods" is to apply throughout the chapter is the only point of difficulty that I found. But I have come to the conclusion that it is not relevant. The relief under FA 1990 s 41 was for companies carrying on a trade which consisted of or included the manufacture of goods and then selling on the goods. It was essential for this purpose that "goods" be given a statutory meaning. But there is nothing to prevent the Oireachtas deeming any kind of activity to be "the manufacture within the State of goods" and for the purposes of interpreting any such statutory provision the definition of "goods" itself becomes irrelevant because the entire activity is deemed to be the "manufacture of goods". That is effectively the kind of legislation which s 39(2) is.

The question of law submitted to this Court by the Appeal Commissioners in the Case Stated is whether they were entitled on the evidence as set out in the Case Stated to hold that the company qualified for relief under Chapter VI of Part I of the Finance Act 1980 for the accounting period ended 31 October. 1991. The answer to that question must be "yes".

I therefore dismiss the appeal.

Sean MacAonghusa (Inspector of Taxes) v Ringmahon Company

High Court - 26 November 1999 - Budd J

Corporation tax - case stated - whether loan interest was money wholly and exclusively expended for the purpose of trade of the company - company redeemed £6 million Redeemable Preference shares - company raised a loan of £6 million - whether loan for purpose of restricting share capital and paying off shareholders - whether loan a temporary and fluctuating borrowing - purposes of trade is to serve purposes of the trade - object in making the payment is based on the intentions of the taxpayer - whether incidental consequences - question of degree - whether Inspector can direct company on how to finance its business - whether loan needed to continue trade - whether company entitled to a deduction for annual loan interest - whether judge's determination properly within the evidence adduced before him.

The net point of law in this case stated on which the Inspector of Taxes appealed to the High Court arose on the question of whether or not the annual interest on a bank loan raised by Ringmahon Company ("the respondent") was an allowable deduction against the trading profits of the respondent.

Facts

The share capital of the respondent included £6 million Redeemable Preference Shares held by a related company Dunnes Stores Ireland Company. The share capital was used for the purposes of the respondent's trade of "Retailing of Food, Clothing and other Household Goods". The respondent redeemed the Redeemable Preference Shares and borrowed £6 million from Allied Irish Banks and claimed the annual interest on this bank loan as an allowable deduction against its trading profits.

The law

TCA 1997 s 81(2) provides as follows:

> Subject to the Tax Acts, in computing the amount of profits or gains to be charged to tax under Case I or II of Schedule D no sum shall be deducted in respect of:
>
> (a) any disbursements or expenses not being money wholly and exclusively laid out or expended for the purposes of the trade of profession ...

Submissions

The Inspector contended that the loan was raised for the purpose of restructuring the share capital of the company and was not expenditure wholly and exclusively for the purposes of the company's trade. The respondent argued that the loan was used in the purchase of premises, plant, stock and services and was not retained as a cash sum for investment. The loan was needed to carry on the respondent's business. The Inspector pointed out that the word "exclusively" ruled out any purpose other than trade and that the Circuit Court judge had erred in law by adding words such as "vital to survive" and "only possible option" to the phraseology in s 81(2). The respondent submitted that while the loan itself was not deductible the recurring interest was wholly and exclusively expended for the purposes of the trade.

Held by Budd J in dismissing the appeal that:

(i) the Revenue Commissioners cannot direct a tax paying company as to how it should finance its business;

(ii) the respondent was entitled to redeem the Redeemable Preference Shares;

(iii) the respondent needed funds to continue trading and no new assets other than trading assets were acquired;

(iv) the phrases "vital to service" and "only possible option" were merely illustrative of the statutory requirement of wholly and exclusively laid out for the purposes of the trade;

(v) the decision of the Circuit Court judge was perfectly within the evidence adduced before him and he was entitled to make the findings he made and to come to his rational conclusion that the recurrent cost of the loan was wholly and exclusively laid out for the purposes of the trade of the respondent.

Legislation: TCA 1997 s 81(2)

Cases referred to in judgment: TG Brosnan (Inspector of Taxes) v Mutual Enterprise Ltd [1997] 3 IR 257

Inspector of Taxes (Mara) v Hummingbird [1982] ILRM 421

WS McGarry (Inspector of Taxes) v Limerick Gas Committee [1932] IR 125

McGrath v McDermott (Inspector of Taxes) 3 ITR 683

Mallalieu v Drurnmond (Inspector of Taxes) [1983] STC 665

Prince v Mapp (Inspector of Taxes) [1970] 1 WLR 260

Morgan (HM Inspector of Taxes) v Tate & Lyle Ltd [1955] AC 21

Vodafone Cellular Ltd v Shaw (Inspector of Taxes) [1997] STC 734

Trans- Prairie Ltd v Minister of National Revenue 70 DTC 6351

DWS Corporation v Minister of National Revenue [1968] 2 Ex CR 44

Strong and Company of Romsey Ltd v Woodfield (Surveyor of Taxes) 5 TC 215

CIR v Carron Co 45 TC 18

CIR v Pullman Car Co Ltd 35 TC 221

Case Stated

Case stated for the opinion of the High Court under TCA 1997 s 941 as extended by s 94, (previously ITA 1967 s 428 and s 430) by His Honour, Judge Dominic Lynch, a judge of the Circuit Court assigned to the Dublin Circuit.

1. This matter came before me on 21 October 1997 and 11 November 1997 by way of a re-hearing, pursuant to TCA 1997 s 942 (preciously ITA 1967 s 429), of an appeal by Ringmahon Company (hereinafter called "Ringmahon") against a corporation tax assessment for the accounting period ended 28 December 1991.

2. Shortly stated, the question for my determination was whether in computing the amount of its profits under Case I of Schedule D, Ringmahon was entitled to a deduction in respect of bank interest £435,764 payable on a term loan which was applied to redeem preference share capital.

3. Evidence was given before me by Mr Frank Bowen, Chartered Accountant, accountant and advisor to Ringmahon.

4. The following facts were proved or admitted:

(a) Ringmahon, an unlimited company, is a wholly owned subsidiary of Ringmahon Holdings Ltd, the ordinary shares of which are held by members of the Dunne family.

(b) In 1987 Ringmahon acquired some of the former H Williams supermarkets and began to trade from these stores under the Dunnes Stores brand name.

(c) Ringmahon is engaged in the trade of "Retailing of Food, Clothing and other Household Goods".

(d) The purchase of the H Williams shops was initially financed by way of loan from Dunnes Stores Ireland Company (hereinafter called "DSIC"), but this finance was replaced by the issue by Ringmahon of 11,500,000 Redeemable Preference Shares of 5p at a premium of 95p per share to DSIC on 4 January 1988 (DSIC is ultimately controlled by the Dunne Family Trust, the beneficiaries of which are members of the Dunne family.)

(e) In 1991 the Ringmahon board decided to redeem 6,000,000 of the Redeemable Preference Shares held by DSIC. The company negotiated a loan of £6m with Allied Irish Banks for this stated purpose. The loan was drawn down by Ringmahon on 30 April 1991, and on 2 May 1991 Ringmahon issued a cheque for £6m to DSIC. The journal entries reflect a redemption of 6,000,000 Redeemable Preference Shares in the accounts of Ringmahon for the period ended 28 December 1991.

(f) The proposal to redeem part of the preference share capital was in pursuance of the stated objective at the time that Ringmahon was set up that the company would be financed independently of the Dunne Family trust (including the group companies owned by the trust) and would stand alone as a separate operation.

(g) There was no obligation on Ringmahon to redeem the preference share capital. The Articles of Association provide that the company has sole discretion in the decision to redeem all or part of its Redeemable Preference Shares.

(h) The issued ordinary share capital of Ringmahon at the date of the aforementioned redemption was two ordinary £1 shares fully paid up.

5. It was contended on behalf of Ringmahon that the only way in which it could carry on its trade after the redeemable preference shares had been redeemed was by borrowings and the interest on those borrowings was accordingly wholly and exclusively laid out for the purposes of that trade: in support of that contention the following arguments were made:

(a) The replacement of redeemable preference shares with borrowings from AIB was a refinancing by Ringmahon of its trading operations and interest on those borrowings was as much allowable as if borrowings from its bankers had been the original method of financing the company.

(b) The fact that the bank borrowings replaced the share capital is irrelevant to the wholly and exclusively test laid down in ITA 1967 s 61(a) in a particular accounting period, where the bank liability is supporting the trade and its assets - and there was nothing else to support in Ringmahon.

(c) The relevant test is has the particular expense been laid out in any particular year or accounting period wholly and exclusively in earning the profits of that year or accounting period - it is submitted that the answer to this question is in the affirmative.

(d) The borrowings did no more than continue to support the trading apparatus - that is to say, trading assets such as premises, plant stock and so forth. No new asset was acquired by the company on account of the refinancing - and the company having redeemed the preference shares this new funding was necessary to continue its trade Accordingly it was submitted that interest on the funding was wholly and exclusively laid out for the purposes of the trade, that is to say, the loan funding supported the trading assets and enabled the trade to continue. If that funding were to be withdrawn or were not available, cash to pay creditors would not be available and the company would probably have gone into liquidation.

(e) The interest paid to the bank was paid on borrowings -

> for the purpose of enabling the company to carry on and earn profits in the trade

(*per* Lord Davy in *Strong v Woodfield* 5 TC 215) - the interest was laid out for the purpose of earning the profits (*cf ibid*).

(f) If Ringmahon had financed its business by bank borrowing from the commencement of its trade the interest payable would clearly have been allowable as a trading expense - accordingly it is submitted that there is no basis on which the position should be different merely because there were no borrowings in the period prior to the 1991 accounting period: up to that point the company had financed its business by redeemable share capital - it then substituted that financing by bank borrowings and in the submission of the appellant there is no distinction in principle between interest payable on those bank borrowings and say, interest payable on bank borrowings which had been substituted for other bank borrowings,

(g) Ringmahon was free to finance its trading operations by whatever means it deemed appropriate and the Revenue are not entitled to dictate the means which it from time to time should see fit to adopt - and the bank borrowings were to finance its trading operations as it had no other operations.

(h) The borrowings were necessary to support the company's trade.

(i) Interest due and payable to AIB on the borrowings was laid out solely to enable the company to stay in business and to carry on its trade.

(j) Accordingly the interest amounting to £435,764 was wholly and exclusively laid out for the purposes of the trade of the company and was a proper deduction in arriving at the company's Case I profits for the accounting period ending on 28 December 1991.

(k) The following authorities were cited in support:

Trans-Prairie Pipelines Ltd v Minister of National Revenue 70 DTC 6351 - (Exchequer Court of Canada)

Strong & Company of Romsey Ltd v Woodifield 5 TC 215

Montreal Coke and Manufacturing Co v Minister of National Revenue [1944] 1 All ER 743

CIR v Pullman 35 TC 291

Craddock v Zevo Finance Co Ltd 27 TC 267

CIR v Carron Company 45 TC 18

Westmoreland Investment Ltd v MacNiven [1998] STC 1131

Morgan v Tate and Lyle 35 TC 367

McGarry v the Limerick Gas Committee 1 ITR 375

UK Inspector's Manual IM 777

6. It was contended on behalf of the Inspector of Taxes as follows:

(a) The object of Ringmahon in proceeding to make application for and negotiate the loan agreement with the bank was solely related to the question of redeeming, in part, the Redeemable Preference Shares held by DSIC.

(b) It follows, therefore, that the purpose of the loan was to enable the company to redeem, in part, the Redeemable Preference Shares held by DSIC.

(c) The effect of the receipt by Ringmahon of the loan monies and the immediate application of those monies by way of payment to DSIC (for redemption of preference shares) was that part of the issued share capital of Ringmahon was replaced with loan capital.

(d) The monies borrowed were placed at the disposal of the shareholders of Ringmahon.

(e) The redemption of the share capital did not impact on the day to day trading activities of Ringmahon.

(f) Neither the object of Ringmahon in seeking the borrowings nor the effect of the subsequent payment by Ringmahon to DSIC of the loan monies did in any way serve the purposes of the trade of Ringmahon as distinct from serving the purposes of the company itself

(g) Accordingly. the payment of interest on the borrowings in question was not money wholly and exclusively laid out for the purposes of the trade.

(h) A deduction is therefore prohibited for the full amount of interest claimed of £435,764 under TCA 1997 s 81 (2)(a) [previously ITA 1967 s 61(a)].

(i) The following cases were cited in support:

Montreal Coke and Manufacturing Co v Minister of National Revenue [1944] 1All ER 743
Archibald Thomson, Black Co Ltd v Batty 7 TC 158
Strong and Company of Romsey Ltd v Woodifield 5 TC 215
Patrick McGrath and Ors v JE McDermott (Inspector of Taxes) 3 ITR 653.

7. When the matter was heard by the Appeal Commissioners, they found that:

(a) once a shareholder subscribes money for shares, what he gets in return is confirmation that he owns a portion of the business. It was perhaps acceptable in a loose accounting sense to say that the share capital subscribed might be financing part of the company's assets but, from a legal point of view, it is absolutely not the case that there was anything of a financing nature involved in the subscription for shares;

(b) it was necessary to actually stick with what was planned to happen and what did actually happen. It was not in order to look at what an accountant might say was the effective result of the transactions and,

(c) they concluded that the loan documentation showed that the money was used to redeem the shares and that there was nothing which directed them to conclude that the loan was raised for the purposes of the company's trade.

8. Having considered the facts and arguments presented, it is clear and is common case that the Revenue Commissioners cannot direct a tax paying company as to how it should finance its business and it does appear on the facts that the company found itself in need of funds and so monies had to be borrowed and, therefore, interest was payable. In considering the case made by the Revenue Commissioners I found myself adding words to the section (TCA 1997 s 81(2)(a)) such as "vital to survive" and "only possible option" and, on the interpretation of the statute, that is not something which I was entitled to do.

Accordingly, having considered the matter fully, I held that Ringmahon was entitled to a deduction of £435,764 under the rules of TCA 1997 s 81(2)(a) (previously ITA 1967 s 61(a)), being in respect of money which was wholly and exclusively laid out for the purposes of the trade of Ringmahon.

9. Immediately after my determination the Inspector of Taxes declared dissatisfaction with my decision and in due course required me to state and sign a case for the opinion of the High Court pursuant to TCA 1997 s 943 (previously ITA 1967 s 430) which case I do hereby state and sign accordingly.

10. The question of law for the opinion of the High Court is whether I was correct in holding that Ringmahon was entitled to a deduction of £435,764 in computing the amount of its profits under Case I of Schedule D.

High Court - 26 November 1999

Budd J, This is a case stated for the opinion of the High Court pursuant to the TCA 1997 s 943 from a decision of His Honour, Judge Dominic Lynch given in his judgment delivered on 11 November 1997 with which the Inspector immediately expressed dissatisfaction and required a case to be stated. The Inspector had initially raised an assessment for corporation tax on the respondent, Ringmahon Company ("the company"). On appeal by the company the matter went before the Appeal Commissioners. There was then an appeal to the Circuit Court which heard the matter as a full appeal on the facts and heard the evidence of Frank Bowen, Chartered Accountant, who had acted as advisor to the company. The learned Circuit Court judge held that the company was entitled to a deduction of £435,764.00 in computing the amount of its profits under Case I of Schedule D. The relevant part of TCA 1997 s 81 reads as follows:

> (1) The tax under Cases I and II of Schedule D shall be charged without any deduction other than is allowed by the Tax Acts.
> (2) Subject to the Tax Acts, in computing the amount of the profits or gains to be charged to tax under Case I or II of Schedule D, no sum shall be deducted in respect of -
> (a) any disbursement or expenses, not being money wholly and exclusively laid out or expended for the purposes of the trade or profession;... .

The provisions of ITA 1967 s 61 dealing with the general rule as to deductions is in similar terms:

> Subject to the provisions of this Act, in computing the amount of the profits or gains to be charged, no sum shall be deducted in respect of -
> (a) any disbursements or expenses, not being money wholly and exclusively laid out or expended for the purposes of the trade or profession;...

Since reference will be made to the similar provision in the UK Tax Codes it is helpful to note that the ICTA 1988 s 74 deals with general rules as to deductions not allowable:- (As inserted by virtue of FA 1994 s 144(2) this provision now reads):

> (1) Subject to the provisions of the Tax Acts, in computing the amount of the (profits) to be charged under Case I or Case II of Schedule D, no sum shall be deducted in respect of -
> (a) any disbursements or expenses, not being money wholly and exclusively laid out or expended for the purposes of the trade, profession or vocation;

The facts of the matter as found by the learned Circuit Court judge are vital. The essence of the matter is the purpose for which the company took out a loan. If the cost of that loan, the interest paid thereon from year to year, is held to be money wholly and exclusively laid out or expended for the purpose of the company's trade, then this interest is a deductible expense for the purposes of Corporation Tax and the company would effect a tax saving at about 40%.

The Inspector's case is that the company raised a loan from Allied Irish Banks for the purpose of redeeming six million redeemable preference shares held by Dunnes Stores Ireland Company (called *DSIC*). He argues that the loan was raised for the purpose of a share restructuring of the company rather than for the trade of the company, which is engaged in the trade of *Retailing of Food, Clothing and other Household Goods.* He stresses the "wholly and exclusively" test in the Irish and UK legislation.

The actual findings of the learned Circuit Court judge are important and accordingly I append the wording of the entire case stated. This gives the history of the transactions and also the findings made by the Circuit Court. These are significant because the case made on behalf of the Inspector is that the findings of the learned Circuit Court judge and his conclusions based on primary facts were significantly influenced by a wrong view of the law. No criticism is made of the statements in the Case Stated up to paragraph 8 but the contention made on behalf of the Inspector is that the learned Circuit Court judge fell into error in saying that he would have to add words to the phraseology in s 81(2)(a) in order to be able to find for the Inspector.

The jurisdiction of the High Court in a case stated under the TCA 1997 ss 941, 942 and 943

First, while the proceedings in this tax matter before the Appeal Commissioners and the Circuit Court were in private, this Case Stated is dealt with in open court. Secondly, charging sections are in general construed against the Revenue while relief sections are construed against the taxpayer. Thirdly, a citizen is entitled to look at the wording of the tax statutes and to arrange his affairs so as to minimise the incidence of tax.

In *TG Brosnan (Inspector of Taxes) v Mutual Enterprises Limited* [1997] 3 IR 257, in 1979 the respondent had obtained a loan of monies in sterling payable *on demand* from a bank to facilitate the purchase of a business premises from which it was intended to carry on its trade. The monies were used for the purchase of a premises but the sterling debt was converted from time to time in various European currencies to achieve the best possible rate of interest payable. As a result of these currency dealings the company incurred substantial losses. The respondent sought to include the losses incurred on the foreign currency transactions in computing the trading profits and allowable losses for corporation tax purposes. The appellant argued that, as the monies were borrowed for the purpose of acquiring a capital asset, any losses incurred on foreign currency dealings with the monies were capital losses and were not allowable as trading losses. That issue was determined in favour of the Revenue by the Appeal Commissioner. On appeal to the Circuit Court, the Circuit judge formed the opinion that the losses were not of a capital nature or intended to be employed as capital in the company's trade and that they were connected with the trade and allowable under ITA 1967 s 61(e). The applicant was dissatisfied with the determination and the Circuit Court judge stated a case for the opinion of the High Court as to whether his decision was correct in law. Murphy J in the High Court answered the Case Stated in the affirmative stating that, in deciding whether losses were of a revenue or capital nature, all relevant facts must be taken into account and that an important factor to be considered in determining whether a bank loan was of a revenue nature, rather than of a capital nature, was whether it was a fluctuating and temporary accommodation; the weight to be attached to these factors was a question of fact to be determined by the Appeal

Commissioners as they thought fit. It could not be said that no reasonable judge of first instance could have concluded on the facts as a whole that the loans were a means of fluctuating and temporary accommodation. On appeal to the Supreme Court it was held that where a loan was a capital transaction, then any accompanying currency exchange loss was a capital loss and was not deductible from profits; but where the loan was in the nature of a revenue transaction, then the currency exchange loss was deductible in computing the respondent's profits. In determining whether a loan was a revenue transaction the test was whether it constituted a temporary and fluctuating borrowing and that this was a question of fact and not of law. The Supreme Court went on to say that a finding by a Circuit Court judge in determining whether a loan was temporary or fluctuating may only be disturbed where there was no evidence to support it, or it was a finding which no judge could reasonably have made on the basis of the facts proved or admitted; and, as it was open to the Circuit Court judge to find on the facts proved or admitted, that the loan constituted a temporary or fluctuating accommodation. And as it was not a finding that no reasonable Judge could have made in the circumstances of the case, it was not open to the High Court or Supreme Court to interfere with such a finding. In the High Court, at p 266, Murphy J said:

> To my mind the fact that the purpose of the borrowing was clearly identified and that that purpose was the acquisition of a capital asset and that it was implemented was a factor of very considerable importance. These relevant facts were obvious to the learned trial judge. It may be that he attached less weight to them than I would have done or that he attached greater significance to other factors, such as, the fact that the borrowing was repayable 'on demand'. All one can say is that there were a number of factors to be taken into account and I cannot say that no reasonable judge of first instance could have concluded on the facts as a whole that the loans were a means of fluctuating and temporary accommodation. In the circumstances there are no grounds on which I would be justified in interfering with the decision which he reached.

In the Supreme Court Hamilton CJ at p 283 helpfully sets out a synopsis of the case law and encapsulates the rule as to the approach to be taken. The Circuit Court judge had been dealing with an appeal under the provisions of the ITA 1967. Under s 429 of that Act there is provision for an appeal by way of a rehearing before the Circuit Court judge and the fundamental issue for decision in all the circumstances of the case was whether the AIB loan, made to the respondent, was *fluctuating and temporary accommodation* or an accretion to the capital of the company. At p 283 the Chief Justice said:

> The Circuit Court judge had held that the loan was temporary and fluctuating. Such finding by the Circuit Court judge can only be disturbed if it was a finding in respect of which there was no evidence to support or which no judge could reasonably have made on the basis of the facts proved or admitted before him.

He then set out with approval the views expressed by Murphy J in the passage quoted above and continued:

> In adopting this approach, which was the correct approach, the learned trial judge was applying the principle enunciated in many cases that findings on primary facts should not be set aside by the courts unless there was no evidence whatever to support them.
>
> In the course of his judgment in *Inspector of Taxes (Mara) v Hummingbird* [1982] ILRM 421, Kenny J stated at p 426 of the report that:
>
> > A case stated consists in part of findings on questions of primary fact, eg with what intention did the taxpayers purchase the Baggott Street premises. These findings on primary facts should not be set aside by the courts unless there was no evidence whatever to support them. The commissioner then goes on in the case stated to give his conclusions

or inferences from these primary facts. These are mixed questions of fact and law and the court should approach these in a different way. If they are based on the interpretation of documents, the court should reverse them if they are incorrect for it is in as good a position to determine the meaning of documents as is the commissioner. If the conclusions from the primary facts are ones which no reasonable commissioner could draw, the court should set aside his findings on the ground that he must be assumed to have misdirected himself as to the law or made a mistake in reasoning. Finally, if his conclusions show that he has adopted a wrong view of the law, they should be set aside. If, however, they are not based on a mistaken view of the law or a wrong interpretation of documents, they should not be set aside unless the inferences which he made from the primary facts were ones that no reasonable commissioner could draw. The ways of conducting business have become very complex and the answer to the question whether a transaction was an adventure in the nature of trade nearly always depends on the importance which the judge or commissioner attaches to some facts. He will have evidence some of which supports the conclusion that the transaction under investigation was an adventure in the nature of trade and he will have some which points to the opposite conclusion. These are essentially matters of degree and his conclusions should not be disturbed (even if the court does not agree with them, for we are not retrying the case) unless they are such that a reasonable commissioner could not draw them or they are based on a mistaken view of the law.

The way in which a court should approach the conclusions of the Commissioner was discussed in the House of Lords in *Edwards (Inspector of Taxes) v Bairstow* [1956] AC 14, in which the House reversed the finding of the commissioner that a purchase of plant was not an adventure in the nature of trade. In the course of his speech Viscount Simonds said:

> 'For it is universally conceded that though it is a pure finding of fact, it may be set aside on grounds which have been stated in various ways but are, I think fairly summarised by saying that the court should take that course if it appears that the commissioners have acted without any evidence, or on a view of the facts which could not reasonably be entertained and Lord Radcliffe in the course of his speech said:
>
> > 'I do not think that inferences drawn from other facts are incapable of being themselves findings of fact, although there is value in the distinction between primary facts and inferences drawn from them. When the case comes before the court, it is its duty to examine the determination having regard to its knowledge of the relevant law. If the case contains anything ex facie which is bad law and which bears on the determination, it is, obviously erroneous in point of law. But without any such misconception appearing ex facie, it may be that the facts found are such that no person acting judicially and properly instructed as to the relevant law could come to the determination under appeal. In those circumstances, too, the court must intervene. It has no option but to assume that there has been some misconception of the law, and that this has been responsible for the determination. So too there has been error in point of law. I do not think that it matters much whether this state of affairs is described as one in which there is no evidence to support the determination, or as one in which the evidence is inconsistent with, and contradictory of, the determination or as one in which the true and only reasonable conclusion contradicts the determination. Rightly understood, each phrase propounds the same test. For my part, I prefer the last of the three since I think it is rather misleading to speak of there being no evidence to support a conclusion when in cases such as these, many of the facts are likely to be neutral in themselves and only to take their colour from the combination of circumstances in which they are found to occur.'

> As it was open to the learned Circuit Court judge to find, on the facts proved or admitted, that the AIB loan constituted 'temporary and fluctuating' accommodation, it was not open to the High Court or this Court to interfere with such finding unless it was a finding that no reasonable judge could have made in the circumstances of this case.

Both parties accepted the principles as explained by the Supreme Court in the *Brosnan* case. Counsel for the Inspector on the one hand contended that the findings of the Circuit Court judge and his conclusions, while based on primary facts, were significantly influenced by his erroneous view of the law and that he was in error in saying that he would have to add words such as *vital to survive* or *only possible option* before he would be able to find for the Inspector. Counsel for the company, on the other hand, stressed that the learned Circuit Court judge had set out the facts from which he drew reasonable inferences in paragraph 8 and had then come to the conclusion that the interest incurred on the loan was wholly and exclusively laid out for the purposes of the company's trade. I agree that the findings of fact in the case stated were clearly and sufficiently set out and that there was no need for any further findings of fact.

In an earlier case stated *WS McGarry (Inspector of Taxes) v Limerick Gas Committee* [1932] IR 125 Limerick Corporation, having installed modern plant and machinery in their gas works, dismissed a number of their workmen in consequence of the modernisation. The Corporation had no power to pay any compensation by way of pensions or otherwise to these men and so they promoted a Private Bill in Parliament to authorise them to do this. In computing the liability of the Corporation to income tax for the year in which the Bill was promoted, the Commissioners for the special purposes of the Income Tax Acts were of the opinion that the cost of promoting the Bill was not in the nature of capital expenditure, but was a proper debit item to be set against the income of the undertaking and that it was a necessary trading expense incurred in the course of carrying on the undertaking. The Inspector required the Special Commissioners to state a case for the opinion of the High Court which held that the Commissioners were right in holding that the cost of promoting the Bill was an admissible deduction in the revenue account of the Corporation for the purpose of computing the liability of the Corporation to income tax for the year. The cost of promoting the Bill had been £200 which was allowed by the Special Commissioners. They decided that this item was an admissible deduction because it was a necessary trading expense incurred in the course of carrying on the business. At p 133 Hannah J said:

> Construing paragraph 13, in substance the Special Commissioners found that it was a necessary trading expense incurred in the course of carrying on the undertaking. It was open to them upon the evidence to come to that conclusion, or, on the contrary, to come to the conclusion that the item was not a necessary trading expense. There was evidence of the purpose for which the Bill was promoted and of the circumstances from which there was a moral obligation to be discharged by the Gas Committee in regard to the men who had been previously employed by them. There was evidence upon which the Special Commissioners could have come to a different conclusion, but they have come to this conclusion. The evidence was that in consequence of the changes made in their undertaking and the installation of newer forms of machinery, it was necessary for the Gas Committee to get rid of some of their employees and to make provision for pensions. They had to get legal sanction for certain financial arrangements, which were necessary in order to enable them to discharge this moral obligation. That being so, it was open to the Special Commissioners to come to one or other of two conclusions and they came to the conclusion now in question.
>
> English cases do not assist us much in this matter because our Supreme Court in the case of *Lord Iveagh v Revenue Commissioners* [1930] IR 386 has explained the law which this court

should apply in dealing with appeals from the Special Commissioners. In the first place, we are not bound by the form in which the question to be determined is submitted; the mere words, 'question of law' do not bind the Court to answer the question as such; the Court must look at the case stated to see whether or not, and how far, the question is one of fact, and, if it is a question of fact, the Court can set aside the finding of the Special Commissioners that it is a question of law. In *Lord Iveagh's* case - to which I referred at a very early stage in the argument - the Chief Justice said at p 437: 'Now, by the code of income tax law derived from the British Legislature, and continued in operation with some adaptations and amendments in the Saorstát, the determination of questions of fact for income tax purposes has been consigned to a jury of two official persons, who are final on fact and subject to instruction and correction on questions of law by the High Court on case stated.' The rest of the paragraph is immaterial. He continued at p 438:- 'In my opinion, therefore, the question propounded at foot of the case - "Whether the appellant was domiciled in Saorstát Éireann in the years of assessments" - being, as so stated, a question of fact, was not such a question as the statute authorised to be submitted to the High Court. Moreover, the High Court, misled by the question, was not, in my opinion, authorised by the statute in examining the evidence and dealing with the appeal generally as if it were an appellate tribunal hearing an appeal from a judgment on a trial by a judge without a jury, with full jurisdiction to review determinations of law and fact. Fitzgibbon J in a more detailed judgment, agreed with this view, and cited passages from the authorities to the same effect. At p 441 he cited Lord Sumner in *Levene v Inland Revenue Commissioners* [1928] AC 217 at p 228 as saying: 'The tribunal thus provided is neither bound by the findings of other similar tribunals in other cases nor is it open to review, so long as it commits no palpable error of law, and the Legislature practically transfers to it the function of imposing taxes on individuals, since it empowers them in terms so general, that no one can be certainly advised in advance, whether he must pay or can escape payment. The way of taxpayers is hard, and the Legislature does not go out of its way to make it any easier'. Mr Justice Fitzgibbon continued, in reference to the same case: 'Lord Cave says: "Under the well established rule these findings cannot be disturbed by the Courts unless there was no evidence to support them".

Therefore, having come to the conclusion that the Special Commissioners have found as a fact that this was a necessary trading expense, I have to deal with two points: first, whether there was evidence to support that finding, and, second, whether there was any palpable error of law. I have already indicated the view I have formed as to the finding of fact based on the evidence. In dealing with the other point I am aided by the fact that there was no express prohibition in Rule 3 of the Rules applicable to Cases I and II, Schedule D, of the Income Tax Act 1918, against the Commissioners finding as they have done; they are, therefore, left more at large as to their determination (that this was a proper debit item) than if there had been a definite rule covering this under which they had to act. There is also the further fact that, under this private Act (The Limerick Corporation Gas Undertaking (Pensions) Act 1929), the Corporation were given power to pay all the costs, charges and expenses incurred by them in obtaining the Act out of their revenue and assets. But the right so given by s 12 of the Act to pay the costs out of the revenue and assets does not necessarily bind the Court in its determination, though it is a fact in the case.

Now it has been argued that the Commissioners have made a palpable error of law. We have only one clue to the reasoning of the Commissioners; they say that there is a close analogy between this case and the case of *Mitchell v BW Noble Ltd* [1927] 1 KB 719. Is this so? In *Mitchell's* case a very large sum of money - more than £19,000 - was paid by a company to a director of the company in order to get rid of him, and to make financial arrangements, so that the company might have the benefit of carrying on its business and trade more satisfactorily, and it was held that that money, having been paid for the purpose of discharging an agreed obligation to a director who was leaving for the benefit of the company, was an admissible deduction in the revenue account. The Commissioners might have held the other way, but having so found, they were held by the Court of Appeal to be right.

> Now, in the present case the outlay was necessary in order to obtain power to make legal certain financial arrangements to discharge the obligation which the Committee were under in regard to persons leaving their employment by reason of the changes in their business. I think this shows that there is an analogy in principle between *Mitchell's* case and the present case. I therefore think that the Commissioners have not made any error of law, and accordingly I answer the question submitted in the affirmative.

My understanding from these cases is that there is an onus on Counsel for the Inspector to show that there is palpable or obvious and certain error in the inferences and deductions made by the learned Circuit Court judge from the facts as found. Much of these are in reality common case up to paragraph 8 of the case stated. Counsel for the company also relies on *Patrick McGrath and Ors v JE McDermott (Inspector of Taxes)* 3 ITR 683 which involved a tax avoidance scheme which brought about allowable losses for capital gains tax purposes which losses were utilised to offset taxable gains incurred by the appellant's on previous disposals of assets by the appellants. The Inspector of Taxes had refused to allow the appellants loss claim on the grounds that no real loss was incurred and that the series of transactions had no purpose other than the avoidance of tax and that the doctrine of fiscal nullity as applied by the UK Courts should be followed in this country. It was held by Carroll J in the High Court in allowing the taxpayer's appeal that in determining whether a liability to tax arose from transactions it was necessary to look, not at the substance of the transactions or financial results but at the actual legal effect of each transaction and the rights of the parties thereunder. An exemption from tax is governed by the same principles as a liability to tax. The doctrine of fiscal nullity as developed by the courts in the United Kingdom has not been accepted by the Irish courts. The imposition of tax and the granting of relief is solely a matter for the legislature and if the legislature had failed to legislate against a tax avoidance scheme it was not the function of the courts to intervene. Her decision was upheld by the Supreme Court in dismissing the appeal by the respondent on the grounds that the doctrine of fiscal nullity did not form part of Irish law and that the function of the courts in interpreting a statute is limited to ascertaining the true meaning of each statutory provision. To add to or delete from express statutory provisions so as to condemn tax avoidance schemes would constitute an invasion of the legislative powers of the Oireachtas. At p 703 Finlay CJ said:

> It is clear that successful tax avoidance schemes can result in unfair burdens on other tax payers and that unfairness is something against which the courts naturally lean. The function of the courts in interpreting a statute of the Oireachtas is, however, strictly confined to ascertaining the true meaning of each statutory provision, resorting in cases of doubt or ambiguity to consideration of the purpose and intention of the legislature to be inferred from other provisions of the statute involved, or even of other statutes expressed to he construed with it. The courts have not got a function to add to or delete from express statutory provisions so as to achieve objectives which to the courts appear desirable. In rare and limited circumstances words or phrases may be implied into statutory provisions solely for the purpose of making them effective to achieve their expressly avowed objective. What is urged upon the court by the appellants in this case is no more and no less than the implication into the provisions of either s 12 or s 33 of the Act of 1975 of a new sub-clause or subsection providing that a condition precedent to the computing of an allowable loss pursuant to the provisions of s 35(5) is the proof by the taxpayer of an actual loss, presumably at least coextensive with the artificial loss to be computed in accordance with the subsection. In the course of the submissions such a necessity was denied but instead it was contended that the real as distinct from what is described as the artificial nature of the transactions should be looked at by the court, and that if they were, the section could not apply to them.

> I must reject this contention. Having regard to the finding in the case stated that these transactions were not a sham, the real nature, on the facts by which I am bound, of the scheme was that the shares were purchased and the purchaser became the real owner thereof, that shares were sold and that the vendor genuinely disposed thereof and that an option to purchase shares really existed in a legal person legally determined to be connected to the person disposing of them.
>
> In those circumstances, for this court to avoid the application of the provisions of the Act of 1975 to these transactions could only constitute the invasion by the Judiciary of the powers and functions of the legislature, in plain breach of the constitutional separation of powers.

As to whether the Court should adopt a realistic new approach to the construction of a taxing statute, the Supreme Court declined the invitation of Counsel to depart from Irish precedent. McCarthy J at p 704 reaffirmed the position in Ireland:

> In his argument in reply on behalf of the Revenue, Mr Kelly SC, expressly invited this court to adopt a 'new approach' to the construction of a taxing statute and, for that purpose, where what is admittedly a real transaction in the purchase and sale of shares in a company, but which has resulted in what is termed a 'fiscal nullity', to look to reality and not to allow an unreal result. To do this would be, it is said, to look through realistic spectacles as did the House of Lords in England in *Ramsay Ltd v IRC* and *Furniss v Dawson* [1984] AC 474. The argument is attractive in equity but it is wrong in law. Until the decision of the appeal commissioners in the instant case, it appears to have been accepted that where a taxpayer brought himself within the actual wording of a taxing statute providing for some taxation relief, that was an end to the matter. The court did not look beyond to see what the end result was. This has been identified as the principle in the case of the *IRC v Duke of Westminster* [1936] AC 1 which was expressly accepted in the High Court by Kenny J, in *O'Sullivan v P Ltd* 3 ITC 255. In their closely reasoned decision, the appeal commissioners recount part of Mr McCann's argument 'that Ramsay et seq have, effectively, overruled the Duke of Westminster principle, that this principle is part of Irish law, as a result of the Kenny J decision in *O'Sullivan v P Ltd* and that the Irish Courts up to the High Court level, and specifically this tribunal, are precluded from following this new.' The appeal commissioners found the argument unacceptable on the basis that, since various opinions expressed in the House of Lords had stated words to the effect; the difference is in approach. It does not necessitate the overruling of any earlier decision of this House.
>
> This meant that such a view point must be accepted within this jurisdiction. For myself I am unable to perform the mental gymnastics that I think necessary to conclude that Ramsay did not reverse Westminster. But that is not for me, the practice direction of the House of Lords in [1966] 3 AER 77 expressly qualifies in cases involving fiscal arrangements the stated right of the House to depart from its previous decisions. No tribunal other than the High Court or the Supreme Court may properly review a statement of principle called from a judgment of the High Court.

In the course of his judgment at p 705 McCarthy J referred to *Revenue Commissioners v Doorley, Bishop of Elphin* [1933] IR 750 in which Kennedy CJ cited - with approval the speech of Lord Cairns in *Partington v Attorney General* LR 4 HL 100:

> I am not at all sure that, in a case of this kind, a fiscal case, form is not amply sufficient, because, as I understand the principle of all fiscal legislation, it is this, if the person sought to be taxed comes within the letter of the law he must be taxed, however great the hardship may appear to the judicial mind to be. On the other hand, if the Crown, seeking to recover the tax, cannot bring the subject within the letter of the law, the subject is free, however apparently within the spirit of the law the case might otherwise appear to be. In other words, if there be admissible, in any statute, what is called an equitable construction, certainly such a construction is not admissible in the taxing statute, where you can simply adhere to the words of the statute.

Accordingly Counsel for the company submits that in a tax case the court should confine its gaze to the actual wording of the statute and should not be looking under stones or speculating at the underlying economic reality of the transactions.

Submissions made on behalf of the Inspector

Counsel on behalf of the appellant Inspector urged that the court should scrutinise the real and significant purpose of the transaction. He suggested that the object of taking out the loan was in reality to give benefit to the shareholders and was not only for the purpose of the company's trade. In this instance the loan obtained at the cost of the interest paid to the bank, was not spent on the company's trade but instead was to put cash into the pockets of the shareholders. By way of contrast, he suggested that if the company had lost a major case and was forced to borrow a sum from the bank in order to pay the damages and to keep the business afloat, then the costs of this loan could be *wholly and exclusively for the purposes of such trade.* Likewise if a medical consultant were to visit a patient at his villa in the South of France and to stay there for a fortnight in order to minister to his sick patient, then, provided there was a genuine medical reason for the entire of the stay, the pleasant sojourn could be regarded as merely incidental even though the doctor had dined in a number of excellent restaurants during his stay in Provence. He submitted that a number of principles could be derived from the cases which he proposed to cite:

1. The words *for the purposes of the trade* mean "to serve the purposes of the trade". They do not mean for the purposes of the tax payer;
2. To ascertain whether a payment was made for the purposes of a tax payer's trade, it is necessary to discover his object in making the payment. The test is therefore, an objective one;
3. The object of the taxpayer in making the payment must be distinguished from the effect of the payment;
4. Although the taxpayer's subjective intentions are determinative, they are not limited to the conscious motives which were in his mind at the time of the payment. Some consequences are so inextricably involved in the payment that, unless merely incidental, they must be taken to be a purpose for which the payment was made. However, consequential and incidental effects can be ignored;
5. The primary enquiry is to establish what was the particular object of the taxpayer in making the payment.

He argued that since the loan was taken out to pay off the preference shareholders and was paid to achieve this within a couple of days then the objective of the transaction can be identified as the payment for the shares. In effect the AIB loan went to buy out the preference shares and put cash in the hands of the preference shareholders and this did not affect the trading carried on by the company. The short response of counsel for the company's short response to this is that the company was entitled to redeem the preference shares in the event of the shareholders requiring capital. Once the company had paid over £6,000,000 to redeem the preference shares, then the company needed £6,000,000 in order to carry on its trading business. Since the cost of the loan of £6,000,000 from Allied Irish Banks is the cost of the interest then this recurrent annual cost is a necessary expenditure in order to allow the company to continue its trade. He argues that the loan was necessary and accordingly the cost of interest was wholly and exclusively an expenditure which allowed the trade of the company to continue.

I have had the benefit of both Counsels' comments in respect of a number of cases. The first case referred to was *Mallalieu v Drummond (Inspector of Taxes)* [1983] STC 665. The tax payer, a practising lady barrister, complying with the Bar Council's notes for guidance on dress in court, wore, in court and in chambers and on her way there, black dresses, suits and shoes and white blouses. The clothing although subdued consisted of perfectly ordinary articles of apparel suitable for everyday wear. But for the requirements of her profession that she should be so clothed for her court appearances and for the fact that she would have been barred from pleading in court if she had not been so clothed, the tax payer would have not purchased those clothes. The tax payer had an ample supply of other clothes to keep her in comfort and decency. The preservation of warmth and decency was not a consideration which crossed her mind when she bought the clothes. In computing the profits of her profession in the year of assessment 1977-78, the taxpayer claimed that the sum she had spent on the replacement, laundering and cleaning of the clothes she wore in court was expenditure incurred "wholly and exclusively ... for the purpose of her profession" within s 130(a) of the Income and Corporation Taxes Act 1970. The Inspector of Taxes disallowed the deduction and the General Commissioners dismissed her appeal on the ground that although the taxpayer's sole motive in choosing the particular clothes was to satisfy the requirements of her profession and that if she had been free to do so she would have worn different clothes, the expenditure had a dual purpose, the professional purpose of enabling her to earn profits in her profession and the non-professional purpose of enabling her to be warmly and properly clad while on her way to chambers or court and thereafter while she was engaged in her professional activities. The judge allowed her appeal holding that when the taxpayer spent money on the upkeep of her working clothes, she had nothing in her mind except the requirements of her profession and accordingly the expenditure was incurred exclusively to serve the purposes of her profession. The Court of Appeal affirmed the decision and the Crown appealed to the House of Lords which held (with Lord Elwyn-Jones dissenting:-) the words "expended for the purposes of the ... profession" in s 130(a) meant expended to serve the purposes of the ... profession" and "purposes" in this context referred to the purposes of the business. To ascertain whether money was expended to serve the purposes of the tax payer's business it is necessary to discover the tax payer's object in making the expenditure. Although the tax payer's conscious motive was of vital significance in ascertaining her object, it was not decisive and the Commissioners were entitled to find on the facts that as the taxpayer had to wear something, one object was the provision of the clothing that she needed as a human being. It followed that the expenditure was not incurred wholly and exclusively for the purposes of her profession and the appeal would therefore be allowed. At p 668 Lord Brightman said:

> The effect of para (a) is to exclude, as a deduction, the money spent by the taxpayer unless she can establish that such money was spent exclusively for the purposes of her profession. The words in the paragraph 'expended for the purposes of the trade, profession or vocation' mean in my opinion 'expended to serve the purposes of the trade, profession or vocation', or as elaborated by Lord Davey in *Strong & Co of Romsey Ltd v Woodifield (Surveyor of Taxes)* [1906] AC 448 at 453, 5 TC 215 at 220 'for the purpose of enabling a person to carry on and earn profits in the trade etc.' The particular words emphasised do not refer to 'the purposes' of the taxpayer us some of the cases appear to suggest; (as an example see the report of this case in [I 983] STC 24 at 127/28, [1983] 1 WLR 252 at 256). They refer to 'the purposes' of the business which is a different concept although the 'purposes' (ie the intentions or objects) of the tax payer are fundamental to the application of the paragraph.

> The effect of the word 'exclusively' is to preclude a deduction if it appears that the expenditure was not only to serve the purposes of the trade, profession or vocation of the tax payer but also to serve some other purposes. Such other purposes, if found to exist, will usually be the private purposes of the taxpayer: see for example *Prince v Mapp (Inspector of Taxes)* [1970] 1 WLR 260, 46 TC 169.
>
> To ascertain whether the money was expended to serve the purpose of the taxpayer's business it is necessary to discover the taxpayer's 'object' in making the expenditure: see *Morgan v Tate and Lyle Ltd* [1955] AC 21 at and 47. As the taxpayer's 'object' in making the expenditure has to be found, it inevitably follows that (save in obvious cases which speak for themselves) the commissioners need to look into the taxpayer's mind at the moment when the expenditure is made. After events are irrelevant to the application of s 130 except as a reflection of the taxpayer's state of mind at the time of the expenditure.
>
> If it appears that the object of the taxpayer at the time of the expenditure was to serve two purposes, the purposes of his business and other purposes, it is immaterial to the application of s 130(a) that the business purposes are the predominant purposes intended to be served.
>
> The object of the taxpayer in making the expenditure must be distinguished from the effect of the expenditure. An expenditure may be made exclusively to serve the purposes of the business, but it may have a private advantage. The existence of that private advantage does not necessarily preclude the exclusivity of the business purposes. For example, a medical consultant has a friend in the South of France who is also his patient. He flies to the South of France for a week, staying in the home of his friend and attending professionally on him. He seeks to recover the costs of his airfare. The question of fact will be whether the journey was undertaken solely to serve the purposes of the medical practice. This will be judged in the light of the taxpayer's object in making the journey. The question will be answered by considering whether the stay in the South of France was a reason, however subordinate, for undertaking the journey, or was not a reason but only the effect. If a week's stay on the Riviera was not an object of the consultant, if the consultant's only object was to attend on his patient, his stay on the Riviera was an unavoidable effect of the expenditure on the journey and the expenditure lies outside the prohibition in s. 130.

At page 671 he continued by describing the approach taken in the High Court and the Court of Appeal:

> As the taxpayer according to the undisputed evidence had nothing in her mind except the etiquette of her profession on the several occasions when she spent money on the upkeep of her wardrobe of working clothes, and 'had no thought of warmth and decency', it inevitably followed that the money was spent exclusively to serve the purposes of her business.
>
> The provision of clothing as such, it was held, was nothing more than an incidental, although no doubt welcome, effect of her one and only object. The approach of the Court of Appeal was similar. After summarising the General Commissioner's findings of fact, the learned Master of the Rolls continued [1983] STC 124 at 129 [1983] 1 WLR 252 at 258:
>
>> 'From those findings of fact there is in my judgment only one reasonable conclusion to be drawn, namely, that the taxpayer's sole purpose in incurring the expenditure was a professional purpose, any other benefit being purely incidental.

Unfortunately for Ann Mallalieu, Lord Diplock, Lord Keith and Lord Roskill all agreed with Lord Brightman in his conclusion at p 673:

> My Lords, I find myself totally unable to accept this narrow approach. Of course the taxpayer thought only of the requirements of her profession when she first bought (as a capital expense) her wardrobe of subdued clothing and, no doubt, as and when she replaced items or sent them to the launderers or the cleaners she would, if asked, have repeated that she was maintaining her wardrobe because of those requirements. It is the natural way that anyone incurring such expenditure would think and speak. But she needed clothes to travel to work and clothes to

> wear at work, and I think it is inescapable that one object, though not a conscious motive, was the provision of the clothing that she needed as a human being. I reject the notion that the object of a taxpayer is inevitably limited to the particular conscious motive in mind at the moment of expenditure. Of course the motive of which the taxpayer is conscious is of vital significance, but it is not inevitably the only object which the commissioners are entitled to find to exist. In my opinion the commissioners were not only entitled to reach the conclusion that the taxpayer's object was both to serve the purposes of her profession and also to serve her personal purposes, but I myself would have found it impossible to reach any other conclusion.
>
> It was inevitable in this sort of case that analogies would be canvassed: for example, the self-employed nurse who equips herself with what is conveniently called a nurse's uniform. Such cases are matters of fact and degree. In the case of the nurse, I am disposed to think, without inviting your Lordships to decide, that the material and design of the uniform may be dictated by the practical requirements of the art of nursing and the maintenance of hygiene. There may be other cases where it is essential that the self employed person should provide himself with and maintain a particular design of clothing in order to obtain any engagements at all in the business that he conducts. An example is the self-employed waiter, mentioned by Kerr LJ, who needs to wear 'tails'. In his case the 'tails' are an essential part of the equipment of his trade, and it clearly would be open to the commissioners to allow the expense of their upkeep on the basis that the money was spent exclusively to serve the purposes of the business. I do not think that the decision which I urge on your Lordships should raise any problems in the 'uniform' type of case that was so much discussed in argument. As I have said, it is a matter of degree.

Since the expense of the clothing was not wholly and exclusively laid out for the purposes of the trade, profession or vocation but was laid out in part for the advantage and benefit of the taxpayer as a living human being, in contrast to Ann Mallalieu, barrister-at-law, the cost was not a deductible allowance. In the course of argument before me, it was suggested that the *Mallalieu* case concerned a once off expenditure on purchase of a barrister's clothing. However, Lord Brightman at p 668 makes clear that the initial cost of purchase being a capital expense was not material for present purposes whereas the cost of cleaning and renewing the clothes was the sum claimed as a deduction in computing the profits of her practice chargeable under Sch D. Incidentally it was common ground that the relevant time for determining what were the taxpayer's purposes and what was in her mind when the expenditure was incurred was at the moment the expenditure was made. This has a bearing on Ringmahon and puts significance on the time when the recurrent interest was paid.

Counsel for the respondent argues that the company cannot claim the £6,000,000 as deductible but can claim the cost thereof being the interest paid as a recurrent cost in order to obtain the funds which enabled the company to keep going. The £6,000,000 loan would have been used in the company's trading to buy premises, plant stock or services and thus was used for the purpose of the trade and was not retained as an actual cash sum simply for investment.

Counsel for the Inspector referred me to several cases as illustrating the practical working of the principles involved. In *MacKinlay (Inspector of Taxes v Arthur Young McClelland Moores and Co* [1989] STC 898 the taxpayers were the partners in a large firm of Chartered Accountants (the firm). The firm's policy, agreed to by all the partners was to pay certain specified removal expenses of employees and partners who moved to offices in different parts of the United Kingdom at the firms request. In the year of assessment 1981-82 two partners moved to offices in different parts of the United Kingdom from those where they had hitherto practised and their removal expenses were met by the firm. A claim that the removal expenses of the two partners were deductible in ascertaining the profits of the firm as money wholly and exclusively paid out for the purpose of the firm's business was disallowed. The Crown contended that expenses incurred by a sole practitioner in moving his home for the purposes of his business would not be deductible since, as he had to live somewhere, the expenditure would be regarded as serving the dual purpose of his business and his personal interests and that there was no difference in principle between a sole practitioner and the members of a partnership. The taxpayers accepted that the removal expenses of a sole practitioner would not be deductible, but contended that, in the case of a large partnership implementing a policy adopted by all the partners for the purpose of advancing the interests of the firm, the interests of the partners as partners could be severed from their private interests which could be regarded as incidental to that purpose. The Special Commissioners upheld the taxpayer's contentions and determined the appeal in favour of the taxpayers. An appeal by the Crown was allowed by Vinelott J who upheld its contentions that expenditure which would be treated as having a dual purpose when incurred by a sole trader was likewise to be regarded as having a dual purpose when incurred by a partnership regardless of its size and was therefore precluded from deduction by the provisions of s 130(a) of the Income and Corporation Taxes Act 1970. An appeal by the taxpayers was allowed by the Court of Appeal on the ground that, in paying the removal expenses of two of its partners, the collective purpose of the partnership - which for this purpose was an entity separate its individual partners - was, on the facts, "wholly and exclusively" to promote its professional business: so that the deduction of those expenses was not precluded by s 130(a). On appeal by the Crown to the House of Lords it was held that the payment, or reimbursement, by a partnership of the removal expenses of a partner, although made with the motive of persuading him to move so as to further the business interests of the partnership, must inevitably have the immediate and essentially private purpose of assisting him to establish a new home; so it could not qualify as "money wholly and exclusively laid out and expended for the purposes of the trade (or) profession" within the meaning of s 130(a), so as to be deductible in computing the profits of the partnership for income tax purposes. Some of Lord Oliver of Aylmerton's observations are instructive. At p 900 he said:

> There is a wealth of authority regarding the application of this formula to individual items of expenditure of various kinds, but whilst the cases may be helpful as illustrations or analogues, the question in each case is the simple question whether the facts are capable of fitting and do fit the formula. There is no very difficult issue of construction involved, for it is not in doubt that the word 'exclusively' is used in its ordinary and natural sense. The difficulties, such as they are, lie not in the words 'wholly and exclusively' but in ascertaining whether a particular expenditure is, as a matter of fact, laid out 'for' and only for the purposes of the trade or profession.

At p 905 he continued:

> One is, accordingly brought back, first, last and all the time to the question whether an expenditure on a partner is removing expenses can be said to be laid out not just partly but exclusively for the purposes of the partnership business. That cannot, in my judgment, be answered simply by ascertaining what was the motive with which the move was undertaken. It is inescapable as it seems to me, that the expenditure, motivated no doubt by the fact of moving house, which in turn was motivated by the desire to put the partner concerned in a better position to further the interests of the firm, was an expenditure serving and necessarily and inherently intended to serve the personal interests of the partner in establishing his private residence for himself and his family and it cannot be said to be exclusively for the purposes of the partnership practice. Your Lordships have been referred to what may be regarded as a seminal decision of this house in *Mallalieu v Drummond (Inspector of Taxes)* [1983] STC 665, [1983] 2 AC 861 and much argument has been addressed to the question whether the purpose

> of the particular payment falls to be ascertained objectively or by reference only to the subjective intention of the payer. For my part, I think that the difficulties suggested here are more illusory than real. The question in each case is what was the object to be served by the disbursement or expense? As was pointed out by Lord Brightman in *Mallalieu's* case, this cannot be answered simply by evidence of what the payer says that he intended to achieve. Some results are so inevitably and inextricably involved in particular activities they cannot but be said to be a purpose of the activity. Miss Mallalieu's restrained and sober garb inevitably served and cannot but have been intended to serve the purpose of preserving warmth and decency and her purpose in buying cannot but have been, in part at least, to serve that purpose whether she consciously thought about it or not. So here the payment of estate agents' fees, conveyancing costs and so on, and the provision of carpets and curtains cannot but have been intended to serve the purpose of establishing a comfortable private home for the partner concerned even though his motive in establishing a home in that particular place was to assist him in furthering the partnership interests. Nobody could say with any colour of conviction that in purchasing new curtains he or his wife was acting on partnership business. In my judgment once one escapes from what I regard as the fallacy of confusing the purpose of the expenditure with the motives of the members of the executive committee (and, inferentially, of the other partners) in resolving to reimburse the expenditure, the case presents very little difficulty and is, indeed, a march clearer and easier case than *Mallalieu.*

Counsel also referred me to *Vodafone Cellular Limited and Ors v Shaw (Inspector of Taxes)* [1997] STC 734 which contains a useful summary of the principles involved by Millett LJ. At p 742, under the heading "Was the payment made wholly and exclusively for the purposes of the taxpayer company's trade?", he said:

> Whether a payment is made exclusively for the purpose of the taxpayer company's trade or partly for that purpose and partly for another is a question of fact for the commissioners. The court can interfere only if the commissioners have made an error of law in reaching their conclusion. The principles on which the court acts are to be found in the speech of Lord Radcliffe in *Edwards (Inspector of Taxes) v Bairstow* [1956] AC 14 36 TC 207, and are too well known to repeat. It is sufficient to say that the court will interfere where the true and only reasonable conclusion from the facts found by the commissioners contradicts the determination. In the case of an individual taxpayer, the other purpose is usually a private purpose of his own. In a case like the present, where the taxpayer company is a company forming part of a group, the other purpose is likely to be the purpose of the trade of one or more of the other companies in the group. But the same principles apply. The trade of a parent company is for tax purposes distinct from the trade of its subsidiary. The two companies are separate taxable persons, and the trade or business of one is not the same as the trade or business of the other, however closely it may affect it (*see Odhams Press Limited v Cook (Inspector of Taxes)* [1938] 23 TC 233 at 254, 257).
>
> The leading modern cases on the application of the exclusively test are *Mallalieu v Drummond (Inspector of Taxes)* and *MacKinlay (Inspector of Taxes) v Arthur Young McClelland Moores & Co.* From these cases the following propositions may be derived.
>
> 1. The words for the purposes of the trade mean to serve the purposes of the trade. They do not mean for the purposes of the taxpayer but for the purposes of the trade, which is a different concept. *A fortiori* they do not mean for the benefit of the taxpayer.
> 2. To ascertain whether the payment was made for the purposes of the taxpayer's trade it is necessary to discover his object in making the payment. Save in obvious cases which speak for themselves, this involves an inquiry into the taxpayer's subjective intentions at the time of the payment.
> 3. The object of the taxpayer in making the payment must be distinguished from the effect of the payment. A payment may be made exclusively for the purposes of the trade even though it also secures a private benefit. This will be the case if the securing of the private

> benefit was not the object of the payment but merely a consequential and incidental effect of the payment.
>
> 4. Although the taxpayer's subjective intentions are determinative, these are not limited to the conscious motives which were in his mind at the time of the payment. Some consequences are so inevitably and inextricably involved in the payment that unless merely incidental they must be taken to be a purpose for which the payment was made.
>
> To these propositions I would add one more. The question does not involve an inquiry of the taxpayer whether he consciously intended to obtain a trade or personal advantage by the payment. The primary inquiry is to ascertain what was the particular object of the taxpayer in making the payment. Once that is ascertained, its characterisation as a trade or private purpose is in my opinion a matter for the commissioners, not for the taxpayer. Thus in *Mallalieu v Drummond (Inspector of Taxes)* the primary question was not whether Miss Mallalieu intended her expenditure on clothes to serve exclusively a professional purpose or partly a professional and partly a private purpose, but whether it was intended not only to enable her to comply with the requirements of the Bar Council when appearing as a barrister in court but also to preserve warmth and decency.
>
> Similarly, in my opinion, the present case does not involve an inquiry whether the directors who resolve to enter into the fee cancellation agreement consciously intended to obtain a benefit thereby for one company rather than another. The primary inquiry is to ascertain the particular object which the directors sought to achieve by it. Once that is ascertained the characterisation of that object as serving the purposes of the trade of one particular company or another is not a finding of primary fact but a conclusion based upon the primary facts.

He explained how the Special Commissioners and the judge had fallen into error and concluded:

> In my judgment the case is a simple one. The directors' purpose is self evident: it was to rid the group of a trading liability owed to a third party. The liability in question was a liability of the taxpayer company alone: ergo the directors' intention, whether articulated or not, was exclusively to serve the purposes of the taxpayer company's trade. The elimination of the liability to Millicom would make it unnecessary to put in hand whatever arrangements there might be within the group to enable the taxpayer company to finance the liability. But this was merely a consequential and incidental effect of the elimination of the liability; it cannot possibly have been its purpose. It was, after all, not even necessary to cancel the fee agreement in order to release the subsidiaries from the obligation to reimburse the taxpayer company. That was within the power of the taxpayer company at any time, and did not require Millicoms consent or the expenditure of $30m.
>
> In my judgment the true and only reasonable conclusions from the facts found by the Special Commissioners contradicts their determination.

I derive assistance from this decision. First, it reinforces the proposition that the court will interfere with the finding of the Commissioners, or in this case the findings of fact by the learned Circuit Court judge, where the true and only reasonable conclusion from the facts found by the learned Circuit Court judge contradicts the determination. Secondly, the case emphasises that the object of the taxpayer in making the payment must be distinguished from the effect of the payment and a payment may be made exclusively for the purposes of the trade even though it also secures a private benefit. I remind myself that in the present case the payment involved is that of the recurring interest on the loan secured from the bank which has been used for the financing of the trade of Ringmahon. One must go on then to examine whether the securing of the private benefits in that the owners of the redeemable preference shares were paid off, was merely a consequential and incidental effect of the securing of the loan by the payment of the recurring interest.

Trans-Prairie Pipelines Ltd v Minister of National Revenue 70 DTC 6351 a decision of the Exchequer Court of Canada delivered on 3rd of November 1970 was analysed by both Counsel. The similarity of the facts to those in *Ringmahon* is striking but Counsel for the Inspector cautions that the significance of the comparison is diluted by the difference in the wording of the Canadian statute as the phrase "wholly and exclusively expended for the purposes of the trade" is not used. I set out the facts of this case and the wording of the Canadian Income Tax Act 1952. Section 11(1)(c) for the purposes of analysis as to whether the principles derived are in point or whether, although the facts are similar, the difference in the wording of the statutes are such that the Canadian comparative is worded so as to be of wider application than the Irish phrases and so unhelpful and perhaps misleading. The appellant company was incorporated in 1954 to construct and operate a pipeline, its original issued capital being a number of common shares and 140,000 redeemable preferred shares, the latter having a total par value of $700,000. In 1956 the company issued $700,000 first mortgage bonds and used $400,000 of the amount so borrowed (with $300,000 obtained by issuing additional common shares) to redeem the preferred shares. In 1956 (and subsequent years) the company deducted the interest paid on its bonds; in 1956 it also deducted (under s 11(1)(cb)) legal expenses incurred in connection with the bond issue and the preferred share redemption. The Minister allowed the company to deduct only three-sevenths of the claimed expenses. The Minister took the position that four-sevenths, or $400,000, of the money borrowed through the issue of bonds was used by the company to redeem its preferred shares and not used for the purpose of earning income from its business; that interest on the $400,000 was therefore not deductible under s 11(l)(c); and that legal expenses incurred in the course of borrowing only $300,000 of the $700,000 could be deducted under s 11(1)(cb). The Appeal Board had agreed with the Minister's interpretation and the company had appealed to the Exchequer Court which allowed the appeal holding that the company was entitled to deduct all of the interest paid on its bonds during the years in question and all of the legal expenses claimed under s 11(l)(cb). The whole of the $700,000 borrowed on the bonds was, during those years, borrowed money used for the purpose of earning income from the companies business within the meaning of s 11(1)(c). Prior to the transactions in question, the capital being used for the purpose of earning income from the company's business was the $700,000 subscribed by the preferred shareholders and the amount subscribed by the original common shareholders. After those transactions, the money subscribed by the preferred shareholders had been withdrawn and what the company was using in its business to earn income was the amount subscribed by common shareholders (original and additional) and the $700,000 of borrowed money. As a practical matter of business common sense, the $700,000 of borrowed money went to fill the hole left by the redemption of the $700,000 preferred shares. Surely, what must have been intended by s 11(1)(c) was that the interest should be deductible for the years in which the borrowed money was employed in the business rather than that it should be deductible for the life of the loan as long as its first use was for the purpose of earning income from the business. At p 6352 Jackett P said:

> Accordingly, in 1956, the appellant redeemed its preferred shares and, to do so, paid $700,000 to the holders of those shares. At the same time, it borrowed $700, from the Great West Life Assurance Company by way of a bond issue and raised a further $300,000 by issuing additional common shares.
>
> In the course of carrying out these transactions, the preferred shares were redeemed by using the $300,000 obtained by the new issue of common shares and $400,000 out of the $700,000 received on the floating of the bond issue.

Question of deductibility of interest

In these circumstances, the question arises as to whether the appellant is entitled to a deduction, in computing its income for 1956 and subsequent years, of the whole or only part of the interest payable on such bonds by virtue of s 11(1)(c) of the Income Tax Act, which reads as follows:

11.(1) notwithstanding paragraphs (a), (b) and (h) of subsection 1 of section 12, the following amounts may be deducted in computing the income of a taxpayer for a taxation year:

(c) an amount paid in the year or payable in respect of the year (depending on the method regularly followed by the taxpayer in computing his income), pursuant to a legal obligation to pay interest on

(i borrowed money used for the purpose of earning income from a business or property (other than borrowed money used to acquire property the income from which would be exempt), or ...

or a reasonable amount in respect thereof, whichever is the lesser.

The respondent has disallowed the deduction of four-sevenths of the amount of such interest for each of the years in question on the ground that $400, 000 out of the $700,000 borrowed by the bond issue was used to redeem preferred shares and was not, therefore, used 'for the purpose of earning income' from the business. In this conclusion, the respondent has been upheld by the Tax Appeal Board.

All of interest deductible

The alternative view is that, prior to the transactions in question, the capital being used for the purpose of earning income from the appellant's business was the $700,000 subscribed by the preferred shareholders and the $140,006 subscribed by the common shareholders, and that, after those transactions, the money subscribed by the preferred shareholders had been withdrawn and what the appellant was using in its business to earn income was the $440,006 subscribed by common shareholders and the $700,000 of borrowed money. This in my view is a correct appreciation of the matter. It follows that in my view the whole of the $700,000 of borrowed money was being used by the appellant in its business for the purpose of earning income from the business; and that is my view even though, from another point of view, and in a different sense, some $400, 000 of the $700, 000 was in fact paid on the redemption of the preferred shares.

Interpretation of section

The difficulty arises from the fact that, in ordinary parlance when one talks of the use of money in a business to earn income, one is referring to the mass of capital dedicated to that business, through all the different forms through which it passes while it remains in the business, and, when one talks of using money to acquire property or to pay a debt, one is referring to using money to make a particular payment as a result of which the payer no longer has that money.

When a business person has borrowed money to use in a business, he is, according to the ordinary use of language, using that borrowed money in his business to earn income therefrom even though part of it has been converted into 'bricks and mortar' and part of it was paid out during the first year for inventory and by way of salaries. Indeed, except in very unusual circumstances, he is using that borrowed money in his business to earn income until the loan matures and is paid off. By contrast, the actual money borrowed will, according to the ordinary use of language, have been 'used' to acquire plant and machinery and to pay running expenses and will, in fact, have completely ceased to belong to the business man once it has been so used.

It would not, of course, be completely absurd to attribute the latter sense to the words 'money used' - where they first appear in s 11(1)(c)(i) Whether or not interest is deductible on borrowed money during each year of the life of a loan would then depend upon whether the first expenditure of the money after being borrowed was an expenditure for the purpose of the business. That test would, in most cases produce the right result. However, in my view, such an

> interpretation is not only not in accordance with the ordinary sense of the words as used in the context but it results in a rule that is not sound in principle. For example, a parent company such as the appellant company in *DWS Corporation v Minister of National Revenue* (1968) 2 Ex CR 44 [68 DTC 5045], and 69 DTC 5203 (SC of C) having raised some borrowed capital, could use it on one occasion to acquire inventory for its business and could then, when it comes back in the ordinary course of trade, put it at the disposal a subsidiary for the balance of the term of the loan and charge the interest as an expense of the parent's business. If, on the other hand, the words 'money used for the purpose of earning income in a business' are given their ordinary sense in this context of interest on borrowed capital, the obviously sensible result achieved in the *DWS* case would flow whether borrowed capital was turned over to a related company without ever being used in the borrower's business or was turned over to a related company after being so used for a limited time. Surely, what must have been intended by s 11(1)(c) was that the interest should be deductible for the years in which the borrowed capital was employed in the business rather than that it should be deductible for the life of the loan as long as its first use was in the business. The facts of the present appeal provide an even more striking illustration of the inappropriateness of the meaning of the words 'money used for the purpose of earning income from a business' that is relied on by the respondent. Prior to the 1956 transactions, the appellant's capital used in its business consisted in part of $700,000 subscribed by preferred shareholders. As a result of those transactions, the $700,000 had been repaid to the shareholders and the appellant had borrowed $700,000 which, as a practical matter of business common sense, went to fill the hole left by redemption of the $700,000 preferred Yet, according to the view relied on by the respondent, for the purpose of this provision concerning interest on borrowed capital, $400,000 of the borrowed money cannot be regarded even though being used to earn income from the business.

It seems to me that assistance can be gleaned from this case even though the Canadian Section is narrower in scope. Under the Canadian section the loan could be borrowed and used for the purchase of a luxury yacht, a use of the money which is obviously not for the purpose of earning income from the business. However, if the yacht is then sold and the money gained from this sale is used for the purpose of earning income from the business then the interest paid for such a loan would become deductible. Counsel for the company stresses that in the Canadian case the appellant had borrowed $700,000 and this as a matter of business common sense went to fill the hole left by the redemption of the $700,000 preferred shares. Under the Canadian section the interest on the loan should be deductible for the years in which the borrowed capital was employed in the business and he says that the same principle applies in the very similar situation in *Ringmahon*. Both Counsel have referred to *Morgan (HM Inspector of Taxes) v Tate & Lyle Limited* 35 TC 367 which concerned the deductibility for income tax purposes of the expenses of an anti-nationalisation campaign. The respondent company, which carried on the business of sugar refiners, claimed to deduct in the computation of its trading profits for income tax purposes expenses incurred on a propaganda campaign designed to show that nationalisation of the sugar refining industry would be harmful to "workers, consumers and stock holders alike". On appeal, the General Commissioners accepted evidence that the primary object of the campaign was to prevent the company from losing its business and to preserve its assets intact. The Crown contended, *inter alia,* that so far as this was the object of the campaign the expenditure was incurred not directly for the earning of profits but was the cost of a campaign to decide who should earn the profits, viz the company or the State, and that another purpose was to prevent the acquisition of the company's capital stock by a national body. The Commissioners found that the sum in question was money wholly and exclusively laid out for the purposes of the company's trade and was an admissible deduction. On an appeal by way of Case Stated to the Chancery division Harman J on 18

December 1952 concluded that the City of London Commissioners of Taxes had come to a right conclusion and dismissed the appeal and this was upheld by a majority of the Court of Appeal. The Crown appealed and on 1 June 1954 judgment was given against the Crown in the House of Lords. Counsel for the Inspector sought to derive comfort from a passage near the conclusion of the judgment of Jenkins LJ at p 403 where he said:

> I have only to add, with respect to the Privy Council case of *Ward & Co Lid v Commissioner of Taxes* [1923] AC 145, that while the expenditure in question affords a closer parallel to the disputed expenditure in the present case than is to be found in any of the other cases of which I am aware, the language of the material New Zealand enactment which prohibited the deduction of expenditure "not exclusively incurred in the production of the assessable income" was so markedly different from, and so much narrower than, the language of the enactment governing the present case that I cannot read it as providing any authority against the conclusion to which I have come.
>
> As Lord Cave said at the end of his judgment: "It is only necessary to add that the decisions on the English Income Tax Acts, the language of which is different from that of the New Zealand Act, have no real bearing upon the question now under decision".

The New Zealand wording may be markedly different but Counsel for the company argues cogently that our provision with regard to deductibility stems from the same source as the provision in the United Kingdom and I note that the *WS MacGarry v Limerick Gas Committee* [1932] IR 125 was cited. At p 408 Lord Morton of Henryton said:

> My Lords, the purpose for which a company expends money can only be either the purpose of the directors, if they expend it under the powers conferred upon them by the memorandum and articles without the express sanction of a general meeting, or the purposes of the shareholders if these purposes are expressed at a general meeting. Here there is no conflict between the purpose of the directors and the purpose of the shareholders in general meeting. The passages which I have quoted from the Case Stated show that these bodies had one purpose only, namely, to prevent the seizure of the business and assets of the company. The sum in question was spent for that purpose. It would appear likely, from the documents exhibited to the Case Stated, that part of the sum was spent by the Directors before the 15 September 1949 but to my mind this fact is immaterial, as the purpose for which it was spent was the same throughout. At p 417 Lord Reed said:
>
> > The proposal which the directors were opposing was the transfer to public ownership of their sugar refining concern. If that proposal became law the company would lose its business and assets. I think that it is reasonably clear that the dominant purpose of the directors was to prevent the company from losing its business and to preserve its assets intact. People often have more than one reason for forming a purpose, and I think that the facts found in the case indicate that the directors had two main reasons. They believe that nationalisation would be disastrous to the industry and that it would cause loss to the shareholders. Whether their beliefs were right or wrong is quite immaterial. The question whether their purpose can be held to come within the terms of Rule 3(a) does not depend on whether or not their purpose was misconceived. The shareholders purpose and reasons are set out in the resolution of 15th of September, and there is nothing in the case to indicate that its terms do not reflect their real purpose and reasons. Their purpose was to prevent the assets of the company being seized and their reasons were that such seizure would harm workers, consumers and themselves alike. Again it does not matter whether those reasons were good or bad. It was maintained by the Appellant at one stage that this expenditure was not wholly and exclusively laid out for the purposes of the respondents' trade because their propaganda was directed against nationalisation of the industry of sugar refining as a whole and was not confined to opposition to compulsory acquisition of their own concern. But this argument has now been given up. If the propaganda was to be

> effective it had to be on broad lines, and the fact that it would also benefit other concerns does not matter if the purpose was to preserve the respondents own concern.

At p 425 Lord Reid continued:

> A general test is whether the money was spent by the person assessed in his capacity of trader or in some other capacity, whether on the one hand the expenditure was really incidental to the trade itself or on the other hand it was mainly incidental to some other vocation or was made by the trader in some other capacity than that of trader. It is said that the appellant can succeed in this case on an application of that test because a distinction must be recognised between a person as trader and the same person as owner of his trade. I find that distinction difficult to understand. Whatever may be meant by referring to the trade as an entity, until there is a change of ownership of the trade, the trade only exists because it is being carried on by the trader and the trader is the only owner of the trade because he is carrying it on. I do not see how a person can be owner of the trade unless he is also the trader or how he can be the trader unless he is also the owner of the trade. It therefore appears to me that there is no real distinction between a person in his capacity of trader and that person in his capacity of owner of the trade and that if the appellant is to succeed it must be that the terms of the Rule require, in the special circumstances of this case, some modification of the test generally applicable. I see no sufficient reason for so holding.

Counsel for the company argues that this passage nullifies the distinction between money paid out for the purposes of the trade and money paid for the purposes of the company. However, I read this in the context that Lord Reid was finding that the respondents' expenditure was wholly and exclusively laid out to prevent their business and assets being taken from them. My understanding of the reasoning and outcome in this case is that money expended on such a propaganda campaign can be within the category of money "wholly and exclusively expended for the purposes of the trade" and as such is deductible for income tax purposes. This would seem to be of rather wider ambit than the situation where, on the findings of the learned Circuit Court judge, the company found itself in need of funds and so the company then borrowed money to carry on its trade and had to pay interest as the cost of obtaining the loan.

Counsel for the Inspector referred me to *Archibald Thomson Black and Co Ltd v Batty* 7 TC 158 in which a Company which had made losses in trading carried forward a debit balance from year to year in its balance sheet. The existence of this debit balance stood in the way of the payment of dividends when the company entered on a period of profit earning. To enable dividends to be paid the company applied to the Court to have its capital reduced, and in so doing incurred legal and other expenses. The appellant company claimed to deduct these expenses in computing the balance of profits and gains for the purposes of assessments to income tax, Schedule D, but it was held that the expenditure in question was not expenditure for the purposes of the trade of the company, but was rather for the purpose of distributing the profits of its trade, and was not a proper deduction in computing the profits for the purposes of assessment to income tax. The Court of Session (Scotland) Second Division on 7 January 1919 concluded that the expenditure, while being quite a proper expenditure and quite properly made in the interests of the company, was not, for the purposes of the trade but was made for the purposes of distributing more advantageously, as it was thought, the results of that trade, namely, the profit, which, on a trading account balance, would have been available for distribution among the shareholders, had it not been for the debit balance. They held that it was not, in a proper sense of the term, a disbursement made for the purposes of the trade. It was made for the purpose of dealing with the results of that trade, after these results had been realised; that is to say, it was made for the purpose of distributing the balance of profit and loss among the shareholders instead of, as had previously been the case, by placing it to the credit of the debit balance. They concluded that it was not a deduction made for the purposes of the trade of the company, but for the purposes of distributing the profits of its trade after these profits have been earned.

I think that there is a clear distinction between these legal and other expenses incurred in an application to court to have a company's capital reduced so that it might be able to pay dividends and it is readily understandable why these costs were not deductible as they were not incurred for the purposes of its trade.

Montreal Coke and Manufacturing Company v Minister of National Revenue [1944] 1 REO 743 is relied on by both parties. This case came before the Privy Council in 1944. The appellant company carried on undertakings in Canada which were financed by money borrowed from the public on interest-bearing bonds which were redeemable prior to maturity at a premium. The principal and interest were payable at the bond-holders option in currency other than Canadian dollars. Owing to the state of the exchange the options as to the mode of payment occasioned considerable expense to both companies. Market conditions being favourable, both companies decided in 1935, with a view to reducing their interest charges, to redeem their existing bonds before maturity and to reborrow at lower rates on less onerous conditions as to payment. The carrying through of these financial operations necessarily involved substantial outlays on the part of both companies. The question is whether or not under the Income War Tax Act 1927 s 6(a) the appellants were entitled in computing their respective incomes for the purposes of assessment to income tax for the year 1935-1936 to deduct certain expenses incurred by them respectively in effecting changes in their bonded indebtedness for the purpose of reducing their annual interest payments. It was decided that the expenditure in question incurred by the appellants was in relation to the financing of their businesses and was not incurred in the "earning of the income" within the meaning of s 6(a) of the Act; and, therefore, was not deductible in computing their taxable income. An editorial note helpfully explains that this was a conversion loan which consisted of paying off high interest securities and replacing them by borrowing on more favourable terms. This process necessarily involved considerable incidental expense. It was not, however, a part of the ordinary trading of the company, but an isolated episode and the expense was chargeable to capital account and was not deductible as money spent to earn income. Counsel for the Inspector contends that this is a closely analogous case and so it requires further scrutiny. At p 746 Lord MacMillan said:

> The question at issue turns entirely upon the terms of the Income War Tax Act 1927. Part II of the Act, which is headed "Exemptions and Deductions" contains s 6 which has a subheading "Deductions from income not allowed". So far as relevant to the present purpose s 6 reads as follows:
>
> 6. In computing the amount of the profits or gains to be assessed, a deduction shall not be allowed in respect of (a) disbursements or expenses not wholly, exclusively and necessarily laid out or expended for the purpose of earning the income; (b) any outlay, loss or replacement of capital or any payment on account of capital or any depreciation, depletion or obsolescence, except as otherwise provided in this Act.
>
> By s 9 of the Act the tax is charged upon income and by s 3 income is defined to mean annual net profit or gain.
>
> It is important to attend precisely to the language of s 6. If the expenditure sought to be deducted is not for the purpose of earning the income, and wholly, exclusively and necessarily for that purpose, then it is disallowed as a deduction. If the expenditure is a payment on account

of capital it is also disallowed. The appellants say that the outlays in question were made wholly, exclusively and necessarily for the purpose of earning income and were not payments on account of capital. The respondent maintains the contrary.

The justification for upholding the deductions claimed could not be more attractively presented than it is in the judgement of Rinfret J (now Chief Justice of Canada), with which Taschereau J concurred. The judge says:

> There are two ways of increasing the profits from a trade or commercial or other calling; either by increasing the earnings while the expenses remain the same or by decreasing the expenses while the earnings remain the same. Of course, if the expenses diminish at the same time as the gross earnings are increased the profits will be correspondingly larger and the proposition just mentioned is only made more evident ... In order to pay a lower interest and to get rid of the exchange rates it was necessary to redeem the original bonds; and therefore the expenses required to achieve that result were wholly, exclusively and necessarily laid out or expended for the purpose of decreasing the fixed interest and exchange charges and accordingly 'for the purpose of earning the income'.

Down to the last nine words quoted the statement of Rinfret J is unexceptionable but their Lordships are unable to accompany him in leaping the last fence. If the statute permitted the deduction of expenditure incurred for the purpose of increasing income the appellants might well have prevailed. But such a criterion would have opened a very wide door. It is obvious that there can be many forms of expenditure designed to increase income which would not be appropriate deductions in ascertaining annual net profit or gain. The statutory criterion is a much narrower one. Expenditure to be deductible must be directly related to the earning of income. The earnings of a trader are the product of the trading operations which he conducts. These operations involve out-goings as well as receipts and the net profit or gain which the trader earns is the balance of his trade receipts over his trade out-goings. It is not the business of the appellant to engage in financial operations. The nature of their business is sufficiently indicated by their titles. It is to these businesses that they look for their earnings. Of course, like other business people, they must have capital to enable them to conduct their enterprises, but their financial arrangements are quite distinct from the activities by which they earn their income. No doubt the way in which they finance their businesses will or may reflect itself favourably or unfavourably in their annual accounts but expenditure incurred in relation to the financing of their businesses is not in their Lordship's opinion expenditure incurred in the earning of their income within the statutory meaning. The statute in s 5(b) above quoted significantly employs the expression "capital used in the business to earn the income", differentiating between the provision of capital and the process of earning profits. A faint suggestion was made that the item for overlapping interest might be differentiated from the other items of expenditure in view of the fact that interest on borrowed money is a permissible deduction at such rate as the Minister may allow. But the overlapping interest was paid as part of the cost of the refunding operations and on money borrowed temporarily in excess of what was required for the purpose of the businesses during the overlapping period and was thus properly disallowed by the Minister.

They concluded that the particular expenditure in the case fell clearly within the statutory prohibition against deduction.

This is an important case illustrating the distinctions involved. While the Privy Council did not stress the words "and necessarily", these are an additional reason why there is a very real difference between the *Montreal Coke* transaction and Ringmahon's situation. At issue in *Montreal Coke* was simply the expense of financing being the costs of replacing one loan with another and it was not concerned with interest on a loan to maintain trading finance except peripherally where overlapping interest was mentioned. It was not a decision in which the Privy Council disallowed interest on a new loan in the future incurred for trading purposes. The nub of the distinction is that if a company simply refinances its trading operations then it has not acquired any new asset. If, for example, Ringmahon were to buy a luxurious yacht and refinances this expenditure by way of a loan from a bank then Ringmahon has acquired an asset and this floating gin palace could hardly be described as being for the purpose of its trade in household goods and so the interest on the loan would not be deductible. On the other hand if the cost of the raising of the loan to keep the company trading is the interest on the loan then it is this cost of interest which permits the company's trade to continue. The costs of such interest is a recurrent item each year.

At p 747 there is a further passage in the judgment of Lord MacMillan which clarifies the distinction between refinancing involving the costs of replacing one loan with another on the one hand, and on the other hand taking out a loan for the sole and exclusive purpose of using the funds therefrom in order to continue in trade and to earn profits:

> It was conceded in the courts in Canada, and in any event it is clear, that the expenses incurred by the appellants in originally borrowing the money represented by the bonds subsequently redeemed were properly chargeable to capital and so were not incurred in earning income. If the bonds had subsisted to maturity the premiums and expenses then payable on redemption would plainly also have been on capital account. Why then should the outlays in connection with the present transactions, described as 'refunding operations', not also fall within the same category? The Lordships are unable to discern any tenable distinction. In the history of both companies the financial readjustment of their borrowed capital was an isolated episode, unconnected with the day to day conduct of their businesses, and the benefit which they derived was not 'earned' by them in their businesses.

This may be contrasted with the finding at para 8 of the Case Stated that the deduction claimed by Ringmahon was in respect of money which was wholly and exclusively laid out for the purposes of the trade of Ringmahon.

I was referred to *Strong and Company of Romsey Limited v Woodifeld (Surveyor of Taxes)* 5 TC 215 as illustrating where the line should be drawn. The appellants were a brewery company who owned an inn in Poole called the Lion and Lamb Inn. On 2 March 1901 a guest at the inn was injured by the falling of a chimney during a gale. On behalf of the appellants it was contended that as in the course of their business as brewers it became necessary at times to carry on business as innkeepers and that the profits of such business as innkeepers were included in the accounts of the company that as the expenditure was incurred by the appellants in the course of and incidental to the conduct of the concern the profits of which were assessed, allowance must be made on account of such expenditure of £1,490, being damages and costs incurred by them in defending the action brought by the injured guest. In agreeing with his colleagues that this sum was not allowable as a deduction at p 215 Lord Davey said:

> My Lords the question in this Appeal is whether a sum of £1,490 which the Appellants have had to pay for costs and damages occasioned to a person staying in their inn by the fall of a chimney is a proper deduction in arriving at the profits of the appellant's trade for the purpose of the income tax. The answer to that question, in my opinion, depends on the answer to be given to another question, whether the deduction claimed was a disbursement or expense wholly and exclusively laid out or expended for the purpose of the appellants' trade, within the meaning of Rule 1 applying to both cases 1 and 2 of Schedule D in section 100 of the Income Tax Act 1842. It has been argued that the deduction claimed was a loss connected with or arising out of the appellants' trade within Rule III, applying to Case 1 only. Case 1 relates to trades, manufactures, adventures or concerns in the nature of trade, and I think that the word 'loss' in Rule III means what is usually known as a loss in trading or in speculation. It contemplates a case in which the result of the trading or adventure is a loss, wholly or partially of the capital employed in it. I doubt whether the damages in the present case can properly be

> called a trading loss. I prefer to decide the case upon Rule 1, which applies to profits of trades and also to professions, employments or vocations. I think that the payment of these damages was not money expended 'for the purpose of the trade'. These words are used in other rules, and appear to me to mean for the purpose of enabling a person to carry on and earn profits in the trade, & C. I think the disbursements permitted are such as are made for that purpose. It is not enough that the disbursement is made in the course of, or arises out of, or is connected with, the trade or is made out of the profits of the trade. It must be made for the purpose of earning the profits.

The logic of the judgment is that the loss sustained by the appellants was not really incidental to their trade as innkeepers but fell upon them in their character not of traders but of householders. Since the appellant was carrying on the business of an innkeeper one might have thought that the court might have been sympathetic to the suggestion that, as it was a customer of the inn who was injured while in premises where the appellant was carrying on the business of an innkeeper there might have been a tenable argument that this was an expense incurred in the course of trade. However, the costs and damages incurred in dealing with the claim by the customer fell on the wrong side of the line. Counsel for the respondent contrasts the use made of the sum of £1,490 expended in this case with the cost of financing a loan which was used to maintain Ringmahon's trading operations.

In a Scottish case *Commissioners of Inland Revenue v Carron Company* 45 TC 18 the respondent company, which carried on the business of iron founders, was incorporated by charter in 1773. The company's constitution remained virtually unaltered until revised in 1963. By the late 1950s many of its features had become archaic and unsuited to modern conditions, and the company's commercial performance was suffering a progressive decline. The most significant disadvantages were the restriction of the company's borrowing powers to £25,000, restrictions on the issue and transfer of shares and the restriction of voting rights to certain members holding at least ten £250 shares. The restrictions relating to shares and voting rights prevented the manager of the company's day to day commercial business from being given the status of a managing director and so made it difficult to obtain a suitable person for the post. It was accordingly decided to petition for a supplementary charter under which, *inter alia*, (a) responsibility for management could be vested in a board of directors, so that management could proceed on lines similar to that of a company incorporated under the Companies Act, (b) the limitation of the company's borrowing powers to £25,000, the restrictions on the issue and transfer of shares and the restriction of voting rights would all be removed, and (c) the members' liability would be limited. A number of the points covered by the proposed charter had little to do with the company's trade.

The Company petitioned for the supplementary charter in December 1959, but proceedings were suspended pending the outcome of an action by a shareholder claiming that the procedure adopted in deciding to petition was invalid. After winning the action before the Lord Ordinary and in the First Division of the Court of Session, the company was advised that its prospects of success in the House of Lords were dubious, and the shareholder threatened to raise a further action on new grounds which would once more indefinitely postpone consideration of the petition. Consequently the company settled the action on the terms that it should pay the pursuer's costs in the action and buy out part of her holding and the whole holding of another shareholder, her nephew, who had for many years been at variance with the company, and, on the other hand, that she and her nephew should desist from future obstruction and he should never again acquire shares in the company. A supplementary charter was granted in January 1963 substantially in the form proposed; the company's affairs were then reorganised and its commercial performance improved. On appeal against an assessment to income tax under Case 1 of Schedule D for the year 1964-65 the company claimed to deduct the costs of obtaining the charter (£3,107) and defending the action (£2,641) and the amounts paid to the two dissenting shareholders in respect of their shares (£83,800) and expenses in the actions (£1,666). For the Crown it was contended that the sums in question were not incurred wholly and exclusively for the purposes of the trade; alternatively, that they were incurred on capital account. The Special Commissioners found that the significant objects of the new charter were the removal of the restrictions on borrowing and the issue and transfer of shares and qualification for voting, which were obstacles to the proper management and conduct of the business, and that the object of the other expenses was the removal of the obstruction to the charter; they held that the company was entitled to the deductions claimed. In the Courts it was conceded by the Crown that if the cost of obtaining in the charter was deductible, so were the other sums in question. It was held by the House of Lords that the objects of the new charter (a) being to remove obstacles to profitable trading, anything in it beyond that could be disregarded; and (b) that, since the engagement of a competent manager and the removal of restrictions on borrowing facilitated the day to day trading operations of the company, the expenditure was on income account.

At p 48 Lord President Clyde in the Court of Session had said:

> In the present case the Special Commissioner have held that the expenditure in question was all incurred by the company to modernise its structure by securing additional borrowing powers and as a means of engaging managerial staff of the required calibre. These purposes are obviously purposes which are in their nature capable of being for the purposes of the trade, and as these are the purposes which the Commissioners held were in fact the company's purposes their conclusion is one of fact for them....
>
> The Crown's contention was that the purpose of the company in occurring this expenditure was in order to obtain a supplementary charter. But the findings of the Commissioners are against this view, and a commercial company would not spend money on a mere piece of paper as an end in itself. The supplementary charter was a mere stepping stone to the real practical purpose of improving their trading potential. The Crown also argued that, even although the Special Commissioners were entitled to find, as they did, what were the company's purposes in obtaining the supplementary charter, yet this conclusion was vitiated because that charter also contains incidental provisions not directly concerned with trading. But there is no finding in the case that such incidental provisions were attributable to any other purpose than a trading purpose, and in any event such merely incidental benefits will not prevent the whole and exclusive purpose of the expenditure in question being for the purpose of the expander's trade ...

At p 62 Lord Cameron said:

> The business of the company was not to obtain or trade in charters; to obtain a supplementary charter was not an end in itself. I think the Crown's contention confuses purpose, objects and means of achieving the objects. As I read the facts, the purpose of the company was to improve its capacity to trade profitably under modern conditions. The company's object was to modernise its machinery, to give it adequate power to finance its day-to-day trading transactions and to obtain the requisite managerial skill. The method of execution was by way of obtaining a supplementary charter, with the necessarily corollary of getting rid of obstruction in the way of doing so presented by the activities of Mr Stevenson and Mrs Brown. The findings of the Commissioners as to the objects of the respondents, which are set out in their decision as findings on the evidence, are in my opinion critical. The object of the operation was found to be: (1) to remove the limitation on the company's borrowing power and

> (2) to deal with the restriction on the shares and the qualification for voting which were obstacles to the proper management and conduct of the business. These are unchallenged facts. The plain purpose in pursuing these objects was to enable the company to finance its trade and to obtain a management fit and qualified for its trade. It is found as a fact in paragraph VI (5) of the Case that the 'only remedy which would remove the obstacles ... was the grant of a supplementary royal charter'. In my opinion, upon these facts the Commissioners were well entitled to find that the sums expended were expended wholly and exclusively for the purposes of the trade. The expenses of the petition would plainly come within such a purpose, because it was only by means of such a charter that the operative machinery of the company could be repaired and modernised, and in my opinion the other sums fall within it.

The Crown appealed to the House of Lords from this decision of the First Division of the Court of Session and lost again. Lord Wiberforce relied on the findings of the Special Commissioners that the objects of Carron were to remove obstacles to profitable trading. If such was their object, the expenditure was brought within s 137(a), and it is immaterial that other advantages came in its train. He said that it would in fact be in accordance with normal practice and legal prudence to use the opportunity of obtaining new powers for essential trading purposes to introduce other convenient constitutional amendments, and he agreed with the Commissioners that this action could not disqualify the expenditure.

Counsel for Ringmahon relies on the principles involved in this case which concerned the costs incurred by a company which needed to change the terms of its charter in order to obtain modem efficiency. It had discretion to remain as it was but opted for improved commercial efficiency and was allowed to deduct the costs of obtaining the alteration of the charter and the cost of buying out the dissident shareholders. Counsel points out that the allowance of these once off payments as a deduction is a weaker case in principle than Ringmahon's recurrent payment of interest as the cost of obtaining finance which has been used for trading purposes.

Counsel for the respondent admitted that if the loan was taken out for the purpose of purchasing a luxury yacht or a race horse irrelevant to the trade of the company, then the cost of this loan would not be deductible. However, if the yacht or the racehorse were then sold the money gained from such a sale could be brought in and used for the purpose of the company's trade and then the interest payable on this sum would be deductible since this would be the cost of money being used to fund the trading business.

Finally Counsel referred me to *Commissioners of Inland Revenue v Pullman Car Company Ltd* 35 TC 221 in which in 1938 the respondent Company, as part of a scheme of reduction and reorganisation of its share capital, substituted cumulative income stock for part of its cumulative preference shares. The income stock was redeemable under certain conditions and carried cumulative interest at 5% per annum, subject to the adequacy of the cumulative net profits of the company. In assessments to profits tax on the company for the chargeable accounting period ending 30 September 1949, interest paid on the income stock was not deducted in computing the profits and was treated as part of the gross relevant distributions to proprietors. On appeal to the Special Commissioners the company contended that the interest was a proper deduction in computing profits by virtue of paragraph 4, Fourth schedule, Finance Act 1937 and that, in any event, it was not a distribution. The Special Commissioners accepted the company's first contention, expressed no opinion on the second and allowed the appeal. Harman J sitting in the Chancery division of the High Court on 26 May 1954 held that the interest was not a distribution of profits and was allowable as a deduction in computing profits for profit tax purposes. He decided that the payments were interest on money and not distribution of profits and dismissed the appeal brought by the Crown. In effect the company had reduced the share capital and these funds were replaced by borrowings from the shareholders. Thus the interest payable was a charge which fell to be made against the profits of the company. Harman J at p 227 said:

> It seems to me that holders of income stock are in the position of people who have lent money to the company, and they are not proprietors nor sharers in the profits as such.

It would seem that there is no real distinction whether the loan is from an individual, a shareholder or from the bank. The crucial question is was the money lent used to support and maintain the trade of the company.

Conclusion

It was accepted by the learned Circuit Court judge that the Revenue Commissioners cannot direct a taxpaying Company as to how it should finance its business. Up to 1991 Ringmahon had financed its business by redeemable share capital. It was quite reasonable for the learned Circuit Court judge, who had heard the evidence, to conclude that Ringmahon, having redeemed the 6,000,000 redeemable preference shares then found itself in need of funds and so had to arrange to borrow funds for the purpose of keeping its trade going. The recurrent interest paid was the cost of obtaining this finance. It seems to me that Ringmahon was entitled to redeem the preference shares. It was then faced with the need to plug the gap in its finances by acquiring trading funds which it did by acquiring a loan from the bank at the recurrent cost of interest. Since these funds were used for trading, and no new asset was acquired from these funds other than trading assets, applying the principles deduced from the cases cited, it seems to me that the learned Circuit Court judge was quite correct in holding that Ringmahon was entitled to a deduction of £435,764 in computing the amount of its profits under Case I, Schedule D. I should add that it seems to me that the hypothetical added further words were only postulated by the learned Circuit Court judge in order to illustrate his point that "wholly and exclusively expended for the purposes of the trade" embraced the cost of the loan of the funds which gave Ringmahon working finance to maintain its trade. When he mentioned the phrases "vital to survive" and "only possible option", this phraseology was merely illustrative that an added proviso to the effect that the taking out of the loan was vital to the survival of Ringmahon and the only possible option for the company would have been a necessary further hurdle for the taxpayer achieving deductibility and since Ringmahon need not have redeemed the preference shares, it would not have satisfied this further criterion. The decision of the learned Circuit Court judge was perfectly within the evidence adduced before him and he was entitled to make the findings he made and to come his rational conclusion that the recurrent cost of the loan was wholly and exclusively laid out for the purposes of the trade of Ringmahon.

Hibernian Insurance Company Limited v MacUimis (Inspector of Taxes)

High Court - 25 July 1997 - Carroll J

Supreme Court - 20 January 2000 - Murphy J, Barron J

Corporation Tax - Case stated - investment company - expenses of management deductible - interpretation of expenses of management for corporation tax purposes - expenses incurred in respect of investment appraisals and advices with a view to acquisitions of investments - whether expenses incurred prior to the date on which a decision was made to acquire the particular investment - whether character of expenditure alters depending upon whether the investment was purchased or not - whether expenses were of a revenue or capital nature - Corporation Tax Act 1976, s 15

This appeal by the Hibernian Insurance Company Limited ("the appellant") raises the issue whether certain expenses incurred by this group of investment companies constituted management expenses within the meaning of CTA 1976, s 15 ("the Act") and as such deductible in computing liability to corporation tax.

The Group consists of four principal operating subsidiary companies carrying on business of general insurance, life insurance, international insurance and fund management involved in making investments which require the maintenance and evaluation of existing investments and of potential future investments. During the period 1986-1990 costs amounting to £404,000 were incurred on services provided by investment bankers, leading accountants and lawyers for the purpose of exploring and evaluating three significant investment opportunities namely the PMPA and ICI in Ireland and VIMAR in Spain. In the events none of these companies were acquired by the Group.

Section 15 of the Act provides for the deduction of any sums disbursed "as expenses of management (including commissions)" while it is accepted that these words have no special meaning for the purposes of the Act nonetheless certain expenses are granted to an investment company which would not be allowed to other taxpayers. The Inspector contends that a distinction is to be drawn between expenditure on capital and revenue transactions and that only revenue expenses should be regarded as expenses of management. The appellant rejects this approach and says that the management of an investment company goes beyond the management of existing investments and must include the cost of appraising potential investments. In that regard a line should be drawn between expenses incurred up to the time when a decision is made to acquire or dispose of an investment and all expenses incurred thereafter. The former are expenses of management.

Held by Murphy J in disallowing the appeal that:

(i) Section 15 does not expressly direct the deduction of expenses of management without reference to the revenue or capital character of the expenditure;

(ii) It would require the clearest words in fiscal legislation to justify the deduction of a capital payment from a revenue receipt;

(iii) The test of differentiating between expenditure incurred prior to making a decision and thereafter is too imprecise and too difficult to apply;

(iv) From the date on which the Group focused its attention on the acquisition of prospective investments the expenditure incurred thereafter has to be considered to be capital costs notwithstanding that the purchase was frustrated or aborted.

Held by Barron J in dismissing the appeal that:

(i) "Expenses of management" has no special meaning for the purposes of the Act;

(ii) Investment companies are allowed certain expenses over and above the entitlement of an individual;

(iii) Investment companies maintain their capital investments on which the best return is sought;

(iv) Expenditure on the appraisal of existing investments and on the scope on new investment must equally be expenses of management;

(v) Once an appraisal becomes specific in relation to a particular investment the expenditure is no longer management but part of the acquisition or disposal cost of the investment.

Legislation: CTA 1976, ss 15(1), 15(6); FA 1915, ss 21(2), 41(1); FA 1918 s 33

Cases referred to in judgment: Sunlife Assurance Society v Davidson (Inspector of Taxes) 37 TC 330

Capital & National Trust Ltd v Golder 31 TC 265

Hoechst Finance Ltd v Gumbrell (Inspector of Taxes) [1983] STC 150

Stephen Court Ltd v JA Browne [1984] IRLM 231, 5 ITR 680

Southwell v Savill Brothers Ltd (1901) 2 KB 349

Sargeant (Inspector of Taxes) v Eayers 48 TC 573

Lothian Chemical Company Ltd v Rogers (1926) 11 TC 508

Cases Stated

Case Stated for the opinion of the High Court under ITA 1967 s 428 as applied by CTA 1976 s 146.

1. On 10 March 1995 at Circuit Court No 16 in the matter of Hibernian Insurance Company Ltd (appellant) and MacUimis (Inspector of Taxes) (respondent), the appellant appealed against an assessment raised on them by the respondent by Notice dated 22 April 1993 and confirmed by the Appeal Commissioners on 14 September 1994 for the period 1 January 1990 to 31 December 1990. The appeal arises out of the refusal by the Inspector of Taxes to allow excess management expenses incurred by Hibernian Group Plc (the Group) and surrendered by the Group to the appellant pursuant to CTA 1976 s 107.

2. It was agreed between the parties that the entitlement to surrender excess management expenses from the Group to the appellant was not in issue, that the Group is an investment company within the meaning of CTA 1976 s 15 and that the only question for decision was whether certain expenses totalling £404,720 incurred by the Group in the year ended 31 December 1990 constituted management expenses for the purposes of s 15.

3. Oral evidence was given by Mr Eamon Walsh, who was managing director of the Group at the date of the expenditure which was the subject matter of the appeal.

4. The following facts were admitted or proved at the hearing before me:

(a) The Group was incorporated on 7 April 1986 and on 30 May 1986 adopted a new Memorandum of Association authorising it to carry on the business of an investment company. The Group was set up with the objective of facilitating the expansion of life and general insurance business and other financial services activities to be carried on through subsidiary companies, both through organic growth and through investments when suitable opportunities arose.

(b) The business of the Group consisted wholly or mainly in the making of investments and the principal part of its income has been derived from the making of investments. The Group's business of making investments required:

(i) the maintaining and evaluating of its existing investments; and

(ii) evaluating potential investment opportunities.

(c) On 30 May 1986 the Group was established and acquired the entire shareholding in the previous existing Hibernian Insurance Company Limited which became an operating subsidiary. On 21 August 1987, the Group acquired 50% of the shares in Hibernian Life Association from Hibernian Insurance. This was effectively a reorganisation within the Group, a change in the way in which Hibernian Life Association was held rather than a change in the business of Hibernian Group Plc. The Group incorporated Hibernian Reinsurance on 20 December 1988 and Hibernian Investment Managers on the 29 June 1989, which was essentially a recognition of existing activities in Hibernian Insurance in that these companies were formed effectively by the upgrading of departments within the general company (Hibernian Insurance) to the status of separate companies. The structural developments in the Group, between 1986 and 1990, were in effect reorganisations of the business that was there into a different corporate structure. In the case of *Hibernian Reinsurance and Hibernian Investment Managers* the purpose of the creation of separate companies was to enable them to invest more resources and expand the businesses previously carried on by departments of Hibernian Insurance. In the case of Hibernian Reinsurance this required the investment of approximately £12m share capital in the new company. The Group had therefore as a consequence of the above, four principal operating subsidiaries involved in:

(i) general insurance in Ireland and the UK;

(ii) life assurance in Ireland;

(iii) international reinsurance; and

(iv) fund management.

Hibernian Group Plc has been accepted by the Revenue Commissioners as an investment company within the meaning of CTA 1976 s 15(b). The Corporation Tax Returns made by Hibernian Group Plc described the company as an investment holding company.

(d) In the period since 1986, apart from the activities mentioned at (c), two significant investment opportunities arose for the Group in Ireland viz PMPA and ICI and one in Spain viz Vimar. In addition over this time, consideration was being given to acquiring the remaining 50% of Hibernian Life Association Limited, a transaction which subsequently took place in November 1991.

(e) In 1990, costs amounting to £.404m were charged in the accounts of the Group as management expenses. A breakdown of these costs is as follows:

		IR£
Investment Bank of Ireland	PMPA and ICI	187,500
Buck Paterson	ICI	16,441
Coopers & Lybrand	HLA	9,269
Coopers & Lybrand	ICI	6,620
Coopers & Lybrand	Vimar	70,443

		IR£
William Fry	Vimar	25,980
Jones Lang Wootton	Vimar	3,967
Stibbe Blaisse & De Jong	Vimar	3,325
Other Costs	Vimar	81,175
Total		404,720

(f) The business of the Group was managed by the Board of Directors which in the year ended 31 December 1990 comprised Mr Eamon Walsh, Group Chief Executive and other executive and non-executive directors. In practice, the function of management was delegated to a sub-committee of the Board which then procured the necessary appraisal skills and advice from professional experts, both internally within the Group structure and also externally.

(g) A number of advisors were retained to assist management in the appraisal of these potential investments and to advise and assist the board in its deliberations on making any or all of such potential acquisitions. Details of the costs and the work involved are set out in the annexed Schedule.

(h) In assessing any potential investment opportunities, it was the Group's policy to exercise considerable care and appraisal skills in order to protect the existing investments of the Group. The costs for the Group of evaluating potential acquisitions varied enormously depending on the size and complexity of the transaction and depending on whether the acquisition was actually made or, alternatively, a decision was made at some point not to proceed. The process required an active role for the management beginning with the identification of possible acquisitions, setting the evaluation process in train, co-ordinating the efforts of the management team and the professional advisers involved in considering the acquisition, investigating the possible sources of finance and deciding how the investment would fit in with the Group's current portfolio of investments. At any stage the process could be discontinued whether due to the investment turning out to be unsuitable, the breakdown in negotiations or otherwise.

(i) The appraisal and investigation carried out in respect of the investment opportunities set out in (d) above was detailed and involved of necessity understanding the nature of the business underwritten by the target enterprise, in particular the long term nature of risks and the quality of the rating applied to these risks, the adequacy of claims reserves involving both a case by case review, assessment of financial provisions and supporting actuarial appraisal and assessment.

(j) This type of evaluation activity continued in years subsequent to 1990.

(k) At the time of the proposed acquisitions of ICI, PMPA and Vimar, the valuation of Hibernian Group Plc was in the region of £100m. The purchases of ICI, PMPA and Vimar would have involved sums of approximately £100m, £50m and £10m respectively. In the event, none of these companies were ultimately acquired by Hibernian Group Plc.

5. It was argued on behalf of the appellant that:

(a) The acquisition and disposal of investments was an ordinary part of the business of an investment company.

(b) In this case, the expenses were not abnormal expenses. It was the normal business of the Group to evaluate on a more or less continuing basis the making of investments.

(c) "Management Expenses" is a term which is not defined in the statutes. However, case law suggests that the definition is a wide one, that the words must bear their ordinary meaning and that the phrase is not confined to the directors' costs of devising and directing the policy of the company.

(d) Expenses incurred by the Group up to the time when a decision has been made to purchase or sell investment constitute management expenses.

(e) The correct test to be applied in deciding whether or not expenses of this nature are expenses of management is whether or not the expenditure was severable from the actual expenditure on the proposed acquisition. Applying this test, the expenses are clearly expenses of management.

6. On behalf of the Inspector of Taxes it was contended that:

(a) The expenditure in question related to the evaluation of significant investment opportunities. In the Revenue view, this expenditure is capital in nature, not revenue. The acquisitions being contemplated were of such magnitude, that the expenses incurred in connection with them could not be regarded as being properly expenses in the management of the company because they bore no relationship to the ordinary management of the company.

(b) The Sun Life Assurance Company case is not authority for the contention that in *any* company, expenditure on the evaluation of proposed acquisitions of investments is revenue and hence allowable. Since, in Life Assurance cases, investments are held in the course of the trade, expenditure in relation to these trading items may be revenue. The Sun Life case is authority for the allowability of such revenue/trading expenses as Management Expenses in the Life Assurance regime. It does not broaden the scope of Management Expenses' to include expenditure in relation to specific capital projects outside the normal business activity of the company.

Hibernian Group PLC is an investment company and investment companies do not trade, therefore, they cannot hold investments in the course of a trade. Investments must be held as capital assets, hence expenditure in relation to the acquisition or disposal of investments will be capital, not revenue.

(c) There is no logical reason for the distinction drawn by the appellants between expenditure up to the point where a decision is made on whether or not to proceed with the proposed acquisition and expenditure following the decision to buy: the first, they say, being management expenses, and the second, capital. The distinction is solely one between revenue and capital expenditure.

7. Having considered the evidence of fact and heard the arguments advanced by the parties, I decided as follows:

A four year period of intense and sustained research and consultation took place between 1986 and 1990 which I am unable to classify or describe as management, either in the generally accepted sense of the term or within the thrust or context of the reference to which I have been directed and the evidence which I have heard. I believe that the £404,720, the subject of the claim, was expended in looking at projects which I would regard as being in the category of mergers/takeovers and would be in the category of capital expenditure. I find against the appellant and for the Revenue.

8. Question of Law

The question of law for the opinion of the Court is whether I was correct in holding that the expenses of £404,720 incurred by way of expenses by the appellant were not expenses of management within the meaning of s 15(1) of the Corporation Tax Act 1976.

9. Cases referred to by the appellant and respondent

Appellant:

Stephen Court Limited v JA Browne (Inspector of Taxes) [1984] IRLM 23.

Sun Life Assurance Society v Davidson (HM Inspector of Taxes) 37 TC 330. Decision of High Court

Hoechst Finance Limited v Gombrell (Inspector of Taxes) [1981] STC 11127. Decision of the Court of Appeal

Hoechst Finance Limited v Gombrell (Inspector of Taxes) [1983] STC 11150.

London County Freehold and Leasehold Properties Limited v Sweet (HM Inspector of Taxes) [1942] 167 LT 175.

Capital and National Trust Limited v Golder (HM Inspector of Taxes) [1949] 65 TLR 772.

Respondent:

Sun Life Assurance Society v Davidson (HM Inspector of Taxes) 37 TC 330.

Hoechst Finance Limited v Gombrell (Inspector of Taxes) [1981] STC 11127. Decision of the High Court.

10. *Other authorities cited*

Appellant: Extract from Butterworth's UK Tax Guide 1994/1995, pp 1419, 1420 and 1421.

Extract from MacLeod & Levitte Taxation of Insurance Business (3rd ed) pp 88 - 90.

Respondent: None.

Schedule

(Comment on the purpose and nature of the work for which the expenditure the subject of the appeal was incurred):

1. *Investment Bank of Ireland (IBI)*

   IBI were retained to assist management in providing critical appraisals and advice to the Board of the Group on the proposed investments in ICI and PMPA. Detailed consultations took place between the Group's management and IBI and detailed reports were prepared by IBI for the Group board. Both of these companies were very sizeable operators in the Irish market and all of the enquiries referred to in the opening paragraphs above had to be carried out. This involved a very substantial amount of collaboration with the Group's management. In the case of PMPA, circumstances were such that a bid did not emerge. In the case of ICI, an offer was made and this was not accepted. In both cases the sale involved purchase of shares in a new company which would have become a subsidiary of the Group.

2. *Buck Paterson*
Buck Paterson carried out an examination and verification of aspects of the pension scheme of ICI for the Group.
3. *Coopers & Lybrand - HLA*
The original 50% investment in Hibernian Life was made by Hibernian Insurance Company Limited. Following the set up of the Group in 1986, the investment was transferred to the Group in 1987. This fee was charged for an actuarial review and valuation of "in force" business of HLA. As HLA was at this time 50% owned by Hibernian and 50% by Life Association of Scotland, this appraisal was carried out in 1990 both to give assurance on the existing investment of 50% and to assist in forming a preliminary view on the potential acquisition of the remaining 50%.
4. *Coopers & Lybrand- ICI*
This fee related to advisory services on taxation matters relating to the proposed acquisition of ICI.
5. *Coopers & Lybrand - VIMAR*
These fees were incurred for detailed audit and evaluation work carried out by Coopers & Lybrand's Madrid office on this potential Spanish general insurance acquisition. This work was carried out at an early stage to enable a view to be formed on the state of work and its potential value and generally appraise its suitability and value in an investment context. In addition, taxation and legal structure aspects of such an investment were considered.
6. *William Fry - VIMAR*
These fees were incurred in investigating and evaluating a proposal to acquire the Spanish company Vimar Sequros y Reaseguros SA. drafting the purchase agreement which could be used if the transaction proceeded and all other work and correspondence.
7. *Jones Lang & Wootton - VIMAR*
These costs were incurred in obtaining an independent professional property evaluation on the properties of Vimar in Spain.
8. *Stibbe Blaisse & De Jong*
Fees incurred here related to investigation of aspects of the structure of the acquisition of Vimar, particularly its being held through a Dutch holding company structure.
9. *Other Costs*
Other costs related to salary costs and direct general expenses incurred in investigating Vimar. The other costs relate to salary costs and direct general expenses incurred in investigating Vimar. The salary costs relate to time spent by a number of Hibernian Insurance Company management staff in evaluating Vimar. Included were underwriting, finance, data processing and general management. The charge is based on a time apportionment of the staff involved. Costs included are direct salary and on costs re pension and PRSI costs made up as set out below along with direct travel costs.

	£
Salary	54,922
Pension	11,808
PRSI	3,989

	£
	70,719
Travel Costs re airfares and hotel accommodation	10,456
	81,175

In January of 1990, it was agreed in principle to proceed with an offer for an 80% holding in Vimar subject to satisfactory finalisation of their 1989 trading results. It subsequently emerged that their 1989 trading was significantly worse than had been anticipated and a decision was taken not to proceed.

High Court - 25 July 1997

Carroll J, This is a Case Stated under ITA 1967 s 428 as applied by CTA 1976 s 146 concerning a refusal by the respondent to allow excess management expenses incurred by the Hibernian Group Plc (the Group) and surrendered by the Group to the appellant pursuant to CTA 1976 s 107 which was confirmed by the Appeal Commissioners and on appeal, by the Circuit Court on 10 March 1995.

It was agreed that the entitlement to surrender excess management expenses from the Group to the appellant was not in issue and that the Group is an investment company within the meaning of CTA 1976 s 15. It was further agreed that the only question for a decision was whether certain expenses totalling £404,720.00 incurred by the Group in the year ended 31 December 1990, constituted management expenses for the purposes of CTA 1976 s 15.

The facts admitted or proved before the learned Circuit Judge are set out at paragraph 4 of the Case Stated as follows:

(a) The Group was incorporated on 7 April 1986 and on 30 May 1986 adopted a new Memorandum of Association authorising it to carry on the business of an investment company. The Group was set up with the objective of facilitating the expansion of life and general insurance business and other financial services activities to be carried on through subsidiary companies, both through organic growth and through investments when suitable opportunities arose.

(b) The business of the Group consisted wholly or mainly in the making of investments and the principal part of its income has been derived from the making of investments. The Group's business of making investments required:

(i) the maintaining and evaluating of its existing investments; and

(ii) evaluating potential investment opportunities.

(c) On 30 May 1986 the Group was established and acquired the entire shareholding in the previous existing Hibernian Insurance Company Limited which became an operating subsidiary. On 21 August 1987, the Group acquired 50% of the shares in Hibernian Life Association from Hibernian Insurance. This was effectively a reorganisation within the Group, a change in the way in which Hibernian Life Association was held rather than a change in the business of Hibernian Group Plc. The Group incorporated Hibernian Reinsurance on 20 December 1988 and Hibernian Investment Managers on the 29 June 1989, which was essentially a recognition of existing activities in Hibernian Insurance in that these companies were formed effectively by the upgrading of departments within the general company (Hibernian Insurance) to the status of separate companies. The structural developments in the Group, between 1986 and 1990, were in effect reorganisations of the business that was there into a different corporate structure. In the case of *Hibernian Reinsurance and Hibernian Investment Managers* the purpose of the creation of separate companies was to enable them to invest more resources and expand the businesses previously carried on by departments of Hibernian Insurance. In the case of Hibernian Reinsurance this required the investment of approximately £12m share capital in the new company. The Group had therefore as a consequence of the above, four principal operating subsidiaries involved in:

(i) general insurance in Ireland and the UK;

(ii) life assurance in Ireland;

(iii) international reinsurance; and

(iv) fund management.

Hibernian Group Plc has been accepted by the Revenue Commissioners as an investment company within the meaning of CTA 1976 s 15(b). The Corporation Tax Returns made by Hibernian Group Plc described the company as an investment holding company.

(d) In the period since 1986, apart from the activities mentioned at (c), two significant investment opportunities arose for the Group in Ireland viz PMPA and ICI and one in Spain viz Vimar. In addition over this time, consideration was being given to acquiring the remaining 50% of Hibernian Life Association Limited, a transaction which subsequently took place in November 1991.

(e) In 1990, costs amounting to £.404m were charged in the accounts of the Group as management expenses. A breakdown of these costs is as follows:

		IR£
Investment Bank of Ireland	PMPA and ICI	87,500
Buck Paterson	ICI	16,441
Coopers & Lybrand	HLA	9,269
Coopers & Lybrand	ICI	6,620
Coopers & Lybrand	Vimar	70,443
William Fry	Vimar	25,980
Jones Lang Wootton	Vimar	3,967
Stibbe Blaisse & De Jong	Vimar	3,325
Other Costs	Vimar	81,175
Total		404,720

(f) The business of the Group was managed by the Board of Directors which in the year ended 31 December 1990 comprised Mr. Eamon Walsh, Group Chief Executive and other executive and non-executive directors. In practice, the function of management was delegated to a sub-committee of the Board which then procured the necessary appraisal skills and advice from professional experts, both internally within the Group structure and also externally.

(g) A number of advisors were retained to assist management in the appraisal of these potential investments and to advise and assist the board in its deliberations on making any or all of such potential acquisitions. Details of the costs and the work involved are set out in the annexed Schedule.

(h) In assessing any potential investment opportunities, it was the Group's policy to exercise considerable care and appraisal skills in order to protect the existing investments of the Group. The costs for the Group of evaluating potential acquisitions varied enormously depending on the size and complexity of the transaction and depending on whether the acquisition was actually made or, alternatively, a decision was made at some point not to proceed. The process required an active role for the management beginning with the identification of possible acquisitions, setting the evaluation process in train, co-ordinating the efforts of the management team and the professional advisers involved in considering the acquisition, investigating the possible sources of finance and deciding how the investment would fit in with the Group's current portfolio of investments. At any stage the process could be discontinued whether due to the investment turning out to be unsuitable, the breakdown in negotiations or otherwise.

(i) The appraisal and investigation carried out in respect of the investment opportunities set out in (d) above was detailed and involved of necessity understanding the nature of the business underwritten by the target enterprise, in particular the long term nature of risks and the quality of the rating applied to these risks, the adequacy of claims reserves involving both a case by case review, assessment of financial provisions and supporting actuarial appraisal and assessment.

(j) This type of evaluation activity continued in years subsequent to 1990.

(k) At the time of the proposed acquisitions of ICI, PMPA and Vimar, the valuation of Hibernian Group Plc was in the region of £100m. The purchases of ICI, PMPA and Vimar would have involved sums of approximately £100m, £50m and £10m respectively. In the event, none of these companies were ultimately acquired by Hibernian Group Plc.

In the Schedule to the Case Stated, the purpose and nature of the work for which the expenditure was incurred is dealt with. In summary these were:

1. Investment Bank of Ireland

IBI were retained to assist management in providing critical appraisals and advice to the Board of the Group on the proposed investments in ICI and PMPA. In the case of PMPA, a bid did not emerge. In the case of ICI, two offers were made but not accepted. In both cases the sale involved purchase of shares in a new company which would have become a subsidiary of the Group.

2. Buck Paterson

Buck Paterson carried out an examination and verification of aspects of the pension scheme of ICI for the Group.

3. Coopers & Lybrand

This fee was charged for an actuarial review and valuation of "in force" business of HLA which was 50% owned by Hibernian. The appraisal was carried out to give assurance on the existing investment of 50% and to assist in forming a preliminary view on the potential acquisition of the remaining 50%.

4. Coopers & Lybrand- ICI

This fee related to advisory services on taxation matters relating to the proposed acquisition of ICI.

5. Coopers & Lybrand - VIMAR

These fees were incurred for detailed audit and evaluation work on this potential Spanish general insurance acquisition.

6. William Fry - VIMAR

These fees were incurred in investigating and evaluating a proposal to acquire Vimar and in drafting correspondence and other work.

7. Jones Lang & Wootton - VIMAR

These costs were incurred in obtaining an independent professional property evaluation on the properties of Vimar in Spain.

8. Stibbe Blaisse & De Jong

These fees related to investigation of aspects of the structure of the acquisition of Vimar.

9. Other costs

Other costs related to salary costs and direct general expenses incurred in investigating Vimar.

In January of 1990, it was agreed in principle to proceed with an offer for an 80% holding in Vimar subject to satisfactory finalisation of the 1989 trading results. These results turned out to be worse than had been anticipated and a decision was taken not to proceed.

The learned Circuit Judge decided that he could not classify or describe the four year period of intense and sustained research and consultation between 1986 and 1990 as management expenses. He said the subject of the claim, £404,720.00, was expended in looking at projects which he would regard as being in the category of merger/takeovers and would be in the category of capital expenditure.

The question of law for the opinion of the Court is whether the learned Circuit Judge was correct in holding that the expenses of £404,720.00 incurred by way of expenses by the appellant were not expenses of management within the meaning of CTA 1976 s 15(1).

CTA 1976 s 15(1) provides:

> In computing for purposes of corporation tax the total profits for any accounting period of an investment company resident in the State there shall be deducted any sums disbursed on or after the 6 April 1976 as expenses of management (including commissions) for that period, except any such expenses as are deductible in computing income for the purposes of Case V of Schedule D.

The proviso to the sub-section does not apply.

It is also relevant to consider CTA 1976 s 11. Subsection (1) provides:

> Except as otherwise provided by this Act and any other enactment relating to income tax or corporation tax, the amount of any income shall for the purposes of corporation tax be computed in accordance with income tax principles, all questions as to the amounts which are or are not to be taken into account as income, or in computing income, or charged to tax as a person's income, or as to the time when any such amount is to be treated as arising, being

> determined in accordance with the income tax law and practice as if accounting periods were years of assessment.

Group relief and kinds of Group relief are dealt with in ss 107 and 116. Since the only question is whether the sum of £404,720.00 was disbursed as "expenses of management" for the purposes of s 15, nothing turns on these sections.

ITA 1967 s 61 provides for the general rule as to deductions and in particular states:

> (1) Subject to the provisions of this Act in computing the amount of profits or gains to be charged, no sum shall be deducted in respect of ....
>
> (f) any capital withdrawn from, or any sum employed or intended to be employed as capital in such trade or profession.

Mr O'Keeffe for the appellant made the point that CTA 1976 s 15 stands on its own. Section 11 says "except as otherwise provided" by the Act and s 15 provides "otherwise". ITA 1967 s 61 sets out matters to be deducted in calculating profits/gains of trade under Schedule D/Case 1. It is only when these are calculated that the profits are known. The structure of s 15 is totally different. It provides for calculating the total profits and then deducting the expenses of management. Therefore there are two distinct matters, what are total profits and what are expenses of management. He said capital considerations do not arise where expenses of management are being considered. He said the Group is on the lookout for investments. In order to make acquisitions they have to have investigation and evaluation. Expenses has a broad meaning. Whether the acquisition is completed or not, on-going expenses are expenses of management. If appraisals lead to investment, expenses of management up to the moment of decision can be severed. He said the Judge's finding was a mistake of law. A company whose business is mergers/takeovers is not protected by s 15. The business in question is the making of investments and the income derived. It is open to the Court to find on the basis of the facts found, that these are expenses of management and therefore allowable. The expenses are the expenses of evaluation and appraisal up to the time of decision. They are management expenses whether carried out by management or delegated to outside experts. The principles apply whether the investments are part of circulating capital or fixed assets. The words should be given a wide meaning.

Mr Clarke for the respondent argued that the principles of Income Tax are borrowed under ITA 1967 s 11(1). He said that the company for the first time in four years were looking at buying in from outside new substantial businesses. The case comes down to whether the capital/revenue distinction is properly made in the phrase "expenses of management". The relevant consideration comes down to the interpretation of "expenses of management". It is appropriate to distinguish between capital and revenue expenses. Management implies something of regular expenditure in the same way as trade implies regular business. One manages in an active way, not by leaving it there. A live company with a portfolio of investments needs to keep it under constant review and to "manage it", as implied in the term "fund manager". For a life assurance company, ss 33 to 50 provide a special and curious tax requirement. It puts them into a different category and creates a hybrid. It is treated in the same way as a bank that makes current profits. Here it is not a regular general management of assets. These are manifestly one off transactions. Management would not include consideration of those types of investments. Taking over a company that is the same size or half the size or one-tenth the size is not managing it; it is the consideration of a take-over. The authorities do not decide in absolute terms. From first principles these are not management expenses. By their nature they are designed to achieve capital. The cases cited do not have an application where the acquisition would not be a regular acquisition but a major increase equal to capital. The expense is not related to management at all. The legal test to be applied is whether capital or revenue is relevant. If it is capital it cannot be considered as revenue. The distinction is a matter of law. If it was capital expenditure and the Court was satisfied that expenditure in considering investments of a capital nature was not allowable, there was ample evidence on which the learned Circuit judge could reach a conclusion. The scale of the acquisition is undisputed. If this submission in law is correct, the factual decision of the learned Circuit Judge stands up to scrutiny. The appropriate test is whether it was a decision that the learned Circuit Judge could have come to. There is only one issue: whether the revenue/capital issue is imported into consideration by use of the words "expenses of management".

In the course of argument the following cases were referred to:-

In *London County Freehold and Leasehold Properties Limited v Sweet (HM Inspector of Taxes* 24 TC 412, the appellant was an investment company. It was held that the Special Commissioners were correct in deciding that expenses incurred in the issue of new stock were not expenses of management within the meaning of ITA 1918 s 33(1). In that case MacNaughton J at p 416 referred to the fact that the Special Commissioners held that the disbursements claimed were (1) disbursements of capital and (2) were not expenses of management within the meaning of ITA 1918 s 33. He said:

> The statement that they were disbursements of capital has been criticised. Its meaning is not quite clear but I think it means that if the company were assessed to tax in accordance with the rules under Case 1 of Schedule D, that then those expenses would be regarded as capital expenses and not as income expenses. The statement that the expenses were disbursements of capital is, however, I think, immaterial. The question is whether they were expenses of management, for if they were not expenses of management then no claim can be made under s 33.

He held that the expenses incurred in the rearrangement of the loan capital of a company stand on the same footing as expenses incurred in raising loan capital. They could not be regarded as expenses of the management of the business of the appellant company and the appeal was dismissed.

Capital and National Trust Limited v Golder (HM Inspector of Taxes) 31 TC 265. This was a case where brokerage and stamp duties on changes of investments were claimed for relief in respect of management expenses under the ITA 1918. In this case it was held that the brokerage and stamp duty on change were not management expenses. In the Court of Appeal, Tucker LJ at p 773 referring to an argument that the expenses were "expenses of management" because they were expenses incurred by the management in carrying out the business of the company, said "that seems to me a totally different thing from that with which we are concerned in the present case, namely the expenses *of* management not expenses incurred *by* the management in carrying out the proper business of the company".

In *Sun Life Assurance Society v Davidson (HM Inspector of Taxes)* 37 TC 330, the appellant carried on a life assurance business and made claims to relief from income tax in respect of brokerage and stamp duties disbursed in connection with purchases and sales of investments as being expenses of management. It was held by the House of Lords that the Special Commissioners were correct in holding that the sums were not admissible as expenses of management. Lord Morton of Henryton said at p 357:

> It has been common ground between the parties throughout all Courts that 'expenses of management' do not include the price of investments brought by the society in the course of its business. Now it is clear that the sums now in question are not part of the price, for the price of

> an investment, purchased or sold, is the sum which is paid by the purchaser to the seller. These expenses are, however, so closely linked with the transaction of purchase that they may naturally be considered as items in the total cost of a purchase which has already been resolved upon by the management of the company and not as expenses of management. This is the short and simple ground upon which the Commissioners decided the case in favour of the Crown and I have arrived at the conclusion, though with considerable doubt, that it is a sound ground.

Lord Reid said at p 360:

> I do not think it is possible to define precisely what was meant by 'expenses of management'. It has not been argued that these words have any technical or special meaning in this context. They are ordinary words of the English language and like most words their application in a particular case can only be determined on a broad view of all relevant matters. I cannot accept the argument for the appellants that every sum spent by the company is an expense of management unless it can be brought within certain limited classes of expenditure which are admittedly not expenses of management, such as payments to policy holders and the purchase price of investments acquired by the company. It is not enough to show negatively that a particular sum does not fall into any other class; it must be shown positively that it ought to be regarded as an expense of management. But looking to the purpose and content of the section it appears to me that the phrase has a fairly wide meaning, so that, for example, expenses of investigation and consideration whether to pay out money either in settlement of a claim or in an acquisition of an investment must be held to be expenses of management. And the collocation of the words '(including commissions)' shows that a sum can be an expense of management whether the work in question is done by the company's staff or done by someone else on a commission basis and it must follow that if work of an appropriate kind is done for a fixed fee that fee may also be an expense of management.

And later:

> It seems to me more reasonable to ask with regard to a payment, whether it should be treated as part of the cost of acquisition on the one hand or on the other hand something severable from the costs of acquisition which can properly be regarded as an expense of management.

In *Hoechst Finance Limited v Gumbrell (Inspector of Taxes)* 1983 STC 150, the taxpayer company had to obtain a guarantee in order to raise the money for financing the other UK subsidiaries and to obtain the guarantee it had to agree to pay the parent company continuing commission. It was held by the Court of Appeal that the commission could not be severed from the cost of acquisition of the funds. It followed that the commission payments were not management expenses within the meaning of s 304(1) of the Income and Corporation Taxes Act 1970. Lord Justice Dillon at p 155 said that the commission could not be severed from the cost of acquisition and Lord Justice May at p 156 referring to the Sun Life Assurance Society case said:

> In my opinion the result of that case is that in this type of situation one has to ask whether the relevant payment can be regarded as properly severable from the costs of acquisition of an investment or the issue of loan stock on the one hand or a direct and necessary part of the cost of a normal method of purchase or issue on the other. If, posing that question, the answer is that it is the latter, then the payment is not an expense of management.

In *Stephen Court Limited v JA Browne (Inspector of Taxes)* 1984 ILRM 231. The capital asset of the appellant consisted of the premises known as Stephen Court and the business of the company was both the letting of the premises and the collection of the rent. It was held that the auctioneers commission and the solicitors' costs incurred with the creation of the lease could not be said to be expenses of a capital nature. The expenses of negotiating the lease and preparing the necessary documents were expenses of management within the meaning of ITA 1967 s 81(5)(d) and were an authorised deduction in calculating the appellant's profits. McWilliam J said at p 236:

> I am of opinion that the view of Lord Reid (in the Sun Life case) is correct when he indicated that if expenses incurred for work performed by a member of the staff of a business would be classed as management expenses, such expenses would not cease to be management expenses because independent qualified persons were employed for the same work.

In *Commissioners of Inland Revenue v Wilson's Executors* 18 TC 465, the respondent claimed relief from Income Tax in respect of the cost of maintenance, repairs, insurance and management of his estate. He contended that a sum paid to a farm tenant in settlement of an action and the amount of his own expenses in the litigation were admissible deductions. The General Commissioners allowed the claim insofar as it related to compensation for disturbance and the expenses of the litigation. But it was held by the Court of Session (Scotland) that these payments were not costs of "management" within the meaning of Rule 8 of No 5 of Schedule A of the Income Tax Act 1918.

In *Atherton v British Insulated and Helsby Cables Limited* 10 TC 155, the respondent company contributed a loan sum of £31,784.00 irrevocably as the nucleus of a pension fund established by trust deed for the benefit of its clerical and technical salaried staff. It was held that it was not an admissible deduction for income tax purposes. Viscount Cave LC said at p 192:

> But when an expenditure is made not only once and for all, but with the view to bringing into existence as asset or an advantage for the enduring benefit of a trade, I think that there is a very good reason (in the absence of special circumstances leading to an opposite conclusion) for treating such an expenditure as properly attributable not to revenue but to capital.

In *Sergeant (HM Inspector of Taxes) v Eayrs* 48 TC 573 the respondent visited Australia to investigate conditions with a view to emigrating and buying a farm there. On appeal against an assessment to income tax the General Commissioners allowed his travelling expenses as a deduction. In the High Court it was contended that the expenditure in question was capital expenditure being expenditure for the purpose of setting up a new or extended business. Goff J at p 577 said the respondent had really no answer to that way of putting the matter. At p 578 he cited the dictum of Viscount Cave LC in *Atherton v British Insulated and Helsby Cables Limited* (see above).

He also referred *to Commissioners of Inland Revenue v Granite City Steamship Company Limited* 13 TC 1 where Lord Sands said at p 14:

> Broadly speaking, outlay is deemed to be capital when it is made for the initiation of a business or extension of a business or for a substantial replacement of equipment.

Goff J then said:

> What the respondent did in this case appears to me, applying the principles so laid down, to have been something in which he incurred not revenue but capital expenditure. In the result the business was not extended because he found prices in Australia prohibitive and therefore the expenditure was abortive. But *Lothian Chemical Company Limited v Rogers* (1926) 11 TC 508 shows, as one would expect, that this is an irrelevant consideration. The expenditure does not change its nature according to whether it be successful or unsuccessful.

In *Tucker (Inspector of Taxes) v Granada Motorway Services Limited* [1979] STC 393 where the question was whether a lump sum paid to the landlord to get rid of an annual charge against revenue in the future thus reducing the rent payable was capital expenditure, Lord Fraser of Tullybelton said at p 403:

> The question whether particular payment is of capital or of revenue character has had to be decided in many recorded cases including several in your Lordship's House. The reasons for the decisions having been related to the particular facts of each case have naturally differed widely.

He cited the statement by Viscount Cave LC in *Atherton* case (already quoted) and then continued:

> That statement was the foundation of the argument for the appellant in this instant appeal. The expenditure of £122,220.00 was evidently made once and for all and thus satisfies the first limb of the test but it was said that it did not satisfy the second limb because it was not made with a view to bringing into existence an asset or an advantage for the enduring benefit of the appellant's trade. I cannot accept that argument. In my opinion it represents the wrong approach to the problem because it treats what I may call the Atherton test as if it were the only one capable by itself of providing an answer to the question without regard to other factors. That is not so. There is high authority for the view that no single rule or touchstone has been devised for distinguishing between capital and revenue payments ... On the contrary there are many factors some or all of which may be relevant in the circumstances of each particular case. In the present case the fact that the payment was made once and for all is an indication though not a conclusive indication that the payment was of a capital nature. The second limb of the Atherton test seems to me inappropriate in respect that it tends to concentrate attention too much on the reason why the expenditure was incurred ("with a view to" what purpose?). A more relevant test to the present case is to see for what the payment was made. It was made for commuting part of the liability for additional rent payable under the lease. That fact goes a long way to stamp it with the character of a capital payment because the lease is, in my opinion, a capital asset of the appellant, as indeed was conceded.

In my opinion certain guidelines can be extracted from these cases. No single rule has been devised for distinguishing between capital and revenue payments. The phrase "expenses of management" does not have a technical or special meaning. They are ordinary words whose application in a particular case should be determined on a broad view of all relevant matters. Expenses of management are not all expenses incurred by management in carrying out the business of the company. There is a distinction between expenses *of* management and the expenses incurred by management. Expenditure does not change its nature according to whether the project on which it is made is successful or unsuccessful. If expenses incurred for work performed by a member of the staff would be classified as management expenses, they do not cease to be management expenses because independent qualified persons were employed for the same work.

Expenses so closely linked with the transaction of purchase that they may naturally be considered as items in the total costs of a purchase are not expenses of management. It is possible to sever from the costs of acquisition, costs which are not a direct and necessary part of the cost of a normal method of purchase and can properly be regarded as an expense of management.

In order to answer the question for determination in the Case Stated it is necessary to decide whether the various items of work included in the sum of £404,720.00 are so closely linked with the proposed acquisitions that they should be naturally considered as items in the total cost of the purchases or whether they are not a direct and necessary part of the cost of a normal method of purchase. No submissions were made that differing considerations vis-à-vis revenue/capital, applied to the various items of expenditure that made up the sum in question. Accordingly I have dealt with the case on that basis.

Outlay is deemed to be capital when it is made for the initiation of a business or extension of a business (see *Sergeant v Eayrs* 48 TC 573 and *Commissioners for Inland Revenue v Granite City Steamship Company* 13 TC 1). In this case the expenditure was made for the extension of a business. The dictum of Lord Reid in *Sun Life* case that the expenses of investigation in the acquisition of an investment must be held to be an expense of management would appear to qualify this proposition. However, I think Lord Reid's dictum must be interpreted in the context of a life assurance company which is a trading company unlike an investment company which is not a trading company. In this case the expenditure was made once and for all with a view to bringing assets into existence (see *Atherton v British Insulated and Helsby Cables Limited*).

While Mr O'Keeffe submitted that capital/revenue considerations do not apply and that only the question of what are expenses of management has to be considered, it seems to me that the expenses of management cannot be examined without analysing whether the expenditure is so closely linked with the acquisition of assets that it can be categorised as a capital payment.

I do not think it could be said that the various items of expenditure were not a direct and necessary part of the proposed capital acquisitions. The learned Circuit Judge had evidence on which he could hold that the expenditure would be in the category of capital expenditure. He also said he considered the subject of the claim as being in the category of merger/takeovers. While mergers might not apply, it appears to me that the learned Circuit Judge could severally describe the transactions as being in the category of take-overs and this did not detract from his finding of capital expenditure.

Accordingly, the question whether the learned Circuit Judge was correct in holding that the expenses of £404,720.00 incurred by way of expenses by the appellant were not expenses of management within the meaning of CTA 1976 s 15(1) must be answered in the affirmative.

Supreme Court - 20 January 2000

Murphy J, This appeal raises the issue whether certain disbursements by Hibernian Group Plc (the Group) and surrendered by it to Hibernian Insurance Company Ltd (Hibernian) constitute management expenses within the meaning of CTA 1976 s 15, and as such deductible in computing liability to corporation tax.

The issue arises in this way. The Group was incorporated on the 7 April 1986, with the object of facilitating the expansion of life and general insurance business carried on through subsidiary companies both by organic growth and through investments when suitable opportunities arose. By its memorandum the Group was authorised to carry on the business of an investment company and in fact its business consisted wholly or mainly in the making of investments and the principal part of its income was derived from the making of such investments. That business required the maintenance and evaluation of the existing investments of the Group and the evaluation of potential investment opportunities.

In May 1986 the Group acquired the entire share holding in Hibernian. On the 21 August 1987 the Group acquired 50% of the shares in Hibernian Life Association. On the 20 December 1988 the Group incorporated Hibernian Reinsurance and on the 29 June 1989 Hibernian Investment Managers was incorporated. In the period between 1986 and 1990 three significant investment opportunities arose, two in Ireland, namely, PMPA and ICI and one in Spain, namely, Vimar. These were insurance companies the purchase of shares in which was explored and evaluated by or on behalf of the Group. In so doing the Group incurred expenditure of £404,720 largely in respect of advice from investment bankers and leading accountants as well as legal advice. In the event none of the three companies was ultimately acquired by the Group.

The Group contended that the expenditure constituted management expenses within the meaning of s 15. It was not disputed that the Group was entitled and did surrender to Hibernian those expenses pursuant to CTA 1976 s 107. Furthermore, it was claimed by the Group, and conceded by the Inspector, that the Group was at all material times an investment company within the meaning and for the purposes of s 15 aforesaid. Accordingly, the expenditure totalling £404,720 would have been available to Hibernian as a deduction in computing its total profits for the purposes of corporation tax if and to the extent that such disbursements constituted "expenses of management" within the meaning of that section. The claim by the Group to such a deduction having been refused by the Inspector of Taxes it was appealed to the Circuit Court in Dublin where Judge Devally found against Hibernian and in favour of the Inspector expressing his views in the following terms:

> A four-year period of intense and sustained research and consultation took place between 1986 and 1990 which I am unable to classify or describe as management, either in the generally accepted sense of the term or within the thrust or context of the reference to which I have been directed and the evidence which I have heard. I believe that the £404,720, the subject of the claim, was expended in looking at projects which I would regard as being in the category of mergers/takeovers and would be in the category of capital expenditure.

The learned Judge then, at the request of Hibernian, stated a case for the opinion of the High Court under ITA 1967 s 428, as applied by CTA 1976 s 146. The question on which the opinion of the Court was sought was whether the Judge was correct in holding that the expenditures aforesaid were not expenses of management within the meaning of CTA 1976 s 15(1). In the body of the Case Stated the Judge of the Circuit Court set out with commendable clarity the facts which he had found or were admitted in relation to the manner in which the business of the Group was managed and in the schedule to the Case Stated he set out details of the services rendered in respect of the payments claimed to be expenses of management.

The findings and admissions in relation to the business of the company are set out in lettered paragraphs of which the most important were as follows:

> (B) The business of the Group consisted wholly or mainly in the making of investments and the principal part of its income has been derived from the making of investments. The Group's business of making investments required:
>
> (I) The maintaining and evaluating of its existing investments, and
>
> (II) Evaluating potential investment opportunities.
>
> (F) The business of the Group as managed by the Board of Directors which in the year ended the 31 December 1990 comprised Mr Eamon Walsh, Group Chief Executive and other executive and non executive directors. In practice, the function of management was delegated to a subcommittee of the Board which then procured the necessary appraisal skills and advice from professional experts, both internally and within the group structure and also externally.
>
> (H) ... The process [of evaluating potential investment opportunities] required an active role for the management beginning with the identification of possible acquisitions, setting the evaluation process in train, co-ordinating the efforts of the management team and the professional advisors involved in considering the acquisition, investigating the possible sources of finance and deciding how the investment would fit in with the current portfolio of investments. At any stage the process could be discontinued whether due to the investment turning out to be unsuitable, the breakdown in negotiations or otherwise.

Particulars set out in the Schedule in the Case Stated in numbered paragraphs relating to the fees or costs paid for expert advice in relation to potential investments included the following:

1 Investment Bank of Ireland

IBI were retained to assist management in providing critical appraisals and advice to the Board of the Group on the proposed investments in ICI and PMPA. Detailed consultation took place between the Group's management and IBI and detailed reports were prepared by IBI for the Group Board. Both of these companies were very sizeable operators on the Irish market and all of the inquiries referred to in the opening paragraphs above had to be carried out. This involved a very substantial amount of collaboration with the Group's management. In the case of PMPA, circumstances were such that a bid did not emerge. In the case of ICI, an offer was made and this was not accepted. The Group was invited to make a second offer which was also ultimately not accepted. In both cases, the sale involved purchase of shares in a new company which would have become a subsidiary of the Group.

5 Coopers & Lybrand - Vimar

These fees were incurred where details of it and the evaluation work carried out by Coopers & Lybrand's Madrid office on this potential Spanish general insurance acquisition. This work was carried out at an early stage to enable a view to be formed under the state of work and administration in the company, its net asset value and its potential value and generally appraise its suitability and value in an investment context. In addition, taxation and legal structure aspects of such an investment were considered.

6 William Fry - Vimar

These fees were incurred in investigating and evaluating the proposal to acquire the Spanish company Vimar Saseguros y Reaseguros SA, drafting the purchase agreement which could be used if the transaction proceeded and all other work and correspondence.

9 Other Costs:

... In January of 1990, it was agreed in principle to proceed with an offer for an 80% holding in Vimar subject to satisfactory finalisation of their 1989 trading results. It subsequently emerged that their 1989 trading was significantly worse than had been anticipated and a decision was taken not to proceed.

Ms Justice Carroll answered the question raised in the Case Stated in the affirmative for the reasons set out in a comprehensive judgment delivered by her on the 25th day of July 1997. It is from that judgment and the order made thereon that Hibernian appeals to this Court.

The phrase "expenses of management" was introduced into the income tax code by the FA 1915 ss 41(l) and 21(2). Those sections were subsequently repealed by the ITA 1918 but re-enacted by s 33 thereof. As some of the authorities cited to this Court concerned the interpretation and application of that section it is appropriate to quote the material parts thereof as follows:

> 33(1) Where an assurance company carrying on life assurance business, or any company whose business consists mainly in the making of investments, and the principal part of whose income is derived therefrom, or any savings bank or other bank for savings, claims and proves to the satisfaction of the Special Commissioner that, for any year of assessment, it has been charged to tax by deduction or otherwise, and has not been charged in respect of its profits in

accordance with the rules applicable to Case figure 1 of Schedule D, the company or bank shall be entitled to repayment of so much of the tax paid by it as is equal to the amount of the tax on any sums dispersed as expenses of management (including commissions) for that year: Provided that -

(a) Relief shall not be given under this section so as to make a tax paid by the company or bank less than the tax which would have been paid if the profits had been charged in accordance with the said rules; and

(b) …

(c)

(2) ....

(3) A company or bank shall not be entitled to any relief under this section in respect of any expenses as to which relief may be claimed or allowed under rules 7 and 8 of No 5B of Schedule A.

Section 33 aforesaid remained part of the system under which the liability of the companies to which it applied was determined for the purposes of Income Tax from 1918 and Corporation Profits Tax from 1920 until the assessment of companies to Income Tax was terminated and Corporation Profits Tax abolished by the CTA 1976. However, in computing the corporation tax chargeable under that Act on the "profits" of a company a similar, though not identical relief was granted by s 15 of the 1976 Act in respect of management expenses. That Act made separate provision for life assurance companies (s 33) and investment companies (s 15).

CTA s 15(6) defines an investment company as meaning:

Any company whose business consists wholly or mainly in the making of investments, and the principal part of whose income is derived therefrom, but includes any savings bank or other bank for savings.

The material provisions of s 15 are contained in subsection 1 thereof which is as follows:

15.(1) In computing for purposes of corporation tax the total profits for any accounting period of an investment company resident in the State there shall be deducted any sums disbursed on or after the 6th day of April 1976, as expenses of management (including commissions) for that period, except any such expenses as are deductible in computing income for the purposes of Case V of Schedule D:

PROVIDED that there shall be deducted from the amounted treated as expenses of management the amount of any income derived from sources not charged to tax, other than franked investment income.

Profits in general are required to be determined in accordance with the provisions of s 11 (1) of the Act of 1976 on the basis provided therein, namely:

11(1) Except as other wise provided by this Act or any other enactment relating to income tax or corporation tax, the amount of any income shall for purposes of corporation tax be computed in accordance with income tax principles, all questions as to the amounts which are or are not to be taken into account as income, or in computing income, or charged to tax as a person's income, or as to the time when such amount is to be treated as arising, being determined in accordance with income tax law and practice as if accounting periods were years of assessment.

Section 14(1) dealt with deductions (and additions) in the computation of profits in respect of capital allowances in the following terms:

In computing for purposes of corporation tax a company's profits for any accounting period there shall be made in accordance with this section all such deductions and additions as are

> required to give effect to the provisions of the Income Tax Acts which relate to allowances (including investment allowances) and charges in respect of capital expenditure, as those are applied by this Act.

Section 14 then goes on to deal with the manner in which such allowances are applied for the purposes of corporation tax.

Having regard to the fact that "expenses of management" may be deductible in computing the liability to tax of one type or another of a variety of companies it is surprising how few decisions have been reported in relation to the meaning of that expression. Helpful observations offered by leading authors do not appear to be supported by authority. In *Wheatcroft's Law of Income Tax, Sur Tax and Profits Tax* 1952 Edition at paragraph 1/688 the author says:

> An investment holding company can recover tax on its management expenses including office expenses, salaries and directors fees where an individual or trustee holding investments has no similar rights.

Again, Messrs Brennan, Moore & Carr in their book on *Corporation Tax* published by the Institute of Taxation in Ireland provide examples of management expenses which include rent, stationery, electricity, secretarial expenses and directors salaries. That analysis apparently based on the function of management as opposed to other aspects of commercial enterprise does not appear to have been pursued in the authorities to which this Court was referred.

Perhaps the most important single decision was one relied on in this Court by both the appellant and the respondent, namely, the *Sunlife Assurance Society v Davidson (Inspector of Taxes)* 37 TC 330 (the *Sunlife* case). The plaintiff in that case was, as its name indicates, a life assurance company. It claimed relief from tax in respect of two categories of disbursements, first, brokerage charges and secondly stamp duties arguing that those disbursements constituted expenses of management within the meaning of s 33 of the ITA 1918. Harman J in the High Court and all of the judges of the Court of Appeal decided that neither category of disbursement constituted expenses of management. They did so because they felt bound by the decision of the Court of Appeal in *Capital & National Trust Ltd v Golder* 31 TC 265 (*Golder*'s case). The judges of the Court of Appeal believed that "expenses of management" should be given a wide meaning - perhaps a very wide meaning - and for that reason were reluctant to disallow the two items in issue. Singleton LJ explained his views (at p 346) in the following terms:

> If the purchase is part of the ordinary day to day business of the Society it is difficult at first sight to see why something which the Society has to pay in order to carry out the purchase is not an expense of the ordinary running of the Society business. It is argued that the expenses of management end when a decision is made to buy, and thus that the cost of a stamp or brokerage which takes place later is not an expense of management. That cannot be right, for someone on behalf of the Society has to receive and to check the securities and the broker is under the duty of seeing to the transfers and forwarding the securities. That is a part of his work in return for the remuneration he receives by way of brokerage or commission. It seems to me to be impossible to split the transaction in this way: to do so is to depart from common sense.

The House of Lords upheld the unanimous conclusion of that Court of Appeal and sought to lay to rest in the misgiving which the members of the Court had felt in arriving at their decisions. In particular Viscount Simons in the House of Lords, having quoted the passage already cited from the judgment of Singleton LJ, went on to say (at p 357):

> The case is thus put by the learned Lord Justice as cogently as it can be put. But it is, I think, vitiated by the initial mistake that he regards 'management' as equivalent to running the company's business in a wide and almost colloquial sense. If it had this meaning, it would cover the price of the investment equally with the brokerage and the stamp duties. But *ex concessis* it does not, and I would say with the greatest respect that it would be to depart from common sense to treat the three constituents of the cost of purchase differently.

On the other hand Lord Reid made clear that expenses of management were not confined to expenses involved in taking managerial decisions nor exclude expenses involved in carrying out such decisions in individual cases (p 359). The passage cited from the judgment of Lord Reid and relied on in most subsequent cases was expressed (at p 360) in the following terms:

> I do not think that it is possible to define precisely what is meant by 'expenses of management'. It has not been argued that these words have any technical or special meaning in this context. They are ordinary words of the English language, and, like most such words, their application in a particular case can only be determined on a broad view of all relevant matters. I cannot accept the argument for the appellant that every sum spent by the company is an expense of management unless it is brought within certain limited classes of expenditure which are admittedly not expenses of management, such as payments to policy holders and the purchase of investments acquired by the company. It is not enough to show negatively that a particular sum does not fall into any other class; it must be shown positively that it ought to be regarded as an expense of management. But looking to the purpose and content of the section it appears to me that the phrase has a fairly wide meaning, so that, for example, expenses of investigation and consideration whether to pay out money either in settlement of a claim or in acquisition of an investment must be held to be expenses of management. The collocation of the words '(including commissions)' shows that a sum can be an expenses of management whether the work in question is done by the company staff or done by someone else on a commission basis. It must follow that if work of an appropriate kind is done for a fixed fee that fee may also be an expense of management.
>
> Admittedly the price paid for an investment is not an expense of management, and counsel for the appellants did not and could not reasonably withhold the admission that a sum spent on enhancing the value of a trading asset is not an expense of management. I do not think that it is practicable or reasonable to draw a rigid line between payments which enhance the value of an asset and payments which do not ... It seems to me more reasonable to ask, with regard to a payment, whether it should be regarded as part of the cost of acquisition on the one hand or, on the other, something severable from the cost of acquisition which can properly be regarded as an expense of management.

On those criteria a particular disbursement would fail to qualify for deduction either because it could not be severed from the cost of acquisition of an asset or if it could be so severed, it could not properly be regarded as an expense of management.

Whilst it is easy to accept, as Lord Reid pointed out, that expenses of management cannot be defined with precision, one might have thought the general concept of management and the expenses thereof could be identified with some measure of clarity. I would have hoped that Viscount Simons was correct when he said at p 354:

> It is in fact very clear that an expression like 'expenses of management' is insusceptible of precise definition and that there must be a border line or twilight area in which a conclusion one way or another could (not) easily be reached. That does not mean that there is not on either side of it an area of sunshine and of darkness.

Unfortunately very little guidance is available as to where these areas of sunshine and darkness may be found. Certainly it would appear that the area of twilight is extensive. The decision of the House of Lords in that case affirming the hesitant decision of the Court of Appeal therein effectively subsumed the judgment in the *Golder*'s case. There are, however, two points of note remaining from the earlier case. First, to note that that judgment was expressly directed to an investment company rather than an assurance company and, secondly, the simple but helpful reminder provided by Tucker LJ (at p 273 of the report) in the following terms:

> He [counsel for the appellant] says these expenses were 'expenses of management' because they were expenses incurred by the management in carrying out the business of the company. That seems to me a totally different thing. What we are concerned with here is the expenses of management, not expenses incurred by the management in carrying out the proper business of the company.

The decision in *Hoechst Finance Ltd v Gumbrell (Inspector of Taxes)* is helpful in that it examines the phrase "expenses of management" in the context of s 304(l) of the Income and Corporation Tax Act 1970, which is similar in its concept and its terms to s 15 of the 1976 Act. In that case the taxpayer company was incorporated to raise and provide finance for its fellow subsidiary companies. It raised a substantial loan on the stock exchange but only on terms that the parent company guaranteed repayment thereof. For so doing the parent company charged a commission of.25% per annum on the amount of the loan outstanding for the time being. The tax payer contended that the commission so payable was deductible "as an expense of management". Mr Justice Nourse allowed that claim but his decision was unanimously overruled by the Court of Appeal.

A passage from the judgment of Dillon LJ (at page 155) is material for the analysis which it provides both in relation to expenses of management and expenditure of a capital nature. He said:

> In the present case it seems to me that the guarantee had to be obtained by the company from its parent in order to raise the money to invest by advances to the other United Kingdom subsidiaries and the company had to agree to pay the parent the continuing commission in order to obtain the guarantee and therefore realistically as part of the price of raising the money. The commission cannot be severed from the cost of acquisition and so equally the annual payments of the commission cannot be severed from the cost acquisition. It is unreal to regard each annual payment as merely a payment for the current year or the current six months to keep the guarantee on foot as part of the continuing management of the company's business, because the whole obligation in respect of the loan stock and the obligation of the guarantee was undertaken once and for all when the stock was raised and the guarantee was entered in to and, as shown by the letter from the parent company, the commission was charged by the parent company for giving the guarantee. It all relates back to the giving of the guarantee.

Stephen Court Ltd v JA Browne [1984] IRLM 231 did involve the consideration of the concept of "management" but only in the context of the ITA 1967 s 81(5)(d) which provided for the deduction from rents of certain payments including:

> (d) The cost of maintenance, repairs, insurance and management of the premises borne by the person chargeable and relating to and constituting an expense of the transaction or transactions under which the rents or receipts were received, not being an expense of a capital nature.

Whilst McWilliam J did analyse and derive some assistance from the judgments in the *Sunlife* case, *Golder*'s case and *Hoechst Finance* it is clear that the word "management" was used in s 81 of the 1967 Act in a very different context from that in which it appears in CTA 1976 s 15. First, it appears in the context with the words "maintenance repairs and insurance" and, secondly, it is expressly concerned with "management of the premises". In the circumstances I think there is little assistance to be derived from that judgment in determining the issues which arise in the present case. I would, however, note that McWilliam J approved, in my view correctly, the observation of Lord Reid that if expenses incurred for work performed by a member of the staff the business could be classed as management expenses should expenses would not cease to be management expenses because independent and qualified persons were employed for the same work.

In *Golder*'s case it was conceded that the cost of purchasing an investment which formed part of the current or circulating capital of the tax payer company was not and could not be an expense of management. If that concession was correctly made - and I believe that it was - *a fortiori* expenditure incurred in purchasing a capital asset would not qualify as expenses of management. In the present case the appellant did not in the High Court nor does he in this Court contend otherwise. The essence of his argument is, and has been, that no costs or expenses which the Group might have incurred in respect of any of the potential investments subsequent to the date upon which the Board of Directors decided to purchase the particular investment would qualify as expenses of management but all expenditure prior to that date would so qualify. The respondent on the other hand contended that all of the expenses of investigating and evaluating the potential investments were so closely linked with the proposed purchase that they would fall to be considered as the cost of purchase if the transactions had proceeded. The respondent contended that the character of the expenditure could not alter depending upon whether the purchase was successful or not. Moreover, the respondent argued, the relationship between the expenditure which was incurred and the nature of the asset which would have been acquired if the transaction had proceeded brought the expenditure into the category of capital and as such was not deductible in calculating profits whatever other characteristics it might have possessed.

Unquestionably the respondent is correct is saying that different judges, and in particular Lord Reid in the *Sunlife Assurance* case, had referred to the severability of certain items from the cost of purchase. Other judges spoke of "divorcing" particular sums from the price paid or the amount received when changes took place in the investments of a tax payer company. There is no doubt that such distinctions can be made. In fact it must be possible to identify a variety of phases between the stage when one company considers the desirability acquiring all of or a substantial share holding in another company and the ultimate completion of such an acquisition. The question arises, however, as to why one should classify differently work of the same character but carried on in different phases or stages of such an acquisition. Undoubtedly the Group is entitled to pray in aid the observations of Lord Reid both as to the severability and deductibility of the costs incurred in relation to such activities. The other judges in the *Sunlife Assurance* case placed a different emphasis on the relationship between expenditure and acquisition. Their views might be summarised by saying that a particular expenditure could not constitute an expense of management if it formed an "integral part" of the acquisition of an asset. Whilst taxes and duties imposed on transactions are inescapably associated with such transactions and professional advice in relation thereto are, in theory at any rate, optional, it would be impossible in practice to suggest that the legal costs of, say, investigating the title to land the subject matter of a contract for sale or professional advice in relation to a "due diligence" investigation for a take over could be dispensed with. Indeed the appellants would not suggest otherwise. The argument on their behalf is that such costs and expenses are deductible when incurred before the decision to purchase but not if incurred after it. In my view such a decision cannot change the nature of the service provided. If a purchase were completed I do not doubt that it would be universally accepted that all of the costs incurred in relation to the exploration, evaluation and investigation of the company to be acquired, would be "costs of the purchase". I believe that it would be impossible to justify any distinction as the nature of those costs depending upon whether the work done on behalf of the purchaser was carried out before any agreement was reached: after an option had been obtained: or before or after a conditional or unconditional agreement signed. The problems to which these variations and refinements could give rise is exemplified by the present case. In the findings made by Judge Devally and quoted above in relation to the fees paid to the Investment Bank of Ireland it is explained that the Group made not one but two offers for ICI and neither of which was ultimately accepted. Those offers would appear to indicate that the time had been reached "when a decision was made by the Group to proceed with the acquisition". In relation to Vimar the lawyers actually drafted the purchase agreement: The findings made by the Circuit Court Judge contained the following statement:

> In January of 1990, it was agreed in principle to proceed with an offer for and 80% holding in Vimar subject to satisfactory finalisation of their 1989 trading results. It subsequently emerged that their 1989 trading was significantly worse than had been anticipated and a decision was taken not to proceed.

It would seem that even on the test proposed by the Group that at least some of the costs would have been incurred after a decision was made to acquire the shares in question but more particularly the facts illustrate how difficult it would be to rely on such an imprecise event to differentiate between the nature of an expenditure incurred. In my view one cannot go further than saying that a close relationship between a proposed acquisition and expenditure incurred in respect thereof would necessarily deprive that expenditure of the characteristics of a management disbursement. The relationship between the disputed expenses in the present case and the potential purchases was such as to deprive that expenditure of the character of expenses of management.

The respondent had also disputed the right of the Group to deduct the expenditure incurred in evaluating the putative investments on the ground that such expenditure constituted capital payments and that payments of that character were not deductible in computing profits for corporation tax. The Group denied that the payments were capital in their nature but argued more particularly that s 15 of the 1976 Act authorised the deduction of management expenses, whatever their nature, in computing profits. The Group accepted that "income" for the purposes of corporation tax must, in general, be determined in accordance with the principles of income tax law and practice. The Group pointed out that the requirement is to be applied "except as otherwise provided by this Act". Whilst the application of income tax principles would exclude capital payments from deduction in computing income the Group argues that s 15 expressly and unequivocally directed the deduction of sums disbursed "as expenses of management" without reference to any other quality or characteristic of the disbursement. It was contended that this amounted to a statutory exception from s 11 of the 1976 Act. That is a proposition which I do not accept.

Even allowing for the technical and artificial nature of fiscal legislation it would require the clearest words to justify the inference that the legislature intended to arrive at taxable profits or income for an accounting period by deducting a capital payment from a revenue receipt. It can be done, and is done, in various ways for different capital allowances but I would not infer from the general terms of s 15 of the 1976 Act that the legislature intended for such a radical change in the concept of profits. If expenses of management constitute capital disbursements they are not, in my view, deductible in computing profits and it may be that the converse is likewise the case: if disbursements constitute capital payments they would not constitute expenses of management. The decided cases tend to support this view.

Whether an expenditure incurred in relation to the proposed acquisition of a capital asset would lose the character of a capital payment acquired by association with the purpose of which it was expended has been considered in a number of cases.

In *Southwell v Savill Brothers Ltd* [1901] 2 KB 349 a brewing company was in the habit of making applications to licensing justices for new licenses in respect of premises owned by it. As the licensing justices sometimes required the applicant to surrender an existing licence the brewers made a practice of paying annual sums to the holders of certain existing licenses in return for the right to call for a surrender of such licenses in case they were required by the Justices. The brewery accepted that where an application for a new licence was successful no part of the annual payments were deductible. In that event the payments were treated as capital. They contended, however, that where the licence was refused they should be allowed to deduct from their profits the annual expenditure. Kennedy J in delivering his judgment disallowing the deduction said (at p 353):

> The fact that the expenditure does not turn out to be a profitable investment cannot alter the nature of the expenditure, or make it any less an investment of capital.

Similarly in *Sargeant (Inspector of Taxes) v Eayrs* 48 TC 573 Goff J held that a tax payer who carried on a farming business in England incurred costs in travelling to Australia with a view to buying a farm was not entitled to deduct the costs in computing his taxable income.

The costs constituted capital expenses even though no farm was ever bought. The judgment of Goff J was summarised (at p 578) in the following terms:

> In the result the business was not extended, because he found prices in Australia prohibitive, and therefore the expenditure was abortive. But *Lothian Chemical Company Ltd v Rogers* [1926] 11 TC 508 shows, as one would expect, that that is an irrelevant consideration. The expenditure does not change its nature according to whether it is successful or unsuccessful.

In my view the very substantial costs incurred by the Group in procuring the expert and specific evaluation of the three investment opportunities referred to in the Case Stated did not constitute management expenses. It is not necessary to make a positive finding as to the category into which the expenditure does fall. I am satisfied, however, that from the date on which the Group focused its attention on the acquisition of the prospective investments the expenditure incurred in respect of them would properly have been considered to be costs of acquisition of an investment in the event of the purchase being completed and that it would not have a different characterisation simply because the plans to purchase were frustrated or aborted. In my view Judge Devally was entitled to conclude that the disbursements in question did not constitute management expenses and the learned High Court Judge was correct in deciding that there was ample evidence to justify that conclusion.

Accordingly I would dismiss the appeal and affirm the order of the High Court.

Barron J**,** The appellant is an investment company within the meaning of CTA 1976 s 15. Section 15(1) is as follows:

> In computing for purposes of corporation tax the total profits for any accounting period of an investment company resident in the State there shall be deducted any sums dispersed on or after the 6th day of April 1976 as expenses of management (including commissions) for that period, except any such expenses as are deductible in computing income for the purposes of Case V of Schedule D:

> Provided that there shall be deducted from the amount treated as expenses of management the amount of Any income derived from sources not charged to tax, other than franked investment income.

This provision recognises that in the case of investment companies there are expenses which should be allowable against the income from its investments for tax purposes. To this extent the section is a successor of ITA 1918 s 33.

The issue which arises on this appeal is as to the meaning of the expression "expenses of management" as it occurs in the statutory provision. It is accepted by both parties that these words have no special meaning for the purposes of the Act. Some assistance in their meaning might have been obtained from a consideration of the words "including commissions", these words clearly indicating that commissions were to be regarded as part of expenses of management. However, no arguments have been addressed to the Court as to the assistance, if any, which might be derived in the interpretation of the words "expenses of management" from the reference to commissions. For the same reasons there is no need to consider what expenses would have been deductible if income was being computed for the purposes of Case V of Schedule D.

Counsel for the respondent has submitted that in considering expenses of management one must have regard to the distinction between capital and revenue and that only revenue expenses should be regarded as expenses of management.

The respondent further submits that management in this sense only involves management of its existing investments and taking such steps as may be necessary to obtain the best return from such investments.

Counsel for the appellant on the other hand rejects the notion of a division between capital and revenue expenses. He submits that this is a principle relating to the taxation of traders, which is not what is involved in the instant case. He also maintains that management goes beyond the management of existing investments and must include the cost of appraising potential investments. He submits that a line should be drawn when a decision is made either to acquire or to dispose of an investment and that all expenses up to the time of making such a decision are expenses of management.

ITA 1918 s 33 was considered in *Sun Life Assurance Society v Davidson* 37 TC 330. The facts in that case were whether or not brokerage and stamp duty incurred on the purchase of shares should be allowed as expenses of management. Two passages from the judgment of Viscount Simonds indicate the differing views as to what expenses should or should not be allowed under the heading *Expenses of Management.*

The first is at p 354 where he quotes a passage from the judgment of the special commissioners in the same case. This passage was as follows:

> And we so hold, that the brokerage and stamp duties payable on the purchase of an investment, being not general expenses of conducting the Society's business but expenses specifically referable to and only incurred by reason of the purchase, are expenses of the purchase and not expenses of management. If we draw a line between the moneys admittedly laid out by the Society or expenses of management and the moneys laid out for the price of an investment, we hold that the brokerage and stamp duties fall on the same side of the line as the latter. The fact that the purchase is necessarily made in the ordinary course of carrying on the Society's business does not of itself determine whether the sums in question are expenses of management of that business. In our view the disputed items are so closely linked with the transaction of purchase (being necessarily incurred in the course thereof) as to be considered part of the expenses of the purchase and not expenses of management of the Society's business. We hold also that the brokerage and stamp duties paid by the Society on the sale of an investment are not expenses of management.

At p 356 he quoted the views of Singleton LJ to the contrary where the latter said:

> If the purchase is part of the ordinary day to day business of the Society it is difficult at first sight to see why something which the Society has to pay in order to carry out the purchase is not an expense of the ordinary running of the Society's business. It is argued that the expenses of management end when a decision is made to buy, and thus that the cost of stamp or brokerage which takes place later is not an expense of management. That cannot be right, for someone on behalf of the Society has to receive and to check the securities and the broker is under the duty of seeing to the transfers and forwarding the securities. That is part of his work in return for the remuneration he receives by way of brokerage or commission. It seems to me to lie impossible to split up the transaction in this way; to do so is to depart from common sense.

In my view, these positions could equally have been taken in relation to the proper construction of the expression "expenses of management" in s 15 of the 1976 Act.

Since an investment company is not being taxed on the basis of being a trading company it seems to me to be inappropriate to consider the distinction between the costs of trading and the costs of obtaining a capital asset. Having regard to what is the purpose of the section it seems to me to be appropriate to consider those expenses which it would be unfair to disallow as against investment income.

An investment company maintains its capital in its investments. In the course of its management, its managers have to consider not only whether such capital is best employed but also whether it is providing the best return. I do not accept that only expenditure in relation to getting the best return from existing investments is what is intended by the expression "expenses of management". Expenditure relating to the appraisal of existing investments or the scope of new investment must equally be expenses of management. However, once an appraisal becomes specific in the sense of relating to a particular investment, this is not management, but possible acquisition or disposal as the case may be.

In the *Sun Life* case Lord Somervell of Harrow referred to the brokerage and stamp duty in that case as being a direct and necessary part of the cost of a normal method of purchase. In regard to the two views cited by Viscount Simonds, I prefer the test formulated by the Revenue that such expenses were not only specifically referable to, but only incurred by reason of the purchase and so could not have been expenses of management. It seems to me that the fact that the duties of management still existed in relation to a purchase is insufficient as a test of whether expenditure comes within the expression "expenses of management".

In a sense the issue in the present case is where to draw the line between management on the one hand and investment in the sense of acquisition or disposal on the other. There must be a distinction between the general expenses of management and expenses incurred specifically in relation to a particular investment. The former involves general day to day activity of the company. The latter relax such day to day involvement. This is exemplified by the passage from *Wheatcroft's Law of Income Tax, Surtax and Proper Tax* referred to by Murphy J:

> An investment holding company can recover tax on its management expenses including office expenses, salaries and directors' fees where an individual or trustee holding investments has no similar rights.

What we are dealing with is a privilege granted to an investment company not available to other taxpayers. Tax is paid on the income generated regardless of the cost of administration whether of the fund or of the income generated by the fund. Such costs are the real costs of management. In the instant case, the proposed investments were never made, but that did not change the nature of what was being done. The decision which it is submitted creates the dividing line between costs of management and costs of acquisition was in fact taken before any other disputed expenditure was incurred. It may be part of day to day management to appraise the possibility of acquisitions or disposals, but it ceases to be such when a specific situation is pursued.

The costs of management come to an end when a decision is taken to acquire or dispose of an investment as the case may be. This does not relate to the entering into of a binding commitment. Once steps are taken which may lead to a binding commitment and which are necessary for management to make a full and informed decision then management ceases and acquisition or disposal as the case may be commences.

I would dismiss the appeal.

Patrick J O'Connell (Inspector of Taxes) v Thomas Keleghan

High Court - 10 February 2000 - McCracken J

Capital gains tax/income tax - case stated - sale of shares - sale price in the form of loan notes - loan notes not transferable or assignable - "paper for paper" transaction - whether capital gains tax deferred pending redemption of loan notes - whether loan notes a simple debt or a debt on a security - whether CGT 1975 Sch 2 para 2 is based on "two fictions" - whether fictions are no more than rules of computing tax - "no disposal fiction" and "composite simple asset fiction" - whether marketability is the essence of a loan note - inducement payment to enter into service contract - whether payment liable to income tax - whether taxpayer ever took up employment on foot of the service contract

This appeal by the Inspector of Taxes against the determination of the Appeal Commissioners raises two issues. The first issue is whether an inducement payment of £250,000 to take up employment with Siucre Éireann cpt was subject to income tax pursuant to ITA 1967 s 110. The second issue turned on the question of whether the redemption of a loan note was subject to capital gains tax in accordance with CGT 1975 Sch 2 para 2/4 or CGT 1975 s 46(1).

The relevant facts as set out in the case stated were:

(i) Thomas Keleghan ("the respondent") entered into a share purchase agreement dated 8 February 1990 whereby he sold his shareholding in Gladebrook Ltd to Siucre Éireann CPT for a consideration of £1,867,068 in the form of a loan note which he redeemed for cash in February 1993. The loan note was not transferable or assignable.

(ii) On 8 February 1990 the respondent who was sales director of Sugar Distribution entered into a service contract with Siucre Éireann cpt ("the company") whereby for a consideration of £250,000 he agreed to serve the company as sales director. However, he never became an employee of the company but remained as sales director of Sugar Distributors until his retirement in June 1991.

Income tax

ITA 1967 s 110 is a wide provision aimed at taxing all manner of payments to employees but since the Appeal Commissioners determined that the respondent never became an employee of the company he could not be liable to income tax on the inducement payment of £250,000.

Capital gains tax

The sale of the shares in Gladebrook Ltd in return for a loan issued by the purchaser gave rise to a capital gain but that gain was not chargeable by virtue of the "paper for paper" relieving provision of CGT 1975 Sch 2 para 2. The interpretation of this provision has resulted in considerable case law. The point in issue is whether the original shares and the new asset (the loan note) must continue to be treated as the same asset. The correct interpretation of this provision is that it is limited to the computation of tax and does not have the effect of changing the nature of the new asset such as the loan note for other purposes of the Act.

Accordingly the disposal of loan notes is governed by s 46(1) of the Act which deals with the disposal of a debt or of a debt on a security. No chargeable gains arises on the disposal of a first time acquired debt whereas a chargeable gain may apply to the disposal of a debt on a security. However the essential elements required for a debt on a security is that it be marketable and be capable of becoming more valuable than its nominal value. In the absence of these elements the loan note could not be considered to be a debt on a security.

Note

The statutory definition of a debt on a security was amended by FA 1996 s 61 (TCA 1997 s 541(7)) to provide that debentures or loan notes issued in relieved "paper for paper" exchanges are treated as chargeable assets on subsequent disposals.

Held by McCracken J in dismissing the appeal that:

(i) A liability to income tax could not arise on the inducement payment under ITA 1967 s 110 whose recipient never became an employee;

(ii) The correct interpretation of CGT 1975 Sch 2 para 2 is that it is limited to the computation of tax and does not alter the nature of the loan note in the context of its subsequent disposal;

(iii) Section 11(1) provides that chargeable gains shall be computed subject to Sch 2;

(iv) The loan note does not contain the essential elements of a debt on a security that it be marketable and capable of becoming more valuable;

(v) The redemption of the loan note constitutes the non chargeable disposal of a debt within the meaning CGT 1975 s 46(1).

Legislation: FA 1965 s 23; ITA 1967 ss 110, 428; CGT 1975 s 11(1), (2), Sch 2 para 2

Cases referred to in judgment: Floor v Davis (Inspector of Taxes) [1978] STC 436

Westcott v Woolcombers Ltd [1987] STC 600

WT Ramsey v CIR 54 TC 101

Clevely's Investment Trust v CIR (1971) 47 TC 300

Aberdeen Construction Group v IRC [1987] AC 885

Mooney (Inspector of Taxes) v McSweeney 5 ITR 163, [1997] IR 424

Case stated

Case stated under ITA 1967 s 428 by John O'Callaghan and Ronan Kelly, Appeal Commissioners, for the opinion of The High Court.

1. At an appeal hearing held at 14 St Stephen's Green, Dublin 2 on 1, 3 and 10 March 1995, the respondent appealed against an assessment to income tax under Schedule E for the year of assessment 1991/92 and an assessment to capital gains tax for the year of assessment 1992/93. The appeals were heard at the same time as many of the facts are common to both appeals.

2. Shortly stated the questions for our decision were as follows;

(a) Income Tax: whether the IR£250,000 paid under the Share Purchase Agreement (Exhibit 1) which payment is the subject of the "side letter" (Exhibit 2), is assessable to income tax under Schedule E for the year of assessment 1991/92;

(b) Capital Gains Tax: whether the loan note is a "debt on a security" for the purposes of CGTA 1975, s 46(1) and if it is not such a debt does the said s 46(1) apply to its redemption so that no chargeable gain accrues on that redemption.

(c) whether, for the purposes of CGTA 1975 Sch 2 para 2, the redemption of the loan note is a disposal of the original shares.

3. The following documents were proved or admitted before us:

(a) Agreement dated 8 February 1990 ("Share Purchase Agreement") between Siuicre Éireann cpt, the respondent and others. A copy of this document is annexed hereto as Exhibit 1 and forms part of the Case Stated.

(b) Letter dated 8 February 1990 ("Side Letter") from the respondent to Siuicre Éireann cpt. A copy of this letter is annexed hereto as Exhibit 2 and forms part of the Case Stated.

(c) Agreement dated 8 February 1990 ("Service Agreement") between Siuicre Éireann cpt and the respondent. A copy of this document is annexed hereto as Exhibit 3 and forms part of the Case Stated.

(d) Loan Note (Certificate No 3 in the amount of IR£1,867,068) issued to the respondent by Siuicre Éireann cpt. A copy of this document is annexed hereto as Exhibit 4 and forms part of the Case Stated.

4. The following witnesses gave evidence before us:

(a) the respondent and

(b) Mr Charles Lyons, former director of Sugar Distributors Ltd and former shareholder in Gladebrook Ltd.

5. As a result of the evidence, both oral and documentary, adduced before us we found the following facts proved or admitted;

(a) The respondent acquired 2,151 IR£1 ordinary shares in Gladebrook Ltd in December 1988. Gladebrook Ltd held 49% of the share capital of Sugar Distributors (Holdings) Ltd which in turn held 100% of the share capital of Sugar Distributors Ltd.

(b) By way of the Share Purchase Agreement dated 8 February 1990, the respondent and others sold their shares in Gladebrook Ltd to Siuicre Éireann cpt for a total consideration of IR£8.6m to be satisfied by the issue of loan notes by Siuicre Éireann cpt.

(c) The nominal amount of the loan note received by the respondent was IR£1,867,068.

(d) A chargeable gain did not accrue to the respondent on the sale of his shares in Gladebrook Ltd to Siuicre Éireann cpt as it was accepted that the provisions of to the CGTA 1975 Sch 2 para 4 applied to that transaction.

(e) On 8 February 1990, the respondent signed a service agreement (Exhibit 3) with Siuicre Éireann opt.

(f) On 8 February 1990, the respondent also signed a "side letter" (Exhibit 2) addressed to Siuicre Éireann cpt.

(g) Prior to the signing of the Service Agreement, the respondent was Sales Director of Sugar Distributors Limited. He never became an employee of Siuicre Éireann cpt but remained as Sales Director of Sugar Distributors Limited until his retirement in June 1991, when he was 65 years of age.

(h) The respondent's loan note was redeemed for cash in February 1993.

Income tax assessment

6. It was contended on behalf of the respondent that:

(a) the IR£250,000, the subject of the side letter, is not an emolument. In order for a payment to be assessable to tax as an emolument it must be paid in return for acting or being an employee. The respondent never became an employee of Siuicre Éireann cpt. The IR£250,000 payment is accordingly not liable to income tax under Schedule E;
ITA 1967 s 110(1), is the charging section in respect of Schedule E. In order to be liable to income tax under s 110(1), a taxpayer must possess an office or employment and must receive a salary, fee, or perquisite which derived from that office or employment. As the respondent never held an employment with Siuicre Éireann the sum of £250,000 cannot arise from an employment. There cannot be a charge to income tax in the absence of a source.

(b) ITA 1967 s 110(2) applies only where an employment was held. As an employment was never held s 110(2) has no relevance;

(c) The sum of £250,000 was assessed to income tax in the year of assessment 1991/1992. Even if the IR£250,000 is an emolument, it is not assessed for the correct year of assessment under ITA 1967 s 110(2);
The only possible years of assessment in which the £250,000 might be assessable to income tax are 1989/90 (the year in which respondent became entitled to receive the payment in the future) or 1992/93 (the year in which the loan note was redeemed).

(d) The IR£250,000 was paid in respect of the non competition clauses in the Service Agreement. The IR£250,000 does not come within the scope of ITA 1967 s 525 as the respondent was never an employee of Siuicre Éireann. Accordingly the payment is not within the charge to income tax under Schedule E.

7. It was contended on behalf of the Inspector of Taxes that:

(a) the respondent exercised an office or employment in accordance with the terms of the Service Agreement as a director of Sugar Distributors Ltd from 1 January 1990 until his retirement in June 1991;

(b) the inducement payment of IR£250,000 comes within the term "prequisite or profit whatsoever therefrom" in ITA 1967 s 110(1).

(c) the inducement payment is correctly assessed in the year of assessment 1991/92.

(d) if the "side letter" (Exhibit 2) is ineffective then the IR£250,000 referred to therein, forms part of the consideration in computing the amount of the chargeable gain arising on the redemption of the loan note.

8. The following cases were cited by the parties:

Bray v Best 1989 STC 159
Hochstrasser v Mays 38 TC 637
Beak v Robson 25 TC 33
Prichard v Arundale 47 TC 680
Brumby v Milner 51 TC 583
McKeown v Roe 1 ITC 206
Bedford v H 2 ITR 588
Vaughan-Neil v IRC 1979 STC 644

9. Having adjourned the case to consider the matters, we gave our reserved decision on 31 May 1995. We came to the conclusion that:

> in respect of the IR£250,000, we do not believe there is a Schedule E assessment appropriate to 1991/92.

10.The following figures were then determined:

Emoluments	IR£26,591

11. Immediately after the determination the Inspector of Taxes expressed dissatisfaction therewith as being erroneous in law and asked for a case stated for the opinion of the High Court, which we duly state and sign accordingly.

12. The question of law for the opinion of the High Court is whether, on the foregoing facts and evidence, our decision as set out at Paragraph 9 is correct in law.

Capital gains tax assessment

13. It was contended on behalf of the respondent that:

(a) Under the CGTA 1975 a charge to capital gains tax cannot arise unless a chargeable gain exists. Section 46(1) states that a disposal of a debt by the original creditor does not constitute a chargeable gain unless the debt is a "debt on a security". The Siucre Éireann loan note is not a debt on a security. Therefore, a chargeable gain, the element necessary for a charge to capital gains tax to accrue, does not exist.
The bedrock of the charge to tax under the capital gains tax system is contained s 3(1), the charging section of the Act. It is as follows:

> Tax shall be charged in accordance with this Act in respect of capital gains, that is, in respect of chargeable gains, computed in accordance with this Act and accruing to a person on the disposal of assets"

A chargeable gain is defined in s 11(2) as:

> Every gain accruing on or after the 6th day of April 1974, shall, except so far as otherwise expressly provided be a chargeable gain.

The basic concept contained in these two sections is that one must have a chargeable gain and not merely a capital gain in order for tax to fall due. If this element is missing the Act has no application whatsoever.

(b) The loan note is not a "debt on a security" for the purposes of CGTA 1975 s 46(1). The expression "debt on a security" is not defined in the Capital Gains Tax Acts. The UK courts considered the expression in, inter alia, the cases *Aberdeen Construction Group Ltd v CIR* 52 TC 281 and *WT Ramsey Ltd v CIR* 54 TC 101. The decisions in these cases held that for a debt to constitute a debt on a security it must be transferable and marketable and capable of earning a profit. The Siuicre Éireann loan note was not transferable and was not assignable. Neither did it have any profit-earning capability. Accordingly, it is not a debt on a security.

Lord Wilberforce stated in *WT Ramsey Ltd v CIR* 54 TC 101:

> With all this lack of certainty as to the statutory words, I do not feel any doubt that in this case the debt was a debt on a security. I have already stated its terms. It was created by contract whose terms were recorded in writing; it was designed, from the

> beginning, to be capable of being sold, arid indeed, to be sold at a profit. This was a contractual loan, with a structure and permanence such as fitted it to be dealt in and to have market value.

Lord Fraser of Tullybelton held in the same case:

> The reason for the provision that no chargeable gain should accrue on a disposal of a simple debt by the original creditor must have been to restrict allowable losses ... because the disposal of a simple debt by the original creditor or his legatee will very seldom result in a gain. No doubt it is possible to think of cases where a gain may result, but they are exceptional. On the other hand it is all too common for debts to be disposed of by the original creditor at a loss, and if such losses were allowed for capital gains tax it would be easy to avoid tax by writing off bad debts - for example those owed by impecunious relatives. But debts on a security, being of the nature of investments, are just as likely to be disposed of by the original creditor at a gain as they are at a loss, and they are subject to the ordinary rule.

(c) If the loan note is a simple debt then the disposal of the debt by its redemption is not subject to capital gains tax in accordance with CGTA 1975 s 46(1).

(d) Points (a), (b) and (c) above are sufficient to determine this appeal in favour of the respondent. CGTA 1975 Sch 2 para 2 has no relevance to the operation of CGTA 1975 s 46. In the event that this point was not accepted, the respondent put forward the following arguments with regard to CGTA 1975 Sch 2 para 2;

(e) CGTA 1975 Sch 2 para 2 does not deem the redemption of the loan note to be a disposal of the original shares.

(f) There is nothing to indicate that para 2 operates in primacy to s 46. The opposite is indicated. The opening phrase of s 46(2) is "Subject to the provisions of the said paragraph 3 and paragraph 4 of Schedule 2 …". Nowhere in the section is it stated that s 46 is subject to Sch 2 generally.
The fact that it is stated within the section that the section is subject to two specific paragraphs of Sch 2 demonstrates that s 46 is not subject to Sch 2 generally.

(g) Paragraph 2 does not deem that no disposal of the original share holding has occurred for all purposes. The first limb of para 2 states that a reorganisation of share capital "shall not be treated" as involving any disposal or acquisition of shares. However, the second limb states that, taking both the original holding and the new holding as a single asset, the original holding and the new holding shall be treated as the same asset acquired as the original shares were acquired. The wording of this second limb clearly indicates that a disposal of the original shares has occurred and that an actual acquisition of the new holding has also occurred. Buckley LJ stated in *Floor v Davis (IOT)* 52 TC 609 at 635 (CA):

> FA 1965 Sch 7 paras 4(2) and 6(1), ... as I read them, provide that a disposal of assets to which they apply shall not for the purposes of the charge to tax be treated as a disposal. This does not mean that such a disposal is not a disposal within the meaning of that term in the Act, but that, notwithstanding that it is a disposal, it shall not be taxed as such.

(h) Paragraph 2 only applies at the time of the reorganisation. Paragraph 2 is dealing only with the taxation implications at the time of the reorganisation. It simply provides that at that point in time no disposal is to be treated as occurring. It has no other implications. The fiction is confined to the instant of the reorganisation itself.

(i) Paragraph 2 is not an authority for treating the new shares as having the same identity and characteristics as the original shares at the time of the reorganisation.

Paragraph 2 does not treat the new shares as having the same identity and characteristics as the original shares, much less as treating the original shares as retaining the characteristics which the old shares had when originally acquired.

The absurdity of treating the new shares as having the same characteristics as the original shares can be seen in the application of other provisions of CGTA 1975:

(i) CGTA 1975 s 4(2)

This provision states that, where an individual is neither resident nor ordinarily resident in the state in a year of assessment, a chargeable gain shall not accrue to him on a disposal of assets unless thin gain has accrued, inter alia, in respect of a disposal of land in the state.

The respondent's argument is best illustrated by an example. An individual, resident in the state, originally owned shares in a trading company. Over the years the business of the company changed and it developed into a property dealing company. At this stage the individual exchanged these shares on a reorganisation for new shares in a trading company and later became non-resident. If one asks what characteristics these shares have at the time of their disposal, it would be impossible to argue that they have the characteristics of the original trading shares or the property dealing shares at the time of the reorganisation.

(ii) CGTA 1975 s 26

This section exempts or limits gains where an individual disposes of a family company. The individual must, inter alia, own 25% of the voting control of the family company or 10% of the voting rights and his family, including himself, must own 75% of the voting rights, in order to qualify for the relief on disposal.

An individual, who owns 25% of the voting control of his company, exchanges his shares for shares in another company on a reorganisation. After the exchange he owns 5% of the voting control of the acquiring company. If he later disposes of his 5% holding, he will not be eligible for retirement relief, even though he may satisfy all other conditions of the section. If paragraph 2 deemed that no disposal of the original holding had occurred for all purposes, it would be impossible to argue that he was not entitled to the relief. The individual would be deemed to still hold 25% of the voting control in his original company.

This problem has been recognised in the United Kingdom.

TCGA 1992 Sch 6 para 2 recognises that, on a reorganisation, a shareholder, disposing of his original shares, may lose his entitlement to retirement relief, as the new shares may not be qualifying shares, even though the original shares were qualifying shares. Sch 6 para 2 allows the shareholder to elect to take retirement relief at the time of the reorganisation.

(j) All para 2 seeks to do is to postpone the calculations of capital gains tax until the new holding has been disposed of. It achieves this by treating the new holding as having the same base cost and acquisition date as the original holding. It does not do anything else. Paragraph 2 is part of Sch 2, which along with Schs 1 and 3, contain the provisions under which capital gains tax is calculated.

(i) *Westcott (IOT) v Woolcombers Ltd* [1987] STC 600

This is the interpretation given to the UK equivalent of para 2 and para 4 in *Westcott (IOT) v Woolcombers Ltd* [1987] STC 600. The basis for Sir Denys Buckley's decision in favour of the taxpayer was that FA 1965 Sch 7 paras 4(2) and 6(1) (the then UK equivalent of paras 2 and 4) were concerned with computational rules only. He states at page 607:

> The purposes of para 4(2) appear to me to be: (1) to ensnare that no shareholder of the company shall be treated as having realised a chargeable gain or sustain an allowable loss in consequence of the reorganisation or reduction of capital and (2) to ensure that on any subsequent disposal by any shareholder of any part of the 'new holding', that the cost to him of the shares so disposed of shall, for capital gains tax purposes, be treated as having been the historical cost to him of acquiring the 'original shares 'represented by the shares disposed of

He states further [at page 609]:

> The function of Schs 6, 7 and 8 of this Act is to regulate the computation of the amount of any chargeable gains or allowable losses arising in any particular circumstances (Finance Act 1965, ss 22(g) and 23(1)). Paragraph 4(2) of Sch 7 does not provide that any disposal or acquisition of an asset which shall have actually occurred shall for all purposes, be deemed not to have occurred. It is one of a collection of miscellaneous rules regulating how the amounts of gains and losses are computed. It must be construed in that light.

(ii) *Floor v Davis (IOT)* 52 TC 609

This case was concerned with the interpretation of the UK equivalent of CGTA 1975 Sch 2 paras 2 and 4. Sir John Pennycuick, in the Court of Appeal, stated at page 630:

> Perhaps one should mention, in order to avoid possible misunderstanding, that where paras 4(2) and 6(2) provide that the share transaction is not to be treated as involving a disposal that expression clearly notes a disposal giving rise to a charge to tax. It is not suggested that the transaction its to be disregarded in the sense that the acquiring company is to be treated as a mere emanation of the other company.

The decision was not commented upon in the House of Lords. The argument before that Court was confined to a different point.

(iii) *NAP Holdings UK Limited v Whittles (IOT)* [1994] STC 979

Lord Keith of Kinkel gave the leading judgment in this case in the House of Lords. He summarised the taxpayers contention as follows:

> The argument for the taxpayer is that the effect of s 78, as applied by s 85(3) to the case where a persona acquires shares in company A in exchange for shares in company B, is that for all capital gains tax purposes that person is to be treated as not having disposed, of the shares in company B, and as not having acquired the shares in company A.

He dismissed the company's contention. Section 78 did not have such general and wide ranging effect. A disposal of shares had actually occurred. He approved the reasoning in *Westcott.*

(k) The wording of s 46(1) is clear and unambiguous. The wording of para 2 is not. Paragraph 2 relies on the application of fictions. One must treat notional shares as having been held by notional shareholders in a fictional company. It is a well established principle of tax law that a clear and unambiguous provision should be applied in primacy to a provision which is nebulous. Section 46(1) should therefore be applied in primacy to paragraph 2.

(l) Schedule 2 para 4 applies "with any necessary adaptations". It is submitted that should it be necessary, the recognition of a founding principle of the legislation is such an adaption.
Section 46(1) contains a founding principle of the legislation - a chargeable gain shall not accrue on the disposal of certain assets. The recognition of a founding principle of the capital gains tax legislation is such a necessary adaptation.
In any event paragraph 4 provides that paragraph 2 is to apply "as if the two companies were the same company and the exchange were a reorganisation of its share capital". Paragraph 4 is, therefore, not even dealing with the original shares (ie the Gladebrook shares in this instance) but rather with a new fictional entity. This is discussed in detail in *Westcott (IOT) v Woolcombers* [1987] STC 600, by Sir Denys Buckley, at p 608:

> It appears to me that para 6(1) requires the fictional company to comprise both Topmakers and the relevant other company. The share capital of the fictional company must consequently, I think, be assumed to consist of shares representing all the shares of Topmakers in issue at the time of the notional reorganisation and shares representing all the shares of the other company concerned, and its notional corporators will be the holders of all those shares of Topmakers and the holders of all the shares in the other company. The consequence of the notional reorganisation of the notional share capital must, I think, be assumed to be that thereafter the notional holders of shares of the fictional company derived from actual holdings of shares in Topmakers will have acquired all the notional shares of the fictional company assumed to be held by actual holders of shares of the other company. Simultaneously, Holdings will have acquired some new Topmakers shares credited as fully paid up, but that acquisition cannot, in my view, form any part of the notional reorganisation of the notional share capital of the fictional company. That notional reorganisation must, as it appears to me, consist exclusively of the notional transfer of part of the notional share capital of the fictional company. This would not in truth involve any reorganisation of the notional share capital of the fictional company; it would merely alter the identities of the notional holders of that notional share capital. Paragraph 6(1), however, requires this fictional transaction to be treated as if it were a reorganisation of the notional share capital of the fictional company.
>
> I now proceed to consider how far the provisions of para 4(2) can be regarded as appropriate to this supposed state of affairs, and what adaptations of those provisions, if any, are necessary to make them appropriate to such a state of affairs.
>
> It seems to me that all the notional shares of the fictional company would be recognisably 'original shares' of the fictional company: they would be shares notionally held before and concerned in the notional reorganisation. In the supposed

state of affairs to be assumed in the instant case pursuant to para 6(1) in accordance with my preceding analysis, those 'original shares' after the supposed reorganisation will all still notionally exist, although some of them will notionally have been transferred by the notional holders of one part of the notional share capital of the fictional company to the notional holders of the rest of that notional share capital. Accordingly, in my judgment, that notional share capital as a whole which in consequence of the so-called reorganisation must be assumed all to be held by actual holders of Topmakers' shares in issue at the date of the supposed reorganisation, must be regarded as constituting the 'new issue' for the purposes of para 4(2). A possible alternative view might be that only part of the notional share capital which is to be assumed to have beets transferred should be regarded as constituting the 'new issue'. I do not think that it matters which of these two views is correct.

Viewing the matter in this way, it does not seem to me that any adaptation of the language of para 4(2) is required in the instant case. It is merely necessary to apply that language to the fictions imposed by para 6(1), and then to treat the actual shares in each of the three companies as the substance of the notional shares in the notional share capital of the fictional company derived from those actual shares. This final step is, as it seems to me, essential to giving factual effect to para 6(2).

(m) In a single company reorganisation the original shares are retained, and co-exist with the new shares subsequent to the reorganisation. The legislation treats the transaction as not involving any disposal of the old shares when in fact no such disposal has taken place. This demonstrates that the section is not seeking to disturb the normal rules of disposal and acquisition but is merely a computational provision whereby the cost base of the old shares (still retained) is applied to the aggregation of the old shares and the new shares.

In a dual company reorganisation the original shares are actually disposed of. Accordingly paragraph 2 is not an authority for the proposition that the original shares are not deemed to have been disposed of.

This is clearly recognised in subparas 4 and 5 of para 2, which deal, respectively, with situations where the old holding is exchanged partly for cash and partly in consideration of new shares and where the new holding consists of different classes of shares

(n) The transformation of assets for CGT purposes frequently occurs The respondent disposed of his original asset, on which a chargeable gain could accrue, his shareholding in Gladebrook, in exchange for an asset, a loan note, the disposal of which cannot cause a chargeable gain to accrue. This transformation of a gain, depending of the type of asset involved, from chargeable to non-chargeable is not unique and has precedents in other areas of capital gains tax law.

(i) CGTA 1975 s 25

This section provides that a gain shall not be a chargeable gain where an individual disposes of:

> … dwelling-house or part of a dwelling-house which is or has been occupied by him as his only or main residence.

Therefore, if an individual disposes of a house which was occupied by him as his only or main residence, but at the time of the disposal he has rented it to tenants, the gain which arises on this disposal is transformed from a non-chargeable gain into a chargeable gain and a liability to capital gains tax will accrue to the individual on this disposal.

In the alternative, if an individual owns a house which he rents, and later occupies the house as his sole or main residence, the house is now transformed into an asset on whose disposal no chargeable gain will accrue.

(ii) CGTA 1975 s 20

Section 20 states:

> (1) This section has effect as respects any policy of assurance or contract for a deferred annuity on the life of any person.
>
> (2) No chargeable gain shall accrue on disposal of, or of an interest in, the rights under any such policy of assurance or contract except where the person making the disposal is not the original beneficial owner and acquired the rights or interests for a consideration in money or money's worth.

Therefore, if the original policy holder disposes of the policy, no chargeable gain accrues on this disposal. If on the other hand, the person disposing of the policy of insurance has acquired the policy from the original holder, a chargeable gain will accrue on this disposal. A non-chargeable gain has transformed into a chargeable gain, and vice versa, depending on the status of the disponer.

(iii) CGTA 1975 s 46(1)

Section 46(1) provides:

> where a person incurs a debt to another (that is, the original creditor, whether in Irish currency or in some other currency, no chargeable gain shall accrue to that creditor or his personal representative or legatee on the disposal of the debt:

A chargeable gain does not accrue on the disposal of a debt which is not a debt on a security, only where it is disposed of by the original creditor. However, if the original creditor, A, sold the debt to a third party, B, a chargeable gain could accrue in B's hands, as B is not the original creditor. Taking this example a step further, if B sold the debt back to A the debt would revert to it's previous status.

(o) The legislature has recognised that, on a reorganisation, the original shares have actually been disposed of and that a new shareholding has been acquired which may have different characteristics from the original shares. Provisions have been enacted which take account of the problems which may arise from the fact that the new holding and the old holding are different shareholdings with different characteristics.

(i) FA 1986 s 12(6):

Section 12 grants relief from capital gains tax to employees who purchase shares in their employer company. The shares must have certain characteristics in order for the relief to apply. Section 12(6) recognises that after a reorganisation, the original holding, which had been disposed of may have comprised of qualifying shares, whereas the new holding acquired in exchange may not. Section 12(6)(a) states that where such a reorganisation has occurred "the new holding shall be treated as shares in respect of which relief under this section has been given".

If the appellant's submission were correct, s 12(6) would be entirely unnecessary and the new shares would retain the characteristics of the original qualifying shares.

(ii) FA 1994 s 66:

This section provides for a 27% rate of capital gains tax for chargeable gains on disposals of certain shares by individuals. The shares disposed of must be "qualifying shares" within the meaning of the section.

The company in which the shares are held must also have certain characteristics. It must be resident in the state throughout a specified period. It must be unquoted and the value of its issued share capital must not exceed a certain figure.

Sub-sections 7 and 8 of the section clearly recognise that an individual who held qualifying shares in a qualifying company may exchange these shares on a reorganisation, and receive in their place non-qualifying shares in a non-qualifying company. Sub-sections 7 and 8 contain provisions which allow such an individual to still benefit from the 27% rate of capital gains tax. Sub-sections 7 and 8 are a clear recognition that the respondent's interpretation is correct. If no disposal had occurred and the original shares were qualifying shares then the new holding would also constitute qualifying shares. Sub-sections 7 and 3 would be totally unnecessary.

The explanatory memorandum to the Finance Bill 1994 as passed states:

> Measures are included to cater for cases involving the disposal of ordinary shares which had been acquired in the context of the reorganisation of a company's share capital or in situations importing company amalgamations or takeovers

Finally, the Finance Bill 1994, as initiated makes no reference to shares acquired under reorganisations, takeovers or amalgamations under Sch 2 para 2. It is obvious from this omission that the Revenue Commissioners realised that a disposal would actually take place if paragraph 2 was invoked and that measures would have to be included in section 66 to take account of this.

(p) A review of capital gains tax case law shows that the courts have applied a narrow meaning to statutory fictions where the word "treat", as opposed to the word "deem" is used in legislation.

The word "treat" is used in para 2 and therefore a narrow interpretation should be given to the fictions contained in this paragraph. This can be seen from the following cases:

(i) *Marshall (IOT) v Kerr* [1994] STC 638

This case concerned inter alia s 24 and in particular FA 1965 s 24(7) [now s 62 of the TCGA 1992] which is as follows:

> On a person acquiring any asset as legatee
>
> (a) no chargeable gain shall accrue to the personal representatives, and
>
> (b) the legatee shall be treated as if the personal representatives' acquisition of the asset had been his acquisition of it

Lord Templeman [at p 641] interprets s 24(7) as follows:

> Section 24(7) applies when a personal representative assents to the vesting in a legatee of an asset comprised in the estate at the date of death. The assent does not constitute a disposal for the purposes of the tax. The legatee is treated as if he had acquired the asset on the death of the testator at market value. When the legatee disposes of the asset his chargeable gain will be measured by the difference between the market value of the asset at the death of the testator and the price of value of the asset when the legatee disposes of the asset.

Lord Lowry agreed with Lord Templeman and stated as follows on the effect of s 24 [at p 646]:

> On reading s 24, whether in its original form or as amended, I think it is clear that the section is simply concerned with consequences of death and that its provisions, including the deeming provisions, lay down time and levels and value by reference to which the liability for capital gains is to be calculated.

(ii) *de Rothschild v Lawrenson (IOT)* [1994] STC 8

This case concerned FA 1981 s 80 [now s 87, as amended, of the TCGA 1992] and FA 1988 Sch 10. The facts of this case were that the taxpayer had created two offshore settlements, but retained a life interest in possession. The taxpayer himself was resident and domiciled in the UK. In the tax year 1988/1989 the trustees of the settlement paid the whole of the trust fund to the taxpayer and he was assessed to capital gains tax on the proceeds. He appealed the assessment on the basis that s 80(2) provided that if the conditions contained in s 80(1) in any year of assessment were fulfilled there was to be computed the amount on which the trustees would have been chargeable if they had been resident and ordinarily resident in the UK. The trust gains so computed under s 80(2) were to be treated as accruing to the beneficiaries who received capital distributions. Sch 10, para 4 stated that para 1 would not apply to resident trustees of settlements in which the settler had an interest. The taxpayer claimed that due to the interaction of these provisions he had escaped liability to tax. He was unsuccessful before Vinelott J in the House of Lords. Vinelott J held against the taxpayer on two alternate grounds. He states as follows at p 18:

> To my mind para 1(2) of Sch 10 deals with a case where the trustees are in fact chargeable to tax on realised gains. In a case within s 80(2) gains are to be completed as the amount on which the trustees would have been chargeable to tax if they had been resident or ordinarily resident in the United Kingdom. However, the trustees are not made chargeable; the gains so computed are to be treated as chargeable gains accruing to the beneficiaries.

In this case the deeming provisions were given a narrow interpretation by the learned judge.

(iii) *Van-Arkadie (IOT) v Plunket* [1983] STC 54

This case involved in part the interpretation of the former FA 1965 s 41(2), now s 13 of the TCGA 1992. This sub-section is as follows:

> Subject to this section, every person who at the time when the chargeable gain accrues to the company is resident or ordinarily resident in the United Kingdom Who, if an individual, is domiciled in the United Kingdom and who holds shares in the complicity shall be treated for the purposes of this Part of the Act as if part of the chargeable gain had accrued to him

Vinelott J at p 58 states as follows:

> It is important to bear in mind that the effect of s 41 is to attribute directly to a person within sub-s (2) … a proportion of a gain accruing to a non-resident close company. He is to be treated as if that par t of the gain had accrued to him. He is not to be treated as hinting disposed of an interest in hits shares or, indeed, of any other property

(q) The appellant is attempting to apply a "roll-over" type approach to para 2.

"Roll-over relief' is governed by CGTA 1975 s 28. This relief is granted where an individual disposes of qualifying assets ("the old assets") and reinvests the proceeds of sale in other qualifying assets ("the new assets"). The gain on the original assets is calculated at the time of its disposal, but does not accrue to the individual until the new assets are disposed of. The gain on the original assets is put into storage, so to speak, until the subsequent disposal occurs.

The appellant's argument is that where Sch 2 para 2 applies, the liability to tax on the disposal of the original shares is some how also put into storage, and then calculated, when the new shares are disposed of. This could not be the case. The wording of para 2 and s 28 is entirely different. Section 28 states that where the old assets have been disposed of and the proceeds reinvested in new assets:

> then the person carrying on the trade shall, on making a claim in that behalf; be treated for the purposes of this Act as if the chargeable gain accruing on the old assets did not accrue until he ceases to use the new assets for the purposes of the trade.

Had it been intended that a similar procedure apply with regard to reorganisations under para 2, it would have been quite simple to import into para 2 wording similar to that contained in s 28.

(r) An often used phrase in tax legislation is "shall for all purposes be deemed to be". This phrase means that a certain set of facts or a certain situation shall exist for all purposes of the Act or tax in question.

Paragraph 2 does not contain this phrase. This implies that the fictions contained therein are to be applied in a specific manner and not generally for all the purposes of the CGTA 1975.

Had it been intended that para 2 would apply for all purposes of the Act it would have been quite easy to include the above phrase within the paragraph. The tax acts abound with examples of the use of this phrase. Examples are as follows:

FA 1974 s 57(1)	Transfer of assets abroad
FA 1989 s 88(3)	Schemes to avoid liability to tax under Schedule F
ITA 1967 s 449(i)(a)	Transfer of income arising from securities
ITA 1967 s 438(1)	Covenants
CGTA 1975 s 15(3)	Trustees
CTA 1976 s 135(3)	Companies leaving a group
ITA 1967 s 194(1)	Assessment of husband in respect of the income of both spouses

(s) A well established principle of statutory interpretation is that where a specific provision exists which is applicable to a certain set of circumstances, where those circumstances occur, the specific principle must be applied over other general provisions. Section 46(1) is such a specific provision. It sets out the rules which apply when debts, either debts on a security or simple debts, are disposed of. It governs exclusively the capital gains tax consequences of the disposal of a debt. In the present ease the respondent has disposed of a debt. Section 46(1) therefore applies in primacy to other provision of the CGTA 1975 such as Sch 2 para 2.

This principle was recently applied in the Northern Irish ease *IRC v McGuekian* [1994] STC 888. The question which had to be answered in this ease, inter alia, was whether the *Ramsay* principle should be applied to the transaction which had occurred, or whether the anti-avoidance provision specifically enacted to counteract transactions of that type should be applied. The Court of Appeal for Northern Ireland held that the specific anti-avoidance provision, ICTA 1970 s 470, was the only applicable provision.

(t) The appellant's interpretation gives rise to anomalous results.

(u) The appellant's interpretation of the interaction between para 2 and s 46(1) is at variance with their UK counterparts interpretation of the British equivalent legislation.

FA 1993 s 84(3) was brought in to amend both TCGA 1992 s 251 (the UK equivalent of s 46) and the UK reorganisation provisions. It deems certain simple debts to be debts on a security when they are issued on a reorganisation of a company's share capital. The UK legislature has recognised that if, on a reorganisation, original shares in a company were exchanged for a new holding of debentures that were simple debts, no charge to capital gains tax would accrue either at the time of the reorganisation itself or when the debentures were later disposed of.

14. It was contended on behalf of the Inspector of Taxes that:

(a) the loan note complies with the provisions of CA 1963 s 86. The loan note is not a simple debt as envisaged by CGTA 1975 s 46(1). Despite its limited marketability it comes within the term "debt on a security";

(b) as the provisions of CGTA 1975 Sch 2 paras 2 and 4 applied to the acquisition of the loan note by the respondent, the redemption of the loan note is treated for capital gains tax purposes by virtue of the provisions of the said paras 2 and 4, as if it were the disposal of the original shares in Gladebrook;

(c) as a consequence of the redemption being treated as a disposal of the original shares, CGTA 1975 s 46(1) which deals with the disposal of debts, cannot apply.

15. The following cases were cited by the parties:

Aberdeen Construction Group Ltd v CIR 52 TC 281
WT Ramsey Ltd v CIR 54 TC 101.
Cleveley Investment Trust Co v CIR 47 TC 300
Westcott v Woolcombers 1987 STC 600
Nap Holdings v Whittles 1994 STC 979
Floor v Davis 52 TC 609
Marshall v Kerr 1994 STC 638
CIR v Metrolands 54 TC 679
Murphy v Ingram 49 TC 410
Van Arcadie v Plunket 1983 STC 54
Glenrothers v IRC 1994 STC 74

De Rothschild v Lawrenson 1995 STC 623
Cape Brandy Syndicate v CIR 12 TC 358
Woltson v CIR 31 TC 141
IRC v Duke of Westminster 19 TC 490
Patrick McGrath and Ors v JE McDermott 3 ITR 863
Canadian Eagle Oil Company Ltd v The King [1945] 2 All ER 499
Wilcox v Smith (1857) 4 Drew 49 (Ch)
IRC v McGuckian, McGuckian v IRC [1994] STC 888

16. Having adjourned the case to consider the matters, we gave our reserved decision on 31 May 1995. We came to the conclusion that:

> As the cases cited in the course of the appeal show the meaning of the phrase "debt on a security" is unclear. A series of decided cases in the Irish Courts (so well known as to be unnecessary to quote) has established the principle that tax legislation should be construed by giving words their ordinary meaning. In determining the "legislative intent" of the statute there should be no immediate resort to considering the public policy underlying the enactment of the provision under consideration. However, this latter statement must be qualified in cases where ambiguity or uncertainty clouds the meaning of the legislation. In such cases it is appropriate to adopt a "purposive" or "teleological" approach to construing the legislation.
>
> In this case we are firmly of the view that there is considerable uncertainty about the meaning of the phrase "debt on a security" so we concluded that we must therefore consider the meaning of the phrase by taking into account matters of policy underlying the scheme of the Gains Tax Act.
>
> The exclusion of simple debts or loans from the definition of chargeable assets is clearly logical within the context of determining what gains of a capital nature should be taxed and what losses should be allowed. Debts or loans do not have the same characteristics as other assets, such as land, shares and many other categories of assets. These latter items have the capacity to increase and decrease in value: and thereby realise gains or losses. Typically debts or loans do not have this symmetrical aspect to them. Debts do not normally increase in value over time, although they may decrease in value through not being repaid, and similar comments apply to loans. (Ignoring foreign currency implications which we do not consider to be relevant here).
>
> A trader may obtain a deduction for income tax purposes in respect of a bad debt but this clearly has no implication for capital gains tax. Similarly, a bank may claim relief in relation to an irrecoverable loan but it is not at all clear that loans advanced to individuals should be treated as realisable assets of that individual that may give rise to profits or losses of a capital nature in his hands. These comments would seem to apply *a fortiori* in the case of loans advanced by one individual to another or by a company other than a bank.
>
> In general, the legislative provisions of the Capital Gains Tax Act reflect the above "common sense" approach. The question then arises as to why a debt on a security, whatever the precise meaning of the phrase might mean, is treated differently.
>
> Although that the phrase is surely not confined to the financial instruments known as "Government Securities" - also described as gilts, bonds, punts etc - it seems to

us to be worthwhile to consider the nature of those instruments in a small amount of detail.

Government securities are issued at rates of interest that reflect the rates prevailing in the economy at the time of their issue. They may then be bought and sold on the stock market during the period prior to their redemption. If interest rates change following the issue of the security the capital value of the instrument is likely to change. For example, a government security issued at par and with an interest rate of 5% with a redemption date very far into the future might almost halve in value if interests rates were to increase to 10% - because securities being issued at the later rate of 10% would produce twice the income of the earlier issue and the investor has a very long time to wait before he or she will get back their original investment. Short-dated securities are not so sensitive to interest rate movements because the imminent receipt of the original capital advanced to the government on issue, or given to a vendor of the security in the market, is a large component of the quoted value of the security.

These instruments are essentially debts owed by the government to the holder but they are traded in the financial markets between the date of their issue and redemption and real gains and losses are made in respect of their capital values - quite apart from any income that may be derived from them, which is, obviously, liable to be taxed as income.

It seems from the above that it was definitely intended that assets in the nature of government securities should be treated as coming within the meaning of the phrase "debt on a security". (The fact that capital gains arising on some such securities may be exempted from capital gains tax does not appear to upset the argument here.) While this does not bring us to the point of being able to adopt an exhaustive definition of the phrase it does lead us very directly to the idea that the asset in question must be capable of being realised and that when it is so realised that such an event may give rise to either a gain or a loss of a capital nature.

The previous comments do little more than to explain in a somewhat simplified way the rationale of the judges who have emphasised that point that the transferability of the item in question may be very important since without transferability it is not immediately clear how it is possible to realise a gain or a loss.

One way of looking at the matter which we found of some help was to consider, in the light of the decided cases, whether the loan note in this case was closer to a straightforward cheque or promissory note issued by a bank than it was to an asset in the nature of an investment such as but not necessarily in an exclusive sense, a government security. In our view the loan note in this case, being specifically non-assignable, and having been issued effectively as deferred consideration for the sale of shares, is much closer to a simple debt than to an asset in the nature of an investment that is capable of generating a capital profit or loss.

The case was exhaustively argued before us. Quite a number of the arguments advanced referred to legislative provisions that were not directly related to the point in this case and then proceeded to argue by analogy. We did not find that these matters assisted us greatly in coming to our conclusions. However, we wish to state that we are in agreement with the following matters advanced on behalf of the taxpayer and they were relevant to the decision we reached.

Paragraph 13(g)

We have concluded that paragraph 2 of the Second Schedule to the Capital Gains Tax Act does indicate that a disposal of the original shares has occurred.

Paragraph 13(h)

We accept that "Paragraph 2 only applies at the time of the reorganisation ... It simply provides that at that point in time no disposal is to be treated as occurring." We also agree with the argument of the respondent; that a proper construction of Sch 2 para 2 to the Capital Gains Tax Act does not result in some kind of transformation or metamorphosis of the old shares into the new shares so that the old shares remain extant, and capable of being sold and thereby chargeable to Capital Gains Tax, but in a new form.

We further accept the argument of the respondent that para 2 merely seeks to postpone the calculation of the capital gain until the new holding is disposed of.

It is for these reasons that we have held, as stated above, that the loan note in this case is not a "debt on a security" so that no chargeable gain arise on its encashment.

17. The following figures were then determined:

Chargeable Gain	Nil

18. Immediately after the determination the Inspector of Taxes expressed dissatisfaction therewith as being erroneous in law and asked for a case stated for the opinion of the High Court, which we duly state and sign accordingly.

19. The question of law for the opinion of the High Court is whether, on the foregoing facts and evidence, our decision as set out at para 16 is correct in law.

Agreement for Sale and Purchase of Shares of GladeBrook Limited

Dated the 8 February 1990
Siuicre Éireann cpt
With Charles M Lyons
Michael Tully
Thomas P Keleghan
Charles P Garavan
Talmino Limited

Clause

1. Parties
2. Recitals
3. Definitions
4. Sale and purchase
5. Waivers of pre-emption
6. Purchase consideration
7. Conditions precedent
8. The warranties
9. Provisions to apply between signing and completion
10. Recision
11. Intellectual property rights

12. Completion
13. Directors' loans
14. Public flotation
15. Placing
16. Restrictive covenants
17. Indemnity
18. Confidentiality
19. Announcements
20. Applicable law
21. Non-assignability
22. Survival after completion
23. Entire agreement
24. No general waiver
25. Release or compromise
26. Further assurance
27. Notice
28. Sale of shares

List of schedules

Schedule I	The vendors
Schedule II	Details of SDL's subsidiaries
Schedule III	Deed of indemnity
Schedule IV	Details of the directors
Schedule V	Details of the properties
Schedule VI	Service agreements
Schedule VII	Warranties
Schedule VIII	The loan notes

List of annexures

Annexure A	The 1989 accounts
Annexure B	The company's accounts
Annexure C	The memoranda and articles of association
Annexure D	The management accounts

1. Parties

(1) THE PERSONS WHOSE NAMES AND ADDRESSES ARE SET OUT IN SCHEDULE 1 AND TALMINO LTD having its registered office at Portman House, Hue Street, Jersey Channel Islands (hereinafter called the "vendors")

(2) SIUICRE ÉIREANN cpt having its registered office at St Stephens Green House, Dublin 2 (hereinafter called the "purchaser")

and

GLADEBROOK COMPANY LIMITED having its registered office at 50 South Mall, Cork (hereinafter called "the company").

2. Recitals

2.1 The company is a private company with limited liability incorporated under the Companies Acts (as hereinafter defined) on the 25th day of July 1988 Number 134099 and has at the date hereof an authorised share capital of IR£1,000,000 divided into 1,000,000 ordinary shares of IR£1 each of which 10,000 of such shares have been issued and are credited as fully paid.

2.2 The vendors are the beneficial owners of the entire issued share capital of company as detailed opposite their names in Schedule 1 and have the right, power and authority to sell and transfer the said shares free from any claims, options, charges, liens, encumbrances or equities.

2.3 The vendors have agreed to sell or to procure the transfer and the purchaser has agreed to purchase all the said shares subject to and on the terms and conditions hereinafter appearing.

2.4 Sugar Distributors (Holdings) Limited is a private company with limited liability incorporated under the Companies Acts (as hereinafter defined) on the 25th day of January 1967 Number 24563 and has at the date hereof an authorised share capital of IR£500,000 divided into 245,000 "A" ordinary shares of IR£1 each and 255,000 "B" ordinary shares of IR£1 each all of which have been issued and are fully paid.

2.5 The company is the beneficial owner of 245,000 "A" ordinary shares of £1 each representing 49% of the entire issued share capital of Sugar Distributor (Holdings) Limited and has the right, power and authority to sell and transfer the said shares free from any claims, options, charges, liens, encumbrances or equities.

3 Definitions

3.1 In this agreement and in the schedules to this agreement unless otherwise expressly stated or unless the context otherwise requires the following words and expressions shall bear the following meanings:

"**SDL**" **accounts**": the consolidated audited balance sheet of SDL and its subsidiaries as at the 29th day of September 1989 and the consolidated audited profit and loss account for the period ended on the 29th day of September 1989 and the notes thereto, the directors' report and other documents annexed thereto, copies of which are attached hereto as Annexure "A".

"**accounts dates**": the 29th day of September 1989 in relation to SDL and its subsidiaries and the 31st day of December 1989 in relation to the company.

"**Company's accounts**": the audited balance sheet of the company for the year ended on the 30th day of June 1989.

"**management accounts**": the management accounts of the company as at the 31st day of December 1989 a copy of which is annexed hereto as Annexure "D".

"**accounts**": the SDL accounts, the company's accounts and the management accounts collectively referred to.

"**Group companies**": the company and SDL and SDL's subsidiaries particulars of which are set forth in Schedule II.

"**Group company**": any one of the group companies.

"**Companies Acts**": the Companies Acts 1963 to 1986.

"**Group company's auditors**": Messrs Pannell Kerr Forster of 17 Percy Place, Dublin 4.

"**completion**": Completion of the sale and purchase of the shares in accordance with Clause 12.

"**completion date**": the date of completion.

"**CGTA**": Capital Gains Tax Act 1975.

"**CTA**" Corporation Tax Act 1976.

"**deed of indemnity**": the deed of indemnity contained in Schedule III.

"**disclosure letter**": the letter of even date herewith from the vendors' solicitors to the purchaser's solicitors

"**Directors**" the persons who are directors of the company and SDL and whose names and addresses are set forth in Schedule IV.

"**indemnities:** the indemnities and covenants contained in the Deed of Indemnity

"**intellectual property rights**": all patents, patent applications, trade mark applications, trade names, designs, copyright, know-how, technical knowledge and information or other similar industrial or commercial rights used by or available to any of the group companies at any stage in connection with any part of the business of any of the group companies anywhere in the world and whether registered or not.

"**IR£**": Irish Punts being the currency denomination of the Republic of Ireland.

"**Loan notes**": Loan notes set out in Schedule VIII.

"**Memoranda and articles of association**": the memorandum and articles of association of each of the group companies, true copies of which are annexed hereto as Annexure C.

"**Properties**": the properties of SDL and its subsidiaries particulars which are contained in Schedule V.

"**Placing**": an event whereby a broker or issuing house purchases or subscribes for shares in the purchaser and then places such shares with its clients in connection with a listing of the share capital of the purchaser or a recognised Stock Exchange.

"**Public flotation**": an event whereby the share capital of the purchaser offered to the public for sale and/or subscription are listed on a recognised stock exchange.

"**Purchaser's solicitors**": Matheson Ormsby Prentice of 3 Burlington Road, Dublin 4.

"**Service agreements**": the service agreements between each of the vendors and SDL in the form set out in Schedule VI.

"**SDL**": Sugar Distributors (Holdings) Limited having its registered office at Athy Road, Carlow.

"**Shares**": the issued ordinary shares of IR£1 each in the capital of the company comprising the whole of its issued and allotted share capital and agreed to be sold to the purchaser hereunder.

"**Subsidiary**": a subsidiary as defined in CA 1963 s 155.

"**Taxation**": all forms of taxation, duties, imposts, levies and rates wherever and whenever imposed including without limitation, income tax, PAYE, corporation tax (including surcharge), advance corporation tax, capital gains tax, capital acquisitions tax, rates, value added tax, customs duty, excise duty, capital duty, stamp duty, pay-related social insurance, or other similar contributions and including the loss of any relief or allowances of any capital or other expenditure or on the selling of any assets, and generally any tax, duty, impost, levy or rate or other amount and any interest, penalty or fine in connection therewith and cognate words such as "tax, "taxes", "taxation liability' and similar words shall be similarly defined.

"**Vendors' solicitors**": Messrs MJ Horgan & Sons of 50 South Mall, Cork.

"**Warranties**" the warranties, representations and statements contained in Schedule VII

"**Warrantors**": the vendors.

In this agreement and in the Schedules hereto:

(A) Save as herein otherwise expressly provided expressions defined in the Companies Acts have the same meanings herein.

(B) Reference to any statute or statutory provision includes a reference to that statute or statutory provision as amended, extended or re-enacted prior to the date hereof and all statutory instruments or orders made pursuant thereto.

(C) Reference to the singular includes reference to the plural and vice versa and reference to the masculine gender includes reference to the feminine and neuter genders and vice versa.

(D) Unless the context otherwise requires, reference to any clause, sub-clause, paragraph, recital, Schedule or Annexure is to a clause, sub-clause, paragraph, recital, Schedule or Annexure (as the case may be) of or to this agreement.

(E) Any reference to a document as being in agreed terms shall mean a document in terms agreed between the parties or their respective solicitors and initialled by them for the purpose of identification.

(F) The headings contained in this agreement and the schedules are inserted for convenience of reference only and shall not in any way form part of nor affect or be taken into account in the construction or interpretation of any provision of this agreement or the schedules.

4 Sale and purchase

4.1 Subject to the terms and conditions hereof and for the consideration hereinafter appearing the vendors as beneficial owners hereby agree to sell and the purchaser hereby agrees to purchase the shares with effect from completion free from all claims, options, charges, liens, encumbrances or equities and with the benefit of all rights attaching thereto.

4.2 The purchaser shall not be obliged (but shall be entitled at its sole discretion) to complete the purchase of any of the shares unless the purchase of all the shares is completed simultaneously but may instead rescind this agreement without prejudice o any other remedy it may have.

5 Waivers of pre-emption

For the purposes of completion each of the vendors hereby waives all rights of pre-emption conferred on him in relation to the shares.

6. Purchase consideration

6.1 The total purchase consideration payable by the purchaser for the purchase of the shares shall be the sum of IR£8,680,000 (eight million six hundred and eighty thousand

Irish pounds) which shall be paid to the vendors in the proportions set out in the third column of Schedule 1.

6.2 The purchase consideration shall be satisfied by the issue by the purchaser on Completion of the loan notes to the vendors.

7. Conditions Precedent

7.1 Notwithstanding anything else contained in this agreement, this agreement is conditional upon compliance with the following conditions to the satisfaction of the purchaser.

(A) The granting on terms acceptable to the parties hereto by all other third parties or any regulatory authorities of any permissions, consents or licences which may be necessary or advisable in relation to the transaction contemplated therein.

(B) No governmental or state agency or regulatory body or Authority or trade union or supplier or customer or any other person having:

  (i) instituted or threatened any action suit or investigation to restrain, prohibit or otherwise challenge the acquisition of the shares by purchaser; or

  (ii) threatened to take any action as a result of or in anticipation of such acquisition; or

  (iii) proposed or enacted any statute or regulation which would prohibit, restrict or delay the implementation of such acquisition.

(C) The vendors having exercised or refrained from exercising their voting rights in respect of the shares in accordance with instructions reasonably necessary to complete this transaction given to them by the purchaser and exercised or refrained from exercising such rights without first obtaining instructions from the purchaser.

(D) The vendors having procured the unconditional release without any continuing liability of any guarantees or indemnities given by any of the group companies for any obligation of the vendors, the directors or any of them or any third parties.

(F) The vendors and the directors at all times pending completion using their best endeavours to maintain the goodwill and carrying on the business of each of the group companies in a proper and efficient manner.

(G) The vendors providing the purchaser with such information financial or otherwise concerning all aspects of the business of each of the group companies as the purchaser may reasonably request and access to all the facilities of each of the group companies at all reasonable times on business days.

(H) No breach of any of the warranties having been committed or incurred.

(I) No material point or factor having occurred, arisen or come to light which would or would be likely materially to decrease the value of the shares.

(J) Without prejudice to any claim under the indemnities contained in Clause 17 the purchaser being satisfied that the liabilities of the company less cash on deposit and on hand do not exceed 1R£1,755,000 (one million seven hundred and fifty five thousand Irish pounds).

(K) Compliance by the parties with the terms of Clause 12.

(L) The disclosure letter not disclosing any matter is unacceptable to the purchaser in its sole discretion.

(M) The purchaser being satisfied in his absolute discretion as to the adequacy of the funding level of the group company's pension scheme(s).

7.2 The warrantors shall use their best endeavours to obtain the fulfilment of the aforesaid conditions on or before the 28th day of February 1989 (or such later date(s) as the parties may agree in writing).

7.3 Provided always that the purchaser may at its option in writing waive compliance with any of the foregoing conditions other than the condition set out in paragraph (B) of Clause 7.1 and upon such waiver, the condition(s) thereby waived shall be deemed to have been complied with.

8 Warranties

8.1 In consideration of the purchaser entering into this agreement the warrantors hereby jointly and severally represent, warrant and undertake to the purchaser, each of the group companies and their and each of their successors in title that (subject to Clause 12) the warranties are and will at completion be true and accurate in all respects and so that "now", "the date hereof' and other like expressions when used in relation thereto shall refer both to the date of this agreement and to the completion date.

8.2 The warrantors hereby jointly and severally agree and declare that each of the warranties shall be construed as separate and independent and save as otherwise expressly provided shall not be limited by reference to any other warranty, clause, sub-clause, paragraph, sub-paragraph or anything in this agreement, the annexures or schedules.

8.3 If there shall be any misrepresentations or non-fulfilment of or any breach of any of the warranties, then the warrantors shall be jointly and severally liable to pay to the purchaser or at the discretion of the purchaser pay to any one or more of the group companies:

(A) An amount equal to 100 per cent of all and any losses, damages, or expenses directly or indirectly suffered or incurred by the purchaser or by any of the group companies as a result of or in relation to such misrepresentation of non-fulfilment or such breach of the warranty in question.

(B) If the result of any such misrepresentation or non-fulfilment or breach of either that some asset of any of the group companies is worth less than its value would have been had such misrepresentation, non-fulfilment or breach not arisen, or that any of the group companies is or will be under a liability of increased or substituted liability which would not have arisen had such misrepresentation, non-fulfilment or breach not arisen, then (and upon being so required by the purchaser) as an alternative to making any payment under paragraph 8.3(A) an amount equal to 100 per cent of any depletion or diminution in the value of the asset in question or 100 per cent of all loss occasioned to the relevant group company by such liability or increased or substituted liability; and

(C) All costs on a full indemnity basis which the purchaser or any of the group companies may suffer or incur by reason of such misrepresentation non-fulfilment or breach of the warranty in question.

8.4 It shall not be a defence to any claim whether in respect of the warranties or the indemnities that the purchaser ought to have known or did know about the matter the subject of the claim and completion shall not in any way constitute a waiver of the purchaser's rights under the warranties and the indemnities or otherwise under this agreement.

8.5 Promptly upon the warrantors or any of them becoming aware of the impending or threatened occurrence of any event which would or might reasonably be expected to cause or constitute a breach of any of the warranties or be inconsistent with the contents of the disclosure letter or which would have caused or constituted a breach of any of the warranties or an inconsistency with the contents of the disclosure letter had such event occurred or been known to the warrantors or any of them prior to the date hereof the vendors shall give written notice thereof to the purchaser and shall use their best endeavours to prevent or remedy the same.

8.6 If after completion the purchaser shall become aware of any claim by any third party (other than a claim by the purchaser or any affiliate parent or subsidiary company of the purchaser) which may result in the purchaser and/or any of the group companies having any claim under the warranties, the purchaser shall forthwith give notice in writing to the warrantors and the warrantors shall be entitled to defend such claims in the name of the relevant group company, but at the expense of the warrantors, and to have the conduct of any action, dispute, compromise or defence thereof and of an incidental negotiation: and the purchaser and the group companies shall give to the vendor all reasonable co-operation, access and assistance for the purpose of resisting such claim.

8.7 Provided always, however, that save as provided in Clause 17 the purchaser shall not be entitled to claim that any fact constitutes a breach of the warranties to the extent:

(A) that such fact has been fully and fairly disclosed in the disclosure letter; or

(B) that such fact has been reserved or provided for in the accounts.

8.8 The total liabilities of the vendors in respect of any of the warranties shall not exceed the purchase price payable hereunder and insofar as any claim arises in connection with a breach of warranties in relation to SDL or any of its subsidiaries such claim shall be limited to 49% of the loss arising due to such breach of warranties relating to SDL or any of its subsidiaries.

8.9 The vendors shall not be liable under the warranties unless the aggregate amount of the liabilities arising thereunder exceeds 1R£50,000.

9 Provisions to apply between signing and completion

9.1 The vendors hereby jointly and severally undertake to the purchaser that they will procure that, prior to completion and save as otherwise provided in this agreement, the group companies will refrain from doing any act or thing whereby any of the warranties would not be true if given at any time down to and including completion.

9.2 The vendors hereby jointly and severally undertake to the purchaser that they will forthwith disclose in writing to the purchaser any matter or thing which may arise or become known to them or any of them after the date of this agreement and prior to completion which is inconsistent with any of the warranties or the contents of the disclosure letter or which ought to be known by a purchaser for value of the shares.

9.3 The vendors shall procure that forthwith upon the signing of this agreement the purchaser, its agents, representatives, accountants and solicitors are given promptly on request all such facilities and information regarding the business assets, liabilities, contracts and affairs of each of the group companies and the documents of title and other evidence of ownership of its assets as the purchaser may require.

10 Recision

10.1 If before completion any breach of any of the warranties has been committed or occurred and the purchaser shall not have agreed in writing to disregard such breach or if on or before the 28th day of February 1990 or such later date as the parties may agree the conditions contained in Clause 7.1 are not complied with to the purchasers satisfaction then the purchaser shall be entitled to rescind this agreement whereupon the purchaser shall be wholly freed from all liabilities and other obligations hereunder.

10.2 Any right of recision conferred upon the purchaser by this agreement shall be in addition to and without prejudice to all other rights and remedies available to the purchaser and no exercise or failure to exercise such right of rescission shall constitute a waiver by the purchaser of any such other rights or remedies.

10.3 Upon exercise by the purchaser of any right of recision hereunder, all monies paid to the purchaser to the vendors or any of them or to any other persons hereunder, shall be repayable forthwith to the purchaser, together with any interest earned thereon and if not so repaid, shall be recoverable as a simple contract debt in any court or competent jurisdiction.

11. Intellectual property rights

Each of the vendors hereby assigns to each of the group companies any interest held by any of them in any intellectual property rights as and from the completion date.

12 Completion

12.1 Subject to Clause 10 the completion date shall be the date which will be seven days after the last of the conditions contained in Clause 7.1 have been complied with.

12.2 On completion:

(A) The vendors shall:

- (i) deliver to the purchaser evidence satisfactory to the purchaser that the conditions referred to in sub clause 7.1 have been complied with.
- (ii) deliver to the purchaser duly executed transfers in favour of the purchaser (or as the purchaser in writing directs) accompanied by the relative certificates in respect of all the shares.
- (iii) deliver to the purchaser duly executed transfers in favour of the purchaser (or as the purchaser in writing directs) of all shares of any of the other group companies which are not registered in the name the company together with the relative share certificates.
- (iv) deliver to the purchaser the relevant share certificates in respect of the shares held by the company in the other group companies.
- (v) deliver to the purchaser in relation to the company the statutory body (duly written up-to-date), the common seal, the certificate incorporation, any unissued or cancelled share certificates, all available copies of the memorandum and articles of association, the title deeds of the properties, all other documents, contracts, licenses, easements, agreements, insurance policies, records, correspondence, paper files and books of trading and account.
- [(vi) procure the passing of board resolutions of each of the group companies revoking all existing authorities to bankers in respect of the operation of all bank accounts and giving authority in favour of such persons as the

purchaser may nominate to operate such accounts and appointing such persons as the purchaser may nominate as directors and secretary of each of the group companies and hand to the purchaser duly certified copies of such resolutions.]

(vii) cause such of the directors (if any) required by the purchaser to resign from their directorships in and all offices of profit under the group companies without any payment under the Redundancy Payments Act or otherwise and deliver to the purchaser their written resignation under seal containing an acknowledgement that each has no claim against any of the group companies in respect of breach of contract, compensation for loss of office or otherwise howsoever (except only for any accrued remuneration and expenses remaining to be reimbursed details of which have been supplied to the purchaser) together also with the written resignation of the secretary of each of the group companies containing an acknowledgement in the like terms.

(viii) deliver to the purchaser such waivers or consents as the purchaser may require signed by the vendors or other persons to enable the purchaser or its nominees to be registered as the holder(s) of the shares or any shares or any of the other group companies not registered in the name of the vendors.

(ix) discharge or procure the discharge (as the case may be) of all monies due to any of the group companies by the vendors or the directors or any of them.

(x) Procure the release of any guarantees given by any of the group companies in favour of any of the vendors or the directors or any third party.

(xi) satisfy the purchaser that one or more of the group companies has good marketable title to each of the properties and deliver to the purchaser the title deeds relating to each of the properties.

(xii) deliver to the purchaser the deed of indemnity duly executed by the parties thereto.

(B) The purchaser shall issue the loan notes in accordance with Clause 6.2

(C) The service agreements shall be executed and exchanged between the parties thereto.

13 Directors loans

On Completion each of the directors shall make the following loans to the purchaser:

	IR£
C Lyons	250,000
M Tully	250,000
TP Keleghan	250,000
CP Caravan	250,000
Total	1,000,000

13.2 Subject to Clause 13.3 such loans shall be interest free and shall be repayable at any time after the earlier of the 31 October 1991 or the date of public flotation at the times and in the amounts as may be required by the vendors.

31.3 In the event that all or any part of such loans are not repaid on or before the 1 November 1991 interest shall accrue thereon from the 1 November 1991 to the date of actual repayment at the rate equal to the Dublin Inter Offered Bank Rate for 6 month funds calculated on the 1st day of January and the 1st day of July in each year.

14. Public flotation

14.1 In the event of a public flotation occurring on or after the 1 October 1991 and in the event of the vendors being allocated shares for subscription in such public flotation the vendors shall be enticed in lieu of subscribing for such shares to convert the loan notes into ordinary shares in the purchaser on the basis of IR£100 of loan note converted for every IR£100 of shares issued and in calculating the issue price of such shares the price per share shall be the same price as the shares are offered to the public on the public flotation and not at any concessionary price as may be offered to any suppliers or employees or any other special class of persons.

14.2 In the event of a public flotation occurring before the 1 October 1991 and in the event of the vendors being allotted shares for subscription in such public flotation the vendors shall be enticed in lieu of subscribing for such shares to convert the loan notes into ordinary shares in the purchaser provided that the loan notes so converted prior to the 1 October 1991 shall be converted at a discount on their amount such discount to be calculated in accordance with the following table depending on the date conversion:

Date of Public Flotation	*Conversion rate per IR£100 amount of loan notes prior to 1 October 1991*
	IR£
1 January 1990 - 31 October 1990	88.84
1 November 1990 - 30 November 1990	89.72
1 December 1990 - 31 December 1990	90.60
1 January 1991 - 31 January 1991	91.53
1 February 1991 - 28 February 1991	92.41
1 March 1991 - 31 March 1991	93.34
1 April 1991 - 30 April 1991	94.27
1 May 1991 - 31 May 1991	95.20
1 June 1991 - 30 June 1991	96.13
1 July 1991 - 31 July 1991	97.06
1 August 1991 - 31 August 1991	98.04
1 September 1991 - 30 September 1991	99.02
after 30th September 1991	100.00

14.3 Provided, however, that in any public flotation each of the vendors shall be treated to the same basis as all other applicants for shares and nothing contained herein shall oblige the purchaser to allot any number of shares in such public flotation to any of the vendors or restrict the numbers of shares which any of the vendors may subscribe for and be allotted in any public flotation.

15. Placing

15.1 In the event of a placing on or after the 1 October 1991 the purchaser will direct the brokers to the placing to offer such number of shares in itself to each of the vendors so that the subscription monies payable by the vendors for such subscription shall equal the amount of the loan notes and the vendors shall be entitled in lieu subscribing for such shares to convert loan notes into ordinary shares in the purchaser on the basis of IR£100 of loan note converted for every IR£100 of conversion shares issued. For the purposes of calculating the price of such shares shall be the same price payable by the other places in the placing and not at any concessionary price as may be offered to any supplier, employees or any other class of persons.

15.2 In the event of a placing before the 1 October 1991 the same provisions as in Clause 15.1 shall apply provided that the loan notes so converted prior to the 1 October 1991 shall be converted at a discount on their amount such discount to be calculated in accordance with the following table depending on the date of conversion:

Date of public flotation	*Conversion rate per IR£100 amount of loan notes prior to 1 October 1991*
	IR£
1 January 1990 - 31 October 1990	88.84
1 November 1990 - 30 November 1990	89.72
1 December 1990 - 31 December 1990	90.60
1 January 1991 - 31 January 1991	91.53
1 February 1991 - 28 February 1991	92.41
1 March 1991 - 31 March 1991	93.34
1 April 1991 - 30 April 1991	94.27
1 May 1991 - 31 May 1991	95.20
1 June 1991 - 30 June 1991	96.13
1 July 1991 - 31 July 1991	97.06
1 August 1991 - 31 August 1991	98.04
1 September 1991 - 30 September 1991	99.02
after 30th September 1991	100.00

15.3 In the event of a placing prior to 1 October 1991 the vendors shall be entitled to subscribe in cash for such number of additional shares in the purchaser as shall equal the difference between the number of shares in the purchaser actually received pursuant to Clause 15.2 and the number of shares they would have been entitled to pursuant to Clause 15.1.

16. Restrictive covenants

Each of the vendors hereby undertakes to the purchaser that:

(A) He will not within the relevant territory during the relevant period carry on or be concerned directly or indirectly or be engaged, concerned or interested, whether as principal, shareholder, partner, employee, agent or otherwise (except as a shareholder in a public company whose shares are quoted or dealt in or any recognised Stock Exchange and holding not more than 5% of the share capital of such public company) in any business competing with the business or businesses of any of the group companies as carried on at any time prior to the completion date.

(B) He will not within the relevant territory during the relevant period either on his own account or on behalf of any other person, firm or company directly or indirectly solicit, interfere with or endeavour to entice away from any of the group companies any person, firm or company who has been a client, customer or subscriber of any of the group companies during the two years immediately prior to completion or who is in the habit of dealing with any of the group companies.

(C) He will not at any time hereafter either on his own account or on behalf of any other person, firm or company directly or indirectly endeavour to entice away any consultant, executive or employee from any of the group companies.

(D) He will not at any time after completion disclose to any person or himself use for any purpose, and shall use his best endeavours to prevent the publication or disclosure of, any information concerning the business, accounts or finance of any of the group companies or of any of the group companies' clients customers, transactions or affairs, which may, or may have, come to his knowledge.

16.2 The benefits of each and every of the provisions set out in this clause, and each and every part of each such provision thereof, shall be deemed to be separate and severable and enforceable accordingly. While the restrictions contained in this clause are considered by the parties to be reasonable in all the circumstances as at the date hereon it is acknowledged that restrictions of such a nature may be invalid because of changed circumstances or other unforeseen factors and accordingly it is hereby agreed that in the event of any provision of this clause being found to be void as going beyond what is reasonable in all the circumstances for the protection of the interests of the purchaser and/or each of the group companies but would be valid if some part thereof were deleted or the period of application reduced or the range of activities or area covered limited such provision shall apply with such modification and shall be given effect to such modified form as may be necessary to make it valid and effective.

16.3 In this Clause 16

(A) The "relevant territory" shall mean the Republic of Ireland, Northern Ireland and Great Britain.

(B) The "relevant period" shall mean the period of five years from the completion date.

17. Indemnity

The vendors hereby acknowledge that the purchaser has entered into this agreement on the basis inter alia that the liabilities of the company do not exceed IR £1,755,000 (one million seven hundred and fifty five thousand Irish pounds) net of cash on deposit and in hand and accordingly in addition to any other right of indemnity which the purchaser may have under this agreement or under the deed of indemnity and separate therefrom to the intent that the indemnity contained in this clause shall not be affected, restricted or limited by anything contained in the disclosure letter or elsewhere in this agreement the vendors hereby jointly and severally undertake to indemnify and keep the purchaser and the company indemnified from and against all losses, damages and expenses directly or indirectly incurred by the purchaser or any of the group companies as a result of or in relation to the liabilities of the company whether actual, contingent or otherwise exceeding IR£1,755,000 (one million seven hundred and fifty five thousand Irish pounds) net of cash on deposit and in hand.

18. Confidential

Save as which has to be disclosed in connection with a public flotation or placing the purchaser agrees that all documents including this agreement and information furnished by the vendor or any of the group companies to the purchase prior to the date hereof or pursuant hereto are to be kept strictly confidential to the parties hereto their respective employees, subsidiaries, subsidiaries' employees and professional advisers and shall not be disclosed by the purchaser to third parties without the prior written consent of the vendors.

19 Announcements

No announcement, public or otherwise, concerning the sale and purchase hereby agreed or any matter ancillary thereto shall be made by any party hereto without the prior written approval of the others.

20 Applicable law

This agreement shall governed by and construed in accordance with the laws of the Republic of Ireland and each of the parties hereto submits to the non-exclusive jurisdiction of the Courts of the Republic of Ireland. The purchaser hereby appoints the company to accept service of any proceedings on its behalf and each of the vendors hereby appoints the vendors' solicitors to accept serge of any proceedings on his behalf respectively.

21 Non-assignability

This agreement shall be binding upon and enure to the benefit of the successors of the parties but shall not be assignable.

22 Survival after completion

The provisions of this agreement insofar as the same shall not have been performed at completion shall remain in full force and effect notwithstanding completion.

23 Entire agreement

This agreement shall supersede, cancel and replace any and all previous agreements made between any of the parties hereto relative to its subject matter. No variation of this agreement shall be effective unless made in writing and signed by or by a duly authorised signatory of each of the parties hereto.

24 No general waiver

A waiver by any of the parties hereto of any breach by any or all of the other parties hereto of any of the terms provisions or conditions of this agreement, or the acquiescence of any of the parties hereto in any act (whether of commission or omission) which but for such acquiescence would be a breach as aforesaid shall not constitute a general waiver of such term provision or condition or of any subsequent act contrary thereto.

25 Release or compromise

The purchaser may release or compromise the liability of any of the vendors hereunder or grant to any of the vendors any other indulgence without affecting the liability of any of the other vendors or any other third party hereto.

26 Further assurance

At the request and at the cost of the purchaser, the vendor shall execute all such documents and do all such acts and things as may reasonably be required subsequent to completion by the purchaser in order to perfect the right, title and interest of the purchaser to the shares or any at the group companies to any asset.

27. Notice

Notices or other communications given pursuant to this agreement by any party hereto to any other party hereto shall be in writing and shall be sufficiently given;

(A) if delivered by hand or sent by post to the address set forth herein of the part to which the notice or communication is being given or to such other address as such party shall communicate in writing to the party giving the notice of communication.

(B) if sent by telex to the correct telex number of the party to which it is being sent.

(C) if sent by post, hereunder, it shall be sent by registered post.

(D) if sent by facsimile message to the correct facsimile number of the party to which it is being sent.

every notice or communication given in accordance with this Clause shall be deemed to have been received as follows:

Means of despatch	*Deemed received*
Delivery by hand	The day and time of delivery
Post	10 business days after posting
Telex	Answerback received
Facsimile	The day and time of sending

28 Sale of shares

In further consideration of the purchaser purchasing the shares each of the vendors hereby agrees that they will not for a period of three years from the date of Public Flotation or placing as the case may be dispose in any manner any share acquired by any of them in any such public flotation or placing and shall only dispose of any such shares thereafter in consultation with the purchaser's brokers.

In witness whereof the parties hereto have executed these presents in manner hereinafter appearing the day, month and year first herein written.

Schedule I The Vendors

Names and addresses of the vendors	*No of shares held in company*	*Proportion of purchase consideration*
		IR£
Charles M Lyons "Woodside" Oak Park Carlow	2,151	1,867,068
Michael Tully "Cluain Mhuire" Oak Park Carlow	1,122	973,896
Thomas P Keleghan 98 Kincora Grove Clontarf Dublin	2,151	1,867,068

Charles P Garavan Curragrean Oranmore Galway	2,151	1,867,068
Talmino Limited having its registered office at Portman House Hue Street Jersey Channel Islands	2,425 10,000	2,104,900 8,680,000

Schedule II SDL'S Subsidiaries

Subsidiary companies	*Nature of business*	*Percentage owned*	*Registered office*
Sugar Distributors Ltd	Wholesalers	100	Carlow
Sugar Distributors (Export) Ltd	Exporters	100	Carlow
ISM (Investments) Ltd	Finance company	100	Carlow
Hyspin Ltd	Non trading	100	Carlow
Fleet Care Ltd	Non trading	100	Carlow
Lumley Packers Ltd	Non trading	90	Carlow
Milltown Packaging Company Ltd	Wholesalers	100	Carlow (non-trading)
Wm McKinney (1975) Ltd	Wholesalers	70	Belfast
Chambers & Sons Ltd	Wholesalers	51	Belfast
Trilby Trading Ltd	Food industry suppliers	51	Drogheda
Trilby Commodity Trading Ltd	Food industry suppliers	100	Jersey
Gosford Ltd	Food industry suppliers	51	Belfast
J & J Peden Ltd	Wholesalers	51	Belfast
Associated companies			
Tanktrans Limited	Specialist tank haulage	49	Carlow
Cregagh Foods Limited	Wholesalers	49	Belfast
James Budgett & Son Limited	Wholesalers	33 1/3	London

All of the above companies are incorporated in the Republic of Ireland with the exception of Wm McKinney (1975) Limited, Gosford Limited, Chambers & Sons Limited and Cregagh Foods Limited are incorporated in Northern Ireland, Trilby Commodity Trading Limited which is incorporated in Jersey and James Budgett & Son Limited which is incorporated in England. All shares in subsidiary and associated companies consist of ordinary shares.

Schedule III Form of Deed of Indemnity

THIS DEED OF INDEMNITY made the ____________ day of ____________ One Thousand Nine Hundred and Ninety

BETWEEN: (1) CHARLES M LYONS of ____________

and

MICHAEL TULLY of ____________

and

THOMAS P KELEGHAN of ____________

and

CHARLES P GARAVAN of ____________

and

TALMINO LIMITED having its registered office at Plan House, Hue Street, Jersey, Channel Islands (hereinafter called "the Covenantors") of the First Part,

(2) SIUICRE ÉIREANN cpt having its Registered Office at St Stephens Green House, Dublin 2 ("the purchaser") of the Second Part

and

(3) GLADEBROOK LIMITED having its registered office at 50 South Mall, Cork

and

SUGAR DISTRIBUTORS (HOLDINGS) LIMITED having its registered office at Athy Road, Carlow (hereinafter collectively called "the group companies" and each a "group company") of the third part.

WHEREAS

This deed is entered into pursuant to the provisions of an agreement for sale and purchase of shares of even date herewith made between the parties hereto (hereinafter called "the agreement").

NOW THIS DEED WITNESSETH as follows:

1. Definitions

(a) Save as herein otherwise expressly stated to the contrary all words and expressions defined in the agreement shall have the same meaning wherever used herein.

(b) References to taxation shall be deemed to include any tax, duty or levy in respect of income or profits or gains deemed to have been or treated as or regarded as, earned, accrued or received and any references to claims, demands or assessments to tax, duty or levy on the happening of any event shall include claims, demands or assessments to tax, duty or levy where such events are deemed to have or treated or regarded as having occurred.

(c) The expression "claim" includes any notice, demand, assessment, letter or other document issued or action taken by the Revenue Commissioners or any governmental authority or body whatsoever in any part of the world whereby any group company is or may be placed or sought to be placed under liability to make a payment and whether or not the same is primarily payable by any group company and whether or not any group company has or may have any right of reimbursement against any other person or persons.

(d) The expression "claim for taxation" shall include not only liabilities of any group company to make payments of or in respect of taxation but shall also be deemed to include:

A. The loss or counteracting or clawing back of any relief, allowance deduction or credit in relation to the taxation which would (except for the claim in question) have been available to or which has been claimed by any group company; and

B. The nullifying or cancellation or set-off of a right to repayment of taxation which would (except for the claim in question) have been available to any group company;

and in such a case the amount of the relief allowance deduction or credit so lost or counteracted or clawed back or the amount of repayment which would otherwise have been obtained shall be treated as an amount of taxation for which a liability has arisen and fallen due.

(e) Any reference to a statutory provision shall include such provision and any regulations made in pursuance thereof as from time to time modified or re-enacted whether before or after the date of this deed insofar as such modification applies or is capable of applying to any transactions entered into prior to completion and (so far as liability thereunder may exist or can arise) shall include past statutory provisions or regulations (as from time to time modified or re-enacted) which such provisions or regulations have directly or indirectly replaced.

(f) Words and expressions defined for the purpose of the relevant taxing or other legislation shall herein bear the same meanings.

(g) The expression "the shares" shall mean all shares in the capital of the Company purchased or agreed to be purchased by the purchaser or which the purchaser shall have a right to subscribe for pursuant to the terms of the agreement.

2. Indemnities

Subject as provided in Clause 3 the Covenantors hereby jointly and severally agree with and undertake to the purchaser for itself and as Trustee for each of the group companies to indemnify and keep indemnified the purchaser and each of the group companies from and against any depletion in or reduction in value of its or their net assets in consequence of or as a result of:

(a) any claim for taxation made against any of the group companies; and

(b) to the extent only that the same is not taken into account for the purpose of paragraph (a) above any depletion of the assets of any group company arising by reason of or in consequence of or in connection with any claim (other than a frivolous or vexatious claim) for any taxation;

(c) to the extent only that the same have not resulted in a depletion of assets of any group company for the purpose of paragraph (b) above any reasonable costs and expenses properly incurred or payable by any group company in connection with or in consequence of any claim made against any group company for any taxation where any such claim for any taxation has been made or may hereafter be made wholly or partly in respect of or in consequence of any operations, activities, acts, omissions, transactions or arrangements whatsoever of any group company or of the covenantors (and including also any operations, activities, acts, omissions, transactions, arrangements by whomsoever made or any other events whatsoever giving rise to any claim for any taxation against any group company) occurring or entered into before completion, and including instances where such claim arises from the combined effects of two or more such operations, activities, acts, omissions, transactions or arrangements or other events only the first or some of which shall have taken place before completion;

(d) any matter or thing to which the warranties relate not being in fact in accordance or in conformity with the warranties.

3 Exclusions

The covenantors shall not be liable under the provisions of Clause 2.

(a) to the extent (if any) to which provisions or allowance has been made in the accounts in respect of the claim or liability in question;
(b) to the extent that the matter thing or claim has been disclosed by the covenantors to the purchaser in the disclosure letter.
(c) to the extent that any claim shall arise as a result of any provision or reserve made by any of the group companies being insufficient by reason of any increase in the rates of taxation made after the date hereof with retrospective effect.

4 Notice

In the event of the purchaser becoming aware of any claim or liability or penalty falling within Clause 2.01 of which the covenantors may not be aware the purchaser shall procure that notice thereof is given to the covenantors in the manner provided in the agreement and as regards any relevant claim the purchaser and the covenantors shall procure so far as they are reasonably able that the relevant group company shall at the request of the covenantors take such action as they may reasonably request to avoid dispute, resist appeal, compromise or defend the claim, liability or penalty and any adjudication in respect thereof but subject to the relevant group company being indemnified and secured to its reasonable satisfaction by the Covenantors against all losses (including additional taxation) costs, damages and expenses which may be thereby incurred.

5 Dispute

In the event of any dispute as to the quantum of the liability of the covenantors then the purchaser or the covenantors may require the matter to be determined by an independent auditor to be appointed by the President for the time being of the Institute Chartered Accountants in Ireland. Accordingly, either the purchaser or the covenantors may request such President to nominate an independent auditor for the purpose of this clause and any such request shall include a request that such auditor shall determine the quantum of the liability of the covenantors within two months of the matter being referred to the said President. The determination of such auditor shall be final and binding on the parties and such auditor shall be deemed to be an expert and not an arbitrator and accordingly the provisions of the Arbitration Acts 1954 and 1980 (or any modification or amendment thereof) shall not apply. The costs and charges of such auditor shall be paid by such of the parties concerned and in such proportions as such auditor may in his absolute discretion consider fair and reasonable.

6 Binding on successors

This deed shall enure to the benefit of and be binding upon the respective parties hereto and their respective personal representatives or successors.

7. Liability joint and several

The liability of the covenantors hereunder shall be joint and several.

IN WITNESS whereof these presents have been entered into the day month and year first herein WRITTEN

Signed sealed and delivered by in the presence of:

Signed sealed and delivered by in the presence of:

Signed sealed and delivered by in the presence of:

Signed sealed and delivered by in the presence of:

Present when the common seal of TALMINO Limited was affixed hereto

Present when the common seal of ____________ was affixed hereto:

Present when the common seal of ____________ was affixed hereto:

Schedule IV Details of Directors

GLADEBROOK LIMITED
Charles Mark Lyons "Woodside" Oak Park Carlow
Charles Caravan Curragrean Oranmore Galway
Thomas Gerard Keleghan 93 Kincora Grove Clontarf Dublin 3
Michael Tully "Cluain Mhuire" Oak Park Carlow

SUGAR DISTRIBUTORS LIMITED
Christopher Kieran Comerford 87 Ailesbury Road Dublin 4
John Patrick Gray 34 Shrewsbury Lawn Cabinteely Co Dublin
Charles Mark Lyons "Woodside" Oak Park Carlow
Charles Caravan Curragrean Oramnore Galway
Thomas Gerard Keleghan 98 Kincora Grove Clontarf Dublin 3
Michael Tully "Cluain Mhuire" Oak Park Carlow

Schedule V Details of the Properties

(1) All that and those that are the freehold properties of SDL at Carlow comprising of approximately 1 acre together with the buildings thereon.

(2) all that and those the property of Chambers & Sons Limited at Knockmore Industrial Estate, Marine Road, Lisburn, Co Antrim BT28 2EJ.

(3) All that and those the property Trading Limited, Lawrence Street, Drogheda, Co Louth.

Schedule VI Service Agreements

AN AGREEMENT made the ____________day of ____________ 1990

BETWEEN SIUICRE ÉIREANN cpt having its registered offices at St. Stephens Green House Dublin 2 ("the company") of the one part

and

CHARLES LYONS

of ____________

(the executive) of the other part

WHEREBY IT IS AGREED as follows:

1. The company shall employ the executive and the executive shall serve the company as group general manager of the flour division and also with responsibility for sales and distribution of sugar or such similar type position within the group as the managing director for the time being of the company (the "managing director") shall in his absolute discretion decide. Subject to the provisions for determination of this agreement hereinafter contained such employment shall be for a period of 5 years commencing on the 1st day of January 1990 and expiring on the 31st day of December 1994 and shall continue thereafter unless and until terminated by either party by the service of six months prior notice on the other party.

2. As an executive of the company the executive shall:

(a) undertake such duties and exercise such powers in relation to the company and its business as the managing director shall from time to time assign or vest in him;

(b) in the discharge of such duties and in the exercise of such powers observe and comply with all resolutions regulations and directions from time to time made or given by the managing director;

(c) devote substantially the whole of his time and attention during business hours to the discharge of his duties hereunder;

(d) conform to such hours of work as may from time to time reasonably be required of him and shall not be enticed to receive any remuneration for work performed outside his normal hours;

(e) in pursuance of his duties hereunder perform such services for subsidiary companies or any parent company of the company and (without further remuneration unless otherwise agreed) accept and hold for the duration of this agreement such offices or appointments in such subsidiary companies as the managing director may from time to time reasonably require.

3 (a) The executive shall forthwith on the signing of this agreement cease (except in pursuance of his duties in SDH) all activities in connection with the buying, selling, importing, transporting or distribution of sugar and flour and shall not without the consent of the company during the term of this agreement be engaged or interested either directly or indirectly in any capacity in any trade business or occupation whatsoever other than the business of the company but so that this provision shall not prohibit the holding whether directly or through nominees of quoted investments so long as not more than five per cent of the share or stock of any class of any one company shall be so held. In this clause the expression "occupation" shall include membership of the Oireachtas or any other public or private work which in the opinion of the company may hinder or otherwise interfere with the performance by the executive of his duties under this agreement.

3. (b) The executive hereby undertakes to the company that:

(i) He will not within the relevant territory during the relevant period carry on or be concerned directly or indirectly or be engaged, concerned or interested whether as principal, shareholder, partner, employee, agent or otherwise (except as a shareholder in a public company whose shares are quoted or dealt in or any recognised Stock Exchange and holding not more than 5% of the share capital of such public company) in any business competing with the business or businesses of the company or any of its subsidiaries or associate companies as carried on at any time prior to the termination of this agreement.

(ii) He will not within the relevant territory during the relevant period either on his own account or on behalf of any other person, firm or company directly or indirectly solicit, interfere with or endeavour to entice away from the company or any of its subsidiaries or associated companies any person, firm or company who has been a client or customer of the company or any of its subsidiaries or associate companies during any time up to the termination of this agreement or who is in the habit of dealing with the company or any of its subsidiaries or associate companies.

(iii) He will not at any time hereafter either on his own account or on behalf of any other person, firm or company directly or indirectly endeavour to entice away any consultant, executive or employee from the company or any of its subsidiaries or associate companies.

3. (c) The benefits of each and every of the provisions set out in this Clause, and each and very part of each such provision thereof, shall be deemed to be separate and severable and enforceable accordingly. While the restrictions contained in this Clause are considered by the parties to be reasonable in all the circumstances as at the date hereof it is acknowledged that restrictions of such a nature may be invalid because of changed circumstances or other unforeseen factors and accordingly it is hereby agreed that in the event of any provision of this Clause being found to be void as going beyond what is reasonable in all the circumstances for the protection of the interests of the company, its subsidiaries or associated companies but would be valid if some part thereof were deleted or the period of application reduced or the range of activities or area covered limited such provision shall apply with such modification and shall be given effect to in such modified form as may be necessary to make it valid and effective.

3. (d) In this Clause 3:

(A) The "relevant territory" shall mean the Republic of Ireland, Northern Ireland and Great Britain

(B) The "relevant period" shall mean the period of three years from the termination of this agreement.

4. The executive shall not except as authorised or required by his duties reveal to any person or company any trade secrets or confidential information concerning the organisation business finances transactions or affairs of the company or of its parent or any of its subsidiaries which may come to his knowledge during his employment hereunder and shall keep with complete secrecy all confidential information entrusted to him and shall not use or attempt to use any such information in any manner which may injure or cause loss either directly or indirectly to the company or its business or may be likely so to do. This restriction shall continue to apply after the termination of this agreement without limit in point of time but shall cease to apply to information or knowledge which may come into the public domain.

5. The executive shall not during the continuance of this agreement make otherwise than for the benefit of the company any notes or memoranda relating to any matter within the scope of the business of the company or concerning any of its dealings or affairs nor shall the executive either during the continuance of this agreement or afterwards use or permit to

be used any such notes or memoranda otherwise than for the benefit of the company it being the intention of the parties hereto that all such notes or memoranda made by the executive shall be the property of the company and left at its registered office upon the termination of this agreement.

6. Subject as hereinafter provided the company shall pay to the executive during the continuance of this agreement salary at the rate of IR£39,850 annum subject to annual review by the managing director. In the event of any increase of salary being agreed or notified as the result of such review such increase shall thereafter have effect as if it were specifically provided for as a term of this agreement. The said salary shall be payable by equal monthly instalments (and proportionately for any lesser period each monthly instalment being deemed to accrue rateably from day to day) in arrear on the last day of each month.

7. (a) The company shall provide and maintain for the sole use of the executive while on the business of the company a motor car of suitable type and shall pay all expenses in connection with such use, such motor car to be changed from time to time in accordance with the company's policy regarding vehicle replacements, and the executive shall ensure that at all times when the car is driven it is in the state and condition required by law.

7. (b) As an alternative to 7(a) the company shall if so required by the executive pay a mileage allowance for use of the executive's car on business at rates agreed between the parries from tune to time.

8. The executive shall be reimbursed all travelling hotel and other out-of-pocket expenses properly vouched and reasonably incurred by him in or about the discharge of his duties hereunder.

9. The executive shall be entitled to twenty six days holidays (exclusive of statutory public holidays) in each holiday year to be taken at such time or times as the managing director shall consider most convenient having regard to the requirements of the company's business and otherwise in accordance with the Holidays (Employees) Act 1973. The "holiday year" is 12 calendar months starting on 1 January.

10.(1) If the executive shall at any time be prevented by illness injury accident or any other circumstances beyond his control (such prevention being hereinafter referred to as "the illness") from discharging in full his duties hereunder for a total of six or more months in any twelve consecutive calendar months the company may by notice in writing to the executive given at any time so long as the illness shall continue discontinue payment in whole or part of the said salary on and from such date as may be specified in the notice until the illness shall cease.

(2) Subject as hereinbefore provided the said salary shall notwithstanding the illness continue to be paid to the executive in accordance with clause 7 hereof in respect of the period of the illness prior to such discontinuance.

(3) Provided that if the illness shall be or appear to be occasioned by actionable negligence of a third party in respect of which damages are or may be recoverable the executive shall forthwith notify the managing director of that fact and of any claim, compromise, settlement or judgment made or awarded in connection therewith and shall give to the company all such particular of such matters as the company may reasonably require and shall if so required by the company refund to the company such sum (not exceeding the amount of damages recovered by him

under such compromise, settlement or judgment less any costs in or in connection with or under such claim compromise settlement or judgment borne by the executive and not exceeding the aggregate of the remuneration paid to him by way of salary in respect of the period of the illness) as the company may determine.

(4) Except as expressly provided by this clause the executive shall not be entitled to any salary in respect of any period during which he shall fail or be unable from any cause to perform all or any of his duties hereunder without prejudice to any right of action accruing or accrued to either party in respect of any breach of this agreement.

(5) Any payment receivable from the Department of Social Welfare in respect of illness shall be claimed by the executive and immediately refunded to the company.

11.(1) This agreement may be terminated forthwith by the company without prior notice if the executive shall at any time:

(a) commit any serious breach of this agreement;

(b) be guilty of dishonesty or incompetence or poor performance or any grave misconduct or wilful neglect in the discharge of his duties hereunder;

(c) become bankrupt or commit any act of bankruptcy or make any arrangement or composition with his creditors;

(d) become of unsound mind;

(e) be convicted of any criminal offence other than road traffic offences or such offences which in the reasonable opinion of the company do not affect his position as an executive of the company;

(f) be absent or unable through illness to discharge in full his duties hereunder for a period of six consecutive months;

(g) if for any other reason become incapable of performing his duties under this agreement;

(2) Upon the termination of this agreement the executive shall forthwith give to the company formal letters of resignation from all offices and appointments held by him hereunder and in the event of his failure to do so the company is hereby irrevocably authorised to appoint some person as his attorney in his name and on his behalf to execute any documents and to do all things requisite to give effect thereto.

12.(1) Since the executive has obtained and is likely to obtain in the course of his employment with the company knowledge of trade secrets of the company and other confidential information of the company the executive hereby agrees with the company in addition to any other restrictions contained in this agreement that if the company shall have obtained trade secrets or other confidential information from any third party under an agreement including restrictions on disclosure known to him he will not without the consent of the company at any time (whether during the continuance of this agreement or after the termination thereof) infringe such restrictions.

(2) Since the executive also may obtain in the course of his employment by reason of services rendered for or offices held in any subsidiary company of the company knowledge of the trade secrets or other confidential information of such company the executive hereby agrees that he will at the request and cost of the company enter into a direct agreement or undertaking with such company whereby he will

accept restrictions corresponding to the restrictions herein contained (or such of there as may be appropriate in the circumstances) for such period as such company may reasonably require for the protection of its legitimate interests.

13. The executive hereby undertakes with the company that he shall not dispose of any shares received by him in the company consequent upon any Public Flotation of the company or any placing by it of any of its shares for a period of three years from the date of such public flotation or placing and shall only dispose of such shares thereafter in consultation with the company's brokers.

14 (1) Any notice under this agreement shall be in writing and shall be signed by or on behalf of the party giving it.

(2) Any such notice may be served by leaving it or sending it by telex, facsimile, prepaid recorded delivery or registered post:

(a) in the case of the executive at his address hereinbefore set out or at such other address which he may notify in writing to the company; or

(b) in the case of the company at its registered office for the time being.

(3) Any notice so served by post shall be deemed to have been served 48 hours after the letter containing the same was sent by recorded delivery or registered post. Any notice given by telex or cable shall be deemed to have been served at the time at which such telex or cable would be received in the ordinary course of transmission and in proving such service it shall be sufficient to prove that the notice was properly addressed and was posted or sent in accordance with sub-clause (2) above.

15. The termination of this agreement shall not affect such of the provisions hereof as are expressed to operate or have effect thereafter and shall be without prejudice to any right of action already accrued to either party in respect of any breach of this agreement by the other party.

16. The executive shall during the continuance of this agreement account to the company for any remuneration or other benefit received by him as executive or other officer of or shareholder in any company promoted by the company or any subsidiary of the company.

17. If before the termination of this agreement the employment of the executive hereunder shall be determined by reason of the liquidation of the company for the purpose of reconstruction or amalgamation and he shall be offered employment with any concern or undertaking resulting from such reconstruction or amalgamation on terms and conditions not less favourable than the terms of this agreement then the executive shall have no claim against the company in respect of the determination of his employment hereunder.

18. Every dispute or difference arising between the parties hereto with regard to this agreement or the duties powers or liabilities of either party hereunder or with regard to the construction of any clause hereof or any act or thing to be done in pursuance thereof or arising out of anything herein contained whether during the continuance of this agreement or upon or after its termination shall be referred to a single arbitrator in accordance with the provisions of the Arbitration Acts 1954 or any re-enactment or modification thereof for the time being in force.

19. A waiver by any of the parties hereto of any breach by the other party or any of the terms provisions or conditions of this agreement or the acquiescence by any such party in any act (whether commission or omission) which but for such acquiescence would be a

breach as aforesaid shall not constitute a general waiver of such term provision or condition or of any such act.

20. This agreement is the substitution for all previous contracts of service between the company and the executive which shall be deemed to have been terminated by mutual consent as from the date on which this agreement commences.

21. For the purposes of this agreement any reference to the group shall refer to the company and its subsides including SDH.

22. For the avoidance of doubt the executive shall continue to participate in the SDH Pension Scheme as heretofore pending alternative arrangements being agreed between the parties.

IN WITNESS WHEREOF the parties hereto or their duly representative have hereunder executed this agreement the day and year first herein written.

Present when the common seal of SIUICRE ÉIREANN cpt was affixed hereto:

Signed sealed and delivered by the said CHARLES LYONS

in the presence of ____________

AGREEMENT made the ____________ day of ____________ 1990

BETWEEN SIUICRE ÉIREANN cpt having its registered office at St Stephens Green House, Dublin 2 ("the company") of the one part

AND

CHARLES GARAVAN

(the executive) of the other part

WHEREBY IT IS AGREED as follows:

The company shall employ the executive and the executive shall serve the company as deputy managing director of Odium Group Limited and also with a developmental role for sales and distribution of sugar or such other similar type position within the group as the managing director for the time being of the company (the "managing director") shall in his absolute discretion decide. Subject to the provisions for determination of this agreement hereinafter contained such employment shall be for a period of 5 years commencing on the 1st day of January 1990 and expiring on the 31st day of December 1994 and shall continue thereafter unless and until terminated by either party by the service of six months prior notice on the other party.

As an executive of the company the executive shall:

(a) undertake such duties and exercise such powers in relation to the company and its business as the managing director shall from time to time assign to or vest in him;
(b) in the discharge of such duties and in the exercise of such powers observe and comply with all resolutions regulations and directions from time to time made or given by the managing director;
(c) devote substantially the whole of his time and attention during business hours to the discharge of his duties hereunder;

(d) conform to such hours of work as may from time to time reasonably required of him and shall not be entitled to receive any remuneration for work performed outside his normal hours;

(e) in pursuance of his duties hereunder perform such services for subsidiary companies or any parent company of the company and (without further remuneration unless otherwise agreed) accept and hold for the duration of this agreement such offices or appointments in such subsidiary companies as the managing director may from time to time reasonably require.

3 (a) The executive shall forthwith on the signing of this agreement cease (except in pursuance of his duties in SDH) all activities in connection with the buying, selling, importing, transporting or distribution of sugar and flour and shall not without the consent of the company during the term of this agreement be engaged or interested either directly or indirectly in any capacity in any trade business or occupation whatsoever other than the business of the company but so that this provision shall not prohibit the holding whether directly or through nominees of quoted investments so long as not more than five per cent of the share or stock of any class of any one company shall be so held. In this clause the expression "occupation" shall include membership of the Oireachtas or any other public or private work which in the opinion of the company may hinder or otherwise interfere with the performance by the executive of his duties under this agreement.

3 (b) The executive hereby undertakes to the company that:

(i) He will not within the relevant territory during the relevant period carry on or be concerned directly or indirectly or be engaged, concerned or interested whether as principal, shareholder, partner, employee, agent or otherwise (except as a shareholder in a public company whose shares are quoted or dealt in or any recognised Stock Exchange and holding not more than 5% of the share capital of such public company) in any business competing with the business or businesses of the group or any of its subsidiaries or associate companies as carried on at any time prior to the termination of this agreement.

(ii) He will not within the relevant territory during the relevant period either on his own account or on behalf of any other person, firm or company directly or indirectly solicit, interfere with or endeavour to entice away from the company or any of its subsidiaries or associated companies any person, firm or company who has been a client or customer of the company or any of its subsidiaries or associate companies during any time up to the termination of this agreement or who is in the habit of dealing win the company or any of its subsidiaries or associate companies.

(iii) He will not at any time hereafter either on his own account or on behalf of any other person, firm or company directly or indirectly endeavour to entice away any consultant, executive or employee from the company or any of its subsidiaries or associate companies.

3. (c) The benefits of each and every of the provisions set out in this Clause, and each and every part of each such provision thereof, shall be deemed to be separate and severable and enforceable accordingly. While the restrictions contained in this Clause are considered by the parties to be reasonable in all the circumstances as at the date hereof it is acknowledged that restrictions of such a nature may be invalid

because of changed circumstances or other unforeseen factors and accordingly it is hereby agreed that in the event of any provision of this Clause being found to be void as going beyond what is reasonable in all the circumstances for the protection of the interests of the company, its subsidiaries or associated companies but would be valid if some part thereof were deleted or the period of application reduced or the range of activities or area covered limited such provision shall apply with such modification and shall be given effect in such modified form as may be necessary to make it valid and effective.

(d) In this Clause 3:

(A) The "relevant territory" shall mean the Republic of Ireland, Northern Ireland and Great Britain.

(B) The "relevant period" shall mean the period of three years from the termination of this agreement.

4. The executive shall not except as authorised or required by his duties reveal to any person or company any trade secrets or confidential information concerning the organisation business finances transactions or affairs of the company or of its parent or any of its subsidiaries which may come to his knowledge during his employment hereunder and shall keep with complete secrecy all confidential information entrusted to him and shall not use or attempt to use any such information in any manner which may injure or cause loss either directly or indirectly to the company or its business or may be likely so to do. This restriction shall continue to apply after the termination of this agreement without limit in point of time but shall cease to apply to information or knowledge which may come into the public domain.

5. The executive shall not during the continuance of this agreement make otherwise than for the benefit of the company any notes or memoranda relating to any matter within the scope of the business of the company or concerning any of its dealings or affairs nor shall the executive either during the continuance of this agreement or afterwards use or permit to be used any such notes or memoranda otherwise than for the benefit of the company it being the intention of the parties hereto that all such notes or memoranda made by the executive shall be the property of the company and left at its registered office upon the termination of this agreement.

6. Subject as hereinafter provided the company shall pay to the executive during the continuance of this agreement salary at the rate of IR£37,100 and subject to annual review by the managing director. In the event of any increase of salary being agreed or notified as the result of such review such increase shall thereafter have effect as if it were specifically provided for as a term of this agreement. The said salary shall be payable by equal monthly instalments (and proportionately for any lesser period in monthly instalment being deemed to accrue rateably from day to day), in arrear on last day of each month.

7. (a) The company shall provide and maintain for the sole use of the executive while the business of the company a motor car of suitable type and shall pay all expenses in connection with such use, such motor car to be changed from time to time in accordance with the company's policy regarding vehicle replacements, and executive shall ensure that at all times when the car is driven it is in the state and condition required by law.

7. (b) As an alternative to 7(a) the company shall if so required by the executive pay mileage allowance for use of the executive's car on business at rates agreed between the parties from time to time.

8. The executive shall be reimbursed all travelling hotel and other out-of-pocket expenses properly vouched and reasonably incurred by him in or about the discharge of his duties hereunder.

9. The executive shall be enticed to twenty six days holidays (exclusive of statutory public holidays) in each holiday year to be taken at such time or times as the managing director shall consider most convenient having regard to the requirements of the company's business and otherwise in accordance with the Holidays (Employees) Act 1973. The "holiday year" is 12 calendar months starting on 1 January.

10.(1) If the executive shall at any time be prevented by illness, injury, accident or any other circumstances beyond his control (such prevention being hereinafter referred to as "the illness") from discharging in full his duties hereunder for a total of six or more months in any twelve consecutive calendar months the company may by notice in writing to the executive given at any time so long as the illness shall continue, discontinue payment in whole or part of the said salary on and from such date as may be specified in the notice until the illness shall cease.

(2) Subject as hereinbefore provided the said salary shall notwithstanding the illness continue to be paid to the executive in accordance with clause 7 hereof in respect of the period of the illness prior to such discontinuance.

(3) Provided that if the illness shall be or appear to be occasioned by actionable negligence of a third party in respect of which damages are or may be recoverable the executive shall forthwith notify the managing director of that fact and of any claim compromise settlement or judgment made or awarded in connection therewith and shall give to the company all such particulars of such matters as the company may reasonably require and shall if so required by the company refund to the company such sum (not exceeding the amount of damages recovered by him under such compromise settlement or judgment less any costs in or in connection with or under such claim compromise settlement or judgment borne by the executive and not exceeding the aggregate of the remuneration paid to him by way of salary in respect of the period of the illness) as the company may determine.

(4) Except as expressly provided by this clause the executive shall not be entitled to any salary in respect of any period during which he shall fail or be unable from any cause to perform all or any of his duties hereunder without prejudice to any right of action accruing or accrued to either party in respect of any breach of this agreement.

(5) Any payment receivable from the Department of Social Welfare in respect of illness shall be claimed by the executive and immediately refunded to the company.

11.(1) This agreement may be terminated forthwith by the company without prior notice if the executive shall at any time:

(a) commit any serious breach of this agreement;

(b) be guilty of dishonesty or incompetence or poor performance or any grave misconduct or wilful neglect in the discharge of his duties hereunder;

(c) become bankrupt or commit any act of bankruptcy or make any arrangement or composition with his creditors;

(d) become of unsound mind;

(e) be convicted of any criminal offence other than road traffic offences or such offences which in the reasonable opinion of the company do not affect his position as an executive of the company;

(f) be absent or unable through illness to discharge in full his duties hereunder for a period of six consecutive months;

(g) if for any other reason become incapable of performing his duties under this agreement;

(2) Upon the termination of this agreement the executive shall forthwith give to the company formal letters of resignation from all offices and appointments held by him hereunder and in the event of his failure to do so the company is hereby irrevocably authorised to appoint some person as his attorney in his name and on his behalf to execute any documents and to do all things requisite to give effect thereto.

12.(1) Since the executive has obtained and is likely to obtain in the course of his employment with the company knowledge of trade secrets of the company and other confidential information of the company the executive hereby agrees with the company in addition to any other restrictions contained in this agreement that if the company shall have obtained trade secrets or other confidential information from any third party under an agreement including restrictions on disclosure known to him he will not without the consent of the company at any time (whether during the continuance of this agreement after the termination thereof) infringe such restrictions.

(2) Since the executive also may obtain in the course of his employment by reason of services rendered for or offices held in any subsidiary company, of company knowledge of the trade secrets or other confidential information of such company the executive hereby agrees that he will at the request and order the company enter into a direct agreement or undertaking with such company whereby he will accept restrictions corresponding to the restrictions herein contained (or such of them as may be appropriate in the circumstances) for such period as such company may reasonably require for the protection of its legitimate interests.

13. The executive hereby undertakes with the company that he shall not dispose of any shares received by him in the company consequent upon any public flotation of the company or any placing by it of any of its shares for a period of five years from the date of such public flotation or placing and shall only dispose of his shares thereafter in consultation with the company's brokers.

14.(1) Any notice under this agreement shall be in writing and shall be signed by them on behalf of the party giving it.

(2) Any such notice may be served by leaving it or sending it by telex, facsimile, prepaid recorded delivery or registered post:

(a) in the case of the executive at his address hereinbefore set out or at such other address which he may notify in writing to the company; or

(b) in the case of the company at its registered office for the time being.

(3) Any notice so served by post shall be deemed to have been served 48 hours after the letter containing the same was sent by recorded delivery or registered post. Any notice given by telex or cable shall be deemed to have been served at the time at which such telex or cable would be received in the ordinary course of

transmission and in proving such service it shall be sufficient to prove that the notice was properly addressed and was posted or sent in accordance with sub-clause (2) above.

15. The termination of this agreement shall nor affect such of the provisions hereof as are expressed to operate or have effect thereafter and shall be without prejudice to any right of action already accrued to either party in respect of any breach of this agreement by the other party.

16. The executive shall during the continuance of this agreement account to the company or any remuneration or other benefit received by him as executive or other officer of the shareholder in any company promoted by the company or any subsidiary of the company.

17. If before the termination of this agreement the employment of the executive hereunder shall be determined by reason of the liquidation of the company for the purpose of reconstruction or amalgamation and he shall be offered employment with any concern or undertaking resulting from such reconstruction or amalgamation on terms and conditions not less favourable than the terms of this agreement then the executive shall have no claim against the company in respect of the determination of his employment hereunder.

18. Every dispute or difference arising between the parties hereto with regard to the agreement or the duties powers or liabilities of either party hereunder or with regard to the construction of any clause hereof or any act or thing to be done in pursuance thereof or arising out of anything herein contained whether during the continuance of this agreement or upon or after its termination shall be referred to a single arbitrator in accordance with the provisions of the Arbitration Acts 1954 or any re-enactment or modification thereof for the time being in force.

19. A waiver by any of the parties hereto of any breach by the other party or any of the terms provisions or conditions of this agreement or the acquiescence by any such party in any act (whether commission or omission) which but for such acquiescence would be a breach as aforesaid shall not constitute a general waiver of such term, provision or condition or of any such act.

20. This agreement is the substitution for all previous contracts of service between the company and the executive which shall be deemed to have been terminated by mutual consent as from the date on which this agreement commences.

21. For the purposes of this agreement any reference to the group shall mean the company and its subsidiaries including SDL.

AGREEMENT made the ____________ day of ____________ 1990

BETWEEN SIUICRE ÉIREANN cpt having its registered office at St Stephens Green House, Dublin 2 ("the company') of the one part

AND

MICHAEL TULLY

of

(the executive) of the other part

WHEREBY IT IS AGREED as follows:

The company shall employ the executive and the executive shall serve the company as group general manager finance or in such other executive position of a similar type in the financial and/or secretarial area as the managing director for the time being of the company (the "managing director") shall in his absolute discretion decide. Subject to the provisions for determination of this agreement hereinafter contained such employment shall be for a period of 5 years commencing on the 1st day of January 1990 and expiring on the 31st day of December 1994 and shall continue thereafter unless and until terminated by either party by the service of six months prior notice on the other party.

As an executive of the company the executive shall:

(a) undertake such duties and exercise such powers in relation to the company and its business as the managing director shall from time to time assign to or vest in him;

(b) in the discharge of such duties and in the exercise of such powers observe and comply with all resolutions regulations and directions from time to time made or given by the managing director;

(c) devote substantially the whole of his time and attention during business hours to the discharge of his duties hereunder;

(d) conform to such hours of work as may from time to time reasonably be required of him and shall not be entitled to receive any remuneration for work performed outside his normal hours;

(e) in pursuance of his duties hereunder perform such services for subsidiary companies or any parent company of the company and (without further remuneration unless otherwise agreed) accept and hold for the duration of this agreement such offices or appointments in such subsidiary companies as the managing director may from time to time reasonably require.

3. (a) The executive shall not without the consent of the company during the term of this agreement be engaged or interested either directly or indirectly in any capacity in any trade business or occupation whatsoever other than the business of the company but so that this provision shall not prohibit the holding whether directly or through nominees of quoted investments so long as not more than five per cent of the share or stock of any class of any one company shall be so held. In this Clause expression "occupation" shall include membership of the Oireachtas or any other public or private work which in the opinion of the company may hinder or otherwise interfere with the performance by the executive of his duties under this agreement.

3. (b) executive hereby undertakes to the company that:

(i) He will not within the relevant territory during the relevant period carry on or be concerned directly or indirectly or be engaged, concerned or interested whether as principal, shareholder, partner, employee, agent or otherwise (except as a shareholder in a public company whose shares are quoted or dealt in or any recognised Stock Exchange and holding not more than 5% of the share capital of such public company) in any business competing with the business or businesses of the company or any of its subsidiaries or associate companies as carried on at any time prior to the termination of this agreement

(ii) He will not within the relevant territory during the relevant period either on his own account or on behalf of any other person, firm or company directly or indirectly solicit, interfere with or endeavour to entice away from the company or any of its subsidiaries or associated companies any person, firm or company who has been a client or customer of the company or any of its subsidiaries or associate companies during any time up to the termination of this agreement or who is in the habit of dealing with the company or any of its subsidiaries or associate companies.

(iii) He will not at any time hereafter either on his own account or on behalf of any other person, firm or company directly or indirectly endeavour to entice away any consultant, executive or employee from the company or any of its subsidiaries or associate companies.

3. (c) The benefits of each and every of the provisions set out in this Clause, and each and every part of each such provision thereof, shall be deemed to be separate and severable and enforceable accordingly. While the restrictions contained in this Clause are considered by the parties to be reasonable in all the circumstances as at the date hereof it is acknowledged that restrictions of such a nature may be invalid because of changed circumstances or other unforeseen factors and accordingly it is hereby agreed that in the event of any provision of this Clause being found to be void as going beyond what is reasonable in all the circumstances for the protection of the interests of the company its subsidiaries or associated companies but would be valid if some part thereof were deleted or the period of application reduced or the range of activities or area covered limited such provision shall apply with such modification and shall be given effect in such modified form as may be necessary to make it valid and effective.

3. (d) In this Clause 3:

(A) The "relevant territory" shall mean the Republic of Ireland, Northern Ireland and Great Britain.

(B) The "relevant period" shall mean the period of three years from the termination of this agreement.

4. The executive shall not except as authorised or required by his duties reveal to any person or company any trade secrets or confidential information concerning organisation business finances transactions or affairs of the company or of its parent or any of its subsidiaries which may come to his knowledge during his employment hereunder and shall keep with complete secrecy all confidential information entrusted to him and shall not use or attempt to use any such information in any manner which may injure or cause loss either directly or indirectly to the company or its business or may be likely so to do. This restriction shall continue to apply after the termination of this agreement without limit in point of time but shall cease to apply to information or knowledge which may come into the public domain.

5. The executive shall not during the continuance of this agreement make otherwise than for the benefit of the company any notes or memoranda relating to any matter within the scope of the business of the company or concerning any of its dealings or affairs nor shall the executive either during the continuance of this agreement or afterwards use or permit to be used any such notes or memoranda otherwise than for the benefit of the company it being the intention of the parties hereto that all such notes or memoranda made by the

executive shall be the property of the company and left at its registered office upon the termination of this agreement.

6. Subject as hereinafter provided the company shall pay to the executive during the continuance of this agreement salary at the rate of IR£39,850 per annum subject to annual review by the managing director. In the event of any increase of salary being agreed or notified as the result of such review such increase shall thereafter have effect as if it were specifically provided for as a term of this agreement. The said salary shall be payable by equal monthly instalments (and proportionately for any lesser period each monthly instalment being deemed to accrue rateably from day to day) in arrear on the last day of each month.

7. (a) The company shall provide and maintain for the sole use of the executive while on the business of the company a motor car of suitable type and shall pay all expenses in connection with such use, such motor car to be changed from time to time in accordance with the company's policy regarding vehicle replacements and the executive shall ensure that at all times when the car is driven it is in the state and condition required by law.

7. (b) As an alternative to 7(a) the company shall if so required by the executive pay a mileage allowance for use of the executive's car on business at the following rates:

Mileage	Pence Per Mile

8. The executive shall be reimbursed all travelling hotel and other out-of-pocket expenses properly vouched and reasonably incurred by him in or about the discharge duties hereunder.

9. The executive shall be entitled to five weeks' holidays (exclusive of statutory public holidays) in each holiday year to be taken at such time or times as the managing director shall consider most convenient having regard to the requirements of the company's business and otherwise in accordance with the Holidays (Employees) Act 1973. The "holiday year" is 12 calendar months starting on 1 January.

10.(1) If the executive shall at any time be prevented by illness injury accident or any other circumstances beyond his control (such prevention being hereinafter referred to as "the illness") from discharging in full his duties hereunder for a total of six or more months in any twelve consecutive calendar months the company may by notice in writing to the executive given at any time so long as the illness shall continue discontinue payment in whole or part of the said salary on and from such date as may be specified in the notice until the illness shall cease.

(2) Subject as hereinbefore provided the said salary shall notwithstanding the illness continue to be paid to the executive in accordance with clause 7 hereof in respect of the period of the illness prior to such discontinuance.

(3) Provided that if the illness shall be or appear to be occasioned by actionable negligence of a third party in respect of which damages are or may be recoverable the executive shall forthwith notify the managing director of that fact and of any claim, compromise, settlement or judgment made or awarded in connection therewith and shall give to the company all such particulars of such matters as the company may reasonably require and shall if so required by the company refund to the company such sum (not exceeding the amount of damages recovered by him under such compromise, settlement or judgment less any costs in or in connection with or under such claim, compromise, settlement or judgment borne by the

executive and not exceeding the aggregate of the remuneration paid to him by way of salary in respect of the period of the illness) as the company may determine.

(4) Except as expressly provided by this clause the executive shall not be entitled to any salary in respect of any period during which he shall fail or be unable from any cause to perform all or any of his duties hereunder without prejudice to any right of action accruing or accrued to either party in respect of any breach of this agreement.

(5) Any payment receivable from the Department of Social Welfare in respect of illness shall be claimed by the executive and immediately refunded to the company.

11.(1) This agreement may be terminated forthwith by the company without prior notice if the executive shall at any time:

(a) commit any serious breach of this agreement;
(b) be guilty of dishonesty or incompetence or poor performance or any grave misconduct or wilful neglect in the discharge of his duties hereunder;
(c) become bankrupt or commit any act of bankruptcy or arrangement or composition with his creditors;
(d) become of unsound mind:
(e) be convicted of any criminal offence other than road traffic offences or such offences which in the reasonable opinion of the company do not affect his position as an executive of the company;
(f) be absent or unable through illness to discharge in full his duties hereunder for a period of six consecutive months;
(g) if for any other reason become incapable of performing his duties under this agreement;

(2) Upon the termination of this agreement the executive shall forthwith give to the company formal letters of resignation from all offices and appointments held by him hereunder and in the event of his failure to do so the company is hereby irrevocably authorised to appoint some person as his attorney in his name and on his behalf to execute any documents and to do all things requisite to give effect thereto.

12.(1) Since the executive has obtained and is likely to obtain in the course of his employment with the company knowledge of trade secrets of the company and other confidential information of the company the executive hereby agrees with the company in addition to any other restrictions contained in this agreement that if the company shall have obtained trade secrets or other confidential information from any third party under an agreement including restrictions on disclosure known to him he will not without the consent of the company at any time (whether during the continuance of this agreement or after the termination thereof) infringe such restrictions.

(2) Since the executive also may obtain in the course of his employment by reason of services rendered for or offices held in any subsidiary company of the company knowledge of the trade secrets or other confidential information of such company the executive hereby agrees that he will at the request and cost of the company enter into a direct agreement or undertaking with such company whereby he will accept restrictions corresponding to the restrictions herein contained (or such of them as may be appropriate in the circumstances) for such period as such company may reasonably require for the protection its legitimate interests.

13. The executive hereby undertakes with the company that he shall not dispose of any shares received by him in the company consequent upon any public flotation of the company or any placing by it of any of its shares for a period of five years from the date of such public flotation or placing and shall only dispose of any such shares thereafter in consultation with the company's brokers.

14.(1) Any notice under this agreement shall be in writing and shall be signed by or on behalf of the party giving it.

(2) Any such notice may be served by leaving it or sending it by telex, facsimile, prepaid recorded delivery or registered post:

(a) in the case of the executive at his address hereinbefore set out or at such other address which he may notify in writing to the company; or

(b) in the case of the company at its registered office for the time being.

(3) Any notice so served by post shall be deemed to have been served 48 hours after the letter containing the same was sent by recorded delivery or registered post. Any notice given by telex or cable shall be deemed to have been served at the time at which such telex or cable would be received in the ordinary course of transmission and in proving such service it shall be sufficient to prove that the notice was properly addressed and was posted or sent in accordance with sub-clause (2) above.

15. The termination of this agreement shall not affect such of the provisions hereof as are expressed to operate or have effect thereafter and shall be without prejudice to any right of action already accrued to either party in respect of any breach of this agreement by the other party.

16. The executive shall during the continuance of this agreement account to the company for any remuneration or other benefit received by him as executive or other officer of or shareholder in any company promoted by the company or any subsidiary of the company.

17. If before the termination of this agreement the employment of the executive hereunder shall be determined by reason of the liquidation of the company for the purpose of reconstruction or amalgamation and he shall be offered employment with any concern or undertaking resulting from such reconstruction or amalgamation on conditions not less favourable than the terms of this agreement then the executive shares have no claim against the company in respect of the determination of his employment hereunder.

18. Every dispute or difference arising between the parties hereto with regard to this agreement or the duties powers or liabilities of either party hereunder or with regard to the construction of any clause hereof or any act or thing to be done in pursuance thereof or arising out of anything herein contained whether during the continuance of this agreement or upon or after its termination shall be referred to a single arbitrator in accordance with the provisions of the Arbitration Acts 1954 or any re-enactment or modification thereof for the time being in force.

19. A waiver by any of the parties hereto of any breach by the other party or any of the terms provisions or conditions of this agreement or the acquiescence by any such party in any act (whether commission or omission) which but for such acquiescence would be a breach as aforesaid shall not constitute a general waiver of such term provision or condition or of any such act.

20. This agreement is the substitution for all previous contracts of service between the company and the executive which shall be deemed to have been terminated by mutual consent as from the date on which this agreement commences.

21. For the avoidance of doubt it is hereby agreed between the parties that the executive shall continue to participate in the company's staff pension scheme as heretofore.

IN WITNESS WHEREOF the parties hereto or their duly representative have hereunder executed this agreement the day and year first herein written.

Present when the common seal of SIUICRE ÉIREANN cpt affixed hereto:

Signed sealed and delivered by the said MICHAEL TULLY in the presence of:

AGREEMENT made the _____________ day of _____________ 1990

BETWEEN SIUICRE ÉIREANN cpt having its registered office at St Stephens Green House, Dublin 2 ("the company") of the one part

THOMAS KELEGHAN (the executive) of the other part

WHEREBY IT IS AGREED as follows:

1. The company shall employ the executive and the executive shall serve the company as sales director responsible for selling sugar and such other sales as the group general manager of the flour division for the time being of the company (the "general manager") shall decide. Subject to the provisions for determination of this agreement hereinafter contained such employment shall be for a period of 18 months commencing on the 1st day of January 1990 and expiring on the 30th day of June 1991 and shall continue thereafter unless and until terminated by either party by the service of three months written notice on the other party.

2. As an executive of the company the executive shall:

(a) undertake such duties and exercise such powers in relation to the company and its business as the general manager shall from time to time assign to or vest in him;

(b) in the discharge of such duties and in the exercise of such powers observe and comply with all resolutions regulations and directions from time to time made or given by the general manager;

(c) devote substantially the whole of his time and attention during business hours to the discharge of his duties hereunder;

(d) conform to such hours of work as may from time to time reasonably be required of him and shall not be entitled to receive any remuneration for work performed outside his normal hours;

(e) in pursuance of his duties hereunder perform such services for subsidiary companies or any parent company of the company and (without further remuneration unless otherwise agreed) accept and hold for the duration of this agreement such offices or appointments in such subsidiary companies as the general manager may from time to time reasonably require.

3. (a) The executive shall forthwith on the signing of this agreement cease pursuance of his duties in the group) all activities in connection with the buying selling, importing, transporting or distribution of sugar and/or flour and shall not without the consent of the company during the term of this agreement be engaged or

interested either directly or indirectly in any capacity in any trade business or occupation whatsoever other than the business of the company but so that this provision shall not prohibit the holding whether directly or through nominees of quoted investments so long as not more than five per cent of the share or stock of any class of any one company shall be so held. In this clause the expression "occupation" shall include membership of the Oireachtas or any other public or private work which in the opinion of the company may hinder or otherwise interfere with the performance by the executive of his duties under this agreement.

3. (b) The executive hereby undertakes to the company that:

(i) He will not within the relevant territory during the relevant period carry on or be concerned directly or indirectly or be engaged, concerned or interested whether as principal, shareholder, partner, employee, agent or otherwise (except as a shareholder in a public company whose shares are quoted or dealt in or any recognised Stock Exchange and holding not more than 5% of the share capital of such public company) in any business competing with the business or businesses of the company or any of its subsidiaries or associate companies as carried on at any time prior to the termination of this agreement.

(ii) He will not within the relevant territory during the relevant period either on his own account or on behalf of any other person, firm or company directly or indirectly solicit, interfere with or endeavour to entice away from the company or any of its subsidiaries or associated companies any person, firm or company who has been a client or customer of the company or any of its subsidiaries or associate companies during any time up to the termination of this agreement or who is in the habit of dealing with the company or any of its subsidiaries or associate companies.

(iii) He will not at any time hereafter either on his own account or on behalf of any other person, firm or company directly or indirectly endeavour to entice away any consultant, executive or employee from the company or any of its subsidiaries or associate companies.

3. (c) The benefits of each and every of the provisions set out in this Clause, and each and every part of each such provision thereof, shall be deemed to be separate and severable and enforceable accordingly. While the restrictions contained in this Clause are considered by the parties to be reasonable in all the circumstances as at the date hereof it is acknowledged that restrictions of such a nature may be invalid because of changed circumstances or other unforeseen factors and accordingly it is hereby agreed that in the event of any provision of this Clause being found to be void as going beyond what is reasonable in all the circumstances for the protection of the interests of the company, its subsidiaries or associated companies but would be valid if some part thereof were deleted or the period of application reduced or the range of activities or area covered limited such provision shall apply with such modification and shall be given effect to in such modified form as may be necessary to make it valid and effective.

3. (d) In this Clause 3:

(A) The "relevant territory" shall mean the Republic of Ireland, Northern Ireland and Great Britain.

(B) The "relevant period" shall mean the period of three years from the termination of this agreement.

4. The executive shall not except as authorised or required by his duties reveal to any person or company any trade secrets or confidential information concerning the organisation business finances transactions or affairs of the company or of its parent or any of its subsidiaries which may come to his knowledge during his employment hereunder and shall keep with complete secrecy all confidential information entrusted to him and shall not use or attempt to use any such information in any manner which may injure or cause loss either directly or indirectly to the company or its business or may be likely so to do. This restriction shall continue to apply after the termination of this agreement without limit in point of time but shall cease to apply to information or knowledge which may come into the public domain.

5. The executive shall not during the continuance of this agreement make otherwise then for the benefit of the company any notes or memoranda relating to any matter within the scope of the business of the company or concerning any of its dealings or affairs nor shall the executive either during the continuance of this agreement or afterwards use or permit to be used any such notes or memoranda otherwise than for the benefit of the company it being the intention of the parties hereto that all such notes or memoranda made by the executive shall be the property of the company and left at its registered office upon the termination of this agreement.

6. Subject as hereinafter provided the company shall pay to the executive during the continuance of this agreement salary at the rate of IR£37,100 annum subject to annual review by the general manager. In the event of any increase of salary being agreed notified as the result of such review such increase shall thereafter have effect as if it were specifically provided for as a term of this agreement. The said salary shall be payable by equal monthly instalments (and proportionately for any lesser period each monthly instalment being deemed to accrue rateably from day to day) in arrear on the last day of each month.

7. (a) The company shall provide and maintain for the sole use of the executive while on the business of the company a motor car of suitable type and shall pay all expenses in connection with such use, such motor car to be changed from time to time in accordance with the company's policy regarding vehicle replacements, and the executive shall ensure that at all times when the car is driven it is in the state condition required by law.

7. (b) As an alternative to 7(a) the company shall if so required by the executive pay a mileage allowance for use of the executive's car on business at rates as agreed between the company and the executive from time to time.

8. The executive shall be reimbursed all travelling hotel and other out-of-pocket expenses properly vouched and reasonably incurred by him in or about the discharge of his duties hereunder.

9. The executive shall be entitled to twenty six days holidays (exclusive of statutory public holidays) in each holiday year to be taken at such time or times as the general manager shall consider most convenient having regard to the requirements of the company's business and otherwise in accordance with the Holidays (Employees) Act 1973. The "holiday year" is 12 calendar months starting on 1 January.

10.(1) If the executive shall at any time be prevented by illness, injury, accident or any other circumstances beyond his control (such prevention being hereinafter referred to as "the Illness") from discharging in-full his duties hereunder for a total of six or more months in any twelve consecutive calendar months the company may by notice in writing to the executive given at any time so long as the illness shall continue discontinue payment in whole or part of the said salary on and from such date as may be specified in the notice until the illness shall cease.

(2) Subject as hereinbefore provided the said salary shall notwithstanding the illness continue to be paid to the executive in accordance with clause 7 hereof in respect of the period of the illness prior to such discontinuance:

(3) Provided that if the illness shall be or appear to be occasioned by actionable negligence of a third party in respect of which damages are or may be recoverable the executive shall forthwith notify the general manager of that fact and of any claim, compromise, settlement or judgment made or awarded in connection therewith and shall give to the company all such particulars of such matters as the company may reasonably require and shall if so required by the company refund to the company such sun (not exceeding the amount of damages recovered by him under such compromise, settlement or judgment less any costs in or in connection with or under such claim, compromise, settlement or judgment borne by the executive and not exceeding the aggregate of the remuneration paid to him by way of salary in respect of the period of the illness) as the company may determine.

(4) Except as expressly provided by this clause the executive shall not be entitled to any salary in respect of any period during which he shall fail or be unable from any cause to perform all or any of his duties hereunder without prejudice to any right of action accruing or accrued to either party in respect of any breach of this agreement.

(5) Any payment receivable from the Department of Social Welfare in respect of illness shall be claimed by the executive and immediately refunded to the company.

11.(1) This agreement may be terminated forthwith by the company without prior notice if the executive shall at any time:

(a) commit any serious breach of this agreement;

(b) be guilty of dishonesty or incompetence or poor performance or any grave misconduct or wilful neglect in the discharge of his duties hereunder;

(c) become bankrupt or commit any act of bankruptcy or arrangement or composition with his creditors;

(d) become of unsound mind:

(e) be convicted of any criminal offence other than road traffic offences or such offences which in the reasonable opinion of the company do not affect his position as an executive of the company;

(f) be absent or unable through illness to discharge in full his duties hereunder for a period of six consecutive months;

(g) if for any other reason become incapable of performing his duties under this agreement;

(2) Upon the termination of this agreement the executive shall forthwith give to the company formal letters of resignation from all offices and appointments held by him hereunder and in the event of his failure to do so the company is hereby irrevocably authorised to appoint some person as his attorney in his name and on

his behalf to execute any documents and to do all things requisite to give effect thereto.

12.(1) Since the executive has obtained and is likely to obtain in the course of his employment with the company knowledge of trade secrets of the company and other confidential information of the company the executive hereby agrees with the company in addition to any other restrictions contained in this agreement that if the company shall have obtained trade secrets or other confidential information from any third party under an agreement including restrictions on disclosure known to him he will not without the consent of the company at any time (whether during the continuance of this agreement or after the termination thereof) infringe such restrictions.

(2) Since the executive also may obtain in the course of his employment by reason of services rendered for or offices held in any subsidiary company of the company knowledge of the trade secrets or other confidential information of such company the executive hereby agrees that he will at the request and cost of the company enter into a direct agreement or undertaking with such company whereby he will accept restrictions corresponding to the to the restrictions herein contained (or such of them as may be appropriate in the circumstances) for such period as such company may reasonably require for the protection of its legitimate interests.

13. The executive hereby undertakes with the company that he shall not dispose of any shares received by him in the company consequent upon any public flotation company or any placing by it of any of its shares for a period of five years from the date of such public flotation or placing.

14.(1) Any notice under this agreement shall be in writing and shall be signed by or on behalf of the party giving it.

(2) Any such notice may be served by leaving it or sending it by telex, facsimile, prepaid recorded delivery or registered post:

(a) in the case of the executive at his address hereinbefore set out or at such other address which he may notify in writing to the company, or

(b) in the case of the company at its registered office for the, time being.

(3) Any notice so served by post shall be deemed to have been served 48 hours after the letter containing the same was sent by recorded delivery or registered post. Any notice given by telex or cable shall be deemed to have been served at the time at which such telex or cable would be received in the ordinary course of transmission and in proving such service it shall be sufficient to prove that the notice was properly addressed and was posted or sent in accordance with sub-clause (2) above.

15. The termination of this agreement shall not affect such of the provisions hereof as are expressed to operate or have effect thereafter and shall be without prejudice to any right of action already accrued to, either party in respect of any breach of this agreement by the other party.

16. The executive shall during the continuance of this agreement account to the company for any remuneration or other benefit received by him as executive or other officer of or shareholder in any company promoted by the company or any subsidiary of the company.

17. If before the termination of this agreement the employment of the executive hereunder shall be determined by reason of the liquidation of the company for the purpose of reconstruction or amalgamation and he shall be offered employment with any concern or undertaking resulting from such reconstruction or amalgamation on terms and conditions not less favourable than the terms of this agreement then the executive shall have no claim against the company in respect of the determination of his employment hereunder.

18. Every dispute or difference arising between the parties hereto with regard to this agreement or the duties powers or liabilities of either party hereunder or with regard to the construction of any clause hereof or any act or thing to be done in pursuance thereof or arising out of anything herein contained whether during the continuance of this agreement or upon or after its termination shall be referred to a single arbitrator in accordance with the provisions of the Arbitration Acts 1954 or any re-enactment or modification thereof for the time being in force.

19. A waiver by any of the parties hereto of any breach by the other party or any of the terms provisions or conditions of this agreement or the acquiescence by any such party in any act (whether commission or omission) which but for such acquiescence would be a breach as aforesaid shall not constitute a general waiver of such term provision or condition or of any such act.

20. This agreement is the substitution for all previous contracts of service between the company and the executive which shall be deemed to have been terminated by mutual consent as from the date on which this agreement commences.

21. For the purposes of this agreement any reference to group shall mean the company and its subsidiaries including Sugar Distributors (Holdings) Limited.

22. For the avoidance of doubt the executive shall continue to participate in the SDH Scheme as heretobefore.

WITNESS WHEREOF the parties hereto or their duly representative have hereunder executed this agreement the day and year first herein written.

Present when the common seal of SIUICRE ÉIREANN cpt was affixed hereto:

Signed sealed and delivered by the said THOMAS KELEGHAN in the presence of:

Schedule VII Warranties Information

Disclosure of information

1. All information produced or given by or on behalf of the vendors or any of the group companies to the purchaser or any accountant, lawyer or agent thereof in the course of the negotiations leading to this agreement was when given and is at the date hereof true and accurate in all material respects and so far as such information is expressed as a matter of opinion such opinions are truly and honestly held and not given casually or recklessly, or without due regard for their accuracy. After making all proper enquiries there is to the best of the knowledge information and belief of each of the group companies and the vendors no fact or matter which has not been disclosed in writing to the purchaser which renders such information untrue or misleading (in any material respect) at the date of the agreement or completion or which on the basis of the utmost good faith ought to be disclosed to any intending purchaser of shares in the company or the disclosure of which

might reasonably affect the willingness of a purchaser to purchase the shares on the terms contained herein.

Disclosure letter

2. The information contained in the disclosure letter is true, complete and accurate in all respects.

Recitals and schedules

3. The information set out in the recitals, schedules and annexures to this agreement is true complete and accurate in all respects.

Memorandum and articles of association

4.(A) The Memorandum and Articles of Association of the company is true and complete and embodies therein or has annexed thereto a copy of every resolution or agreement amending or modifying the same and fully set out all rights attaching to each class of the share capital of the company.

Shares

5. The shares constitute the entire issued share capital of the company all of which are registered in the name of and beneficially owned by the vendors. Particulars of the issued share capital of SDL's subsidiaries set out in Schedule II constitute the whole of the issued share capital of such subsidiaries all of which are registered in the name of SDL or nominees on behalf of SDL and all of which are beneficially owned by the SDL. The vendors have good and proper title to and there is no mortgage, charge, pledge, lien or other form of security, encumbrance on, or restriction on transfer over or affecting any of the shares or the shares in any of the other group companies or over any unissued share capital of any of the group companies and there is no agreement or commitment to give any of the foregoing and no claim by any person to be entitled to any of the foregoing.

No options or similar risks

6. There are no options, rights to call for or acquire, pre-emption rights or other agreements or arrangements (including conversion rights) in force in relation to the shares which call or may call for the present or future issue, allotment, or transfer of or accord to any person the right to call for the issue, allotment or transfer of any share or loan capital of any of the group companies or affect the right to transfer the registered and/or beneficial ownership in any shares in the capital of any of the group companies.

No other shares or business

7. Other than as regards the company holding shares in SDL or SDL holding shares in the other group companies none of the group companies are nor have ever been, nor agreed to become, the holder(s) or beneficial owner(s) of any class of the share or other capital of any company or corporation wherever incorporated and none of the group companies is, was or has agreed to become a member of any joint venture or partnership or other unincorporated association (other than trade associations) and none of the group companies have any branch, place of business or any assets outside Ireland.

No issue of shares or loan capital

8. No share or loan capital has been issued or agreed to be issued by any companies since the accounts date of such group company.

Assets

Ownership of assets

9. All the assets (including fixtures, fittings, equipment and vehicles) included in the accounts (and which are not shown therein or in the disclosure letter to be on lease or hire purchase) are the property of the group companies free from encumbrance and on completion all such assets shall be in the possession of the group companies.

No encumbrance

10. There is no option, right to acquire, mortgage, charge, pledge, lien or other form of security or encumbrance or equity on or over or affecting the whole or any part of the assets or undertaking of any of the group companies and there is no agreement or commitment to give or create any of the foregoing and no claim has been made by any person to be entitled to any of the foregoing.

Register of members

11. The register of members of each of the group companies accurately and sufficiently records its members from time to time and none of the group companies have received any notice of any intended application or proceedings to rectify the said register.

Accounts books records etc

12. All the accounts, books, ledgers, financial and other records, of whatsoever kind, of each group company:

(a) have been fully, properly and accurately kept and completed;
(b) do not contain any material inaccuracies or discrepancies of any kind;
(c) give and reflect a true and fair view of its trading transactions, and its financial contractual and trading position.

Insurances

13. The business and assets of each of the group companies of an insurable nature have been adequately and properly insured against loss or injury and all other such risks (including public liability insurance) which in accordance with sound commercial practice should have been insured against by companies carrying on business such as the group companies all such insurances have been, are and will remain in full force and effect up to and including completion. Nothing has been done or omitted to be done which would make any policy of insurance void or voidable and there is no claim outstanding, pending or threatened against any of the group companies by any person in respect of death or injury or loss or damage to property which is not covered by insurance.

Pension and Employees

List of pension schemes

14. The disclosure letter contains a complete and accurate list and a fair summary description of all existing pension schemes ("the pension schemes") of each of the group companies.

No other schemes

15. With the exception of the pension schemes there are not in existence nor has any proposal been announced to establish any retirement, death or disability benefit schemes for officers or employees or any dependent of any of them of any of the group companies nor are there any obligations to or in respect of present or former officers or employees or any dependent of any of them with regard to retirement, death or disability pursuant to which any of the group companies is or may become liable to make payments and no pension or retirement or sickness gratuity is currently being paid or has been promised by any of the group companies to or in respect of any former director or former employee or any dependent of any of them.

Schemes are exempt

16. The Pension Schemes are exempt approved Schemes within the meaning of FA 1972, ss 15 and 16.

Trust deed and rules

17. True copies of all the trust deeds and rules constituting and governing the pension schemes have been delivered to the purchaser and except as may be expressed otherwise therein such documents are up-to-date and satisfactory to ensure continued treatment of the pension schemes as exempt approved schemes as aforesaid.

Explanatory booklets and announcements

18. True copies of all explanatory booklets and announcements and other communications to employees relating to the pension schemes have been delivered to the purchaser and none of the group companies have any obligation under the pension schemes in respect of any present or former employee or director or any dependent of any of them other than under the documents referred to in the above paragraphs.

Employment terms

19. (i) The particulars shown in the schedule of employment annexed to the disclosure letter give full particulars of all collective agreements, customs and practices for the time being dealing with relations between each of the group companies and its employees or any trade union and show the name, job description, age and date of commencement of service of each officer and employee of each of the group companies (all of whom are in the full time employment of the relevant group company) and give details of the wages or salary and all other benefits (including those regarding holidays, bonus entitlements and company cars) and rights to which each officer and employee is entitled or with which they are each provided.

(ii) Pending completion no group companies shall engage or offer to engage or dismiss (whether with or without notice, constructively or otherwise) any officer or employee without the prior written consent of the purchaser.

No commissions

20. There are no schemes in operation by or in relation to any of the group companies whereunder any officer or employee of any group company is entitled to a commission or remuneration of any sort calculated by reference to the whole or part of the turnover, profits or sales of any group company. None of the group companies in existence or are proposing to introduce any share incentive scheme for any of their officers or employees.

Benefit-in- kind

21. No monies other than in respect of remuneration or emoluments of employment are payable by any of the group companies to or for the benefit of any of their officers or executives. None of the group companies have made or agreed to make any payment to, or provided or agreed to provide any benefit for any present or former officer or employee or any dependent of any of them which was not allowable as a deduction for the purposes of taxation.

Termination of employment

22. There are no subsisting contracts of service to which any of the group companies are a party which cannot be terminated by twelve weeks notice or less without giving rise to any claim for damages or compensation other than a statutory redundancy payment or under the Unfair Dismissals Act 1977.

No breach of employment terms

23. No liability has been incurred by any of the group companies for breach of any contract of service or for services or for compensation for wrongful or unfair dismissal or discrimination or for failure to comply with an order for the reinstatement or re-engagement of any employee.

No gratuitous payments

24. No gratuitous payment has been made or promised by any of the group companies in connection with the actual or proposed termination or suspension of employment or variation of any contract of employment of any present or former director or employee.

Litigation and Offences

No Litigation or similar action

25. None of the group companies are engaged in any litigation as plaintiff or defendant or in any criminal or arbitration proceedings or any proceedings before any tribunal or before any enquiry and there are no proceedings of any of the aforesaid kinds pending or threatened either by or against any of the group companies and there are no facts which are likely to give rise thereto nor is there any dispute with any revenue authority in relation to the affairs of any of the group companies.

No breaches

26. None of the group companies are committing or have committed any breach of contract or statutory duty or any law or any tortious or other act which could lead to a successful claim or an injunction being made or granted against it and no event has occurred as regards any of the group companies which would entitle any third party to terminate any contract or call in any money before the normal due date thereof.

No conflicts

27. Each of the group companies are entitled to carry on the business now carried on by it without conflict with any valid rights of any other person and none of the group companies are a party to any joint venture, consortium or other joint partnership arrangement or agreement, and there are no claims against any of the group companies for the breach of any such agreement.

Obligations Contracts, Licences Etc

Obligations

28. None of the group companies are party to or have any liability (present or future) under any deed, debenture, instrument, guarantee, warranty or indemnity of any sort other than those specified in the disclosure letter (full details of which are therein disclosed to the purchaser). None of the group companies are in default or has been called upon to pay under or in respect of any such deed, debenture, instrument, guarantee, warranty or indemnity.

Contracts

29.(A) The disclosure letter contains accurate particulars of all the contracts and other engagements, whether written or oral to which any group company is a party at the date of this agreement which:

(a) is of an unusual or abnormal nature or outside the ordinary and proper course of business;

(b) is of a loss-making nature (that is, known to be lively to result in a loss to it on completion of performance);

(c) involves or is likely to involve the supply of goods the aggregate sales value of which will represent in excess of 10 per cent of its turnover for the preceding financial year;

(d) involves or is likely to involve obligations or liabilities which by reason of their nature or magnitude ought reasonably to be made known to an intending purchaser of the shares;

(e) the vendors or any parent, subsidiary of the vendors or any or person or company associated with the vendors are a party to or entitled to benefit thereunder.

(B) None of the group companies are in default under any such contract agreement or commitment.

(C) Pending completion no such agreement, or commitment will be entered into by any of the group companies.

Restrictions on freedom

30. No agreements or arrangements are in force which in any way restrict the freedom of any of the group companies to conduct their day to day business or which provide for the furnishing, receipt or exchange of information or assistance in relation to the conduct of any of the group companies' businesses.

31. All necessary licences, consents, permits and authorities (public and private) have at all times been obtained by each of the group companies to enable each of them to carry on its business effectively in the places and in the manner in which such business is and has been

from time to time carried on and all such licences, consents, permits and authorities are valid and subsisting and none of the group companies are in breach of any of the terms and conditions thereof and none of the group companies or the vendors know of reason why any of them should be suspended, can revoked.

Disclosure of information

32. None of the group companies and/or the vendors have disclosed or permitted to be disclosed, or undertaken or arranged to disclose, confidential information or lists of customers or suppliers to any person.

Restrictive practices/EEC

33. To the best of the vendors' information, knowledge and belief, there are no proceedings, claims, enquiries, or investigations whatsoever threatened or pending against any of the group companies in respect of or in connection with or arising from the Restrictive Practices Act 1972, the Restrictive Practices (Amendment) Act 1987 or Articles 85 or 86 of the Treaty of Rome and there is no agreement, arrangement or concerted practice which has been notified to the Commission of the European Communities for an exemption or in respect of which an application has been made for negative clearance.

Consumer protection legislation

34. No practices, procedure, labelling, packaging, arrangement or form of agreement followed, adopted or used by any of the group companies or any of their agents in the course of their business contravenes in any way any provision of the Merchandise Marks Acts 1887 to 1970, the Consumer Information Act 1978, The Packaged Goods (Quality Control) Act 1980, The Dangerous Substances Acts 1972 to 1979, The Hire Purchase Acts 1946 to 1960, the Sale of Goods and Supply of Services Act 1980, the European Communities Act 1972 or any applicable regulation or directive of the European Commission.

Customers

35. No group company has within two years prior to the date hereof been and is not in prospect of being materially and adversely affected by the loss of any important customer or supplier or by any abnormal factor relating to a customer or supplier or by any dispute or matter which would affect the relationship of it with any of its customers or suppliers or any trade association to which it belongs or is a member thereof.

Debtors

36. Excluding the bad and doubtful debts for which full and adequate provision was made in the accounts all advances to customers and other accounts and all book debts of each of the group companies on completion will be good for the full face value thereof and will be paid in the ordinary course of business within three calendar months after completion or one month after the expiration of normal credit terms whichever is the later.

Position since the accounts dates

37.(a) Since the accounts dates:

(i) there has been no material adverse change in the turnover profits financial position or prospects of SDL or any of its subsidiaries or of the company.

(ii) the business of the SDL and etch of its subsidiaries has been continued so as to maintain the same as a going concern and in its ordinary and usual course and without prejudice to the generality of the foregoing the policies and practices as regards capital expenditure, trade, debts, prepaid expenses, stocks of raw materials and spare parts, trade and expense creditors and accrued trade expenses have not b or altered in any way;

(iii) SDL nor any of its subsidiaries have not done or omitted to do anything to prejudice their goodwill;

(iv) SDL and each of its subsidiaries have paid their creditors in accordance with their respective credit terms;

(v) the trading prospects of SDL and each of its subsidiaries have not been adversely affected as a result of any event or circumstance;

(vi) there has not been any damage, destruction or loss (whether or not covered by insurance) affecting the assets of SDL, any of its subsidiaries or of the company or of any of their businesses;

(vii) there has not been and there is not threatened any labour trouble, strike or other occurrence event or condition of a similar character which adversely affects or may hereafter adversely affect the assets, properties, business or prospects of SDL or any of its subsidiaries;

(viii) none of SDL nor any of its subsidiaries nor the company have disposed of any part of their or any of their assets or assumed or incurred any material liabilities (including contingent liabilities), except in the ordinary and proper course of is business;

(ix) none of SDL nor any of its subsidiaries nor the company have paid or agreed to pay or provide to their or any of their officers or employees any increase in fees, remuneration or benefits;

(x) none of SDL nor any of its subsidiaries nor the company have released any debtor on terms that he pays less than the book value of his debt (except for settlement discounts on the usual terms which have been disclosed to the purchaser in writing) and no debt owing to any of the group companies has been deferred, subordinated or written off or has proved to any extent irrecoverable;

(xi) no dividend or other distribution has been or is treated as having been declared made or paid by SDL any of its subsidiaries or by the company; and

(xii) The business of SDL or any of its subsidiaries has not been materially and adversely affected by the loss of any important customer or source of supply or by any abnormal factor not affecting similar businesses to a like extent and after making due and careful enquiries none of the warrantors is aware of any facts likely to affect such company is manner.

(b) The consolidated net asset value of SDL and its subsidiaries is not and as not been less than the amount of the net consolidated asset value of SDL and each of its subsidiaries as at the 29 September 1989.

Vendors other interests and liabilities to group companies

38.(a) The vendors do not have any rights or interests, directly or indirectly, in any business other than those now carried on by the group companies which are or are likely to be or become competitive with the businesses of the group companies, save as registered holder or beneficial owner of any class of securities of any company which is listed on the stock exchange or dealt in on the unlisted securities market, and in respect of which a vendor holds and is beneficially interested in less than 5 per cent of any single class of the securities in the company;

(b) There is no outstanding amount due by any of the vendors to any of the group companies or by any of the group companies to any of the vendors.

Accounts

Accuracy of accounts

39. The accounts are true and fair in all respects and have been prepared in accordance with the Companies Acts and other applicable statutes and regulations and on a consistent basis and in accordance with good and current accounting standards including (without limitations) the statements of standard accounting practice of the Institute of Chartered Accountants in Ireland and to the extent required by such standards:

(a) set out fairly the assets and liabilities of each of the group companies and the amounts thereof and show a true and fair view of the financial position of each of the group companies and of the results of each of the group companies for the financial years/periods ended on dates referred to therein and of the profit or losses for the periods ending on such dates;

(b) make adequate provision for depreciation of the fixed assets of the each of the group companies having regard to their original cost and estimated life;

(c) include no intangible assets except for goodwill at IR£181,000;

(d) make full provision for all liabilities and capital commitments in the case of SDL and its subsidiaries as at the 29 September 1989 and in the case of the company as at the 31 December 1989 including contingent, unquantified or disputed liabilities;

(e) contain in accordance with generally accepted accounting standards either provisions therein adequate to cover or essential particulars in notes thereto of all liabilities of each of the group companies (whether qualified, contingent, unascertained or otherwise);

(f) make full provision or reserve for taxation anticipated to be due from or to be assessed on each of the group companies.

(g) make reasonable provision or reserve for deferred taxation in accordance with generally accepted accounting principles and standard as of their respective dates;

(h) do not take account of any revaluations of the fixed assets of any of the group companies;

(i) include all stock-in-trade and work-in-progress of each of the group companies at the lower of cost or net realisable value and write off all redundant, obsolete and slow-moving stock-in-trade; and

(j) have been prepared in accordance with the same accounting principles and bases and valuing stock and raw materials in the same manner as have been applied in prior years.

Guarantees, charges etc

40. The accounts disclose all loans, guarantees, indemnities, mortgages, charges, debentures, or unusual liabilities (including contingent liabilities) which have been given or

made or incurred by or assigned to or vested in or were outstanding on behalf of each of the group companies.

Capital commitments

41. None of the group companies have any commitments on capital account outstanding at the accounts dates and since the accounts dates none have been created and none will be created prior to completion.

No liabilities

42. The group companies have at the accounts dates no liabilities (absolute, accrued, contingent or otherwise), other than those included in the accounts and since the accounts dates no such liabilities have been incurred other than in the ordinary course of business.

No extraordinary items

43. The financial position and profits shown by the accounts have not (except as therein disclosed) to a material extent been affected by any extraordinary or exceptional items or by inconsistencies of accounting practice or by the inclusion of non-recurring items of income or expenditure or by transactions entered into otherwise than on normal commercial terms or by any other factor rendering such financial position and profits unusually good or bad or high or low as the case may be.

Net asset value

44. On completion the total value of the net assets of the group companies shall not be less than that shown by the accounts.

Taxation

45.(a) Without prejudice to the generality of any other provision of the warranties, all liabilities (whether actual, contingent or disputed) of each group company for taxation as at accounts dates are fully provided for in the relevant group company's accounts;

(b) No group company has since the accounts dates made nor is to be regarded as having given any such loan or advance as is mentioned in CTA 1976 s 98 (loans to participators) nor has any group company since the accounts dates made any relevant payment (within the meaning of CTA 1976 s 151 and pending completion no such loan, advance or relevant payment will be made or given;

(c) all taxation of any nature whatsoever or other sums imposed, charged, assessed, levied or payable under the provisions of applicable legislation relating to taxation for which the company is liable as a result of any act or omission by the company prior to completion wig if and insofar as such taxation or other sums ought to be paid prior to or on completion have been paid at or before completion and in particular but without prejudice to the generality of the foregoing at completion all amounts for due payment to the Revenue Commissioners in respect of value added tax or in respect of goods imported or in respect of income tax deductible under Schedule F or in respect of the PAYE regulations from time to time in force will have been paid by the relevant due dates and at completion all social welfare and pay related social insurance (PRSI) contributions (both employer's and employees') due in respect of the employees of the company will have been duly pad on their due payment date;

(d) each group company has for each accounting period up to and including the accounting period ending on the accounts dates furnished the company's Inspector of Taxes with full and accurate particulars relating to the affairs of the company, and has also within the prescribed periods of time made all returns given or delivered all notices accounts and information required for the purpose of taxation and all such have been correct in all material respects and on a proper basis and none such are disputed by the Revenue Commissioners or other authority concerned and there are no grounds or circumstances which might cause any such dispute;

(e) no group company is liable and has not at any time since the accounts dates been liable to pay interest on overdue taxation;

(f) no group company owns any shares or securities acquired as a "new holding" under the provisions of CGTA 1975 Sch 2 para 2-5;

(g) no group company has at any time:

  (i) repaid or redeemed or agreed to repay or redeem any shares of any class of its share capital or otherwise reduced or agreed to reduce its issued share capital or any class thereof; or

  (ii) capitalised or agreed to capitalise in the form of shares, debentures or other securities or in paying up any amounts unpaid on any shares debentures or other securities any profits or reserves of any class or description or passed or agreed to pass any resolution to do so; or

  (iii) provided capital to any company on terms whereby the company so capitalised has in consideration thereof issued shares, loan-stock or other securities where the terms of any such capitalisation were otherwise than by way of a bargain made at arm's length or where the shares, loan-stock or other securities acquired are shown in the accounts at a value in excess of their market value at the time of acquisition;

(h) no person is liable to capital acquisitions tax attributable to the value of any of the shares and in consequence no person has the power to raise the amount of such tax by sale or mortgage of or by a terminable charge on any of the shares;

(i) no group company has been a party to or involved in any share for share exchange nor any scheme or reconstruction or amalgamation such as are mentioned in CGTA 1975 Sch 2 and CTA 1976 s 127 under which shares or debentures have been issued or any transfer of assets effected;

(j) no act or transaction has been effected, nor will have been effected prior to completion, in consequence of which any group company is or may become liable for any taxation primarily chargeable against some other company;

(k) no group company has acquired or disposed of any asset or entered into any transaction otherwise than by way of bargain at arm's length;

(l) no group company has entered into any financing or leasing agreement in which or in connection with which it has indemnified any other party against any claim, loss or other liability arising from any change in taxation legislation or in the interpretation of taxation legislation;

(m) there are set out in the disclosure letter full particulars of all difference between the accounting and taxation treatments of all items in the 19[ ] accounts and the audited accounts for each of the three preceding financial years;

(n) there has not been in respect of any accounting period ended prior to the accounts dates any excess of distributable investment or distributable income within the meaning of CTA 1976 s 100.

(o) where full provision for deferred taxation (in accordance with standard statement of accounting practice No 15 of the Institute of Chartered Accountants in Ireland) is not made in the accounts full details of the amounts have been disclosed in the disclosure letter.

(p) No group company has any liability arising out of the provisions of FA 1983 ss 44 to 48 (advance corporation tax), FA 1983 s 56 (chargeable gains - secondary liability), FA 1983 s 97 (revenue offences), FA 1970 s 17 (sub-contractors tax).

(q) where fixed assets have been stated in the accounts in excess of their cost any potential liability to corporation tax on chargeable gains that would accrue on the sale of these assets at their values stated are either provided for in the deferred tax account or are disclosed by way of note in the accounts.

The properties

46.(a) The properties described in Schedule V hereto comprise all the lands and buildings owned leased or occupied by the company and Schedule V contains full particulars of the title of each group company thereto.

(b) The group companies have a good and marketable title to the properties and have in their possession or under their control all relevant deeds and documents and where the title to the properties is registered in the Land Registry it is so registered with absolute title.

(c) The present user of the properties is that permitted under the Local Government (Planning & Development) Acts 1963 to 1983 ("the Planning Acts") and all conditions attached to any permission thereunder have been complied with and no use or development thereof or building, erection or improvement thereon or disposal or effluent or waste therefrom in any way contravenes the Planning Acts the Local Government (water Pollution) Act 1977, the European Communities Act 1972 or any bye-laws or building regulations or other relevant and applicable legislation or creates any nuisance to any person.

Schedule VIII The Loan Notes

Dated ______________ February 1990

SIUICRE ÉIREANN cpt

INSTRUMENT

Constituting

Certificate No *Amount of*

£

Issued pursuant to a Resolution of the Board of Directors of SIUICRE ÉIREANN cpt having its registered office at St Stephens Green House, Dublin 2 passed on February 1990.

NAME:

ADDRESS:

This is to certify that the above-mentioned is/are the registered holder(s) of IR£ ___ in nominal amount of the loan notes of Siuicre Éireann cpt. The holders of the loan notes entitled to the benefit of, and are subject to the conditions hereinafter contained

Given under the common seal of SIUICRE ÉIREANN cpt

Dated

Note or any part thereof is transferable or assignable by any noteholder.

Conditions of issue

In these conditions unless there be something in the subject matter or context inconsistent therewith:

"Company":	Siuicre Éireann cpt
"Interest Payment Date":	1st day of November and the 1st day of May each year

2. (a) If the loan notes are not redeemed on or after the 31 October 1991 the company will pay to the noteholder's interest (less any applicable tax) on the principal amount of the loan notes outstanding at a rate equal to the Dublin Inter Bank Offered Rate for six month funds ("DIBOR") calculated on the relevant interest payment date in respect of the six months beginning on and including an Interest Payment Date and ending on but excluding the next following interest date (and "interest period") save that in respect of any part of a loan note redeemed prior to any interest payment date interest shall cease to be payable in respect of such redeemed part of the loan note as and from such date of redemption.

(b) Interest payable hereunder shall accrue from day to day and be computed on the basis of a year of 365 days and the actual number or days elapsed in each relevant interest period.

(c) Whenever any payment hereunder shall become due on a day which is not a week day on which clearing banks in Dublin are open for normal banking business (a "business day") payment shall be made on the next succeeding business day but no adjustment shall be made to the amount of interest payable for the relevant interest period.

(d) In the event that the company shall fail to pay to the noteholders any sum due and payable hereunder on the date on which such sum is expressed to be due and payable pursuant to these conditions the company shall (without prejudice to all other rights and remedies of the noteholders in respect of such failure) pay to the noteholders interest at DIBOR on such overdue amount from the date of such failure up to the date of actual payment (as well after as before judgment) calculated on a day to day basis for so long as such amount remains unpaid in full.

3. The following provisions shall have effect as to the repayment of the loan notes:

(a) noteholders may elect at any time to have loan notes redeemed in whole or in part by giving to the company not less than 30 days notice stating the amount of the loan notes they lavish to have redeemed; the earliest date for redemption shall be 1 November 1991 and the latest date for redemption shall be 31 October 1997; loan notes not redeemed by 31 October 1997 shall be redeemed in full on that date;

(b) the principal amount of any loan note then outstanding shall immediately become repayable on demand together with interest accrued thereon (subject to deduction of any applicable tax) in accordance with condition 2 above up to the date of actual repayment upon the happening of any of the following events:

(i) the company failing to pay interest in respect of any loan note within 28 days of the date for payment thereof;

(ii) the company failing to pay within 28 days of the due date for payment any part of the principal amount of any loan note;

(iii) an order is made or an effective resolution is passed for the winding-up of the company or the guarantor (other than a voluntary winding-up for the purpose of amalgamation or reconstruction); or

(iv) an encumbrances shall take possession or a receiver shall be appointed over the whole or any substantial part of the assets or undertaking of the company or the guarantor.

4. The company shall give notice in writing to each of the noteholders of the happening of the events specified in conditions 3(b)(iii) or (iv) above.

5. Any loan notes repaid or purchased by the company shall forthwith be cancelled and shall not be available for re-issue.

6. Every noteholder will be entitled without charge to one certificate stating the amount of the loan notes held by him, every certificate shall bear a serial number and refer to the instrument. Joint holders of loan notes will be entitled only to one certificate in respect of the loan notes held by them jointly and the same will be delivered the first named of such of the joint holders unless all such joint holder otherwise specify in writing.

7. A register of holders of the loan notes will be kept by the company at its registered office or at such other place in the Republic of Ireland as it may from time to time decide, and there shall be entered in such register:

(a) The names and addresses of the holders for the time being of the loan notes;

(b) the nominal amount of the loan notes held by every registered holder; and

(c) the date at which the name of every such registered holder is entered in respect of the loan notes standing in his name.

Any change of address on the part of the noteholder shall forthwith be notified to the company in writing and thereupon the register shall be altered accordingly. A noteholder and any person authorised by any noteholder shall be at liberty at all reasonable times during office hours to inspect the register.

8. Except in the case of the death of a noteholder no loan note or any part thereof shall be transferable or assignable by any noteholder.

9. The company shall be entitled provided it guarantees repayment at its discretion to assign any or all of its obligations and rights relating to the loan notes and the noteholder consents to such assignment, as soon as practicable after such assignment the company shall give notice thereof to the noteholder at the address recorded for such noteholder in the register of holders of loan notes.

10. Except as provided by statute or as required by any order of a Court of competent jurisdiction, the company shall recognise the registered holder of any loan note as the absolute owner thereof, and shall not be bound to take notice of, or to see to the execution of, any trust whether express, implied or constructive to which any loan note may be subject, and the receipt of such person (or in the case of joint holdings of any one of such

holders) for the interest on, or for the moneys payable upon the repayment of, the same shall be a good discharge to the company notwithstanding any notice it may have, whether express or otherwise of the right, title, interest or claim of any other person to or in such loan note or interest or moneys. No notice of any trust, express, implied or constructive shall (except as aforesaid) be entered on the register in respect of any loan note.

11. Subject to Clause 14 the executors or administrators of a deceased holder of a loan note (not being one of several joint holders) shall be the only persons recognised by the company as having any title to or interest in such loan note.

12. In the case of the death of any of the joint holders of a loan note the survivor(s) shall be the only person(s) recognised by the company as having any title to or interest on such loan note.

13. Any person becoming entitled to any loan note in consequence of the death or bankruptcy of any holder of such loan note may, upon producing such evidence of his title as the directors shall think sufficient, be registered himself as the holder of such loan note.

14. Any interest or other moneys payable on or in respect of any loan note may be paid by cheque or warrant sent though the post to the registered address of the holder or in the case of joint holdings, to the registered address of that one of such joint holders who is the first named on the register or to such person and at such address as the holder or joint holders may in writing from time to time direct. Every such cheque or warrant shall be to the satisfaction of the monies represented thereby. Every such cheque or warrant shall be sent at the risk of the persons entitled to the monies represented thereby.

15. If any certificate be worn out or defaced then, upon production thereof to the directors, they may cancel the same and may issue a new certificate in lieu thereof, and if any such certificate be lost or destroyed then upon proof thereof to the satisfaction of the directors, or in default of proof on such indemnity as the directors may deem adequate being given, a new certificate in lieu thereof may be given to the persons entitled to such lost or destroyed certificate. An entry as to the issue of a new certificate and indemnity (if any) shall be made in the register.

Given under the common seal of SIUICRE ÉIREANN cpt was affixed hereto:

Sugar Distributors (Holdings) Limited

Report and Financial Statements for the 52 Weeks ended 29 September 1989

Contents

2 Directors and other information
3 Directors' report
4 Auditors' report
5 Profit and loss account
6 Balance sheet
7 Statement of source and application of funds
8 Notes and accounting policies management information
13 Detailed profit and loss account

Directors and other information

Directors	C K Comerford (Chairman)
	C M Lyons (Managing Director)
	C P Garavan
	J P Gray
	T G Keleghan
	M Tully
Secretary	M Tully
Registered Office	Athy Road
	Carlow
Auditors	Pannell Kerr Forster, 17 Percy Place, Dublin 4
Solicitors	M J Horgan & Sons 50 South Mall Cork
Bankers	Allied Irish Banks plc
	Ulster Bank Limited

Directors' report

The directors submit their report together with the audited financial statements for the 52 weeks ended 29 September 1989.

1. Results and dividends

The profit for the period amounts to IR£246,811 which has been transferred to reserves. The directors do not recommend the payment dividend.

2. Review of the business and future developments

The principal activity of the company during the period continued to the marketing of sugar, other foods and products and the management group activities. The directors anticipate that any future development would relate to these activities.

3. Events since the period end

There have been no significant events since the balance sheet date would affect the company.

4. Group companies

The information concerning group companies, as required by CA 1986 s 16, is set out in Note 8 of the financial statement.

On 29 September 1989, 66,351 ordinary IR£1 shares were sold Tanktrade Limited. The company bought and sold during the period, its interest in Gaywood Sugars Limited. During the period the company bought shares in subsidiary and associated companies as follows:

	Date of acquisition	*Number*	*Description*
William McKinney (1975) Ltd	11/1/89	5,000	Ord £1 share
Chambers & Sons Ltd	23/3/89	255,000	Ord £1 share
James Budgett & Son Ltd	17/5/89	83,333	Ord £1 share
Milltown Packaging Co Ltd	28/6/89	10	Ord £1 share

Directors

Mr JF Punch, Mr TH O'Neill and Mr HN McKeown resigned on 8 December 1988. Mr JM Lepere resigned as a director and chairman on 14 April 1989. Mr CK Comerford was appointed chairman on 4 July 1989

Auditors

The auditors, Pannell Kerr Forster, have indicated their willingness to be reappointed under CA 1963 s 160(2).

By order of the Board on 7 December 1989
Directors C K Comerford, C M Lyons

Auditors' report to the members

We have audited the financial statements on pages 5 to 12 in accordance with auditing standards.

In our opinion the financial statements give a true and fair view of the state of the company's affairs at 29 September 1989 and of its profit and source and application of funds for the period then ended and give, in requisite manner, the information required by the Companies Acts 1963 to 1986.

The net assets of the company, as stated in the balance sheet on page 6 are more than half of the amount of its called-up share capital and, in our opinion, on that basis there did not exist at 29 September 1989 a financial situation which under the Companies (Amendment) Act 1983 s 40(1) would require the convening of an extraordinary general meeting of the company.

In our opinion the information given in the directors' report on page 3 is consistent with the financial statements.

We have obtained all the information and explanations we considered necessary for the purposes of our audit. In our opinion proper books of account have been kept by the company. The financial statements are in agreement with the books of account.

Pannell Kerr Forster, Chartered Accountants

Dublin December 1989

Profit and loss account 52 weeks ended 29 September 1989

	Notes	*1989*
		IR£
Operating loss	2	(36,575)
Interest receivable and Similar income	4	457,226
Interest payable and similar charges	4	(76,493)
Profit on ordinary activities	5	344,158
Tax on profit on ordinary activities	6	(97,347)
Profit on ordinary activities after taxation		246,811
Extraordinary Item	7	-
Profit for the period		246,811
Movements on profit and loss account		

At beginning of period	90,426
Profit for the period	246,811
At end of period	337,237

CK Comerford, C M Lyons, Directors

Balance sheet 29 September 1989

	Notes		1989
		IR£	IR£
Fixed assets			
Financial assets	8		2,777,729
Current assets			
Debtors	9	900	
Cash at bank and in hand		38	
		938	
Creditors: amounts falling due within one year	10	653,709	
Net current liabilities			(652,771)
Total assets less current liabilities			2,124,958
Creditors: amounts falling due after more than one year	10		1,287,721
Capital and reserves			
Called up share capital	11		500,000
Profit and loss account			337,237
			2,124,958

Approved by the board on 7 December 1989

Directors: K Comerford, CM Lyons

Statement of source and application of funds 52 weeks ended 29 September 1989

		1989
	IR£	IR£
Source of funds		
Profit on ordinary activities before taxation		344,158
Adjustment for items not involving the movement of funds:		
Write back of provision for inter-company loans and balances	(50,000)	
Profit on disposal of subsidiary	(1,000)	
Write off of investment in subsidiary	5,000	
Tax credit on dividends receivable	(97,222)	
		(143,222)
Total generated from operations		200,936
Funds from other sources		
Sale of associated company		-

Sale of subsidiary company	1,000	
		1,000
Application of funds		
Tax paid	228	
Investment in subsidiary companies	333,987	
Investment in associated company	2,646,688	
		2,980,903
		(2,778,967)
Movement in working capital		
Debtors	(2,185)	
Creditors	(1,936,430)	
Amount due from subsidiary companies	(840,363)	
		(2,778,978)
Movement in net liquid funds		
Bank balances and cash		11
		(2,778,967)

Notes and accounting policies 52 weeks ended 29 September 1989

1. Accounting policies

(a) *Historical cost convention* The financial statements have been prepared under the historical cost convention.

(b) *Pensions* Annual contributions are based on actuarial advice obtained at intervals of five years and are charged to the profit and loss account on an accruals basis.

2. Operating loss

	1989
	IR£
Management fees	254,002
Administrative expenses	(290,577)
Operating loss	(36,575)
Analysis of staff costs	
Wages and salaries	114,104
Social welfare costs	6,784
Pension costs	11,677
	132,565

	Number
Average number employed in the period	3

3. Interest receivable and similar income

	1989
	IR£
Interest on overpayment of tax	-
Dividends receivable from group companies	347,222

Interest from group companies	110,004
	457,226

4. Interest payable and similar charges

	1989
	IR£
Interest payable on bank borrowings repayable within five years	
	76,493

5. Profit on ordinary activities before taxation is shown after charging/(crediting)

	1989
	IR£
Directors' remuneration:- for services as directors	132,565
Auditors remuneration	16,000
Provision for inter-company loans	(50,000)
Loss on disposal of associated company	-
Profit on disposal of subsidiary	(1,000)

6. Taxation

	1989
	IR£
Based on profit on ordinary activities	
Corporation Tax at 45% (1988 at 48 ½%)	-
Underprovision in previous period	125
	125
Tax credit applicable to dividends receivable from group companies	
	97,222
	97,347

7. Extraordinary item

	1989
	IR£
Loss on disposal of associated company	-

8. Financial fixed assets

	1989
	IR£
Group companies - unlisted	
Shares at cost	381,435
Additions	333,987
Disposals	(66,351)
Amounts written off	(188,012)
Amounts owed (to)/by group companies	461,059
	(379,240)

	1989
	IR£
	81,819
Associated companies - unlisted	
Shares at cost	102,797
Additions	2,646,688
Amounts written off	(53,575)
	2,695,910
	2,777,729

In the opinion of the directors the value to the company of the unlisted investments is not less than the book amount shown above.

Subsidiary company	*Nature Of Business*	*Percentage Owned*	*Registered Office*
Sugar Distributors Ltd	Wholesalers	100	Carlow
Sugar Distributors (Export) Ltd	Exporters	100	Carlow
ISM (Investments) Ltd	Finance Co	100	Carlow
Hyspin Ltd	Non trading	100	Carlow
Fleet Care Ltd	Non trading	100	Carlow
Lumley Packers Ltd	Non trading	90	Carlow
Milltown Packaging Co Ltd	Wholesalers	100	Carlow
Trilby Trading Ltd	Food industry suppliers	51	Drogheda
Gosford Ltd	Food industry suppliers	51	Belfast
Wm McKinney (1975) Ltd	Wholesalers	70	Belfast
Trilby Commodity Trading Ltd	Food industry suppliers	100	Jersey
Chambers & Sons Ltd	Wholesalers	51	Belfast
Associated companies			
James Budgett & Son Ltd	Wholesalers	33 1/3	London
Cregagh Foods Ltd	Wholesalers	49	Belfast
Tanktrans Ltd	Specialist tank haulage	49	Carlow

All of the above companies are incorporated in the Republic of Ireland with the exception of Wm McKinney (1975) Limited, Chambers & Sons Limited and Cregagh Foods Limited which are incorporated in Northern Ireland, Trilby Commodity Trading Limited which is incorporated in Jersey and James Budgett & Son Limited which is incorporated in England. All shares in subsidiary and associated companies consist of ordinary shares.

Sugar Distributors (Export) Limited and ISM (Investments) Limited, who are wholly owned subsidiaries of the company have availed of the exemption available under the Companies (Amendment) Act 1986 s 17, whereby they will annex the group financial statements to their annual return rather than their own.

9. Debtors

	1989
	IR£
Prepayments and accrued income	900
All debtors are due within one year	

10. Creditors

	1989
	IR£
Amounts falling due within one year:	
Bank loans	633,00
Corporation tax	-
Accruals and deferred income	20,709
	653,709
Amounts falling due after more than one year:	
Bank loans repayable within five years	1,287,721

11. Called up share capital

	1989
Authorised, allotted, called up and fully paid:	IR£
A Ordinary shares of IR£1 each	245,000
B Ordinary shares of IRE1 each	255,000
	500,000

12. Pensions

The company operates an externally funded defined benefit contributory pension scheme for the majority of employees. The most recent actuarial review was undertaken as at 1 February 1986. The actuarial report is not available for public inspection. The advice of a professionally qualified actuary is taken in assessing pension costs and liabilities.

13. Holding company

The company is a member of the Siuicre Éireann cpt group of companies.

Detailed profit and loss account
52 weeks ended 29 September 1989

Income	1989
	IR£
Management fees receivable	254,002
Expenditure	
Profit on disposal of subsidiary	(1,000)
Write off investments	5,000
Audit fees and expenses	13,985
Professional fees	855
Pensions	61,400
Legal	47,414
Consultancy	92,035
Provision for inter-company loans and balances	(50,000)
Directors' salaries	120,888
	290,577
Operating Loss	(36,575)

Gladebrook Company Limited

Report and Financial Statements for the Period ended 30 June 1989

Contents

2 Directors and other information
3 Directors' report
4 Auditors' report
5 Profit and loss account
6 Balance sheet
7 Notes and accounting policies

Directors and other information

Directors:	C Caravan
	T Keleghan
	C Lyons
	M Tully
Secretary:	M Tully
Registered Office	50 South Mall Cork
Auditors:	Pannell Kerr Forster 17 Percy Place Dublin 4
Solicitors:	M J Horgan & Sons 50 South Mall Cork
Bankers:	Allied Irish Banks plc

Directors' report

The directors submit their report together with the audited financial statements for the period from incorporation to 30 June 1989.

Results and Dividends

Loss on ordinary activities after tax for the period amounted to IR£89,899. Dividends were paid or proposed and, accordingly, this amount is retained in the profit and loss account.

Review of the business

The company, which was incorporated on 25 July 1988, acts as an investment holding company.

Events since the period end

There have been no significant events since the balance sheet date which would affect the company.

Related company

The company's only related company is Sugar Distributors (Holdings) Limited

Directors

The directors are not required to retire by rotation.

Auditors

The auditors, Pannell Kerr Forster, have indicated their willingness to be re-appointed under the Companies Act 1963, 160(6)(b).

By order of the Board
Directors: M Tully, T Keleghan 8 February 1990

Auditors' report to the members

We have audited the financial statements on pages 5 to 9 in accordance with auditing standards.

In our opinion, the financial statements give a true and fair view of the state of the company's affairs at 30 June 1989 and of its loss for the period then ended and give, in requisite manner, the information required by the Companies Acts 1963 to 1986.

The balance sheet on page 6 shows an excess of liabilities over assets and, in our opinion, on that basis there existed at 30 June 1989, a financial situation which under the Companies (Amendment) Act 1983 s 40(1), would require the convening of an extraordinary general meeting of the company.

In our opinion, the information given in the directors' report on page 3 is consistent with the financial statements.

We have obtained all the information and explanations we considered necessary for the purposes of our audit. In our opinion, proper books of account have been kept by the company. The financial statements are in agreement with the books of account.

Dublin
3 February 1990
Pannell Kerr Forster Chartered Accountants

Balance sheet as at 30 June 1989

	Notes		*30 June 1989*
		IR£	*IR£*
Fixed assets			
Financial assets	5		1,701,850
Current assets			
Cash at bank and in hand		127,939	
Creditors: Amounts falling due within one year	6	1,909,688	
Net current liabilities			(1,781,749)
Total-assets less current liabilities			(79,899)
Share capital	7		10,000
Profit and loss account			(89,899)
			(79,899)

Approved by the board on 8 February 1990
Directors: M Tully, T Keleghan

Notes and accounting policies for the period ended 30 June 1989

1. Accounting policies

(a) Historical cost convention: The financial statements are prepared under the historical cost convention.

(b) Income from shares in related companies: Income from shares in related companies is taken to the profits and loss account on a cash receipts basis.

2. Interest payable and similar charges

	30 June 1989
	IR£
Payable on bank borrowings repayable within five years	30,000
Interest receivable	

3. Loss on ordinary activities before taxation

This is arrived at after charging: Auditors' remuneration	30,000

4. Tax on loss on ordinary activities

Corporation tax based on tax adjusted profits for the period	30,000

5. Financial fixed assets

Shares in unlisted related company at cost	1,701,850

In the opinion of the directors the value of the shares in the unlisted related company is not less than the amount stated above.

The shares in the unlisted related company comprise 49% of the issued ordinary share capital of Sugar Distributors (Holdings) Limited, a company engaged in the marketing and distribution of sugar and other food products and having its registered office at Athy Road, Carlow.

Sugar Distributors (Holdings) Limited prepares its annual financial statements up to the last working day in September The directors consider - that it would involve expense and delay out of proportion to the value to the members to prepare consolidated financial statements under the equity method of accounting.

The aggregate amount of capital and reserves of Sugar Distributors (Holdings) Limited at its last accounting date, 30 September 1988, amounted to IR£2,944,000 and its loss for the financial year then ended, amounted to IR£247,000.

6. Creditors: amounts falling due within one year

	30 June 1989
	IR£
Bank loan	850,000
Amount due to related company	1,000,000
Accruals and deferred income	58,886
Corporation tax	802
	1,909,688

The bank loan is secured by guarantees from the directors and by equitable deposit of the ordinary shares which the company holds in Sugar Distributors (Holdings) Limited.

The amount due to the related company is subordinated in favour of any amounts outstanding on the bank loan.

7. Share capital

Authorised:	
Ordinary shares of IR£1 each	1,000,000
Allotted, called up and fully paid: Ordinary shares of IR£1 each	10,000

During the period the company issued 10,000 ordinary shares of IR£1 each.

8. Contingent liability

There is a legal case pending against the company in respect of an indemnity which the company has given to Allied Irish Banks plc in respect of a cheque for a specified amount to be drawn on the bank by a third party. A cheque for such an amount was subsequently drawn on the bank by a fourth party and the bank is now seeking to enforce the indemnity. The company holds that its indemnity was not intended to cover the fourth party concerned and, consequently, does not have any liability.

The financial statements do not include provision in respect of any liability which may ultimately be payable by the company. The directors consider that a liability will not materalise for the company in respect of this claim, and that in any event, the worst possible outcome for the company is IR£50,000.

Management Accounts for the Period ended 31 December 1989

Contents

2 Directors and other information
3 Auditors' report to the members
4 Profit and loss account
5 Balance sheet
6 Notes and accounting policies

Directors and other information

Directors:	C Caravan
	T Keleghan
	C Lyons
	M Tully
Secretary:	M Tully
Registered Office	50 South Mall Cork
Auditors:	Pannell Kerr Forster 17 Percy Place Dublin 4
Solicitors:	M J Horgan & Sons 50 South Mall Cork
Bankers:	Allied Irish Banks plc

Auditors' report to the members

We have audited the financial statements on pages 4 to 8 in accordance with Auditing Standards.

In our opinion, the financial statements give a true and fair view of the state of the company's affairs at 31 December 1989 and of its profit for the period then ended.

We have obtained all the information and explanations we considered necessary for the purposes of our audit. In our opinion, proper books of account have been kept by the company. The financial statements are in agreement with books of account.

Dublin

8 February 1990

Pannell Kerr Forster Chartered Accountant

Profit and loss account for the period ended 31 December 1989

	Notes	*6 Months ended 31 Dec 1989*	*49 Weeks ended 30 June 1989*
		IR£	*IR£*
Administrative expenses		(20,820)	(51,370)
Income from shares in related companies		150,000	(36,029)
Interest payable and similar charges	2	(44,862)	-
Profit/(loss) on ordinary activities before taxation	3	84,318	(87,399)
Tax on profit/(loss) on ordinary activities	4	(3,000)	(2,500)
Profit/(loss) on ordinary activities after taxation		81,318	(89,899)
Balance at beginning of period		(89,899)	-
Balance at end of period		(8,581)	(89,899)

Directors: M Tully, T Keleghan

	Notes	*31 December 1989*		*30 June 1989*	
		IR£	*IR£*	*IR£*	*IR£*
Fixed assets					
Financial assets	5		1,701,850		1,701,850
Current assets					
Debtors	6	1,038		-	
Cash at bank and in hand		217,653		127,939	
		218,691		127,939	
Creditors amounts falling due within one year	7	1,919,122		1,090,688	
Net current liabilities			(1,700,431)		(1,781,749)
Total assets less current liabilities			1,419		(79,899)
Share capital	8		10,000		10,000
Profit and loss account			(8,581)		(89,899)
			1,419		(79,899)

Approved by the board on 8 February 1990

Directors M Tully, T Keleghan

Notes and accounting policies for the period ended 31 December 1989

1. Accounting policies

(a) Historical cost convention: The financial statements are prepared under the historical cost convention

(b) Income from shares in related companies is taken to the profit and loss account on a cash receipts basis.

2. Interest payable and similar

	31 December 1989	30 June 1989
	IR£	IR£
Payable on bank borrowings repayable five years	51,988	41,323
Interest receivable	(7,126)	(5,294)
	44,862	36,029

3. Profit/(loss) on ordinary activities before taxation

	31 December 1989	30 June 1989
	IR£	IR£
This is arrived at after charging:		
Auditors' remuneration	375	375

Tax on profit/(loss) on ordinary activities

	31 December 1989	30 June 1989
	IR£	IR£
Corporation tax based on tax adjusted profits for the period	3,000	3,000

5. Financial fixed assets

	31 December 1989	30 June 1989
	IR£	IR£
Shares in unlisted related company at cost	1,701,850	1,701,850

In the Opinion of the directors the value of the shares in the unlisted related company is not less than the amount stated above.

The shares in the unlisted related company comprise 49% of the issued ordinary share capital of Sugar Distributors (Holdings) Limited, a company engaged in the marketing and distribution of sugar and other food products and having its registered office at Athy Road, Carlow.

Sugar Distributors (Holdings) Limited prepares its annual financial statements up to the last working day in September. The directors consider that it would involve expense and delay out of proportion to the value to the members to prepare consolidated financial statements under the equity method of accounting.

The aggregate amount of capital and reserves of Sugar Distributors (Holdings) Limited at its last accounting date, 29 September 1989, amounted to IR£1,954,000 and its profit for the financial year then ended, amounted to IR£833,000

6. Debtors

	31 December 1989	30 June 1989
	IR£	IR£
Prepayments and accrued income	1,038	-

7. Creditors: amounts falling due within one year

	31 December 1989	*30 June 1989*
	IR£	*IR£*
Bank 1oan and Overdraft	869,698	850,000
Amount due to related company	1,000,000	1, 000, 000
Accruals and deferred income	47,570	58,886
Corporation tax	1,854	802
	1,919,122	1,909,658

The bank 1oan is secured by guarantees from the directors and by equitable deposit of the ordinary shares which the company holds in Sugar Distributors (Holdings) Limited.

The amount due to the related company is subordinated in favour of any amounts outstanding on the bank loan.

8. Share capital

Authorised:		
Ordinary shares of IR£1 each	1,000,000	1,000,000
Allotted, called up and fully paid:		
Ordinary shares of IR£1 each	10,000	10, 000

9. Contingent liability

There is a legal case pending against the company in respect of an indemnity which the company has given to Allied Irish Banks plc in respect of a cheque for a specified amount to be drawn on the bank by a third party. A cheque for such an amount was subsequently drawn on the bank by a fourth party and the bank is how seeking to enforce the indemnity. The company holds that its indemnity was not intended to cover the fourth party concerned and, consequently, it does not have any liability.

The financial statements do not include provision in respect of any liability which may ultimately be payable joy the company. The directors consider that a liability will not materalise for the company in respect of this claim, and that in any event, the worst possible outcome for the company is IR£50,000.

Loan Notes 1990

Certificate No	Amount of loan note
3	1,867,068

Issued pursuant to a Resolution of the Board of Directors of SIUICRE ÉIREANN cpt having its registered office at St Stephen's Green Dublin 2 passed on ____________ February 1990

Name	Thomas G Keleghan
Address	98 Kincora Grove, Clontarf, Dublin

This is to certify that the above-mentioned is/are registered holder(s) of IR£1,867,068 in nominal amount of the Loan notes of Siuicre Éireann cpt. The holder of the loan notes is entitled to the benefit of, and are subject to the conditions hereinafter contained.

Given under the common seal of Siuicre Éireann cpt.

Dated February 1990

SIUICRE ÉIREANN cpt INSTRUMENT

Conditions of Issue

1. In these conditions unless there be something in the subject matter or context inconsistent therewith:

Company	Siuicre Éireann cpt
Interest Payment Dates	1st day of November and 1st day of May each year

2. (a) If the loan notes are not redeemed on or after the 31st October 1991 the company will pay to the noteholder's interest (less any applicable tax) on the principal amount of the loan notes outstanding at a rate equal to the Dublin Inter Bank Offered Rate for six months funds ("DIBOR") calculated on the relevant interest payment date in respect of the six months begging on and including an interest payment date and ending on but excluding the next following interest date (and interest period) save that in respect of any part of a loan note redeemed prior to any interest payment date interest shall cease to be payable in respect of such redeemed part of the loan note as and from such date of redemption.

(b) Interest payable hereunder shall accrue from day to day and be computed on the basis of a year of 365 days and the actual number of days elapsed in each relevant interest period.

(c) Whenever any payment hereunder shall become due on a day which is not a week day on which clearing banks in Dublin are open for normal banking business (a "business day") payment shall be made on the next succeeding business day but no adjustment shall be made to the amount of interest payable for the relevant interest period.

(d) In the event that the company shall fail to pay to the noteholders any sum due hereunder on the date on which such sum is expressed to be due and payable pursuant to these conditions the company shall (without prejudice to all other rights and remedies of the noteholders in respect of such failure) pay to the noteholders interest at DIBOR on such overdue amount from the date of such failure up to the date of actual payment (as well after as before judgment) calculated on a day to day basis for so long as such amount remains unpaid in full.

3. The following provisions shall have effect as to the repayment of the loan notes:

(a) noteholders may elect at any time to have loan notes redeemed in whole or in part by giving to the company not less than 30 days notice stating the amount of the loan notes they wish to have redeemed; the earliest date for redemption shall be 1 November 1991 and the latest date for redemption shall be 31 October 1997; loan notes not redeemed by 31 October 1997 shall be redeemed in full on that date;

(b) the principal amount of any loan note then outstanding shall immediately become repayable on demand together with interest accrued thereon (subject to deduction of any applicable tax) in accordance with condition 2 above up to the date of actual repayment upon the happening of any of the following events:

(i) The company failing to pay interest in respect of any loan note within 28 days of the due date for payment thereof;

(ii) the company failing to pay within 28 days of the due date for payment any part of the principal amount of any loan note;

(iii) an order is made or an effective resolution is passed for the winding-up of the company or the guarantor (other than a voluntary winding-up for the purpose of amalgamation or reconstruction); or

(iv) an encumbrance shall take possession or a receiver shall be appointed over the whole or any substantial part of the assets or undertaking of the company or the guarantor.

4. The company shall give notice in writing to each of the noteholders of the happening of the events specified in conditions 3(b)(iii) or (iv) above.

5. Any loan notes repaid or purchased by the company shall forthwith be cancelled and shall not be available for re-issue.

6. Every noteholder will be entitled without charge to one certificate stating the amount of the loan notes held by him. Every certificate shall bear serial number and refer to the instrument. Joint holders of loan notes will be entitled only to one certificate in respect of the loan notes held by them jointly and the same will be delivered to the first named of such of the joint holders unless all such joint holders otherwise specify in writing.

7. A register of holders of the loan notes will be kept by the company at its registered office or at such other place in the Republic of Ireland as it may from time to time decide, and there shall be entered in such register:

(a) The names and addresses of the holders for the time being of the loan notes;

(b) the nominal amount of the loan notes held by every registered holder; and

(c) the date at which the name of every such registered holder is entered in respect of the loan notes standing in his name.

Any change of address on the part of the noteholder shall forthwith be notified to the company in writing and thereupon the register shall be altered accordingly. A noteholder and any person authorised by any noteholder shall be at liberty at all reasonable times during office hours to inspect the register.

8. Except in the case of the death of a noteholder no loan note or any part thereof shall be transferable or assignable by any noteholder.

9. The company shall be entitled provided it guarantees repayment at its discretion to assign any or all of its obligations and rights relating to the loan notes and the noteholder consents to such assignment. As soon as practicable after such assignment the company shall give notice thereof to the noteholder at the address recorded for such noteholder in the register of holders of loan notes.

10. Except as provided by statute or as required by any order of a Court of competent jurisdiction, the company shall recognise the registered holder of any loan note as the absolute owner thereof, and shall not be bound to take notice of, or to see to the execution of, any trust whether express, implied or constructive to which any loan note may be subject, and the receipt of such person (or in the case of joint holdings of any one of such holders) for the interest on, or for the moneys payable upon the repayment of, the same shall be a good discharge to the company notwithstanding any notice it may have, whether express or otherwise of the right, title, interest or claim of any other person to or in such loan note or interest or moneys. No notice of any trust, express, implied or constructive shall (except as aforesaid) be entered on the register in respect of any loan note.

11. Subject to Clause 14 the executors or administrators of a deceased holder of a loan note (not being one of several joint holders) shall be the only persons recognised by the company as having any title to or interest in such loan note.

Given under the common seal of SIUICRE ÉIREANN cpt was affixed hereto:

Dated day of _____________ 19.

BETWEEN SIUICRE ÉIREANN cpt one part

and

THOMAS KELEGHAN other part

Service Agreement

8 February 1990

An agreement made 8 day of February 1990

BETWEEN SIUICRE ÉIREANN cpt having its registered office at St Stephens Green House, Dublin 2 ("the company") of the one part

AND

THOMAS KELEGHAN

Of (the executive) of the other part

WHERRY IT IS AGREED as follows:

1. The company shall employ the executive and the executive shall serve the company as sales director responsible for seeing sugar and such other sales as the group general manager of the flour division for the time being of the company (the "general manager") shall decide. Subject to the provisions for determination of this agreement hereinafter concerned such employment shall be for a period of 18 months commencing on the 1st day of January 1990 and expiring on the 30th day of June 1991 and shall continue thereafter unless and until terminated by either party by the service of three months' written notice on the other party.

2. As an executive of the company the executive shall:

(a) undertake such duties and exercise full powers in relation to the company and its business as the general manager shall from time to time assign to or vest in him;

(b) the discharge of such duties and in the exercise of such powers observe and comply win all resolutions regulations and directions from time to time made or given by the general manager;

(c) devote substantially the whole of his time and attention during business hours to the discharge of his duties hereunder;

(d) conform to such hours of work as may from time to time reasonably be required of him and shall not be entitled to receive any remuneration for work performed outside his normal hours;

(e) in pursuance of his duties hereunder perform such services for subsidiary companies or any parent company or the company and (without further remuneration unless otherwise agreed) accept and hold for the duration of this agreement such offices or appointments in such subsidiary companies as the general manager may from time to time reasonably require.

3. (a) The executive shall forthwith on the signing of this agreement cease (except in pursuance of his duties in the group) all activities in connection with the buying, selling, importing, transporting or distribution or sugar and/or flour and shall not without the consent of the company during the term of this agreement be engaged or interested either directly or indirectly in any capacity in any trade, business or occupation whatsoever other than the business of the company but so that this provision shall not prohibit the holding whether directly or through nominees of quoted investments so long as not more than five per cent of the share or stock of any class of any one company shall be so held. In this clause the expression occupation shall include members of the Oireachtas or any other public or private work which in the opinion of the company may hinder or otherwise interfere with the performance by the executive of his duties under this agreement.

3. (b) The executive hereby undertakes to the company that:

(i) He will not within the relevant territory during the relevant period carry on or be concerned directly or indirectly or be engaged, concerned or interested whether as principal shareholder, partner, employee, agent or otherwise (except as a shareholder in a public company - whose shares are quoted or dealt in or any recognised stock exchange and holding not more than 5% of the share capital of such public company) in any business competing with the business or businesses of the company or any of its subsidiaries or associate companies as carried on at any time prior to the termination of this agreement.

(ii) He will not within the relevant territory during the relevant period either on his own account or on behalf of any other person, firm or company direct or indirectly solicit, interfere with or endeavour to entice away from the company or any of its subsidiaries or associated companies any person, firm or company who has been a client or customer of the company or any of its subsidiaries or associate companies during any time up to the termination of this agreement or who is in the habit of dealing with the company or any of its subsidiaries or associate companies.

(iii) He will not at any time hereafter either on his own account or on behalf of any person, firm or company directly or indirectly endeavour to entice away any consultant, executive or employee from the company or any of its subsidiaries or associate companies.

3. (c) The benefit of each and every of the provisions set out in this clause, and each and every part of each such provision thereof, shall be deemed to be separate and severable and enforceable accordingly. While the restrictions contained in this clause are considered by the parties to be reasonable in all the circumstances as at the date hereof it is acknowledged that restrictions of such a nature may be invalid because of changed circumstances or other unforeseen factors and accordingly it is hereby agreed that in the event of any provision of this clause being found to be void as going beyond what is reasonable in all the circumstances for the protection of the interests of the company, its subsidiaries or associated companies but would be valid if some part thereof were deleted or the period or application reduced or the range of activities or area covered limited such provision shall apply with such modification and shall be given effect to in such modified form as may be necessary to make it valid and effective.

3. (d) In this Clause 3:
   (A) The "relevant territory" shall mean the Republic of Ireland, Northern Ireland and Great Britain.
   (B) The "relevant period" shall mean the period of three years from the termination of this agreement.

4. The executive shall not except as authorised or required by his duties reveal to any person or company any trade secrets or confident information concerning the organisation, business finances, transactions or affairs of the company or of its parent or any of its subsidiaries which may come to his knowledge during his employment hereunder and shall keep with complete secrecy all confidential information entrusted to him and shall not use or attempt to use any such information in any manner which may injure or cause loss either directly or indirectly to the company or its business or may be likely so to do. This restriction shall continue to apply after the termination of this agreement without limit in point of time but shall cease to apply to information or knowledge which may come into the public domain.

5. The executive shall nor during the continuance of this agreement make otherwise than for the benefit of the company any notes or memoranda relating to any matter within the scope or the business of the company or concerning any or its dealings or affairs nor shall the executive either during the continuance of this agreement or afterwards use or permit to be used any such notes or memoranda otherwise than for the benefit of the company it being the intention of the parties hereto that all such notes or memoranda made by the executive shall be the property of the company and left at its registered office upon the termination of this agreement.

6. Subject as hereinafter provided the company shall pay to the executive during the continuance of this agreement salary at the rate or IR£37,100 annually subject to annual review by the general manager. In the event of any increase of salary being agreed or notified as the result of such review such increase shall thereafter have effect as if it were specifically provided for as a term of this agreement. The said salary shall be payable by equal monthly instalments (and proportionately for any lesser period each monthly instalment being deemed to accrue rateably from day to day) in arrear on the last day of each month.

7. (a) The company shall provide and maintain for the sole use of the executive while on the business of the company a motor car of suitable type and shall pay all expenses in connection with such use, such motor car to be changed from time to time in accordance with the companies policy regarding vehicle replacements, and the executive shall ensure that at all times when the car is driven it is in the state and condition required by law.

7. (b) As an alternative to 7(a) the company shall if so required by the executive pay a mileage allowance for use of the executive's car on business at rates agreed between the company and the executive from time to time.

8. The executive shall be reimbursed all travelling, hotel and other out-of-pocket expenses properly vouched and reasonably incurred by him in or about the discharge of his duties hereunder.

9. The executive shall be entitled to twenty six days holidays (exclusive of statutory public holidays) in each holiday year to be taken at such time or times as the general manager shall consider most convenient having regard to the requirements of the company's

business and otherwise in accordance with the Holidays (Employees) Act 1973. The "holiday year" is 12 calendar months starting on 1 January.

10.(1) If the executive shall at any time be prevented by illness injury accident or any other circumstances beyond his control (such prevention being hereinafter referred to as "the illness") from discharging in full his duties hereunder for a total of six or more months in any twelve consecutive calendar months the company may by notice in writing to the executive given at any time so long as the illness shall continue discontinue payment in whole or part of the said salary on and from such date as may be specified in the notice until the illness shall cease.

(2) Subject as hereinbefore provided the said salary shall notwithstanding the illness continue to be paid to the executive in accordance with clause 7 hereof in respect of the period of the illness prior to such discontinuance.

(3) Provided that if the illness shall be or appear to be occasioned by actionable negligence of a third party in respect of which damages are or may be recoverable the executive shall forthwith notify the general manager of that fact and of any claim, compromise, settlement or judgment made or awarded in connection therewith and shall give to the company all such particulars of such matters as the company may reasonably require and shall if so required by the company refund to the company such sum (not exceeding the amount of damages recovered by him under such compromise, settlement or judgment less any costs in or in connection with or under such claim, compromise, settlement or judgment borne by the executive and not exceeding the aggregate of the remuneration paid to him by way of salary in respect of the period of the illness) as the company may determine.

(4) Except as expressly provided by this clause the executive shall not be entitled to any salary in respect of any period during which he shall fail or be unable from any cause to perform all or any of his duties hereunder without prejudice to any right of action accruing or accrued to either party in respect of any breach of this agreement.

(5) Any payment receivable from the Department of Social Welfare in respect of illness shall be claimed by the executive and immediately refunded to the company.

12.(1) This agreement may be terminated forthwith by the company without prior notice if the executive shall at any time:

(a) commit any serious breach of this agreement;

(b) be guilty of dishonesty or incompetence or poor performance or any grave misconduct or wilful neglect in the discharge of his duties hereunder;

(c) become bankrupt or commit any act of bankruptcy or make any arrangement or composition with his creditors;

(d) become of unsound mind;

(e) be convicted any criminal offence other than road traffic offences or such offences which in the reasonable opinion of the company do not affect his position as an executive of the company,

(f) be absent or unable through illness to discharge in full his duties hereunder for a period of six consecutive months;

(g) if for any other reason become incapable of performing his duties under this agreement;

(2) Upon the termination of this agreement the executive shall forthwith give to the company formal letters of resignation from all offices and appointments held by

him hereunder and in the event of his failure to do so the company is hereby irrevocably authorised to appoint some person as his attorney in his name and on his behalf to execute any documents and to do all things requisite to give effect thereto.

13.(1) Since the executive has obtained and is likely to obtain in the course of his employment with the company knowledge of trade secrets of the company and other confidential information of the company the executive hereby agrees with the company in addition to any other restrictions contained in this agreement that if the company shall have obtained trade secrets or other confidential information from any third party under an agreement including restrictions on disclosure known to him he will not without the consent of the company at any time (whether during the continuance of this agreement or after the termination thereof) infringe such restrictions.

(2) Since the executive also may obtain in the course of his employment by reason of services rendered for or offices held in any subsidiary company of the company knowledge of the trade secrets or other confidential information of such company the executive hereby agrees that he will at the request and cost of the company enter into a direct agreement or undertaking with such company whereby he will accept restrictions corresponding to the restrictions herein confined (or such of them as may be appropriate in the circumstances) for such period as such company may reasonably require for the protection of its legitimate interests.

13. The executive hereby undertakes with the company that he shall not dispose of any shares received by him in the company consequent upon any public flotation of the company or any placing by it of any of its shares for a period of five years from the date of such public flotation or placing.

14.(1) Any notice under this agreement shall be in writing and shall be signed by or on behalf of the party giving it.

(2) Any such notice may be served by leaving it or sending it by telex, facsimile, prepaid recorded delivery or registered post:

(a) in the case of the executive at his address hereinbefore set out or at such other address which he may notify in writing to the company; or

(b) in the case of the company at its registered office for the time being.

(3) Any notice so served by post shall be deemed to have been served 48 hours after the letter containing the same was sent by recorded delivery or registered post. Any notice given by telex or cable shall be deemed to have been served at the time at which such telex or cable would be received in the ordinary course of transmission and in proving such service it shall be sufficient to prove that the notice was properly addressed and was posted or sent in accordance with sub-clause (2) above.

15. The termination of this agreement shall not affect such of the provisions hereof as are expressed to operate or have effect thereafter and shall be without prejudice to any right of action already accrued to either party in respect of any breach of this agreement by the other party.

16. The executive shall during the continuance of this agreement account to the company for any remuneration or other benefit received by him as executive or other officer of shareholder in any company promoted by the company or any subsidiary of the company.

17. If before the termination of this agreement the employment of the executive hereunder shall be determined by reason of the liquidation of the company for the purpose or reconstruction or amalgamation and he shall be offered employment with any concern or undertaking resulting from such reconstruction or amalgamation on terms and conditions not less favourable than the terms of this agreement then the executive shall have no claim against the company in respect of the determination of his employment hereunder.

18. Every dispute or difference arising between the partners hereto with regard to this agreement or the duties, powers or liabilities of either party hereunder or with regard to the construction of any clause hereof or any act or thing to be done in pursuance thereof or arming our of anything herein contained whether during the continuance of this agreement or upon or after its termination shall be referred to a single arbitrator in accordance with the provisions of the Arbitration Acts 1954 or any re-enactment or modification thereof for the time being in force.

19. A waiver by any of the parties hereto of any breach by the other party or any of the terms, provisions or conditions of this agreement or the acquiescence by any such party in any act (whether commission or omission) which but for such acquiescence would be a breach as aforesaid shall not constitute a general waiver or such term, provision or condition or of any such act.

20. This agreement is the substitution for all previous contracts of service between the company and the executive which shall be deemed to have been terminated by mutual consent as from the dare on which this agreeably commences.

21. For the purposes of this agreement any reference to group shall mean the company and its subsidiaries including Sugar Distributors (Holdings) Limited.

22. For the avoidance of doubt the executive shall continue to participate m the SDH scheme as heretobefore.

BY WITNESS WHEREOF the panics hereto or their duly representative have hereunder executed this agreement the day and year first herein written.

SIUICRE ÉIREANN cpt

Signed up sealed and delivered by the said THOMAS KELEGHAN

in the presence of:

To: Siuicre Éireann cpt St Stephens Green House Dublin 2 8 February 1990

In relation to the sale of my shares in Gladebrook Limited to Siuicre Éireann cpt I confirm that notwithstanding the terms of the share purchase agreement dated the 8th day of February 1990 between among others, myself, Siuicre Éireann cpt, Gladebrook Limited and Talmino Limited that IR£250,000 of the purchase consideration stated therein was paid as an inducement for me to enter into the service contract (as defined in the said share purchase agreement) and accordingly in the event of my not complying with the terms of the said service contract that portion of the IR£250,000 purchase consideration attributable to the sale of my shares in Gladebrook Limited will become repayable by me to Siuicre Éireann cpt.

In the event of any such repayment becoming due, I hereby acknowledge that Siuicre Éireann cpt and Talmino Limited can set-off such amount against any sums becoming payable to the defaulting party under any loan notes or alternatively can sell any shares held by it on our behalf, the subscription monies for which, have been satisfied by the redemption of loan notes.

Your faithfully

High Court - 10 February 2000

This is a Case Stated by the Appeal Commissioners pursuant to ITA 1967 s 428 for the decision of the High Court.

There are in fact, two separate assessments which basically arise out of the same series of transactions, one being an income tax assessment and the other being a capital gains tax assessment.

The Facts

In the Case Stated the Appeal Commissioners found the following facts proved or admitted:

(a) The respondent acquired 2,151 IR£1 Ordinary shares in Gladebrook Limited in December 1988. Gladebrook Limited held 49% of the share capital of Sugar Distributors (Holdings) Limited, which in turn held 100% of the share capital of Sugar Distributors Limited.

(b) By way of a share purchase agreement dated 8 February 1990, the respondent and others sold their shares in Gladebrook Limited to Siucre Éireann cpt for a total consideration of IR£8.6 million to be satisfied by the issue of loan notes by Siucre Éireann cpt.

(c) The nominal amount of the loan note received by the respondent was IR£1,867,068.00.

(d) A chargeable gain did not accrue to the respondent on the sale of his shares in Gladebrook Limited to Siucre Éireann CPT as it was accepted that the provisions of CGTA 1975 Sch 2 para 4 applied to that transaction.

(e) On the 8 February 1990 the respondent signed a service agreement with Siucre Éireann CPT.

(f) On 8 February 1990 the respondent also signed a "side letter" addressed to Siucre Éireann CPT.

(g) Prior to the signing of the service agreement, the respondent was Sales Director of Sugar Distributors Limited. He never became an employee of Siucre Éireann CPT but remained as Sales Director of Sugar Distributors Limited until his retirement in June 1991, when he was 65 years of age.

(h) The respondent's loan note was redeemed for cash in February 1993.

The basic transaction was the purchase by Siucre Éireann CPT (hereinafter called the "purchaser") of the entire issued share capital of Gladebrook Limited, which transaction is governed by an agreement dated 8 February 1990 between the purchaser and the five shareholders of Gladebrook Limited, one of whom is the respondent. This agreement provided that the total consideration payable by the purchaser would be the sum of IR£8,680,000.00 and further provided that:

> The purchase consideration shall be satisfied by the issue by the purchaser on completion of the loan notes to the vendors.

The form of loan note was set out in a schedule to the agreement. The loan notes themselves provided that they could be redeemed in whole or part on 30 days notice, the earliest date for redemption being 1 November 1991 and the latest date for redemption being 31 October 1997. Interest was to be payable from 31 October 1991 on the amount outstanding. There were detailed provisions in the loan notes as to registration and the issue of certificates and it was expressly provided in the conditions of issue of the loan notes that:

> Except in the case of the death of a note holder no loan note or any part thereof shall be transferable or assignable by any note holder.

Furthermore, on the face of the loan note itself it was stated:

> No loan note or any part thereof is transferable or assignable by any note holder.

The share purchase agreement also contained certain provisions whereby the holder of a loan note could convert the note into shares in the purchaser in the event of a public flotation or in the event of a placing, but if such a flotation or placing took place prior to 1 October 1991 the loan note would be converted at a discount calculated on a sliding scale.

In addition to the share purchase agreement, the respondent also signed a side letter with the purchaser on 8 February 1990 the relevant portion of which reads as follows:

> In relation to the sale of my shares in Gladebrook Limited to Siucre Éireann CPT I confirm that notwithstanding the terms of the share purchase agreement dated the 8 February 1990 between amongst others, myself, Siucre Éireann CPT, Gladebrook Limited and Talmino Limited that IR£250,000 of the purchase consideration stated therein was paid as an inducement for me to enter into the service contract (as defined in the said share purchase agreement) and accordingly, in the event of my not complying with the terms of the said service contract that portion of the IR£250,000 purchase consideration attributable to the sale of my shares in Gladebrook Limited will become payable by me to Siucre Éireann CPT.

On the same day the respondent entered into a service agreement with the purchaser which provided, *inter alia*:

1. The company shall employ the executive and the executive shall serve the company as sales director responsible for selling sugar and such other sales as Group Manager of the flour division for the time being of the company (the general manager) shall decide. Subject to the provisions for the determination of this agreement hereinafter contained such employment shall be for a period of 18 months commencing on the 1st day of January 1990 and expiring on the 30th day of June 1991 and shall continue thereafter unless and until terminated by either party by the service of three months written notice on the other party.
2. As an executive of the company the executive shall:
   (a) undertake such duties and exercise such powers in relation to the company and its business as the general manager shall from to time assign to or vest in him.

The service agreement also contained a detailed non-competition clause and other provisions which it is not necessary to set out in detail by reason of the finding of fact by the Appeal Commissioners that the respondent never became an employee of the purchaser.

Assessment for income tax

The appellant claims that the £250,000 referred to in the side letter is liable to income tax under Schedule E. The charging section in respect of Schedule E tax is set out ITA 1967 s 110 as amended. Subsection 1(1) reads as follows:

> Tax under Schedule E shall be annually charged on every person having or exercising an office or employment of profit mentioned in that schedule, or to whom any annuity, pension or stipend, chargeable under that schedule, is payable, in respect of all salaries, fees, wages, perquisites or profits whatsoever therefrom and shall be computed on the amount of all such salaries, fees, perquisites or profits whatsoever therefrom for the year of assessment.

This being a Case Stated, I am bound by the facts as found by the Appeal Commissioners, and in particular I must accept that the respondent was never employed by the purchaser. The section imposes the charge on persons having or exercising an office for employment of profit in respect of income of various kinds received by him "therefrom", that is from the office or employment of profit. If he had no such office or employment, he could have received no income therefrom, and therefore could have no liability under Schedule E.

Capital gains tax assessment

The issue in this case is whether the redemption of the loan notes for cash in February 1993 gave rise to a chargeable gain upon which capital gains tax is payable. Capital gains tax is payable in respect of chargeable gains on the disposal of assets, and the scheme of the Act as set out in s 11(2) is that all such gains are chargeable unless there is a provision to the contrary in the Act. There are in fact a number of provisions to the contrary in the Act, two of which fall to be dealt with in the present case. The first point which arises is the nature of the asset which was disposed of in February 1993, and the second point is whether, if such disposal was the disposal of a debt, it gave rise to a chargeable gain.

Nature of the disposal

The original transaction in this case was one whereby the respondent sold his shares in Gladebrook Limited and received in return for those shares a loan note issued by the purchaser. This undoubtedly gave rise to a capital gain, but that gain was not a chargeable gain by virtue of the provision of CGTA 1975 Sch 2 para 2. That paragraph dealt with the reorganisation or reduction of share capital of a company, and subparagraph 2 thereof reads as follows:

> Subject to the following subparagraphs, a reorganisation or a reduction of a company's share capital shall not be treated as involving any disposal of the original shares or any acquisition of the new holding or any part of it but the original shares (taken as a single asset) and the new holding (taken as a single asset) shall be treated as the same asset acquired as the original shares were acquired.

It is common case that the sale of the shares and the acquisition of the loan note is governed by this paragraph, and that no tax was payable on that transaction. However, there is considerable dispute over the effect of this provision, and in particular over the meaning of the phrase "the original shares (taken as a single asset) and the new holding (taken as a single asset) shall be treated as the same asset acquired as the original shares were acquired."

The primary intention of this provision is quite clear. It is to ensure that, while no tax shall be payable on the substitution of one asset for another on the reorganisation of a company, nevertheless where there is an ultimate realisation of the secondly acquired asset, the amount of the gain should be assessed by reference back to the cost of the original asset. It is contended by the appellant that the effect of this paragraph is that one must treat the secondly acquired asset for all purposes as if it were still the original asset, and therefore that what is being redeemed in February 1993 must in effect be treated as if it were the original shares. If this contention is correct, there is no doubt that Capital Gains Tax is payable on that disposition.

The equivalent sections in the United Kingdom legislation have been considered in several cases there. In *Floor v Hovis (Inspector of Taxes)* [1978] STC 436 at 447 Buckley LJ commented on these provisions and said:

> ... as I read them, provided that a disposal of assets to which they apply shall not for the purposes of the charge to tax be treated as a disposal. This does not mean that such a disposal is not a disposal within the meaning of that term in the Act, but that, notwithstanding that it is a disposal, it shall not be taxed as such.

Similar views were expressed in the Court of Appeal by Sir Denys Buckley in *Westcott v Woolcombers Limited* [1987] STC 600 at 609 where he said:

> The function of Schedule 6, 7 and 8 of the Act is to regulate the computation of the amount of any chargeable gains or allowable losses arising in any particular circumstances (FA 1965 ss 22(9) and 23(1). Paragraph 4(2) of Schedule 7 does not provide that any disposal or acquisition of an asset which shall have actually occurred shall, for all purposes, be deemed not to have occurred. It is one of a collection of miscellaneous rules regulating how the amounts of gains and losses are to be computed. It must be construed in that light.

This case refers to "the two fictions", the first being the "no disposal fiction", and the second being "the composite single asset fiction". These cases make it clear that these fictions are what I might call selective fictions, in that they do not have general application, but only apply when considering the computation of tax.

This seems to me to be the correct approach, as I think becomes clear if one looks at this problem in stages. There could be no question that the provisions of a schedule of a Capital Gains Tax Act could change the nature of the loan notes in this case so that they in fact remain shares in the company, with the same rights attached to them as were attached to the original shares. Were it otherwise, the holder of the notes would be entitled to notice of and to attend general meetings of the company and to participate in dividends of the company. This is, of course, absurd. Therefore, there must be some limit to the fictions. The next step is to consider whether the fictions apply to all the provisions of the Capital Gains Tax legislation. This again cannot be so, as the fictions could not be intended to apply, for example, to the calculation of shareholdings for the purposes of s 26 of the Act. One is, therefore, driven to the inevitable conclusion that the fictions only apply to the limited objects of the schedule, namely to the calculation of the amount of tax payable. This is confirmed by the wording of s 11(1) which provides that the amount of the gains accruing on the disposal of assets shall be computed subject to the provisions of, *inter alia*, Sch 2. This is the whole purpose of the schedule, and there is no logical reason why the provisions of that schedule should apply to matters other than the computation of the gain. Accordingly, when considering whether there has been a chargeable gain on the disposal of the loan notes, they must be treated as loan notes and not as the original shares in the company other than for the purpose of computing the actual amount of tax payable.

Nature of the Loan Note

Section 46(1) of the Capital Gains Tax Act reads as follows:

> Where a person incurs a debt to another (that is the original creditor) whether in Irish currency or in some other currency, no chargeable gain shall accrue to that creditor or his personal representative or legatee on a disposal of the debt:
>
> Provided that this subsection shall not apply in the case of the debt on a security as defined in paragraph 3 of Schedule 2 (Conversion of Sureties).

While the word "security" is defined in paragraph 3 of Schedule 2, unfortunately the definition does not in itself resolve the difficulties. Security is therein defined as:

> Includes any loans, stock or similar security whether of any government or of any public or local authority or of any company and whether secured or unsecured but excluding securities falling within s 19.

Section 19 refers to a number of government and similar securities which are not to be treated as chargeable assets, and some reliance is placed by the appellant on the fact that this includes savings certificates issued under the authority of the Minister for Finance. It is argued that these are very similar to a loan note, in that they are simply an acknowledgement of a debt by the Minister for Finance to the holder, and that the implication of the definition of "security" is that were it not for the fact they fell within s 19, savings certificates would be considered to be a security, and therefore they would constitute a debt on a security. I do not think this argument is of great assistance to the appellant as certainly on one view all acknowledgements of monies due by the State could be considered to be securities, in that they are in effect secured by the assets of the State.

Unfortunately, the Act gives no further assistance in defining the words "a debt on a security". It is quite clear, however, that a debt on a security is treated differently from an ordinary debt. It must have some distinctive feature. This feature has been defined in several United Kingdom cases as being that of marketability or the fact that it can be dealt in. In *WT Ramsey v Commissioners of Inland Revenue* 54 TC 101, Lord Frasier of Tullybelton said at p 194:

> Further consideration has satisfied me that the existence of a document or a certificate cannot be the distinguishing feature between the two classes of debt. If Parliament had intended it be so, that could easily have been stated in plain terms and there would have been no purpose in using the strange phrase 'the debt on a security" in paragraph 11(1) of Schedule 7, or in referring to the "definition" of security in paragraph 5. The distinction in paragraph 11(1) is, I think between a simple unsecured debt and a debt of the nature of an investment, which can be dealt in and purchased with a view to being held as an investment. The reason for the provision that no chargeable gain should accrue on disposal of a simple debt by the original creditor must have been to restrict allowable losses (computed in the same way as gains - FA 1965 s 23, which was the relevant statute in 1973) because a disposal of a simple debt by the original creditor or his legatee will very seldom result in a gain. No doubt it is possible to think of cases where a gain may result, but they are exceptional. On the other hand it is all too common for debts to be disposed by the original creditor at a loss, and if such losses were allowed for Capital Gains Tax it would be easy to avoid tax by writing off bad debts - for example those owed by impecunious relatives. But debts on a security, being of the nature of investments, are just as likely to be disposed of by the original creditor at a gain as they are at a loss, and they are subject to the ordinary rules.

Similar definitions have been applied in several United Kingdom cases, and in particular *Cleveley's Investment Trust v CIR* [1971] 47 TC 300, and *Aberdeen Construction Group v IRC* [1978] AC 885. These cases all emphasise that a debt on a security ought to be a marketable asset worth more than its face value.

The phrase has also been considered by Morris J (as he then was) in *McSweeney v Mooney* [1997] 3 IR 424 where, after considering the English authorities, he expressed the view at p 429 that:

> The essence of a loan on a security must be whether the additional 'bundle of rights' acquired with the granting of the loan, to use Wilberforce LJ's phrase, enhances the loan so as to make it marketable and potentially more valuable than the value of the repaid loan upon repayment. This potential increase in value must not be illusory or theoretical. It must be realistic at the time when the loan and the rights are acquired by the lender.

In the present case the loan notes quite clearly are not marketable. Both on the face of the note itself and in the conditions of issue it is provided that neither the note or any part thereof shall be transferable or assignable and accordingly if marketability is an essential element of a debt on a security, then this loan note cannot come within the definition, and it is a simple promise to repay a debt, which cannot constitute a chargeable gain by virtue of the provisions of s 46.

I also think that the loan note in the present does not come within the second test suggested in the passage quoted above, namely that it has, or even has the capability of having, an enhanced value. This loan note was issued in February 1990 and initially carried no interest at all. If it was not redeemed on or after 31 October 1991 it would carry interest at the Dublin Inter Bank offered rate for six month funds, but this is of course, a very low interest rate, and the loan note would be redeemed at its face value by October 1997 at the latest. In my view payment of interest at this rate would not enhance the value of the loan note as an investment. The only other advantage attached to the loan note is that it could be converted into ordinary shares in the company in the event of a public flotation or placing. However, if either of these events take place prior to 30 September 1991, this conversion will take place at a discount, and in any event the price at which the shares are to be subscribed for is their full issue price, and therefore it seems to me that these conversion rights do not in fact add anything to the value of the loan note, because at the time of conversion the loan note will still be worth only its face value.

Based on these facts, I do not think that the loan note could be considered to be a debt on a security within the meaning of s 46(1), and therefore no chargeable gain accrues.

Accordingly, in my view the Appeal Commissioners were correct in their decisions both in relation to the income tax issue and the capital gains tax issue.

Cases reported

A

A & B v WJ Davis (Inspector of Taxes) .... Vol II p 60
AB Ltd v Mac Giolla Riogh (Inspector of Taxes) .... Vol II p 419
AB v JD Mulvey (Inspector of Taxes) .... Vol II p 55
Action Aid Ltd v Revenue Commissioners .... Vol V p 392
AE v The Revenue Commissioners .... Vol V p 686
Agricultural Credit Corporation Ltd, The v JB Vale (Inspector of Taxes) .... Vol I p 474
Airspace Investments Ltd v M Moore (Inspector of Taxes) .... Vol V p 3
Alliance & Dublin Consumers' Gas Co, The v Davis (Inspector of Taxes) .... Vol I p 104
Alliance and Dublin Consumers' Gas Co, The v McWilliams (IOT) .... Vol I p 207
Allied Irish Banks plc v James Bolger & Joan Bolger .... Vol V p 1
Associated Properties Ltd v The Revenue Commissioners .... Vol II p 175
Attorney General v Hamilton [1993] 2 IR 250 .... 1998 p 120
Attorney General v Power & Anor .... Vol V p 525
Attorney General, The v Sun Alliance & London Insurance Ltd .... Vol III p 265
Attorney-General, The v Irish Steel Ltd and Vincent Crowley .... Vol II p 108

B

Bairead, MA (Inspector of Taxes) v Martin C Carr .... Vol IV p 505
Bairead, MA (Inspector of Taxes) v Maxwells of Donegal Ltd .... Vol III p 430
Bairead, MA v M McDonald .... Vol IV p 475
Bank of Ireland Finance Ltd v The Revenue Commissioners .... Vol IV p 217
Bedford (Collector-General) v H .... Vol II p 588
Beirne (Inspector of Taxes) v St Vincent De Paul Society (Wexford Conference) .... Vol I p 383
Belville Holdings Ltd (in receivership and liquidation) v Cronin (Inspector of Taxes) .... Vol III p 340
Birch (Inspector of Taxes) v Denis Delaney .... Vol I p 515
BKJ v The Revenue Commissioners .... Vol III p 104
Boland's Ltd v Davis (Inspector of Taxes) .... Vol I p 86
Boland's Ltd v The Commissioners of Inland Revenue .... Vol I p 34
Bourke (Inspector of Taxes) v Lyster & Sons Ltd .... Vol II p 374
Bourke (Inspector of Taxes) v WG Bradley & Sons .... Vol IV p 117
Breathnach (Inspector of Taxes) v MC .... Vol III p 113
Brosnan (Inspector of Taxes) v Mutual Enterprises Ltd .... Vol V p 138
Brosnan (Inspector of Taxes) v Leeside Nurseries Ltd .... Vol V p 21
Brosnan, TJ (Inspector of Taxes) v Cork Communications Ltd .... Vol IV p 349
Browne, JA (Inspector of Taxes) v Bank of Ireland Finance Ltd .... Vol III p 644
Browne Paul and Others v The Revenue Commissioners & Ors .... Vol IV p 323
Burke & Sons Ltd v Revenue Commissioner, Ireland and Attorney General ... Vol V p 418
Byrne v Conroy .... 1998 p 75
Byrne (Terence) v The Revenue Commissioners .... Vol V p 560

C

Carbery Milk Products Ltd v The Minister for Agriculture & Ors .... Vol IV p 492

Carroll Industries Plc (formerly PJ Carroll & Co Ltd) and
PJ Carroll & Co Ltd v S O'Culachain (Inspector of Taxes) .... Vol IV p 135
Casey (Inspector of Taxes) v AB Ltd .... Vol II p 500
Casey (Inspector of Taxes) v The Monteagle Estate Co .... Vol II p 429
CD v JM O'Sullivan (Inspector of Taxes) .... Vol II p 140
Cherry Court v The Revenue Commissioners .... Vol V p 180
City of Dublin Steampacket Co, The (In liquidation) v The Revenue
Commissioners .... Vol I p 318
City of Dublin Steampacket Co, The v Revenue Commissioners .... Vol I p 108
Cloghran Stud Farm v AG Birch (Inspector of Taxes) .... Vol I p 496
Colclough v Colclough .... Vol II p 332
Collins, Daniel & Ors (as executor of the will of Michael Byrne (Deceased))
and Daniel Collins v J D Mulvey (Inspector of Taxes) .... Vol II p 291
Commissioners of Inland Revenue v The Governor and Company of The
Bank of Ireland .... Vol I p 70
Commissioners of Inland Revenue, The v The Dublin and Kingstown
Railway Co .... Vol I p 119
Companies Act 1963-1983, The v Castlemahon Poultry
Products Ltd .... Vol III p 509
Companies Act 1963-1983, The v M F N Construction Co Ltd
(in liquidation) .... Vol IV p 82
Connolly (Inspector of Taxes) v Denis McNamara .... Vol II p 452
Connolly (Inspector of Taxes) v WW .... Vol II p 657
Connolly, Edward v AG Birch (Inspector of Taxes) .... Vol I p 583
Connolly, Peter v The Collector of Customs and Excise .... Vol IV p 419
Coombe Importers Ltd (In Liq), Re & Re the Companies Acts 1963-1990, Re ... 1998 p 59
Corr, F (Inspector of Taxes) v F E Larkin .... Vol II p 164
Criminal Assets Bureau v Gerard Hutch .... 1999-2000 p 65
Cronin (Inspector of Taxes) v C .... Vol II p 592
Cronin (Inspector of Taxes) v Cork & County Property Co Ltd .... Vol III p 198
Cronin (Inspector of Taxes) v IMP Midleton Ltd .... Vol III p 452
Cronin (Inspector of Taxes) v Lunham Brothers Ltd .... Vol III p 363
Cronin (Inspector of Taxes) v Strand Dairy Ltd .... Vol III p 441
Cronin (Inspector of Taxes) v Youghal Carpets (Yarns) Ltd .... Vol III p 229
Crowe Engineering Ltd v Phyllis Lynch and Others .... Vol IV p 340
Cummins (Decd), In Re Estates of, O'Dwyer & Charleton v Keegan & Ors .... Vol V p 367
Cunard Steam Ship Co Ltd, The v Herlihy (Inspector of Taxes), and
The Cunard Steam Ship Co Ltd v The Revenue Commissioners .... Vol I p 330
Curtin (Inspector of Taxes) v M Ltd .... Vol II p 360
Curtis, Gerard and Brendan Geough v The Attorney General and
The Revenue Commissioners .... Vol III p 419
Cusack, Patrick v Evelyn O'Reilly and The Collector General .... Vol IV p 86

D

Daly, Michael v The Revenue Commissioners & Ors .... Vol V p 213
Davis (Inspector of Taxes) v Hibernian Bank Ltd .... Vol I p 503
Davis, RG (Inspector of Taxes) v The Superioress, Mater Misericordiae
Hospital, Dublin .... Vol I p 387

Davis, WJ (Inspector of Taxes) v X Ltd .... Vol II p 45
Davoren, Estate of Mary Davoren, Thomas O'Byrne v Michael Davoren & Anne Coughlan .... Vol V p 36
De Brun (Inspector of Taxes) v K .... Vol III p 19
Deighan, Michael v Edward N Hearne, Attorney General & Ors .... Vol III p 533
Denny & Sons (Ireland) Ltd T/A Kerry Foods v Minister for Social Welfare .. Vol V p 238
Dilleen, TA (Inspector of Taxes) v Edward J Kearns .... Vol IV p 547
Diners Club Ltd, The v The Revenue and The Minister for Finance .... Vol III p 680
Director of Public Prosecutions v Martin McLoughlin .... Vol III p 467
Director of Public Prosecutions v Michael Cunningham .... Vol V p 691
Director of Public Prosecutions v Robert Downes .... Vol III p 641
Director of Public Prosecutions, The v Seamus Boyle .... Vol IV p 395
Dolan (Inspector of Taxes) v AB Co Ltd .... Vol II p 515
Dolan, JD (Inspector of Taxes) v "K" National School Teacher .... Vol I p 656
Donovan (Inspector of Taxes) v CG Crofts .... Vol I p 115
Downing, Estate of Teresa (Owner) .... Vol I p 487
Doyle & Ors v An Taoiseach & Ors .... Vol III p 73
Dunnes Stores (Oakville) Ltd v MC Cronin (Inspector of Taxes) .... Vol IV p 68

E

EG v Mac Shamhrain (Inspector of Taxes) .... Vol II p 352
Erin Executor and Trustee Co Ltd (as trustee of Irish Pension Fund Property Unit Trust) v the Revenue Commissioners .... Vol V p 76
Evans & Co v Phillips (Inspector of Taxes) .... Vol I p 43
Executors and Trustees of AC Ferguson (Deceased) v Donovan (IOT) .... Vol I p 183
Exported Live Stock (Insurance) Board, The v TJ Carroll (IOT) .... Vol II p 211

F

Fennessy (Inspector of Taxes) v John McConnellogue .... Vol V p 129
Fitzgerald, Martin v Commissioners of Inland Revenue .... Vol I p 91
Flynn, W (Inspector of Taxes) v (1) John Noone Ltd, and Flynn, W (Inspector of Taxes) v (2) Blackwood & Co (Sligo) Ltd .... Vol II p 222
Forbes (Inspector of Taxes) v GHD .... Vol II p 491
Forde, Michael Decision by Appeal Commissioners .... Vol IV p 348
Frederick Inns Ltd, The Rendezvous Ltd, The Graduate Ltd, Motels Ltd (In Liquidation) v The Companies Acts 1963-1983 .... Vol IV p 247

G

G O'C & A O'C, In the Matter of, (Application of Liam Liston (Inspector of Taxes)) .... Vol V p 346
GH Ltd v Browne (Inspector of Taxes) .... Vol III p 95
Gilbert Hewson v JB Kealy (Inspector of Taxes) .... Vol II p 15
Gilligan v Criminal Assets Bureau, Galvin, Lanigan & Revenue Commissioners .... Vol V p 424
Governor & Co of the Bank of Ireland v MJ Meeneghan & Ors .... Vol V p 44
Great Southern Railways Co, The v The Revenue Commissioners .... Vol I p 359
Green & Co (Cork) Ltd v The Revenue Commissioners .... Vol I p 130
Guinness & Mahon Ltd v Browne (Inspector of Taxes) .... Vol III p 373

Guinness, Arthur Son & Co Ltd v Commissioners of Inland Revenue
Arthur Guinness Son & Co Ltd v Morris (Inspector of Taxes) .... Vol I p 1

H

Hammond Lane Metal Co Ltd, The v S O'Culachain (IOT) .... Vol IV p 187
Haughey and Others v Attorney General and Others .... 1998 p 119
Hayes, C (Inspector of Taxes) v RJ Duggan .... Vol I p 195
Healy, John v SI Breathnach (Inspector of Taxes) .... Vol III p 496
Hearne, EN (Inspector of Taxes) v O'Cionna & Ors
t/a JA Kenny & Partners .... Vol IV p 113
Heron, Peter C & Ors v The Minister For Communications .... Vol III p 298
HH v MJ Forbes (Inspector of Taxes) .... Vol II p 614
Hibernian Insurance Company Limited v MacUimis (Inspector of Taxes)
.... Vol V p 495, 1999-2000 p 113
Hibernian Transport Companies Ltd, In re .... Vol V p 194
Hodgins, JT (Inspector of Taxes) v Plunder & Pollak (Ireland) Ltd .... Vol II p 267
Howth Estate Co v WJ Davis (Inspector of Taxes) .... Vol I p 447
HT Ltd, In re (In Liquidation) & Ors .... Vol III p 120
Hughes, HPC (Inspector of Taxes) v Miss Gretta Smyth
(Sister Mary Bernard) & Ors .... Vol I p 411
Hussey, J (Inspector of Taxes v M J Gleeson & Co Ltd .... Vol IV p 533
H Williams (Tallaght) (In Receivership and Liquidation) and
the Companies Act 1963-1990, In the Matter of .... Vol V p 388

I

Irish Agricultural Machinery Ltd v O'Culachain (IOT) .... Vol III p 611
Irish Nationwide Building Society v The Revenue Commissioners .... Vol IV p 296
Irish Provident Assurance Co Ltd (In Liquidation) v Kavanagh (IOT) .... Vol I p 45
Irwin, Liam J v Michael Grimes .... Vol V 209

J

JW v JW .... Vol IV p 437

K

K Co v Hogan (Inspector of Taxes) .... Vol III p 56
Kealy, J B (Inspector of Taxes) v O'Mara (Limerick) Ltd .... Vol I p 642
Kearns (Edward J) v Dilleen (Inspector of Taxes) .... Vol V p 514
Keller, Karl v The Revenue Commissioners & Ors .... Vol IV p 512
Kelly, HF (Inspector of Taxes) v H .... Vol II p 460
Kelly, JF (Inspector of Taxes) v Cobb Straffan Ireland Ltd .... Vol IV p 526
Kennedy (Inspector of Taxes) v The Rattoo Co-operative Dairy
Society Ltd .... Vol I p 315
Kennedy, Giles J v EG Hearne, the Attorney General & Ors .... Vol III p 590
Kenny, J v Revenue Commissioners, Goodman & Gemon Ltd
(Notice Parties) .... Vol V p 363
Kerrane, JG (Inspector of Taxes) v N Hanlon (Ireland) Ltd .... Vol III p 633
Kill Inn Motel Ltd (In Liquidation) v The Companies Acts 1963/1983 .... Vol III p 706
King (Evelyn Spain), The v The Special Commissioners .... Vol I p 221

King (Harris Stein), The v The Special Commissioners .... Vol I p 62
Kinghan, Albert v The Minister for Social Welfare .... Vol III p 436
Knockhall Piggeries v JG Kerrane (Inspector of Taxes) .... Vol III p 319

L

Louth, James & Ors v Minister for Social Welfare .... Vol IV p 391
Lynch, Mary v Moira Burke & AIB Banks plc .... Vol V p 271

M

MacAonghusa (Sean) (Inspector of Taxes) v Ringmahon Company .... 1999-2000 p 81
MacCarthaigh, DA (Inspector of Taxes) v Francis Daly .... Vol III p 253
MacDaibheid (Inspector of Taxes) v SD .... Vol III p 1
MacDermott (Inspector of Taxes) v BC .... Vol III p 43
MacGiolla Mhaith (Inspector of Taxes) v Cronin & Associates Ltd .... Vol III p 211
MacGiolla Riogh (Inspector of Taxes) v G Ltd .... Vol II p 315
MacKeown (Inspector of Taxes) v Patrick J Roe .... Vol I p 214
Madigan, PJ & Or v The Attorney General, Revenue Commissioners & Ors .. Vol III p 127
Manning, David v John R Shackleton & Cork County Council .... Vol IV p 485
Mara (Inspector of Taxes) v GG (Hummingbird) Ltd .... Vol II p 667
Masser, AH Ltd (In receivership) & Ors v Revenue Commissioners .... Vol III p 548
Maye, John v Revenue Commissioners .... Vol III p 332
McAuliffe, Tony v The Minister for Social Welfare .... Vol V p 94
McCabe (Inspector of Taxes) v South City & County Investment Co Ltd
.... Vol V p 107, 1998 p 183
McCall (Deceased) v Commissioners of Inland Revenue .... Vol I p 28
McCann, Charles Ltd v S O'Culachain (Inspector of Taxes) .... Vol III p 304
McCrystal Oil Co Ltd v The Revenue Commissioners & Ors .... Vol IV p 386
McDaid, Charles v His Honour Judge David Sheehy, DPP & Ors .... Vol IV p 162
McDaid, Charles v His Honour Judge Sheehy & Ors .... Vol V p 696
McElligott p & Sons Ltd v Duigenan (Inspector of Taxes) .... Vol III p 178
McGarry (Inspector of Taxes) v Limerick Gas Committee .... Vol I p 375
McGarry, L v W S (Inspector of Taxes) .... Vol II p 241
McGarry, W S (Inspector of Taxes) v EF .... Vol II p 261
McGarry, WS (Inspector of Taxes) v JA Spencer .... Vol II p 1
McGrath, Patrick & Ors v JE McDermott (Inspector of Taxes) .... Vol III p 683
McGurrin, L (Inspector of Taxes) v The Champion Publications Ltd .... Vol IV p 466
McHugh (Inspector of Taxes) v A .... Vol II p 393
McLoughlin, Edward and Thomas Marie Tuite v Revenue
Commissioners and The Attorney General .... Vol III p 387
McMahon,T & Ors v Rt Hon Lord Mayor Alderman & Burgess of Dublin ..... Vol V p 357
McMahon, J (Inspector of Taxes) v Albert Noel Murphy .... Vol IV p 125
McNally, Daniel v S O Maoldhomhniagh .... Vol IV p 22
McNamee, Estate of Thomas & Or, v The Revenue Commissioners .... Vol V p 577
Milverton Quarries Ltd v The Revenue Commissioners .... Vol II p 382
Minister for Labour, The v PMPA Insurance Co Ltd
(Under administration) .... Vol III p 505
Minister for Social Welfare v John Griffiths .... Vol IV p 378
Molmac Ltd v MacGiolla Riogh (Inspector of Taxes) .... Vol II p 482

Moloney (Inspector of Taxes) v Allied Irish Banks Ltd as executors of the estate of Francis J Doherty (Deceased) .... Vol III p 477
Monahan, Patrick (Drogheda) Ltd v O'Connell (Inspector of Taxes) .... Vol III p 661
Mooney, TB v EP O'Coindealbhain and The Revenue Commissioners .... Vol IV p 62
Mooney (Inspector Of Taxes) v McSweeney .... Vol V p 163
Most Honourable Frances Elizabeth Sarah Marchioness Conyngham, The v Revenue Commissioners .... Vol I p 231
Moville District Board Of Conservators v D Ua Clothasaigh (Inspector of Taxes) .... Vol II p 154
Muckley, Bernard and Anne, v Ireland, AG & Revenue Commissioners .... Vol III p 188
Mulvey, JD (Inspector of Taxes) v Denis J Coffey .... Vol I p 618
Mulvey, JD (Inspector of Taxes) v RM Kieran .... Vol I p 563
Murnaghan Brothers Ltd v S O'Maoldhomhnaigh .... Vol IV p 304
Murphy (Inspector of Taxes) v Asahi Synthetic Fibres (Ireland) Ltd .... Vol III p 246
Murphy, Frances & Mary Murphy v The Attorney General .... Vol V p 613
Murphy, John B v District Justice Brendan Wallace & Ors .... Vol IV p 278
Murphy, S (Inspector of Taxes) v Dataproducts (Dublin) Ltd .... Vol IV p 12
Murphy, Sean (Inspector of Taxes) v The Borden Co Ltd .... Vol III p 559

N

Navan Carpets Ltd v S O'Culachain (Inspector of Taxes) .... Vol III p 403
Noyek, A & Sons Ltd (In voluntary liquidation) v Edward N Hearne .... Vol III p 523

O

O'Broin, SP (Inspector of Taxes) v (1) Mac Giolla Meidhre, and O'Broin, SP (Inspector of Taxes) v (2) Finbar Pigott .... Vol II p 366
O'C, JB v PCD and A Bank .... Vol III p 153
O'Cahill (Inspector of Taxes) v Albert Harding & Ors .... Vol IV p 233
O'Callaghan, Thomas v JP Clifford & Ors .... Vol IV p 478
O'Cleirigh (Inspector of Taxes) v Jacobs International Ltd Inc .... Vol III p 165
O'Coindealbhain (Inspector of Taxes) v Breda O'Carroll .... Vol IV p 221
O'Coindealbhain (Inspector of Taxes) v KN Price .... Vol IV p 1
O'Coindealbhain (Inspector of Taxes) v TB Mooney .... Vol IV p 45
O'Coindealbhain, EP (Inspector of Taxes) v The Honourable Mr Justice Sean Gannon .... Vol III p 484
O'Conaill (Inspector of Taxes) v JJ Ltd .... Vol III p 65
O'Conaill (Inspector of Taxes) v R .... Vol II p 304
O'Conaill (Inspector of Taxes) v Z Ltd .... Vol II p 636
O'Connell, Patrick J (Inspector of Taxes) v Fyffes Banana Processing Ltd 1999-2000 p 71
O'Connell (Patrick J) (Inspector of Taxes) v Thomas Keleghan .... 1999-2000 p 143
O'Connlain (Inspector of Taxes) v Belvedere Estates Ltd .... Vol III p 271
O'Culachain (Inspector of Taxes) v McMullan Brothers Ltd .... Vol V p 200
O'Culachain, S (Inspector of Taxes) v Hunter Advertising Ltd .... Vol IV p 35
O'Culachain, S v McMullan Brothers .... Vol IV p 284
O'Dwyer (Inspector of Taxes) and the Revenue Commissioners v Irish Exporters and Importers Ltd (In Liquidation) .... Vol I p 629
O'Dwyer, JM (Inspector of Taxes) v Cafolla & Co .... Vol II p 82

O'Dwyer, JM (Inspector of Taxes) v The Dublin United Transport Co Ltd .... Vol II p 115
O'Grady (Inspector of Taxes) v Laragan Quarries Ltd .... Vol IV p 269
O'Grady (Inspector of Taxes) v Roscommon Race Committee .. Vol IV p 425, Vol V p 317
O'Laoghaire (Inspector of Taxes) v CD Ltd .... Vol III p 51
O'Leary, Edward v The Revenue Commissioners .... Vol IV p 357
O'Loan, HA (Inspector of Taxes) v Messrs M J Noone & Co .... Vol II p 146
O'Reilly, Gerald v W J Casey (Inspector of Taxes) .... Vol I p 601
O'Rourke v Revenue Commissioners .... Vol V p 321
O'Shea (Inspector of Taxes) v Michael Mulqueen .... Vol V p 134
O'Siochain, Sean (Inspector of Taxes) v Bridget Neenan .... Vol V p 472, 1998 p 111
O'Siochain, S (Inspector of Taxes) v Thomas Morrissey .... Vol IV p 407
O'Srianain (Inspector of Taxes) v Lakeview Ltd .... Vol III p 219
O'Sullivan (Inspector of Taxes) v p Ltd .... Vol II p 464
O'Sullivan JM (Inspector of Taxes) v Julia O'Connor, as Administratrix of Evelyn H O'Brien (Deceased) .... Vol II p 61
O'Sullivan v The Revenue Commissioners .... Vol V p 570
O hArgain, L (Inspector of Taxes) v B Ltd .... Vol III p 9
O Laochdha, (Inspector of Taxes) v Johnson & Johnson (Ireland) Ltd .... Vol IV p 361
Orange, James G v The Revenue Commissioners .... Vol V p 70
Orr, Michael (Kilternan) Ltd v The Companies Act 1963-1983, and Thornberry Construction (Irl) Ltd v The Companies Act 1963-1983 .... Vol III p 530

P

Pairceir (Inspector of Taxes) v EM .... Vol II p 596
Pandion Haliaetus Ltd, Ospreycare Ltd & Or v Revenue Commissioners .... Vol III p 670
Parkes (Roberta) v David Parkes .... 1998 p 169
Pharmaceutical Society of Ireland, The v Revenue Commissioners .... Vol I p 542
Phillips (Inspector of Taxes) v Keane .... Vol I p 64
Phillips (Inspector of Taxes) v Limerick County Council .... Vol I p 66
Phonographic Performance (Ireland) Ltd v J Somers (IOT) .... Vol IV p 314
Pine Valley Developments Ltd & Ors v Revenue Commissioners .... Vol IV p 543
Prior-Wandesforde, Captain RH v Revenue Commissioners .... Vol I p 249
Proes v Revenue Commissioners .... Vol V p 481
Property Loan & Investment Co Ltd v Revenue Commissioners .... Vol II p 25
Private Motorists Provident Society Ltd & WJ Horgan v Minister for Justice .... Vol V p 186
Purcell v Attorney General .... Vol IV p 229
Purcell, Joseph v AG Ireland & The Minister for the Environment .... Vol V p 288

Q

Quigley, JJ (Inspector of Taxes) v Maurice Burke .... Vol IV p 332, Vol V p 265

R

Racing Board, The v O'Culachain .... Vol IV p 73
Rahinstown Estates Co v M Hughes, (Inspector of Taxes) .... Vol III p 517
Revenue Commissioners v ORMG .... Vol III p 28
Revenue Commissioners v Arida Ltd .... Vol IV p 401, Vol V p 221

Revenue Commissioners v Associated Properties Ltd..Vol II p 412
Revenue Commissioners v Colm O Loinsigh ....Vol V p 98
Revenue Commissioners v Daniel Anthony Moroney & Ors ....Vol V p 589
Revenue Commissioners v Edward Doorley ....Vol V p 539
Revenue Commissioners v Henry Young ....Vol V p 294
Revenue Commissioners v HI.. Vol III p 242
Revenue Commissioners v L & Co...Vol II p 281
Revenue Commissioners v Latchford & Sons Ltd.. Vol I p 240
Revenue Commissioners v Orwell Ltd ....Vol II p 326
Revenue Commissioners v R Hilliard & Sons Ltd ....Vol II p 130
Revenue Commissioners v Sisters of Charity of the Incarnate Word .... 1998 p 65
Revenue Commissioners v Switzer Ltd ....Vol II p 19
Revenue Commissioners v Y Ltd ....Vol II p 195
Right Hon Earl of Iveagh v The Revenue Commissioners .... Vol I p 259
Robinson, WA T/A James Pim & Son v JD Dolan (IOT) .... Vol I p 427
Rowan, In the Goods of Bernard Louis (Deceased) Joseph Rowan v
Vera Agnes Rowan & Ors.. Vol III p 572

S

S Ltd v O'Sullivan ....Vol II p 602
S W Ltd v McDermott (Inspector of Taxes) ....Vol II p 661
Saatchi & Saatchi Advertising Ltd v McGarry (Inspector of Taxes)
.... Vol V p 376, 1998 p 99
Smyth EA & Weber Smyth v The Revenue Commissioners ....Vol V p 532
Stamp (Deceased) In the matter of, v Noel Redmond & Ors........................... Vol IV p 415
State, The (at the Prosecution of Patrick J Whelan) v Michael Smidic
(Special Commissioners of Income Tax)... Vol I p 571
State, The (Calcul International Ltd and Solatrex International Ltd)
v The Appeal Commissioners and The Revenue Commissioners .... Vol III p 577
State, The (FIC Ltd) v O'Ceallaigh (Inspector of Taxes) .... Vol III p 124
State, The (Melbarian Enterprises Ltd) v The Revenue
Commissioners... Vol III p 290
State, The (Multiprint Label Systems Ltd) v The Honourable Justice
Thomas Neylon .... Vol III p 159
Stephen Court Ltd v JA Browne (Inspector of Taxes) ....Vol V p 680
Sugar Distributors Ltd v The Companies Acts 1963-90 ....Vol V p 225
Sunday Tribune Limited (in Liquidation)... 1998 p 177
Swaine (Inspector of Taxes) v VE ....Vol II p 472
Swan (Deceased), In re Hibernian Bank Ltd v Frances Munro & Ors ....Vol V p 565

T

Taxback Limited v The Revenue Commissioners ....Vol V p 412
Texaco Ireland Ltd v S Murphy (Inspector of Taxes).. Vol IV p 91
Tipping, WJ (Inspector of Taxes) v Louis Jeancard ....Vol II p 68
Travers, John v Sean O'Siochain (Inspector of Taxes) ....Vol V p 54
Trustees of The Ward Union Hunt Races, The v Hughes (IOT) .... Vol I p 538

U

Ua Clothasaigh, D (Inspector of Taxes) v Patrick McCartan .... Vol II p 75
United Bars Ltd (In receivership), Walkinstown Inn Ltd
(In receivership) and Raymond Jackson v Revenue Commissioners ....Vol IV p 107
Urquhart D (Decd), In Re the Estate of, & The Revenue Commissioners
v AIB Ltd ....Vol V p 600

V

Vale, JB (Inspector Of Taxes) v Martin Mahony & Brothers Ltd........................ Vol II p 32
Veterinary Council, The v F Corr (Inspector of Taxes)...................................... Vol II p 204
Viek Investments Ltd v The Revenue Commissioners......................................Vol IV p 367

W

W Ltd v Wilson (Inspector of Taxes) .... Vol II p 627
Warnock & Ors practicing as Stokes Kennedy Crowley & Co
v The Revenue Commissioners ....Vol III p 356
Waterford Glass (Group Services) Ltd v The Revenue Commissioners ....Vol IV p 187
Wayte (Holdings) Ltd (In Receivership) v EN Hearne (IOT) ....Vol III p 553
Wiley, Michael v The Revenue Commissioners ....Vol IV p 170
Williams Group Tullamore Ltd v Companies Act 1963-1983 ....Vol III p 423
Wing v O'Connell (Inspector of Taxes) .... Vol I p 155
WLD Worldwide Leather Diffusion Ltd v Revenue Commissioners ....Vol V p 61

Cases reported and considered

A

A & B v WJ Davis (Inspector of Taxes) 2 ITC 350, Vol II p 60

A G Moore & Co v Hare 6 TC 572, [1915] SC 91, Vol II p 32, 515

AB Ltd v Mac Giolla Riogh (Inspector of Taxes) 3 ITC 301, Vol II p 419

AB v JD Mulvey (Inspector of Taxes) 2 ITC 345, [1947] IR 121, Vol II p 55
Cited also at: Vol III p 373

Abbey Films Ltd v Ireland [1981] IR 158, Vol III p 533

Abbot Laboratories Ltd v Carmody 44 TC 569, Vol III p 65

Aberdeen Construction Co Ltd v CIR [1978] 52 TC 281 Vol V p 163

Aberdeen Construction Group v IRC [1987] AC 885, 1999-2000 p 144

Absalom v Talbot 26 TC 166, [1944] AC 204, Vol II p 281

Action Aid Ltd v Revenue Commissioners Vol V p 392

Adams, Re [1967] IR 424, Vol III p 572

Addie, Robert & Sons' Collieries v CIR 8 TC 671, [1924] SC 231, Vol I p 91, Vol II p 32, 382

Administration des Douanes v Societe Anonyme Gondrant Freres and Societe Anonyme Garancini (Case 169/80) [1981] ECR 1931 1998 p 76

AE v The Revenue Commissioners [1984] ILRM 301, Vol V p 686

AG (New South Wales) v Quin [1990] 170 CLR 1, Vol IV p 170

AG for Manitoba v AG for Canada [1925] AC 561, Vol III p 73

AG of Hong Kong v NG Yuen Shiu [1983] 2 AC 629, Vol IV p 170

AG v Black IR 6 Ex 308, Vol II pp 154, 204

AG v Carlton Bank [1899] 2 QB 158 Vol V p 539

AG v Casey [1930] IR 163, Vol III p 387

AG v De Preville [1900] 1 QB 223 Vol V p 539

AG v Delaney [1876] IR 10 CL 125, Vol I p 542, Vol V p 539

AG v Doorley [1933] IR 750, Vol II p 326

AG v Great Eastern Co 5 AC 473, Vol II p 241

AG v Hamilton [1993] 2 IR 250, 1998 p 120

AG v Hope IR 2 CL 308 Vol V p 539

AG v Jameson [1905] 2 IR 218 Vol V p 532, 577

AG v London County Council No 1 4 TC 265, [1901] AC 26, Vol I pp 447, 487, 515

AG v London County Council No 2 5 TC 242, [1907] AC 131, Vol I p 487

AG v Metropolitan Water Board 13 TC 294, [1928] 1 KB 833, Vol II p 332, Vol III p 229

AG v Pettinger 6 H & N 733, Vol I p 259

AG v Southern Industrial Trust Ltd [1947] ILTR 174, Vol III pp 127, 387

AG v Sun Alliance & London Insurance Ltd [1985] ILRM 522, Vol III p 265

AG v The v Irish Steel Ltd and Vincent Crowley 2 ITC 402, Vol II p 108

AG v Seccombe [1990] 2 KB 688 1999-2000 p 63

AG v Till 5 TC 440, Vol III p 229

Agricultural Credit Corporation Ltd, The v JB Vale (Inspector of Taxes) 2 ITC 46 [1935] IR 681, Vol I p 474

Cited also at: Vol III, Vol I p 629, Vol III p 1, 373,

Aikman v Aikman 3 Macq HL 877, Vol I p 259

Ainsworth v Wilding [1896] 1 Ch 673, Vol III p 340

Airspace Investments Ltd v M Moore (Inspector of Taxes) Vol V p 3
Ajayi v RT Briscoe (Nig) Ltd [1964] 1 WLR 1326 Vol V p 589
Alianze Co Ltd v Bell 5 TC 60, 172 [1904] 2 KB 645, [1905] 1 KB 184, [1906] AC 18 Vol II p 515
Allchin v Coulthard 25 TC 430, [1943] AC 607, Vol II p 332
Alliance & Dublin Consumers' Gas Co, The v RG Davis (Inspector of Taxes) 1 ITC 114, [1926] IR 372, Vol I p 104
Cited also at: Vol I pp 474, 629
Alliance and Dublin Consumers' Gas Co v McWilliams 1 ITC 199, [1928] IR 1, 1 LTR 201, Vol I p 427
Cited also at: Vol I p 164, 207
Allied Irish Banks Ltd v Ardmore Studios International [1972] unrep Vol V p 226
Allied Irish Banks plc v James Bolger & Joan Bolger Vol V p 1
Almeida-Sanchez v US [1973] 413 US 266 Vol V p 614
Amalgamated Meat Packers Ltd, In re the [unrep], Vol III p 452
Amalgamated Property Co v TENAS Bank [1982] QB 84, Vol IV p 492
American Thread Co v Joyce 106 LT 171, 29 LTR 266, 6 TC 1 & 163, Vol I pp 28, 583, Vol II p 68
Ammonia Soda Co v Chamberlain [1918] 1 Ch 266, Vol II p 515
Anderson v Laneville 9 Moo PC 325, Vol I p 259
Anderton and Halstead Ltd v Birrell (Inspector of Taxes) [1932] I KB 271, Vol II pp 195, 627, Vol IV p 505
Anderton v Lambe [1981] 43 Ch D, Vol IV p 1
Andrews v Astley [unreported], Vol I p 64
Andrews v Partington [1791] 3 Bro CC 401 Vol V p 37
Anglo Persian Oil Co Ltd v Dale 16 TC 253, [1932] 1 KB 124, Vol I p 642, Vol II p 515
Anheuser Busch v The Controller of Patents Design and Trade Marks [1987] IR 329, Vol IV p 485
Antelope, The, 10 Wheaton 66 Vol V p 45
Appenroot v Central Middlesex Assessment Committee [1937] 2 KB 48, Vol II p 515
Archbishop of Thyateira v Hubert 168 LT 190, 25 TC 249, Vol II p 68
Archer-Shee v Baker 11 TC 749, 759, [1927] 1 KB 109, [1927] AC 844, Vol II p 393 Vol III p 477
Arthur Guinness Son & Co Ltd v CIR Arthur Guinness Son & Co Ltd v Morris (Inspector of Taxes) 1 ITC 1, [1923] 2 IR 186, Vol I p 1
AS v RB, WS and Registrar General [1984] ILRM 66, Vol IV p 437
Ashbury Railway Carriage and Iron Co v Riche, Vol IV p 247
Ashcroft, Clifton-V-Strauss, Re (1927) 1 Ch 313 Vol V p 295
Ashton Gas Co v Attorney General [1906] AC 10 Vol V p 565
Ashwander v Tennessee Valley Authority 297 US 288 Vol V p 696
Assets Co Ltd v Forbes 34 SLR 486, 3 TC 542
Associated Portland Cement Manufacturers Ltd v Kerr 27 TC 103, [1945] 2 AER 535, [1946] 1 AER 68, Vol II p 515
Associated Portland Cement Manufacturers Ltd v The Prices Commission [1975] 119 So 30, 63, [1975] ICR 34, Vol IV p 135
Associated Properties Ltd v The IRC 3 ITC 25, [1951 IR 140, Vol II p 175
Athenaeum Life Assce Society, In re [1858] Ch 4 Kay & J 304 Vol V p 226

Atherton v British Insulated & Helsby Cables Ltd 10 TC 155, [1925] 1 KB 421, [1926] AC 205, Vol I p 642, Vol II pp 32, 45, 222, 267, 360, 500, 515, 602, Vol III p 95, Vol IV p 425, Vol V p 496
Atkinson, In re, 31 Ch D 577 Vol V p 526
Attorney General of New Zealand v Ortiz [1984] AC 1 Vol V p 45
Attorney General v Power & Anor Vol V p 525
Cited also at: [1906] 2 IR 272, Vol III p 104
Ayerst v C & K (Construction) Ltd [1974] 1 AER 670, Vol IV p 247
Aylmer v Mahaffy 10 TC 594 & 598, [1925] NIR 167, Vol II p 374

B

Bach v Daniels 9 TC 183, [1925] 1 KB 526, Vol 1 p 515, Vol II pp 315, 636
Bagge v Whitehead [not reported], Vol III p 387
Bairead, MA (Inspector of Taxes) v Martin C Carr Vol IV p 505
Bairead, MA (Inspector of Taxes) v Maxwells of Donegal Ltd [1986] ILRM 508, Vol III p 430
Bairead, MA v M McDonald Vol IV p 475
Balgownie Land Trust Ltd v CIR 14 TC 684, Vol III p 1
Balkan-Import-Export GmbH v Hauptzollamt Berlin-Packhof (Case 118/76) [1977] ECR 1177 1998 p 76
Bank of Ireland Finance Ltd v The IRC Vol IV p 217
Bank of Ireland v Caffin [1971] IR 123, Vol IV p 437
Bank of Ireland v Kavanagh [Judgment delivered 19 June 1987], Vol IV p 407
Bank of Ireland v Rockfield Ltd [1979] IR 21 Vol V p 226
Bankline Ltd v CIR 49 TC 307, Vol III p 633
Barclays Bank v Siebe Gorman [1979] 2 Lloyd's Rep 142, Vol III p 548
Barker (Christopher) & Sons v CIR [1919] 2 KB 222, Vol III p 211
Barnardo's Homes v CIR 7 TC 646, [1921] 2 AC 1, Vol III p 477
Baroness Wenlock v River Dee Co [1885] 10 AC, Vol II p 241
Barrington's Hospital v Commissioner of Valuation [1975] IR 299, Vol II p 661
Bartlett v Mayfair Property Co [1898] 2 Ch 28, Vol II p 130
Baxendale v Murphy 9 TC 76 [1924] 2 KB 494, Vol I p 601
Baytrust Holdings Ltd v IRC [1971] 1 WLR 1333, Vol III p 661
Beak v Robson 25 TC 33, [1943] AC 352, Vol II p 515
Bean v Doncaster Amalgamated Collieries 27 TC 296, [1944] 2 AER, Vol II p 515
Beauchamp v FW Woolworth Plc [1989] STC 510 HL Vol V p 138
Beaumont, In Re, deceased [1980] Ch 444, [1979] 3 WLR 818 Vol V p 614
Bebb v Bunny 8 TC 454, 1 K & J 217, Vol II p 332
Bede Steam Shipping Co Ltd, In re [1917] 1 Ch 123 Vol V p 532
Bedford (Collector-General) v H [1968] IR 320, Vol II p 588
Beechor v Major [1865] BLT 54 Vol V p 271
Beirne (Inspector of Taxes) v St Vincent De Paul Society (Wexford Conference) 1 ITC 413 Vol I p 383
Beke v Smith (1836) 2 M & W 191 1998 p 76
Belgian State and Grand Duchy of Luxembourg v Martens (Cases 178, 179 and 180/73) [1974] ECR 383 1998 p 76
Belgium and Luxembourg v Mertens [1974] ECR 1998 p 76
Bell Bros Ltd, Re, ex parte Hodgson (1) 65 TLR 245 Vol V p 532
Bell Bros Pty Ltd v Shire of Serpentine-Jarrahdale [1969] 121 CLR 137 Vol V p 614

Bell v Kennedy LR 1 SC Appeal p 307, I S & D 307, LRIA SC 441, Vol I p 259
Belmont Farm v Minister for Housing 60 LGR 319 Vol V p 357
Belmont Finance Corporation Ltd v Williams Furniture Ltd (No 2) [1980] 1 AER 393, Vol IV p 247
Beloff v Pressdram Ltd [1973] 1 All ER 241 1998 p 177
Belville Holdings Ltd (Receivership and liquidation) v Cronin (Inspector of Taxes) [1985] IR 465, Vol III p 340
Beni Felkai Mining Co Ltd, Re [1934] 1 Ch 406, Vol III p 523
Bennet v Marshall 22 TC 73, [1938] 1 KB 591, Vol II pp 68, 393
Benson (Inspector of Taxes) v Yard Arm Club Ltd 53 TC 67, [1979] STC 266, Vol III p 219, Vol IV p 284
Benyon & Co Ltd v Ogg 7 TC 125, Vol I p 629
Berry v Farrow [1914] 1 IR 358, Vol II p 332
Berry v Fisher [1903] IR 484, Vol IV p 415
Best v Samuel Fox & Co Ltd [1952] AC 716, Vol IV p 437
Beynon and Co Ltd v Ogg 7 TC 125, Vol I pp 1, 28
Bickerman v Mason per Reps TL 2976, Vol IV p 22
Biddell Brothers v Clemens Horst Company [1911] 1 KB 934, Vol I p 130
Birch (Inspector of Taxes) v Denis Delaney 2 ITC 127, [1936] IR 517, 531, Vol I p 515
Cited also at: Vol I p 583, Vol II pp 315, 429, 472, 596, Vol III pp 1, 9
Birmingham v District Land Co v London & North Investment Railway Co [1888] 40 Ch D 268 Vol V p 589
BKJ v The IRC Vol III p 104
Blake and Others v AG [1982] IR 117, [1981] ILRM 34, Vol III p 127, Vol IV pp 187, 323.
Blakiston v Cooper 5 TC 347, [1907] 1 KB 702, 2 KB 688, [1909] AC 104, Vol I p 155
Bolam v Regent Oil Co Ltd 37 TC 56, Vol II p 515
Boland v An Taoiseach [1974] IR 338 Vol V p 614
Boland's Ltd v Davis (Inspector of Taxes) 1 ITC 91, [1925] ILTR 73, Vol I p 86
Cited also at: Vol III p 363.
Boland's Ltd v The CIR 1 ITC 42, Vol I p 34
Bolson J & Son Ltd v Farrelly 34 TC 161, Vol III p 253
Bomford v Osborne [1942] AC 14, 23 TC 642, Vol II pp 241, 515
Bonner v Basset Mines Ltd 6 TC 146, Vol II p 382
Bord na gCon v Stokes [November 1975], Vol IV p 73
Boulton v Bull [1795], Vol III p 441
Bourke (Inspector of Taxes) v Lyster & Sons Ltd 3 ITC 247, Vol II p 374
Bourke (Inspector of Taxes) v WG Bradley & Sons [1990] IR 379, Vol IV p 117
Bourne and Hollingsworth v the CIR 12 TC 483, Vol II p 429
Bowers v Harding 3 TC 22, Vol II p 366
Bowlby, In re, [1904] 2 Ch 685 Vol V p 526
Bowles v The AG and Others 5 TC 685, [1912] 1 Ch 123 p 135, Vol I p 583
Boyd v Shorrock [not reported], Vol III p 332
BP Australia Ltd v Commissioner of Taxation of the Commonwealth of Australia [1966] AC 224, Vol II p 515
Bradbury v The English Sewing Cotton Co Ltd 8 TC 481, [1923] AC 744, Vol I p 583
Bradbury v United Glass Bottle Manufacturers Ltd 38 TC 369, Vol II p 515
Bradshaw v Blundon 36 TC 397, Vol III p 373
Bray v Best [1989] STC 159, Vol IV p 407

Breathnach v McCann 3 ITR 112, [1984] ILRM 679 Vol V p 200
Breathnach, SI (Inspector of Taxes) v MC [1984] IR 340, Vol III p 113
Cited also at: Vol III p 219
Breen v The Minister for Defence [unreported, SC 20 July 1990], Vol IV p 170
Brennan and Others v AG and Wexford Co Co [1983] ILRM 449 (HC), [1984] ILRM 355 (SC), Vol III p 127
Brennan v AG [1984] ILRM 355, Vol IV pp 229, 323
Brice v The Northern Association Co [1911] 2 KB 577, [1912] 2 KB 41, [1913] AC 610, 6 TC 327, Vol I p 474
Brickwood & Co v Reynolds 3 TC 600, [1898] 1 QB 95, Vol I p 642
Brighton College v Marriott 10 TC 213, [1925] 1 KB 312, [1926] AC 192, Vol I pp 387, 542, Vol II p 211
Bristow (Inspector of Taxes) v Dickinson and Co Ltd 27 TC 157, 62 TLR 37, [1946] KB 321, Vol II pp 140, 374
British Airways v C & E Commissioners [1989] STC 182, Vol IV p 349
British American Tobacco Co v The IRC [1943] AC 335, [1941] 2 KB 270, Vol II p 175
British Broadcasting Corporation v Johns 41 TC 471, Vol IV p 73
British Insulated & Helsby Cables Ltd v Atherton [1926] AC 205 Vol V p 680
British Legion peterhead Branch v CIR 35 TC 509, Vol III p 253
British Mexican Petroleum Co v Jackson 16 TC 570, Vol II p 281
British Railways Board v C & E Commissioners [1977] STC 221, Vol IV p 349
British Sugar Manufacturers Ltd v Harris (Inspector of Taxes) [1938] 2 KB 220, Vol II p 195, Vol IV p 505
Briton Ferry Steel Co Ltd v Barry 23 TC 414, [1940] 1 KB 463, Vol II p 315
Brocklebank, Re, 23 QBD 461, Vol II p 130
Broken Hill Property Co Ltd v Commissioners of Taxation 41 ALJR 377, Vol III pp 113, 120, 219, Vol IV p 284.
Brosnan (Inspector of Taxes) v Leeside Nurseries Ltd Vol V p 21
Brosnan (Inspector of Taxes) v Mutual Enterprises Ltd Vol V p 138
Cited also 1999-2000 p 82
Brosnan, TJ (Inspector of Taxes) v Cork Communications Ltd Vol IV p 349
Brown v Donegal County Council [1980] IR 132, 146, Vol III p 19
Browne & Bank of Ireland Finance Ltd [1991] 1 IR 431, 3 ITR 644 Vol V p 139
Browne Paul and Others v The IRC and Others [1991] 2 IR 58, Vol IV p 323
Cited also at: Vol IV p 125
Browne v Burnley Football & Athletic Co Ltd 53 TC 357, [1980] STC 424, Vol IV p 425, Vol V p 317
Browne v Burnley Football and Athletic Co Ltd 53 TC 537
Browne, JA (Inspector of Taxes) v Bank of Ireland Finance Ltd [1987] IR 346 [1991] 1 IR 431, Vol III p 644
Browns Transport Ltd v Kropp (1958) 100 CLR 263, Vol III p 73
BSC Footwear Ltd v Ridgeway 47 TC 495, Vol IV p 135
Buchanan Ltd, Peter v McVey [1954] IR 89 Vol V p 45, 226, 1998 p 76
Buckley v AG [1950] IR 67 Vol V p 696
Bucks v Bowers [1970] Ch D 431, Vol III p 633
Bula Ltd v Tara Mines Ltd [1994] ILRM 111 Vol V p 266
Bullcroft Main Collieries Ltd v O'Grady [1932] 17 TC 93, Vol II p 267, 360
Bullimore v C & E Commissioners MAN/86/145, Vol IV p 349

Burke & Sons Ltd v Revenue Commissioner, Ireland and Attorney General Vol V p 418
Burmah Steamship Co Ltd v CIR [1931] SC 156, [1931] SLT 116, 16 TC 67, Vol I p 427
Burman v Thorn Domestic Appliances (Electrical) Ltd [1982] STC 179, Vol III p 165
Button v West Cork Railway [1883] 23 Ch D, Vol III p 706
Byrne (Terence) v The Revenue Commissioners Vol V p 560
Byrne v Conroy 1998 p 75
Byrne v Ireland [1972] IR 241 Vol V p 614

C

C & E Commissioners v Zinn and Others [1988] STC 57, Vol IV p 349
Cadwalader 12 SC LTR 499, 5 TC 101, Vol I p 259
Café Brandy Syndicate v CIR 12 TC 358 1998 p 100
Cafolla v AG [1985] IR 486, Vol IV p 323
Cahill v Harding 4 ITR 233 Vol V p 134
Cahill v Sutton [1980] IR 269, Vol III p 127, 419
California Copper Syndicate v Harris 5 TC 159, [1904] 41 SLR 691, 6F 894, Vol I pp 474, 503, 629, Vol III p 644
Campbell v Hall [1774] 1 Cowp 204 ([1558-1774] AER Rep 252 Vol V p 322
Camille and Henry Dreyfus Foundation v CIR (1955) 36 TC 126 1998 p 66
Cannon Industries Ltd v Edwards 42 TC 265, [1966] 1 AER 456, Vol II p 614
Cape Brandy Syndicate v CIR 12 TC 358
Cape Brandy Syndicate v CIR 12 TC 358, [1921] 1 KB 64, Vol I pp 1, 28, Vol III pp 56, 477, Vol IV p 91, Vol V p 376, 472
Capital and National Trust Ltd v Golder 31 TC 265, Vol III p 95, Vol V p 496, 680, 1999-2000 p 114
Carbery Milk Products Ltd v The Minister for Agriculture and Others Vol IV p 492
Carlisle and Silloth Golf Club v Smith 6 TC 198, [1912] 2 KB 177, [1913] 3 KB 75 Vol I pp 387, 515
Carr v CIR [1944] 2 AER 163, Vol III p 211
Carroll Group Distributors Ltd v GAJF Bourke Ltd Vol V p 108, 1998 p 183
Carroll Industries Plc (formerly PJ Carroll & Co Ltd) and PJ Carroll & Co Ltd v S O'Culachain (Inspector of Taxes) [1988] IR 705, Vol IV p 135
Cited also at: Vol IV p 304
Carroll v Mayo County Council [1967] IR 364, Vol II p 636
Carson v Cheyney's Executor 38 TC 240, [1959] AC 412, [1958] 3 AER 573, Vol III p 484, Vol IV p 135
Cary v Cary 2 Sch and Lef 173, Vol I p 601
Casdagli v Casdagli [1919] AC p 177, Vol I p 259
Casey (Inspector of Taxes) v AB Ltd [1965] IR 575, Vol II p 500
Casey (Inspector of Taxes) v The Monteagle Estate Co 3 ITC 313, [1962] IR 106, Vol II p 429
Cassidy v Minister for Industry and Commerce [1978] IR 297, Vol III p 73, Vol V p 288
Cassidy v Minister of Health (1978) IR 207 Vol V p 239
Cayzer Irvine & Co Ltd v CIR 24 TC 491, Vol II p 472
CCSV v Minister for the Civil Service [1984] 3 AER 935, Vol IV p 170
CD v JM O'Sullivan (Inspector of Taxes) 2 ITC 422, [1949] IR 264, Vol II p 140
Cecil v CIR [1919] 36 TLR 164, Vol III p 211
Cenlon Finance Co Ltd v Ellwood 40 TC 176, [1961] 2 AER 861, [1961] Ch 634, [1962] AC 782, [1974] ITC No 10, Vol II p 627, Vol III p 56, Vol IV p 187

Central London Property Trust Ltd v High Trees House Ltd [1947] KB 130, Vol V p 589
Chambers v Fahy Supreme Court, unrep, 1931 Vol V p 472
Chamney v Lewis [1932] 17 TC 318, Vol II pp 393, 491
Chancery Lane Safe Deposit and Office Co Ltd v CIR 43 TC 83, Vol II p 627
Chantrey Martin & Co v Martin [1952] 2 AER 691, Vol IV p 332, Vol V p 266
Charente Steamship Co v Wilmot 24 TC 97, [1941] 2 KB 386, Vol II p 602
Charge Card Services Ltd, Re, Vol III p 680
Charles Brown & Co v CIR 12 TC 1256, Vol I p 427
Charles McCann v O'Culachain [1985] IR 298, [1986] IR 196, 3 ITR 304 Vol V p 21, 515
Charleston Federal Savings and Loan Assn v Alderson [1945] 324 US 182, Vol III p 127
Charterbridge Corporation v Lloyds Bank [1969] 2 AER, Vol IV p 247
Chaulk v R [1990] 3 Scr 13 Vol V p 213
Cherry Court v The Revenue Commissioners Vol V p 180
Chettiar v Chettiar [1962] 2 WLR 548; [1962] AC 294 1998 p 169
Chevron Oil Co v Huson [1971 404 US 97 Vol V p 614
Chibett Robinson 9 TC 48, 132 LTR 31, Vol I p 155
Chicago, Indianapolis & Louisville Railway Co v Hackett [1931] 228 US 559 Vol V p 614
Chicot County Drainage District v Baxter State Bank [1940] 308 US 371 Vol V p 614
Chinn v Collins [1981] AC 533, [1981] 2 WLR 14, [1981] 1 AER 189, [1980] 54 TC 311, Vol III p 683
Cipriano v City of Houma [1969] 395 US 701 Vol V p 614
CIR v Alexander von Glehn & Co [1920] 2 KB 553, Vol II p 515
CIR v Anderstrom 13 TC 482, [1928] SC 224, Vol II pp 393, 491
CIR v Barclay Curle and Co Ltd 45 TC 221, Vol III pp 113, 120, 219
CIR v Birmingham Theatre Royal Estate Co Ltd 12 TC 580, Vol I p 447, Vol III p 253
CIR v Brender and Cruickshank 46 TC 574, Vol IV p 45
CIR v Buchanan 37 TC 365, [1957] 3 WLR 68, Vol II p 352
CIR v Burrell 9 TC 27, [1924] 2 KB 52, Vol I p 318
CIR v Carron Co 45 TC 18 1999-2000 p 82
CIR v Cock Russel & Co Ltd 29 TC 387, Vol IV p 135
CIR v Cola 38 TC 334, [1959] SLT 122, Vol II p 515
CIR v Dalgety & Co 15 TC 216, Vol III p 403
CIR v Forrest 3 TC 117, 15 AC 334, Vol I p 542
CIR v Forsyth Grant 25 TC 369, [1943] SC 528, Vol II p 636, Vol IV p 1
CIR v Forth Conservancy Board [1930] SC 850, [1931] AC 540, 47 TLR 429, 16 TC 103, Vol I p 656, Vol II p 154, Vol IV p 73
CIR v Fraser 24 TC 498, Vol III p 253
CIR v Gas Lighting Improvement Co Ltd [1922] KB 381, 12 TC 503, Vol I p 447
CIR v George Burrell and William Burrell 9 TC 27, [1924] 2 KB 52, 129 LTR 542, Vol I p 45
CIR v Granite City Steamship Co [1927] Sess Cas 705, 13 TC 1, Vol II p 515, Vol III p 165
CIR v Gribble [1913] 3 KB 212, Vol III p 611
CIR v Hendersons Executors 16 TC 282, Vol III p 477
CIR v Hyndland Investment Co Ltd 14 TC 694, Vol III p 1
CIR v Kingston Railway Co 1 ITC 131, Vol I p 387
CIR v Lambhill Ironworks Ltd 31 TC 393, Vol III p 65
CIR v Land Securities Investment Trust Ltd 45 TC 495 Vol III p 95, Vol V p 139

CIR v Livingston and Others 11 TC 538, Vol III pp 1, 253, 373
CIR v Lysaght 13 TC 511, [1928] AC 234, Vol I p 259
CIR v Mackinlay's Trustees 22 TC 305, [1938] SC 765, Vol II p 627
CIR v Maxse 12 TC 41, Vol III pp 178, 211
CIR v Morton [1941] SC 467, 24 TC 259, Vol II p 82
CIR v Newcastle Breweries 12 TC 926, 95 LJ, KB 936, 97 LJ, KB 735, Vol II p 515, Vol III p 165
CIR v Payne 110 LJKB 323, 23 TC 610, Vol II p 82
CIR v Peebleshire Nursing Association 11 TC 335, [1927] SC 215, Vol I p 387
CIR v Pullman Car Co Ltd 35 TC 221, 1999-2000 p 82
CIR v Ramsay [1935] 154 LT 141, 20 TC 79, Vol II p 222, 464, 602
CIR v Ransom (William) & Son Ltd 12 TC 21, Vol III p 178
CIR v Reinhold 34 TC 389, Vol III p 1
CIR v Robins Brothers Ltd 43 TC 266, Vol IV p 425
CIR v Saunders & Pilcher 31 TC 314, Vol III p 304
CIR v Scott Adamson 17 TC 679, [1933] SC 23, Vol II p 482
CIR v Scottish & Newcastle Breweries Ltd 55 TC 252, Vol III pp 113, 120, 219
CIR v Scottish Central Electric Power Co 13 TC 331, [1930] SC 226, 15 TC 761, Vol II p 32, Vol III p 403
CIR v Sneath [1932] 2 KB 362, 17 TC 149, Vol II p 326
CIR v Sneath 17 TC 149, [1932] 2 KB 362, Vol I p 571
CIR v South Behar Railway Co Ltd 12 TC 657, [1925] AC 476, Vol I p 387
CIR v Sparkford Vale Co-operative Society Ltd 133 LT 231, 12 TC 891, Vol I p 315
CIR v The Budderpore Oil Company Ltd 12 TC 467, Vol I p 629
CIR v The Dublin and Kingstown Railway Co [1930] IR 317, 1 ITC 131, Vol I p 359
CIR v The Edinburgh and Bathgate Railway Co 12 TC 895, [1926] Sess Cas 862, Vol I p 359
CIR v The Governor & Co of The Bank of Ireland 1 ITC 74, [1925] 2 IR 90, Vol I p 70
CIR v The Korean Syndicate Ltd [1920] 1 KB 598, 12 TC 181 p 205, Vol I p 447
CIR v The Scottish Automobile & General Insurance Co Ltd [1932] SC 87, 16 TC 381, Vol I p 474, 629
CIR v The Tyre Investment Trust Ltd 132 LT 59, 12 TC 646 pp 655 and 656, Vol I p 447
CIR v The Yorkshire Agricultural Society 13 TC 58, [1928] 1 KB 611, Vol I p 542
CIR v Toll Property Co Ltd 34 TC 13, Vol III p 1
CIR v Trustees of Joseph Reid, Deceased 30 TC 431, [1947] SC 700, [1949] LJR 701, Vol II p 464
CIR v Von Glehn & Co Ltd 12 TC 232, [1920] KB 553, Vol I p 195
CIR, The v The Dublin and Kingstown Railway Co [1930] IR 317, Vol I p 119
City of Dublin Steampacket Co, The (in liquidation) v The Revenue Commissioners 1 ITC 285, [1930] IR 217, Vol I p 318
City of Dublin Steampacket Co, The v IRC 1 ITC 118, [1926] IR 436, Vol I p 108
Cited also at: Vol I p 387
City of London Contract Corporation v Styles [1887] 2 TC 239, Vol II p 515
City of London Real Property Co Ltd v Jones 15 TC 266, [1930] AC 432, Vol I pp 487, 515
Cityview Press Ltd v An Chomhairle Oiliuna [1980] IR 381, Vol III p 127, Vol IV p 162
Clerical, Medical and General Life Assurance Society v Carter 2 TC 437, 22 QBD 444, Vol I p 45
Cleveleys Investment Trust Company v CIR 1975 TC 300 Vol V p 163,1999-2000 p 144

Clifford & O'Sullivan, Re [1921] 2 AC 570, Vol III p 290
Clinch v IRC [1974] IQB 76, Vol III p 356
Clitheroes Estate, In re, 31 Ch D 135 Vol V p 526
Cloghran Stud Farm v AG Birch (Inspector of Taxes) 2 ITC 65, [1936] IR 1, Vol I p 496
Cited also at: Vol I p 515, Vol II p 315
Clover Clayton & Co v Hughes [1910] AC 242 (p 256), Vol I p 427
CM v TM (No 2) [1990] 2 IR 52, [1991] ILRM 268, Vol IV p 437
CM v TM [1987] IR 152, [1988] ILRM 456, Vol IV p 437
Coates v Holker Estates Co [1961] 40 TC 75, Vol II p 657
Codman v Hill [1919], Vol III p 253
Colclough v Colclough [1965] IR 668, Vol II p 332
Cole Bros Ltd v Phillips (Inspector of Taxes) [1981] STC 671, [1982] STC 311, Vol IV pp 68, 284
Cole Bros v Phillips [1980] Ch D 518, 55 TC 188, Vol III p 219
Cole Bros v Phillips [1981] STC 671 Vol V p 200
Coleman's Depositaries Ltd and Life and Health Assurance Association, Re [1907] 2 KB 798, Vol III p 159
Collco Dealings Ltd v IRC 39 TC 509, [1961] 1 AER 762, Vol III p 246
Collins v Adamson 21 TC 400, [1937] 4AE 236, [1938] 1 KB 477, Vol II p 515
Collins v IRC 12 TC 773, [1925] SC 151, Vol I p 240
Collins, Daniel and Michael Byrne, Daniel Collins and Redmond Power as executor of the will of Michael Byrne, deceased, and Daniel Collins v J D Mulvey (Inspector of Taxes) 3 ITC 151, [1956] IR 233, Vol II p 291
Collyer v Hoare & Co Ltd [1931] 1 KB 123, 17 TC 169, [1932] AC 407, Vol I pp 447, 515
Colquohoun v Brooks 2 TC 490, [1889] 14 AC 493, Vol I p 183, Vol II pp 393, 491
Coltness Iron Co v Black 1 TC 287, Vol II p 382
Colville v CIR 8 TC 422, [1923] SC 423, 60 SCLR 248, Vol I p 601
Combe v Combe [1951] 2 KB 215 Vol V p 589
Commercial Structures Ltd v Briggs 30 TC 477, [1948] 2 AER 1041, Vol II pp 195, 627
Commission of the European Communities v Council of the European Communities [1973] ECR 575, Vol IV p 170
Commission of the European Communities v Denmark C47/88, Vol IV p 512
Commissioner of Inland Revenue v Granite City Steamship Co Ltd 13 TC 1 Vol V p 496
Commission v France and UK (Cases 92and 93/87) [1989] ECR 405 1998 p 76
Commissioners of Inland Revenue v Dowdall O'Mahony & Co Ltd 33 TC 259 1998 p 66
Commissioners of Inland Revenue v Gull 21 TC 374 1998 p 66
Commissioner of Inland Revenue v Wilsons Executors 18 TC 465 Vol V p 496
Commissioner of Taxes v Nchanga Consolidated Copper Mines [1964] 2 WLR 339, 1 AER 208, Vol II pp 515, 602
Commissioners for Special Purposes of Income Tax v Pemsel 3 TC 53, [1891] AC 531, Vol I pp 221, 387, 542, Vol II p 661
Commissioners of Inland Revenue v Land Securities Investment Trust Ltd 45 TC 495 Vol V p 680
Commissioners of Taxes v Melbourne Trust Ltd [1914] AC 1001, 84 LJPC 21, 30 TLR 685, Vol I p 474
Companies Act 1908 v Ross & Boal Ltd [1924] 1 IR 129, Vol III p 332
Companies Act 1963-1983, The v Castlemahon Poultry Products Ltd [1986] IR 750, [1987] ILRM 222, Vol III p 509

Companies Act 1963-1983, The v MFN Construction Co Ltd (in liquidation) Vol IV p 82
Compton, In re [1945] Ch 123; [1945] 1 AER 198; 114 LJ Ch 99; 172 LT 158; 61 TLR 167; 89 SJ 142, Vol V p 37.
Connolly (Inspector of Taxes) v Denis McNamara 3 ITC 341, Vol II p 452
Connolly (Inspector of Taxes) v WW Vol II p 657
Connolly Peter v The Collector of Customs and Excise Vol IV p 419
Connolly, Edward v AG Birch (Inspector of Taxes) 2 ITC 201, [1939] IR 534, Vol I p 583
Cited also at: Vol II p 472, Vol III p 9
Construction Industry Training Board v Labour Force Ltd [1970] 3 AER 220, Vol III p 505, Vol IV p 391
Cook, Exparte, 29 LJQ B 68, Vol I p 221
Cooke v Beach Station Caravans Ltd [1974] 49 TC 514, [1974] STC 402, Vol IV pp 68, 425, Vol V p 317
Cooke v Walsh [1984] IR 710 Vol V p 696
Cookson v Lee 23 LJ Ch NS p 473, Vol II p 241
Coombe Importers Ltd (In Liq) & Re the Companies Acts 1963-1990, 1998 p 59
Cooper v Stubbs 10 TC 29, [1925] 2 KB 753, Vol I p 629, Vol II pp 204, 614
Cooper, In re, [1911] 2 KB 550, Vol II p 332
Co-operative Insurance Society v Richardson [1955] CLY 1365, Vol III p 43
Copeman v Coleman 22 TC 594, [1939] 2 KB 484, Vol II p 82
Cormacs Trustees v The Commissioners of Inland Revenue [1924] SC 819 Vol V p 181
Corporation of Birmingham v Barnes 19 TC 195, Vol III pp 165, 253
Corr, F (Inspector of Taxes) v F E Larkin 3 ITC 13, [1949] IR 399, Vol II p 164
Costa v ENEL [1964] ECR 585 1998 p 76
Costa Rica Railway Co Ltd v CIR 29 TC 34, Vol II p 429
Cottin v Blane [1975] 2 ANSTR 544, Vol III p 265
Courtauld v Leigh LR 4 Ex at 149 Vol V p 570
Cowan v Seymour 7 TC 372, [1920] 1 KB 500, Vol I pp 155, 618
Cox v Glue 5 CB 533, Vol II p 636
Cox v Hickman 8 HCL 268, Vol III p 467
Cox v Murray [1919] 1 IR 358, Vol II p 332
Cox v Rabbits 3 AC 478, Vol I p 601
Craddock v Zevo Finance Co Ltd 27 TC 267, [1944] 1 AER 566, 174 LT 385, Vol II p 419
Craignish, Re, [1892] 3 Ch 192, Vol I p 259
Craven's Mortgage, Re, 8 TC 651, [1907] 2 Ch 448, Vol II p 332
Criminal Assets Bureau v Gerard Hutch 1999-2000 p 65
Croft v Sywell Aerodrome 24 TC 126, [1942] 1 AER 110, Vol II p 315
Cronin (Inspector of Taxes) v C [1968] IR 148, Vol II p 592
Cronin (Inspector of Taxes) v Cork & County Property Co Ltd [1986] IR 559, Vol III p 198
Cited also at: Vol III p 271, Vol IV p 135
Cronin (Inspector of Taxes) v IMP Midleton Ltd Vol III p 452
Cronin (Inspector of Taxes) v Lunham Brothers Ltd [1986] ILRM 415, Vol III p 363
Cronin (Inspector of Taxes) v Strand Dairy Ltd Vol III p 441
Cited also at: Vol III p 611, Vol IV p 35, 533, 526, Vol V 21
Cronin (Inspector of Taxes) v Youghal Carpets (Yarns) Ltd [1985] IR 312, [1985] ILRM 666, Vol III p 229
Cronin v Strand Dairy 3 ITR 441 Vol V p 21
Cronk, John & Sons Ltd v Harrison [1936] 120 TC 112, Vol III p 683

Crosby v Wadsworth [1805] 6 East 602, Vol II p 636
Crowe Engineering Ltd v Phyllis Lynch and Others Vol IV p 340
Crowley v Ireland [1980] IR 102 Vol V p 614
Cullen v AG LR 1 HL 190 Vol V p 539
Cullen v Cullen [1962] IR 268 Vol V p 589
Cummins, In the Matter of the Estates of: O'Dwyer & Charleton v Keegan & Ors Vol V p 367
Cunard Steam Ship Co Ltd, The v Herlihy (Inspector of Taxes), and The Cunard Steam Ship Co Ltd v IRC 1 ITC 373, [1931] IR 287, 307, Vol I p 330
Currie v CIR & Durant v CIR [1921] 12 TC 245, Vol III p 211
Curtin (Inspector of Taxes) v M Ltd 3 ITC 227, [1960] IR 59, Vol II p 360
Curtis, Gerard & Brendan Geough v AG &IRC [1986] ILRM 428, Vol III p 419
Cusack Patrick v Evelyn O'Reilly and The Collector General Vol IV p 86
Cyril Lord Carpets Ltd v Schofield 42 TC 637, Vol III p 165

D

D & GR Rankine v CIR 32 TC 520, [1952] SLT 153, Vol II p 429, Vol IV p 135
Dagnall, In re, 12 TC 712, [1896] 2 QB 407, Vol I p 108
Dale v CIR [1953] 34 TC 468, Vol II p 596
Dale v Johnson 32 TC, Vol III p 661
Daly, Michael v The Revenue Commissioners & Ors Vol V p 213
Daphne v Shaw [1926] 11 TC 256, Vol II p 602, Vol III pp 113, 120
Date v Mitcalfe [1928] 1 KB 383, 13 TC 41, [1927] WN 271, Vol I p 221
Davis (Inspector of Taxes) v Hibernian Bank Ltd 2 ITC 111, Vol I p 503
Cited also at: Vol II p 419, Vol III p 373
Davis (Inspector of Taxes) v The Superioress, Mater Misericordiae Hospital Dublin [1933] IR 481, 1 ITR 387 Vol V p 6
Davis v Adair [1895] 1 IR 379, Vol I p 259
Davis v Johnson [1978] 1 AER 841, CA 1132 HL (E), Vol III p 113, 120
Davis v M 2 ITC 320, [1947] IR 145, Vol II p 500, 515
Davis, RG (Inspector of Taxes) v The Superioress, Mater Misericordiae Hospital, Dublin 2 ITC 1, [1933] IR 480, 503, Vol I p 387
Cited also at: Vol III p 178, Vol V p 6
Davis, WJ (Inspector of Taxes) v X Ltd 2 ITC 320, [1946] ILTR 57, [1947] ILTR 157 Vol II p 45
Davoren, Estate of Mary Davoren Vol V p 36
Dawson v Dawson 11 Jur 984, Vol II p 332
De Brun (Inspector of Taxes) v K [1981] IR 117, [1982] ILRM 13, Vol III p 19
Cited also at: Vol III pp 56, 113, 120, 304, 319, 441, 477, 533, 611, 683, Vol IV pp 91, 349, 526, 547
De Burca v The Attorney General [1976] IR 38 Vol V p 614
De Nicolls v Saunders LR 5, CP 589, Vol II p 222
Dearle v Hall 15 TC 725, 3 Russell Reports 1, Vol II p 592
Deaton v AG [1963] IR 170, [1962] 98 ILTR 99, Vol III pp 419, 533, Vol IV p 278
Defrenne v Sabena [1976] 2 CMLR 98 Vol V p 614
Deighan, Michael v Edward N Hearne, AG and Others [1986] IR 603, [1990] IR 499, Vol III p 533
Cited also at: Vol III p 590, Vol IV p 505,1999-2000 p 65
Dennehy v Minister for Social Welfare [Unreported HC 26 July 1984], Vol IV p 437

Denny & Sons (Ireland) Ltd T/A Kerry Foods v Minister for Social Welfare Vol V p 238
Depoix v Chapman 28 TC 462, [1947] 2 AER 649, Vol II p 241
Derry v Inland Revenue [1927] SC 714 Vol V p 614
Derry v The CIR [1927] Sess Cas 714, 13 TC 30, Vol II p 75
Deuchar v Gas Light & Coke Co [1925] AC, Vol II p 241
Dewar v IRC 19 TC 561, Vol III p 484
Dickson v Fitch's Garage [1975] STC 480 Vol V p 200
Diggines v Forestal Land, Timber and Railways Co Ltd 15 TC 630, [1931] AC 380, Vol II p 304
Dilleen, TA (Inspector of Taxes) v Edward J Kearns Vol IV p 547
Diners Club Ltd, The v The Revenue and The Minister for Finance [1988] IR 158, Vol III p 680
Dinning v Henderson 3 de G & S 702, Vol II p 332
Diplock v Wintle [1948} Ch 465, Vol IV p 247
Ditcher v Denison 11 Moore PC 325 p 337, Vol II p 108
Diver v McCrea [1908] 42 ILTR 249 Vol V p 271
Diver v McCrea [1908] 42 ILTR 249.
Dixon v Fitch's Garage Ltd 50 TC 509, [1975] STC 480, [1975] 3 AER 455, Vol III p 219, Vol IV pp 68, 284, 425
Dixon, Heynes v Dixon, Re, [1900] 2 Ch 561, Vol III p 265
Dolan (Inspector of Taxes) v AB Co Ltd [1969] IR 282, 104 ILTR 101, Vol II p 515
Cited also at: Vol II p 602
Dolan v Corn Exchange [1975] IR 315 Vol V p 322
Dolan v Joyce and Kirwan [1928] IR 559, Vol II p 1
Dolan v Neligan [1967] IR 247, Vol III p 403, Vol V p 322, 614
Dolan, JD (Inspector of Taxes) v "K" National School Teacher 2 ITC 280, [1944] IR 470, Vol I p 656
Cited also at: Vol II p 592, Vol III p 484, Vol IV p 221
Donald v Thomson 8 TC 272, [1922] SC 237, Vol II p 636
Donovan (Inspector of Taxes) v CG Crofts 1 ITC 214, [1926] IR 477, Vol I p 115
Cited also at: Vol I p 183, Vol II p 75
Douglas v Douglas CR 12 Eq 643, Vol I p 259
Downing, Estate of Teresa (Owner) 2 ITC 103, [1936] IR 164, Vol I p 487
Downing's Estate, Re, 1 ITC 103, [1936] IR 164, Vol II p 332
Doyle & Others v An Taoiseach & Others [1986] ILRM 522, Vol III p 73
Cited also at: Vol IV p 162
Doyle and Others v Government of Ireland and Others [1981] ECR 735, Vol III p 73
Doyle, In Re Evelyn (SC) 21 Dec 1955 Vol V p 614
DPP v Humphrys [1977] AC 1, [1976] 2 WLR 837, [1976] 2 AER 497, Vol III p 419
DPP v Luft & Anor 2 AER 569, [1976] 3 WLR 32, Vol III p 28
DPP v Lynch [1982] IR 64, [1981] ILRM 389, Vol III p 419
DPP v Martin McLoughlin [1986] IR 355, [1986] ILRM 493, Vol III p 467
Cited also at: Vol IV p 378
DPP v Michael Cunningham Vol V p 691
DPP v Ottewell [1970] AC 642, 649, Vol III p 19
DPP v Robert Downes [1987] IR 139, [1987] ILRM 665, Vol III p 641
Cited also at: Vol IV p 395
DPP v Seamus Boyle Vol IV p 395

Draper v AG [1984] IR 277, [1984] ILRM 643, Vol IV p 437
Drexl, In re, No 299/86, Vol IV p 512
Drummond v CIR 32 TC 263, [1951] SC 482, Vol II p 636
Dublin Corporation v Building and Allied Trade Union & Ors [SC] unrep 24 July 1996 Vol V p 322
Dublin Corporation v Flynn [1980] IR 357, Vol III p 419
Dublin Corporation v M'Adam 20 LR IR 497, Vol II p 211
Duggan & Others v An Taoiseach & Others [unreported 11 April 1988], Vol IV pp 170, 229
Duke of Westminster v CIR 151 LTR 489, 51 TLR 467, 19 TC 490, [1936] AC 1, Vol I pp 601, 618, 629, Vol II pp 222, 515
Duncan's Executors v Farmer [1909] Sess Cas 1212, 46 SCLR 857, 5 TC 417, Vol I p 618
Dunn Trust (In Voluntary Liquidation) v Williams 31 TC 477, Vol III p 373, 644
Dunne v Hamilton [1982] ILRM 290, Vol III p 356
Dunnes Stores (Oakville) Ltd v MC Cronin (Inspector of Taxes) Vol IV p 68
Duple Motor Bodies Ltd v IRC [1961] 1 WLR 739, Vol III p 198
Duple Motor Bodies Ltd v Ostime 39 TC 537, Vol IV p 135
Durbeck's, Re, [1981] ECR 1095, Vol IV p 492
DWS Corporation v Minister of National Revenue [1968] 2 Ex CR 44, 1999-2000 p 82

E

Eadie v CIR 9 TC 1, [1924] 2 KB 198, Vol I p 115, Vol II p 75
Earl Beatty v CIR 35 TC 30, Vol II p 627
Earl Howe v CIR 7 TC 289 Vol V p 108
Earl of Derby v Aylmer 6 TC 665, Vol III p 113, 120
East Cork Foods v O'Dwyer Steel [1978] IR 103 Vol V p 322, 614
East Donegal Co-operative Livestock Marts Ltd v AG [1970] IR 317, 104 ILTR 81, Vol III pp 73, 127, 590, Vol V p 614, 1998 p 120
East India Trading Co Inc v Carmel Exporters and Importers Ltd [1952] 1 AER 1053, Vol II p 281
East Realty and Investment Co v Schneider Granite Co [1916] 240 US 55, Vol III p 127
Eastmans Ltd v Shaw 43 TLR 549, 14 TC 218, Vol II pp 32, 515, Vol III p 95, Vol V p 680
Ebrahimi v Westbourne Galleries Ltd [1973] AC 379 Vol V p 226
Edinburgh Life Assurance Co v Lord Advocate 5 TC 472, Vol IV p 135
Educational Company v Fitzpatrick No 2 [1961] IR 345 1998 p 120
Edward J Kearns v Dilleen (Inspector of Taxes) Vol V p 514
Edwards (Inspector of Taxes) v Bairstow [1956] AC 14
Edwards (Inspector of Taxes) v Bairstow 36 TC 207, [1956] AC 14, Vol II pp 515, 614, 636, Vol III pp 1, 178, 211, 219, 253, 644, Vol IV p 135, Vol V p 139, 200
EG v Mac Shamhrain (Inspector of Taxes) 3 ITC 217, [1958] IR 288, Vol II p 352
Eglinton Silica Brick Co Ltd v Marrian [1924] Sess Cas 946, 61 SC LR 601, 9 TC 92, Vol II p 115
Egyptian Delta Land and Investment Co Ltd v Todd 14 TC 119, [1929] AC 1, Vol I p 259
Egyptian Hotels Ltd v Mitchell 6 TC 542, CA [1914] 3 KB 118, [1915] AC 1022, Vol I p 359, Vol II p 68
Eisher v Macomber 252 US 207, Vol IV p 135
Ellerker v Union Cold Storage Co Ltd 22 TC 195, Vol III p 304
Elliott v Elliott 9 M & W 23, Vol I p 130
Elmhirst v The CIR 21 TC 381, [1937] 2 KB 551, Vol I p 563

Emery, John & Sons v CIR 20 TC 213, [1935] SC 802, [1937] AC 91, Vol I p 515, 583, Vol II pp 429, 472
Emery's Investment Trusts, In re [1959] 1 Ch 410 1998 p 169
English Crown Spelter Co Ltd v Baker 5 TC 327, 99 LTR 353, Vol I p 642
Ensign Tankers (Leasing) Ltd v Stokes (Inspector of Taxes) [1989] STC 705, [1992] 2 AER 275 Vol V p 6
Erichsen v Last 4 TC 422, 8 QBD 414, Vol I p 330, 387
Erin Executor and Trustee Co Ltd (as trustee of Irish Pension Fund Property Unit Trust) v the Revenue Commissioners Vol V p 76
Essex County Council v Ellman (1989) STC 31T Vol V p 108, 1998 p 183
Estate of Persse, Re, [1888, unreported, Land Judges Court], Vol II p 332
Estate of Peter Kelly, Re, [1908, unreported], Vol II p 332
European Communities v Hellenic Republic [1989] ECR 2965 1998 p 76
Evans & Co v Phillips (Inspector of Taxes) 1 ITC 38, Vol I p 43
Evans Medical Supplies Ltd v Moriarty 37 TC 540, [1956] 1 WLR 794, Vol II p 602
Evans v Wheatley 38 TC 216, Vol II p 515
Executors and Trustees of AC Ferguson, The (deceased) v Donovan (Inspector of Taxes) 1 ITC 214, [1927] ILTR 49, [1929] IR 489, Vol I p 183
Exham v Beamish [1939] IR 336, Vol II p 154
Exparte Brett [1897] 1 IR 488, Vol I p 28
Exported Live Stock (Insurance) Board, The v TJ Carroll (Inspector of Taxes) 3 ITC 67, [1951] IR 286, Vol II p 211
Cited also at: Vol IV p 73

F

Faccini Dore v Recreb [1995] All ER European Cases 1998 p 76
Falcke v Scottish Imperial Insurance Co 34 Ch D 234, Vol I p 601
Fall v Hitchen 49 TC 433, Vol III p 43, Vol IV p 45
Farmer v The Juridicial Society of Edinburgh [1914] Sess Cas 731, 6 TC 467 [1914], Vol I p 542
Farmer v The Scottish North American Cross Ltd Vol V p 139
Farrell v Alexander [1975] 3 WLR 642, 650-1, [1977] AC 59, Vol III p 19, 229
Federal Commissioner of Taxation v Westraders Pty Ltd [1980] 114 CLR 35, Vol III p 683
Federal Commissioners of Taxation v ICI Australia Ltd [1972] 127 CLR 529, 3 ATR 321, Vol IV p 68
Fee v Collendars Trustees [1927] SLT (Sh Ct) 17, Vol II p 32
Feeny v Pollexfen and Co Ltd [1931] IR 589, Vol III p 661
Fennessy (Inspector of Taxes) v John McConnellogue Vol V p 129
Ferguson v Dawson & Partners CA [1976] Vol V p 239, 1998 p 177
Ferguson v Noble [1919] 2 SC LT 49, 7 TC 176, [1919] SC 534, Vol I p 231
Ferguson, Re [1935] IR 21, Vol II p 332
Figgis Deceased, In re [1969] 1 Ch 123, [1968] 2 WLR 1173, [1968] 1 All ER 999, Vol V p 272
Finden v Stephens 2 Ph 142, Vol I p 601
Findlay's Trustees v IRC [1938] 22 ATC 437 Vol V p 577
Finlay v Murtagh [1979] IR 249, Vol IV p 117
Finucane v McMahon [1990] 1 IR 165 Vol V p 272
Firma A Racke v Hauptzollamt Mainz (Case 98/78) [1979] ECR 69 1998 p 76
Firman, Re, [not rep], Vol III p 387

First National Commercial Bank plc v Angland [1996] IR 75, 1999-2000 p 65
Fitzgerald v Persse Ltd [1908] IR 279, Vol II p 130
Fitzgerald, Martin v CIR 1 ITC 100, [1926] IR 182, 585 , Vol I p 91
Cited also at: Vol II pp 32, 45, 222, 267, 360, Vol IV p 425
Fleming v Wilkinson 10 TC 416, Vol II p 393, 491
Floor v Davis (Inspector of Taxes) [1978] STC 436, 1999-2000 p 144
Flynn, W (Inspector of Taxes) v (1) John Noone Ltd, and Flynn, W (Inspector of Taxes) v (2) Blackwood & Co (Sligo) Ltd 3 ITC 79, Vol II p 222
Cited also at: Vol II pp 222, 464, 515, Vol III p 683
Foley v Fletcher [1858] 3 H & N 769 Vol V p 108, 1998 p 183
Food Controller v Cork [1923] AC 647, Vol I p 45
Forbes (Inspector of Taxes) v GHD 3 ITC 365, [1964] IR 447, Vol II p 491
Forbes v Forbes Kay 341, Vol I p 259
Forde, Michael Decision by Appeal Commissioners Vol IV p 348
Forsyth v Thompson 23 TC 374, Vol I p 164
Foster v Elsley 19 Ch D 419, Vol I p 601
Franconini v Franconini 11 Jur NS 124, Vol I p 427
Fraser (Inspector of Taxes) v London Sportscar Centre Ltd [1985] STC 688, [1985] 59 TC 63, Vol III p 611, Vol IV p 304
Frasers (Glasgow) Bank Ltd v CIR 40 TC 698, Vol III p 373
Frederick Inns Ltd, The Rendezvous Ltd, The Graduate Ltd, Motels Ltd (In Liquidation) v The Companies Acts 1963-1983 Vol IV p 247
Freidson v Glynn Thomas [1922] WN 251, Vol I p 64
Fry v Burma Corporation Ltd 15 TC 113, [1930] 1 KB 249, [1930] AC 321, Vol I p 571, 583
Fry v IRC [1959] Ch 86, Vol III p 56
Fry v Salisbury House Estate Ltd [1930] 1 KB 304, 143 LT 77, [1930] AC 432, Vol II p 429, 596, Vol V p 680
Furniss v Dawson [1984] AC 474, [1984] 2 WLR 226, [1984] 1 AER 530, [1984] 55 TC 324, [1984] STC 153, Vol III p 670, 683, Vol IV p 547, Vol V p 6, 108, 163, 515 1998 p 183
Furse, In re (1980) 3 AER 344 Vol V p 481
Furtado v Carndonald Fening Co [1907] SC 36, 20 TC 223, Vol I p 515

G

G O'C & A O'C (Application of Liam Liston (Inspector Taxes)), In the Matter of Vol V p 346
G v An Bord Uchtala [1980] IR 32, [1979] 113 ILTR 25, Vol IV p 437
G v Director of Public Prosecutions [1994] 1 IR 374
G v DPP [1994] 1 IR 374, Vol V p 362
Gaffney v Gaffney [1975] IR 133, Vol IV p 437
Garforth v Tankard Carpets Ltd 53 TC 342, Vol III p 340
Gartside v IRC [1968] 2 WLR 277, Vol III p 104
Garvey v Ireland [1981] IR 75 Vol V p 696
Gascoigne v Gascoigne [1918] 1 KB 223 1998 p 169
Gason v Rich 19 LR (Irl) 391 Vol V p 272
Gatien Motor Co v Continental Oil [1979] IR 406, Vol IV p 269
General Medical Council v CIR 13 TC 819, [Reported 139 LTR 225], Vol I p 542
General Nursing Council for Scotland v The CIR 14 TC 645, [1929] SC 664, Vol I p 542

General Reversionary Interest and Investment Co Ltd v Hancock 7 TC 358, [1939] 1 KB 25, Vol II p 515

George Ingelfield Ltd, In re [1933] Ch 1 Vol V p 515

Germyn Street Turkish Baths Ltd [1971] 3 AER 184, Vol III p 423

GH Ltd v Browne (Inspector of Taxes) [1984] ILRM 231, Vol III p 95

Gibbon v Pearse [1905] 1KB 816, Vol IV p 332

Gibbs v Mersey Docks Trustees [Not reported], Vol II p 241

Gilbert Hewson v JB Kealy (Inspector of Taxes) 2 ITC 286, Vol II p 15

Gilbert v CIR [1957] 248 F 2d 399, Vol III p 683

Gillies v CIR 14 TC 329, [1929] SC 131, Vol I p 411

Gilligan v Criminal Assets Bureau, Galvin, Lanigan & Revenue Commissioners Vol V p 424

Gisbourne v Gisbourne [1877] 2 AC 300, Vol IV p 340

Glamorgan Quarter Sessions v Wilson 5 TC 537, [1910] 1 KB 725, Vol II p 332

Glanely v Wightman 17 TC 634, [1933] AC 613, Vol II p 315

Glasgow Corporation v Inland Revenue [1959] SLT 230 Vol V p 614

Glenboig Union Fireclay Co Ltd v CIR 12 TC 427, [1922] Sess (HL) 112, Vol I p 1, 427, Vol II p 515

Gliksten 14 TC 364, Vol I p 164

Global Plant Ltd v Secretary of State for Health and Social Security [1971] 3 AER 385, [1971] 2 WLR 269, [1972] 1 QB 139, Vol III p 43, Vol IV p 45

Gold Coast Selection Trust v Humphrey 30 TC 209, [1948] AC 459, [1946] 2 AER 742, [1948] 2 AER 379, Vol II p 419

Golden Horse Shoe Ltd v Thurgood [1934] 1 KB 548, Vol II p 515

Golder v Great Boulder Proprietary Gold Mines Ltd 33 TC 75, [1952] 1 AER 360, Vol II p 500

Golding (Inspector of Taxes) v Kaufman [1985] STC 152, Vol IV p 547, Vol V p 515

Goldstein v CIR [1966] 364 F 2nd 734, Vol III p 683

Goodman International and Anor v Hamilton [1992] IR 54 1998 p 120

Gordon and Blair Ltd v Cronin 40 TC 358, Vol III p 363

Gordon v Dunleavy [1928] IR 595, Vol II p 291

Goslings and Sharpe v Blake 2 TC 450, 23 QBD 324, Vol II p 332

Gould v Curtis 6 TC 293, [1913] 2 KB 84, Vol II p 661

Governor & Co of the Bank of Ireland v MJ Meeneghan & Ors Vol V p 44

Governors of Rotunda Hospital v Coman 7 TC 517, [1921] 1 AC 1, 36 TLR 646, Vol I p 387, 515

Government of India, Ministry of Finance (Revenue Division) v Taylor [1955] AC 491 1998 p 76

Gowers and Others v Walker and Others 15 TC 165, [1930] 1 Ch p 262, Vol II p 108

Graham v District Justice Carroll (unreported, HC 9 December 1987), Vol IV p 278

Graham v Greene [1925] 9 TC 309, Vol II p 614, Vol III p 363

Graham v Minister for Industry and Commerce [1933] IR 156, Vol III p 43, Vol IV p 45, Vol V p 239

Grainger v Gough 3 TC 462, [1896] AC 325, Vol I p 330

Granite Supply Association Ltd Kitton 5 TC 168, 43 SCLR 65, [1905] 8F 5, Vol I p 91, Vol II pp 32, 45, 382, 515

Granville Building Co Ltd v Oxby 35 TC 245, Vol III p 1

Gray & Co Ltd v Murphy 23 TC 225, Vol I p 164

Gray and Gillet v Tiley 26 TC 80, Vol III p 1
Gray v Formosa [1963] p 259, Vol IV p 437
Gray v Holmes 30 TC 467, [1949] TR 71, Vol II p 452
Great Northern Railway Co v Sunburst Oil & Refining Co [1932] 287 US 358 Vol V p 614
Great Southern Railways Co, The v The IRC 1 ITC 298, [1930] IR 299, Vol I p 359
Green & Co (Cork) Ltd v The IRC 1 ITC 142, [1927] IR 240, Vol I p 130
Green & Others v Minister for Agriculture [1990] ILRM 364, Vol IV p 323
Green v Favourite Cinemas Ltd 15 TC 390, Vol II p 464
Green v IRC ITC 142, [1927] IR 240, Vol I p 240
Green v J Gliksten & Sons Ltd [1928] 2 KB 193, [1929] AC 381, 14 TC 364, Vol I p 427
Green, JW & Co Ltd v the IRC [1927] IR 240, [1927] ILTR 145, Vol IV p 304
Greene v Louisville and Interurban Railway Co [1917] 244 US 499, Vol III p 127
Greenhalgh v Arderne Cinemas Ltd & Others [1950] 2 AER 1120, Vol III p 423
Greenore Trading Co Ltd [unreported] 28 March 1980, Vol III p 423
Gresham Life Assurance Society Ltd v Bishop 4 TC 464, [1903] 2 KB 171, Vol III p 484
Gresham Life Assurance Society v AG [1916] 1 Ch 228, Vol I p 34
Gresham Life Assurance Society v Styles 3 TC 185, [1892] AC 309, Vol I pp 1, 515, Vol IV p 135
Griffin v Illinois [1956] 351 US 12 Vol V p 614
Griffiths (Inspector of Taxes) v Harrison (Waterford) Ltd, JP [1962] 1 AER 909, Vol V p 6
Griffiths v Mockler 35 TC 135; [1953] 2 AER 805, Vol II p 366
Grimes v Wallace [1994] unrep, 4 March 1994 Vol V p 210
Grocock v Grocock [1920] 1 KB 1, Vol I p 629
Groome v Fodhla Printing Co [1943] IR 380, Vol II p 360
Grove v Young Men's Christian Association 88 LT 696, 4 TC 613, Vol I p 387
Guardians of Parish of Brighton [1891] 2 QN 157, Vol II p 175
Guardians of the Banbury Union v Robinson 4 QB 919 Vol V p 560
Guildford Corporation v Brown [1915] 1 KB 256, Vol III p 441, 611
Guinness & Mahon Ltd v Browne (Inspector of Taxes) Vol III p 373
Cited also at: Vol III p 644
Gulbenkian Settlement Trusts, In re [1970] AC 508; [1968] 3 WLR 1127; [1968] 3 AER 785; Vol V p 37

H

H & G Kinemas Ltd v Cooke 18 TC 116, Vol III p 178
H Williams (Tallaght) (in Receivership and Liquidation), In the Matter of Vol V p 388
Hall v IRC 12 TC 382, [1921] LJ 1229, Vol I p 240
Hallett's Estate, Re, [1879] 13 Ch D 696, Vol IV p 247
Hallstrooms Pty Ltd v Federal Commissioners of Taxation [1946] 72 CLR 634, Vol II p 515
Hamerton v Overy 35 TC 73, Vol II p 366
Hamilton v CIR 16 TC 28, Vol III p 229
Hamilton v Hamilton [1982] IR 466, [1982] ILRM 290, Vol III p 73, Vol IV p 162
Hamilton v Linaker [1923] IR 104, Vol II p 332
Hammond Lane Metal Co Ltd, The v S O'Culachain (Inspector of Taxes) [1990] IR 560, Vol IV p 187
Cited also at: Vol V p 6
Hampton (IOT) v Fortes Auto-Grill Ltd [1980] STC 80, 53 TC 691, Vol IV pp 68, 284
Hanbury, In re 38 TC 588 Vol V p 108, 1998 p 183

Hancock v General Reversionary and Investment Co 7 TC 358, [1919] 1 KB 25, Vol II p 32
Hanlon v North City Milling Co [1903] 2 IR 163 Vol V p 532
Harling v Celynen Collieries Workmen's Institute 23 TC 558, [1940] 2 KB 465, Vol II p 482
Harrision, JP (Watford) Ltd v Griffith 40 TC 281, Vol III p 373
Hartland v Diggines 10 TC 247, [1926] AC 289, Vol II p 452
Harvey v Caulcott 33 TC 159, Vol II p 472, Vol III p 1, 9, 373
Harvey v Minister for Social Welfare [1990] ILRM 185 Vol V p 696
Haughey, Re [1971] IR 217, Vol III p 590, Vol V p 614, 1998 p 120
Haughey and Others v Attorney General and Others 1998 p 119
Hay v O'Grady 1 IR 210 Vol V p 272
Hayes, C (Inspector of Taxes) v RJ Duggan 1 ITC 269, [1929] IR 406, Vol I p 195
Cited also at: Vol II p 291
Healy, John v SI Breathnach (Inspector of Taxes) [1986] IR 105, Vol III p 496
Cited also at: Vol V p 98
Heaney v Ireland [1994] 2 ILRM 420 Vol V p 213
Hearne, EN (Inspector of Taxes) v O'Cionna and Others T/A JA Kenny & Partners Vol IV p 113
Heather v p E Consulting Group Ltd 48 TC 293, Vol IV p 135
Helby v Matthews [1895] AC 471 Vol V p 515
Helby v Rafferty [1979] 1 WLR 13 Vol V p 614
Henderson v Folkestone Waterworks Co [1885] 1 TLR 329 Vol V p 614
Henley and Co 1 TC 209, 9 Ch D 469, Vol I p 45
Henriksen v Grafton Hotels Ltd 24 TC 453, [1942] 1 KB 82, [1942] 2 KB 184, Vol II p 515
Herbert v McQuade 4 TC 489, [1902] 2 KB 631, Vol I pp 155, 427, 618, Vol II p 261
Heron peter C and Others v The Minister For Communications [1985] IR 623, Vol III p 298
Heydon's case 3 Rep 75 Vol V p 539
HH v MJ Forbes (Inspector of Taxes) Vol II p 614
Cited also at: Vol III p 178
Hibernian Insurance Company Limited v MacUimis (Inspector of Taxes) Vol V p 495,1999-2000 p 113
Hibernian Transport Companies Ltd, In re Vol V p 194
High Wycombe Squash Club Ltd v C & E Commissioners [1976] VAT TR 156, Vol IV p 349
Highland Railway Co v Balderston 26 SC LR 657, 2 TC 485, Vol II p 32
Hill v East and West India Dock Co 9 AC 448, Vol II p 130
Hill v Gregory 6 TC 39, [1912] 2 KB 70, Vol I p 515
Hill v Mathews 10 TC 25, Vol II p 115
Hinchcliffe (Inspector of Taxes) v Crabtree 47 TC 419, Vol IV p 125
Hinches, Dashwood v Hinches, Re, [1921] 1 Ch 475, 19 TC 521, Vol I p 515
Hinton v Madden and Ireland Ltd 38 TC 391, [1959] 3 AER 356, 1 WLR 875, Vol II p 602, Vol III pp 113, 120
Hitchcock v Post Office [1980] ICR 100, Vol IV p 45
Hochstrasser v Mayes 38 TC 673, [1958] 3 WLR 215, [1959] Ch 22, [1960] AC 376, Vol II p 452, Vol IV p 407

Hodgins, JT (Inspector of Taxes) v Plunder & Pollak (Ireland) Ltd 3 ITC 135, [1957] IR 58, Vol II p 267
Cited also at: Vol II pp 382 500, 515, 602, Vol III p 65
Hoechst Finance Ltd v Gumbrell [1983] STC 150, Vol III p 95, Vol V p 496, 680, 1999-2000 p 114
Hoeper v Tax Commission of Wisconsin [1931] 284 US 206 Vol V p 615
Holland v Hodgson [1872] LR 7 CP 328, Vol III p 332
Holroyd v Wyatt 1 de G & S 125, Vol II p 332
Holt v IRC [1953] 1 WLR 1488 Vol V p 295, 577
Hood Barrs v CIR 27 TC 385, [1945] 1 AER 500 (on appeal [1946] 2 AER 768), Vol II p 82
Hope-Edwards v Blackburne [1901] 1 Ch 419, Vol I p 487
Horsfall, exparte [1827] 108 ER 820, Vol IV p 332
Houghland v RR Low (Luxury Coaches) Ltd [1962], Vol III p 253
Howe (Earl) v CIR 7 TC 289 1998 p 184
Howe, Ex parte Brett, Re, [1871] 6 Ch App 838, 841, Vol III p 265
Howth Estate Co v WJ Davis (Inspector of Taxes) 2 ITC 74, [1936] ILTR 79, Vol I p 447
Cited also at: Vol II p 429
HT Ltd, Re (in Liquidation) and Others [1984] ILRM 583, Vol III p 120
Cited also at: Vol III p 523
Hudson Bay Co Ltd v Stevens 101 LT 96, 25 TLR 709, 5 TC 424, Vol I pp 1, 474
Hudson v Wrightson 26 TC 55, Vol III p 9
Hughes v Metropolitan Railway Co [1877] 2 AC 439 Vol V p 589
Hughes v Utting and Co Ltd 23 TC 174, [1940] AC 463, Vol II p 472
Hughes, HPC (Inspector of Taxes) v Miss Gretta Smyth (Sister Mary Bernard) and Others 1 ITC 418, [1933] IR 253, Vol I p 411
Cited also at: Vol II p 82
Humble v Humble 12 Beav 43, Vol II p 332
Humphrey v Peare 6 TC 201, [1913] 2 IR 462, Vol I p 1, 155
Huntington v Attrill [1893] AC 150 Vol V p 45
Huntley v Gaskell [1906] AC 56, Vol I p 259
Hussey, J (Inspector of Taxes v M J Gleeson & Co Ltd Vol IV p 533, Vol V p 22
Hutton v The West Cork Railway Co [1883] 23 Ch D 654, Vol III p 706, Vol IV p 247
Hyam v CIR [1929] SC 384, 14 TC 479, [1929] SC LT 361, Vol II p 32

I

Iarnrod Eireann v Ireland unrep, 28 April 1995 Vol V p 213
Imperial Chemical Industries of Australia & New Zealand Ltd v Federal Commissioner of Taxation [1970] 120 CLR 396, 1 ATR 450, Vol IV p 68
Imperial Tobacco Co Ltd v Kelly 25 TC 292, [1943] 1 AE 431, [1943] 2 AE 119, Vol II p 281
Income Tax Commissioners of Bihar and Orissa Singh [1942] 1 AER 362, Vol II p 500
Industrie en Handelsonderreming Vreugdenhil BV v Commission (Case 282/90) [1992] ECR 1937 1998 p 76
Indyka v Indyka [1966] 3 AER 583 (CA), [1967] 2 AER 689, [1969] 1 AC 33, Vol IV p 437
Ingram v IRC [1986] Ch 585, [1986] 2 WLR 598, Vol III p 683
Ingram, JG & Son Ltd v Callaghan 45 TC 151, Vol III p 363
Inland Revenue Commissioners v Duke of Westminster [1979] 3 AER 775 Vol V p 6

Inland Revenue Commissioners v Plummer [1935] AER 295 Vol V p 6

Inspector of Taxes v Kiernan [1981] IR 117, 3 ITR 19 Vol V p 22, 108, 515, 1998 p 183, 1999-2000 p 72

Inspector of Taxes (Mara) v Hummingbird [1982] ILRM 421, 1999-2000 p 82

International Fishing Vessels Ltd v The Minister for the Marine [1989] IR 149, Vol IV p 485

Inwards v Baker [1965] 2 QB 29 Vol V p 589

Ioannides v Republic of Cyprus 6 Nov 1978 Vol V p 615

IRC v Barclay Curle & Co [1969] 45 TC 221, Vol IV pp 68, 425

IRC v Blott [1921] 2 AD 171, Vol IV p 135

IRC v Broadway Cottages Trust [1955] CJ 20; [1954] 3 WLR 438; [1954] 3 AER 120; 98 SJ 588; 47 R & IT 574; 35 TC 577, Vol V p 37

IRC v Burmah Oil Co Ltd [1981] 54 TC 200, [1982] STC 30, Vol III p 683

IRC v City of Glasgow Police Athletic Association 34 TC 76, [1953] AC 380, Vol II p 393

IRC v Clay [1914] 3 KB 466 Vol V p 577

IRC v Cock Russell 29 TC 387, 28 ATC 393, [1949] 2 AER 889, Vol II p 419

IRC v Crossman & Ors [1937] AC 26 Vol V p 577

IRC v Doorley [1933] IR 750, Vol II p 25, 195, Vol III p 683, Vol IV p 22, 91

IRC v Duke of Westminster [1936] AC 1, [1935] 104 LJ (KB) 383, 153 LT 223, 51 TLR 467, 19 TC 490, Vol II p 464, Vol III p 683, Vol V p 163

IRC v Europa Oil (NZ) Ltd [1971] AC 760, [1971] 2 WLR 55, Vol III p 683

IRC v Falkirk Temperance Cafe 11 TC 353, [1927] SC 261, Vol I p 387

IRC v Fraser 24 TC 498, Vol III p 178

IRC v Frere [1965] AC 402, Vol III p 403

IRC v Lysaght 13 TC 511, [1928] AC 234, Vol II p 32

IRC v Metrolands Property Finance Ltd [1981] STC 195 Vol V p 347

IRC v N 101 ILTR 197, Vol III p 319

IRC v National Federation of Self Employed and Small Businesses Ltd [1982] AC 617, Vol IV p 229

IRC v Newcastle Breweries Ltd 12 TC 927, 42 TLR 609, Vol I p 207

IRC v Paterson 9 TC 163, Vol III p 484

IRC v Plummer [1980] AC 896, [1979] 3 WLR 689, [1979] 3 AER 775, [1979] 54 TC 1, [1979] STC 793, Vol III p 683, Vol V p 108, 1998 p 183

IRC v Ramsey (1935) 20 TC 70 Vol V p 108, 1998 p 184

IRC v Reid's Trustees [1949] AC 361, Vol III p 56

IRC v Scottish & Newcastle Breweries Ltd [1981] STC 50, [1982] STC 296, Vol IV pp 68, 284, 425

IRC v Sneath 17 TC 149, 48 TLR 241, [1932] 2 KB 362, Vol II p 374

IRC v Strong 15 SLR 704, Vol I p 155, 427

IRC v The Duke of Westminster [1936] AC p 19 & 24, Vol II p 175

IRC v Thompson [1937] 1 KB 290, Vol III p 553

IRC v Wesleyan and General Assurance Society [1946] 2 AER 749, [1946] 62 TLR 741 (CA), [1948] 1 AER 555, [1948] 64 TLR 173, 30 TC 11 (HL), Vol II p 464, Vol III p 683

IRC v Wolfson [1949] WN 190, Vol II p 175

Irish Agricultural Machinery Ltd v O'Culachain (Inspector of Taxes) [1987] IR 458, [1990] IR 535, Vol III p 611, Vol V p 22

Cited also at: Vol IV pp 35, 125, 361, 533, Vol V p 22

Irish Creamery Milk Suppliers Association and Others v The Government of Ireland and Others [not reported], Vol III p 73
Irish Nationwide Building Society v The IRC Vol IV p 296
Irish Permanent Building Society v Registrar of Building Societies, Irish Life Building Society and Others [1981] ILRM 242, Vol III p 28
Irish Provident Assurance Co Ltd (In Liquidation) v Kavanagh (Inspector of Taxes) 1 ITC 52, [1930] IR 231, Vol I p 45
Cited also at: Vol I p 318
Irish Shell and BP Ltd v Costello [1981] ILRM 66, Vol IV p 269, Vol V p 108, 515, 1998 p 184
Irwin v Michael Grimes Vol V p 209

J

James, Ex parte [1874] 8 Ch App 609 Vol V p 615
Jarrold v Good 40 TC 681
Jarrold v John Good & Sons Ltd 40 TC 681, Vol III p 219, Vol IV p 68, Vol V p 200
JB O'C v PCD and A Bank 3 ITR 153 Vol V p 347
Jeffrey v Rolls-Royce Ltd 40 TC 443, [1960] 2 AER 640, Vol II p 602
Jenkins Productions Ltd v CIR 29 TC 142, EPT Leaflet No 21 [1944] 1 AER 610, Vol II p 130
Jennings v Kinder 38 TC 673, [1959] Ch 22, [1958] 3 WLR 215, Vol II p 452
Jennings v Middlesborough Corporation 34 TC 447, Vol III p 253
Johnson v New Jersey [1966] 384 US 719 Vol V p 615
Jones v CIR 7 TC 310 Vol V p 108, 1998 p 184
Jones v Cwmmorthin Slate Co 1 TC 267, Vol II p 382
Jones v Flint 19 Ad & E 753, Vol II p 636
Jones v Leeming [1930] AC 415, Vol II p 204
Jones v Nuttall 10 TC 349, Vol III p 319
Jones v The Mersey Docks 11 HL Ca 480, Vol II p 211
Jones v The South West Lancashire Coal Owners' Association Ltd [1927] AC 827, Vol II p 211
Jones v Wright 13 TC 221, 44 TLR 128, 139 LTR 43, Vol I p 601
Jones, In re [1933] Ch 842 Vol V p 565
Jones, In re, 26 Ch D 736 Vol V p 526
Jones, Samuel & Co (Devondale) Ltd v CIR 32 TC 513, [1952] SLT 144, Vol II p 267, Vol III p 65
Jordan and Harrison v MacDonald and Evans [1952] ITLR 101, Vol IV p 45
Joyce, Re [1946] IR 277, Vol III p 572
Julius v The Bishop of Oxford 5 AC 214 p 222, Vol I p 104
JW v JW Vol IV p 437

K

K Co v Hogan (Inspector of Taxes) [1985] ILRM 200, Vol III p 56
Cited also at: Vol IV p 547
Kahn v Shevin [1974] 416 US 351 Vol V p 615
Kealy, JB (Inspector of Taxes) v O'Mara (Limerick) Ltd 2 ITC 265, [1942] IR 616, Vol I p 642
Cited also at: Vol II pp 25, 45, 222, 500, 602
Keenan Brothers Ltd [1985] ILRM 641, Vol III p 548, Vol V p 108, 1998 p 184

Keir v Gillespie 7 TC 473, 478, Vol III p 319
Keller, Karl v The IRC and Others Vol IV p 512
Kelly, HF (Inspector of Taxes) v H 3 ITC 351, [1964] IR 488, Vol II p 460
Kelly, JF (Inspector of Taxes) v Cobb Straffan Ireland Ltd Vol IV p 526, Vol V p 22
Kellystown Co v Hogan [1985] ILRM 200 Vol V p 515
Kelsall Parsons & Co, v CIR 21 TC 608, [1938] SC 238, Vol II p 515
Kemp (as Hawkins' Executor) v Evans 20 TC 14, Vol II p 393
Kennard Davis v CIR 8 TC 341, Vol II p 326, Vol III pp 229, 403
Kennedy (Inspector of Taxes) v The Rattoo Co-operative Dairy Society Ltd 1 ITC 282, Vol I p 315
Cited also at: Vol III p 533
Kennedy, Giles J v EG Hearne, AG and Others [1987] IR 120, [1988] IR 481, [1988] ILRM 53, 531, Vol III p 590
Cited also1998 p 120
Kenny J v Revenue Commissioners, Goodman & Gemon Ltd (Notice Parties) Vol V p 363
Kenny v AG 11 LR IR 253 Vol V p 539
Kenny v Harrison & Anor [1902] 2 KB 168, Vol III p 661
Kensington Income Tax Commissioners v Aramayo 6 TC 279 & 613, [1916] 1 AC 215, Vol II p 291
Kent v Sussex Sawmills Ltd (1947) IR 177 Vol V p 108, 1998 p 184
Kerrane, JG (Inspector of Taxes) v N Hanlon (Ireland) Ltd [1987] IR 259, Vol III p 633
Kidston v Aspinall [1963] 41 TC 371, Vol II p 627, Vol IV p 187
Kiely v Minister for Social Welfare (No 2) [1977] IR 267 1998 p 120
Kill Inn Motel Ltd (In Liquidation) v The Companies Acts 1963/1983 Vol III p 706
Kilmarnock Equitable Co-operative Society Ltd, Re, 42 TC 675, Vol III p 65, 304
Kilroy v Parker [1966] IR 309 Vol V p 37
King (Harris Stein), The v The Special Commissioners 1 ITC 71, Vol I p 62
King v AG [1981] IR 233, Vol III p 127
King v Foxwell 3 Ch D 518, Vol I p 259
King, The v British Columbia Fir and Cedar Timber Co Ltd [1932] AC 441, Vol I p 164
King, The v Earl Cadogan [1915] 3 KB 485, Vol II p 464
King, The v The Commissioners for Special Purposes of Income Tax (ex parte King (Evelyn Spain), The v The Special Commissioners 1 ITC 227, [1934] IR 27, Vol I p 221
Kinghan, Albert v The Minister for Social Welfare Vol III p 436
Kinsela v Russell Kinsela Property in Liquidation [1986] 4 NSWLR 722, Vol IV p 247
Kiriri Cotton Co Ltd v Dewani [1960] AC 192 Vol V p 615
Kirke's Trustees v CIR (Supra) 11 TC 323, [1927] SC HL 56, 136 LT 582, Vol II p 115
Kirkness v John Hudson & Co Ltd 36 TC 28, Vol III p 477
Knetsch v US [1960] 364 US 361, Vol III p 683
Knight v Calder Grove Estates 35 TC 447, Vol II p 382
Knight's, Re, 5 Coke Rep 54B, Vol II p 222
Knockhall Piggeries v JG Kerrane (Inspector of Taxes) 1985] ILRM 655, Vol III p 319
Knowlton v Moore [1900] 178 US 41, 77 Vol V p 615
Knox v Guidea 11th ILR 482, Vol I p 583

L

L v W S McGarry,(Inspector of Taxes), Vol II p 241
Lady Beresford v Driver [1851] 2 OLJ (Ch) 476, Vol IV p 332
Lands Allotment, Re, [1894] 1 Ch 616\1986 4 NSWLR 722, Vol IV p 247

Larkins v National Union of Mineworkers [1985] IR 671 Vol V p 45
Larner v London County Council [1949] 2 KB 683 Vol V p 615
Lauderdale Peerage, Re, 10 AC 692, Vol I p 259
Law Shipping Co Ltd v CIR 12 TC 621, [1924] SC 74, Vol II p 267
Lawrie, Wm p v CIR 34 TC 20, [1952] SLT 413, Vol II p 360, Vol IV p 425
Laycock v Freeman Hardy and Willis Ltd 22 TC 288, [1939] 2 KB 1, Vol II p 315
Le Mesurier v Le Mesurier [1985] AC 517, Vol IV p 437
Le Soleil Ltd v Minister of National Revenue 73 DTC 5093, Vol IV p 466
Leach v Pogson 40 TC 585, Vol III p 253
Lean and Dickson v Ball 10 TC 345, 655, Vol III p 319
Lee v Dangar Grant & Co [not reported], Vol III p 387
Leeder v Counsel [1942] 1 KB 264, Vol II p 204
Leeds Permanent Benefit Building Society v Mallandaine 3 TC 577, [1897] 2 QB 402,
Leeds Permanent Building Society v Proctor [1982] STC 821, [1982] 3 AER 925, Vol IV pp 68, 284
Lehnhausen v Lake Shore Auto Parts Co [1973] 410 US 356 Vol V p 615
Leicestershire County Council v Faraday [1941] 2 KB 205, Vol IV p 332, Vol V p 266
Leigh v Dickson 15 QBD 85, Vol I p 601
Leigh v IRC 11 TC 590, [1928] 1 KB 73, Vol III p 484
Leigh v Taylor [not reported], Vol III p 332
Leitch v Emmott 14 TC 633, [1929] 2 KB 236, Vol I p 563, Vol IV p 1
Levene v IRC 13 TC 486, [1928] AC 217, Vol I pp 259, 375, 387
Lewis Merthyr Consolidated Collieries Ltd [1929] 1 Ch 498, Vol IV p 107, Vol V p 388
Lewis, Exparte, 21 QBD 191, Vol I p 221
Lincoln Wagon and Engine Co Ltd v CIR 12 TC 494, Vol II p 429
Linkletter v Walker [1965] 381 US 618 Vol V p 615
Liquidator of Irvine and Fullerton Property Investment Society v Cuthbertson 43 SC LR 17, Vol II p 25
Lismore RDC v O'Malley 36 ILTR 54, 56, Vol II p 241
Liverpool & London & Globe Insurance Co v Bennett [1911] 2 KB 577, [1913] AC 610, 6 TC 327, Vol I p 447, Vol III pp 633, 644
Lloyd v Sulley 21 SC LR 482, 2 TC 37, Vol I p 259
Lomax v Newton 24 TC 558, 216 LT 419, [1953] 1 WLR 1123, [1953] 2 AER 801, Vol II pp 366, 460
London and Northern Estates Co v Harris 21 TC 197, [1937] 3 AER 252, 106 LJKB 823, Vol II p 429
London County Council v AG 4 TC 265, [1901] AC 26, Vol II pp 222, 332, 393
London County Freehold and Leasehold Properties Ltd v Sweet 24 TC 412, [1942] 2 AER 212, 58 TLR 281, Vol II p 429, Vol V p 496
London Investment & Mortgage Co v Worthington 38 TC 86, Vol III p 165
London Library v Carter 2 TC 594, Vol II p 661
London School Board v Northcraft [1889] 2 Hudsons BC 4 Ed 147, Vol IV p 332
Lord Advocate v Jaffrey [1921] 1 AC 146, Vol IV p 437
Lord Chetwode v IRC [1977] 1 WLR 248, Vol III p 403
Lord Cromwell v Andrews Cro Eliz 15, Vol II p 222
Lord Glanely v Wightman 17 TC 634, [1933] AC 618, Vol I p 496
Lord Inverclyde's Trustees v Inland Revenue [1924] SC 14, Vol II p 195
Lord Inverclyde's Trustees v Millar 9 TC 14, [1924] SC 14, Vol II p 25, Vol III p 246

Lord Massey v CIR [1918] 2 KB 584 Vol V p 108, 1998 p 184
Lord Mostyn v London 3 TC 294, [1895] 1 QB 170, Vol I p 515
Lord Sudeley's, Re, [unrep], Vol III p 477
Lord Vestey's Executors and Vestey v IRC [1951] Ch 209, [1950] 2 AER 891 (HL), [1949] 1 AER 1108, [1949] 31 TC 1 (CA), Vol III p 683
Lothian Chemicals v IRC 11 TC 508, Vol IV p 135
Lothian Chemical Company Ltd v Rogers (1926) 11 TC 508 1999-2000 p 114
Louisville Gas and Electric Co v Coleman [1928] 277 US 32, Vol III p 127
Louth, James & Others v Minister for Social Welfare Vol IV p 391
Loveridge, Drayton v Loveridge, Re, [1902] 2 CH 865, Vol I p 427
Lowe and Others v IRC [1983] STC 816, Vol IV p 135
Lowndes v de Courcy (SC) 7 April 1960 Vol V p 589
Lucas and Chesterfield Gas & Water Board, Re, [1909] 1 KB 16, Vol III p 298
Luipaard's Vlei Estate and Gold Mining Co Ltd v IRC 15 TC 573, [1930] 1 KB 593, Vol I pp 487, 583, Vol II p 332, Vol III p 229
Luke v IRC [1963] AC 557, Vol IV p 162
Lumsden v IRC [1914] AC 877 Vol V p 539
Lupton v Cadogan Gardens Developments 47 TC 1, [1971] 3 AER 460, Vol III p 253
Lupton v RA and AB Ltd [1968] 2 AER 1042, Vol III p 253
Lupton v SA and AB 47 TC 598 Vol V p 61
Lurcott v Wakely and Wheeler [1911] 1KB 905, Vol II p 267
Lynch, Mary v Moira Burke & AIB Banks plc Vol V p 271
Lynham v Butler (No 2) [1933] IR 74, [1932] 67 ILTR 75, [1932] LJ IR 72, Vol III p 533
Lyons, J & Co Ltd v AG [1944] Ch D 281, 1 AER 477, [1944] Cr 287, Vol III p 219, Vol IV p 68, Vol V p 200
Lysaght v CIR 13 TC 511, [1928] AC 234, Vol I pp 249, 387

M

M v An Bord Uchtala [1975] IR 140, [1977] IR 287, Vol V p 615, 696
MacAonghusa (Sean) (Inspector of Taxes) v Ringmahon Company 1999-2000 p 81
MacAuley v The Minister for Post and Telegraphs [1966] IR 345, Vol III p 533
MacCarthaigh, DA (Inspector of Taxes) v Francis Daly [1985] IR 73, [1986] ILRM 24, 116, Vol III p 253
MacDaibheid (Inspector of Taxes) v SD Vol III p 1
MacDermott (Inspector of Taxes) v BC Vol III p 43
Macduff, Re, 13 TC 846, [1896] Second Chancery p 466 and 467, Vol I p 542
MacGiolla Mhaith (Inspector of Taxes) v Cronin & Associates Ltd Vol III p 211
MacGiolla Riogh (Inspector of Taxes) v G Ltd 3 ITC 181, [1957] IR 90, Vol II p 315
MacKeown (Inspector of Taxes) v Patrick J Roe 1 ITC 206, [1928] IR 195, Vol I p 214
Cited also at: Vol I p 618
MacLaine & Co v Eccott [1926] AC 424, 10 TC 481, Vol I pp 330, 571
Maclaine v Gatty [1921] 1 AC 376 Vol V p 615
MacLennan, In re [1939] 1 Ch 750 Vol V p 565
Macsaga Investments Co Ltd v Lupton 44 TC 659, Vol III p 253
Madeleine Vionnet et Cie v Wills [1940] 1 KB 72, Vol II p 281
Madigan PJ & p Madigan v AG, The Revenue Commissioners and Others [1986] ILRM 136, Vol III p 127
Cited also at: Vol IV p 323
Maher and Nugent's Contract, In re (1910) IR 167 Vol V p 560

Maher v The Attorney General [1973] IR 140 Vol V p 615
Mahoney's, Re, [1910] 2 IR 741, Vol I p 221
Maire v Wood and Others [1958] SLT 326, Vol III p 467
Malcolm v Lockhart 7 TC 99, [1919] AC 463, Vol I p 496, Vol II p 315
Mallalieu v Drurnmond (Inspector of Taxes) [1983] STC 665, 1999-2000 p 82
Mallandin Investments Ltd v Shadbolt 23 TC 367, Vol I p 164
Mallett v Stavely Coal & Iron Co Ltd [1928] 2 KB 405, 13 TC 772, Vol II p 222, 515
Malone & Others v Manton 131 LTR 144, Vol II p 222
Malone v Harrison [1979] 1 WLR 1353 Vol V p 615
Mann Crossman & Paulin Ltd v Compton [1947] 1 AER 742, 28 TC 410, Vol II p 515
Manning, David v John R Shackleton & Cork County Council Vol IV p 485
Mara (Inspector of Taxes) v GG (Hummingbird) Ltd [1982] ILRM 421, Vol II p 667
Cited also at: Vol III pp 9, 43, 178, 211, 219, 253, 373, 441, 496, 644, Vol IV pp 117, 125, 233, 269, 284, 349, Vol V p 6, 22, 98, 139, 201, 239
Marbury v Madison [1803] 5 US 49 Vol V p 615
Marchioness of Ormonde v Brown 17 TC 333, Vol II p 491
Margerison v Tyre Soles Ltd 25 TC 59 (not reported elsewhere), Vol II p 515
Margrett v Lowestoft Water and Gas Co 19 TC 481, Vol II p 267
Mark Fishing Co v United Fishermen and Allied Workers Union 24 DLR (3 ed) p 585, Vol III p 467
Market Investigations Ltd v Minister for Social Security [1968] 2 AER 732, [1969] 2 QB 173, Vol III p 43, Vol IV p 45,Vol V p 239
Marleasing SA v La Commercial Internacional de Alimentacionsia [1990] 1 ECR 4135 1998 p 76
Marron v Cootehill (No 2) Rural District Council [1915] AC 792 Vol V p 539
Marsden & Sons Ltd v CIR [not reported] 12 TC 217, Vol I p 642
Marshall (IOT) v Kerr [1983] STC 360 Vol V p 347
Marshall v Crutwell [1875] LR 20 Eq 328, 44 LJ Ch 504, 39 JP 775 Vol V p 272
Martin v Lowry [1926] 1 KB 550, [1927] AC 312, 41 TLR 574, 11 TC 297, Vol I pp 155, 629
Mason v New South Wales [1959] 102 CLR 108 Vol V p 615
Masser, AH Ltd (Receivership) & Others v The Revenue Commissioners Vol III p 548
Massey v Crown Life Insurance [1978] 2 AER 576 Vol V p 239
Mathews v Cork County Council 5 TC 545, [1910] 2 IR 521, Vol I p 45
Matthews v Chicory Marketing Board (1938) 60 CLR 263, Vol III p 73
Maxwell v McLure 6 Jur NS 407, 8 WR 370, Vol I p 259
Maye, John v The IRC [1986] ILRM 377, Vol III p 332
Mayfair Property Co, Re, [1898] 2 CH 28, Vol II p 326
Mayo Perrott v Mayo Perrott [1958] IR 336, [1958] 93 ILTR 195, Vol IV p 437
McAuliffe, Tony v The Minister for Social Welfare Vol V p 94 (1995) ILRM 189 Vol V p 239
McC v KED [1985] IR 697, [1987] ILRM 189, Vol IV p 437
McCabe (Inspector of Taxes) v South City & County Investment Co Ltd Vol V p 107, 1998 p 183
McCall (deceased) v CIR 1 ITC 31, Vol I p 28
McCall v Bradish-Ellames [1950] IJR 16, 84 LTR 78, Vol IV p 367
McCann, Charles Ltd v S O'Culachain (Inspector of Taxes) [1985] IR 298, [1986] IR 196, Vol III p 304,1999-2000 p 144

Cited also at: Vol III pp 441, 611, Vol IV p 35, 361, 466, 526, 533 p 547, Vol V p 21
McCausland, Samuel v Ministry of Commerce [1956] NILR 36, Vol III pp 304, 441, 611, Vol IV p 35, 533, Vol V p 22
McConnells Trustees CIR [1927] SLT 14 Vol V p 295, 532
McCrystal Oil Co Ltd v The IRC and Others Vol IV p 386
McDaid, Charles v His Honour Judge David Sheehy, the Director of Public Prosecutions & Ors [1991] IR 1, Vol IV p 162, Vol V p 696
McDonald v Bord Na gCon [1964] IR 350, [1965] IR 217, Vol III pp 387, 577, 590, Vol V p 288, 615, 696, 1998 p 120
McDonald v Shand 39 TLR 444, 8 TC 420, Vol I p 214
McDougall v Smith [1918] 7 TC 134, Vol II p 596
McElligott p & Sons Ltd v Duigenan (Inspector of Taxes) [1985] ILRM 210, Vol III p 178
McEnery, In re [1941] IR 323 Vol V p 37
McEvoy v Belfast Banking Co [1935] Ac 24, [1834] NI 67; [1933] 68 ILTR 3, [1934] All ER 800, [1934] 103 LJPC 137, 151 LT 501, 40 Com Cas 1, Vol V p 272, 1998 p 169
McGarry (Inspector of Taxes) v Limerick Gas Committee 1 ITC 405, [1932] IR 125, Vol I p 375
Cited also at: Vol II pp 500, 515, 1999-2000 p 82
McGarry, W S (Inspector of Taxes) v EF 3 ITC 103, [1954] IR 64, Vol II p 261
McGarry, WS (Inspector of Taxes) v JA Spencer 2 ITC 297, [1946] IR 11, Vol II p 1
McGee v The Attorney General [1974] IR 284 Vol V p 615
McGlinchey v Wren [1982] IR 154, [1983] ILRM 169, Vol III p 533
McGrath Patrick & Ors v JE McDermott (Inspector of Taxes) [1988] IR 258, [1988] ILRM 181, 647, Vol III p 683, Vol V p 6, 108, 163, 295, 472, 515, 1998 p 184
Cited also at: Vol III p 271, Vol IV pp 91, 547, Vol V pp 6, 108, 163, 295, 472, 515 1999-2000 p 63, 72, 82
McGurrin, L (Inspector of Taxes) v The Champion Publications Ltd Vol IV p 466
McHugh (Inspector of Taxes) v A 3 ITC 257, [1958] IR 142, [1959] ILTR 125, Vol II p 393
McIntyre v CIR 12 TC 1006, Vol III p 211
McKenna v Eaton Turner 20 TC 566, [1937] AC 162, Vol II p 68
McKenna v Herlihy [1920] 7 TC 620, Vol II p 636
McKinlay v H T Jenkins & Son Ltd 10 TC 372, Vol II p 281
McKinley v Minister for Defence [1992] 2 IR 333, Vol IV p 437
McLaren v Needham 39 TC 37, Vol II p 515
McLaughlin v Mrs Blanche Bailey 7 TC 508, [1920] IR 310 & 316, Vol I p 496, Vol II p 315
McLellan Rawson and Co Ltd v Newall 36 TC 117, Vol III p 1
McLoughlin, Edward and Thomas Marie Tuite v The Revenue Commissioners and AG [1986] IR 235, [1986] ILRM 304, [1990] IR 83 , Vol III p 387
Cited also at: Vol III p 533, 641, Vol IV p 395
McMahon v The Attorney General [1972] IR 69 Vol V p 615
McMahon, J (Inspector of Taxes) v Albert Noel Murphy Vol IV p 125
McMahon,T & Ors v Rt Hon Lord Mayor Alderman & Burgess of Dublin Vol V p 357
McMillan v Guest [1941] 1 KB 258, [1942] AC 561, 24 TC 190, Vol II p 68
McNally, Daniel v S O Maoldhomhniagh Vol IV p 22, Vol V p 515
Cited also at: Vol IV p 547
McNamee & Ors v The Revenue Commissioners, In the Matter of the Estate of Vol V p 577

McPhail v Doulton [1971] AC 424; [1970] 2 WLR 1110; [1970] 2 AER 228; 114 SJ 375 Vol V p 37
McRae v CIR [1960] 34 Tax Court of US Reports 20, Vol III p 683
McTaggart v Strump 10 TC 17, [1925] SC 599, Vol II p 464
Meenaghan v Dublin County Council [1984] ILRM 616, Vol IV p 485
Melling v O'Mathghamhna and Anor [1962] IR 1, Vol III p 387, Vol IV p 395
Mersey Docks and Harbour Board v Lucas 2 TC 25, [1903] 8 AC 891, Vol I pp 387, 601, 656, Vol II pp 154, 211, 592, Vol III p 484, Vol V p 539
Mersey Docks v Cameron 11 HL Ca 443, Vol II p 211
Mesco Properties Ltd, Re, [1979] 1 WLR 558, Vol III p 523
Michelham, Re, [1921] 1 Ch 705, Vol II p 332
Middlesex Justices 2 QBD 510, Vol I p 221
Mikrommatis v Republic of Cyprus [1961] 2 RSCC 125 Vol V p 615
Miley v Rooney 4 TC 344, [1918] 1 IR 455, Vol I p 542
Millheim v Barewa Oil & Mining Co NL [1971] WAR 65 Vol V p 226
Milnes v J Beam Group Ltd 50 TC 675, Vol III p 340
Milverton Quarries Ltd v The IRC 3 ITC 279, [1960] IR 224, Vol II p 382
Minister for Agriculture v Norgo Ltd [1980] IR 155 Vol V p 691
Minister for Fisheries v Sealy [1939] IR 21 Vol V p 221
Minister for Industry and Commerce v Hale and Others [1967] IR 50, Vol III p 43
Minister for Justice v Siucre Eireann [1992] IR 215 Vol V p 226
Minister for Labour, The v PMPA Insurance Co Ltd (under administration) [1990] IR 284, Vol III p 505
Cited also at: Vol IV p 391
Minister for Social Welfare, The v John Griffiths Vol IV p 378
Minister of Finance v Smith [1927] AC 193, Vol I p 195
Minister of National Revenue v Anaconda American Brass Ltd [1956] 1 AER 20, [1956] AC 85 Vol II p 515; Vol III p 198, Vol IV p 135
Mitchell v B W Noble Ltd 43 TLR 102, [1927] 1 KB 719, 137 LTR 33, 11 TC 372, Vol I p 375, Vol II p 500, 515
Mitchell v CIR 25 TC 380, [1943] SC 541, Vol II p 636
Mitchell v Egyptian Hotels Ltd [1915] AC 1022; 6 TC 542, Vol I p 183
Mitchell v Ross 40 TC 11, Vol III p 43
Mogul of Ireland v Tipperary (NR) CC [1976] IR 260 Vol V p 272
Mohanlal Hargovino of Jubbulpore v Commissioners of Income Tax [1949] AC 521, 28 ATC 287, Vol II p 515
Molmac Ltd v MacGiolla Riogh (Inspector of Taxes) 3 ITC 376, [1965] IR 201, 101 ILTR 114, Vol II p 482
Moloney (Inspector of Taxes) v Allied Irish Banks Ltd as executors of the estate of Francis J Doherty deceased [1986] IR 67, Vol III p 477
Monahan Patrick (Drogheda) Ltd v O'Connell (Inspector of Taxes) Vol III p 661
Mooney (Inspector Of Taxes) v McSweeney Vol V p 163,1999-2000 p 144
Mooney v O'Coindealbhain (No 2) [1992] 2 IR 23 Vol V p 326
Mooney, TB v EP O'Coindealbhain & The Revenue Commissioners Vol IV p 62
Cited also at: Vol V p 326
Moore & Co v Hare [1915] Sess Cas 91, 52 SC LR 59, 6 TC 572, Vol II p 45, 500
Moorhouse v Lord 10 HC Cas 272, Vol I p 259
Morant v Wheal Grenville Mining Co 3 TC 298, Vol II p 382

Morgan v Tate and Lyle 35 TC 367, [1953] Ch 601, [1955] AC 21, Vol II p 500, 515, 1999-2000 p 82
Morgan, In re, 24 Ch D 114 Vol V p 526
Morice v The Bishop of Durham 10 TC 86 p 539, [1925] 10 Vesey 522, Vol I p 542
Morrow v Carty [1957] NI 174 Vol V p 589
Morse v Stedeford 18 TC 457, Vol II p 515
Moses v Macferlan [1760] 2 Burr 1005, Vol IV p 247, Vol V p 615
Most Honourable Frances Elizabeth Sarah Marchioness Conyngham, The v IRC 1 ITC 259, [1928] ILTR 57, 136, Vol I p 231
Moville District Board Of Conservators v D Ua Clothasaigh (Inspector of Taxes) 3 ITC 1, [1950] IR 301, Vol II p 154
Mowleim, Re, 43 LJ CH 354, Vol I p 427
Moynihan v Greensmyth [1977] IR 55 Vol V p 615
Muckley, Bernard and Anne Muckley v Ireland, The Attorney General and The IRC [1985] IR 472, [1986] ILRM 364, Vol III p 188
Mullingar RDC v Rowles 6 TC 85, [1913] 2 IR 44, Vol I pp 1, 427
Mulloy v Minister for Education [1975] IR 88, Vol III p 127
Multipar Syndicate Ltd v Davitt (Inspector of Taxes) [1945] 1 AER 298, Vol IV p 505
Mulvey, JD (Inspector of Taxes) v Denis J Coffey 2 ITC 239, [1942] IR 277, Vol I p 618
Mulvey, JD (Inspector of Taxes) v RM Kieran 2 ITC 179, [1938] IR 87, Vol I p 563
Munby v Furlong 50 TC 491, Vol III pp 113, 120
Municipal Mutual Insurance Ltd v Hills Vol XVI TC p 448, Vol II p 211
Murnaghan Brothers Ltd v S O'Maoldhomhnaigh [1991] 1 IR 455, Vol IV p 304
Murph's Restaurants, In re [1979] ILRM 141 Vol V p 226
Murphy & Ors v AG [1982] IR 241, Vol III pp 127, 188, Vol V p 424
Murphy (Inspector of Taxes) v Asahi Synthetic Fibres (Ireland) Ltd [1985] IR 509, [1986] IR 777, Vol III p 246
Murphy v Dublin Corporation [1972] IR 215, [1972] 107 ILTR 65, Vol III p 533
Murphy v Minster for Industry and Commerce [1987] IR 295, Vol IV p 378
Murphy v Roche [1987] IR 106 Vol V p 696
Murphy, Frances & Mary Murphy v The Attorney General Vol V p 613
Murphy, John B v District Justice Brendan Wallace and Others Vol IV p 278
Murphy, S (Inspector of Taxes) v Dataproducts (Dublin) Ltd [1988] IR 10, Vol IV p 12
Murphy, Sean (Inspector of Taxes) v The Borden Co Ltd, Vol III p 559
Murray v Ireland & AG [1985] IR 532, [1985] ILRM 542, Vol IV p 437
Murtagh Properties Ltd v Cleary [1972] IR 330, Vol III p 127, Vol IV p 323, Vol V p 615
Musker v English Electric Co Ltd 41 TC 556, (Ch D) 106 SJ 511, Vol II p 602

N

N McS v Inspector of Taxes Vol V p 294
Narich Property Ltd v Commissioner of Payroll Tax [1984] ICR 286, Vol IV p 45
Nashville, Chattanooga & St Louis Railway v Browning [1940] 310 US 362 Vol V p 615
Nathan, Re, 12 QBD 461, Vol I p 221
National Bank of Scotland v The Lord Advocate 30 SL Rep 579 Vol V p 560
National Bank of Wales, Re, [1897] 1 Ch 298, Vol II p 175
National Bank v Baker 17 TC 381, [1932] 1 KB 668, Vol I pp 474, 503
National Irish Banks Ltd v Radio Telefís Éireann SC, 20 March 1998 1998 p 120
National Provident Institution v Brown 8 TC 57, [1921] 2 AC 222, Vol I p 515
National Provincial Bank of England v Jackson 33 Ch D 1 Vol V p 560

Naval Colliery Co Ltd v CIR 12 TC 1017, Vol III p 95
Navan Carpets Ltd v S O'Culachain (Inspector of Taxes) [1988] IR 164, Vol III p 403 Vol V p 326
Neale v City of Birmingham Tramways Company [1910] 2 Ch 464, Vol II p 175
Nesbitt v Mitchell 11 TC 211, Vol II p 115
Nestor v Murphy [1979] IR 326, Vol IV p 162
Nevile Reid & Co Ltd v CIR 12 TC 545, Vol I p 130, Vol III p 611
New York Life Assurance Co v Styles 2 TC 460 [1914] 14 AC 381 (p 389), Vol I p 387
Newcastle City Council v Royal Newcastle Hospital [1959] AC 248, Vol II p 636
Newman Manufacturing Co v Marrable [1931] 2 KB 297 Vol V p 539
Nicoll v Austin 19 TC 531, Vol II p 452
Nixon v Commissioner of Valuation [1980] IR 340, Vol III p 319
Noble, BW Ltd v IRC 12 TC 923, Vol II p 175
Nolder v Walters 15 TC 380, Vol II p 366
Nord Getreide v Haupdzolla MT Hamburg-Jones [1985] ECR 3127 1998 p 76
Norris v AG [1984] IR 36, Vol IV p 437, 1998 p 120
Northend v White & Leonard [1975] 1 WLR 1037, Vol III p 633
Northern Association Co v Russell 26 SLR 330, 2 TC 551, Vol I p 474
Northern Bank Finance Co Ltd v Quinn & Anor [1979] ILRM 221 Vol V p 226
Northern Insurance Co v Russell 2 TC 571, Vol III p 373
Norton v Shelby County [1886] 118 US 425 Vol V p 615
Noyek, A & Sons Ltd (in Voluntary liquidation) v Edward N Hearne [1988] IR 772, Vol III p 523
Nugent-Head v Jacob 30 TC 83, [1947] 1 KB 17, Vol II p 75

O

O hArgain, L (Inspector of Taxes) v B Ltd [1979] ILRM 56, Vol III p 9
O Laochdha, (Inspector of Taxes) v Johnson & Johnson (Ireland) Ltd [1991] 2 IR 287, Vol IV p 361
O'B v S [1984] ILRM 86, Vol IV pp 415, 437
O'Brien v Bord na Mona [1983] IR 255, [1983] ILRM 314, Vol III pp 533, 590, Vol IV p 512
O'Brien v Commissioner for Tipperary (South Riding) Board of Health [1938] IR 761, Vol III p 43
O'Brien v Keogh [1972] IR 144, Vol III p 127, Vol V p 615
O'Brien v Manufacturing Engineering Co Ltd [1973] IR 334, 108 ILTR 105, Vol III p 127, Vol V p 615
O'Broin, SP (Inspector of Taxes) v (1) Mac Giolla Meidhre, and O'Broin, SP (Inspector of Taxes) v (2) Finbar Pigott 3 ITC 235, [1959] IR 98, Vol II p 366
O'Byrne v Minister for Finance [1959] IR 1, 94 ILTR 11, Vol III p 127, Vol V p 615
O'C, JB v PCD and A Bank [1985] IR 265, Vol III p 153
O'Cahill (Inspector of Taxes) v Albert Harding and Others Vol IV p 233
O'Callaghan, Thomas v JP Clifford and Others Vol IV p 478
O'Cleirigh (Inspector of Taxes) v Jacobs International Ltd Incorporated [1985] ILRM 651, Vol III p 165
O'Coindealbhain (Inspector of Taxes) v Breda O'Carroll [1989] IR 229, Vol IV p 221, Vol V p 472, 1998 p 111
O'Coindealbhain (Inspector of Taxes) v KN Price [1988] IR 14, Vol IV p 1
O'Coindealbhain (Inspector of Taxes) v TB Mooney [1990] IR 422, Vol IV p 45,

Cited also at: Vol V p 239, 323, 326
O'Coindealbhain, EP (Inspector of Taxes) v The Honourable Mr Justice Sean Gannon [1986] IR 154, Vol III p 484
O'Conaill (Inspector of Taxes) v JJ Ltd Vol III p 65
O'Conaill (Inspector of Taxes) v R 3 ITC 167, [1956] IR 97, Vol II p 304
O'Conaill (Inspector of Taxes) v Z Ltd Vol II p 636
O'Connell, Patrick J (Inspector of Taxes) v Fyffes Banana Processing Ltd 1999-2000 p 71
O'Connell (Patrick J) (Inspector of Taxes) v Thomas Keleghan 1999-2000 p 143
O'Connlain (Inspector of Taxes) v Belvedere Estates Ltd [1985] IR 22, Vol III p 271
O'Croinin and Quinn v Brennan [1939] IR 274, Vol III p 387
O'Culachain, S (Inspector of Taxes) v Hunter Advertising Ltd Vol IV p 35
Cited also at: Vol IV p 466, 533, Vol V p 22 376
O'Culachain (Inspector of Taxes) v McMullan Brothers Ltd Vol IV, p 284, 1998 p 100
Cited also at: Vol IV p 425, Vol V p 200, 317, 482
O'Dwyer (Inspector of Taxes) & IRC v Irish Exporters and Importers Ltd (In Liquidation) 2 ITC 251, [1943] IR 176, Vol I p 629
Cited also at: Vol II p 82
O'Dwyer, JM (Inspector of Taxes) v The Dublin United Transport Co Ltd 2 ITC 437, [1949] IR 295, Vol II p 115
O'Farrell & Another, Re, [1960] IR 239, [1958] 95 ILTR 167, Vol III p 533
O'Flaherty v Browne [1907] 2 IR 416 Vol V p 272
O'G, T v AG [1985] ILRM 61, Vol IV p 437
O'Grady (Inspector of Taxes) v Laragan Quarries Ltd [1991] 1 IR 237, Vol IV p 269
O'Grady (Inspector of Taxes) v Roscommon Race Committee Vol IV p 425, Vol V p 317
O'Grady v Bullcroft Main Collieries 17 TC 93, Vol III p 65, Vol IV p 425
O'Kane, J & R & Co v CIR 12 TC 303, HL 126 LT707, 56 ILTR 57, Vol I p 1
O'Keeffe v An Bord Pleanala [1992] ILRM 69, Vol IV pp 170, 512
O'Laoghaire (Inspector of Taxes) v CD Ltd Vol III p 51
O'Leary, Edward v The IRC Vol IV p 357
O'Loan, HA (Inspector of Taxes) v Messrs M J Noone & Co 2 ITC 430, [1949] IR 171, Vol II p 146
Cited also at: Vol III p 178
O'R v O'R [1985] IR 367, Vol III p 533
O'Reilly, Gerald v W J Casey (Inspector of Taxes) 2 ITC 220, [1942] IR 378, Vol I p 601
O'Rourke v Revenue Commissioners Vol V p 321
O'Shea (Inspector of Taxes) v Michael Mulqueen Vol V p 134
O'Siochain, Sean (Inspector of Taxes) v Bridget Neenan Vol V p 472, 1998 p 111
O'Siochain, Sean (Inspector of Taxes) v Thomas Morrissey Vol IV p 407
O'Srianain (Inspector of Taxes) v Lakeview Ltd Vol III p 219
Cited also at: Vol IV pp 68, 284, Vol V p 317
O'Sullivan (Inspector of Taxes) v p Ltd 3 ITC 355, Vol II p 464
Cited also at: Vol III p 683, Vol V p 295
O'Sullivan JM (Inspector of Taxes) v Julia O'Connor, as Administratrix of Evelyn H O'Brien, Deceased 2 ITC 352, [1947] IR 416, Vol II p 61
O'Sullivan v The Revenue Commissioners Vol V p 570
Oakey Abattoir Pty Ltd v Federal Commissioner of Taxation 84 ATC 4718, Vol III p 683
Oakthorpe Holdings Ltd, In Re [1989] ILRM 62 Vol V p 388

Odeon Associated Theatres Ltd v Jones 48 TC 257, [1971] 1 WLR 422, [1972] 2 AER 407, ITR Vol III p 198, Vol IV pp 135, 304
Odhams Press Ltd v Cook 56 TLR 704, [1938] 2 AER 312, 4 AER 545, 23 TC 233, Vol I p 642
Ogilvie v Kitton [1908] Sess Cas 1003, 5 TC 338, Vol I p 183
Old Battersea and District Building Society v The CIR [1898] 2 QBD 294, Vol IV p 296
Old Bushmills Distillery Company Ltd, Exparte Brydon, Exparte Bank of Ireland [1896] 1 IR 301, Vol I p 28
Olive & Partington Ltd v Rose 14 TC 701, Vol II p 115
Oppenheim v Tobacco Securities Trust Co Ltd [1951] AC 297; [1951] 1 AER 31; [1951] 1 TLR 118 Vol V p 37
Orange, James G v The Revenue Commissioners Vol V p 70
Oriental Inland Steam Co, Re, [1874] Ch App 557, Vol IV p 247
Ormond Investment Co Ltd v Betts 13 TC 400, [1927] 2 KB 326, [1928] AC 143, 138 LT 600, Vol I p 447, Vol II p 429, 482, 1998 p 66
Orr, Michael (Kilternan) Ltd v The Companies Act 1963-1983, and Thornberry Construction (Irl) Ltd v The Companies Act 1963-1983 [1986] IR 273, Vol III p 530
Osler v Hall & Co [1923] 1 KB 720, 17 TC 68, Vol II p 55
Ostime v Australian Mutual Provident Society 39 TC 492, [1959] 3 AER 245, Vol III p 246
Oughtred v IRC [1959] 3 WLR 906, Vol IV pp 187, 367
Ounsworth v Vickers Ltd 6 TC 671, [1915] 3 KB 267, Vol I pp 91, 642, Vol II p 32, 45, 515, Vol IV p 425
Overseers of the Savoy v Art Union of London 12 TC 798, [1894] 2 QB 62, Vol I p 542
Owen v Sassoon 32 TC 101, Vol III p 633
Owens v Greene and Freeley v Greene [1932] IR 225, [1932] 67 ILTR 161 Vol V p 272
Oxford Benefit Building & Investment Society [1896] 35 Ch 502 Vol V p 186, 195

P

Paddington Burial Board v CIR 13 QBD 9, Vol II p 211
Page v The International Agency & Industrial Trust Ltd [1893] 62 LJ Ch 610 Vol V p 186, 195
Pairceir (Inspector of Taxes) v EM Vol II p 596
Palmer v Johnson 13 QBD 351 Vol V p 539
Palser v Grinling Property Holding Co Ltd [1948] AC 291 Vol V p 686
Panama, New Zealand and Australian Royal Mail Co, Re, 5 Ch App 318, Vol III p 661
Pandion Haliaetus Ltd, Ospreycare Ltd, Osprey Systems Design Ltd v The IRC [1987] IR 309, [1988] ILRM 419, Vol III p 670
Paperlink v AG [1984] ILRM 373, Vol IV p 323
Parchim [1918] AC 157, Vol I p 130
Parke v Daily News [1962] 2 AER 929, Vol III p 706, Vol IV p 247
Parker & Cooper Ltd v Reading & Anor [1926] 1 Ch 975 Vol V p 226
Parker v Chapman 13 TC 677, Vol III p 484
Parker v Great Western Railroad Co [1856], Vol III p 441
Parker v Walker and Others [1961] SCT 252, Vol III p 467
Parkes (Roberta) v David Parkes 1998 p 169
Parsons v AG [1943] Ch 12 Vol V p 600
Parsons v Kavanagh [1990] ILRM 560, Vol IV p 323
Partington v AG [1869] LR 4 HL 100, Vol I p 601, Vol II p 332, Vol III p 683, Vol V p 163, 539

Partington, Ex parte, 6 QB 649, Vol II p 130
Partridge v Mullandaine 2 TC 179, [1886] 18 QBD 276, Vol I pp 155, 195, Vol III p 484
Paterson, John (Motors) Ltd v CIR 52 TC 39, Vol III p 559
Patrick v Broadstone Mills [1954] 1 AER 163, [1954] 1 WLR 158, 35 TC 44, Vol II p 515, Vol IV p 135
Patterson v Marine Midland Ltd [1981] STC 540 Vol V p 139
Pattinson Deceased, In re, Graham v Pattinson [1885] 1 TLR 216 Vol V p 272
Pattison v Marine Midland Ltd [1984] 2 WLR 11 Vol V p 139
Pearse v Woodall-Duckham Ltd [1978] STC 372, Vol IV p 135
Pearson v IRC [1980] 2 WLR 871, Vol III p 104
Peel v London North Western Rly [1907] 1 Ch D p 5, Vol II p 241
Penrose v Penrose [1933] Ch 793 Vol V p 600
People (AG), The v Bell [1969] IR 24 Vol V p 221
Perkins Executor v IRC 13 TC 851, Vol III p 484
Perrin v Dickson 14 TC 608, [1929] 2 KB 85, [1930] 1 KB 107, Vol II p 464, Vol V p 10, 1998 p 184
Perry v Astor [1943] 1 KB 260, 19 TC 255, [1935] AC, Vol II p 82
Peter Dodson 77 Cr App Reps 1983, Vol III p 153
Peter Merchant Ltd v Stedeford 30 TC 496, Vol II p 515
Petrotim Securities Ltd v Ayres [1964] 1 AER 269, 41 TC 389, Vol III p 253, 340, 373
Pharmaceutical Society of Ireland, The v The Revenue Commissioners 2 ITC 157 [1938] IR 202, Vol I p 542
Philips v Bourne 27 TC 498, [1947] 1 KB 533, Vol III p 19, 319
Phillips (Inspector of Taxes) v Keane 1 ITC 69, [1925] 2 IR 48, Vol I p 64
Cited also at: Vol II p 460
Phillips (Inspector of Taxes) v Limerick County Council 1 ITC 96, [1925] 2 IR 139, Vol I p 66
Phillips v Whieldon Sanitary Potteries Ltd 65 TLR 712, 33 TC 213, Vol II pp 267, 360
Phonographic Performance (Ireland) Ltd v J Somers (Inspector of Taxes) [1992] ILRM 657, Vol IV p 314
Pickford v Quirke 13 TC 251, Vol III p 253
Pickles v Foulsham 9 TC 261, [1923] 2 KB 413, [1925] AC 458, Vol I p 259, Vol II p 68
Pigs and Marketing Board v Donnelly (Dublin) Ltd [1939] IR 413, Vol III p 127, Vol IV p 162
Pilcher v Logan [1914] 15 SR NSW 24, Vol III p 484
Pine Valley Developments Ltd, Daniel Healy and Others v The IRC Vol IV p 543
Platt v AG of New South Wales 3 AC 336, Vol I p 259
PMPA Garages Ltd, In re [1992] IR 332 Vol V p 323
Pooley, Re, 40 Ch D 1, Vol I p 601
Potts' Exeuctors v IRC [1951] AC 443, [1951] 1AER 76, [1951] 1 TLR 152, [1950] 32 TC 211, Vol III p 683
Power Lane Manufacturing Co v Putnan [1931] 2 KB 309 Vol V p 540
Poynting v Faulkner 5 TC 145, 93 LT 367, Vol I p 155
Prestcold (Central) Ltd v Minister of Labour [1969] 1 AER 69, Vol III p 611
Preston, Re, [1985] 2 WLR 836, Vol III p 356
Pretore di Cento v A person or persons unknown (Case 110/76) [1977] ECR 851 1998 p 76
Pretoria-Pietersburg Railway Co Ltd v Elwood 95 LT 468, 98 LT 741, 6 TC 508, Vol I p 427

Prince v Mapp (Inspector of Taxes) [1970] 1 WLR 260 1999-2000 p 82
Prior-Wandesforde, Captain RH v The IRC 1 ITC 248, Vol I p 249, Vol V p 481
Private Motorists Provident Society Ltd (in liquidation) and WJ Horgan v Minister for Justice Vol V p 186
Private Motorists Provident Society Ltd (in liquidation), In the Matter of, 23 June 1995, 1995 ITR 159 Vol V p 195
Proes v The Revenue Commissioners Vol V p 481
Property Loan & Investment Co Ltd v The IRC 2 ITC 312, [1946] IR 159, Vol II p 25
Proprietary Articles Trade Association v AG of Canada [1931] AC 310, Vol IV p 395
Pryce v Monmouthshire Canal Co 4 AC 197 Vol V p 540
Punjab Co-Operative Bank Ltd Amritsar v Income Tax Commissioner Lahore [1940] AC 1055, Vol III p 373
Punton v Ministry of Pensions and National Insurance [1963] 1 AER 275, Vol II p 491
Purcell, Joseph v AG Ireland & The Minister for the Environment
Purcell, Joseph v Attorney General & Ors Vol IV p 229, Vol V p 288
Pyrah v Annis 37 TC 163, [1956] 2 AE 858, [1957] 1 AER 186, Vol II p 515

Q

Queen v The Pharmaceutical Society of Ireland [1896] 2 IR 384 and 385, Vol I p 542
Queen, The v Bishop of Oxford 4 QBD 245 p 261, Vol II p 108
Queensland Stations Property Ltd v Federal Commr of Taxation (1945) 70 CLR 539 Vol V p 239
Quigley, JJ (Inspector of Taxes) v Maurice Burke [1991] 2 IR 169, Vol IV p 332 Vol V p 265
Quinn v Leathen [1901] AC 495, Vol II p 500
Quinn's Supermarket v AG [1972] IR 1, Vol III p 127, Vol IV pp 323, 437, Vol V p 615

R

R (County Councils North Riding and South Riding County Tipperary) v Considine [1917] 2 IR 1, Vol I p 221
R v Buttle 39 LJ MC 115, Vol II p 175
R v Chief Metropolitan Magistrate ex parte Secretary of State for the Home Department [1989] 1 AER 151 1998 p 76
R v Commissioners for Special Purposes of Income Tax 2 TC 332, 21 QBD 313, Vol I p 221
R v Commissioners for Special Purposes of Income Tax 7 TC 646, [1920] 1 KB 26, Vol I p 221
R v Commissioners of Income Tax for the City of London 91 LTR 94, Vol I p 221
R v Cotham [1898] 1 QB 802, Vol III p 290
R v Crawshaw Bell C C 303, 8 Cox 375, Vol I p 195
R v Criminal Injuries Compensation Board, ex parte Lain [1967] 2 QB 864, [1967] 3 WLR 348, [1967] 2 AER 770, Vol III p 290
R v General Income Tax Commissioners for Offlow 27 TLR 353, Vol I p 221
R v Gregory 5 B and AD 555, Vol I p 195
R v Inland Revenue Commissioners ex p Unilever Plc (1996) STC 681 Vol V p 418
R v National Insurance Commissioner; ex parte Hudson [1972] AC 944 Vol V p 615
R v Peters [1886] 16 QBD 636, Vol III p 19
R v R [1984] IR 296, [1985] ILRM 631, Vol III p 533, 590

R v The Governor of Pentonville Prison ex parte Khubchandani (1980) 71 Crim App R 241 1998 p 76
R v Waller [1910] 1 KB 364 Vol V p 691
R v Woodhouse [1906] 2 KB 501, Vol III p 290
R & V Haegeman v Commission (Case 96/71) [1972] ECR 1005 1998 p 76
Rabbitt v Grant [1940] IR 323, Vol II p 32
Racing Board v Inspector of Taxes, Vol IV p 73
Radio Pictures Ltd v CIR 22 TC 106, Vol II p 281
Rahill v Brady [1971] IR 69, Vol III p 19
Rahinstown Estates Co v M Hughes, (Inspector of Taxes) [1987] ILRM 599, Vol III p 517
Ramsay, WT Ltd v Inland Revenue Commissioners [1981] 1 AER 165 Vol V p 6
Ramsay, WT Ltd v IRC [1982] AC 300, [1981] 2 WLR 449, [1981] 1 AER 865, [1981] 54 TC 101, [1981] STC 174, Vol III p 104, 683, Vol IV p 547, Vol V p 108, 295, 164 1998 p 184
Ramsey v Liverpool Royal Infirmary [1930] AC 588, Vol III p 572
Ramsey, WT Ltd v CIR 54 TC 101 Vol V p 515,1999-2000 p 144
Ranelaugh (Earl) v Hayes [1683] 1 Vern 189, Vol III p 265
Ransom v Higgs [1973] 2 AER 657, [1974] 1 WLR 1594, [1974] 3 AER 949, [1974] 50 TC 1, Vol II p 614, Vol III pp 572, 683
Re Cavan Co-Operative Society [1917] 2 IR 608, Vol III p 319
Re Inverclyde [1924] SC 18, Vol II p 326
Reade v Brearley [not reported] 17 TC 687, Vol I p 656
Readymix (Eire) Ltd v Dublin County Council and the Minister for Local Government [SC] unrep, 30 July 1974 Vol V p 357
Readymix Concrete v Commissioner of Taxation (Australia) [unreported], Vol III p 441
Readymix Concrete v Minister for Pensions [1968] 1 AER 433, Vol IV p 45, Vol V p 239
Reed v Cattermole 21 TC 35, [1937] 1 KB 613, Vol II p 452
Reed v Seymour 11 TC 625, [1906] 2 KB 594, [1926] 1 KB 588, 42 TLR 514, 135 LTR 259, Vol I p 155, 618
Rees Roturbo Development Syndicate Ltd v Ducker (CIR) 13 TC 366, Vol I p 474, 629
Reg v Bow Road Justices, ex parte Adedigba [1968] 2 QB 572, Vol III p 19
Reg v Commissioners of Woods and Forests 15 QB 767, Vol I p 221
Reg v Galsworthy [1892] 1 QB 348, Vol II p 241
Reg v IRC, ex parte Fed of Self-Employed [1982] AC 617, Vol IV p 170
Reg v Labourchere 12 QBD 328, Vol I p 427
Reg v Lords of the Treasury 16 QB 357, Vol I p 221
Regent Oil Co Ltd v Strick [1966] AC 295 Vol V p 139
Regina and Jones [1978] 1 WLR 195, Vol III p 153
Regina v Inspector of Taxes ex parte Clarke [1974] 1 QB 220, Vol III p 159
Reid, re [1921] 64 DLR 598, 50 OLR 595 Vol V p 272
Reid's Trustees v Dawson (1915) SC (HL) 47 Vol V p 540
Reids Trustees v CIR [1929] 14 TC 512, Vol III p 477
Reilly v McEntee [1984] ILRM 572 Vol V p 366
Religious Tract and Book Society of Scotland v Forbes 33 SLR 289, 3 TC 415, Vol I p 387
Rellim Ltd v Vise 32 TC 254, Vol III p 1
Republic of Cyprus v Demetriades [1977] 12 JSC 2102 Vol V p 615
Revenue Commissioners, The v ORMG [1984] ILRM 406, Vol III p 28
Revenue Commissioners, The v Arida Ltd Vol V p 221

Revenue Commissioners, The v Associated Properties Ltd 3 ITC 293, Vol II p 412
Revenue Commissioners, The v Colm O Loinsigh Vol V p 98
Revenue Commissioners, The v Daniel Anthony Moroney & Ors Vol V p 589
Revenue Commissioners, The v Doorley [1933] IR 750, Vol V p 539, 1998 p110, 184
Cited also at: Vol II p 25, 195, 326, Vol III p 683, Vol IV p 22, 91, Vol V p 108, 376
Revenue Commissioners, The v Henry Young Vol V p 294
Revenue Commissioners, The v HI Vol III p 242
Cited also at: Vol V p 393
Revenue Commissioners, The v L & Co 3 ITC 205, Vol II p 281
Revenue Commissioners, The v Latchford & Sons Ltd 1 ITC 238, Vol I p 240
Revenue Commissioners, The v Orwell Ltd 3 ITC 193, Vol II p 326
Revenue Commissioners, The v R Hilliard & Sons Ltd 2 ITC 410, Vol II p 130
Revenue Commissioners, The v Sisters of Charity of the Incarnate Word 1998 p 65
Revenue Commissioners, The v Switzer Ltd 2 ITC 290, [1945] IR 378, Vol II p 19 Vol II p 130
Revenue Commissioners, The v Y Ltd 3 ITC 49, Vol II p 195
Rex (Waterford County Council) v Local Government Board [1902] 2 IR 349, Vol III p 590
Rex v BC Fir and Cedar Lumber Co Ltd 17 TC 564, 147 LT 1, Vol I p 427
Rex v Dibdin [1910] p 57, Vol II p 130
Rex v General Commissioners of Income Tax for the City of London (ex parte Gibbs and Others) [1940] 2 KB 242, [1942] AC 402, 24 TC 221, Vol II p 55
Rex v James Whitney 1 Moody 3, Vol III p 19
Rex v Sarah Chapple [1804] Russell & Ryan 77, Vol III p 19
Rex v Special Commissioners of Income Tax 20 TC 381, (ex parte Elmhirst [1936] 1 KB 487), Vol I p 571
Rhodesia Railways Ltd v Collector of Income Tax, Bechuanaland Portectorate [1933] AC 368, Vol II p 32, 267
Rhymney Iron Co Ltd v Fowler [1896] 2 QB 79, Vol I p 164
Richardson, Re, 50 LJ Ch 488, Vol I p 130
Richmond's Trustees v Richmond [1935] SC 585 Vol V p 565
Ricketts v Colquhoun 10 TC 118, KBD [1924] 2 KB 347, CA [1925] 1 KB 725, HL [1926] AC 1, Vol I p 64, Vol II pP 366, 460
Ridge Securities Ltd v CIR 44 TC 373, Vol III p 253, 373
Right Hon Earl of Iveagh, The v IRC 1 ITC 316, [1930] IR 386, 431, Vol I p 259
Cited also at: Vol I p 375, 387
River Estates Ltd v Director General of Inland Revenue [1984] STC 60, Vol III p 178
River Estates, Re, [1984] STC 60, Vol III p 178
Roberts v Williamson 26 TC 201, [1944] 60 TLR 561, Vol II p 241
Robertson v MacDonagh [1880] 6 LR IR 433, Vol III p 484
Robinson v Corry 18 TC 411, [1934] 1 KB 240, Vol II p 452
Robinson v Scott Bader Co Ltd 54 TC 757, Vol IV p 73
Robinson, WA, t/a James Pim & Son v JD Dolan (Inspector of Taxes) 2 ITC 25, [1935] IR 509, Vol I p 427
Cited also at: Vol III p 165
Roche v Minister for Industry & Commerce [1978] IR 149 Vol V p 696
Roche v p Kelly & Co Ltd [1969] IR 100, Vol IV p 45, Vol V p 239
Rodgers v ITGWU and Others [1978] ILRM 51, Vol IV p 323
Rogers v Inland Revenue 16 SC LR 682, 1 TC 225, Vol I p 259

Rolled Steel Ltd v British Steel Corporation [1986] 1 Ch 246, Vol IV p 247
Rolls v Miller [1884] 27 Ch D 71 Vol V p 686
Rolls-Royce Ltd v Jeffrey 40 TC 443, [1962] 1 AER 801, Vol II p 602
Rompelman v Minister Van Financien, case 268/83 Vol V p 76
Rondel v Worsley [1969] 1 AC 191, Vol III p 484
Roper v Ward [1981] ILRM 408, Vol IV p 247
Rorke v CIR [1960] 1 WLR 1132, 39 TC 194, Vol II p 515
Rosyth Building and Estates Co Ltd v p Rogers (Surveyor of Taxes) [1921] Sess Cas 372, 58 SLR 363, 8 TC 11, Vol I p 447, 515
Routledge & Co Ltd [1904] 2 Ch 474, Vol II p 130
Rowan, In the Goods of Bernard Louis, Deceased, Joseph Rowan v Vera Agnes Rowan and Others [1988] ILRM 65, Vol III p 572
Rowan's Trustees v Rowan [1940] SC 30 Vol V p 565
Rownson, Drew & Clydesdale Ltd v CIR 16 TC 595, Vol I pp 164, 427
Rowntree & Co v Curtis 8 TC 678, [1925] 1 KB 328, Vol II p 32
Royal Bank of Canada v IRC [1972] 1 Ch 665, Vol III p 356
Royal Bank of Ireland & O'Shea [1943] 77 ILTR Vol V p 1
Royal College of Surgeons of England v CIR 4 TC 344, [1899] 1 QB 871, Vol I p 542
Royal Crown Derby Porcelain Co Ltd v Russell [1949] 2 KB 417, Vol III p 19, 533
Royal Insurance Co Ltd v Stephen 14 TC 22, 44 TLR 630, Vol I p 503, Vol III p 373
Royal Insurance Co Ltd v Stephen 44 TLR 630, 14 TC 22, Vol I p 474, Vol II p 419
Royal Liver Friendly Society [1870] LR 5 Exch 78, Vol IV p 296
Royster Guano Co v Virginia [1920] 253 US 412, Vol III p 127
Russell v Aberdeen Town and County Bank 2 TC 321, 13 AC 418, Vol II p 515
Russell v Russell [1985] 315, Vol IV p 437
Russell v Scott [1936] 55 CLR 440, [1936] 36 SR NSW 454, 53 NSWWN 178 Vol V p 272
Russell v Scott [1948] AC 422, Vol III p 56
Russell v Wakefield Waterworks Co [1875] LR 20 Eq 474, Vol IV p 247
Russian Petroleum Co Ltd [1907] 2 Ch 540, Vol II p 130
Rustproof Metal Window CoLtd v CIR 29 TC 243, 177 LT 657, Vol II p 602
Ryall v Hoare 8 TC 521, [1923] KB 447, Vol I p 155, 474
Ryan v Asia Mill 32 TC 275, Vol II p 515
Ryan v Oceanic Steam Navigation Co Ltd [1914] 3 KB 731, Vol I p 330
Ryan v The Attorney General [1965] IR 294 Vol V p 615
Ryans Car Hire v Attorney General [1965] IR 642 Vol V p 272
Ryle Brehon Airlines v Ming (1995) 3 WLR 64 Vol V p 412

S

S Ltd v O'Sullivan Vol II p 602
S v S [1983] IR 68, Vol IV p 437
S W Ltd v McDermott (Inspector of Taxes) Vol II p 661
SA Roquette Freres v French State (Case 145/79) [1980] ECR 3333 1998 p 77
Saatchi & Saatchi Advertising Ltd v Kevin McGarry (Inspector of Taxes) Vol V p 376 1998 p 99
Salisbury House Estate Ltd v Fry [1930] 1 KB 304, [1930] AC 432, 15 TC 266, Vol I pp 447, 487, 515, Vol II p 315, Vol III p 95, Vol IV p 1
Salvesen's Trustee's v CIR [1930] SLT 387 Vol V p 532, 577
San Paulo (Brazilian) Railway Co v Carter 73 LT 538, 3 TC 407, Vol I p 183
Sargeant (Inspector of Taxes) v Eayers 48 TC 573, 1999-2000 p 114

Sargood Bros v The Commonwealth [1910] 11 CLR 258 Vol V p 615
Saunders (GL) (in liquidation), in Re [1986] 1 WLR 215 Vol V p 387
Saunders v Dixon 40 TC 329, Vol II p 515
Saunders, GL Ltd (in liquidation), Re, [1986] 1 WLR 215, [1985] 130 SJ 166, [1985] 83 LS Gaz 779, Vol IV p 107
Saxone Lilley and Skinner Holdings Ltd v CIR 44 TC 122, Vol III p 65
Scales v George Thompson & Co Ltd 13 TC 83, Vol III p 178
Schofield v Hall 49 TC 538, [1975] STC 353, Vol III pp 113, 120, 219, Vol IV pp 68, 284, 425
Scoble v Secretary of State for India 4 TC 618 Vol V p 108, 1998 p 184
Scottish Co-operative Wholesale Society v Meyer [1958] 3 AER 66, Vol III p 423
Scottish Golf Club [1913] 3 KB 75, Vol I p 515
Scottish Investment Trust Co v Forbes 3 TC 231, Vol I p 474, Vol II p 419, Vol III p 373
Scottish Provident Institution v Farmer [1912] Sess Case 452, 6 TC 34 p 38, Vol I p 1
Scottish Widows Fund Life Assurance Society Ltd v Farmer 5 TC 502, Vol III p 484
Seaham Harbour Dock Co v Crook 16 TC 333, Vol III p 165
Sebel Products Ltd v Commissioners of Customs and Excise [1949] Ch 409 Vol V p 615
Sebright, Re, [1944] 1 Ch 287, Vol II p 332
Secretan v Hart 45 TC 701, Vol IV p 135
Secretary of State for India v Scoble 4 TC 618, [1903] AC 299, Vol II p 464
Sergeant (Inspector of Taxes) v Eayrs 48 TC 573 Vol V p 496
Severn Fishery Board v O'May [1919] 2 KB 484, 7 TC 194, Vol II p 154, 204, Vol IV p 73
Shadford v H Fairweather and Co Ltd 43 TC 291, Vol III p 1
Sharkey v Wernher 36 TC 275, [1954] 2 AER 753, [1955] 3 AER 493, Vol II p 315, Vol III p 253, 340
Shaw v Lawless 5 CI & F 129, Vol I p 601
Shell-Mex v Manchester Garages [1971] 1 WLR 612, Vol IV p 269
Shepherd v Harrison LR 5 HL 116, Vol I p 130
Sherdley v Sherdley [1987] STC 217, Vol III p 683
Sherry [not rep], Re, Vol III p 387
Sillar, Re, [1956] IR 344, Vol III p 572
Simmons v Heath Laundry Company [1910] 1 KB 543 1998 p 177
Simpson v Tate 9 TC 314, Vol II p 366
Simpson v The Grange Trust Ltd 19 TC 231, [1934] 2 KB 317, and in the House of Lords 50 TLR 389, Vol I p 447
Simpson v The Grange Trust Ltd 19 TC 231, 51 TLR 320, [1934] 2 KB 317, Vol II p 429
Sinclair v Brougham [1914] AC 415, Vol IV p 247
Sinclair v Cadbury Brothers 18 TC 157, Vol III p 65
Singer v Williams [1918] 2 KB 432, [1921] 1 AC 41, 7 TC 419, Vol I p 583, Vol II pp 82, 491
Small v Easson 12 TC 351, [1920] SC 758, Vol II p 500
Smart v Lincolnshire Sugar Co Ltd 20 TC 643, Vol III p 165
Smidth and Co v Greenwood 8 TC 193, [1920] 3 KB 275, [1921] 3 KB 583, [1922] 1 AC 417, Vol I p 330
Smith v Incorporated Council of Law Reporting for England and Wales 6 TC 477, [1914] 3 KB 674, Vol II p 32, 393, 515
Smith v Lion Brewery Co Ltd 5 TC 568, [1911] AC 155, Vol I p 515, 642
Smith v The Law Guarantee and Trust Society Ltd [1904] Ch 569, Vol I p 45

Smith, John & Son v Moore 12 TC 266, [1921] 2 AC 13, Vol II p 515
Smyth EA & Weber Smyth v The Revenue Commissioners [1931] IR 643, Vol V p 532
Smyth v Revenue Commissioners [1931] IR 643, Vol V p 577
Smyth v Stretton 20 TLR 443, 5 TC 41, Vol I p 155
Society of the Writers to the Signet v CIR 2 TC 257, [1886] 14 Sess Cas 34, Vol I p 542
Solamon v Solamon & Co Ltd [1897] AC 22, Vol IV p 247
Solicitors Act 1954, Re, [1960] IR 239, Vol III p 577
Solomon v Commissioners of Customs and Excise 2 QB 116, Vol III p 246
Somerville v Somerville 5 Ves 750, 758, Vol I p 259
Sother Smith v Clancy 24 TC 1 Vol V p 108, 1998 p 184
South Australia v The Commonwealth [1941] 65 CLR 373 Vol V p 615
South Behar Railway Co v IRC 12 TC 657, [1925] AC 485, Vol I p 108, 318
Southampton & Itchen Bridge Co v Southampton Local Board [Not reported], Vol II p 241
Southern Railway of Peru v Owen 36 TC 602, [1957] AC 334, Vol II p 515
Southern v Aldwych Property Trust Ltd 23 TC 707, [1940] 2 KB 266, 56 TLR 808, Vol II pp 95, 429, Vol V p 680
Southern v Borax Consolidated Ltd 23 TC 597 [1940] 4 AER 412, [1941] 1 KB 111, Vol II pp 45, 267, 500, 515
Southwell v Savill Bros 4 TC 430, [1901] 2 KB 349, Vol II pp 32, 45, 515, 1999-2000 p 114
Spaight v Dundon [1961] IR 201, Vol IV p 437
Spanish Prospecting Co Ltd [1911] 1 Ch 92, Vol I p 1
Spencer v McGarry 2 ITC 297, [1946] IR 11, Vol II p 241
Spencer v Metropolitan Board of Works LR 22 Ch Div 149 Vol V p 570
Spurway v Spurway [1894] 1 IR 385, Sel and 28 ILTR 2, Vol I p 259
Spyer v Phillipson [1931] 2 Ch 183, Vol III p 332
St Andrew's Hospital (Northampton) v Shearsmith 2 TC 219, 19 QBD 624, Vol I p 387
St John's School Mount Ford & Knibbs v Ward 49 TC 523 Vol V p 201
St Johns School v Ward 49 TC 524, Vol III p 219
St Lucia Usines and Estates Co Ltd v Colonial Treasurer of St Lucia 131 LT 267, [1924] AC 508, Vol I p 214
Stainers Executors v Purchase 32 TC 408, Vol IV p 135
Stamp deceased, In the matter of John Patrick Stamp v Noel Redmond & Ors Vol IV p 415
Standing v Bowring [1885] 31 Ch D 282, 55 LJ Ch 218, 54 LT 191, 34 WR 204, 2 TLR 202 Vol V p 272
Stanley v Gramaphone and Typewriter Ltd 5 TC 358, [1908] 2 KB 89-95, Vol I p 28
State (at the prosecution of Brookfield Securities Ltd) v The Collector Customs and Excise [Unreported], Vol IV p 419
State (Carmody), The v De Burca (HC) 1970, unrep Vol V p 691
State (Creedon) v Criminal Injuries Compensation Tribunal [1988] IR 51, Vol IV p 485
State (Daly) v Minister for Agriculture [1987] IR 1965, Vol IV p 485
State (DPP) v Walsh [1981] IR 412, Vol IV p 437
State (Elm Developments Ltd) v An Bord Pleanala [1981] ILRM 108, Vol IV p 505
State (Healy) v Donoghue [1976] IR 325, Vol IV p 478, Vol V p 615
State (Hully) v Hynes 100 ILTR 145 1998 p 77
State (Keegan and Lysaght) v Stardust Victims Compensation Tribunal [1986] IR 642, Vol IV p 170, Vol IV p 512
State (Keller) v Galway County Council and Another [1958] IR 142, Vol III p 290

State (McFadden) v The Governor of Mountjoy Prison [1981] ILRM 113 1998 p 77
State (Multiprint Label System Ltd) v President of Circuit Court [1984] ILRM 545, Vol IV p 505
State (Nicolaou) v An Bord Uchtala [1966] IR 567, [1966] 102 ILTR 1, Vol III p 127, Vol IV p 437, Vol V p 615
State (O'Duffy) v Bennet & Ors [1935] IR 70 Vol V p 691
State (O'Rourke) v Kelly [1983] IR 58, Vol IV p 278
State (Quinn) v Ryan [1965] IR 70 1998 p 120
State (Ryan) v IRC [1934] IR 13, Vol I p 563, Vol II p 326
State (Walsh) v An Bord Pleanala [1981] ILRM 535, Vol IV p 505
State Board of Tax Commissioners v Jackson [1931] 283 US 527, Vol III p 127
State v Sealy [1939] IR 21, Vol IV p 401
State, (Sheerin) v Kennedy [1966] IR 379, Vol V p 615, 1998 p 120
State, The (at the prosecution of Patrick J Whelan) v Michael Smidic (Special Commissioners of Income Tax) 2 ITC 188, [1938] IR 626, Vol I p 571
Cited also at: Vol II p 374
State, The (Calcul International Ltd and Solatrex International Ltd) v The Appeal Commissioners and The Revenue Commissioners Vol III p 577
State, The (FIC Ltd) v O'Ceallaigh (Inspector of Taxes) Vol III p 124
State, The (Melbarian Enterprises Ltd) v The Revenue Commissioners [1985] IR 706, Vol III p 290
State, The (Multiprint Label Systems Ltd) v The Honourable Justice Thomas Neylon [1984] ILRM 545, Vol III p 159
State, The State (Sheerin) v Kennedy [1966] IR 379 Vol V p 615
Stedeford v Beloe 16 TC 505, [1931] 2 KB 610, [1932] AC 388, Vol I p 618, Vol II p 393
Steer, Re, 3 H & N 599, Vol I p 259
Stephen Court Limited v JA Browne (Inspector of Taxes) (1984) ILRM 231 Vol V p 496
Stephen Court Ltd v JA Browne (Inspector of Taxes) Vol V p 680
Cited also at 1999-2000 p 114
Stevens (Inspector of Taxes) v Tirard [1940] 23 TC 321, Vol IV p 221
Stevenson, Jordon & Harrison Ltd v Macdonald [1952] 1 TLR 101 1998 p 177
Stockport Schools [1898] 2 Ch 687, Vol IV p 296
Strong and Company of Romsey Ltd v Woodfield (Surveyor of Taxes) 5 TC 215 , 1999-2000 p 82
Stovall v Denno [1967] 388 US 293 Vol V p 615
Strick v Regent Oil Co 43 TC 1, [1964] AC 295, [1966] 1 AER 585, Vol II p 515, Vol IV p 135
Stubart Investments Ltd v The Queen [1984] CTC 294, 84 DTC 6305, Vol III p 683
Styles v The New York Life Insurance Co LR 14 AC 381, Vol II p 211
Sugar Distributors Ltd v The Companies Acts 1963-90 Vol V p 225
Sulley v AG 29 LJ Ex 464, 2 TC 149, Vol I pp 183, 330
Sulley v Royal College of Surgeons Edinburgh 29 SC LR 620, [1892] 3 TC 173, Vol I p 542
Sunday Tribune Limited (in Liquidation), Re, 1998 p 177
Sun Insurance Officer v Clark 6 TC 59, [1912] AC 443, Vol II pp 211, 515, Vol IV p 135
Sun Life Assurance Society v Davidson 37 TC 330, Vol III p 95, Vol V p 496, 680, 1999-2000 p 114
Sun Newspapers v Federal Commissioner of Taxation [1938] 61 CLR 337, Vol II p 515

Sunday Tribune Ltd (in liquidation), In the matter of the [1984] IR 505 Vol V p 239
Superwood Holdings v Sun Alliance Insce Group [1995] unrep Vol V p 226
Sutherland v CIR 12 TC 63, 55 SC LR 674, EPD Leaflet No 9, Vol I p 1, Vol III p 253
Swaine (Inspector of Taxes) v VE 3 ITC 387, [1964] IR 423, 100 ILTR 21, Vol II p 472
Cited also at: Vol III p 1, 9
Swan Brewery Co Ltd (No 2) ACLR 168 Vol V p 226
Swan, Deceased; Hibernian Bank Ltd v Frances Stewart Munro & Ors Vol V p 565
Swedish Central Railway Co Ltd v Thompson 9 TC 342, [1925] AC 495, Vol II p 68
Swire, Re, 30 Ch D 239, Vol III p 340
Switzer v Commissioners of Valuation [1902] 2 IR 275, Vol II p 241
Symons v Weeks [1983] STC 195, Vol IV p 135

T

T v T [1983] IR 29, [1982] ILRM 217, Vol IV p 437
Tasker, W & Sons Ltd [1905] 1 Ch 283, Vol II p 130
Taxback Limited v The Revenue Commissioners Vol V p 412
Taylor Clarke International Ltd v Lewis (Inspector of Taxes) 1997 STC 499 Vol V p 164
Tebrau (Johore) Rubber Syndicate Ltd v Farmer [1910] SC 906, 47 SLR 816, 5 TC 658, Vol I pp 1, 474
Tempany v Hynes [1976] IR 101, Vol IV p 304, 367
Temperley v Visibell Ltd 49 TC 129, Vol IV p 1
Tennant v Smith 3 TC 158, [1892] AC 150, Vol II p 452, Vol V p 540
Texaco (Ireland) Ltd v Murphy (No 2) [1992] 1 IR 399 Vol V p 326
Texaco (Ireland) Ltd v Murphy (No.3) [1992] 2 IR 300, 4 ITR 91 Vol V p 323
Texaco Ireland Ltd v S Murphy (Inspector of Taxes) [1989] IR 496, [1991] 2 IR 449, Vol IV p 91,
Cited also at: Vol V p 376
Thomas Merthyr Colliery Co Ltd v Davis [1933] 1 KB 349, Vol I p 164
Thomas v Richard Evans & Co Ltd 11 TC 790, Vol I p 164
Thomas, In re [1982] 4 AER 814 Vol V p 45
Thomas, Weatherall v Thomas, In re [1900] 1 Ch 319, Vol II p 32
Thompson Magnesium Elektron Ltd [1944] 1 AER 126, 26 TC 1, Vol II p 515
Thomson v Goold & Co [1910] AC 409 1998 p 77
Thomson Hill Ltd v Comptroller of Income Tax [1984] STC 251, Vol IV p 135
Thomson v Bensted 7 TC 137, [1919] Sess Cas 8, Vol I p 259
Thomson v St Catherines College, Cambridge [1919] AC 468 Vol V p 615
Thorley, Re, [1891] 2 Ch 613, Vol I p 601
Tilley v Wales [1943] AC 386, Vol IV p 407
Tillmans and SS Knutsford [1908] 2 KB 385, Vol IV p 296
Tilson, In re [1951] IR 1 Vol V p 615
Timpson's Executors v Yerberry 20 TC 155, Vol II p 592
Tinker v Tinker [1970] p 136 1998 p 169
Tipping, WJ (Inspector of Taxes) v Louis Jeancard 2 ITC 360, [1948] IR 233, Vol II p 68
Todd v Egyptian Delta Land & Investment Co Ltd 14 TC 119, [1929] AC 1, Vol II p 68
Tomadini v Administrazione delle Finanze dello Steto [1979] EC Vol II 1814, Vol IV p 492
Tool Metal Manufacturing Co Ltd v Tungsten Electric Co Ltd [1955] 1 WLR 761 Vol V p 589
Tormey v Ireland & AG [1985] IR 289, [1985] ILRM 375, Vol III p 577, Vol IV p 437
Trans- Prairie Ltd v Minister of National Revenue 70 DTC 6351, 1999-2000 p 82

Travers v Holley [1953] p 246, [1953] 3 WLR 507, [1953] 2 AER 794, Vol IV p 437
Travers, John v Sean O'Siochain (Inspector of Taxes) Vol V p 54
Trevor v Whitworth [1887] 12 Appeal Cases 414, Vol IV p 247
Trinidad Petroleum Development Co v IRC 21 TC 1, [1937] 1 KB 408, Vol II p 332, Vol III p 229
Trustees of Psalms and Hymns v Whitwell 7 TLR 164, 3 TC 7, Vol I p 387
Trustees of the Tollemach Settled Estates v Coughtrie 30 TC 454, [1961] AC 880, Vol II p 491
Trustees of The Ward Union Hunt Races, The v Hughes (Inspector of Taxes) 2 ITC 152, Vol I p 538
Tryka Ltd v Newall 41 TC 146, Vol III p 363
Tuck & Sons v Priester [1887] 19 QBD 629, 638, Vol III p 19
Tucker (Inspector of Taxes) v Granada Motorway Services Ltd (1979) STC 393 Vol V p 496
Turner v Cuxson 2 TC 422, 22 QBD 150, Vol I p 155
Turner v Last 42 TC 517, Vol III p 1
Turton v Cooper 5 TC 138, 92 LTR 863, [1907] 2 KB 694, Vol I p 155, 618
Tyler, In Re [1907] 1 KB 865 Vol V p 615
Tzu Tsai Cheng v The Governor of Pentonville Prison [1973] AC 931 1998 p 77

U

Ua Clothasaigh, D (Inspector of Taxes) v Patrick McCartan 2 ITC 367, [1948] IR 219, Vol II p 75,
Cited also at: Vol V p 615
Udny V Udny LR 1 SC Appeals 441, Vol I p 259, Vol V p 481
Ulster Investment Bank Ltd v Euro Estates & Drumkill Ltd [1982] ILRM 57 Vol V p 226
Union Cold Storage Co v Jones 8 TC 725, 129 LTR 512, Vol I p 642, Vol II p 500
United Bars Ltd (Receivership), Walkinstown Inn Ltd (Receivership) and Raymond Jackson v The IRC [1991] IR 396
Cited also at: Vol V p 388
United Collieries Ltd v The Commissioners of the Inland Revenue 12 TC 1248, Vol II p 382
United States of America v Inkley [1989] 1 QB 255 Vol V p 45
United States v Peltier [1975] 422 US 531 Vol V p 615
United Steel Companies Ltd v Cullington (No 1) 23 TC 71, 162 LT 23, Vol II p 515
University of London Press Ltd v University Tutorial Press Ltd [1916] 2 Ch 601, [1916] WN 321, Vol III p 496
Unwin v Hanson [1891] 2 QB 115, Vol III p 19
Urquhart, D & Revenue Commissioners v AIB Ltd [1979] IR 197 Vol V p 366
Urquhart, D (Decd) & Revenue Commissioners v AIB Ltd, In the Matter of the Estate of Vol V p 600
Cited also at: [1979] IR 197, Vol V p 366
Usher's Wiltshire Brewerey Ltd v Bruce [1915] AC 433, 6 TC 399, [1919] 1 KB 25, Vol I pp 91, 642, Vol II p 222, 267, 500, 515, Vol III p 198, Vol IV p 135

V

Vacuum Oil Co Proprietaries v Comrs of Taxation (25 February 1964), Vol II p 515
Vale, JB (Inspector Of Taxes) v Martin Mahony & Brothers Ltd 2 ITC 331, [1947] IR 30, Vol II p 32

Cited also at: Vol II p 267, 360, 515
Vallambrosa Rubber Co Ltd v Farmer 5 TC 529, [1910] SC 519, Vol I pp 91, 642, Vol II p 32, 382, 515, Vol IV p 425
Vestey v IRC (1962) 2 WLR 221 1998 p 184
Von Colson v Landnordhein-Westfalen Case 14/83 [1984] ECR 1891 1998 p 77
Van Den Berghs Ltd v Clark [1935] AC 431, 19 TC 390, Vol I p 642, Vol II pp 32, 222, 515
Van Hool McArdle Ltd (in liquidation), Re, IRC v Donnelly [1983] ILRM 329, Vol III p 523
Vestey v IRC (1962) 2 WLR 221 Vol V p 108
Veterinary Council, The v F Corr (Inspector of Taxes) 3 ITC 59, [1935] IR 12, Vol II p 204
VIEK Investments Ltd v The IRC [1991] 2 IR 520, Vol IV p 367
Cited also at: Vol III p 9, Vol IV pp 323, 437
Vodafone Cellular Ltd v Shaw (Inspector of Taxes) [1997] STC 734,1999-2000 p 82

W

W Ltd v Wilson (Inspector of Taxes) Vol II p 627
Cited also at: Vol IV p 187
W v W [1993] 2 IR 476 Vol V p 482
Wagner Miret v Fondo de Grantia Salaril case [1993] ECR I 6911 1998 p 77
Waldie & Sons Ltd v Commissioners of IR [1919] Sess Cas 697, 12 TC 113 p 118, Vol I p 447
Wales v Graham 24 TC 75, Vol II p 366
Wales v Tilley [1943] AC 386, Vol IV p 407
Walker v Boyd [1932] LJ 402, Vol II p 32
Walker v Giles [1848] 6 CB 662, Vol IV p 296
Wandesforde's 1 ITC 248, [unreported 23 May 1928], Vol I p 259
Warnock and Others practising as Stokes Kennedy Crowley & Co v The IRC [1985] IR 663, [1986] ILRM 37, Vol III p 356
Warrender v Warrender [1835] 2 C & F 488, Vol IV p 437
Waterford Glass (Group Services) Ltd v The Revenue Commissioners [1990]1 IR 334, Vol IV p 187
Cited also at: Vol IV p 367, Vol V 181
Watkins v US (1956) 354 US 178 1998 p 120
Watson v Everitt v Blunden 18 TC 402, Vol I p 601
Watson v Hornby 24 TC 506, [1942] 2 AER 506, Vol II p 315
Watson v Rowles 95 LJKB 959, 42 TLR 379, 11 TC 171, Vol II p 68
Wayte (Holdings) Ltd (Receivership) v EN Hearne (Inspector of Taxes) [1986] IR 448, Vol III p 553
Webb v Ireland [1988] IR 353, Vol IV p 170, 492
Wedick v Osmond and Co [1935] IR 838 p 845, Vol I p 542
Welbeck Securities v Powlson [1986] STC, [1987] STC 468, Vol IV p 547, Vol V p 515
Wellaway v Courtier [1918] 1 KB 200, Vol II p 636
Wemyss v Wemyss Trustee [1921] SC p 40-41, Vol I p 259
Werle & Co v Colquhoun 2 TC 402, 20 QBD 753 (p 759), Vol I p 28, 387
Westcott v Woolcombes Ltd [1987] STC 600
West Mercia Safetyware Ltd (In Liquidation) v Dodd and anor [1988] Butterworths Company Law Cases 250, Vol IV p 247
West v Phillips 38 TC 203, Vol III p 1, 373
Westcombe v Hadnock Quarries Ltd 16 TC 137, Vol III p 165

Westminister Bank Ltd v Osler 17 TC 381, 146 LTR 441, 148 LTR 41, Vol I p 474, 503, Vol II p 419, Vol III p 373
Westminster Bank Ltd v Riches 28 TC 159, Vol II p 332
Westminster v CIR 19 TC 490, [1936] AC 1, Vol I p 515
Weston v Hearn 25 TC 425, [1943] 2 AER 421, Vol II p 452
Westwinds Holdings Co Ltd [unreported] 21 May 1974, Vol III p 423
Whelan, Norah and Others v Patrick Madigan [High Court, 18 July 1978], Vol III p 332
Whicker v Hume 7 HLC p 160, Vol I p 259
Whimster & Co v CIR 12 TC 813, Vol IV p 135, Vol II p 419, Vol III p 198
White, In re, [1892] 2 Ch 217, Vol I p 601
Whiteley Ltd, William v The King [1909] 101 LT 741 Vol V p 615
Wiley, Michael v The IRC [1989] IR 351, Vol IV p 170
Wilks v Heeley [1832] 1 Cr & M 249, Vol III p 265
William's Executors v CIR 26 TC 23, Vol I p 164
Williams Group Tullamore Ltd v Companies Act 1963-1983 Vol III p 423
Williams v Corbet 8 Sim 349, Vol I p 601
Williams v Grundys Trustees 18 TC 271, [1934] 1 KB 524, Vol II p 627
Williams v Singer 7 TC 387, [1921] 1 AC 65, Vol III p 477
Wilson (Inspector of Taxes) v Dunnes Stores (Cork) Ltd Vol III p 403
Wilson Box (Foreign Rights) Ltd v Brice 20 TC 736, Vol III p 1
Wilson v John Lane [unreported], Vol III p 441
Wilson v West Sussex Co Council [1963] 2 QB 764 Vol V p 357
Wimpey International Ltd v Warland, Associated Restaurants Ltd v Warland [1987] Simons Tax Intelligence since reported [1988] STC 149, [1989] STC 273, Vol IV p 284, Vol V p 201
Winans v AG [1904] AC 287, Vol I p 259
Wing v O'Connell (Inspector of Taxes) 1 ITC 170, [1927] IR 84, Vol I p 155
Cited also at: Vol I pP 427, 618, Vol II p 261, Vol III p 165
Winget Ltd: Burn v The Company, Re [1924] 1 Ch p 550, Vol II p 108
Winsconsin v Pelican Insurance Co [1887] 127 US 265 Vol V p 45
Wisdom v Chamberlain [1969] 1 AER 332, 45 TC 92, Vol III p 253, Vol V p 6
WLD Worldwide Leather Diffusion Ltd v The Revenue Commissioners Vol V p 61
Wolmershausen v Gullick [not reported], Vol III p 265
Woolwich Building Society v IRC [1993] AC 70 Vol V p 323

X

Xenos v Wickham LR 2 HL 296 Vol V p 560
XX Ltd v O hArgain, Judgment of Kenny J, 20/6/75, Vol III p 1

Y

Yarmouth v France [1880] 19 QBD 646, [1887] 19 QBD 647, Vol II p 602, Vol III pp 113, 120, 219, Vol IV pp 68, 425, Vol V p 201, 317
Yates (Inspector of Taxes) v Starkey (1951) Ch 465 Vol V p 472
Yates v Starkey 32 TC 38, [1951 Ch 465, Vol IV p 221
Yeates and Others v the Minister for Posts and Telegraphs and Others [1978] ILRM 22,
Young v IRC 12 TC 827, [1926] SC 30, Vol I p 240
Young v Racecourse Betting Control Board 38 TC 426, Vol IV p 73
Young v Robertson 4 Macq HL 314 Vol V p 540

Young v Sealey [1949] Ch 278, [1949] 1 All ER 92, [1949] LJR 529, [1948] 93 SJ 58 Vol V p 272
Young's Estate, Re [1918] 1 IR 30, Vol II p 332
Yuill v Wilson STC 1980, Vol III p 340

Statutes considered

Adaptation of Enactments Act 1922
.... 1998 p 120
Adoption Act 1952
.... Vol V p 696
s 4 .... Vol IV p 415
s 26(2) .... Vol IV p 415
Acquisition of Land (Assessment of Compensation) Act 1919
.... Vol IV p 485
s 2 .... Vol III p 298
Capital Acquisition Tax Act 1976
s 2 .... Vol III p 104
s 15-18 .... Vol V p 295, 680
s 21 .... Vol V p 200
s 39 .... 1999-2000 p 62
(4) .... Vol V p 295
s 52(2) .... Vol V p 295
s 56 .... Vol IV p 340
s 58(3) .... Vol V p 221
s 146 .... Vol V p 138
Sch 2 Pt 1 para 9 .... Vol V p 686
Central Bank Act 1971
s 2 .... Vol III p 559, 664
ss 7 to 31 .... Vol III p 559, 664
s 58 .... Vol III p 559, 664
Capital Gains Tax Act 1975
s 3 .... Vol IV p 515, 547
s 8 .... Vol IV p 515, 547
(2) .... Vol IV p 543
(5) .... Vol IV p 217
s 11(1), (2) .... 1999-2000 p 144
s 12 .... Vol III p 683, Vol V p 163
s 19 .... Vol III p 559, 664
s 28 .... Vol IV p 1
s 33 .... Vol II p 683
s 46 .... Vol V p 163
s 47 .... Vol IV p 515, 547
s 49(1) .... Vol IV p 125
Sch 2 para 2 .... 1999-2000 p 144
Sch 4 paras 6, 7, 11(4) .... Vol IV p 217
Sch 4 para 8(2)(*b*) .... Vol IV p 125
Sch 4 para 11(1), (6) .... Vol IV p 543
Common Law Procedure (Ireland) Act 1854
.... Vol V p 70

Companies (Consolidation) Act 1908
s 69 .... Vol V p 532
s 82(2) .... Vol V p 532
s 107 .... Vol II p 108
s 209 .... Vol II p 108
Companies Act 1963
s 8 .... Vol IV p 247
s 89 .... Vol V p 226
s 98 .... Vol III p 548, Vol IV p 91, Vol V p 388
s 147 .... Vol IV p 247
s 150 .... Vol IV p 247
s 201(3) .... Vol IV p 82
s 202 .... Vol IV p 82
s 205 .... Vol III p 423
s 225 .... Vol V p 186
s 230 .... Vol V p 186
s 235 .... Vol V p 186
s 244 .... Vol III p 120
s 281 .... Vol III p 523
s 285 .... Vol III p 120, 509, 548
.... Vol IV p 82, Vol V p 388
Companies Act 1990
s 8 .... Vol V p 226
s 14 .... Vol V p 226
s 134 .... Vol V p 388
s 227 .... Vol V p 226
Companies Consolidation Act 1908
s 69 .... Vol V p 532
s 82(2) .... Vol V p 532
Constitution of Ireland 1937
.... Vol V p 70
Article 6 .... 1998 p 120
Article 15 .... 1998 p 120
Article 18 .... 1998 p 120
Article 28 .... 1998 p 120
Article 30 .... 1998 p 120
Article 34 .... Vol V p 70, 1999-2000 p 65
Article 34(1) .... Vol III p 590
Article 34.3.4 .... Vol III p 419
Article 37 .... 1999-2000 p 65
Article 38.1 .... Vol III p 387, 419
Article 38.2 .... Vol III p 419
Article 38.5 .... Vol III p 419
Article 40 .... Vol V p 70, 614, 1998 p 120, 1999-2000 p 65
Article 40.1 .... Vol III p 188, Vol IV p 437, Vol V p 481
Article 40.3 .... Vol III p 188, 590
.... Vol IV p 437

Constitution of Ireland 1937 (contd)
Article 41 .... Vol III p 188, Vol IV p 437
.... Vol V p 614
Article 43 .... Vol V p 70
Article 50 .... Vol V p 481, 1998 p 120

Conveyancing Act 1881
s 14 .... Vol V p 589

Conveyancing Act 1891
s 7 .... Vol V p 181

Copyright Act 1963
s 1 .... Vol IV p 314
s 17 .... Vol IV p 314

Corporation Tax Act 1976
.... Vol III p 611
s 1 .... Vol III p 53
(1) .... Vol V p 107, 1998 p 183
s 2 .... Vol IV p 415
s 4 .... Vol III p 670
s 6 .... Vol III p 553, Vol V p 107, 1998 p 183
s 8 .... Vol I p 330
(1) .... Vol IV p 12
(2) .... Vol IV p 12
s 9 (1) .... Vol V p 107, 1998 p 183
s 10 .... Vol V p 107, 1998 p 183
s 11 .... Vol III p 553
(i) .... Vol V p 107, 1998 p 183
(iii) .... Vol V p 107, 1998 p 183
s 13 .... Vol V p 107, 1998 p 183
s 15 .... Vol I p 447, Vol II p 429, Vol V p 680
(1) .... 1999-2000 p 114
(6) .... 1999-2000 p 114
s 16(1) .... Vol III p 363
(2) .... Vol III p 340
s 21 .... Vol IV p 91, Vol V p 200
s 25 .... Vol I p 86, Vol III p 340
s 27(1) .... Vol III p 363
s 28 .... Vol III p 430
s 37 .... Vol IV p 475
s 52 .... Vol IV p 401
s 54 .... Vol III p 304
s 58 .... Vol IV p 633
(3) .... Vol III p 229, Vol V p 221
s 59 .... Vol IV p 633
s 78 .... Vol III p 304
s 83 .... Vol III p 246
s 84 .... Vol III p 246
(1) .... Vol III p 517
s 87(8) .... Vol III p 246

Corporation Tax Act 1976 (contd)
s 100 .... Vol III p 517
s 101 .... Vol III p 517
s 107 .... 1999-2000 p 114
s 131 .... Vol III p 373
s 140 .... Vol III p 533
s 142 .... Vol III p 553
s 143 .... Vol III p 120
s 145 .... 1999-2000 p 72
s 146 .... Vol III p 559, 644, Vol V p 138, 1999-2000 p 114
s 147 .... Vol III p 553
s 151 .... Vol III p 246
s 155 .... Vol IV p 12, Vol III p 246
.... Vol V p 226
s 156 .... Vol V p 226
(1)(*b*) .... Vol III p 246
s 162 .... Vol III p 211
s 182 .... Vol III p 363
s 184 .... Vol III p 363
s 307 .... Vol III p 253
Sch 1 para 10 .... Vol IV p 91
Sch 3 s 164 .... Vol III p 56

Courts of Justice Act 1936
s 38 .... Vol V p 322
s 65 .... Vol V p 195

Courts (Supplemental Provisions) Act 1961
.... Vol III p 641, Vol IV p 395
s 52 .... Vol V p 221

Courts Acts 1924-1981
.... Vol III p 641

Courts Act 1981
s 22 .... Vol III p 403
(1) .... Vol V p 322

Court Officers Act 1926
.... Vol V p 186, 195

Courts of Justice Act 1924
s 38(3) .... Vol IV p 437
s 94 .... Vol III p 387

Courts of Justice Act 1936
s 38 .... Vol V p 322
s 65 .... Vol V p 186, 195
s 76 .... Vol IV p 278

Courts of Justice Act 1961
.... Vol V p 221

Criminal Assets Bureau Act 1996
s 8 .... 1999-2000 p 65
Criminal Justice Act 1988 (UK)
s 71 .... Vol V p 45
s 77(8) .... Vol V p 45
Customs Consolidation Act 1876
s 186 .... Vol IV p 395
s 204 .... Vol IV p 386
Customs and Inland Revenue Regulation Act 1890
s 30 .... Vol IV p 386
Customs Act 1956
.... Vol V p 348
Debtors (Ireland) Act 1840
s 26 .... Vol V p 322
Domicile and Recognition of Foreign Divorces Act 1986
.... Vol IV p 437
Double Taxation Relief (Taxes on Income and Capital Gains) [UK] Order 1976 (SI 319/1976)
.... Vol V p 129
Article 15 .... Vol V p 54
Article 18(2) .... Vol V p 54
Enforcement of Court Orders Act 1926
s 2 .... Vol IV p 86
s 13 .... Vol IV p 86
Ethics in Public Office Act 1995
.... 1998 p 120
Excise Management Act 1827
s 86 .... Vol IV p 278
s 90 .... Vol IV p 278
Excise Collection and Management Act 1841(4 & 5 Vict c 20)
s 24 .... Vol III p 265
Executive Power (Consequential Provisions) Act 1937
.... 1998 p 120
Extradition Act 1965
s 50 .... 1998 p 76
Farm Tax Act 1985
.... Vol III p 229
s 3 .... Vol V p 288
s 9 .... Vol V p 288
Finance Act 1894
s 1 .... Vol V p 600
s 2(1)(a) .... Vol V p 600
s 5(3) .... Vol V p 526

s 7(5) .... Vol V p 294, 532, 577
s 10 .... Vol V p 577
s 22(2)(a) .... Vol V p 600

Finance (1909-1910) Act 1910
s 59(2) .... Vol V p 589
s 74(5) .... Vol IV p 187

Finance Act 1910 Pt V
ss 73-75 .... Vol V p 570

Finance Act 1915
s 21(2) .... 1999-2000 p 114
s 41(1) .... 1999-2000 p 114

Finance Act (No 2) 1915
s 45(5) .... Vol I p 1
Sch IV Pt I
rule 1 .... Vol I p 240
Sch IV Pt III .... Vol I p 34

Finance Act 1918
s 33 .... 1999-2000 p 114
s 35 .... Vol I p 28

Finance Act 1920
s 16 .... Vol II p 596
s 17 .... Vol V p 539
s 52 .... Vol III p 56
(2) .... Vol I p 70, 108
(I) .... Vol I p 359
(*a*) .... Vol I p 108, 119
(*b*) .... Vol I p 330
s 53 .... Vol I p 629, Vol II p 382
.... Vol III p 56
(2)(*b*) .... Vol II p 412
(*h*) .... Vol II p 195
s 54(1) .... Vol II p 130
Pt V .... Vol I p 627

Finance Act 1921
s 21 .... Vol IV p 386
s 30(1)(*c*) .... Vol I p 383
s 53 .... Vol I p 315, Vol II p 195
Sch 2 Pt II
rule 1 .... Vol I p 130

Finance Act 1922
s 18 .... Vol II pp 393, 452
s 20 .... Vol II p 82
(1) .... Vol II p 352
(1)(*c*) .... Vol I p 411

Finance Act 1923
s 17 .... Vol V p 539
Finance Act 1924
s 10 .... Vol I p 656
Finance Act 1925
s 11 .... Vol V p 565
s 12 .... Vol I pp 249, 259
Finance Act 1926
s 24(*a*) .... Vol IV p 395
s 25(1) .... Vol IV p 395
Sch 1 Pt II .... Vol II p 491
s 1(3) .... Vol II p 304
s 2(2) .... Vol II p 304
Finance Act 1929
s 5 .... Vol I p 571
s 8(1) .... Vol I p 146
s 9 .... Vol II p 515
(2) .... Vol I p 146
s 10 .... Vol I p 563, Vol II p 304
.... Vol III p 568
s 11 .... Vol I pp 563, Vol II p 393
.... Vol II pp 304, 464, 491
s 12 .... Vol II pp 55, 115
s 14 .... Vol II p 482
s 17 .... Vol I p 618
s 18 .... Vol II p 304
s 33(1)(*d*) .... Vol II p 25
Sch 1 Pt II .... Vol I p 393, Vol II p 61
Sch 2 para (3) .... Vol II p 304
Finance Act 1932
s 3(4) .... Vol V p 565
s 4 .... Vol I p 393
s 46 .... Vol V p 539
Finance Act 1935
s 6 .... VOL I p 583
(1) .... Vol II p 472
s 21 .... Vol V p 696
(8) .... Vol IV p 162
Finance Act 1937
s 2 .... Vol II p 82
(1) .... Vol II p 352
Finance Act 1939
s 3 .... Vol V p 565
s 7 .... Vol II p 315
Finance Act 1940
s 3 .... Vol V p 393

s 18 .... Vol IV p 386

Finance Act 1941

s 32 .... Vol V p 589
s 36(4) .... Vol II p 175
s 39 .... Vol II p 19

Finance Act 1944

s 14 .... Vol II p 175

Finance Act 1946

s 24 .... Vol II p 195

Finance Act (No 2) 1947

s 13(1) .... 1998 p 169
(4) .... 1998 p 169
(5) .... 1998 p 169
s 23 .... Vol V p 570

Finance Act 1956

Pt V .... Vol II p 602

Finance Act 1958

s 23 .... Vol IV p 323
s 24 .... Vol IV p 323
s 25 .... Vol IV p 323
s 26 .... Vol IV p 323

Finance Act (No 2) 1959

.... Vol IV p 82
s 13(1) .... Vol II p 588

Finance Act 1962

s 22 .... Vol IV p 162

Finance Act 1963

s 34(4)(*d*)(i) .... Vol III p 419
(iii) .... Vol III p 419

Finance Act 1964

s 26 .... Vol III p 56

Finance Act 1965

s 23 .... 1999-2000 p 144

Finance Act 1967

s 12 .... Vol V p 393
s 138-143 .... Vol V p 393
s 153 .... Vol V p 393
s 241 .... Vol V p 317
s 439 .... Vol V p 393

Finance Act 1968

s 7 .... Vol III p 590
s 8 .... Vol III p 590, 1998 p 59
s 11 .... 1998 p 59
s 14 .... Vol IV p 91

s 43(1) .... Vol IV p 170

Finance Act 1969

s 2.......... Vol III p 496, Vol V p 98
s 3.......... Vol V p 393
s 65(1) .... Vol III p 533

Finance Act 1970

s 17.......... Vol IV p 269, 304
s 20.......... Vol III p 484
s 24.......... Vol IV p 187
s 26.......... Vol IV p 68

Finance Act 1971

s 22.......... Vol IV p 22
s 25.......... Vol IV p 22
s 26.......... Vol V p 200

Finance Act 1972

ss 14-25 .... Vol IV p 340
Sch 1 .... Vol IV p 340

Finance Act 1973

s 34.......... Vol III p 670

Finance Act 1974

s 8.......... Vol V p 393
s 13.......... Vol IV p 1
(1).......... Vol III p 319
s 15.......... Vol IV p 1
s 17.......... Vol IV p 1
s 21.......... Vol IV p 1
s 22.......... Vol V p 680
s 31.......... Vol III p 246
s 59.......... Vol III p 356

Finance Act 1975

s 12.......... Vol IV p 1
s 25.......... Vol V p 348
s 31.......... Vol I p 130, Vol III pp 51, 178
(1).......... Vol IV p 304
(2).......... Vol IV p 135

Finance Act 1976

s 21.......... Vol IV p 269
s 26.......... Vol III p 51
s 30.......... Vol IV pp 62, 91
(4).......... Vol V p 322
s 41.......... 1999-2000 p 59
s 46.......... Vol IV p 162, Vol V p 696

Finance Act 1977

s 43.......... Vol III p 611
Pt V Sch 1 .... Vol III p 611

Finance Act 1978

.... Vol V p 322
s 46 .... Vol IV p 91
ss 138-142 .... Vol V p 614

Finance Act 1980

s 1 .... Vol V p 393
s 2 .... Vol V p 393
s 8 .... Vol V p 129
s 18 .... Vol V p 129
s 21 .... Vol III p 188
s 38-51 .... Vol V p 226
s 39 .... Vol III p 611, Vol IV p 35
.... Vol IV pp 361, 526
(1), (2) and (5) .... 1999-2000 p 72
s 41(2) .... Vol III p 304, Vol IV p 35
.... Vol IV p 466
(4) .... Vol IV p 466
(8) .... Vol V p 376, 1998 p 99
s 42 .... Vol IV p 361, Vol V p 221
s 57 .... Vol IV p 478
s 79 .... Vol III p 73
Pt I Ch VI .... Vol III p 441, Vol V p 21

Finance Act 1982

Sch 2 .... Vol IV p 35
s 4. .... Vol IV p 323
s 26 .... Vol IV p 35
s 69(1) .... Vol IV p 395

Finance Act 1983

s 3 .... Vol IV p 437
s 9 .... Vol III p 533
s 18 .... Vol III p 153, Vol V p 348
s 19 .... Vol I p 195, Vol II p 291, Vol V p 424
s 56 .... Vol III p 120
s 94 .... Vol III p 387, Vol IV p 395
(2) .... Vol IV p 478
(4) .... Vol IV p 478
(9) .... Vol IV p 478
s 95 .... Vol III p 127

Finance Act 1983 (No 15)

s 9 .... Vol III p 533

Finance Act 1984

s 12 .... 1999-2000 p 58

Finance Act 1986

s 46 .... Vol III p 253
s 48(2) .... Vol V p 210
s 96(1) .... Vol IV p 187

Finance Act 1987
s 14 .... Vol V p 213
s 15 .... Vol V p 213
s 17-19 .... Vol V p 213
s 53 .... Vol IV p 278
Finance Act 1988
s 1 .... Vol V p 424
s 7 .... Vol V p 424
s 16 .... Vol V p 210
s 73 .... Vol V p 70
Finance Act 1989
s 86 .... Vol V p 6
s 92 .... 1999-2000 p 55
Finance Act 1990
s 14 .... Vol V p 213
s 26 .... Vol V p 213
s 41(1) .... Vol V p 376, 1998 p 99
(5) .... 1999-2000 p 72
Finance Act 1992
s 15 .... Vol V p 472
s 242 .... Vol IV p 419
Finance Act 1995
s 10 .... Vol V p 472
s 105 .... 1999-2000 p 59
Finance Act (Miscellaneous Provisions) 1956
s 13(3) .... Vol III p 452
Finance Act (Miscellaneous Provisions) 1968
s 17 .... Vol II p 667
s 18 .... Vol III p 271
(2) .... Vol III p 198
Finance Act (Miscellaneous Provisions) 1968 (No 7)
s 17 .... Vol III p 9
Finance (Excise Duties) (Vehicles) Act 1952
.... Vol IV p 170
Finance (Taxation of Profits of Certain Mines) Act 1974
.... Vol IV p 91
Fraudulent Conveyances Act 1635
.... Vol III p 706
Garda Síochána Pension Order 1981
.... 1998 p 113
Holidays (Employees) Act 1973
.... Vol III p 505

Imposition of Duties Act 1957

.... Vol IV p 162

Industrial Development Act 1969

s 33 .... Vol IV p 22

Interpretation Act 1937

s 11 .... Vol III pp 559, 644

Income Tax Act 1843

.... 1998 p 183

Income Tax Act 1918

Sch B .... Vol II p 636

rule 8 .... Vol II p 1, Vol II p 241

Sch D .... Vol I p 330, 474, 496, 515

.... Vol II p 32, 45, 140, 164

.... 360, 374, 419

Sch D Case I .... Vol I p 427, 629

.... Vol II p 211, 291, 315, 500,

rule 3 & 6 602

Sch D Cases I & II .... Vol I p 86

rule 1(1) .... Vol I p 642

rule 2 .... Vol II p 382

rule 3 .... Vol I p 375, 642, Vol II p 515

(*a*) .... Vol II p 222

(*d*) and (g) .... Vol II p 267

rule 4 .... Vol II p 115

rule 7 .... Vol I p 43 rule 11

.... Vol II p 55

Sch D Cases II & VI .... Vol I p 195

Sch D Case III .... Vol I pp 45, 393, 491

.... Vol II pp 15, 393, 464, 568, 592

rule 2 (s 17) .... Vol II p 304

rule 4 .... Vol III p 19

rule 5 .... Vol II p 222

Sch D Case IV

rule 2(*a*) .... Vol I p 259

Sch D Case V

rule 3 .... Vol I p 249

Sch D Case VI .... Vol II p 204, 261

Sch E .... Vol I p 155, 601

.... Vol II p 68, 452

rule 1 .... Vol I p 214, 618

rule 5 .... Vol I p 214

rule 7 .... Vol II p 261

rule 9 .... Vol I p 64, Vol II pp 366, 460

Case VI .... Vol II p 154

rule 16 .... Vol I pp 115, 563, Vol II p 75

rule 21 .... Vol I p 487

s 5 .... Vol I p 231

Income Tax Act 1918 (contd)

s 16 .... Vol V p 565
s 25 .... Vol I p 221
s 29 .... Vol V p 565
s 33 (1) .... Vol I p 447, Vol II p 429
s 100(2) .... Vol I p 642
s 133 .... Vol I p 571
s 137 .... Vol I p 571
s 149 .... Vol I p 1, 571, 656
(1)(*e*) .... Vol II p 60
s 186 .... Vol II p 1, 241
s 187 .... Vol II pp 1, 241
s 202 .... Vol I p 221
s 209 .... Vol I p 642, Vol II p 515
Sch 1 .... Vol III p 56

Income Tax Act 1967
.... Vol II pp 366, 460, Vol III p 1
Sch E .... Vol III p 467
s 1 .... Vol III p 559, 644
.... Vol IV p 73
s 4 .... Vol V p 108, 1998 p 183
s 7(*a*) .... Vol III p 533
s 11 .... Vol III p 9
(1) .... Vol V p 496
s 12 .... Vol III p 9
s 17 .... Vol II p 641
s 25 .... Vol II p 393
s 52 .... Vol V p 108, 1998 p 183
s 53 .... Vol I pp 1, 28, 45, 115, 119, 207, 231, 231
.... Vol I pp 318, 427, 474, 629
.... Vol II pp 60, 164, 204, 304, 393, 491, 592, 614
.... Vol III pp 165, 484, 568, Vol IV pp 45, 73, 135, 1998 p 183
.... Vol V p 108
s 53(1) .... Vol III pp 559, 644
s 54 .... Vol V p 21
s 57 .... Vol I p 130
s 58 .... Vol I p 146
.... Vol I p 91
s 61 .... Vol I pp 104, 375, 503, 642
.... Vol II pp 32, 45, 267, 281, 360
.... Vol II pp 382, 500, 515, 602
.... Vol IV p 187, 425, Vol V p 496
.... 1999-2000 p 55, 1999-2000 p 56
s 61(*a*) .... Vol IV p 22
(*e*) .... Vol V p 138
(*f*) .... Vol V p 138
s 62(2) .... Vol IV p 304
s 76 .... Vol I pp 249, 259, Vol II p 304, Vol V p 481

Income Tax Act 1967 (contd)

s 80 .... Vol IV p 187
s 81 .... Vol IV p 187
(5)(*d*) .... Vol III p 95, Vol V p 680
(6)(a)(i) .... Vol V p 680
s 83 .... Vol IV p 187
s 91 .... Vol IV p 187
s 105 .... Vol III p 477, 553
s 109 .... 1998 p 113
s 110 .... Vol I pp 214, 601, 656, Vol II pp 261, 452
.... Vol III p 43, 505, Vol IV p 45
.... Vol IV p 221, 391, 407, 1999-2000 p 144
s 111 .... Vol IV p 221
s 114 .... Vol I p 618, Vol IV pp 233, 407
.... Vol V p 134
s 115 .... Vol IV p 221
(1)(*a*) .... Vol V p 134
s 117 .... Vol II p 452, Vol IV p 323
s 118 .... Vol IV p 323
s 119 .... Vol IV p 323
s 120 .... Vol IV p 323
s 126 .... Vol III p 590, Vol V p 322
s 127 .... Vol II p 641
s 128 .... Vol II p 641
s 129 .... Vol III p 590
s 131 .... Vol III p 590
s 133(1) .... Vol II p 588
s 138 .... Vol V p 129, 614
s 146 .... Vol V p 496
s 161(1) .... Vol III p 670
s 162 .... Vol III p 290, 298
s 169 .... Vol V p 348
(4) .... Vol III p 387
s 172 .... Vol IV p 478
(4) .... Vol V p 348
s 174(1) .... Vol IV p 332
(*a*) .... Vol V p 265
s 176 .... Vol IV p 221
s 178(1) .... Vol III p 387
s 184 .... 1999-2000 p 65
(2) .... Vol III p 533
s 186 .... Vol I p 34, Vol II p 627
.... Vol IV p 187
s 192 .... Vol IV p 188, Vol V p 129, 614
s 193 .... Vol I p 115
s 194 .... Vol I p 563, Vol II p 75
.... Vol V p 424

Income Tax Act 1967 (contd)

s 195 ..... Vol V p 424, 614
(1) ..... Vol V p 129
s 196 ..... Vol V p 614
s 197 ..... Vol V p 614
s 198 ..... Vol V p 614
s 200 ..... Vol I p 183
s 207 ..... Vol III p 553
s 212 ..... Vol III p 553
s 220(5) ..... Vol II p 661
s 224 ..... 1998 p 113
s 238 ..... Vol III p 387
s 239 ..... Vol V p 108, 1998 p 183
s 240 ..... Vol III p 387
s 241 ..... Vol III p 113, 219
..... Vol IV p 68, 425, Vol V p 6
(1) ..... Vol V p 200
(5) ..... Vol III p 253
s 244 ..... Vol IV p 91
s 245 ..... Vol IV p 91
s 252 ..... Vol III p 253
s 254 ..... Vol III p 65
s 255 ..... Vol III p 65, 661, 1999-2000 p 56
(1)(d) ..... Vol V p 357
s 282 ..... Vol III p 253
s 296 ..... Vol III p 253, 387
s 307 ..... Vol III p 332
s 333 ..... Vol I p 542, 1998 p 66
s 334 ..... Vol I p 383, 1998 p 66
s 348 ..... Vol I p 538
s 349 ..... Vol III p 28
s 361 ..... Vol III p 246
s 416 ..... Vol I p 221, 571, 618, 629
..... Vol II p 55, Vol III pp 332, 577
..... Vol IV pp 62, 73, 91, 125, 187
s 416 ..... 1999-2000 p 65
(6) ..... Vol III p 533, Vol V p 210
s 428 ..... Vol III p 159, 198, 611, 1998 p 111
..... Vol IV p 401, 505
..... Vol V p 54, 76, 163, 221, 481, 496
..... 1999-2000 p 72, 1999-2000 p 144
s 428(*b*) ..... Vol III p 340
(9) ..... Vol IV p 91, Vol V p 322
s 429 ..... Vol II p 374, Vol III p 219
..... Vol IV pp 125, 401, 407, 505
s 430 ..... Vol I p 487, Vol II p 332
..... Vol III pp 159, 198, 496, 559, 611, 644
..... Vol IV pp 62, 125, 401, 425, 505
..... Vol V p 54, 138, 221, 481

Income Tax Act 1967 (contd)
s 438 .... Vol I p 411
s 439 .... Vol III p 242
s 440 .... Vol II p 82
s 443 .... Vol II p 352
.... Vol IV p 221
s 448 .... Vol II p 82
s 478 .... Vol V p 424
s 485 .... Vol III p 533, 590,1999-2000 p 65
s 488 .... Vol III p 577
s 496 .... Vol III p 559, 644
s 498 .... Vol V p 322
s 500 .... Vol III p 387, 641
.... Vol IV p 395, 478
s 501 .... Vol III p 577, Vol IV p 478
s 502 .... Vol IV p 478
s 503 .... Vol IV p 395
s 506 .... Vol IV p 478
s 507 .... Vol IV p 478
s 508 .... Vol III p 387
s 527 .... Vol IV p 73
s 542(2) .... Vol V p 348
s 550 .... Vol V p 322
(1) .... Vol IV p 91
(2A)(*c*) .... Vol IV p 62
Pt XXVI .... Vol III p 577
Sch 2 para 3 .... Vol I p 64
Income Tax Act 1970 (UK)
s 130(*f*) .... Vol V p 138
Inland Revenue Regulations Act 1890
s 21 .... Vol V p 691
Labour Exchange Act 1909
.... Vol III p 253, Vol IV p 45
Limited Partnerships Act 1907
.... Vol III p 253
Local Government (Planning and Development) Act 1963
s 5 .... Vol V p 357
s 528(6) .... Vol V p 357
Local Government (Planning and Development) Act 1976
.... Vol IV p 543
Local Government (Planning and Development) Act 1982
.... Vol IV p 543
Minerals Development Act 1940
s 14 .... Vol V p 696

Partnership Act 1890
.... Vol III p 253
Petty Sessions (Ireland) Act 1851
s 22 .... Vol IV p 278
s 42 .... Vol IV p 278
Poor Law Act 1834 (4 & 5 Wm 4 c 76)
s 86 .... Vol V p 560
Poor Relief (Ireland) Act 1838 (1 & 2 Vict c 56)
s 96 .... Vol V p 560
Preferential Payments in Bankruptcy (Ireland) Act 1889
.... 1998 p 59
Prosecution of Offences Act 1974
.... Vol III p 641
s 3 .... Vol IV p 395, Vol V p 691
Racing Board and Racecourses Act 1945
s 4 .... Vol IV p 73
ss 14-16 .... Vol IV p 73
s 27(1) .... Vol IV p 73
Revenue Act 1898 (61 & 62 Vict c 46)
s 13 .... Vol V p 560
Revenue Act 1911
s 15 .... Vol V p 570
Sale of goods Act 1893
.... Vol V p 21
Sea Fisheries Protection Act 1933
s 9 .... Vol IV p 401
Settled Land Act 1882
.... Vol V p 526, 600
Social Welfare Act 1952
s 27(2) .... Vol V p 472
Social Welfare Act 1976
s 18(1) .... Vol V p 472
Social Welfare (Consolidation) Act 1981
.... Vol IV p 113
s 2 .... Vol V p 472
(4) .... Vol IV p 378
s 5(1) .... Vol IV p 378
s 9 .... Vol III p 509
(1),(2) .... Vol IV p 378
s 10 .... Vol III p 509, 1998 p 59
(1),(3) .... Vol IV p 378
s 92 .... Vol IV p 221, Vol V p 472, 1998 p 111
s 94 .... Vol IV p 221, 1998 p 111

Social Welfare (Consolidation) Act 1981 (contd)
s 95 .... Vol V p 472, 1998 p 111
s 111 .... Vol V p 239
s 114 .... Vol IV p 391
s 298 .... Vol V p 239
s 299 .... Vol III p 436, Vol V p 239
Social Welfare Act 1982
s 2 .... Vol V p 472
Social Welfare (Consolidation) Act 1993
.... Vol V p 95
s 16
(1) .... 1998 p 59
(2) .... 1998 p 59
s 301 .... 1998 p 59
Stamp Duties (Ireland) Act 1842
s 38 .... Vol V p 539
Stamp Duties Act 1854
s 1 .... Vol V p 570
Stamp Act 1870
s 17 .... Vol V p 1
ss 96-99 .... Vol V p 570
Stamp Duties Management Act 1891 (54 & 55 Vict c 38)
s 10 .... Vol V p 560
Stamp Act 1891
s 1 .... Vol IV p 187
s 3 .... Vol IV p 187
s 12 .... Vol V p 570
s 13 .... Vol IV p 367, Vol V p 181
s 14 .... Vol V p 363
(4) .... Vol V p 1
s 23 .... Vol V p 570
s 54 .... Vol IV p 187, 367
ss 59-61 .... Vol V p 570
ss 175-78 .... Vol V p 570
Succession Act 1965
.... Vol III p 559
9(2) .... Vol V p 600
10 .... Vol V p 367
67(1) .... Vol V p 367
111 .... Vol V p 600
(1) .... Vol V p 367
115 .... Vol V p 367, 600
120 .... Vol V p 367
Pt VIII .... Vol V p 271

Succession Duty Act 1853
s 18 ... Vol V p 539
Taxes Consolidation Act 1997
s 81(2) ... 1999-2000 p 82
s 112 ... 1999-2000 p 57
s 271 ... 1999-2000 p 57
s 552 ... 1999-2000 p 55
s 573 ... 1999-2000 p 55
s 669 ... 1999-2000 p 57
s 933 ... 1999-2000 p 65
s 955(2)(a) ... 1999-2000 p 65
s 966(5)(a) ... 1999-2000 p 65
s 997 ... 1999-2000 p 61
s 1017 ... 1999-2000 p 58
s 1097 ... 1999-2000 p 65
Taxes Management Act 1880
s 59 ... Vol I p 1
Tribunal of Inquiry (Evidence) Act 1921
... 1998 p 120
Tribunal of Inquiry (Evidence) (Amendment) Act 1979
... 1998 p 120
Unemployment Assistance Act 1933
... Vol III p 253, Vol IV p 45
Unfair Dismissals Act 1977
... Vol V p 239
Value Added Tax Act 1972 (No 22)
Sch 1 ... 1999-2000 p 58
(12) ... Vol III p 680
Sch 2 ... 1999-2000 p 58
Sch 4 ... Vol IV p 117
Sch 6 ... Vol IV p 349, 1999-2000 p 58
s 1(1) ... Vol III p 611
s 2 ... Vol IV p 117, 314
s 3(1)(*f*) ... Vol V p 76
s 4 ... 1999-2000 p 58
(4) ... Vol V p 76
s 5 ... Vol IV p 117, 314
s 8 ... Vol V p 61
s 9 ... Vol V p 61
s 10 ... Vol III p 332, Vol V p 418
(9) ... Vol V p 76
(10) ... Vol V p 76
s 11 ... Vol IV p 117, Vol V p 418
s 12 ... Vol V p 76, 412

Value Added Tax Act 1972 (No 22)
s 16 .... Vol V p 412
s 19 .... Vol V p 412
s 20(1) .... Vol V p 412
s 25 .... Vol III p 332
.... Vol V p 76
s 26 .... Vol IV p 478
s 27 .... Vol IV p 386, 478
s 32 .... Vol V p 76
s 43 .... Vol V p 418
Value Added Tax Act (Amendment) Act 1978 (No 34)
s 3. .... Vol IV p 314
Value Added Tax Act (UK) 1983
s 39(3) .... Vol V p 45
Waiver of Certain Tax, Interest & Penalties Act 1993
s 2 .... Vol V p 210
(2) .... 1999-2000 p 65
s 3 .... Vol V p 210
(6) .... 1999-2000 p 65
Wills Act 1837
.... Vol V p 271

Regulations and Statutory Instruments

Agricultural Levies (Export Control) Regulations 1983 (UK)
.... 1998 p 76
EC Council Directive No 77/388/EEC
.... Vol V p 76
EC Council Directive No 81/77/EEC
.... 1998 p 76
EC Council Directive No 83/182/EEC of 28 March 1983
.... Vol IV p 512
EEC Regulations
804/68 and 2682/72 .... Vol IV p 492
EEC Council Regulations
729/1970, 974/1971 and 667/85 .... 1998 p 76
European Communities (Companies) Regulations 1973
SI 163/1973 .... Vol V p 226
European Communities (Exemption from Import Charges of Certain Vehicles etc Temporarily Imported) Regulations 1983
SI 422/1983 .... Vol IV p 512
Farm Tax (Adjusted Acreage) Regulations
SI 321/1986 .... Vol V p 288

Farm Tax Regulations 1986
SI 237/1986 .... Vol V p 288
Finance Act 1966
SI 152/1970 .... Vol III p 73
SI 160/1979 .... Vol III p 73
Hydrocarbon Oil (Rebated Oil) Regulations 1961 Article 8,
FA 1959 SI 28/1960 .... Vol IV p 113
Imposition of Duties Order 1975
SI 221/1975 .... Vol IV p 162, Vol V p 696
Imposition of Duties (No 236) (Excise Duties on Motor Vehicles etc) 1979
SI 57/1979 para 12 .... Vol IV pp 170, 512
SI 353/1984 .... Vol IV p 512
Income Tax (Employments) Regulations 1960
.... Vol III p 590, Vol V p 322
rule 2 .... Vol IV p 113
SI No 28/1960 .... Vol II p 588, Vol III p 590
Social Welfare (Collection of Employment Contributions by the
Collector General) Regulations 1979
SI 77/1979 .... Vol III p 467, 509
Social Welfare (Collection of Employment Contributions) Regulations 1989
SI 302/1989 .... Vol IV p 378
Superior Court Rules
SI 15/1986 Order 84
r 20(4) .... Vol V p 363
r 25(5) .... Vol V p 363
Supreme Court & High Court (Fees) Order 1984
SI 19/1984 as amended by SI 36/1985 .... Vol III p 530
Treaty of Rome
Article 38 .... 1998 p 76
Article 39 .... 1998 p 76
Article 177 .... Vol III p 73
Article 235 .... 1998 p 76
VAT Regulations 1979
SI 63/1979 .... Vol V p 76
VAT (Refund of Tax)(No 13) Order 1980
SI 263/1980 .... Vol IV p 170
VAT (Exported goods) Regulations 1992
(SI 438/1992) .... Vol V p 412
VAT Registration Regulation 1993
SI 30/1993 .... Vol V p 61

Destination Table (Taxes Consolidation Act 1997)

This table may be used to trace the present location of older legislation as re-enacted in the Taxes Consolidation Act, 1997.

Former Enactment		*Destination in TCA 1997*
Finance Act 1928 (1928 No 11)		
s 34 (2)		s 872(1)
Income Tax Act 1967 (1967 No 7)		
Pt I		
s 1	Definitions of "assurance company", "commencement of this Act", "municipal rate", "National Debt Commissioners" and "repealed enactments" in ITA 1967 s 1(1) unnecessary (obsolete)	ss 2(1), 3(1)
(2)	Unnecessary (construction)	
(3)	Unnecessary (interpretation)	
(4)	Unnecessary (interpretation)	
(5)	Rep by CTA 1976 s 164 and Sch 3 Pt II	
(6)	Unnecessary (obsolete)	
2		s 3(2), (3)
3		s 1(2)
4		s 12
5		s 14(2)
6		s 14(1)
7	Rep by FA 1972 s 46(1) and Sch 4 Pt I	
8		s 1087
Pt II		
ss 9-42	Rep by FA 1969 s 65(1) and Sch 5 Pt I	
43	Rep by FA 1996 s 132(2) and Sch 5 Pt II	
44	Rep by FA 1969 s 65(1) and Sch 5 Pt I	
45	Rep by FA 1969 s 65(1) and Sch 5 Pt I	
46	Rep by FA 1997s 146(2) and Sch 9 Pt II	
Pt III		
s 47		s 17(1)
48		s 33
49 (1), (2)		s 34
49 (3)	Rep by DR&IA 1967 s 4 and Sch 6	
50		s 35
51		ss 17(2), 32
Pt IV		
s 52		s 18(1), (3)
53		s 18(2), (3)
54 (1)		s 654
(2)(a)		s 655(3)
(2)(b),(3), (4)	Rep by FA 1969 s 65(1) and Sch 5 Pt I	
55		s 54
56 (1)-(3)		s 56
(4)-(6)	Rep by FA 1969 s 65(1) and Sch 5 Pt I	
57		s 81(1)
58 (1)		s 65(1)
(2)-(4)		s 66
(5), (6)		s 67

Former Enactment		*Destination in TCA 1997*
Income Tax Act 1967 (1967 No 7) (contd)		
s 58A	(s 58A inserted by FA 1995 s 19)	s 68
59		s 69
60		s 65(2)-(4)
61		s 81(2)
62 (1)(a), (b)		s 89(2)
(b)(proviso)		s 656(2)
(2)		s 89(1)(a), (c)
63		s 84
64	Rep by CTA 1976 s 164 and Sch 3 Pt I	
65	Unnecessary (spent)	
66	Rep by FA 1969 s 65(1) and Sch 5 Pt I	
67 (1)-(3A)		s 85
(4)	Rep by FA 1969 s 31	
68 (1)		s 108
(2)	Rep by FA 1997	ss 146(2) and Sch 9 Pt II
69 (1), (2)	Definition of "capital allowance" rep by FA 1975 s 33 and Sch 1 Pt II	s 1007(1), (2)
69 (3)		ss 880(3), 1007(3)
70 (1)-(3A)		s 880(2)-(6)
(3B)		s 900(3)
(4)		s 1052(4)(a), (c), (e)
(5)		s 880(1)
71 (1)		s 1008(1)
(2)(a), (b)		s 1008(2)
(c)	Unnecessary (spent)	
(3)-(5)		s 1008(3)-(5)
72		s 1010
73		s 1012
74		s 1011
75		s 70(1)
76 (1)		s 71(1)
(2)(a)		s 71(2)
(b)	Rep by CTA 1976 s 164 and Sch 3 Pt I	
(3)		s 71(3)
(4)	Rep by FA 1994 s 157(1)	
(5), (6)		s 71(5), (6)
(7), (8)	Rep by CTA 1976 s 164 and Sch 3 Pt I	
77 (1)		s 70(2)
(2)		s 70(3)
(3), (4)	Ceased by FA 1990 s 17(2)	
(5)		s 70(4)
78	Rep by FA 1969 s 65(1) and Sch 5 Pt I	
79		s 74
80 (1)		ss 96(1), 888(1)
(2)		s 96(2)
(3)	Unnecessary (obsolete)	
(4), (5)		s 96(3), (4)
81 (1)		ss 75(1), 96(1)
(2)		s 75(2)

Former Enactment	*Destination in TCA 1997*
Income Tax Act 1967 (1967 No 7) (contd)	
s 81 (3)(a)	s 75(3)
(b), (c) . . Ceased by FA 1990 s 18(2)	
(4)-(8)	s 97
(9), (10) . . . Unnecessary (spent)	
82 . . . . Rep by FA 1997 s 146(2) and Sch 9 Pt II	
83	s 98
84	s 99
85	s 100
86	s 75(4)
87 . . . . Rep by FA 1969 s 65(1) and Sch 5 Pt I	
88 (1)	s 918(4)
(2), (3) . . . . Rep by FA 1969 s 65(1) and Sch 5 Pt I	
89	s 384
89A . . . . Rep by FA 1996 s 132(2) and Sch 5 Pt II. (s 89A inserted by F(MP)A 1968 s 7)	
90	s 101
91	s 102
92	s 103
93 (1), (2)	s 104
(3)	s 1087(2)
94	s 888
95 . . . . Rep by FA 1969 s 65(1) and Sch 5 Pt I	
96-103 . . . . Unnecessary (obsolete)	
104 . . . . Rep by FA 1969 s 65(1) and Sch 5 Pt I	
105	s 52
106 . . . . Rep by FA 1997 s 146(2) and Sch 9 Pt II	
107	s 107
108 . . . . Rep by CTA 1976 s 164 and Sch 3 Pt I	
Pt V	
s 109	s 19(1)
110	s 112
111 . . . . Deleted by FA 1990 s 19(b) with saver for enactments which refer to s 111	
112	s 113
113	s 948
114(1)-(5)	s 123(1)-(5)
(6) . . . . Unnecessary (spent)	
(7)	s 123(6)
115(1)	s 201(2)
(1A)(a)	s 201(3)
(b) . . . . Unnecessary (operative date)	
(2)-(4)	s 201(4)-(6)
(5)-(7)	s 201(1)
(8)	s 201(7)
116	s 117
117	s 118
118(1), (2)	s 119(1), (2)
(3) . . . . Deleted by FA 1969 s 32(a)	
(4)	s 119(3), (4)
(5) . . . . Deleted by FA 1969 s 32(a)	

Former Enactment		*Destination in TCA 1997*
Income Tax Act 1967 (1967 No 7) (contd)		
s 119(1), (2)		s 116(1)
(3), (4)		s 116(3), (4)
120(1)		s 897(6)
(2)		s 897(7)
(3)	Unnecessary (duplication)	
121	Rep by FA 1973 s 42	
(1), (3)		s 116(1)
122(2)		s 116(2)
123		s 120
124		s 983
125		s 984(1), (2)
126		s 985
127(1)(a)-(f),		s 986(1)(a)-(j), (g), (h)
(ff)	Deleted by FA 1974 s 11 and Sch 1 Pt II	
(2)		s 986(2)
(3)(a)(i)		s 986(3)(a)
(ii)	Deleted by FA 1974 s 11 and Sch 1 Pt II	
(b)		s 986(3)(b)
(c)	Deleted by FA 1974 s 11 and Sch 1 Pt II	
(4)-(5A)		s 986(4)-(6)
(6)	Unnecessary (spent)	
(7)		s 986(7)
127A	(s 127A inserted by FA 1992 s 233)	s 903
128(1),(1A),(2)		s 987(1)-(3)
(3)	Deleted by FA 1982 s 60(2)	
(4)		s 987(4)
129		s 991(1)
130	Ceased by FA 1974 s 71(a)	
131		s 993(1)-(4)
132		s 994
133		s 997
Pt VI		
s 134-136	Rep by FA 1974 s 86 and Sch 2 Pt I	
137		s 458
138		s 461
138A(1)-(6)	(s 138A inserted by FA 1980 s 3. and substituted by FA 1985 s 4)	s 462
(7)	Rep by FA 1996 s 132(2) and Sch 5 Pt II	
138B	(s 138B inserted by FA 1980 s 3)	s 472
139	Ceased by FA 1982 s 2(3) and Sch 1	
140	Ceased by FA 1982 s 2(3) and Sch 1	
141(1)-(6)		s 465
(7)	Rep by FA 1996 s 132(2) and Sch 5 Pt II	
142		s 466
142A	(s 142A inserted by FA 1982 s 5(1))	s 473
143	Ceased by FA 1992 s 4(a)	
144	Rep by FA 1979 s 32(1)	
145(1)-(3)		s 470(1)-(3)
(3A)	Rep by FA 1996 s 132(2) and Sch 5 Pt II	
(4)		s 470(4)
(5)	Rep by FA 1996 s 132(2) and Sch 5 Pt II	
146		s 459(1)

Former Enactment		*Destination in TCA 1997*
Income Tax Act 1967 (1967 No 7) (contd)		
s 147	Rep by FA 1969 s 65(1) and Sch 5 Pt I	
148	Rep by FA 1969 s 65(1) and Sch 5 Pt I	
149		s 459(2)
150	Rep by FA 1969 s 65(1) and Sch 5 Pt I	
151	Ceased by FA 1992 s 4(a)	
152	Ceased by FA 1992 s 4(a)	
153		s 1032
154		s 1016, Sch 32, para 21(1)
Pt VII		
s 155		s 849
156		s 850
157		s 853
158		s 854
159		s 855
160		s 856(1), (2)
161		s 852(1), (2)
162		s 851
163		s 857(1)-(3)
164		s 860
165		s 861(1)
166(1)	Unnecessary (continuity)	
(2)		s 862
Pt VIII		
s 167	Rep by F(MP)A 1968 s 6(1)	
168	Rep by F(MP)A 1968 s 6(1)	
169(1)(a)	Rep by FA 1969 s 65(1) and Sch 5 Pt I	
(b)-(4)		s 877
170		s 878
171	Rep by F(MP)A 1968 s 6(1)	
172(1), (2), (4), (6)		s 879(1)-(4)
(3)	Rep by F(MP)A 1968 s 6(1)	
(5)		s 1052(4)(a), (c), (e)
173(1)-(7), (9)		s 889(10)
173(8)	Deleted by FA 1982 s 60(2)(b)(ii)	
174		s 900(1), (2), (4)
175		s 891
176		s 890
177	Rep by FA 1997 s 146(2) and Sch 9 Pt II	
178		s 897(1)-(5)
179	Rep by F(MP)A 1968 s 6(1)	
180	Rep by FA 1969 s 65(1) and Sch 5 Pt I	
181		s 918(1)-(3)
182		s 920
183(1)(a)		s 921(2)
(b)	Rep by FA 1969 s 65(1) and Sch 5 Pt I	
(2)-(5)(a)		s 921(3)-(6)
183(5)(b)	Rep by FA 1969 s 65(1) and Sch 5 Pt I	
(6)	Rep by FA 1969 s 65(1) and Sch 5 Pt I	
(7)		s 921(1)
184		s 922
185		s 923

Former Enactment		*Destination in TCA 1997*
Income Tax Act 1967 (1967 No 7) (contd)		
s 186		s 924
187(1)		s 928(1)
(2)	Rep by FA 1996 s 132(2) and Sch 5 Pt II	
(3)		s 964(2)
188(1)		s 863
(2)	Rep by FA 1974 s 86 and Sch 2 Pt I	
189		s 867
190		s 929
191(1)-(5)		s 930
(6)	Deleted by FA 1995 s 15(c)	
Pt IX		
s 192		s 1015
193		s 1016
194		s 1017
195		s 1018
195A(1)-(6)	(s 195A inserted by FA 1983 s 6)	s 1020
(7)	Unnecessary (commencement)	
195B	(s 195B inserted by FA 1993 s 10(1))	s 1019
195C	(s 195C inserted by FA 1993 s 10(1))	s 1021
196		s 1022
197		s 1023
198		s 1024
199	Rep by FA 1994 s 157(1)	
200		s 1034
201		s 1035
202		s 1036
203		s 1037
204		s 1038
205		s 1039
206	Rep by FA 1994 s 157(1)	
207		s 1044
208		s 1045
209		s 1046(1), (2)
210(1), (2)		s 1047
(3)	Rep by FA 1969 s 65(1) and Sch 5 Pt I	
211(1)-(3)		s 1048
(4)	Deleted by FA 1973 s 6	
212		s 1049
213		s 1050
Pt X		
ss 214-217	Rep by CTA 1976 s 164 and Sch 3 Pt I	
Pt XI		
218	Definition of "capital allowance" rep by FA 1975 s 33 and Sch 1 Pt II	s 698
219(1)		s 699(1)
(2)	Rep by CTA 1976 s 164 and Sch 3 Pt I	
(3)	Unnecessary (transitional)	
(4)(a)	Unnecessary (spent)	
(b), (c)		s 699(2)
220(1)-(5), (7)	Rep by FA 1978 s 52(1) and Sch 3 Pt I	
(6)	Rep by CTA 1976 s 164 and Sch 3 Pt I	
221	Rep by CTA 197 s 164 and Sch 3 Pt I 6	

Former Enactment		*Destination in TCA 1997*
Income Tax Act 1967 (1967 No 7) (contd)		
Pt XII		
s 222	Rep by FA 1972 s 46(2) and Sch 4 Pt II	
223	Rep by FA 1972 s 46(1) and Sch 4 Pt I	
224(1), (2), (4)		s 126(1), (2)
(3), (5), (6)	Rep by FA 1979 s 6	
225		s 790
226	Rep by FA 1972 s 46(2) and Sch 4 Pt II with saver in FA 1972 Sch 1 Pt III para 4 (substituted by FA 1997 s 146(1) and Sch 9 para 5(3)) for enactments which refer to ITA 1967 Pt XII Ch II	
227	Rep by FA 1972 s 46(2) and Sch 4 Pt II with saver in FA 1972 Sch 1 Pt III para 4 (substituted by FA 1997 s 146(1) and Sch 9 para 5(3)) for enactments which refer to ITA 1967 Pt XII Ch II	
228	Rep by FA 1972 s 46(2) and Sch 4 Pt II with saver in FA 1972 Sch 1 Pt III para 4 (substituted by FA 1997 s 146(1) and Sch 9 para 5(3)) for enactments which refer to ITA 1967 Pt XII Ch II	
229	Rep by FA 1972 s 46(2) and Sch 4 Pt II with saver in FA 1972 Sch 1 Pt III para 4 (substituted by FA 1997 s 146(1) and Sch 9 para 5(3)) for enactments which refer to ITA 1967 Pt XII Ch II	
230	Rep by FA 1972 s 46(2) and Sch 4 Pt II with saver in FA 1972 Sch 1 Pt III para 4 (substituted by FA 1997 s 146(1) and Sch 9 para 5(3)) for enactments which refer to ITA 1967 Pt XII Ch II	
231	Rep by s 46(2) and Sch 4 Pt II FA 1972 with saver in FA 1972 Sch 1 Pt III para 4 (substituted by FA 1997 s 146(1) and Sch 9 para 5(3)) for enactments which refer to ITA 1967 Pt XII Ch II	
232	Rep by FA 1972 s 46(2) and Sch 4 Pt II with saver in FA 1972 Sch 1 Pt III para 4 (substituted by FA 1997 s 146(1) and Sch 9 para 5(3)) for enactments which refer to ITA 1967 Pt XII Ch II	
233	Rep by FA 1972 s 46(2) and Sch 4 Pt II with saver in FA 1972 Sch 1 Pt III para (substituted by FA 1997 s 146(1) and Sch 9 para 5(3)) for enactments which refer to ITA 1967 Pt XII Ch II	
234	Rep by FA 1972 s 46(2) and Sch 4 Pt II with saver in FA 1972 Sch 1 Pt III para 4 (substituted by FA 1997 s 146(1) and Sch 9 para 5(3)) for enactments which refer to ITA 1967 Pt XII Ch II	
235(1)-(5)		s 784(1)-(5)
(6)		s 783(4)
(7)(a)-(c)		s 783(3)
(d)	Rep by FA 1996 s 132(2) and Sch 5 Pt II	
(8)		s 783(2)
(9)		s 783(1)(a), (c)
(10)		s 784(6)

Former Enactment	*Destination in TCA 1997*
Income Tax Act 1967 (1967 No 7) (contd)	
s 235A(1)-(6) . . . (s 235A inserted by FA 1974 s 66)	s 785
(7)	Unnecessary (transitional)
236(1)	s 787(6)
(1A)-(2B)	s 787(8)-(12)
(2C)	Unnecessary (transitional)
(3)-(7)	s 787(1)-(5)
(8)	s 787(13)
(9)	s 787(14)
(10)	Rep by FA 1974 s 86 and Sch 1 Pt I
(11)	s 787(7)
237	Rep by CTA 1976 s 164 and Sch 3 Pt I
238(1), (2)	s 787(15), (16)
(3), (4)	s 783(5), (6)
239	s 788
240	s 789
241(1)(a)	s 284(1)
(b)	s 284(2)(a), (3)
(c)	s 300(1)
proviso	s 284(2)(b)
(1A)	Unnecessary (obsolete)
(2)	s 299(1)
(3)	s 304(4)
(4)	s 304(2)
(5)	s 298(1)
(6)	s 284(4)
(6A)	s 284(5)
(7)-(9)	Rep by FA 1996 s 132(2) and Sch 5 Pt II
(9A)(a)	s 316(1)(a)
(b)	s 316(2)
(10)	ss 284(6), 301(1)
(11)(a)	s 284(7)
(b)	s 406
241A(1), (2) . . . (s 241A inserted by FA 1994 s 24(a))	s 291
(3)	s 301(1)
242	Rep by FA 1996 s 132(2) and Sch 5 Pt II
243	Rep by FA 1996 s 132(2) and Sch 5 Pt II
Pt XIV	
s 244(1)	s 763(2)
(2),(2A)	s 764
(3)-(7)	s 765
(8), (9)	s 763(5), (6)
245	s 670
246	Unnecessary (obsolete)
247	Unnecessary (obsolete)
248	Unnecessary (obsolete)
249	Rep by FA 1996 s 132(2) and Sch 5 Pt II
250	Unnecessary (obsolete)

Former Enactment		*Destination in TCA 1997*
Income Tax Act 1967 (1967 No 7) (contd)		
Pt XV		
s 251(1)		ss 283(2), 300(1)
(2)		s 316(3)
(3)	Unnecessary (operative date)	
(4) (a),(b), (bb)(i),(bbb), (c)	Unnecessary (spent)	
(bb)(ii), (d)		s 283(3)
(5)		s 304(3)(b)
(6)		s 283(1)
(7)		s 283(6)
252		ss 298(1), 299(1), 304(4)
253		ss 301(2), 304(6)(b)
254(1)(a), (b)		s 271(2), (4)
(c)		ss 271(1), 320(1)
(d), (e)		ss 278(1), (2), (6), 305
(2)	Unnecessary (spent)	
(2A)		s 271(4)
(2B)	Unnecessary (spent)	
(3)		s 271(6)
(3A)	Deleted by FA 1994 s 22(1)	
(4)(a)		s 316(3)
(b)		s 317(2)
(5)		s 304(4)
(6)		s 304(2), (3)(a)
(7)		s 271(5)
255(1)-(5)		s 268(1)-(3), (5)-(8)
(6)		s 320(2)
256		s 270
257		s 268(4)
258	Unnecessary (operative date)	
259	Rep by FA 1996 s 132(2) and Sch 5 Pt II	
260		s 316(1)(a)
261		s 316(2)
262	Rep by FA 1996 s 132(2) and Sch 5 Pt II	
263(1)	Unnecessary (interpretation)	
(2), (3)		s 282
(4)		ss 270, 268(4)
264		s 272
265		s 274(1), (3), (4), (5), (8)
266		s 277
267		s 278(1), (3), (4), (5), (6)
268		s 269
269		s 281
270		s 280
271	Definitions of "initial allowance" "wear and tear allowance" unnecessary	s 288(4)(a)
272(1)-(3)		s 288(1)-(3)
(4)		s 288(4)(b)

Former Enactment	*Destination in TCA 1997*
Income Tax Act 1967 (1967 No 7) (contd)	
s 272(5)(a), (b)	s 288(5)
(c)	Unnecessary (spent)
(6)	s 288(6)
273(1)	s 290
(2)	Rep by FA 1996 s 132(2) and Sch 5 Pt II
274	s 292
275	s 293
276	s 294
277	s 289
278	s 295
279	s 296
280	s 297
281	s 298(2)
282	s 300
283(1)	s 301(1)
(2)	Rep by FA 1969 s 65(1) and Sch 5 Pt I
284	s 754
285	s 755
286	s 756
287	Unnecessary (obsolete)
288	s 757
289	Unnecessary (obsolete)
290(1)-(3)	s 758
(4)	Unnecessary (obsolete)
291	s 759
292	s 761
293	s 760
294(1)-(5)	s 303(1)-(5)
(6)	s 302(1)
(7)	s 303(6)
(8)	s 302(2)
(9)	s 303(7)
(10)	s 302(1)
(11), (12)	s 303(8), (9)
295	s 304(2), (4), (5), (6)(a)
296(1)	s 305(1)
(2)	Unnecessary (obsolete)
(3)-(5)	s 305(2)-(4)
297	s 306
298	s 311
299(1)-(3)	s 312(2)-(4)
(4)(a), (b),(i), (b)(ii)	s 312(5)
(b)(iii)	s 762(2)(a)
(5)	s 312(6)
(6)	s 312(1)
300	s 313
301	s 314
302	s 315

Former Enactment		*Destination in TCA 1997*
Income Tax Act 1967 (1967 No 7) (contd)		
s 303(1)		ss 316(1), 762(2)(b)
(2)		s 316(2)
(3)		s 317(2)
304(1)		ss 318, 320(1)
(2)-(6)		s 320(2)-(6)
305		s 769
306	Rep by FA 1996 s 132(2) and Sch 5 Pt II	
(1)		s 381(1)
(1A)	Rep by FA 1997 s 146(2) and Sch 9 Pt II	
(1AA)	Ceased by FA 1990 s 27(2)(a)	
(1AAA)-(6)		s 381(2)-(7)
307(1)		s 381(1)
(1A)	Repealed by FA 1997 s 146(2) and Sch 9 Pt II	
(1AA)	Ceased by FA 1990 s 27(2)	
(1AAA)-(6)		381(2)-(7)
308	Unnecessary (spent)	
309(1), (2)		s 382(1), (2)
(3)	Rep by FA 1969 s 65(1) and Sch 5 Pt I	
310		s 383
311		s 385
312		s 386
313(1), (2)		s 387
(3)	Unnecessary (spent)	
314(1)		s 388
(2)	Rep by FA 1975 s 33 and Sch 1 Pt II	
315		s 389
316		s 390(1), (3)
317(1)	Definition of "capital allowances" deleted by FA 1975 s 33 and Sch 1 Pt II	s 391(1)
(2)(a) from "In paragraph (a)"to end	Rep by FA 1997 s 146(2) and Sch 9 Pt II	
(b)-(d)		s 391(2)
318		s 392
319		s 393
320		s 394
321		s 395
322		s 391(3)
323-328	Rep by CTA 1976 s 164 and Sch 3 Pt I	
329-332	Ceased by FA 1983 s 7	
333		s 207(1), (2)
334(1) (a), (c)		s 208(2)
(b)	Rep by FA 1969 s 65(1) and Sch 5 Pt I	
(2)	Rep by FA 1969 s 65(1) and Sch 5 Pt I	
(2A)		s 208(3)
(3)		s 208(1)
335		s 211(1)-(4)
336		s 213(1), (2)
337	Ceased by FA 1993 s 43(1)	
338		s 206

Former Enactment		*Destination in TCA 1997*
Income Tax Act 1967 (1967 No 7) (contd)		
339 (1)	Rep by F(MP)A 1968 s 3(5) and Sch Pt IV	
(2)		ss 207(3), 211(5), 213(3)
(3)	Rep by F(MP)A 1968 s 3(5) and Sch Pt IV	
(4)		ss 207(4), 211(6), 213(4)
340(1)		s 204(2)
(2)(a)-(c)		s 204(1)
(d), (ff), (g)	Rep by FA 1983 s 120 and Sch 4	
(e), (f)	Rep by FA 1997 s 146(2) and Sch 9 Pt II	
(3)	Rep by FA 1983 s 120 and Sch 4	
341	Rep by DR&IA 1967 s 4 and Sch 6	
342	Rep by DR&IA 1967 s 4 and Sch 6	
343	Rep by FA 1997 s 62(2)	
344	Rep by FA 1996 s 132(2) and Sch 5 Pt II	
345		s 199
346	Rep by FA 1996 s 132(2) and Sch 5 Pt II	
347	Rep by CTA 1976 s 164 and Sch 3 Pt I	
348		s 215
349		s 235
350		s 216
351-352	Rep by FA 1969 s 65(1) and Sch 5 Pt I	
353		s 193 Sch 32, para 2
354		s 194
Pt XXII		
s 355	Rep by FA 1977 s 54(1)(a) and Sch 2 Pt I	
356	Rep by FA 1977 s 54(1)(b) and Sch 2 Pt II	
357	Rep by FA 1977 s 54(1)(a) and Sch 2 Pt I	
358(1)	Unnecessary (saver for FA 1950 s 12)	
(2), (3)		s 833
359		s 834
360	Rep by FA 1996 s 132(2) and Sch 5 Pt II	
361(1)-(7)		s 826(1)-(7)
(8)		s 826(9)
362	Rep by FA 1987 s 23 with saver	
363	Rep by CTA 1976 s 166 and Sch 4 Pt II	
364	Rep by CTA 1976 s 166 and Sch 4 Pt II	
365	Rep by FA 1977 s 146(2) and Sch 9 Pt II	
366	Rep by FA 1977 s 146(2) and Sch 9 Pt II	
Pt XXIII		
s 367		s 748
368		s 749
369(1)		s 750
369(2)	Rep by FA 1977 s 54(1)(a) and Sch 2 Pt I	
370		s 751
Pt XXIV		
s 371		s 752
372		s 753
Pt XXV		
s 373	Rep by CTA 1976 s 164 and Sch 3 Pt I	
374 - 414	Rep by CTA 1976 s 164 and Sch 3 Pt I	
415		s 932
(1)-(7)(f)		s 933(1)-(7)(f)
(7)(g)	Unnecessary (obsolete)	
(8)		s 933(8)

Former Enactment		*Destination in TCA 1997*
Income Tax Act 1967 (1967 No 7) (contd)		
s 415(8A)	Deleted by FA 1983 s 9(a)(i)(IV)	
(9)		s 933(9)
(10)		s 942(9)
(11)	Rep by FA 1974 s 86 and Sch 2 Pt I	
416		s 933(1)-(7)(f)
417	Ceased by FA 1976 s 30(8)	
418	Ceased by FA 1971 s 17(3)	
419	Rep by FA 1997 s 146(2) and Sch 9 Pt II	
420	Deleted by FA 1983 s 9(b)	
421		s 934
422		s 935
423		s 936
424		s 937
425		s 938
426		s 939
427		s 940
428		s 941
429		s 942(1)-(8), (10)
430		s 943
431		s 944
432 (1)		ss 864(1), 949(1)
(2)-(4)		s 949(2)-(4)
Pt XXVII		
s 433		s 237
434 (1)-(5A)		s 238(1)-(6)
(6)	Unnecessary (obsolete)	
(7)	Unnecessary (spent)	
(8)		s 238(7)
435	Rep by CTA 1976 s 164 and Sch 3 Pt I	
436-437	Rep by FA 1969 s 65(1) and Sch 5 Pt I	
Pt XXVIII		
s 438		s 791(2)-(4)
439		s 792(1)-(4)
440	Ceased by FA 1995 s 12(3)	
441		s 793
442		s 791(1)
443(1)		s 795
443(2), (3)		s 794(2), (3)
(4)	Ceased by FA 1995 s 12(3)	
(5)		s 794(4)
444		s 796(1), (2)(a), (b), (c)
445		s 794(5)
446		s 797
447	Definition of "child" rep by FA 1996 s 132(2) and Sch 5 Pt II, definition of "minor" unnecessary (duplication)	s 794(1)s 794(1)
448(1), (3), (4)		s 798(1)-(3)
(2)	Rep by FA 1996 s 132(2) and Sch 5 Pt II	
449		s 812 (1), (2), (4)
Pt XXIX		
s 450		s 799

Former Enactment		*Destination in TCA 1997*
Income Tax Act 1967 (1967 No 7) (contd)		
s 451		s 800
452		s 801(1)-(8)
453		s 802
454		s 803
455		s 804
Pt XXX		
s 456	Rep by CTA 1976 s 164 and Sch 3 Pt I	
457	Rep by CTA 1976 s 164 and Sch 3 Pt I	
458		s 1091
Pt XXXI		
s 459		s 60
460		s 61
461		s 62
462		s 63
462A	(s 462A inserted by FA 1994 s 15)	s 64
463		s 42
464		s 43
465		s 45(1)
466		s 36
467-468(2)	Rep by FA 1997 s 146(2) and Sch 9 Pt II	
468(3)		s 47
469	Rep by FA 1997 s 146(2) and Sch 9 Pt II	
470		s 50
471	Rep by FA 1997 s 146(2) and Sch 9 Pt II	
472(1)		Sch 32, para 1(1)
(2)	Rep by FA 1997 s 146(2) and Sch 9 Pt II	
473	Rep by FA 1997 s 146(2) and Sch 9 Pt II	
474		s 49, Sch 32 para 1(2)
475		s 51
476	Rep by FA 1996 s 132(2) and Sch 5 Pt II	
477 (1)		s 960
(2), (3)	Rep by FA 1996 s 132(2) and Sch 5 Pt II	
478		s 961
479	Rep by FA 1996 s 132(2) and Sch 5 Pt II	
480	Rep by FA 1996 s 132(2) and Sch 5 Pt II	
481	Rep by FA 1969 s 65(1) and Sch 5 Pt I	
482(1), (2)		s 971
(3)	Rep by FA 1996 s 132(2) and Sch 5 Pt II	
483	Rep by IT(A)A 1967 s 1	
484(1)-(4)		s 972(1)-(4)
(5)	Unnecessary (obsolete)	
(6), (7)		s 972(5), (6)
485(1), (2)		s 962(1), (2)
(3), (4)	Rep by FA 1974 s 86 and Sch 2 Pt I	
(5)		s 962(3)
485(6)	Unnecessary (spent)	
486(1), (2), (4)		s 963
(3)	Rep by FA 1997 s 146(2) and Sch 9 Pt II	
487		s 964(1)
488		s 966
489		s 965
490	Rep by FA 1967 s 25 and Sch 3 Pt I	

Former Enactment	Destination in TCA 1997
Income Tax Act 1967 (1967 No 7) (contd)	
s 491	s 998
492	s 968
493	s 969
494 (1)	s 970
(2) .... Rep by FA 1996 s 132(2) and Sch 5 Pt II	
495 .... Rep by FA 1996 s 132(2) and Sch 5 Pt II	
496 .... Rep by FA 1997 s 146(2) and Sch 9 Pt II	
497	s 460
498	s 865
499 .... Unnecessary (operative date)	
500(1)-(3)	s 1052(1)-(3)
(4)	s 1052(4)(a)-(e)
501	s 1053(1)-(4)
502	s 1053(5)-(7)
503	s 1054(2)-(4)
504	s 1060
505	s 1055
506	s 1069(2)
507	s 1068
508	s 1061
509	ss 1054(1), 1069(1)(a)
510	s 1062
511	s 1063
512	s 1065
513	s 1059
514	s 1070
515	s 1057
516	s 1056
517	s 1064
518	s 1066
519	s 874
520	s 1058
521	s 1067
522-524...... Rep by FA 1974 s 86 and Sch 2 Pt I	
525	s 127(1)-(5)
526-527...... Rep by FA 1974 s 86 and Sch 2 Pt I	
528	s 926
529 .... Ceased by FA 1971 s 17(3)	
530-531...... Rep by CTA 1976 s 164 and Sch 3 Pt I	
532 .... Rep by FA 1974 s 86 and Sch 2 Pt I	
533	s 866
534	s 1090
535	s 1088
536	s 868
537	s 870
538	s 875
539	s 901
540 .... Rep by FA 1996 s 132(2) and Sch 5 Pt II	
541	s 873

Former Enactment		*Destination in TCA 1997*
Income Tax Act 1967 (1967 No 7) (contd)		
s 542(1)	Rep by F(MP)A 1968 s 3(5) and Sch Pt IV	
(2)		s 869(1)
(3)	Deleted by FA 1975 s 29	
(4)-(7)		s 869(2)-(5)
543	Rep by FA 1996 s 132(2) and Sch 5 Pt II	
544 (1)		s 837
(2)	Rep by FA 1969 s 65(1) and Sch 5	
545 (1)		s 1096
(2)	Rep by FA 1969 s 65(1) and Sch 5 Pt I	
546	Ceased by FA 1990 s 27(2)(a)	
547		s 483(1)-(3)
548	Rep by FA 1969 s 65(1) and Sch 5 Pt I	
549		s 1004
550 (1)		s 1080(1)
(2)	Ceased by FA 1990 s 24	
(2A)	Rep by FA 1997 s 146(2) and Sch 9 Pt II	
(3)-(5)		s 1080(2)-(4)
551(1), (2)(a)		s 1081
(2)(b)	Rep by FA 1974 s 86 and Sch 2 Pt I	
552	Unnecessary (commencement)	
553		s 111
Pt XXXVIII		
s 554	Unnecessary (commencement and repeals)	
555	Unnecessary (obsolete)	
556	Unnecessary (savings in relation to ITA 1967)	
557	Rep by FA 1996 s 132(2) and Sch 5 Pt II	
558	Rep by FA 1996 s 132(2) and Sch 5 Pt II	
559	Unnecessary (continuity and construction)	
560	Unnecessary (continuity)	
561	Unnecessary (short title)	
Sch 1		Sch 2
Pt I		Pt 2
Pt II	Rep by FA 1997 s 146(2) and Sch 9 Pt II.	
Pts III-V		Pts 3-5
Pt VI		Pt 1
Sch 2		
Rule 1(1), (2)		s 925
(3)	Rep by FA 1996 s 132(2) and Sch 5 Pt II	
2		s 19(2)
3		s 114
4		s 115
5-7	Rep by FA 1976 s 81 and Sch 5 Pt I	
Sch 3		
para1-11		Sch 3
12, 13		s 201(1)(a)
14		Sch 3
Sch 4		
para1(1)		s 459(3)
(2), (3)	Rep by F(MP)A 1968 s 3(5) and Sch Pt IV	
2(1),(3),(4),(5)		s 459(4)
(2)	Rep by F(MP)A 1968 s 3(5) and Sch Pt IV	
3	Rep by F(MP)A 1968 s 3(5) and Sch Pt IV	
Sch 5	Deleted by FA 1996 s 13(b)	

Former Enactment		*Destination in TCA 1997*
Income Tax Act 1967 (1967 No 7) (contd)		
Sch 6		
Pt I	Rep by FA 1977 s 54 and Sch 2 Pt I	
II	Rep by FA 1977 s 54 and Sch 2 Pt I	
III,para 1		s 73
para 2-5	Rep by FA 1977 s 54 and Sch 2 Pt I	
Sch 7	Rep by FA 1977 s 54 and Sch 2 Pt I	
Sch 8		Sch 25
Sch 9	Unnecessary (obsolete)	
Sch 10		Sch 24
para 1-4		para 1-4(1)
5, 6		para 5, 6
7	Rep by CTA 1976 s 166(2) and Sch 4 Pt II	
8-14		para 7-13
Sch 11		Sch 21
Sch 12		Sch 22
Sch 13	Rep by FA 1996 s 132(2) and Sch 5 Pt II	
Sch 14	Rep by FA 1967 s 25 and Sch 3	
Sch 15		Sch 29
Sch 16	Rep by CTA 1976 s 164 and Sch 3 Pt I	
Sch 17		Sch 27
Sch 18		Sch 28
para I	Rep by FA 1969 s 65(1) and Sch 5 Pt I	
II-IX		paras 1-8
Sch 19	Unnecessary (repeals)	
Income Tax (Amendment) Act 1967 (1967 No 7)		
Preamble	Unnecessary (obsolete)	
s 1	Unnecessary (cesser of ITA 1967 ss 480(2), (3), 483)	
2	Unnecessary (short title)	
Finance Act 1967 (1967 No 17)		
s 1	Unnecessary (spent)	
2	Insertion of ITA 1967 s 139(5)	
3	Amendment of ITA 1967 s 141(1)	s 465
4	Amendment of ITA 1967 s 142(1)	s 466
5	Substitution of ITA 1967 s 251(4)	ss 283(2), 300(1)
6 (1)	Substitution of ITA 1967 s 254(1)	s 271(2), (4)
(2)	Insertion of ITA 1967 s 262(4)	s 316(2)
7	Amendment of ITA 1967 s 335	s 211(1)-(4)
8	Amendment of ITA 1967 s 344	
9 (1)	Amendment of ITA 1967 ss 383, 386(2)	s 963
(2)(a)	Amendment of ITA 1967 s 386	s 963
(b)	Amendment of ITA 1967 s 387	s 964(1)
(c)	Amendment of ITA 1967 s 389	
10	Substitution of ITA 1967 s 523	
11 (1),(2),(2A)		s 285(1), (2), (3)
(3)		s 299(2)
(4)		s 285(8)
12 (1)		s 469(1)
proviso to definition of "dependant"		s 469(4)
(2)(a), (c)		s 469(2)
(b)	Deleted by FA 1972 s 9	
(3)		s 469(3)

Former Enactment			*Destination in TCA 1997*
Finance Act 1967 (1967 No 17) (contd)			
s 12	(4)		s 469(5)
	(5)		s 469(6)
	(6)	Amendment of ITA 1967s 153(1)(d)	s 1032
	(7)	Amendment of ITA 1967 s 193	s 1016
Pt V			
s 25		Unnecessary (application of schedule)	
26		Unnecessary (care and management)	
27(2), (6)		Unnecessary (construction and commencement)	
Sch 3, Pt I.		Repeal of ITA 1967 s 490 and Sch 14	
Finance (Miscellaneous Provisions) Act 1968 (1968 No 7)			
s 1	(1)	Substitution of ITA 1967 s 156(1)	s 850
	(2)	Unnecessary (obsolete)	
2		Insertion of ITA 1967 s 181(3)	s 918(1)-(3)
3	(1)	Amendment of ITA 1967 ss 164(2), 416(5), 418(6), 422(3), 429(3)	ss 860, 933(1)-(7)(f), 935, 942(1)-(8), (10)
	(2)-(5)	Unnecessary (application of schedules)	
	(6)	Amendment of SR&O No 48 of 1928 and SIs Nos 152 of 195, 28 of 1960 and 231 of 1961	
4	(1)	Substitution of ITA 1967 s 186(2)	s 920
	(2)	Unnecessary (spent)	
	(3)	Amendment of ITA 1967 s 211	s 1048
	(4)	Substitution of ITA 1967 s 526(6)	
	(5)(a)	Amendment of ITA 1967 s 498	s 865
	(b)	Unnecessary (spent)	
5	(1)		s 876
	(2)	Amendment of ITA 1967 Sch 15	Sch 29
6	(1)	Repeal of ITA 1967 ss 167, 168, 171, 172(3), 179	
	(2)	Amendment of ITA 1967 s 169(1)	s 877
	(3)	Amendment of ITA 1967 s 169(4)	s 877
	(4)	Amendment of ITA 1967 s 170(1)	s 878
	(5)	Amendment of ITA 1967 s 176(1)	s 890
	(6)	Amendment of ITA 1967 s 177	
	(7)	Amendment of ITA 1967s 211(3)	s 1048
7	(1)	Insertion of ITA 1967 s 81(4)(f), s 89A	s 97
	(2)	Unnecessary (spent).	
8		Amendment of ITA 1967 Sch 15	Sch 29
9	(1), (2)		s 200(1)
	(3)	Unnecessary (commencement)	
13		Rep by CTA 1976 s 164 and Sch 3 Pt II	
14		Unnecessary (obsolete)	
15		Rep by CTA 1976 s 164 and Sch 3 Pt II	
Pt IV			
16	(1),(2),(4)	Definition of "control" unnecessary (obsolete)	s 639
	(3)	Ceased by FA 1996 s 131(9)(b)	
17			s 640
18			s 641
19			s 642
20	(1)(a)	Unnecessary (operative date)	
	(b)-(17)		s 643
21			s 644
22			s 645

Former Enactment		*Destination in TCA 1997*
Finance (Miscellaneous Provisions) Act 1968 (1968 No 7)		
s 23 (1)-(3),(5)		s 646
(4)	Rep by FA 1974 s 86 and Sch 2 Pt I	
24 (1)	Unnecessary (commencement)	
(2)	Unnecessary (obsolete)	
Pt V		
27		s 999
29 (2)	Unnecessary (construction)	
Sch Pt I	Amendment of ITA 1967 ss 1(1), 13(1), 37(1)(f)(ii), 38, 41(3), 50(3)(4), 54(4), 60(3), 73(3), 76(5)(6), 81(6), 82(2)(a), 90(2)(3), 113(1)(2), 120(1)(c)(2), 156(2)(3)(4), 164(2), 190(1), 191(4)(5), 194(2)(c), 195(3)(a), 203(1)-(3), 204, 214(2), 228(3), 238(1)(2), 240(1), 241(1), 245(14), 259, 296(3)(4), 301(1), 307(5)(6), 315(1)(2), 367(3), 371(7)(c), 379(1), 382(2), 397, 413(1), 414, 416(1)-(9), 417, 418(1)(2)(3)(6), 421(2), 422(1)(2), 424, 425(1), 426(1), 427(a), 428(1)(9), 429(1)(2), 430(1), 431(1)(2), 432(1)-(4), 437(1)(2), 441(2), 446(2), 462(3)(4), 501(1)(c), 506, 529, 537(2), 542(6), 549(5), 553(2), Sch 6 Pt III para 1(2), 3(2)(3), 4(1)(2), Sch 10 para 13(1), Sch 11 para 3(4), Sch 12 para 2(1)(2), 3(2),(5), Sch 16 paras 1-3, 10	ss 2(1), 3(1), 35, 84, 1012, 71(5)-(6),73, 97, 101, 948, 897(6), 850, 860, 929, 930, 1017, 1018, 1037, 1038, 787(15)-(16),789,284(1), 670, 305(2)-(4), 314, 381(2)-(7), 389, 748, 752, 933(1)-(7)(f),934, 935, 937, 938, 939,940, 941,942(1)-(8)(10), 943, 944,864(1),949(1)-(4), 793, 797, 1053(1)-(4), 1069(2), 870, 869(2)-(5), 1004,111,Sch 21,Sch 22, Sch 24 paras 7-13
Sch Pt II	Amendment of ITA 1967 ss 49(1), 152(6), 181(1)(a), 460(a), 484(3), 530(1), 531(1)-(3), Sch 1 Pt I para 3, 4, Sch1 Pt II para 1, 3, Sch 1 Pt III para 1, 2, Sch 1 Pt IV para 3, 9, Sch 2 para 6(1)(2), Sch 6 Pt II para (3), Sch 16 para 4, 5, 7, 8, 11, Sch 16 para 10	ss 34, 918(1)-(3), 61, 972(1)-(4), Sch 2 Pt 2, Sch 2 Pts 3-5 Sch 2 Pt 1,
Sch Pt III	Amendment of ITA 1967 ss 36(2), 152(4)(b), 163(2), 339(2), 530(5), 536(1), Sch 1 Pt I para 4, 5, Sch 4 para 1(1), 2(3), Sch 17 Pt I,	ss 857(1)-(3); 207(3), 211(5),213(3);1054(2)-(4); 868; Sch 2 Pt 2; 459(4); Sch 27, 459(3),
Sch Pt IV	Repeal of ITA 1967 ss 22(2), 153(3), 339(1)(3), 542(1), Sch 4 para 1(2)(3), 2(2), 3	
	Amendment of ITA 1967 ss 29(1), 30, 35, 36(1), 214(1)(2), 329(1), 332(1), 451(5), 496(1), 530(4), 536(2), 544(2), 553(1)(2), Sch 1 Pt I para 5, Sch 1 Pt IV par1(1), Sch 4 para 2(1), Sch 6 Pt II para (1)	ss 800, 868, 111 Sch 2 Pt 2, Sch 2 Pt 1
Finance Act 1968 (1968 No 33)		
s 1	Unnecessary (spent)	
2		s 768
3		s 480
4	Rep by FA 1996 s 132(2) and Sch 5 Pt II	
5	Rep by FA 1969 s 65(1) and Sch 5	
6 (1)-(5)		s 886
(6)	Amendment of ITA 1967 s 508(1)	s 1061
7 (1), (2)		s 989(2), (3)
(3)	Rep by FA 1974 s 71	
(4), (5)		s 989(4), (5)
(6)	Unnecessary (duplication)	
(7)	Unnecessary (duplication)	

Former Enactment		*Destination in TCA 1997*
Finance Act 1968 (1968 No 33) (contd)		
s 7 (8)	Definition of "income tax month" unnecessary (duplication)	s 989(1)
8 (1),(2) (4)		s 990
(3)	Rep by FA 1974 s 71	
9 (a)		s 991(2)(a)
proviso	Rep by FA 1974 s 71	
(b)		s 991(2)(b)
10		s 992
11		s 1000
12	Amendment of ITA 1967 s 138(1)	s 461
13	Rep by FA 1983 s 17(1)	
14	Amendment of ITA 1967 s 244	s 126(1), (2)
15	Insertion of ITA 1967 s 416(8A)	s 933(1)-(7)(f)
16	Amendment of ITA 1967 s 421(3)	s 944
17	Amendment of ITA 1967 s 523(1)(b)	
27-30	Rep by CTA 1976 s 164 and Sch 3 Pt II	
Pt VIII		
s 34	Rep by CTA 1976 s 164 and Sch 3 Pt III	
35	Rep by CTA 1976 s 166 and Sch 4 Pt II	
36	Rep by CTA 1976 s 164 and Sch 3 Pt III	
37 (1)		ss 203(1), 109(1)
37 (2)		s 203(2)
37 (3)-(7)		s 109(2)-(6)
37 (8)	Unnecessary (duplication)	
37 (9)	Unnecessary (operative date)	
38	Substitution of ITA 1967 s 251(4)	s 283(3)
39	Amendment of ITA 1967 s 254(2)	s 271
41	Rep by Trustee Savings Banks Act 1989	
47	Unnecessary (care and management).	
48 (2), (5)	Unnecessary (construction and commencement)	
Finance (No 2) Act 1968 (1968 No 37)		
s 1	Unnecessary (interpretation)	
8		s 46
10	Unnecessary (care and management)	
11 (4)	Unnecessary (construction)	
Finance Act 1969 (1969 No 21)		
s 1	Unnecessary (spent)	
2		s 195(1)-(11)
3 (1),(2),(4)		s 467
(3)	Rep by FA 1996 s 132(2) and Sch 5 Pt II	
(5)	Amendment of ITA 1967 s 153(1)(d)	s 1032
(6)	Rep by FA 1980 s 19 and Sch 1 Pt III	
(7)	Amendment of ITA 1967 s 497	s 460
(8)	Rep by FA 1980 s 19 and Sch 1 Pt III	
4	Rep by FA 1996 s 132(2) and Sch 5 Pt II	
5	Rep by FA 1996 s 132(2) and Sch 5 Pt II	
6	Unnecessary (obsolete)	
7	Amendment of FA 1967 s 12(2)	s 469(2)
8	Amendment of ITA 1967 s 125(a)	s 984(1), (2)
9	Amendment of ITA 1967 s 138	s 461
10	Amendment of ITA 1967 s 141	s 465
11	Amendment of ITA 1967 s 142(1)	s 466
12	Substitution of ITA 1967 s 157(c)	s 853
13	Insertion of ITA 1967 s 193(2A)	s 1016
14	Insertion of ITA 1967 s 246(1A)	

Former Enactment		*Destination in TCA 1997*
Finance Act 1969 (1969 No 21) (contd)		
s 15	Amendment of ITA 1967 s 374(2)	
16	Amendment of ITA 1967 s 402	
17	Insertion of ITA 1967 s 523(5)	
18 (1)	Definition of "farming" rep by FA 1996 s 132(2) and Sch 5 Pt II	s 232(1)
(2)(a)	Rep by FA 1974 s 14	
(b)		s 231
(c)		s 232(2)
19		s 53
20	Rep by CTA 1976 s 164 and Sch 3 Pt I	
21	Amendment of ITA 1967 Sch 6 Pt III para 1	s 73
22	Substitution of ITA 1967 s 81	ss 75, 96, 97
23	Substitution of ITA 1967 s 82	
24	Substitution of ITA 1967 s 89	s 384
25		s 1041
26 (1)-(4)		s 106
(5)	Unnecessary (duplication)	
(6)	Unnecessary (operative date)	
27	Amendment of ITA 1967 s 80	ss 96, 882
28	Substitution of ITA 1967 s 90	s 101
29	Substitution of ITA 1967 s 93	s 103
30	Amendment of ITA 1967 s 65	
31	Amendment of ITA 1967 s 67	s 85
32	Amendment of ITA 1967 s 118	s 119
33 (1)	Unnecessary (application of schedule)	
51-54	Rep by CTA 1976 s 164 and Sch 3 Pt II	
63 (1)		s 48(2)
(2)		s 48(1)(a)
64 (1), (2)	Amendment of ITA 1967 s 255	s 790
(3), (4)		s 274(6), (7)
(5)	Unnecessary (operative date)	
65	Unnecessary (repeals)	
66	Unnecessary (care and management)	
67 (2), (7)	Unnecessary (construction and commencement)	
Sch 4, Pt I	Amendment of ITA 1967 ss 53(1), 83, 84(1), 86, 89A, 92(1), 94, 162(3)(a), 183(1), 184(1), 214(3), 267(5)(a), 307(1), 316(2), 334(1), 335, 336, 433, 434, Sch 18 and F(MP)A 1967 s 18(2)(g)	ss 18(2)(3), 75(4), 98, 99, 103, 888, 851, 921, 922, 278(1)(3)-(6), 381(1),390 (1)(3), 208(2), 211(1)-(4), 213(1),(2),237,238(1)-(6), Sch 28, 641
Sch 5, Pt I	Repeal of ITA 1967 ss 2(2)(d), 9-42, 44, 45, 54(3)(4), 56(4)(5)(6), 66, 75(2)(ii), 78, 87, 88(2)(3), 95, 104, 106(2), 147, 148, 150, 169(1)(a), 180, 183(1)(b), (5)(b)(6), 210(3), 243(3), 244(6)(b), 245(8)(a), 267(5)(6), 283(2), 309(3), 334(1)(b)(2), 351, 352, 385(2), 436, 437, 477(2)(a), (b), 480(6), 481, 524(3)(a), 545(2),548, Sch 18 para 1 and FA 1968 s 5	
	Amendment of ITA 1967 ss 1(1), 2(1)(c), 4, 52(1)(b), 53(1), 54(2), 60(1), 61(c), 86, 107(1), 169(2), 183(1), 186(1), 219(1), 235(7)(c),251(1),322, 333(1)(a),388, 416(1), 480(1), 485, 533, 544(1), Sch 15	ss 2(1), 3(1); 3(2)(3); 12; 18(1)(3); 18(2)(3); 655(3); 65(2)-(4); 81(2); 75(4); 107;877;921(2);924; 699(1);784(1)-(5); 283(2), 300(1);391(3); 208(2); 933(1)-(7)(f); 866; 837 962(1)(2); Sch 29
Sch 5, Pt III	Repeal of ITA 1967 s 404(7), (8)	

Former Enactment		*Destination in TCA 1997*
Finance Act 1970 (1970 No 14)		
s 1	Unnecessary (spent).	
2 (1), (2)	Ceased by FA 1971 s 2	
(3)	Insertion of ITA 1967 s 153(1)(dd)	s 1032
(4)	Amendment of ITA 1967 s 193(6)	s 1015
2 (5)	Amendment of ITA 1967 s 497	s 460
3 (1)	Amendment of ITA 1967 s 6	s 14(1)
(2)	Unnecessary (operative date)	
4	Amendment of FA 1967 s 11(1) and FA 1969 s 4(1)	s 285(1)-(3)
5	Insertion of ITA 1967 s 127(1)(ff)	
6	Amendment of ITA 1967 s 134	
7	Amendment of ITA 1967 s 135(1)	
8	Amendment of ITA 1967 s 136	
9	Amendment of ITA 1967 s 138(3)	s 461
10	Amendment of ITA 1967 s 141(1A)(a)	s 465
11	Amendment of ITA 1967 s 142(1)	s 466
12	Amendment of ITA 1967 s 221(2)(h)(i)	
13	Amendment of ITA 1967 s 236(1) and Sch 5	s 787(6)
14 (1),(2),(3)		s 287
(4)		s 301(1)
(5)	Amendment of ITA 1967 s 241(7)	
15	Amendment of ITA 1967 s 331(3)	
16	Amendment of ITA 1967 s 332(8)	
17(1)	Definitions of "construction contract", construction paymentscard" and "construction tax deduction card" deleted by FA 1992 s 28(a)(ii)	ss 530(1), 531(11)(c)
(2),(2A),(3) (4),(5), (6), (6A), (6B)		s 531(1), (3), (4), (5), (6), (8), (9), (10)
(7)(a), (b)		s 531(11)(a), (b)
(c)	Deleted by FA 1992 s 28(e)(iii)	
(8), (9), (10)		s 531(12), (13), (14),
(10A),(10B) (11)(12)		(15), (16), (7), (2)
(13)		s 530(2)
(14),(15),(16), (17),(19),(20)	s 531(17), (18)	
17A	(s 17A inserted by FA 1992 s 233)	904
18		s 197
19(1), (2), (2A)		s 279
(3)	Unnecessary (construction)	
(4)	Unnecessary (operative date)	
(5)	Unnecessary (operative date)	
20(1)		s 91(3)
(2)		s 91(1)
(3)(a)-(d)		s 91(2)
(e)	Unnecessary (operative date)	
(4)		s 91(4)
(5)(a)	Rep by FA 1975 s 33 and Sch 1 Pt II	
(b), (c)(d)		s 91(5)
21		s 95
22		s 92

Former Enactment		*Destination in TCA 1997*
Finance Act 1970 (1970 No 14) (contd)		
s 23 (1), (2), (3)		s 90(1)-(3)
(4) s 89(1)(b)		
(5)		s 90(4)
(6)	Unnecessary (operative date)	
24 (1), (2)(a)		s 87
(2)(b)	Rep by CTA 1976 s 164 and Sch 3 Pt II	
24 (3)	Unnecessary (operative date)	
25		s 93
26 (1)-(4)		s 94
(5)	Unnecessary (operative date)	
Pt VI		
s 57 (1)	Unnecessary (duplication)	
(2)-(4)		s 829
(5)	Unnecessary (obsolete)	
58	Amendment of FA 1968 s 35(3)(b)	
59 (1),(2),(3)		ss 38, 48(1)(b)
(5)	Amendment of ITA 1967 s 474(1)	
(6)		s 48(2)
61	Unnecessary (care and management)	
62 (2), (7)	Unnecessary (construction and commencement)	
Finance (No 2) Act 1970 (1970 No 25)		
s 1	Ceased by FA 1972 s 10	
7	Unnecessary (care and management)	
8 (2), (5)	Unnecessary (construction and commencement)	
Finance Act 1971 (1971 No 23)		
Pt I		
s 1	Unnecessary (obsolete)	
2	Unnecessary (cesser of FA 1970 s 2)	
3	Amendment of ITA 1967 s 58 (amendment ceased by FA 1990 s 14(2)	
4 (1)-(4),(6)		s 72
(5)	Unnecessary (operative date)	
5		s 86
6	Amendment of ITA 1967 s 134	
7	Amendment of ITA 1967 s 135	
8	Amendment of ITA 1967 s 136	
9	Insertion of ITA 1967 s 139(6)	
10	Amendment of ITA 1967 s 142(1)	s 466
11 (1), (2)		s 468
(3)	Deleted by FA 1980 s 5	
(4)	Rep by FA 1996 s 132(2) and Sch 5 Pt II	
(5)	Amendment of ITA 1967 s 153(1)(d)	s 1032
(6)	Deleted by FA 1980 s 5	
(7)	Amendment of ITA 1967 s 497	s 460
(8)	Deleted by FA 1980 s 5	
12	Amendment of ITA 1967 s 244	ss 763-765
13	Amendment of ITA 1967 s 251(4)(c)	ss 283(2), 300(1)
14	Amendment of ITA 1967 s 254(2)	
15	Amendment of ITA 1967 s 336	s 213(1), (2)
16 (1)(a), (b)	Amendment of ITA 1967 s 443	
(c)	Amendment of ITA 1967 s 444	
(2), (3)		s 796(2)(d), (e), (f)
17 (1), (2)(a)	Amendment of ITA 1967 s 550	s 1080(1)
(2)(b)	Unnecessary (operative date)	
(3)	Unnecessary (cesser of ITA 1967 ss 418, 529)	

Former Enactment		*Destination in TCA 1997*
Finance Act 1971 (1971 No 23) (contd)		
s 18	Amendment of ITA 1967 s 419	
19	Amendment of ITA 1967 ss 428, 429,	ss 941, 942(1)-(8)(10)
20 (1)-(4), (6)		s 1082
(5)	Unnecessary (operative date)	
21 (1)(a)	Insertion of FA 1970 s 17(2)(aa)	
(b),(c),(d)	Unnecessary (obsolete)	
(2)	Insertion FA 1970 s 17(6A), (6B), (6C)	s 531(5)(6)(8)(9)(10)
(3)	Unnecessary (obsolete)	
22	Unnecessary (spent)	
23	Unnecessary (obsolete)	
24	Unnecessary (obsolete)	
25	Unnecessary (obsolete)	
26 (1),(2),(2A)		s 285(1), (2), (3)
(3)		s 299(2)
(4)		s 285(8)
(5)	Amendment of FA 1970 s 14(1)	s 287
Pt VI		
s 54	Unnecessary (care and management)	
55 (2), (6)	Unnecessary (construction and commencement)	
Finance Act 1972 (1972 No 19)		
Pt I		
s 1 (1)	Rep by FA 1974 s 86 and Sch 2 Pt I	
(2)	Amendment of ITA 1967 s 522	
2	Amendment of ITA 1967 ss 127(1), 128(1)	ss 986(1)(a)-(j), 987(1)-(3)
3	Amendment of ITA 1967 s 135	
4	Amendment of ITA 1967 s 138	s 461
5	Amendment of ITA 1967 s 141	s 465
6	Amendment of ITA 1967 s 142(1)	s 466
7	Amendment of ITA 1967 s 485(5)	s 962(1), (2)
8	Amendment of ITA 1967 s 486	s 963
9	Amendment of FA 1967 s 12(2)	s 469(2)
10	Unnecessary (cesser of F(No 2)A 1970 s 1)	
11	Rep by FA 1997 s 146(2) and Sch 5 Pt II	
12	Unnecessary (repeals)	
13 (1), (2), (4)	Definitions of "ordinary share capital", "proprietary director" and "proprietary employee" rep by FA 1975 s 86 and Sch 2 Pt III, definition of "Revenue Commissioners" unnecessary	s 770
(3)	Rep by FA 1974 s 86 and Sch 2 Pt II	
14		s 771
15 (1)		s 772(1)
(2)(a)-(e),(g)		s 772(2)
(2)(f)	Rep by FA 1974 s 64	
(3)		s 772(3)
(4)	The matter from "In applying this subsection" to end rep by FA 1996 s 132(2) and Sch 5 Pt II	s 772(4)
(5)-(7)		s 772(5)-(7)
15 (8)	Unnecessary (operative date)	
16 (1), (2), (3)		s 774(1), (3), (5)
(4)		s 774(6), Sch 32 para 26
(5)		s 774(7)
(6)	Rep by FA 1996 s 132(2) and Sch 5 Pt II	

Former Enactment	*Destination in TCA 1997*
Finance Act 1972 (1972 No 19) (contd)	
s 16 (7)	s 774(2)
16A .... (s 16A inserted by FA 1997 s 41)	s 775
17 (1), (2)	s 776
(3) .... Rep by FA 1996 s 132(2) and Sch 5 Pt II	
(4) .... Unnecessary (operative date)	
18 (1)(a), (2)-(5)	s 772
(b)..... Rep by FA 1996 s 132(2) and Sch 5 Pt II	
(6) .... Insertion of ITA 1967 s 2(2)(cc)	s 3(2), (3)
(7) .... Unnecessary (operative date)	
19	s 778
20	s 779
21 (1)-(4), .. s 780	
(5)(a), (6), (7)	
(5)(b)..... Unnecessary (operative date)	
22 (1)-(4)	s 781
(5) .... Unnecessary (operative date)	
23	s 782
24 .... Rep by FA 1996 s 132(2) and Sch 5 Pt II	
25 .... Rep by FA 1996 s 132(2) and Sch 5 Pt II	
Pt V	
s 42 (1) .... Amendment of ITA 1967 s 251(4)	
(2) .... Amendment of ITA 1967 s 246(1)	
43	s 212
46 .... Unnecessary (repeals)	
47 .... Unnecessary (care and management)	
48 (2), (5).... Unnecessary (construction and commencement)	
Sch 1, Pt I	Sch 23, Pt I,
para1, 2	para 1, 2
3(1)-(3)	para 3
(4) ...... Unnecessary (operative date)	
4, 5	para 4, 5
Sch 1, Pt II ..... Unnecessary (obsolete)	
Sch 1, Pt III	
para 1........ Amendment of ITA 1967 s 63	s 84
2........ Amendment of ITA 1967 s 115(1)	s 201(2)
3........ Amendment of ITA 1967 Sch 15	Sch 29
4 .... Saver for enactments which contain reference to ITA 1967 Pt XII Ch II (substituted by FA 1997 s 146(1) and Sch 9 para 5(3))	
Sch 1, Pt IV..... Rep by FA 1996 s 132(2) and Sch 5 Pt II	
Sch 1, Pt V ..... Rep by FA 1996 s 132(2) and Sch 5 Pt II	
Sch 1, Pt VI	
paras 1-4 ..... Sch 23, Pt 2, paras 6-9	
5........ Insertion of ITA 1967 s 2(2)(dd)	s 3(2), (3)
Sch 3 .... Amendment of ITA 1967 ss 1(1), 8(1), (2)	ss 2(1), 3(1), s 1087
Sch 4 .... Repeal of ITA 1967 ss 7, 63(a), (b), (c) and proviso, 152(5), 222, 223, Pt XII Ch II	
Finance Act 1973 (1973 No 19)	
s 1 (1) .... Amendment of ITA 1967 s 129	s 991(1)
(2) .... Unnecessary (operative date)	
2 .... Amendment of ITA 1967 s 138(3)	s 461
3 .... Amendment of ITA 1967 s 141	s 465
4 .... Amendment of ITA 1967 s 142(1)	s 466
5	Sch 32, para 21(2)
6 .... Unnecessary (deletion of ITA 1967 s 211(4))	

Former Enactment		*Destination in TCA 1997*
Finance Act 1973 (1973 No 19) (contd)		
s 7	Amendment of ITA 1967 s 229(1)(i)	
8	Amendment of ITA 1967 s 246	
9 (1)	Amendment of ITA 1967 s 251(4)(d)	s 283(3)
(2)		s 283(7)
proviso	Unnecessary (operative date)	
10	Amendment of ITA 1967 s 254(2)	s 316(3)
11	Amendment of ITA 1967 s 272	s 288
12	Amendment of ITA 1967 s 336	s 213(1), (2)
13	Amendment of ITA 1967 s 357(3)	
14	Insertion of ITA 1967 s 387(4)	
15	Insertion of ITA 1967 s 439(1)(ii)(a)	s 792(1)-(4)
16	Amendment of FA 1971 s 22(2)	
17	Amendment of FA 1971 s 26(1)	s 285(1), (2), (3)
18	Amendment of FA 1972 s 21	s 780
19 (1), (2)		s 192
(3)	Unnecessary (operative date)	
20		s 209
21		s 767
22		s 993(5)
23	Deleted by FA 1992 s 4	
24	Rep by FA 1982 s 20(7)	
25		ss 373(2)(a), 374
26		ss 373(2)(a), 375
27		ss 373(2)(a), 377
28		ss 373(2)(a), 378
29		ss 373(2)(a), 379
30 (1), (5), (6)		s 373(1), (2)(a), (3)
(2), (3), (4)		s 380
31	Unnecessary (spent)	
32	Rep by FA 1977 s 54 and Sch 2 Pt I	
33 (1)(a),(b),(c)		s 13(1)
(d)	Unnecessary (duplication)	
(2), (3), (4), (5), (7)	s 13(2)-(6)	
(6)	Unnecessary (commencement)	
34 (1), (2)		s 234(1), (2)(a)
(2A)-(7)		s 234(3)-(8)
35		s 1089(1)
39	Rep by CTA 1976 s 164 and Sch 3 Pt III	
40 (1)-(5)		s 275
(6)	Unnecessary (obsolete)	
(7)	Unnecessary (construction and operative date)	
41	Insertion of ITA 1967 s 117(7), (8)	s 118
42	Unnecessary (cesser of ITA 1967 s 121)	
43	Amendment of ITA 1967 s 128	s 987
44	Insertion of ITA 1967 s 335(2), (3), (4)	s 211(1)-(4)
45	Amendment of ITA 1967 s 413(2)	
46	Amendment of ITA 1967 s 503(2)	s 1054(2)-(4)
92 (1)		ss 39(1), 48(1)(c)
(2)(a)		s 39(2)
(b)		s 48(2)
(4)	Amendment of ITA 1967 s 474(1)	s 49, Sch 32 para 1(2)
97	Unnecessary (care and management)	
98(2), (6)	Unnecessary (construction and commencement)	
Sch 1	Deleted by FA 1992 s 4(b)	

Former Enactment		*Destination in TCA 1997*
Finance Act 1973 (1973 No 19) (contd)		
Sch 2	Rep by FA 1977 s 54 and Sch 2 Pt I	
Sch 3		
paras 1, 3-5,7,8		Sch 1
2	Amendment of ITA 1967 Sch 15	Sch 29
6	Unnecessary (obsolete)	
Sch 4	Rep by FA 1977 s 54 and Sch 2 Pt I	
Sch 5	Deleted by FA 1996 s 13(b)	
Pt I		
para 1-5		Sch 9, para 1to 5
6(a),(c)- (e)		Sch 9, para 6(a)-(d)
(b)	Unnecessary (duplication)	
7, 9		Sch 9 para 7, 8
8, 10	Rep by CTA 1976s 164 and Sch 3	
Pt II	Unnecessary (duplication)	
Finance (Taxation of Profits of Certain Mines) Act 1974 (1974 No 17)		
s 1 (1)	Definition of "tax" unnecessary (duplication)	s 672(1)
(2),(6),(7)		s 672(2), (3), (4)
(3)-(5)	Unnecessary (construction)	
2 (1)		s 673(1)
proviso	Deleted by FA 1990 s 93(a)	
(2)	Unnecessary (spent)	
(3)	Unnecessary (obsolete)	
(4)		s 673(3)
3 (1)	Unnecessary (spent)	
(2)-(5)		s 674(1)(a), (2), (3), (4)
4		s 675
5		s 676
6		s 677
7 (1), (3), (4)		s 678
(2)	Unnecessary (spent)	
7A	(s 7A inserted by FA 1990 s 39(d))	s 679(1)(a),(2)-(5)
8		s 680
8A(1)-(9)	(s 8A inserted by FA 1996 s 34)	s 681
8A (10)	Unnecessary (obsolete)	
9	Rep by CTA 1976 s 164 and Sch 3 Pt II	
10		s 682(1)-(3)
11		s 683
12	Rep by CTA 1976 s 164 and Sch 3 Pt II	
13-15	Rep by CTA 1976 s 164 and Sch 3 Pt I	
16-17	Rep by CTA 1976 s 164 and Sch 3 Pt II	
18	Unnecessary (short title, construction and commencement)	
Finance Act 1974 (1974 No 27)		
Pt I		
s 1	Amendment of ITA 1967 s 1(1)	
2	Amendment of ITA 1967 s 4	
3	Unnecessary (obsolete)	
4		s 59
5 (1)		s 237(1)(b), (2)
proviso	Rep by CTA 1976 s 164 and Sch 3 Pt 1	
(2), (3)		s 16
6	Unnecessary (obsolete)	
7	Amendment of ITA 1967 s 142(1)	

Former Enactment		*Destination in TCA 1997*
Finance Act 1974 (1974 No 27) (contd)		
s 8 (1)		s 464
(2)	Rep by FA 1996 s 132(2) and Sch 5 Pt II	
9	Substitution of ITA 1967 s 152(1)	
10	Unnecessary (cesser of charge to sur-tax)	
11	Unnecessary (supplementary)	
12	Unnecessary (commencement)	
13 (1)		s 654
(2), (3)	Rep by FA 1983 s 120 and Sch 4	
14	Unnecessary (repeal of FA 1969 s 18(2)(a))	
15		s 655(1), (2)
16 (1)		s 657(1)
(2)		s 657(2)
(3)	Deleted by FA 1976s 14(1)(c)	
(4)		s 657(3)
(5)		s 657(1)
17-19	Rep by FA 1983 s 120 and Sch 4	
20	Ceased by FA 1983 s 24	
20A	Unnecessary (spent)	
20B(1)	(s 20B inserted by FA 1981 s 10)	s 657(4)
(2)		s 657(5)
proviso	Unnecessary (obsolete)	
(3)		s 657(6)
(4)		s 657(7)
(5)		s 657(8)
(6)		s 657(9)
(7)		s 657(10)
(8)		s 657(11)
(9)		s 657(12)
21	Ceased by FA 1980 s 24	
Finance Act 1974 (1974 No 27)		
s22(1)	Section 658 is applied on a modified basis by Sch 32 para 23 to reflect the application of FA 1974 s 22 in relation to certain old expenditure	s 658(1)
(2)		s 658(2)(a)
proviso		s 658(2)(b)
(2A)		s 658(3)
(2B)		s 658(4)
(2C)	Deleted by FA 1994 s 23	
(3)		s 658(5)
(4)	Deleted by FA 1982 s 16	
(5)		s 658(6)
(6)		s 658(7)
(7)		s 658(8)
(8)		s 658(9)
proviso		s 658(10)
(9)		s 658(11)
(10)		s 658(12)
(11)		s 658(13)
23	Rep by CTA 1976 s 164 and Sch 3 Pt I	
24	Unnecessary (obsolete)	

Former Enactment		*Destination in TCA 1997*
Finance Act 1974 (1974 No 27) (contd)		
s 25		s 660
26	Amendment of ITA 1967 s 307	s 381(1)
27 (1)-(6)	Definitions of "basis year" unnecessary (obsolete) and "market gardening" unnecessary (duplication)	s 662
(7)	Rep by CTA 1976 s 164 and Sch 3 Pt II	
28	Rep by FA 1983 s 120 and Sch 4	
29	Substitution of ITA 1967 s 496	
30	Rep by FA 1996 s 132(2) and Sch 5 Pt II	
31 (1), (2), (4)		s 246(1), (2), (4)
(3)(a)	Rep by FA 1996 s 132(2) and Sch 5 Pt II	
(3)(b)-(g)		s 246(3)
32		s 245
33		s 247(1)-(3)
34		s 248(1)-(3)
35(1)-(3)		s 249
35(4), (5)		ss 247(4), (5), 248(4), (5)
36		s 253
37		s 254
38	Rep by FA 1997 s 146(2) and Sch 9 Pt II	
39		s 255
40	Rep by FA 1996 s 132 (2) and Sch 5 Pt II	
41 (1)-(6)		s 813
(7)	Unnecessary (obsolete)	
42 (1)	Amendment of ITA 1967 s 61(l)	s 82(2)
(2)	Unnecessary (commencement)	
43	Insertion of ITA 1967 s 75(3), (4)	s 70(1)
44	Rep by FA 1997 s 146(2) and Sch 9 Pt II	
45	Amendment of ITA 1967 s 77(3)	
46		s 71(4)
47	Substitution of ITA 1967 s 219(1)	s 699(1)
48	Amendment of ITA 1967 s 221(2)	
49	Amendment of ITA 1967 ss 231(4)(a), 232(2), 233(2)(a)	
50	Rep by FA 1996 s 132(2) and Sch 5 Pt II	
51 (1)	Amendment of ITA 1967 s 535(1)(b)	s 1088
(2)	Unnecessary (operative date)	
52	Rep by FA 1997 s 146(2) and Sch 9 Pt II	
54	Rep by FA 1997 s 146(2) and Sch 9 Pt II	
55		s 814
56 (1), (2), (3)(b), (c), (4)		s 816
(3)(a)	Rep by CTA 1976 s 164 and Sch 3 Pt II	
57 preamble, (1)-(7) and (8)(a)-(c),(e),(f)		s 806
(d)	Unnecessary (obsolete)	
(9)	Unnecessary (operative date)	
58		s 807
59(1)-(5)		s 808
(6)	Amendment of ITA 1967 Sch 15	Sch 29
60		s 809
61		s 810
62(1), (2)		s 105
(3)	Unnecessary (obsolete)	

Former Enactment		*Destination in TCA 1997*
Finance Act 1974 (1974 No 27) (contd)		
s 63	Amendment of F(MP)A 1968 s 20	s 643
64(1)	Unnecessary (cesser of FA 1972 s 115(2)(f) and ITA 1967 Sch 3 proviso para 4)	
(2)	Substitution of FA 1972 Sch 1 Pt III para 4	
65	Amendment of ITA 1967 s 235	ss 783-784
66	Insertion of ITA 1967 s 235A	s 785
67	Amendment of ITA 1967 s 236 and Sch 5	s 787
69	Amendment of ITA 1967 s 429	s 942(1)-(8), (10)
70	Amendment of ITA 1967 s 489(1)	s 965
71	Unnecessary (cesser of ITA 1967 s 130, FA 1969 ss 7(3), 8(3) and 9(a)(proviso)	
72		s 988
73 (1)-(4)		s 898
(5)	Amendment of ITA 1967 Sch 15	Sch 29
74		s 671
Pt IV		
s 86	Unnecessary (application of schedule)	
87	Unnecessary (care and management)	
88(2), (5)	Unnecessary (construction and commencement)	
Sch 1, Pt I	Amendment of ITA 1967 ss 137-141, 143, 146, 149, 153, 193, FA 1969 s 3, FA 1971 s 11	ss 193, 458, 459(1)-(2), 460, 461, 462, 465, 467, 468, 472, 1032, 1032
Sch 1, Pt II	Amendment of ITA 1967 ss 115(1)(b), 127, 133(1), 195, 233(2), 406(5), 434(1), 435(1), 451(5), 488, 497, 525(1), 528, 530, 543, Sch 1 Pt I para 1(c), Sch 1 Pt II para 1(b), Sch 16 para 8, 9, FA 1967 s 12(2), FA 1968 ss 3, 34(6)	ss 201(2), 986, 997 1018, 238(1)-(6), 800, 966, 460, 127(1)-(5), 926, Sch 2, 469(2), 480
Sch 2, Pt I	Repeal of ITA 1967 ss 134, 135, 136, 144(3), 188(2), 198, 236(10), s 387(4)(c), 396(4), 410(4) , 416(11), 485(3)(4), 522, 523, 524, 526, 527, 532, 551(2)(b), Sch 10 para 5(1)(b) and proviso, F(MP)A 1968 ss 3(6)(a)(b) (c)(i)(c)(vi), 23(4), FA 1972 s 1(1)	
	Amendment of ITA 1967 ss 2(2)(c), 3, 70(1)(c), 116(1), 117(1), 145(1), 162(2), 172(1)(c), 187(1), 191(2), (3), 192(1), 194(1)(a), 196, 231(2)(3), 288(2), 291, 293, 329(1)(b), 332(1)(b), 344(4), 345, 356, 361, 365, 336(b), 387(3)(a), 419, 420, 441(1), 446(1), 465, 486(1), 489(1), 491(1), 492(1), 493, 501(1)(c), 502(2), 505, 511, 521, 539(1), 547(3), 549(1), 550, 552(2), 554(4), 555, 556(1), 559(1), Sch 6 Pt II para 1, 10 Pt III para (3)(1), Sch para 1(1), 5(1)(a), Sch 15, IT(A)A 1967 preamble para 2, FA 1968 ss 6(2)(a), 37(6), 48(2), F(No 2)A 1968 ss 8, 11(4), FA 1969 ss 63(1), 67(2), FA 1970 ss 19(5), 62(2), FA 1971 s 20(2), FA 1972 s 48(2), FA 1973 ss 33(1)(d), (6), 98(2)	ss 1(2), 3(2)(3), 45(1), 48(2), 117, 118, 199, 470(1)-(3),483(1)-(3), 757, 759, 760, 793, 797, 826(1)-(7)(9), 851, 879(1)-(4), 880(2)-(6), 886, 901, 928(1), 930, 963,965, 968, 969, 998, 1000,1004, 1015, 1017, 1022, 1053(1)-(4),1054(2)-(4), 1055, 1063, 1067, 1080(1), 1082, Sch 24 paras 1(1), 6, Sch 29
Sch 2, Pt II	Repeal of definitions of "ordinary share capital", "proprietary director", "proprietary employee" in FA 1972 s 13(1), (3)	
Sch 3	Repealed by FA 1983 s 120 and Sch 4	

Former Enactment		*Destination in TCA 1997*
Finance Act 1975 (1975 No 6)		
s 1	Amendment of ITA 1967 s 142(1)	s 466
2	Amendment of ITA 1967 s 143(3)(b)	
3	Amendment of ITA 1967 s 251(4)(d)	ss 283(2), 300(1)
4	Insertion of ITA 1967 s 254(2A)	s 271(4)
5	Amendment of ITA 1967 s 264	s 272
6	Amendment of FA 1971 s 22(2)	
7	Amendment of FA 1971 s 26(1)	s 285(1)-(3)
8	Amendment of FA 1973 s 8	
9	Amendment of FA 1973 s 19	s 192
10	Amendment of FA 1974 s 3	
11 (1)	Substitution of FA 1974 s 6(1)	
s 11 (2)	Unnecessary (application of schedule)	
12	Substitution of FA 1974 s 13(1)	s 654
13	Amendment of FA 1974 s 15(3)	s 655(1), (2)
14 (1)	Amendment of FA 1974 s 16	s 657(1)
(2)	Unnecessary (operative date)	
15	Amendment of FA 1974 s 17(4)	
16	Amendment of FA 1974 s 20(1)	
17	Amendment of FA 1974 s 21(1)	
18	Amendment of FA 1974 s 22	s 658
19	Amendment of ITA 1967 s 80	ss 96, 888(1)
20	Amendment of ITA 1967 s 83	s 98
21 (1)-(7)		s 947
(8)	Rep by CTA 1976 s 164 and Sch 3 Pt II	
22	Unnecessary (application of schedule)	
25	Amendment of ITA 1967 s 542	s 869
26	Amendment of FA 1968 s 9(b)	s 991(2)(b)
27	Amendment of FA 1973 s 35	s 1089(1)
28	Unnecessary (obsolete)	
29		s 319
30	Rep by CTA 1976 s 164 and Sch 3 Pt I.	
31	Rep by FA 1996 s 132(2) and Sch 5 Pt II	
31A	Rep by FA 1996 s 132(2) and Sch 5 Pt II	
32	Amendment of FA 1974 s 41(7)	
33 (1)		s 2(1)
(2)	Unnecessary (application of schedule)	
34 (1)	Amendment of ITA 1967 s 255(1)	s 268(1)-(3),(5)-(8)
(2)(a)(i)		s 271(4)(b)
(ii)		s 272(3)(b)
(iii)		ss 272(4)(b), 274(1)(b)(ii)
(b)	Unnecessary (spent)	
(3)	Unnecessary (operative date)	
35	Unnecessary (application of schedule)	
56	Unnecessary (care and management)	
57(2), (5)	Unnecessary (construction and commencement)	
Sch 1		
Pt I	Amendment of ITA 1967 ss 138, 139, 140, 141, FA 1969 s 3 FA 1971 s 11, FA 1974 s 8	ss 460,461, 464-466, 467, 1032
Pt II	Amendment of ITA 1967 ss 69(1), 218, 317(1), 236(3), 314, FA 1970 s 20(5)(a), FA 1971 s 22, FA 1973 39(1)(b), (7), FA 1974 s 27(1)	ss 1007(1)-(2), 698,) 391(1), 787(6), 662
Pt III	Amendment of ITA 1967 s 288(2), F(TPCM)A 1974 ss 1, 7(4), 11(2)	ss 757, 59
Sch 2		
Pt I	Unnecessary (obsolete)	
Pt II	Amendment of ITA 1967 Sch 15	Sch 29

Former Enactment		*Destination in TCA 1997*
Finance Act 1975 (1975 No 6) (contd)		
Pt III	Amendment of ITA 1967 ss 81(3), 91(1)(b), 92(2)	
Sch 3	Rep by FA 1996 s 132(2) and Sch 5 Pt II	
Sch 5	Rep by FA 1996 s 132(2) and Sch 5 Pt II	
Finance (No 2) Act 1975 (1975 No 19)		
s 1	Unnecessary (obsolete)	
3	Unnecessary (care and management)	
4	Unnecessary (short title, construction and commencement)	
Capital Gains Tax Act 1975 (1975 No 20)		
s 1	Unnecessary (short title)	
2 (1)(3)(4)		s 5
(2)	Rep by FA 1996 s 132(2) and Sch 5 Pt II	
(5)		s 3(4)
(6)	Unnecessary (construction)	
(7)	Unnecessary (construction)	
(8)	Unnecessary (construction)	
3 (1)-(3)		s 28
(4)	Deleted by FA 1992 s 60(1)(b)	
4(1)-(4)(6)-(8)		s 29(1)-(7)
(2) proviso	Rep by FA 1977 s 54 and Sch 2 Pt I	
(5)		s 30
5 (1)		s 31
(2)		s 979
(3)		s 1042
6	Rep by CGT(A)A 1978 s 17 and Sch 2	
7(1)		s 532(1)
(2)		ss 545(1), 546(1)
8 (1)		s 534
(2)		s 535(2)
(3)		s 567(2)
(4), (5), (6)		s 537
(7)		s 535(1)
9		s 547
10 (1)		s 542(1)
(2)		s 539
(3)		s 542(2)
11		s 545(2), (3)
12 (1)		s 546(2)
(2)		s 546(3)
(3), (4), (5)		s 538
(6)		s 546(4)
(7)		s 546(5)
13		s 1028
14		s 573
15 (1), (9), (11)		s 574
(2)		s 575
(3), (8)		s 576
(4)-(5A)(6)(12)		s 577
(7)		s 578
(10)		s 567(1)

Former Enactment	*Destination in TCA 1997*
Capital Gains Tax Act 1975 (1975 No 20) (contd)	
s 16	s 601(1), (2), (4), (5)
17	s 602
18	s 603
19 (1)	s 607(1)(a), (b), (c), (d), (f)
(2)	s 607(2)
20	s 593
20A .... (s 20A inserted by FA 1993 s 24)	s 594
20B .... (s 20B inserted by FA 1994 s 58)	s 595
21	s 608(2)-(4)
22	s 609
23	s 610, Sch 15, Pt I
24	s 613
25	s 604
26(1)-(6)	s 598
(7) .... Rep by CGT(A)A 1978 s 17 and Sch 2	
27(1)(a)-(c), (2)-(4)	s 599
(d)....... Rep by FA 1996 s 132(2) and Sch 5 Pt II	
28	s 597
29(1)-(3), (5)	s 536
(4) .... Rep by CGT(A)A 1978 s 17 and Sch 2	
30	s 612
31 (1)-(4), (6)	s 731(1)-(5)(a)
(5)	Sch 32, para 25
32	s 732
33 (1)-(6)	s 549
(7) .... Ceased by FA 1996 s 131(9)(a)	
(8) .... Rep by FA 1996 s 132(2) and Sch 5 Pt II	
34	s 550
35 (1)-(3), (5)	s 589
35 (4) .... Deleted by CTA 1976 s 140(2) and Sch 2 Pt II, para 3(2)	
36	s 590(1)-(9)
37	s 579
38	s 828(1)-(3)
39	s 611
40	s 569
41	s 570
42	s 572
43	s 1005
44 (1)	s 981
(2)	s 563(1)
45	s 543
46 (1)-(6)	s 541(1)-(6)
(7)(a)-(d)	s 541(7)(a), (b), (c), (g)
47(1)-(6)(8)-(11)	s 540
(7) .... Rep by CGT(A)A 1978 s 17 and Sch 2	
48	s 533
49 (1)-(6)	s 548(1)-(6)
(7) .... Rep by FA 1997 s 146(2) and Sch 5 Pt II	

Former Enactment		*Destination in TCA 1997*
Capital Gains Tax Act 1975 (1975 No 20) (contd)		
s 50 (1)	Amendment of PCTA 1927 s 1	
(2)	Amendment of IRRA 1890 s 39	
s 51 (1)	For leases only, otherwise unnecessary (application of schedules)	s 566
(2)		s 544(8)
Sch 1, Pt I		
para1		s 544(1)-(6)
Sch 1, Pt I		
para 2		s 551
3(1)-(5)		s 552
(6)		s 828(4)
(7)		s 565
4		s 554
5(1), (2), (4)		s 555
(3)		s 544(1)
6		s 557
7		s 559
8		s 560(1), (2)
9		s 560(3), (4), (5)
10		s 561
11		s 562
12		s 564
13	Rep by CGT(A)A 1978 s 17 and Sch 2	
14(1)-(5)		s 581
(6)	Rep by CGT(A)A 1978 s 17 and Sch 2	
15		s 596
Sch 1, Pt II	Rep by CGT(A)A 1978 s 17 and Sch 2	
Sch 2		
para1		s 583
2(1)-(7)(9)		s 584
(8)	Rep by CGT(A)A 1978 s 17 and Sch 2	
2A	(para 2A inserted by FA 1990 s 87)	s 733
3		s 585
4		s 586(1), (2)
5		s 587(1)-(3)
5A	(para 5A inserted by FA 1997 s 70)	s 588
6		s 600(1)-(5)
Sch 3		Sch 14
para1		para 2
2		para 3
3		para 4(1)-(6)
4		para 5
5		para 6
6		para 7
7		para 8
8		para 9
9		para 10
10		para 1

Former Enactment	*Destination in TCA 1997*
Capital Gains Tax Act 1975 (1975 No 20) (contd)	
Sch 4	
para1(1)	s 849(1), (2)
(2)	s 931(1)
(3)	ss 851, 976(1)
Sch 4	
para2(1)	ss 931(2), 976(2)
(2)	ss 29(8), (9), 567(3), (4), 849(3)-(6), 861(1), 863, 864, 865, 869, 870, 875, 931(3), 949, 976(3), 999, 1043, 1051, 1083, Sch 1
3(1)(3)-(5)	s 913(1), (3)-(5), (7)
(2)	ss 874, 913(2), 1077(1)
(6)	s 1077(2)
para 4	s 914
5	s 915
6	s 916
7	s 917
8(1)	s 945
(2)(a)-(i),(k)	
(2)(j) .... Rep by CGT(A)A 1978 s 17 and Sch 2	
9	s 946
10(1)	s 913(8)
(2)	s 1029
11(1)-(10A)	s 980
(11) .... Unnecessary (operative date)	
12	s 568
13	s 544(7)
14	s 911
15	s 982
16	s 871
17	s 977
18	s 978
19	s 913(6)
Corporation Tax Act 1976 (1976 No 7)	
Pt I	
s 1 (1), (2), (3)	s 21
(4) .... Unnecessary (cesser of corporation profits tax)	
(5)	s 4(1)
2	s 129
3	s 24
4	s 864(2)
5	s 152(1), (2)
Pt II	
6 (1), (2), (3)	s 26(1), (2), (3)
(4) .... Rep by FA 1997s 146(2) and Sch 9 Pt II	
(5)	s 849
(6) .... Amendment of PCTA 1927 s 1	
(7) .... Amendment of IRRA 1890 s 39	
7	s 919(6)

Corporation Tax Act 1976 (1976 No 7) (contd)

Former Enactment		*Destination in TCA 1997*
s 8 (1), (2), (3)		s 25
(4)		ss 1040, 1046(3)
9		s 27
10		s 243(1), (2), (4)-(9)
10A(1)(a), (b)(ii)	(s 10A inserted by FA 1992 s 46(1)(a))	s 454(1)
(b)(i)	Unnecessary (obsolete)	
(2), (3)		s 454(2), (3)
11 (1), (2)(b), (3)-(8)		s 76
(2)(a)	Unnecessary (obsolete)	
12 (1) to(7)		s 77
(8)	Rep by FA 1996 s 132(2) and Sch 5 Pt II	
12A	(s 12A inserted by FA 1994 s 95(a))	s 79
13 (1)		s 78(1)
(1A)	Matter from "and section 132(2) shall have effect" to the end. Unnecessary (obsolete)	s 78(2)
(1B)		s 78(3)(a), (b)
(1C), (2)		s 78(4), (5)
13 (3)(a), (c)		s 78(6)
(b)	Rep by CGT(A)A 1978 s 17 and Sch 2	
(4), (5)		s 78(7), (8)
14(1), (2)		s 307
(3)-(8)		s 308
14A	(s 14A inserted by FA 1994 s 56(b))	s 402
15		s 83
16 (1)-(8)(10)		s 396
(9)	Ceased by FA 1983 s 51	
16A	(s 16A inserted by FA 1992 s 46(1)(c))	s 455
17 (1)	Definitions of "farming" and "market gardening" unnecessary (duplication)	s 663(1)
(2)-(4)		s 663(2)-(4)
(5)	Matter from "In this subsection" to "section 157" unnecessary (obsolete)	s 663(5)
18 (1)-(3)		s 397
(4)	Ceased by FA 1983 s 51	
19		s 399
20		s 400
21 (1)	Unnecessary (application of income tax provisions for purposes of corporation tax)	
(2)	Unnecessary (non-application of income tax provisions)	
(3)	Unnecessary (obsolete).	
(4)		s 309
22 (1)		s 827
(2)		s 826(8)
23 (1)		ss 826(1)-(7), (9), 827
(2)-(4)-(5)		Sch 24, para 4(2)
24		s 156

Former Enactment		*Destination in TCA 1997*
Corporation Tax Act 1976 (1976 No 7) (contd)		
s 25 (1)-(7)		s 157
(8)	Ceased by FA 1983 s 51	
26 (1)-(3), (3) proviso para (a), (4)-(6)		s 158
(3) proviso para (b)	Ceased by FA 1983 s 51	
27 (1)-(7)		s 401
(8)	Unnecessary (obsolete)	
Pt III		
s 28	Ceased by FA 1988 s 33(2)	
28A(1)	(s 28A inserted by FA 1996 s 44)	s 22(1)(a)
(2)-(8)		s 22(2)-(8)
(9)	Unnecessary (obsolete)	
28A(10)		s 457
29		s 844
30 (1)	Unnecessary (interpretation)	
(2)-(4)		s 700
(5)(a)	Amendment of ITA 1967 s 219	s 699(1)
(b)	Unnecessary (obsolete)	
31 (1)-(3)	Ceased by FA 1986 s 34(a)	
(4)	Unnecessary (obsolete)	
(5)		s 702(2)
(6)	Ceased by FA 1986 s 34(a)	
(7)	Unnecessary (obsolete)	
(8)		s 702(1)
(9)	Rep by FA 1992 s 43(4)	
(10)	Unnecessary (spent)	
32 (1), (2)		s 1009(2), (3)
(3)(a)-(d)		s 1009(4)
(c)(proviso)	Unnecessary (spent)	
(4)		s 1009(5)
(5)		s 1009(1)
33 (1)-(1B)(2)		s 707
(3)		s 728
33A(1)-(5), (7), (8)	(s 33A inserted by FA 1992 s 44)	s 708
(6)	Unnecessary (spent)	
33B	(s 33B inserted by FA 1993 s 11(c))	s 712
34		s 709
35		s 710(1)-(5)
35A	(s 35A inserted by FA 1993 s 11(d))	s 711
36		s 713(1)-(6)
36A(1)-(6)(8)	(s 36A inserted by FA 1993 s 11(f))	s 723
(7)		s 706(4)
36B	(s 36B inserted by FA 1993 s 11(f))	s 724
36C	(s 36C inserted by FA 1993 s 11(f))	s 725
37	Deleted by FA 1982 s 42	
38		s 714
39		s 715
40		s 716
41		s 717(1), (3)-(6)
42(1)-(5), (8)		s 718
(6), (7)	Rep by FA 1977 s 54 and Sch 2 Pt I	
43		s 726

Former Enactment		*Destination in TCA 1997*
Corporation Tax Act 1976 (1976 No 7) (contd)		
s 44		s 727
45		s 729(1)-(6)
46		s 730
46A	(s 46A inserted by FA 1992 s 44(d)) Definitions of "collective investment undertaking", "market value", "trading company" and "units" deleted by FA 1993 s 11(j)(i)	s 719
46B(1)	(s 46B inserted by FA 1992 s 44(d))	s 720(1)
(proviso)		s 720(2)
paras (iii)-(v)		
(proviso)	Unnecessary (spent)	
para (i), (ii)		
(2)-(4)		s 720(3)-(5)
47	Deleted by FA 1992 s 44(e)	
48		s 721
49		s 722
50 (1)	Unnecessary (declaratory)	
(2)-(4)		s 706(1)-(3)
51(1)-(3)(a) (4)-(6)		s 845
(3)(b), (c)	Rep by FA 1996 s 132(2) and Sch 5 Pt II	
52 (1)-(4)(6)		s 846
52 (5)	Rep by FA 1996 s 132(2) and Sch 5 Pt II	
Pt IV		
s 53-63	Unnecessary (spent)	
64		s 145(1), (2)(a), (3)-(10)
65		s 146
66	Ceased by CTA 1976 s 66A(3)	
66A(1)(2)(a)	(s 66A inserted by FA 1992 s 35(a)) Definitions of "the adjusted average relieved distribution", "the average relieved distribution" and "the relieved distribution". Unnecessary (spent)	s 145(11)(a)(b)
(2)(b)	Unnecessary (redundant)	
(3)	Unnecessary (cesser of CTA 1976 ss 66 and 67)	
(proviso)	Rep by FA 1997 s 146(2) and Sch 9 Pt II	
(4)	Rep by FA 1997 s 146(2) and Sch 9 Pt II	
67	Ceased by CTA 1976 s 66A(3)	
68	Rep by FA 1996 s 132(2) and Sch 5 Pt II	
69-75	Unnecessary (spent)	
76(1),(2)(a)(ii), (2)(b),(3)-(8)		s 144
(2)(a)(i)	Unnecessary (obsolete)	
76A(1)	Unnecessary (obsolete) (s 76A inserted by FA 1992 s 35(b))	
(2)	Unnecessary (cesser of CTA 1976 s 76(2)(a)(i))	
(proviso)	Rep by FA 1997 s 146(2) and Sch 9 Pt II	
(3)	Rep by FA 1997 s 146(2) and Sch 9 Pt II	
77	Unnecessary (spent)	
Pt VI		
s 78	Unnecessary (spent)	
Pt VII		
s 79	Ceased by FA 1988 s 33(2)	
80	Rep by FA 1997 s 61(2)	

Former Enactment		*Destination in TCA 1997*
Corporation Tax Act 1976 (1976 No 7) (contd)		
Pt VIII		
s 81		s 142
82		s 143
Pt IX		
s 83 (1)	Unnecessary (declaratory)	
(2), (3)		s 20
83 (4)		s 153(1)
(5)		s 152(3)
84		s 130
84A(1)	Section 84A as inserted by FA 1984 s 41 was substituted by FA 1989 s 21(1) but FA 1989 s 21(2) saved provisions of s 84A as it existed before the substitution in respect of certain types of loans. Section 134 of the Bill reflects those provisions while s 133 of the Bill reflects provisions of s 84A as substituted by FA 1989 s 21(1) and as subsequently amended	s 134(3)
(2)		s 134(5)
(3)		ss 134(1)(a), 133(7)
(3A)(a)		s 133(8)(b)
(proviso)	Unnecessary (spent)	
(b)		s 133(8)(c)
(c)		s 133(8)(d)
(d)		s 133(8)(e)
(e)		s 133(8)(a)
(3B)(a)	(s 84A(3B) was substituted by FA 1992 s 40(b) as respects certain loans advanced after 20.12.91; accordingly the original s 84A(3B) (inserted by FA 1991 s 28(a)) still applies for loans advanced before that date)	s 133(9)(a)
(proviso)		133(9)(b)
(3B)(b)		ss 133(9)(c),
(proviso)		s 133(11)
(a)	These three references relate to s 84A(3B) as substituted by FA 1992 s 40(b)	s 133(10)(a)
(b)		s 133(10)(b))
(b)(proviso)		s 133(11))
(4)		s 134(1)(b)
(4A)(a)		s 133(13)(b)
(b)	(s 84A(4A)(b) proviso (para (a) is spent)	s 133(13)(c)
(4A)(c)		s 133(13)(a)
(5)		s 134(1)(a), (c)
(6)		s 134(1)(a)
(7)-(8)	Unnecessary (spent)	
(9)		s 134(4)
(10)		s 134(6)
(9)		s 133(1)(d)
(10)		s 133(4)
85		s 131

Former Enactment		*Destination in TCA 1997*
Corporation Tax Act 1976 (1976 No 7) (contd)		
s 86		s 132
87		s 135
88		s 136
89		s 137
90	Ceased by FA 1983 s 51	
91	Ceased by FA 1983 s 51	
s 92	Unnecessary (spent)	
93		s 140
Pt X		
s 94		s 430
95		s 431
96		s 436
97		s 437
98 (1)-(7), (9)		s 438
(8)	Unnecessary (spent)	
99 (1), (2), (4)		s 439
(3)	Unnecessary (spent)	
100	Section 100(4) definition of "distributable income" para (b). Unnecessary (spent)	s 434
101		s 440
102		s 432
103		s 433
104		s 435
Pt XI		
s 105		s 410
106	Rep by FA 1992 s 50	
107		s 411
108		s 412
109		s 413
110		s 414
111		s 415
112		s 416
113		s 417
114		s 418
115		s 419
116		s 420
116A(1)(a), (b),(ii),(2)-(4) (b), (5)	(s 116A inserted by FA 1988 s 34)	s 456
(b)(i), (4)(a)	Unnecessary (spent)	
117(1)-(3)(a), (b), (d), (4)		s 421
(3)(c)	Unnecessary (spent)	
118		s 422
119		s 423
120	Definition of "connected person" in s 120(5) unnecessary (obsolete)	s 424.
121		s 425
122(1)-(5)		s 426
(6)	Unnecessary (obsolete)	

Former Enactment		*Destination in TCA 1997*
Corporation Tax Act 1976 (1976 No 7) (contd)		
s 123		s 427
124		s 428
125		s 429
Pt XII		
126		s 614
127		s 615
128		s 553
129(1)-(6)(b)		s 616
129(6)(c)(7)		s 590(11)
130		s 617
131		s 618
132		s 619
133		s 620
134		s 626
135		s 623
136		s 624
137		s 625
138		s 621
139(1)-(6)	The matter from "and section 157" to end in s 139(6) unnecessary (obsolete)	s 622
Pt XIII		
s 140(1)	Unnecessary (application of schedule)	
(2)	Unnecessary (application of schedule)	
(3)	Unnecessary (construction)	
Pt XIV		
s 141(1)-(1B)(3)		s 882(2)-(5)
(2)		s 1073
142(1)		s 883
(proviso)	Unnecessary (obsolete)	
(2)		s 1074
143(1)-(6), (7)(a),(b),(d)		s 884
(7)(c), (8)		s 1071
(9)-(11)		s 1072
(12)(a)		s 930
(b)		s 861(2)
(c)		ss 861(2), 884
144		s 919(1)-(5)
145(1), (2)		s 973
145(3)		s 1080
(4)		s 1082
(5)		s 974
146(1)		s 864, Pt 40 Ch I, s 949
(2)		s 856(3)
147(1), (2)		ss 207(3), (4), 211(5), (6), 213(3), (4), 483(1)-(3), 860, 861(1), 862, 863, 865, 868, 869, 870, 873, 874, 875, 886,

Former Enactment		*Destination in TCA 1997*
Corporation Tax Act 1976 (1976 No 7) (contd)		
s 142(1), (2) (contd)		898, 901, 928(1), 929, 947, 998, 1004, 1049, 1055, 1056, 1057, 1058, 1066, 1067, 1068, 1069, 1070, 1081(1)
(3), (4)		ss 1059, 1060, 1061, 1062, 1063, 1065, 1076(2)
147(5)		s 857(4)
148		s 1064
149		s 1075
150		s 647
s 151(1)-(13)		s 239
(14)	Amendment of ITA 1967 s 434	s 238(1)-(6)
152		s 240
153	Rep by FA 1996 s 132(2) and Sch 5 Pt II	
154		ss 882(1), 1076(1)
Pt XV		
s 155(1), (2)		s 1(2)
(3), (4)		s 2(2), (3)
(5)		ss 2(1), 4(1)
(6)-(8)	Unnecessary (construction)	
(9)-(13)		s 4(2)-(6)
156		s 9
157	Ceased by FA 1996 s 131	
158		s 11
159		s 590(10)
160		s 1033
161		s 927
162(1)-(6)		s 441
(7)	Unnecessary (obsolete)	
163		s 830
164	Unnecessary (application of schedule)	
165	Unnecessary (non-application of FA 1924 s 38 for corporation tax)	
166	Unnecessary (application of schedule)	
167	Ceased by FA 1983 s 51(2)	
168	Ceased by FA 1983 s 51(2)	
169	Unnecessary (obsolete)	
170	(s 170(3A)(a) (proviso) is spent)	s 141
171		s 2(4)
172	Unnecessary (relates to introduction of corporation tax)	
Pt XVI		
s 173	Unnecessary (relates to commencement of corporation tax)	
174	Unnecessary (relates to winding up of corporation profits tax)	
174(3)(proviso)		Sch 32, para 18(2)
175		Sch 32, para 19
176	Unnecessary (spent)	
177		Sch 32, para 8
178		s 139
179	Unnecessary (spent)	
180	Unnecessary (commencement)	
181	Unnecessary (spent)	
182(1)-(3), (3)(proviso)		
para (a),(bb),		

Former Enactment	*Destination in TCA 1997*
Corporation Tax Act 1976 (1976 No 7) (contd)	
s 182(4)	Sch 32, para 16(1)-(4)
(3)(proviso) para (b),(c) . . . Unnecessary (obsolete)	
183	Sch 32, para 17
184(1)	Sch 32, para 18(1)
(2)	Sch 32, para 18(3)
184(3)	Sch 32, para 18(4)(a), (b)
(proviso) para (iiA)	Sch 32, para 18(4)(c)
(proviso) para (i)-(iii) . Unnecessary (obsolete)	
(4)	Sch 32, para 18(5)
185 . . . Unnecessary (spent)	
186 . . . Unnecessary (application of schedule)	
187 . . . Unnecessary (obsolete)	
188 . . . Unnecessary (short title and construction)	
Sch 1	
para 1 . . . Definition of "tax" in para 1(3) unnecessary (duplication)	s 321(1)-(7)
2	s 321(8)
3	s 321(9)
4 . . . Unnecessary (obsolete)	
5 . . . Unnecessary (obsolete)	
6 . . . Substitution of ITA 1967 s 241	s 284
7 . . . Substitution of ITA 1967 s 242	
8 . . . Substitution of ITA 1967 s 243	
9 . . . Substitution of ITA 1967 s 244	s 763(2)
10 . . . Substitution of ITA 1967 s 245	s 670
11 . . . Substitution of ITA 1967 s 246	
12 . . . Substitution of ITA 1967 s 247	
13 . . . Substitution of ITA 1967 s 248	
14 . . . Substitution of ITA 1967 s 249	
15 . . . Substitution of ITA 1967 s 251	ss 283(2), 300(1), 316(3)
16 . . . Substitution of ITA 1967 s 252	ss 298(1), 299(1), 304(4)
17 . . . Substitution of ITA 1967 s 254	ss 271(1), (2), (4), 278(1), (2), (6), 305, 320(1)
18 . . . Substitution of ITA 1967 s 256	s 270
19 . . . Substitution of ITA 1967 s 258	
20 . . . Substitution of ITA 1967 s 259	
21 . . . Substitution of ITA 1967 s 260	s 316(1)(a)
22 . . . Substitution of ITA 1967 s 262	
23 . . . Substitution of ITA 1967 s 264	s 272
24 . . . Substitution of ITA 1967 s 265	s 274(1), (3), (4), (5), (8)
25 . . . Substitution of ITA 1967 s 266	s 277
26 . . . Substitution of ITA 1967 s 267	s 278(1), (3), (4), (5), (6)
27 . . . Substitution of ITA 1967 s 270	s 280
28 . . . Substitution of ITA 1967 s 271	s 288(4)(a)
29 . . . Substitution of ITA 1967 s 272	s 288
30 . . . Substitution of ITA 1967 s 274	s 292
31 . . . Substitution of ITA 1967 s 275	s 293
32 . . . Substitution of ITA 1967 s 279	s 296
33 . . . Substitution of ITA 1967 s 280	s 297
34 . . . Substitution of ITA 1967 s 282	s 300
Sch 1	
para 35 . . . Substitution of ITA 1967 s 284	s 754
36 . . . Substitution of ITA 1967 s 285	s 755
37 . . . Substitution of ITA 1967 s 286	s 756
38 . . . Substitution of ITA 1967 s 288	s 757
39 . . . Substitution of ITA 1967 s 290	s 758

Former Enactment		*Destination in TCA 1997*
Corporation Tax Act 1976 (1976 No 7) (contd)		
Sch 1 (contd)		
para 40	Substitution of ITA 1967 s 291	s 759
41	Substitution of ITA 1967 s 292	s 761
42	Substitution of ITA 1967 s 293	s 760
43	Substitution of ITA 1967 s 294	ss 302, 303
44	Substitution of ITA 1967 s 295	s 304(2),(4)-(6)(a)
45	Substitution of ITA 1967 s 297	s 306
46	Substitution of ITA 1967 s 299	ss 312, 762
47	Substitution of ITA 1967 s 301	s 314
48	Substitution of ITA 1967 s 302	s 315
49	Substitution of ITA 1967 s 303	ss 316(1)(2), 317(2), 762(2)(b)
50	Substitution of ITA 1967 s 304	ss 318, 320(1), (2), (6)
51	Substitution of ITA 1967 s 305	s 769
52	Substitution of ITA 1967 s 306	s 381
53	Substitution of FA 1967 s 11	s 285(1), (2), (3), (8), 299(2)
54	Substitution of FA 1968 s 4	
55	Substitution of FA 1969 s 4	
56	Substitution of FA 1970 s 14	ss 287, 301(1)
57	Substitution of FA 1971 s 22	
58	Substitution of FA 1971 s 23	
59	Substitution of FA 1971 s 24	
60	Substitution of FA 1971 s 26	ss 285(1), (2), (3), (8), 288, 299(2)
61	Substitution of FA 1973 s 9(2)	s 283(7)
62	Substitution of FA 1973 s 25	ss 373(2)(a), 374
63	Substitution of F(TPCM)A 1974 s 1	s 672
64	Substitution of F(TPCM)A 1974 s 2	s 673
65	Substitution of F(TPCM)A 1974 s 3	
66	Substitution of F(TPCM)A 1974 s 4	s 675
67	Substitution of F(TPCM)A 1974 s 5	s 676
68	Substitution of F(TPCM)A 1974 s 6	s 677
69	Substitution of F(TPCM)A 1974 s 7	s 678
70	Substitution of FA 1974 s 22	s 658
71	Substitution of FA 1974 s 25	s 660
72	Substitution of FA 1975 s 34	s 248(1)-(3)
Sch 2, Pt I		
para 1	Amendment of ITA 1967 s 1	ss 2(1), 3(1)
2	Amendment of ITA 1967 s 8	s 1087
3	Amendment of ITA 1967 s 83	s 98
4	Amendment of ITA 1967 s 169	s 877
5	Amendment of ITA 1967 s 181(1)	s 918(1)-(3)
6	Amendment of ITA 1967 s 183(1)	s 921
7	Amendment of ITA 1967 s 184(2)(a)	s 922
8	Amendment of ITA 1967 s 186(1)	s 924
9	Amendment of ITA 1967 s 239(6)	
10	Amendment of ITA 1967 s 329	
11	Amendment of ITA 1967 s 331	
12	Amendment of ITA 1967 s 332	
Sch 2, Pt I		
para13	Amendment of ITA 1967 s 333(1)(b)	s 207(1), (2)
14	Amendment of ITA 1967 s 335(1)	s 211(1)-(4)
15	Amendment of ITA 1967 s 336	s 213(1), (2)
16	Amendment of ITA 1967 s 337(2)	
17	Amendment of ITA 1967 s 367(7)	
18	Amendment of ITA 1967 s 369(1)	s 750
19	Amendment of ITA 1967 s 370	s 751
20	Amendment of ITA 1967 s 371	s 752

Former Enactment		*Destination in TCA 1997*
Corporation Tax Act 1976 (1976 No 7) (contd)		
Sch 2 Pt I (contd)		
para 21	Amendment of ITA 1967 s 372	s 753
(1)	Amendment of ITA 1967 s 449(1)	s 812 (1), (2), (4)
(2)		s 812(3)
23	Amendment of ITA 1967 s 450(2)(d)	s 799
24		s 801(9)
25	Amendment of ITA 1967 s 458(1)	s 1091
26		s 51
27		s 483(4)
28	Amendment of ITA 1967 Sch 12	Sch 22
29	Unnecessary (obsolete)	
30		s 109
31		Sch 32, para 26
32	Amendment of FA 1973 s 24	
33		s 375
34		s 23
35		s 234(2)(b)
36(1), (3)		Sch 1, para 1, 2, 5
(2)	Unnecessary (obsolete)	
37	Amendment of F(TPCM)A 1974 s 8(1)	s 680
38		s 682(4)
39	Substitution of F(TPCM)A 1974 s 11	s 682(1)-(3)
40	Amendment of F(TPCM)A 1974 s 18(2)	
41	Amendment of FA 1974 s 4(b)	s 59
42	Amendment of FA 1974 s 31(3)(f)	s 246(1), (2), (4
43	Amendment of FA 1974 s 33(1)	s 247(1)-(3)
44	Amendment of FA 1974 s 38(2)	
45		s 813
46	Amendment of FA 1974 s 54	
47(1)		s 814
(2)	Amendment of FA 1974 s 55	s 814
48		s 671
49	Unnecessary (obsolete)	
50	Unnecessary (spent)	
Sch 2, Pt II		
para 1	Amendment of CGTA 1975 s 2(1)	s 5
2	Amendment of CGTA 1975 s 33(7)(b)	
3	Amendment of CGTA 1975 s 35	s 589
4	Amendment of CGTA 1975 s 36(1), (8)	s 590(1)-(9)
5	Amendment of CGTA 1975 s 36(4)(d)	s 590(1)-(9)
6		ss 563(2), 975(2)
7		s 548(7)
8	Amendment of CGTA 1975 Sch 1 par 2(1)	s 551
9	Amendment of CGTA 1975 Sch 1 par 3(3)(a)(ii), (iii)	s 552
Sch 3, Pt II		
para10	Amendment of CGTA 1975 Sch 1 para 22(1)(a)	
11		Sch 14, para 4(7)
12		s 975(1)
13	Unnecessary (spent)	
Sch 3, Pt I	Repeal of ITA 1967 ss 64, 76(7), (8), 108, Pt X, ss 219(2), 220(6), 221, 237, Pt XIX Ch III, s 347, Pt XXV, s 435, Pt XXX Ch I, Pt XXXVI Ch II, Sch 16, FA 1969 s 20, FA 1973 ss 11, 24(2),	

Former Enactment		*Destination in TCA 1997*
Corporation Tax Act 1976 (1976 No 7) (contd)		
Sch 3, Pt I (contd)	F(TPCM)A 1974 ss 13, 14, 15, 16, FA 1974 ss 4 proviso, 23, 54(4), FA 1975 ss 5, 18, 30	
	Amendment of ITA 1967 ss 1(1), 75(2), 76(2), 316(2), 371(7)(c), 432(3)(a), 543, FA 1972 s 16(4), FA 1973 ss 24(8), 26, FA 1974 s 5(1)	ss 2(1), 3(1); 70(1); 71(2); 390(1), (3); 752 949(2)-(4); s 774(6), Sch 32 para 26; 373(2)(a), 375; s 237(1)(b), (2)
Sch 3, Pt II	Repeal of ITA 1967 s 1(5), FA 1967 s 21, F(MP)A 1968 ss 13, 15, FA 1968 Pt IV, s 48(4), FA 1969 Pt VI, FA 1970 s 24(2)(b), FA 1971 ss 46, 49, 50, FA 1972 s 43 (insofar as it relates to corporation tax), FA 1973 s 37, F(TPCM)A 1974 ss 12, 17, FA 1974 ss 27(7), 53, 56(3)(a), FA 1975 s 21(8)	
	Amendment of ITA 1967 ss 555(1)(e),556, 559(1), FA 1969 s 63 , FA 1970 s 21, FA 1973 ss 30, 33, 34(2), 35, 98(2), Sch 3 para 7, F(TPCM)A 1974 s 10, FA 1974 ss 41(2), 74, FA 1975 s 28, Sch 2	ss 48, 95, 373, 13(1), 234(1)(2)(a), 1089(1), Sch 1, 682(1)-(3), 813, 671, 75(1), 96(1), 97, 102, 103, Sch 29
Sch 3, Pt III	Repeal of FA 1968 ss 34, 36, FA 1973 s 39, FA 1974 s 68	
Sch 4, Pt I	Amendment of ITA 1967 ss 355, 361(1), Sch 10, FA 1970 s 57	s 826(1)-(7), Sch 24, 829
Sch 4, Pt II	Repeal of ITA 1967 ss 363, 364, Sch 10 para 3(1), 7, FA 1968 s 35Sch 24 paras 7-13	
	Amendment of ITA 1967 Sch 10 para 8(3)(c)	Sch 24 paras 7-13
Sch 5	Unnecessary (spent)	
Finance Act 1976 (1976 No 16)		
Pt I		
s 1	Amendment of ITA 1967 s 128(4)	s 987(4)
2	Amendment of ITA 1967 s 142(1)	s 466
3	Amendment of ITA 1967 s 174	s 900(1), (2), (4)
4	Insertion of ITA 1967 s 197(1A)	s 1023
5	Amendment of ITA 1967 s 316(2)	s 390(1), (3)
6 (1)	Amendment of ITA 1967 s 477	s 960
(2)	Amendment of FA 1971 s 20(2)	s 1082
7	Amendment of ITA 1967 s 497	s 460
8	Amendment of ITA 1967 s 525(1)	s 127(1)-(5)
9	Amendment of F(No 2)A 1975 s 1	
10	Unnecessary (obsolete)	
11 (1)-(3)		s 881
(4)	Amendment of ITA 1967 Sch 15	Sch 29
(5)	Amendment of ITA 1967 s 169(1)	s 877
12	Rep by FA 1996 s 132(2) and Sch 5 Pt II	
13		s 805
14	Substitution of FA 1968 s 11	
15	Rep by FA 1996 s 132(2) and Sch 5 Pt II	
16	Rep by FA 1996 s 132(2) and Sch 5 Pt II	
17(1)-(3)(a)(4)(b)		s 996
(3)(b), (4)(a)	Unnecessary (obsolete)	
18	Amendment of FA 1974 s 21	
19	Rep by FA 1983 s 120 and Sch 4	
20	Amendment of FA 1970 s 17	ss 530, 531
21	Substitution of FA 1970 s 17	ss 530, 531
22		s 57
23	Rep by FA 1978 s 5	
24	Amendment of FA 1973 ss 31, 37	

Former Enactment		*Destination in TCA 1997*
Finance Act 1976 (1976 No 16) (contd)		
s 25	Rep by FA 1997 s 146(2) and Sch 9 Pt II	
26	Amendment of FA 1975 s 31(1), insertion of FA 1975 s 31A and Sch 5	
27	Insertion of CTA 1976 s 54(4)	
28	Unnecessary (obsolete)	
29		s 1089(2)
30	Rep by FA 1997 s 146(2) and Sch 9 Pt II	
31		s 373(2)(b)
32		s 376
33	Rep by FA 1978 s 52(1) and Sch 4 Pt I	
34		s 905
Pt VI		
s 81 (1), (3)(a)	Unnecessary (application of schedule)	
82	Unnecessary (care and management)	
83 (2), (6)	Unnecessary (construction and commencement)	
Sch 1, Pt I	Amendment of ITA 1967 ss 138, 141(1A)	ss 458, 465
Sch 5, Pt I	Repeal of ITA 1967 s 125(a) and Sch 2 Rules 5, 6, 7	
	Amendment of ITA 1967 ss 157(c), 557	s 853
Finance Act 1977 (1977 No 18)		
s 1	Amendment of ITA 1967 s 142	s 466
2 (1)	Amendment of ITA 1967 s 236	s 787
(2)	Unnecessary (application of schedule)	
3	Amendment of FA 1974 s 59(3)	s 808
4	Amendment of ITA 1967 s 477(1), (2) and FA 1976 s 6(2)(b)	ss 960, 1082
5 (1)	Unnecessary (obsolete)	
(2)	Unnecessary (application of schedule)	
6 (1), (2)	Unnecessary (obsolete)	
(3)	Unnecessary (application of schedule)	
7	Rep by FA 1980 s 2	
8	Substitution of FA 1974 s 54	
9	Amendment of FA 1974 s 15(3)	s 655(1), (2)
10	Amendment of FA 1974 s 16(1)	s 657(1)
11	Substitution of FA 1974 s 19	
12 (a)	Amendment of FA 1974 s 21	
(b)	Insertion of FA 1974 s 21	
13	Unnecessary (obsolete)	
14		Sch 32, para 23(2)
15	Ceased by FA 1982 s 26(1)	
16 (1), (2)	Amendment of CTA 1976 ss 13, 37	s 78
(3)	Ceased by FA 1982 s 31(2)	
17	Amendment of FA 1982 s 28	
18	Ceased by FA 1982 s 26(1)	
19 (1), (2)	Unnecessary (spent)	
(3)	Rep by FA 1982 s 26(2) and Sch 2	
20-32	Unnecessary (obsolete)	
33	Amendment of CGTA 1975 s 3(3)	s 28
34	Amendment of CGTA 1975 s 31	s 731(1)-(5)(a), Sch 32 para 25
35	Substitution of CGTA 1975 s 32	s 732
36		s 6
37	Unnecessary (spent)	
38	Amendment of FA 1973 s 8(1)	

Former Enactment		*Destination in TCA 1997*
Finance Act 1977 (1977 No 18) (contd)		
s 39 (1)-(5)	Definition of "the former Agreements" unnecessary (obsolete)	s 832
(2)	Unnecessary (spent)	
(4)(b) proviso	Rep by FA 1996 s 132(2) and Sch 5 Pt II	
40	Unnecessary (spent)	
41 (1)	Amendment of CTA 1976 s 171	s 2(4)
(2)	Unnecessary (operative date)	
42	Unnecessary (application of schedule)	
43	Unnecessary (application of schedule)	
53		s 825
54 (1)	Unnecessary (application of schedule)	
55	Unnecessary (care and management)	
56 (2), (7)	Unnecessary (construction and commencement)	
Sch 1, Pt I	Amendment of ITA 1967 Sch 5	
Sch 1, Pt II	Amendment of ITA 1967 ss 1(1), 153(1), 497, 525(1), CTA 1976 ss 66(3)(b), 82(6)	ss 2(1), 3(1); 1032; 460; 127(1)-(5); 143
Sch 1, Pt III	Amendment of ITA 1967 s 138(1), (2)	s 461
Sch 1, Pt IV	Amendment of CTA 1976 ss 58(10), 109(1), 176(6)(a), Sch 5 para 1(6), FA 1968 s 37(4), FA 1972 s16(4), FA 1973 ss 24(9), 26, FA 1974 s 55(4)	s 413; 109(2)-(6); 774(6); Sch 32 para 26; 373(2)(a), 375; 814
Sch 1, Pt V	Amendment of FA 1975 ss 31, 31A, Sch 3, Sch 5, and FA 1976 s 12	
Sch 2, Pt I	Repeal of ITA 1967 ss 355, 357, 369(2), Sch 6 Pts I, II, and III, paras 2, 3, 4, 5, Sch 7, FA 1973 ss 32, 38, and Sch 2, 4, CGTA 1975 s 4(2) proviso, CTA 1976 s 42(6), (7), SI No 143 of 1975 Amendment of FA 1968s 35(2)	
Pt II	Repeal of s 356	
Finance Act 1978 (1978 No 21)		
s 1	Amendment of ITA 1967 s 142	s 466
2	Substitution of ITA 1967 s 143(3)	
3	Amendment of ITA 1967 s 193	s 1016
4 (1)	Amendment of ITA 1967 s 236	s 787
(2)	Unnecessary (application of schedule)	
5	Unnecessary (cesser of FA 1976 s 23)	
6	Unnecessary (obsolete)	
7	Substitution of FA 1973 s 19	s 192
8		s 250
9	Rep by FA 1996 s 132(2) and Sch 5 Pt II	
10 (1)-(6)	Unnecessary (obsolete)	
(7)	Amendment of ITA 1967 s 193(2)	s 1016
11 (1)	Substitution of ITA 1967 s 211(2)	s 1048
(2)	Substitution of ITA 1967 s 504(2)	s 1060
12 (1)	Amendment of FA 1974 s 13	s 654
(2)	Insertion of FA 1974 Sch 3	
13	Amendment of FA 1974 s 15	s 655(1), (2)
14	Amendment of FA 1974 Pt I Ch II	
15 (1), (2)		s 661
(3)	Unnecessary (duplication)	
16 (1)	Amendment of ITA 1967 s 477	s 960
(2)	Unnecessary (obsolete)	
17	Unnecessary (spent)	
18	Unnecessary (obsolete)	
19	Substitution of ITA 1967 s 30	
20	Amendment of FA 1977 Pt I Ch IV	
21	Amendment of CTA 1976 s 28	
22	Amendment of FA 1971 s 26(1)	s 285(1), (2), (3)

Former Enactment			*Destination in TCA 1997*
Finance Act 1978 (1978 No 21) (contd)			
s 23		Amendment of FA 1973 s 8(1)	
24		Amendment of FA 1977 s 40(1)	
25	(1)		s 273(1)
	(2)		s 273(2)
	(2A)		s 273(3)
	(3)		s 273(8)
26			s 310
27	(1)	Amendment of FA 1975 s 31A	
	(2)	Amendment of FA 1976 s 12	
28	(1)	Unnecessary (obsolete)	
	(2)	Unnecessary (obsolete)	
	(3)	Amendment of CTA 1976 s 45	s 729(1)-(6)
	(4)	Amendment of CTA 1976 s 64(3)(c)(ii)	s 145(1), (2)(a), (3)-(10)
	(5)	Amendment of CTA 1976 s 79(6)	
	(6)	Amendment of CTA 1976 s 178(1)	
	(7)	Unnecessary (spent)	
46		Amendment of ITA 1967 ss 129, 550, FA 1970 s 17(6A), FA 1971 s 20(2) , CTA 1976 ss 145, 152	ss 991(1); 1080(1); 531(5)(6)(8)(9); 1082; 973, 974, 1080, 1082; 240
47			s 1092
s 52	(1)	Unnecessary (application of schedule)	
53		Unnecessary (care and management)	
54	(2), (8)	Unnecessary (construction and commencement)	
Sch 1			
Pt I		Amendment of ITA 1967 Sch 5	
Pt II		Amendment of ITA 1967 s 138	ss 461, s 464 and FA 1974 s 8
Pt III		Rep by FA 1996 s 132(2) and Sch 5 Pt II	
Pt IV		Insertion of FA 1974 Sch 3	
Sch 2		Unnecessary (obsolete)	
Sch 4		Repeal of ITA 1967 s 220 (in so far as it is unrep) and FA 1976 s 33	
Capital Gains Tax (Amendment) Act 1978 (1978 No 33)			
s 1	(1)		s 1(2)
	(2)	Unnecessary (interpretation)	
	(3)-(5)	Unnecessary (construction)	
2		Substitution of CGTA 1975 s 3(3)	s 28
3	(1)-(7)		s 556(1)-(7)
4		Ceased by FA 1982 s 30(2)	
5			s 605
6	(1)	Substitution of CGTA 1975 s 14(1)	s 573
	(2)	Unnecessary (operative date)	
7	(1)	Substitution of CGTA 1975 s 15(4)(b)	s 577
	(2)	Unnecessary (operative date)	
8		Substitution of CGTA 1975 s 27	s 599
9		Insertion of CGTA 1975 s 28(2A)	s 597
10		Substitution of CGTA 1975 s 39(1)	s 611
11		Amendment of CTA 1976 ss 13, 37	s 78
12		Amendment of CTA 1976 s 90	
13		Amendment of CTA 1976 s 127(1)	s 615
14		Amendment of CTA 1976 s 132(2)	s 619
15		Amendment of CGTA 1975 Sch 4	ss 29(8)(9), 544(7), 567 (3)(4), 568, 849(1)(2), 849 (3)-(6), 851, 861(1), 863-865, 869-871, 874, 875, 911, 913-917, 931, 945, 946, 949, 976, 977, 978, 980, 982, 999,

Former Enactment		Destination in TCA 1997
Capital Gains Tax (Amendment) Act 1978 (1978 No 33) (contd)		
s 15 (contd)		Sch 1, 1029, 1043, 1051, 1077(1), 1077(2), 1083
16	Unnecessary (application of schedule)	
17	Unnecessary (application of schedule)	
18	Unnecessary (short title, construction and commencement)	
Sch 1		
para 1		s 556(8), (9)
2	Unnecessary (obsolete)	
3	The matter from "and section 4" to the end is unnecessary (obsolete)	s 582
4		s 580
5	Substitution of CGTA 1975 Sch 2 para 2(3)	s 584
6	Unnecessary (obsolete)	
7		s 546(6)
8		s 601(3)
9	Substitution of CGTA 1975 s 32(3)	s 732
10		s 558
Sch 2	Repeal of CGTA 1975 ss 6, 26(7), 29(4), 47(7), Sch 1 Pt I para 13, 14(6) and PtII, Sch 2 para 2(8), Sch 4 para 8(2)(j), CTA 1976 s 13(3)(b)	
	Amendment of CGTA 1975 ss 11(1), (2),16(4), 51(2), Sch 4 para 13, FA 1977 s 16(3)	ss 545(2)(3), 601(1)(2)(4)(5) 544(8), 544(7)
Finance Act 1979 (1979 No 11)		
s 1	Substitution of ITA 1967 s 142(1A)	s 466
2 (1)	Amendment of FA 1977 s 5	
(2)	Unnecessary (application of schedule)	
3 (1), (2)	Unnecessary (obsolete)	
(3)	Unnecessary (application of schedule)	
4	Insertion of ITA 1967 s 138A	s 462
5	Rep by FA 1996 s 132(2) and Sch 5 Pt II	
6	Unnecessary (cesser of ITA 1967 s 224(3), (5), (6), otherwise obsolete)	
7	Unnecessary (spent)	
8 (1		ss 125(1), 471(1)
(2)(a)		s 471(2)
(b)	Rep by FA 1996 s 132(2) and Sch 5 Pt II	
(3)		s 471(3)
(4)		s 125(3)
(4A)		s 125(4)
(5)	Unnecessary (operative date)	
(6)		s 125(2)
9	Amendment of ITA 1967 s 496(2)(b), FA 1974 ss 38(1), 44, 52(b), FA 1978 s 8(2)	s 250
10	Rep by FA 1982 s 8(8)	
11	Rep by FA 1980 s 16	
12	Amendment of ITA 1967 s 488(5)	s 966
13	Amendment of FA 1974 ss 15, 19	s 655(1), (2)
14	Unnecessary (spent)	
15	Amendment of FA 1974 s 20	
16	Amendment of FA 1974 s 21(1)	
17	Amendment of ITA 1967 s 307	s 381(1)
18	Amendment of ITA 1967 s 308	

Former Enactment		Destination in TCA 1997
Finance Act 1979 (1979 No 11) (contd)		
s 19	Substitution of ITA 1967 s 318(1)	s 392
20	Substitution of ITA 1967 s 319(1)	s 393
21	Amendment of CTA 1976 ss 10(6), 169, FA 1978 s 18(5) proviso	s 243(1), (2), (4)-(9)
22	Insertion of FA 1977 s 25A	
23	Amendment of FA 1975 s 31A and FA 1976 s 12	
24	Amendment of FA 1971 s 22	
25	Amendment of FA 1978 s 25(1)	s 273(1)
26	Unnecessary (obsolete)	
27	Substitution of FA 1976 s 25	
28 (1)-(3)		s 786
(4)	Amendment of ITA 1967 s 239(8)	s 788
(5)	Amendment of CTA 1976 s 50(4)(a)	s 706(1)-(3)
29	Amendment of ITA 1967 s 517 and CTA 1976 s 148	s 1064
30	Insertion of ITA 1967 s 70(3A), (3B)	ss 880(2)-(6), 900(3)
31	s 902	
32 (1)	Unnecessary (repeal of ITA 1967 s 144)	
(2)	Unnecessary (declaratory)	
(3)	Unnecessary (obsolete)	
33	Insertion of ITA 1967 s 439(1A)	s 791(2)-(4)
34	Amendment of ITA 1967 Sch 12	Sch 22
35	Insertion of CGTA 1975 s 25(9A)	s 604
36	Amendment of CGTA 1975 s 27(1) s 599	
37 (1)	Unnecessary (CGTA 1975 cesser of s 31(4))	
(2)	Amendment of CGTA 1975 s 31(5)	
58	Unnecessary (care and management)	
59 (2), (6)	Unnecessary (construction and commencement)	
Sch 1		
Pt 1	Amendment of ITA 1967 ss 1(1), 153(1)(dd), 497, 525(1)	ss 2(1), 3(1), 1032, 460, 127(1)-(5)
Pt II	Amendment of ITA 1967 s 138, FA 1974 s 8	ss 461, 464
Sch 2	Unnecessary (obsolete)	
Finance Act 1980 (1980 No 14)		
Pt I		
s 1		s 187
2(1)-(4),(6),(7)		s 188
(5)	Unnecessary (cesser of FA 1977 s 7)	
s 3	Substitution of ITA 1967 ss 138, 138A Insertion of ITA 1967 138B	ss 461, 462, 472
4 (1), (2)	Unnecessary (obsolete)	
(3)	Unnecessary (application of schedule)	
5	Amendment of FA 1971 s 11	s 468
6	Amendment of ITA 1967 ss 143, 152(1)	
7	Rep by FA 1997 s 146(2) and Sch 9 Pt II	
8	Unnecessary (obsolete)	
9	Amendment of ITA 1967 s 3	s 1(2)
10	Amendment of ITA 1967 s 115 and Sch 3	s 201, Sch 3
11	Amendment of ITA 1967 s 336	s 213(1), (2)
12	Amendment of ITA 1967 s 340(2)	s 204(1)
13	Substitution of ITA 1967 s 344(1), (2)	
14	Amendment of ITA 1967 s 447 and FA 1971 s 20(2)	ss 794(1), 1082
15	Amendment of FA 1979 s 7(1) and Sch 2	
16	Unnecessary (FA 1979 cesser of s 11)	

Former Enactment		*Destination in TCA 1997*
Finance Act 1980 (1980 No 14) (contd)		
s 17	Amendment of ITA 1967 ss 58, 72, 77, 241, 244, 245, 296	ss 65(1); 1010; 70(2); 284, 300(1); 763-735; 670; 305(1)
18	Substitution of ITA 1967 Pt IX Ch I	
19	Unnecessary (application of schedule)	
20	Unnecessary (obsolete)	
21	Unnecessary (obsolete)	
22	Amendment of FA 1974 ss 15, 19	s 655(1), (2)
23	Unnecessary (obsolete)	
24	Unnecessary (FA 1974 cesser of ss 20, 21)	
25	Rep by FA 1983 s 120 and Sch 4	
26	Ceased by FA 1988 s 52(3)	
27	Substitution of FA 1974 s 22(2)	s 658(2)(a)
28	Rep by FA 1996 s 132(2) and Sch 5 Pt II	
37	Amendment of FA 1977 Pt I Ch I	
38		s 442(1)
39		s 443
39A(1)-(7)(10)	Definition of "EEC Treaty" unnecessary (obsolete)	s 445
(2) proviso	Deleted by FA 1988 s 35	
(8), (9)	Deleted by FA 1989 s 23	
39B(1)-(7)(a), (b),(8)-(10)		s 446(1)-(12)
(7)(c)	Rep by FA 1988 s 36(1)	
39C		s 449
39D		s 450
40		s 442(2)
41 (1)		s 448(1)
(2)		s 448(2)(a)
(3)-(5)(8)(9)		s 448(3)-(7)
(6), (7)	Unnecessary (obsolete)	
42 (1)-(4)	Unnecessary (obsolete)	
(5)	Substitution of CTA 1976 s 58(10)	
(6)	Amendment of CTA 1976 s 64	s 145(1), (2)(a), (3)-(10)
43	Unnecessary (obsolete)	
44		s 453
45 (1)-(3), (5)-(8)		s 147, Sch 32 para 4
(1A) 1st proviso para (a)	Unnecessary (obsolete)	
(4)	Unnecessary (obsolete)	
46		s 148
47 (1)	Amendment of CTA 1976 s 182	Sch 32, para 16(1)-(4)
(2)		Sch 32, para 5(2)
48 (1)	Amendment of CTA 1976 s 184	Sch 32, para 18
(2)		Sch 32, para 6(2)
49		s 149
50		s 444
51		ss 151, 447
52	Amendment of FA 1977 s 40(1)	
53 (1)	Amendment of FA 1975 s 31A	
(2)	Amendment of FA 1976 s 12	
(3)-(6)	Unnecessary (obsolete)	
54	Amendment of ITA 1967 ss 416(5), 421	ss 933(1)-(7)(f), 934
55	Substitution of ITA 1967 s 4	s 12
56	Amendment of FA 1973 s 24	

Former Enactment		*Destination in TCA 1997*
Finance Act 1980 (1980 No 14) (contd)		
s 57	Amendment of ITA 1967 ss 448(5), 500	ss 798(1)-(3), 1052
58	Amendment of ITA 1967 s 265(4)	s 274(1), (3), (4), (5), (8)
59	Substitution of ITA 1967 s 516	s 1056
60	Substitution of FA 1976 s 34(2)	s 905
61	Amendment of CGTA 1975 ss 2(3), 13(4), 25(9A)(b), Sch 4 para 10(2)	ss 5, 1028, 604, 1029
62	Amendment of CGTA 1975 ss 7(1), 46	ss 532(1), 541
Pt VI		
89	Substitution of FA 1978 s 47(1)	s 1092
95	Unnecessary (care and management)	
96 (2), (7)	Unnecessary (construction and commencement)	
Sch 1		
Pt I	Amendment of ITA 1967 s 141(1A), FA 1969 s 3	ss 465, 467
Pt II	Substitution of ITA 1967 Sch 3	s 201(1)(a), Sch 3
Pt III	Amendment of ITA 1967 ss 82(3), 139, 145(2), 183(7), 307(2)(a)(i), Sch 15, FA 1967 s 12, FA 1969 s 3(1)(a), FA 1974 ss 8(1), 28(6), FA 1976 s 11(3) Repeal of FA 1969 ss 3(6), (8), FA 1978 s 3, FA 1979 s 7(2)(b)	ss 470(1)-(3), 921(1) 381(2)-(7), Sch 29, 469(1), 467, 464, 881
Finance Act 1981 (1981 No 16)		
1	Amendment of FA 1980 ss 1, 2	ss 187, 188
2 (1), (2)	Unnecessary (obsolete)	
(3)	Unnecessary (application of Schedule)	
3	Amendment of FA 1980 s 8	
4	Amendment of ITA 1967 s 128	s 987(1)-(3)
5	Amendment of ITA 1967 s 198(1)	s 1024
6	Rep by FA 1997 s 146(2) and Sch 9 Pt II	
7	Amendment of FA 1970 s 17(2)	s 531(1), (3), (4)
8 (a)	Amendment of FA 1979 s 7	
(b)	Amendment of FA 1979 Sch 2	
9	Amendment of ITA 1967 ss 81(3),111(1)(b), 553(2), FA 1970 s 23(2), F(TPCM)A 1974 s 11(1), (2)	ss 75(3); 111, 90(1)-(3), 683
10	Insertion of FA 1974 s 20B	s 683
11	Insertion of ITA 1967 s 334(2A)	s 208(3)
12	Amendment of ITA 1967 s 477(2)	
13	Rep by FA 1996 s 132(2) and Sch 5 Pt II	
15 (1)	Amendment of CTA 1976 s 6(4)	
(2), (3)	Unnecessary (obsolete)	
16	Substitution of CTA 1976 s 143(1), (2)	s 884
17 (a)	Insertion of FA 1980 s 39(1A)-(1D)	s 443
(b)	Insertion of FA 1980 s 39A	s 445
18	Rep by FA 1997 s 146(2) and Sch 9 Pt II	
19	Amendment of FA 1973 s 34(3)	s 234(3)-(8)
20 (1)	Amendment of FA 1975 s 31A	
(2)	Amendment of FA 1976 s 12	
(3), (5), (6)	Unnecessary (obsolete). There is no s 20(4)	
21	Unnecessary (obsolete)	
22	Insertion of CTA 1976 s 152(4)	s 240
23 (1)(a)		ss 325(1), 326(1), 327(1), 329(1), (2)
(b)		s 329(7)
(c)		s 329(9)(a)
(1)(d)	Unnecessary (obsolete)	

Former Enactment		*Destination in TCA 1997*
Finance Act 1981 (1981 No 16) (contd)		
s 23 (2)		ss 325(2), 326(4), 327(2)
proviso		ss 325(3), 326(5), 327(3)
(3)(a)		ss 325(4), 326(6), 327(4)
(b), (c)		s 329(8)
(4)		s 329(6)
(5)		ss 325(5), 326(7), 327(5)
(6)(a)		ss 325(6)(a), 326(8), 327(7)
(b)		s 325(6)(b)
(7)(a)		ss 325(7)(a), 326(9), 327(7)
(b)		s 325(7)(b)
(8)		s 329(3)
(9)(a)		s 329(4)(a)
(b)		s 329(5)
(10)		s 329(11)
(11)		s 329(12)
23	Sch 32, para 14 . . Sch 32, para 14 of the Bill saves the provisions of s 23 FA 1981 (in so far as that section applied to areas other than the Custom House Docks Area)	
24 (1)		s 326(1)
(2)(a)		s 326(1)
(b)		s 326(1)
(c)	Unnecessary (obsolete)	
(d)	Unnecessary (obsolete)	
s 24 (2) (e)		s 326(8), (9)
(f)		s 326(9)
(g)		s 329(4)(b)
(3)		s 326(10)
24	Sch 32, para 14. . Sch 32, para 14 of the Bill saves the provision of FA 1981 s 24 (in so far as that section applied to areas other than the Custom House Docks Area)	
25		Sch 32, para 9
26		Sch 32, para 10
27	Amendment of ITA 1967 s 254(1)	s 271
28	Substitution of F(MP)A 1968 s 17(1)	s 640
29 (1)	Unnecessary (declaratory)	
(2)(a)	Substitution of F(MP)A 1968 s 18	s 641
(b)	Unnecessary (obsolete)	
(3)	Substitution of F(MP)A 1968 ss 20, 21, 22	ss 643-645
(4)	Amendment of ITA 1967 Sch 15	Sch 29
52		s 1093
53	Unnecessary (care and management)	
54 (2), (7)	Unnecessary (construction and commencement)	
Sch 1	Amendment of ITA 1967 ss 138A, 138B(1), 141(1A), FA 1969 s 3(1), FA 1971 s 11(2)	ss 462, 472, 465, 467, 468
Finance Act 1982 (1982 No 14)		
s 1	Amendment of FA 1980 ss 1(2), 2(6)	ss 187, 188
2 (1), (2)	Unnecessary (obsolete)	
(3)	Unnecessary (application of schedule)	
3	Amendment of FA 1980 s 8	
4 (1)	Unnecessary (commencement)	

Former Enactment		*Destination in TCA 1997*
Finance Act 1982 (1982 No 14) (contd)		
s 4 (2)-(6), (9)		s 121
(7)	Amendment of ITA 1967 s 178(1)	s 897(1)-(5)
(8)	Amendment of ITA 1967 Sch 15	Sch 29
5 (1)	Insertion of ITA 1967 s 142A	s 473
(2)	Amendment of ITA 1967 s 198(1)(a)	s 1024, Sch 29 and Sch 15
6	Rep by FA 1996 s 132(2) and Sch 5 Pt II	
7	Insertion of ITA 1967 s 152(1A)	
8 (1)-(5), (7), (9)		s 122
(6)	Amendment of ITA 1967 s 178(1)	s 897(1)-(5)
(8)	Unnecessary (cesser of FA 1979 s 10)	
9 (1), (2)		s 205
(3)	Unnecessary (commencement)	
10	Amendment of ITA 1967 s 485(5)	s 962(3)
11	Amendment of ITA 1967 s 486	s 963
12	Amendment of FA 1979 s 7(1) and Sch 2	
13	Rep by FA 1996 s 132(2) and Sch 5 Pt II	
14	Amendment of ITA 1967 s 477(2)	s 960
15	Amendment of FA 1974 s 21A(1)	
16	Amendment of FA 1974 s 22	s 658(1)
18		s 225
19 (1)-(2A),		s 482(1)-(4),
(3)-(4A)(5)		(5), (6), (7)
(6)		s 482(10)
20 (1)-(6), (8)		s 840
(7)	Unnecessary (cesser of FA 1973 s 24)	
21	Rep by FA 1997 s 146(2) and Sch 9 Pt II	
22	Rep by FA 1997 s 146(2) and Sch 9 Pt II	
23	Unnecessary (obsolete)	
24 (1)	Amendment of FA 1975 s 31A	
(2)	Amendment of FA 1976 s 12	
25	Unnecessary (obsolete)	
26 (1)(a)	Unnecessary (cesser of FA 1977 ss 15, 17(1)(a), 18)	
(b)	Unnecessary (obsolete)	
(2)	Unnecessary (application of schedule)	
27 (1)	Amendment of CTA 1976 s 6(4)	
(2)	Unnecessary (obsolete)	
(3)	Unnecessary (obsolete)	
(4)	Amendment of ITA 1967 s 550	s 1080(1)
28	Unnecessary (spent)	
29	Unnecessary (interpretation)	
30 (1)	Amendment of CGTA 1975 s 3	s 28
(2)	Unnecessary (cesser of CGT(A)A 1978 s 4)	
(3)	Unnecessary (obsolete)	
31 (1)	Amendment of CTA 1976 s 13	s 78
(2)	Unnecessary (cesser of FA 1977 s 16(3))	
32	Amendment of CGTA 1975 ss 13(4), 16 and CGT(A)A 1978 Sch 1	ss 546(6), 556(8)(9), 558, 580, 582, 584, 601, 732, 1028,
33	Insertion of CGTA 1975 s 5(3)	s 1042
34 (1)	Substitution of CGTA 1975 Sch 4 para 11(5)	s 980
(2), (3)	Unnecessary (obsolete)	
35	Amendment of CTA 1976 s 90(4)	
36 (1)		s 648
(2)-(3A)	Deleted by FA 1992 s 60(2)	
(4)-(6)		s 649
(7)	Deleted by FA 1992 s 68(b)	
37		s 650

Former Enactment		*Destination in TCA 1997*
Finance Act 1982 (1982 No 14) (contd)		
s 38		s 651
39		s 652
40 (1), (2)		s 653
(3)	Insertion of CTA 1976 s 25(8)	
(a)		s 607(1)(e)
(b)	Ceased by FA 1992 s 24(2)	
42 (a)	Substitution of CTA 1976 s 36(3)(a)	s 713(1)-(6)
(b)	Deletion of CTA 1976 s 37	
43	Unnecessary (spent)	
44	Unnecessary (spent)	
45	Unnecessary (spent)	
46	Unnecessary (spent)	
47	Unnecessary (spent)	
48	Unnecessary (spent)	
49	Unnecessary (spent)	
50	Definition of "ordinary share capital" unnecessary (duplication)	s 509
51 (1)-(7)		s 510
(8)	Amendment of ITA 1967 Sch 15	Sch 29
52		s 511
53		s 512
54		s 513
55		s 514
56		s 515
57		s 516
58		s 517
58A	(s 58A inserted by FA 1997 s 50)	s 518
59		s 1082
60	Amendment of ITA 1967 ss 128, 173(6), 426(3), 500, FA 1968 s 6(5), CTA 1976 s 64(9), FA 1976 s 34(4), FA 1979 s 31(5), FA 1980 s 45(8)	ss 987(1)-(3), 889(10) 939, 1052, 886, s 145(1), (2)(a), (3)-(10), 905, 902, s 147, Sch 32 para 4
61	Amendment of ITA 1967 s 371	s 752
62	Insertion of CGTA 1975 s 9(3), (4)	s 547
63		ss 586(3), 587(4)
104	Unnecessary (care and management)	
105(2), (7)	Unnecessary (construction and commencement)	
Sch 1	Amendment of ITA 1967 ss 138, 138A, 141(1A), 142(1), FA 1969 s 3(1), FA 1971 s 11(2), FA 1974 s 8(1). Cesser of ITA 1967 ss 139, 140	ss 461, 462, 464-468
Sch 2, Pt I		
para 1	Unnecessary (cesser of FA 1977 s 19(3))	
2, 3	Unnecessary (spent)	
Sch 2, Pt II		
para 1	Amendment of FA 1980 s 41(2)	s 448(2)(a)
2	Unnecessary (spent)	
3	Amendment of FA 1980 ss 47(2), 48(2)	Sch 32, paras 5(2), 6(2)
4	Unnecessary (spent)	
Sch 3		Sch 11
Finance Act 1983 (1983 No 15)		
Pt I		
s 1	Amendment of FA 1980 s 1(2)	s 187
2	Amendment of FA 1980 s 8	
3		s 1025

Former Enactment		*Destination in TCA 1997*
Finance Act 1983 (1983 No 15) (contd)		
s 4		s 1026(1), (2)
5	Amendment of FA 1982 s 6	
6	Insertion of ITA 1967 s 195A	s 1020
7	Unnecessary (cesser of ITA 1967 Pt XX)	
8	Amendment of ITA 1967 s 344	
9	Amendment of ITA 1967 ss 416, 421, 428, 429, 430, deletion of s 420	ss 933(1)-(7)(f), 934, 941, 942(1)-(8), (10), 943
10	Amendment of ITA 1967 s 496(2A)	
11	Substitution of FA 1974 s 15	s 655(1), (2)
12	Amendment of FA 1974 s 20A	
13	Amendment of FA 1982 s 13(1)	
14	Substitution of ITA 1967 s 307(1A)	
15	Amendment of FA 1974 s 22	s 658
16	Unnecessary (spent)	
17 Preamble	Unnecessary (declaratory).	
(1)	Unnecessary (cesser of FA 1968 s 13)	
(2)	Amendment of ITA 1967 s 175	s 891
18		s 908
19 (1), (2)		s 58
(3)	Unnecessary (duplication)	
(4)	Unnecessary (operative date)	
19A	(s 19A inserted by DCITPA 1996 s 12)	s 859
20		s 909
21 (1), (2)		s 892
(3)	Amendment of ITA 1967 Sch 15	Sch 29
22 (1), (2)		s 885
(3)	Amendment of ITA 1967 Sch 15	Sch 29
23		s 1086
24	Amendment of FA 1982 s 58(1)	s 517
25	Substitution of FA 1982 ss 21(3), 23(3)	
26 (1)	Amendment of FA 1975 s 31A	
(2)	Amendment of FA 1976 s 12	
(3), (4)	Unnecessary (obsolete)	
27	Unnecessary (spent)	
28 (1)	Unnecessary (cesser of FA 1978 s 28(1))	
(2)	Unnecessary (obsolete)	
(3)	Unnecessary (obsolete)	
29	Unnecessary (spent)	
30	Unnecessary (spent)	
31	Amendment of FA 1982 ss 43, 44, 45, 46	
32		s 220
33	Amendment of CTA 1976 s 56(1)	
34	Amendment of FA 1978 Sch 2	
35	Insertion of CTA 1976 s 98(9)	s 438
36	Substitution of CTA 1976 s 143(7)	s 1071
37	Substitution of CTA 1976 s 146(1)	s 864, Pt 40 Ch I, s 949
38		s 159
39		s 160
40		s 161
41		s 162
42 (1)		s 163
(2)	Unnecessary (obsolete)	
43		s 164
44		s 165
45		s 166

Former Enactment		*Destination in TCA 1997*
Finance Act 1983 (1983 No 15) (contd)		
s 46 (1)-(8)		s 167
(9)	Unnecessary (spent)	
47 (1)-(3)		s 168
(4)	Amendment of ITA 1967 s 361(1)	s 826(1)-(7)
47A	(s 47A inserted by FA 1995 s 37)	s 169
48 (1),(2)(a), (3)(4)		s 170
(2)(b)	Unnecessary (spent)	
49	Unnecessary (spent)	
50 (1)-(10), (11)(a)-(d) (12), (13)		s 171
(11)(e)	Rep by FA 1997 s 146(2) and Sch 9 Pt II	
51	Unnecessary (cesser of CTA 1976 ss 16(9), 18(4), 25(8), 26(3) proviso para (b), 90, 91, 167, 168)	
52	Unnecessary (spent)	
53		s 172
54	Rep by FA 1988 s 70(2)	
55	Amendment of CGTA 1975 Sch 4 para 8	s 945
56 (1)	Unnecessary (operative date)	
(2)-(10)		s 571
Pt V		
s 94		s 1078
Pt VII		
s 120	Unnecessary (application of schedule)	
121	Unnecessary (care and management).	
122(2), (6)	Unnecessary (construction and commencement)	
Sch 4	Repeal of ITA 1967 s 340(2)(d)(ff)(g), (3), FA 1974 ss 13(2)(3), 17, 18, 19, 21A, 28, Sch 3, FA 1976 s 19, FA 1980 s 25	
	Amendment of FA 1974 ss 13(1), 20B(3)(b), FA 1978 s 15(2)	ss 654, 657(6), 661
Finance Act 1984 (1984 No 9)		
s 1	Amendment of FA 1980 ss 1(2), 2(6)	ss 187, 188
2	Unnecessary (obsolete)	
3 (1), (2)	Unnecessary (obsolete)	
(3)	Unnecessary (application of schedule)	
4	Amendment of FA 1982 s 6(2)	
5	Amendment of ITA 1967 s 142A(2)(a)(i)	s 473
6	Amendment of ITA 1967 s 432(1)	ss 864(1), 949(1)
7	Unnecessary (cesser of FA 1968 s 41(9))	
8	Amendment of FA 1969 s 3(1)	s 467
9	Substitution of ITA 1967 s 349	s 235
10	Amendment of FA 1983 s 16	
11(1)(3)(4)		s 488(1)-(3)
(2)	Unnecessary (obsolete)	
12 (1)		s 489(1)
1st proviso	Deleted by FA 1991 s 15(1)(a)	
2nd proviso		s 489(2)
(2), (7)		s 488(1)
(3)		s 489(3), (6)
1st proviso		s 489(4)
2nd proviso		s 489(5)

Former Enactment		*Destination in TCA 1997*
Finance Act 1984 (1984 No 9) (contd)		
s 12 (4)		s 489(7)
(5)		s 489(8)
(6)		s 489(9)
(6A)		s 489(10)
(8)		s 489(11)
(9)	Rep by FA 1996 s 132(2) and Sch 5 Pt II	
(10)		s 489(12)
(10A)		s 489(13)
(11)		s 489(15)
proviso	Deleted by FA 1996 s 17(c)(ii)	
13 (1)-(2C)		s 490
(2) proviso	Deleted by s 25(c)(i) FA 1993	
(3)	Amendment of ITA 1967 s 198(1)	s 1024
13A	(s 13A inserted by FA 1989 s 9)	s 491
13B	(s 13B inserted by FA 1996 s 20)	s 492
14		s 493
14A	(s 14A inserted by FA 1995 s 17(1)(d))	s 494
15 (1)-(12)		s 495
(13)	Deleted by FA 1991 s 15(d)	
16 (1)-(3)		s 496
(2)(a)(iii)	Deleted by FA 1991 s 15(e)(i)	
(4)		s 488(4)
16A	(s 16A inserted by FA 1995 s17(1)(g))	s 497
17		s 498
18		s 499
19		s 500
20		s 501
21		s 502
22		s 503
23		s 504
24 (1)-(8)		s 505
(9)	Amendment of ITA 1967 Sch 15	Sch 29
25		s 506
26 (1)-(4)		s 507
(1A)	Deleted by FA 1991 s 15(1)(f)	
27		s 508
28 (1)		ss 45(2), 48(3)
(2)		ss 45(3), 48(4)
(3)		ss 45(4), 48(5)
29 (1)	Definition of "tax" unnecessary (duplication)	s 815(1)
(2)		s 815(2)
(2A)		s 815(3)
(3)(a)		s 815(4)
(b)	Unnecessary (obsolete)	
(4), (5)		s 815(5), (6)
29 (6)	Amendment of ITA 1967 Sch 15	Sch 29
(7)	Unnecessary (operative date)	
30	Amendment of FA 1976 s 30	
31	Amendment of FA 1982 ss 56(1), (2), 58(1) and Sch 3	ss 515, 517, Sch 11
32		s 484
33	Rep by FA 1996 s 132(2) and Sch 5 Pt II	

Former Enactment		*Destination in TCA 1997*
Finance Act 1984 (1984 No 9) (contd)		
s 34	Unnecessary (spent)	
35	Amendment of ITA 1967 ss 251(4)(d), 254(2A)(a), 264(1) proviso para (ii), (3) proviso para (ii), 265(1) proviso para (ii)	ss 271(4), 272, 274(1)(3)-(5),(8)
36		s 268(1)(a)(ii), (9)(a)
37	Amendment of FA 1981 s 23	ss 325, 326, 327, 329 Sch 32, para 14
38	Amendment of FA 1981 s 25	Sch 32, para 9
39	Amendment of FA 1981 s 26(1)	Sch 32, para 10
40 (1)-(10)(a)		s 403
(10)(b)	Unnecessary (obsolete)	
(11)	Unnecessary (obsolete)	
41	Insertion of CTA 1976 s 84A	ss 134, 134(1)(4)
42 (1), (2), (3)		s 138
(4), (5)	Unnecessary (obsolete)	
43	Amendment of FA 1978 Sch 2 Pt I	
44	Amendment of FA 1982 ss 43, 44, 45, 46	
45 (a)	Amendment of FA 1980 s 38	s 442(1)
(b)	Amendment of FA 1980s 39	s 443
46	Amendment of FA 1983s 51(2)	
47	Amendment of FA 1983s 52	
48-65	Rep by FA 1996 s 132(2) and Sch 5 Pt II	
66 (a)		s 607
(b)	Ceased by FA 1988 s 70(2)(b)	
67	Insertion of CGTA 1975 s 25(10A)	s 604
Pt VI		
s 115	Unnecessary (care and management)	
116(2), (7)	Unnecessary (construction and commencement)	
Sch 1		
Pt I	Amendment of ITA 1967 ss 1(1), 153(1)(dd),497, 525(1)	ss 2(1), 3(1), 1032, 460 127(1)-(5)
Pt II	Amendment of ITA 1967 ss 138, 138A	ss 461, 462
Sch 2		Sch 10
Finance Act 1985 (1985 No 10)		
s 1	Amendment of FA 1980 ss 1(2), 2(6),	ss 187, 188
2	Amendment of FA 1984 s 2	
3 (1), (2)	Unnecessary (obsolete)	
(3)	Unnecessary (application of schedule)	
4	Substitution of ITA 1967 s 138A	s 462
5	Amendment of FA 1982 s 6	
6 (1)	Substitution of ITA 1967 s 125	s 984(1), (2)
(2)		s 984(3)
7	Amendment of ITA 1967 s 142A(2)	s 473
8	Amendment of ITA 1967 s 344	
9	Amendment of FA 1968 ss 7(5), 8	ss 989(4), (5), 990
10 (1)(a)		s 664(1)(a)
(b)	Unnecessary (obsolete)	
(2)-(6)		s 664(2)-(6)
11	Amendment of FA 1983 s 16	
12	Amendment of ITA 1967 s 550(4)	s 1080(2)-(4)
13	Amendment of FA 1984 ss 11(1), 12(4), 15(7)(b), 26, 27(8)	ss 488(1)-(3), 489(7) 495, 507, 508
14 (1)	Substitution of FA 1969 s 18(2)(b)	
(2)	Unnecessary (operative date)	
15	Substitution of FA 1973 s 21	s 767
16	Unnecessary (spent)	

Former Enactment		Destination in TCA 1997
Finance Act 1985 (1985 No 10) (contd)		
s 17 (1)	Amendment of FA 1975 s 31A	
(2)	Amendment of FA 1976 s 12	
(3)	Unnecessary (application)	
18	Amendment of FA 1984 ss 49, 51	
19	Unnecessary (spent)	
20	Amendment of ITA 1967 ss 251(4)(d), 254(2A)(a), 264(1) proviso para (ii), 264(3) proviso para (ii), 265(1) proviso para (iii)	ss 283(3), 271(4) 272, 274(1)(3)-(5)(8)
21	Sch 32, para 11. . Sch 32 para 14 of the Bill saves the provisions of FA 1985 s 21 (in so far as that section applied to areas other than the Custom House Docks Area)	
(1)(a)		s 327(1)(a)
(b)	Unnecessary (construction)	
(2)(a)(i)		s 327(1)
(ii)		s 327(3)(a)(ii)
(iii)	Unnecessary (spent)	
(iv)		s 327(1)
(v)	Unnecessary (obsolete)	
(vi)		s 327(1)
(vii)		s 329(9)(b)
(viii)		s 327(4)
(ix)		s 327(6), (7)
(x)		s 327(7)
(xi)		s 329(4)(b)
(xii)		s 329(12)
(b)	Unnecessary (obsolete)	
(3)		s 327(8)
(4)		s 327(9)
(5)		s 329(10)
22 (1)		ss 326(1), 329(1)
(2)		s 326(2)
(3)		s 326(3)
(4)	Unnecessary (spent)	
(5)		s 329(10)
22	Sch 32, para 11 . . Sch 32, para 14 of the Bill saves the provisions of FA 1985 s 22 (in so far as that section applied to areas other than the Custom House Docks Areas)	
23 (1)	Substitution of CTA 1976 s 6(4)	
(2)	Unnecessary (spent)	
24		s 218
25	Amendment of FA 1983 s 52	
Pt V		
s 60	Amendment of ITA 1967 s 143(5)	
Pt VI		
s 69		s 44
70	Unnecessary (care and management)	
71 (2), (7)	Unnecessary (construction and commencement)	

Former Enactment		*Destination in TCA 1997*
Finance Act 1985 (1985 No 10) (contd)		
Sch 1	Amendment of ITA 1967 ss 138, 141(1A),	ss 461, 465, 467, 468 FA 1969 s 3(1), FA 1971 s 11(2)
Finance Act 1986 (1986 No 13)		
s 1	Amendment of FA 1980 s 2(6)	s 188
2	Amendment of FA 1984 s 2	
3 (1), (2)	Unnecessary (obsolete)	
(3)	Unnecessary (application of schedule)	
4	Substitution of ITA 1967 s 141	s 465
5	Amendment of FA 1967 s 12(1)	s 469(1)
6	Amendment of FA 1982 s 6	
7	Insertion of FA 1979 s 8(6)	s 125(2)
8	Rep by FA 1997 s 146(2) and Sch 9 Pt II	
9 (1)(a), (b)(i), (iii)		s 128(1)
(b)(ii)	Unnecessary (obsolete)	
(2)-(11)(a)		s 128(2)-(11)
(11)(b)	Amendment of ITA 1967 Sch 15	Sch 29
10 (1), (2)(a)(b), (6)	Rep by FA 1992 s 12 for share options granted on or after 29.1.92. Section 10 still applies to share options granted before that date	Sch 32, para 7
(2)(c), (3)-(5)	Unnecessary (obsolete)	
11	Substitution of FA 1982 s 52(7), (8)	s 511
12 (1)-(8)	Definitions of "full-time director" and "full-time employee" deleted by FA 1996 s 12 and definition of "ordinary share capital" unnecessary (duplication)	s 479
(9)	Deleted by FA 1996 s 132(2) and Sch 5 Pt II	
13	Amendment of FA 1984 s 12(11)	s 489(15)
14	Ceased by FA 1992 s 13	
15 (1)	Amendment of FA 1975 s 31A	
(2)	Amendment of FA 1976 s 12	
(3)	Unnecessary (application)	
16	Unnecessary (obsolete)	
17-30	Rep by FA 1997 s 146(2) and Sch 9 Pt II	
31	Definition of "operative date" unnecessary (spent)	s 256
32		s 257
33 (1)-(9), (a)-(d), (10)		s 258
(9)(e)	Rep by FA 1997 s 146(2) and Sch 9 Pt II	
33A(1),(2), (2) proviso para (b),(3),(4)	(s 33A inserted by FA 1996 s 42)	s 260
(2) proviso para (a)	Unnecessary (obsolete)	
34 (a)	Unnecessary (cesser of CTA 1976 s 31(1), (2), (3), (6))	
(b)	Amendment of CTA 1976 s 31(4), (9)	
35 (1)(a)-(cc)		s 261
(d), (e)	Deleted by FA 1992 s 22(1)(b)(ii)	
(2)-(4)	Unnecessary (obsolete)	
(5)	Unnecessary (cesser of ITA 1967 s 344)	
36		s 262

Former Enactment		*Destination in TCA 1997*
Finance Act 1986 (1986 No 13) (contd)		
s 37(1)		s 263
(1) proviso para (ii),(2)		
(1) proviso para (i) (3), (4)	Unnecessary (obsolete)	
37A	(s 37A inserted by FA 1992 s 22(1)(c))	s 264
37B	(s 37B inserted by FA 1992 s 22(1)(c))	s 265
38		s 266
39		s 267
40 (1)	Amendment of ITA 1967 Sch 15	Sch 29
(2)	Amendment of FA 1983 s 94(2).	s 1078
41 (1), (2)	Definition of "designated area" unnecessary (obsolete)	s 322(1)
(3)		s 322(4)
42	Sch 32, para 11 of the Bill saves the provisions of FA 1986 s 42 (in so far as that section applied to areas other than the Custom House Docks Area)	Sch 32, para 11
(1)	Definitions of "multi-storey car-park", "qualifying period" and "the relevant local authority" unnecessary (obsolete)	s 323(1)
(2)		s 323(2)(a), (3)(a)
1st proviso		s 323(2)(b)
2nd proviso		s 323(4)
(3)	Deleted by FA 1991 s 22(2)	
(4)	Unnecessary (obsolete)	
(4)proviso		s 323(3)(b)
(5), (6), (8), (9)	Unnecessary (obsolete)	
(7)		s 323(5)
43	Deleted by FA 1994 s 35(1)(b)	
44	Sch 32, para 12 of the Bill saves the provisions of FA 1986 s 44 (in so far as that section applied to areas other than the Custom House Docks Area)	Sch 32, para 12
(1)(a)(b)	Definition of "qualifying period" and "the relevant local authority" unnecessary (obsolete)	s 328(1)
(b) proviso	Deleted by FA 1995 s 32(1)(c)	
44 (1)(c)(f)(g)	Unnecessary (obsolete)	
(d)		s 329(9)(b)
(e)		s 328(3)
(2)		s 328(2)
(3)		s 329(12)
(4)	Rep by FA 1996 s 132(2) and Sch 5 Pt II	
(5)	Amendment of ITA 1967 s 198(1)	s 1024
45	Sch 32, para 13 of the Bill saves the provisions of FA 1986 s 45 (in so far as that section applied to areas other than the Custom House Docks Area)	Sch 32, para 13
(1)(a)(c)		s 324(1)
(b)	Unnecessary (obsolete)	
(2)		s 324(2)
1st proviso para (a)	Unnecessary (obsolete)	
1st proviso para (b)		s 324(3)
2nd proviso	Unnecessary (obsolete)	

Former Enactment		*Destination in TCA 1997*
Finance Act 1986 (1986 No 13) (contd)		
s 46 (1)-(3)		s 1013(1)-(3)
(4)	Rep by FA 1997 s 146(2) and Sch 9 Pt II	
(5)	Unnecessary (obsolete)	
(6)		s 1013(4)(b)
47	Amendment of FA 1985 s 16(1)(b)(i)	
48 (1)-(4)	Definitions of "specified date" (obsolete) and "tax" (duplication) unnecessary	s 1084(1)-(4)
49	Amendment of FA 1976 s 30(1)	
50 (1)		s 373(2)(c)
(2)	Amendment of FA 1976 s 32	s 376
51	Amendment of FA 1981 s 25(1)	Sch 32, para 9
52 (1)		s 317(3)
(2)	Insertion of ITA 1967 s 264(3A)	s 272
53	Amendment of FA 1984 s 40	s 403
54	Insertion of CTA 1976 s 84A(10)	s 133(4)
55 (1)	Amendment of CTA 1976 ss 25(5), 26(4)	ss 157, 158
(2)	Unnecessary (operative date)	
56 (1)	Amendment of CTA 1976 s 70	
(2)	Amendment of CTA 1976 s 39A	
57 (1)	Substitution of CTA 1976 s 155(10)	s 4(2)-(6)
(2)	Unnecessary (operative date)	
58	Unnecessary (spent)	
59 (a)	Insertion of CTA 1976 s 33(1A), (1B)	s 707
(b)	Insertion of CTA 1976 s 39(4A)	s 715
(c)	Insertion of CTA 1976 s 40(1A)	s 716
(d)	Amendment of CTA 1976 s 50	s 706(1)-(3)
60	Amendment of CGTA 1975 s 3(3)	s 28
61	Unnecessary (spent)	
Pt VI		
112(1), (2)		s 7
(3)	Unnecessary (operative date)	
113(1)-(3)	Definition of "tax" in s 113(1) unnecessary (duplication)	s 887
(4)	Unnecessary (cesser)	
(5)		s 928(2), (3)
(6)		s 967
114(1)	Amendment of ITA 1967 s 429	s 942(1)-(8), (10)
(2)	Amendment FA 1976 s 30	
(3)	Amendment of FA 1983 s 107	
(4)	Unnecessary (operative date)	
115		s 1001
116(1)	Substitution of ITA 1967 s 161	s 852(1), (2)
(2)		s 852(3)
117	Unnecessary (care and management)	
118(2), (7), (8)	Unnecessary (construction and commencement)	
Sch 1	Amendment of ITA 1967 ss 138, 138A(2), 138B(1), FA 1974 s 8(1)	ss 461, 462 472, 464
Sch 2	Rep by FA 1992 s 12	
Sch 3	Unnecessary (obsolete)	
Sch 4		
Pt I, II		Sch 5
Pts III, IV, V, VI, VII	Unnecessary (obsolete)	
Income Tax (Amendment) Act 1986 (1986 No 34)		
s 1	Substitution of ITA 1967 s 110	s 112
2	Unnecessary (short title and construction)	

Former Enactment		*Destination in TCA 1997*
Finance Act 1987 (1987 No 10)		
Pt I		
s 1	Amendment of FA 1982 s 6	
2 (1)	Unnecessary (duplication)	
(2)		s 664(1)(a)
proviso		s 664(1)(b)(i)
3	Amendment of FA 1986 s 16	
4	Rep by FA 1994 s 157(1)	
5	Amendment of FA 1986 s 14	
6	Rep by FA 1997 s 146(2) and Sch 9 Pt II	
7 (1)-(4)		s 259
(5)	Unnecessary (construction)	
8	Amendment of FA 1984s 12	ss 488, 489
9	Insertion of FA 1984 s 13(2A), (2B), (2C)	s 490
10	Insertion of FA 1984 s 15(3A), (13)	s 495
11	Amendment of FA 1984 s 16	ss 488(4), 496
12	Insertion of FA 1984 s 26(1A) and substitution of Sch 2 para 1	Sch 10
13		s 520
14		s 521
14A	(s 14A inserted by FA 1988 s 8(c))	s 522
15		s 523
16		s 524
17		s 525
18		s 526
19		s 527
20		s 528
21		s 529
22 (1)	Amendment of FA 1975 s 31A	
(2)	Amendment of FA 1976 s 12	s 77
(3)	Unnecessary (application)	
23 (1)	Unnecessary (repeal of ITA 1967 s 362)	
(2)		s 835
24		s 286
25 (1)		s 317(1)
(2)		s 317(4)
26	Amendment of FA 1984 s 40(10)(a)	s 403
27 (1)(a)	Unnecessary (obsolete)	
(1)(b)		s 322(2)
(2)		s 322(3)
28 (1)	Par (iv) of definition of "qualifying ship" deleted by FA 1990 s 42(1)	s 407(1)
(2)		s 407(3)
(3)	Insertion of FA 1980 s 39(1CC1)	s 443
(4)		s 407(4)
(5)(a)		s 407(6)
(b)		ss 133(1)(d), 134(1)(d)
29	Insertion of FA 1980 s 39(1CC2)	s 443
30	Insertion of FA 1980 s 39B	s 446(1)-(12)
31	Insertion of FA 1980 s 39(1CC3)	s 443
32	Unnecessary (spent)	
33	Amendment of CTA 1976 s 79	
34		s 220

Former Enactment		*Destination in TCA 1997*
Finance Act 1987 (1987 No 10) (contd)		
s 35 (1)-(20)		s 481, Sch 32 para 22
(21)	Unnecessary (obsolete)	
(22)	Rep by FA 1997 s 146(2) and Sch 9 Pt II	
Pt VI		
52	Amendment of ITA 1967 s 162(3)	s 851
54	Unnecessary (care and management)	
55(2), (7)	Unnecessary (construction and commencement)	
Finance Act 1988 (1988 No 12)		
Pt I		
s 1	Amendment of FA 1980 ss 1(2), 2(6)	ss 187, 188
2	Amendment of FA 1986 s 2	
3 (1), (2)	Unnecessary (obsolete)	
(3)	Unnecessary (application of schedule)	
4	Amendment of FA 1982 s 6	
5 (1)	Unnecessary (spent)	
(2)	Unnecessary (construction)	
6	Amendment of FA 1986 Sch 2	
7	Amendment of FA 1984 s 16(2)(a)	
8	Amendment of FA 1987 Pt I Ch III	
9 (1)	Definition of "relevant chargeable period" obsolete except for purposes of s 955(5)	ss 950(1), 955(5)(a)
(2), (3)		s 950(2), (3)
(4)	Deleted by FA 1991 s 45(b)	
10 (1)-(12)	(s 10(12) also provided for the amendment of ITA 1967 Sch 15)	s 951
11		s 952
12		s 953
13		s 954
14 (1), (2)		s 955(1), (2)(a)
(2) proviso		s 955(2)(b)
para (a)-(e)		
para (f)	Unnecessary (obsolete)	
(3), (4)		s 955(3), (4)
(5)		s 955(5)(b)(i)
15		s 956
16		s 1084(1), (5)
17		s 957
18 (1)-(3),		s 958(2)-(5)
(3)1st proviso		
(3) 2nd proviso		
paras (a),(b)		s 958(6)(a), (b)
para (c)	Unnecessary (spent)	
(3A)-(6)		s 958(7)-(10)
(7)		s 958(1)
19 (1)	Rep by FA 1997 s 146(2) and Sch 9 Pt II	
(2)	Amendment of ITA 1967 s 550	s 1080(1)
20 (1) to(4)	Ceased by FA 1990 s 27(2)(b)	
(5)	(The cesser of FA 1988 s 20 by FA 1990 s 27 does not effect the provision of s 20(5))	s 959(7)
21 (1)		s 959(1)
(2)		s 1069(1)(b)
(3), (4), (5)		s 959(2), (3), (4)

Former Enactment		*Destination in TCA 1997*
Finance Act 1988 (1988 No 12) (contd)		
s 21 (6)	Rep by FA 1997 s 146(2) and Sch 9 Pt II	
(7), (8)		s 959(5), (6)
22	Rep by FA 1997 s 146(2) and Sch 9 Pt II	
23 (1)	Amendment of FA 1975 s 31A	
(2)	Amendment of FA 1976 s 12	
(3)	Unnecessary (application)	
24 (1)		s 373(2)(d)
(2)	Unnecessary (obsolete)	
25	Amendment of FA 1986 s 44(1)(a)	s 328(1)
26	Unnecessary (spent)	
27	Amendment of FA 1981 s 23	ss 325(1), 326(1), 327(1), 329(1)(2)
28	Amendment of FA 1985 s 21	ss 326, 327, 329, Sch 32, para 11
29	Amendment of FA 1985 s 22	Sch 32, para 11
30 (1)		ss 774(4)(a), 608(1)(a), 717(2)(a)
(2)(a)		s 774(4)(b)
(b)		s 608(1)(b)
(c)		s 717(2)(b)
31 (1)	Unnecessary (obsolete)	
(2)	Unnecessary (application of schedule)	
32 (1)	Amendment of FA 1980 s 45	s 147, Sch 32 para 4
(2)	Unnecessary (obsolete)	
(3)	Unnecessary (application of schedule)	
33 (1)	Substitution of CTA 1976 s 1(1)	s 21
(2)	Unnecessary (cesser of CTA 1976 ss 28, 79)	
(3)	Unnecessary (application of schedule)	
34	Insertion of CTA 1976 s 116A	s 456
35	Amendment of FA 1980 s 39A(2)	s 445
36 (1)	Rep FA 1980 s 39B(7)(c)	
(2)	Unnecessary (obsolete)	
(3)	Amendment of FA 1980 s 39B(6)	s 446(1)-(12)
(4)		s 451
37		s 452
38	Insertion of FA 1974 s 31(3)(cc)	s 246(3)
39		s 217
40 (1)	Amendment of FA 1987 s 28(1)	s 407(1)
(2)	Unnecessary (obsolete)	
(3)	Amendment of FA 1987 s 28(4)(c)	s 407(4)
41		s 222
42		Sch 32, para 3
43	Amendment of ITA 1967 s 251	ss 283(2)(3)(6), 300(1), 304(3)(b), 316(3)
44	Insertion of ITA 1967 s 254(7)	ss 271(1)(2)(4)-(6), 278(1), (2), (6), 304(2)(3)(a)(4), 305, 316(3), 317(2), 320(1)
45	Amendment of ITA 1967 s 265	s 274(1), (3)-(5), (8)
46	Substitution of FA 1967 s 11(2)	s 285(1), (2), (3)
47	Substitution of FA 1971 s 26(2)	s 285(1), (2), (3)
48	Substitution of FA 1978 s 25(2)	s 273(2)
49	Amendment of FA 1981 s 25(1)	Sch 32, para 9
50	Amendment of ITA 1967 ss 254(2A)(a), 264(1) proviso para (ii), 264(3) proviso para (ii), 265(1) proviso para (iii)	s 271(4), 272, 274(1)(3)-(5)(8)

Former Enactment		*Destination in TCA 1997*
Finance Act 1988 (1988 No 12) (contd)		
s 51 (1)(a)		ss 271(3)(a), 273(5)(a), 283(4)(a), 285(5)(a)
(b)	Unnecessary (obsolete)	
(c)		ss 273(5)(b), 285(5)(b)
(cc)		ss 271(3)(b), 273(5)(c), 285(5)(c)
proviso		ss 271(3)(b), 273(5)(c), 283(4)(b), 285(5)(c)
(d)		ss 274(2), 285(5)(d)
(2)(a),(c),(d)		s 283(3)(a)
(b)	Unnecessary (obsolete)	
(3)		s 285(4)
(4)(a)		s 271(4)(a)
(b)		s 273(4)
(5)		s 274(2)
(6)		ss 271(1), 273(1), 283(1), 285(1)
52 (1)	Amendment of FA 1974 s 22	s 658(1)
(2)	Amendment of FA 1977 s 14(1)	Sch 32, para 23(2)
(3)	Cesser of FA 1980 s 26 (unnecessary)	
70 (1)(a)	Insertion of ITA 1967 s 467A	
(b)	Amendment of ITA 1967 s 474(1)	s 49, Sch 32 para 1(2)
(2)(a)		s 607(1)(d)
(b)	Unnecessary (cesser of FA 1983 s 54 and FA 1984 s 66(6) (in so far as it relates to Bord Telecom Eireann))	
71 (1), (2)(a)		s 1006
(2)(b)	Unnecessary (obsolete)	
72 (1)-(6)	Unnecessary (obsolete)	
(7)	Amendment of FA 1983 s 23(4)	s 1086
73 (1)-(16), (18)		s 1002
(17)	Deleted by FA 1992 s 241(e)	
74 (1), (2)		s 8
(3)	Unnecessary (commencement)	
76	Unnecessary (care and management)	
77 (2), (7), (8)	Unnecessary (construction and commencement)	
Sch 1	Amendment of ITA 1967 ss 138, 138A(2), 138B(1)	ss 461, 462, 472
Sch 2	Unnecessary (obsolete)	
Sch 3	Unnecessary (obsolete)	
Finance Act 1989 (1989 No 10)		
s 1	Amendment of FA 1980 ss 1, 2	ss 187, 188
2	Amendment of FA 1984 s 2	
3	Amendment of FA 1982 s 6	
4 (1)-(6)		Sch 32, para 20
(7)	Rep by FA 1996 s 132(2) and Sch 5 Pt II	
4 (8)	Amendment of ITA 1967 s 198(1)	s 1024
5	Insertion of FA 1969 s 2(5A)-(5D)	s 195(1)-(11)
6	Amendment of FA 1982 s 8(1)(a)	s 122
7	Rep by FA 1997 s 146(2) and Sch 9 Pt II	
8	Ceased by FA 1992 s 4	
9	Amendment of FA 1984 ss 12(1), 16(2)(2A), 17, insertion of s 13A	s 489(1)(2), 493, 496, 498,
10		s 995

Former Enactment		*Destination in TCA 1997*
Finance Act 1989 (1989 No 10) (contd)		
s 11 (1)	Amendment of FA 1975 s 31A	
(2)	Amendment of FA 1976 s 12	
(3)	Unnecessary (spent)	
(4)	Unnecessary (application)	
12 (1)		s 373(2)(e)
(2)	Amendment of FA 1976 s 32	s 376
13	Substitution of ITA 1967 s 251(7)	
14	Substitution of ITA 1967 s 254(7)	s 271(5)
15	Amendment of FA 1974 s 22(2)	s 658(2)(a)
16	Insertion of FA 1978 s 25(3)	s 273(8)
17	Amendment of FA 1981 s 26	Sch 32, para 10
18 (1)		s 734(1)(a), (c)
(2)-(9), (11),(11A),(12)		s 734(2)-(12)
(10)	Deleted by FA 1993 s 20(b)	
19 (1), (2), (3)		s 893
(4)	Amendment of ITA 1967 Sch 15	Sch 29
20	Substitution of CTA 1976 s 36(2)	s 713(1)-(6)
21 (1)	Substitution of CTA 1976s 84A	s 134(3)
(2)(a)		ss 133(3), 134(2)
(2)(b)	Unnecessary (spent)	
22	Amendment of FA 1980 ss 38, 39(1CC)	ss 442(1), 443
23	Deletion of FA 1980 s 39A(8), (9)	
24	Amendment of FA 1980 s 45	s 147, Sch 32 para 4
25 (1)-(3)		s 154(1)-(3)
(4)		s 154(6)
26	Substitution of FA 1984 s 42(1)	s 138
27 (1)	Amendment of CTA 1976 s 100(3)(h)	s 434
(2)	Amendment of FA 1980 s 41(1)	s 448(1)
(3)	Unnecessary (operative date)	
28	Amendment of FA 1987 s 35	s 481, Sch 32, para 22
29	Amendment of CGTA 1975 Sch 4 para 11	s 980
30	Amendment of FA 1986 s 61(1)	
31 (1)	Amendment of FA 1988 s 70(2)	s 607(1)(d)
(2)	Unnecessary (operative date)	
32	Amendment of CGTA 1975 s 19	s 607(1)(a)-(d)(f), (2)
33		s 610, Sch 15, Pt I
Pt VI		
86		s 811
87	Insertion of CGTA 1975 s 33(5A)	s 549
88 (1)-(7)		s 817
(8)	Unnecessary (operative date)	
89 (1)	Amendment of ITA 1967 s 433(1)	s 237
(2)		s 242
Pt VII		
95 (1)(a)	Insertion of ITA 1967 s 467B	
(b)	Amendment of ITA 1967 s 474(1)	s 49, Sch 32 para 1(2)
(2)	Amendment of CGTA 1975 s 19(d)	s 607
98 (1)	Amendment of FA 1973 s 92(1)	ss 39(1), 48(1)(c)
(2)	Amendment of FA 1984 s 66(a)	s 607
99	Unnecessary (care and management)	
100(2), (7), (8)	Unnecessary (construction and commencement)	

Former Enactment		*Destination in TCA 1997*
Finance Act 1989 (1989 No 10) (contd)		
Sch 1 para 1(1)-(6), (7)(a)-(d), (8)	Sch 1 para 1(7)(e) rep by FA 1997 s 146(2) and Sch 9 Pt II	Sch 18 para 1
para 2		para 2
para 3	Amendment of ITA 1967 Sch 15, FA 1983 s 94(2)	Sch 29
Judicial Separation and Family Law Reform Act 1989 (1989 No 6)		
s 26		s 1027(a)
Finance Act 1990 (1990 No 10)		
s 1	Amendment of FA 1980 ss 1, 2	ss 187, 188
2	Amendment of FA 1984 s 2	
3	Amendment of FA 1982 s 6	
4	Amendment of FA 1969 s 3(1)	s 467
5 (1), (2)		s 189
(3)	Unnecessary (commencement)	
6	Amendment of FA 1989 s 8	
7		s 190
8	Amendment of FA 1976 s 13(2)	s 805
9	Amendment of FA 1980 s 28(3)	
10	Amendment of FA 1984 ss 11(1), 12, 16	s 488(1)-(3), 489(1), 496
11		s 251
12	Amendment of ITA 1967 Sch 3	s 201(1)(a), Sch 3
13 (1), (3), (4)		s 214
(2)	Unnecessary (commencement)	
14 (1)	Amendment of ITA 1967 s 58	ss 65(1), 66, 67
(2)	Unnecessary (cesser of FA 1971 s 3)	
15	Substitution of ITA 1967 s 60	s 65(2)-(4)
16	Unnecessary (spent)	
17 (1)(a)	Amendment of ITA 1967 Pt IV Ch IV	
(b)	Amendment of ITA 1967 Sch 6	s 73
(2)	Unnecessary (cesser of ITA 1967 s 77(3)(4))	
18 (1)	Amendment of ITA 1967 ss 81(3), 89	ss 75(3), 384
(2)	Unnecessary (cesser of ITA 1967 s 81(3)(b)(c))	
19 (a)	Substitution of ITA 1967 s 110	s 112
(b)	Unnecessary (deletion of ITA 1967 s 111 with saver for any enactment which refers to ITA 1967 s 111)	
20 (1)	Amendment of ITA 1967 Sch 18	Sch 28
(2)	Amendment of FA 1974 s 20B	s 657(4)(5)
(3)	Unnecessary (cesser of FA 1980 s 17 Table Pt I para (a), (b) and FA 1981s 9(a), (b))	
(4)	Unnecessary (spent)	
21	Unnecessary (spent)	
22 (1)	Amendment of ITA 1967 ss 262(2), 297(2)	s 306
(2)	Amendment of FA 1974 s 22(2A)(c)	s 658(3)
23 (1)	Amendment of ITA 1967 s 70	ss 880(1)-(6), 900(3), 1052(4)(a)(c)(e)
(2)	Amendment of ITA 1967 s 172	ss 879(1)-(4), 1052(4)(a)(c)(e)
(3)	Amendment of FA 1988 ss 9, 10	ss 950, 951, 955(5)(a).
(4)	Unnecessary (spent)	
(5)	Unnecessary (commencement)	
24 (a)	Amendment of ITA 1967 s 477(1)	s 960
(b)	Unnecessary (cesser of ITA 1967 s 550(2) and FA 1982 s 27(4))	
(c)	Amendment of CTA 1976 s 6(4)	
(d)	Amendment of FA 1988 s 18	s 958

Former Enactment			*Destination in TCA 1997*
Finance Act 1990 (1990 No 10) (contd)			
s 25	(1)	Amendment of FA 1986 s 48	s 1084(1)-(4)
	(2)	Unnecessary (operative date)	
	(3)	Unnecessary (spent)	
26	(1)	Unnecessary (invalid)	
	(2)	Unnecessary (spent)	
	(3)	Unnecessary (spent)	
27	(1)	Amendment of ITA 1967 s 236(11)	s 787(7)
	(2)	Unnecessary (cesser of ITA 1967 ss 307(1AA), 546 and FA 1988 s 20)	
28		Substitution of ITA 1967 s 421(2)	s 934
29	(1)(2)(5)(6)		s 1014
	(3)	Amendment of CGTA 1975 s 2(1)	s 5
	(4)	Amendment of CTA 1976 s 1(5)	s 4(1)
	(7)	Unnecessary (operative date)	
30	(1)	Amendment of FA 1986 ss 42(1), 44(1)(a), 45(1)(a)	Sch 32 paras 11, 12, 13
	(2)	Amendment of FA 1989 s 4(1)(a)	Sch 32 para 20
31		Amendment of FA 1987 s 27(1)(a)(ii)	
32		Amendment of FA 1986 s 45(2)	Sch 32 para 13
33	(1)		ss 324(4)(b), 333(4)(b), 345(8)(b), 354(5)(b), 370(8)(b)
	(2)(a)	Definition of "qualifying premises" unnecessary (duplication),	ss 324(4)(a), 333(4)(a), 345(8)(a), 354(5)(a), 370(8)(a)
33	(2)(b)	Unnecessary (obsolete)	
34	(1)(a)		ss 155(1), 489(14)(a)
	(b)(i)	Unnecessary (obsolete)	
	(1)(b)(ii)		ss 155(2)(c), 489(14)(b)
	(2)		ss 155(2)(a), 489(14)(c)(d)
	(3)		s 155(3)
	(4)		s 489(14)(e)
	(5), (6)		s 155(4), (5)
35	(1), (2)		s 735
	(3)	Unnecessary (operative date)	
36		Unnecessary (obsolete)	
37		Unnecessary (obsolete)	
38		Amendment of FA 1989 s 25(3)(a)	s 154(1)-(3)
39	(a)-(c)	Amendment of F(TPCM)A 1974 ss 2(1), 3(2), 4(1)	ss 673(1), 674(1)(a)(2)-(4), 675
	(d)	Insertion of F(TPCM)A 1974 s 7A	s 678
40		Amendment of FA 1980 s 38	s 442(1)
41	(1)	Amendment of FA 1980 s 39	s 443
	(2)	Unnecessary (spent)	
	(3)	Unnecessary (obsolete)	
	(4)(a)		s 133(1)(e)
	(b)	Unnecessary (duplication)	
	(5)		s 403(9)(a)
	(6)		s 442(1)
42	(1)	Amendment of FA 1987 s 28(1)	s 407(1)
	(2)	Unnecessary (obsolete)	
43		Substitution of CTA 1976 s 10(4)	s 243(1), (2), (4)-(9)
44	(1)	Insertion of CTA 1976 s 116(10)	s 420
	(2)	Unnecessary (spent)	
45		Unnecessary (spent)	

Former Enactment			*Destination in TCA 1997*
Finance Act 1990 (1990 No 10) (contd)			
s 46		Amendment of CTA 1976 s 84A	ss 133, 134
47		Amendment of CTA 1976 s 101	s 440
48		Amendment of CTA 1976 s 162	s 441
49		Amendment of CTA 1976 s 151	ss 238(1)-(6), 239
50		Insertion of CTA 1976 s 152(4)	s 240
51	(1), (2)		s 241
	(3)	Substitution of ITA 1967 s 434(5A)	s 238
	(4)	Unnecessary (operative date)	
52		Amendment of FA 1980 s 41(1)	s 448(1)
53		Amendment of CTA 1976 s 58(10)	
54		Substitution of CTA 1976 s 143(1)	s 884
55		Amendment of FA 1983 s 50	s 171
56		Substitution of FA 1983 s 24	s 517
57			s 703
58		Amendment of CTA 1976 s 129(2)	s 616
59			s 704
60			s 705
61		Amendment of ITA 1967 s 337	
62			s 740
63			s 741
64			s 742
65			s 743
66			s 744
67			s 745
68			s 746
69	(1)-(7)		s 747
	(8)	Unnecessary (obsolete)	
70		Amendment of ITA 1967 s 241(1)	s 284(1)(2)(a)(b),(3), 300(1)
71		Amendment of FA 1967 s 11	s 285(1), (2), (3)
72		Amendment of FA 1971 s 26	ss 285(1)(2)(3)(8), 287, 299(2)
73		Amendment of ITA 1967 s 251	ss 283(2), 300(1), 316(3)
74		Amendment of ITA 1967 s 254	ss 271(1)(4)(6), 278(1)(2)(6), 305, 320
75		Insertion of FA 1970 s 19(2A)	s 279
76		Amendment of FA 1978 s 25	s 273(1)(2)(3)(8)
77		Amendment of FA 1974 s 22	s 658
78		Amendment of ITA 1967 s 265(1)	s 274(1)(3)-(5)(8)
79		Amendment of ITA 1967 s 276	s 294
80		Substitution of FA 1988 s 51(2), (3), (4)	ss 283(3)(a), 285(4), 271(4)(a), 273(4)
81	(1)(a)		ss 271(3)(c), 273(7)(a)(i), 283(5), 285(7)(a)(i)
	(b)		s 273(7)(a)(ii)
	(c)		s 285(7)(a)(ii)
	(1) proviso		ss 273(7)(b), 285(7)(b)
	(2)(a), (b)		s 283(3)(b)
	(c)	Unnecessary (obsolete)	
	(3)		s 285(6)
	(4)		s 271(4)(a)
	(5)		s 273(6)
82		Amendment of CGTA 1975 s 3(3)	s 28
83		Amendment of CGTA 1975 s 36	s 590(1)-(9)
84		Amendment of CGTA 1975 s 26	s 598
85		Amendment of CGTA 1975 s 27(3)	s 599

Former Enactment		*Destination in TCA 1997*
Finance Act 1990 (1990 No 10) (contd)		
s 86	Amendment of CGTA 1975 Sch 1 para 15(3)	s 596
87	Insertion of CGTA 1975 Sch 2 para 2A	s 733
Pt VII		
s 131	Insertion of FA 1970 s 17(14)-(17)	s 531(17), (18)
136	Insertion of FA 1982 Sch 3 para 4A	Sch 11
137	Insertion of FA 1986 Sch 2 para 15	
138(1)		ss 45(3),(4)(a), 48(4)(a),(5)(a)
(2)	Amendment of FA 1984 s 28	ss 45(2)-(4), 48(3)-(5)
139	Unnecessary (care and management)	
140(2), (8)	Unnecessary (construction and commencement)	
Sch 1	Unnecessary (obsolete)	
Sch 2	Unnecessary (obsolete)	
Sch 3		Sch 16
Sch 4		Sch 17
Sch 5		Sch 19
Sch 6		Sch 20
Finance Act 1991 (1991 No 13)		
Pt I		
s 1	Amendment of FA 1980 ss 1, 2	ss 187, 188
2 (1), (2)		s 15
(3)	Unnecessary (application of schedule)	
3 (1), (2)	Unnecessary (obsolete)	
(3)	Unnecessary (application of schedule)	
4 (1), (2)		s 463
(3)	Rep by FA 1996 s 132(2) and Sch 5 Pt II	
(4)	Unnecessary (commencement)	
5	Amendment of FA 1989 s 8	
6	Amendment of ITA 1967 s 110	s 112
7	Insertion of ITA 1967 s 138B(3)	s 472
8	Substitution of ITA 1967 s 142A(2)(b)	s 473
9	Amendment of FA 1982 s 6	
10 (1)	Unnecessary (interpretation)	
(2)		s 664(1)(a), (b)(ii)
11	Amendment of FA 1986 s 31(1)	s 256.
12		s 773
13		s 210
14	Amendment of FA 1984 ss 12, 13	ss 488(1), 489, 490, 1024
15 (1)	Amendment of FA 1984 ss 12, 13, 13A, 15, 16, 26	ss 488(1)(4), 489, 490, 491, 495, 496, 507, 1024,
(2)	Amendment of FA 1984 Sch 2 para 1	Sch 10
16	Unnecessary (obsolete)	
17 (1)	Amendment of FA 1984 s 13	s 490
(2)	Amendment of FA 1984 s 15(2)	s 495
(3)(a)	Unnecessary (obsolete)	
(b)	Ceased by FA 1994 s 17	
(4)	Unnecessary (interpretation)	
18 (1)	Amendment of FA 1975 s 31A	
(2)	Amendment of FA 1976 s 12	
(3)	Amendment of FA 1980 s 28	
(4)	Unnecessary (application)	
19 (1)	Amendment of FA 1989 s 18(1)	s 734
(2)		s 734(1)(b)
(3)	Unnecessary (obsolete)	
20 (1), (3)		s 230
(2)		s 610, Sch 15, Pt I

Former Enactment		*Destination in TCA 1997*
Finance Act 1991 (1991 No 13) (contd)		
s 21 (1)	Amendment of FA 1986 s 45	Sch 32, para 13
(2)	Unnecessary (operative date)	
22 (1)		s 271(4)(a)
(2)(a)	Unnecessary (cesser of FA 1986 s 42(3))	
(b)	Unnecessary (operative date)	
23	Amendment of FA 1970 s 19	s 279
24		s 408
25	Amendment of FA 1974 s 22	s 658
26		s 276
27	Amendment of FA 1984 s 29	s 815(1)(2)
28	Amendment of CTA 1976 s 84A	ss 133(7)(13), 134(1)(4)-(6)
29	Insertion of CTA 1976 s 87(4)(e)	s 135
30 (1)	Amendment of CTA 1976 s 35	s 710(1)-(5)
(2)		s 710(6)
31		s 110
32 (1)	Amendment of FA 1980 s 39(3)(a)	s 443
(2)	Unnecessary (operative date)	
33	Amendment of FA 1980 s 39A	s 445
34	Amendment of FA 1980 s 39B(2)	s 446(1)-(12)
35	Amendment of FA 1990 s 41(6)	s 442(1)
36		s 831
37	Unnecessary (obsolete)	
38	Substitution of FA 1988 s 30(1)	ss 774(4)(a), 608(1)(a), 717(2)(a)
39	Amendment of FA 1990 s 45(2)(a)	
40	Amendment of FA 1988 s 41(1)(a)	s 222
41		s 220
42	Amendment of CGTA 1975 s 26	s 598
43 (1), (2)		s 606
(3)	Unnecessary (operative date)	
44	Amendment of FA 1989 s 33(2)	s 610, Sch 15, Pt I
45	Amendment of FA 1988 s 9	ss 950(1)-(3), 955(5)(a).
46	Amendment of FA 1988 s 10	s 951
47	Amendment of FA 1988 s 12	s 953
48	Insertion of FA 1988 s 13(7)	s 954
49	Amendment of FA 1988 s 14(5)	s 955(5)(b)(i)
50	Amendment of FA 1988 s 15(1)	s 956
51	Amendment of FA 1988 s 17(1)	s 957
52	Amendment of FA 1988 s 18	s 958(2)-(5)
53	Amendment of FA 1988 s 21	s 959(1)
54-55	Rep by FA 1997 s 156(1)(a)	
56 (1)(a)(i)		s 325(1)
(ii)	Unnecessary (spent)	
(iii)	Rep by FA 1997 s 156(1)(b)	
(iv)	Unnecessary (spent)	
(b)		s 325(1)
(bb)	Unnecessary (obsolete)	
(c)	Unnecessary (obsolete)	
(2)		s 325(2)
proviso	Rep by FA 1997 s 156(1)(b)	
57 (1)(a)	Rep by FA 1997 s 156(1)(c)	
(b)(i)		s 327(1)
(ii),(iii)	Unnecessary (obsolete)	
(2)	Rep by s 156(1)(c)	
(3)(a)(i)		s 327(1)
(ii)	Unnecessary (obsolete)	
(aa)		s 327(1)
(b)	Unnecessary (obsolete)	

Former Enactment		*Destination in TCA 1997*
Finance Act 1991 (1991 No 13) (contd)		
s 57 (3)(bb)	Unnecessary (obsolete)	
(c)	Unnecessary (obsolete)	
58 (1)(a)	Rep by FA 1997 s 156(1)(d)	
(b)(i)		s 326(1)
(ii)(iii)	Unnecessary (obsolete)	
(2)	Rep by FA 1997 s 156(1)(d)	
(3)(a)		s 326(1)
(b)	Unnecessary (obsolete)	
(c)	Unnecessary (obsolete)	
59	Definitions of "the Act of 1975", "the Act of 1976" unnecessary (duplication) and "relevant day" unnecessary (operative date)	s 173
60		s 174
60A	(s 60A inserted by FA 1997 s 39(b))	s 175
61		s 176
62		s 177
63		s 178
64		s 179
65		s 180
66		s 181
67		s 182
68 (1)-(3)		s 183
(4)	Amendment of ITA 1967 Sch 15	Sch 29
69	Insertion of FA 1983 ss 45(9), 47(1)(c)	ss 166, 168I
70		s 184
71		s 185
72		s 186
Pt VII		
s 126	Amendment of ITA 1967 s 141(4)	s 465
128	Amendment of FA 1970 s 17(5)(a)	s 531(5)(6)(8)(9),
130(1)	Amendment of FA 1988 s 73(1)	s 1002
(2)	Unnecessary (operative date)	
131	Unnecessary (care and management)	
132(2), (8)	Unnecessary (construction and commencement)	
Sch 1, Pt I	Amendment of ITA 1967 s 1(1), FA 1974 s 3(1), and cesser of FA 1974 s 3	ss 2(1), 3(1)
Sch 1, Pt II	Amendment of ITA 1967 ss 138, 138A(2)	ss 461, 462
Sch 2		Sch 6
Oireachtas (Allowance to Members) and Ministerial and Parliamentary Offices (Amendment) Act 1992 (1992 No 3)		
s 4		s 836
Finance Act 1992 (1992 No 9)		
s 1	Amendment of FA 1980 ss 1, 2	ss 187, 188
2 (1)(a)	Amendment of FA 1991 s 2	
(b)	Unnecessary (obsolete)	
(2)(a)	Amendment of ITA 1967 s 198	s 1024
(b)	Unnecessary (spent)	
3	Amendment of FA 1982 s 6	
4	Unnecessary (cesser of ITA 1967 ss 143, 151, 152, FA 1973 s 23 and Sch 1, FA 1989 s 8)	
5	Amendment of ITA 1967 s 432(1)	ss 864(1), 949(1)
6	Amendment of FA 1972 ss 15(3), 21(2), 22	ss 772(3), 780, 781

Former Enactment		*Destination in TCA 1997*
Finance Act 1992 (1992 No 9) (contd)		
s 7 (1)	Insertion of FA 1979 s 8(4A)	s 125(3)
(2)	Unnecessary (operative date)	
8	Amendment of FA 1982 s 4	ss 121, 897(1)-(5), Sch 29
9	Amendment of FA 1982 s 8(1)	s 122
10	Amendment of FA 1987 s 13(1)	s 520
11	Amendment of FA 1987 s 14	s 521
12	Cesser of FA 1986 s 10 and Sch 2, but only as respects share options granted on or after 29 January 1992	Sch 32, para 7(1)
13	Unnecessary (cesser of FA 1986 s 14)	
14 (1)-(3)		s 252
(4)	Insertion of FA 1974 s 34(3)	s 248(1)-(3)
15 (1)		s 126(3)(a)
(2)		s 126(3)(b)
proviso		s 126(4)
(3)		s 126(6)
(4)		s 126(7)
16	Amendment of FA 1977 s 36(a)	s 6
s 17 (1)	Amendment of FA 1982 s 56 and Sch 3 para 1(4)	s 515, Sch 11
(2)	Unnecessary (spent)	
18 (1)	Substitution of ITA 1967 s 525	s 127(1)-(5)
(2)	Substitution of ITA 1967 s 115(1)(b)	s 201(2)
(3)		s 127(6)
19 (1)	Insertion of FA 1973 s 34(2A)	s 234(3)-(8)
(2)	Amendment of CTA 1976 s 170	s 141
20	Amendment of FA 1980 s 28(3)	
21 (1)		s 373(2)(f)
(2)	Amendment of FA 1976 s 32	s 376
22 (1)	Amendment of FA 1986 ss 31, 35, insertion of ss 37A, 37B	ss 256, 261, 264, 265
(2)	Unnecessary (operative date)	
23 (1)	Amendment of FA 1986 s 46(2)	s 1013(1)-(3)
(2)(a)	Unnecessary (operative date)	
(b)		s 1013(5)(a)
23 (3)		s 1013(5)(b)
24 (1)(a)	Insertion of ITA 1967 s 467C	
(b)	Amendment of ITA 1967 s 474(1)	s 49, Sch 32 para 1(2)
(2)(a)	Amendment of CGTA 1975 s 19(d)	s 607
(b)	Unnecessary (cesser of FA 1982 s 41 in so far as it relates to Bord Gais Eireann)	
25		s 405
26 (1)-(3), (5)	Rep by FA 1996 s 132(2) and Sch 5 Pt II	
(4)	Insertion of ITA 1967 s 241(6A)	s 284(5)
27 (1)	Amendment of ITA 1967 s 255(1)(bb)	s 268(1)-(3), (5)-(8)
(2)	Unnecessary (operative date)	
28	Amendment of FA 1970 s 17	ss 530(1)(2), 531
29	Amendment of FA 1986 ss 41(2), 42, 44(1)(a), 45(1)(a)	ss 322(1), s 323(1), 324(1), 328(1), Sch 32, para 11
30	Amendment of FA 1987 s 27(1)(a)(ii)	
31	Amendment of FA 1989 s 4(1)	Sch 32, para 20
32	Amendment of FA 1988 s 18(3)(b)	s 958(2)-(5)
33 (1)	Amendment of FA 1988 s 21	ss 959, 1069(1)(b)
(2)	Unnecessary (operative date)	
34	Amendment of FA 1991 ss 56(1)(a), 57, 58	s 325(1)
35	Insertion of CTA 1976 ss 66A, 76A	s 145(11)(a), (b)
36		s 736

Former Enactment			*Destination in TCA 1997*
Finance Act 1992 (1992 No 9) (contd)			
s 37	(1)		s 154(3)(a), (4)
	(2)		s 154(5)
38	(1)	Substitution of CTA 1976 s 83(4)	s 153(1)
	(2)		s 153(2)
39		Definition of "the definition of scientific research". unnecessary (obsolete)	s 763(1)(3)(4)
40		Amendment of CTA 1976 s 84A	ss 133, 134
41		Substitution of FA 1989 s 21(2)	ss 133(3), 134(2)
	(1)	Amendment of ITA 1967 ss 464, 470, 474(2)	ss 45(1), 49, 50, Sch 32 para 1(2)
42	(2)		s 398(1)
	(3)(a)	Unnecessary (spent)	
	(b)		s 398(2)
	proviso	Unnecessary (spent)	
	(4)	Unnecessary (obsolete)	
43	(1)-(3)	Unnecessary (spent)	
43	(4)	Unnecessary (repeal of CTA 1976 s 31(9))	
44	(a), (b)	Amendment of CTA 1976 s 33	ss 707, 728
	(c), (d)	Insertion of CTA 1976 ss 33A, 46A, 46B	ss 708, 719, 720
	(e)	Unnecessary (deletion of CTA 1976 s 47)	
	(f)	Amendment of CTA 1976 s 50(1)	
45			s 487
46	(1)(a)	Insertion of CTA 1976 s 10A	s 454
	(b)	Amendment of CTA 1976 s 16(1)	s 396
	(c)	Insertion of CTA 1976 s 16A	s 455
	(2)	Amendment of CTA 1976 s 116A	s 456
47		Amendment of FA 1980 s 39	s 443
48		Unnecessary (spent)	
49	(1)	Insertion of CTA 1976 s 25(5A)	s 157
	(2)	Insertion of CTA 1976 s 26(4A)	s 158
50	(1)	Amendment of CTA 1976 s 105	s 410
	(2)	Unnecessary (repeal of CTA 1976 s 106)	
	(3)	Unnecessary (operative date)	
51	(1)	Amendment of FA 1983 s 44	s 165
	(2)	Unnecessary (operative date)	
52		Amendment of FA 1980 s 39A	s 445
53		Amendment of FA 1980 s 39B	s 446(1)-(12)
54		Substitution of FA 1980 s 41(1)	s 448(1)
55	(1), (2)		s 1085(1), (2)
	(3)	Unnecessary (operative date)	
56			s 88
57		Amendment of FA 1988 s 39	s 217
58		Amendment of FA 1987 s 35(1)	s 481, Sch 32, para 22
59		Amendment of CGTA 1975 ss 13(4), 16(1)(2), CGT(A)A 1978 Sch 1 para 8	s 655(1)(2), 601(3)
60	(1)	Substitution of CGTA 1975 s 3(3)	ss 283(2), 300(1)
	(2)	Unnecessary (deletion of FA 1982 s 36(2), (3), (3A))	
61			s 600(6)
62	(1)	Insertion of CGTA 1975 s 9(5)	s 272
	(2)	Unnecessary (operative date)	
63		Amendment of CGTA 1975 s 47	
64			s 630
65			s 631
66			s 632
67			s 633
68		Amendment of FA 1982 s 36	s 648

Former Enactment		*Destination in TCA 1997*
Finance Act 1992 (1992 No 9) (contd)		
s 69		s 634
70		s 635
71		s 636
72		s 637
73	Amendment of CTA 1976 s 132(2).	s 619
74		s 638
75		s 684
76		s 685
77		s 686
78		s 687
79		s 688
80 (1), (2)		s 689
(3)	Unnecessary (operative date)	
81 (1)-(5), (7)		s 690
(6)	Unnecessary (obsolete)	
82		s 691
83		s 692
84		s 693
85		s 694
86		s 695
87		s 696
88		s 697
226	Definition of "relevant chargeable period" unnecessary (obsolete). ITA 1967 s 226(7) also provided for the amendment of Sch 15	s 894
227	Amendment of ITA 1967 ss 94, 173, 176	ss 888, s 889(10), 890
228		s 899
229	Amendment of FA 1989 s 19.	s 893
230(1)-(6)	Definition of relevant chargeable period" unnecessary (obsolete).	s 895
(7)	Unnecessary (operative date)	
230A.	(s 230A inserted by FA 1995 s 41)	s 896
231	Substitution of FA 1986 s 6	
232	Substitution of FA 1976 s 34.	s 905
233	Insertion of ITA 1967 s 127A	s 903
234	Amendment of ITA 1967 s 128(1)	s 987(1)-(3)
235	Insertion of FA 1970 s 17A.	s 904
236		s 906
237		s 912
238	Amendment of FA 1979 s 31	s 902
239	Amendment of FA 1983 s 20	s 909
240	Amendment of FA 1983 s 23	s 1086
241	Amendment of FA 1988 s 73.	s 1002
242		s 1094
243(a)(i), (b)	Amendment of FA 1983 s 94	s 1078
(ii)	Rep by FA 1996 s 132(2) and Sch 5 Pt II	
244	Amendment of FA 1988 s 9(1)	ss 950(1)-(3), 955(5)(a).
245	Insertion of FA 1986 s 48(3)	s 1084(1)-(4)
246	Insertion of CGTA 1975 Sch 4 para 3(4A)	s 913(1), (3)-(5), (7)
247	Amendment of CTA 1976 s 143	ss 861(2), 884, 930, 973, 974, 1071, 1072, 1080, 1082

Former Enactment		Destination in TCA 1997
Finance Act 1992 (1992 No 9) (contd)		
s 248	Amendment of ITA 1967 ss 128(1A), 173(6), 426(3), 500(1)(2), FA 1979 s 31(5), FA 1980 s 45(8), FA 1983 s 112(1)(a)(3)	s 987(1)-(3), 889(10), 939, 1052(1)-(3), 902, 147, Sch 32 para 4
253	Unnecessary (care and management)	
254(2), (8), (9)	Unnecessary (construction and commencement)	
Sch 1	Substitution of Table to FA 1982 s 4(4)	s 121
Sch 2		Sch 13
Finance (No 2) Act 1992 (1992 No 28)		
s 1	Insertion of FA 1980 s 41(9)	s 448(3)-(7)
2	Amendment of FA 1980 s 45(3)	s 147, Sch 32 para 4
3	Amendment of FA 1986 ss 31(1),	s 256, 256, 265 37A(1), 37B(1)
29	Unnecessary (care and management)	
30 (2)	Unnecessary (construction and commencement)	
Finance Act 1993 (1993 No 13)		
Pt I		
s 1	Amendment of FA 1980 ss 1, 2	ss 187, 188
2 (1)	Amendment of FA 1991 s 2	s 15
(2)	Unnecessary (application of schedule)	
3 (1), (2)	Unnecessary (obsolete)	
(3)	Unnecessary (application of schedule)	
4	Amendment of FA 1982 s 6	
5	Rep by FA 1997 s 146(2) and Sch 9 Pt II	
6	Substitution of FA 1990 s 11	
7 (1)	Insertion of ITA 1967 s 115(1A)	s 201(3)
(2)		s 124
8 (a)	Amendment of ITA 1967 s 115	s 201(2)
(b)	Amendment of ITA 1967 Sch 3	s 201(1)(a), Sch 3
9	Unnecessary (spent)	
10	Insertion of ITA 1967 ss 195B, 195C,	ss 1019, 1021
11	Amendment of CTA 1976 ss 33, 36, 38, 43, 46A, 50, substitution of s 46, insertion of ss 33B, 35A, 36A, 36B, 36C	s 706(1)-(3), 707, 711, 712, 713(1)-(6), 714, 719, 726, 724, 725
12 (1)	Unnecessary (spent)	
(2)(a)	Unnecessary (spent)	
(b)		Sch 32, para 24
13		s 737
14 (1)-(3)		s 838(1)-(3)
(4)(a)-(c), (d)-(f)		s 838(4)
(c)proviso	Unnecessary (operative date)	
(5)		s 838(5)
(6)(a), (c)		s 838(6)
(b)	Unnecessary (operative date)	
(7)		s 838(7)
15 (1)	Amendment of FA 1986 ss 31(1),35(1),37A	s 256, 261, 264
(2)	Unnecessary (spent)	
16		s 839
17		s 738
18		s 739
19	Amendment of CGTA 1975 s 31(4)	
20	Amendment of FA 1989 s 18	s 734
21	Amendment of FA 1984 s 29(2A)(b)	s 980
22	Amendment of CTA 1976 s 16(5)	s 396
23	Amendment of CTA 1976 s 33A(1)	s 708
24	Insertion of CGTA 1975 s 20A	s 594

Former Enactment | | | *Destination in TCA 1997*

Finance Act 1993 (1993 No 13) (contd)

Section	Subsection	Description	Destination in TCA 1997
s 25		Amendment of FA 1984 ss 11, 12, 13, 13A, 493, 495, 496, 503 503, 1024,	s 488(1)(2)(3), 489, 490, 14, 15, 16, 22, 23
26		Amendment of FA 1986 s 12(2)	s 479
27	(1)-(3)	Definitions of "full-time working officer or employee" and "personal company" deleted by FA 1995 s 74	s 591(1)-(4)
	(4)(a)(b)(i), (iv)		s 591(5)
	(4)(ii)(iii)	Deleted by FA 1995 s 74	
	(5)		s 591(6)
	proviso	Unnecessary (spent)	
	(6)-(13)		s 591(7)-(14)
	(14)	Unnecessary (obsolete)	
	(15)	Unnecessary (operative date)	
28		Rep by FA 1996 s 132(2) and Sch 5 Pt II	
29	(1)		s 482(1)(a)
	(2)		s 482(9)
30	(1)	Amendment of FA 1986 ss 42, 44(1), 45	s 328(1), Sch 32 paras 11, 13
	(2)	Unnecessary (operative date)	
31		Amendment of FA 1989 s 4(1)	Sch 32, para 20
32		Amendment of FA 1991 ss 56(1)(a), 57, 58	s 325(1), 326(1), 327(1),
33	(1)	Substitution of FA 1988 s 51(1)(a)	ss 271(3)(a), 273(5)(a), 283(4)(a)(5)(a)
	(2)	Unnecessary (operative date)	
34	(1)	Substitution of ITA 1967 ss 254(4)(b),	s 317(2), 317(2), 769 303(3), 305(2)(b)
	(2)	Substitution of FA 1974 s 22(11)	s 658(1)
	(3)	Substitution of FA 1986 s 52(1)(a)(i)	s 317(3)
	(4)	Unnecessary (operative date)	
35	(1)(a), (2)-(6)		s 701
	(b)	Unnecessary (obsolete)	
36		Amendment of FA 1974 s 56	s 816
37			s 223
38		Rep by FA 1997 s 146(2) and Sch 9 Pt II	
39	(1)	Amendment of CTA 1976 s 6(4)	s 26(1), (2), (3)
	(2)	Unnecessary (operative date)	
40		Amendment of FA 1988 s 18	s 958
41		Amendment of FA 1993 s 50(6)	
42	(1)	Amendment of CTA 1976 s 1(5)	s 4(1)
	(2)	Unnecessary (operative date)	
43		Unnecessary (cesser of ITA 1967 s 337)	
44	(1)	Amendment of FA 1980 s 39	s 443
	(2)	Unnecessary (operative date)	
45	(1)	Amendment of CTA 1976 s 84A	s 134(3)
	(2)	Unnecessary (operative date)	
46	(1), (2)		s 150
	(3), (4)	Unnecessary (spent)	
	(5)	Amendment of FA 1980 s 45(7)	s 147, Sch 32 para 4
	(6)	Unnecessary (operative date)	
47	(1), (2)		s 80
	(3)	Insertion of FA 1980 s 39(1CC10)	s 443
	(4)	Unnecessary (commencement)	
48		Amendment of FA 1987 s 35	s 481, Sch 32 para 22
49		Rep by FA 1997 s 146(2) and Sch 9 Pt II	
50		Amendment of CTA 1976 s 10A	s 454(1)
51			s 486
140		Amendment of FA 1992 s 242	s 1094
142		Unnecessary (care and management)	

Former Enactment		*Destination in TCA 1997*
Finance Act 1993 (1993 No 13) (contd)		
s 143(2), (8)	Unnecessary (construction and commencement)	
Sch 1	Amendment of ITA 1967 ss 1(1),138, 38A(2)	ss 2(1), 3(1), 461, 462
Waiver of Certain Tax, Interest and Penalties Act 1993 (1993 No 24)		
s 10	Amendment of ITA 1967 s 512(1)	s 1065
11	Substitution of ITA 1967 s 516	s 1056
12	Amendment of ITA 1967 Sch 15	Sch 29
13		s 907
Finance Act 1994 (1994 No 13)		
Pt I		
s 1	Amendment of FA 1980 ss 1, 2	ss 187,188
2	Amendment of FA 1991 s 2 and FA 1993 Sch 1	ss 2(1), 3(1), 15, 461, 462
3 (1), (2)	Unnecessary (obsolete)	
(3)	Unnecessary (application of schedule)	
4	Insertion of ITA 1967 s 138B(2A)	s 472
5	Amendment of FA 1982 s 6	
6	Rep by FA 1997 s 146(2) and Sch 9 Pt II	
7	Insertion of ITA 1967 s 145(3A)	s 470(1)-(3)
8	Amendment of FA 1967 s 12(2)	s 469(1)
9	Amendment of FA 1982 s 8(1)	s 122
10	Unnecessary (spent)	
11	Amendment of FA 1992 Sch 2	Sch 13
12 (1)	Amendment of FA 1986 ss 35(1), 37A(1)	s 261, 264
(2)	Amendment of FA 1993 s 14(1)(c)	s 838(1)-(3)
13	Amendment of FA 1988 s 18(3)(b)	s 958
14 (1)	Unnecessary (interpretation)	
(2)-(5)		s 195(12)-(15)
15	Insertion of ITA 1967 s 462A	
16 (1)	Amendment of FA 1984 ss 11(1), 14(7A)(a), 16(2)(a)	s 488(1)-(3), 493
(2)	Unnecessary (operative date)	
17	Unnecessary (cesser of FA 1991 s 17(3)(b))	
18 (1)	Substitution of FA 1982 s 19(2)	s 482(1), (2), (3), (4)
(2)		s 482(8)
19 (1)-(6)		s 236
(7)	Unnecessary (commencement)	
20 (1)	Amendment of FA 1987 s 35	s 481, Sch 32 para 22
(2)	Unnecessary (operative date)	
21 (1)		s 373(2)(g)
(2)	Amendment of FA 1976 s 32	s 376
22 (1)	Amendment of ITA 1967 ss 254, 256, 264, 265	s 271, 278(1)(2)(6), 304(4), 305, 316(3), 317(2)
(2)	Unnecessary (operative date)	
23 (1)	Amendment of FA 1974 s 22	s 658
(2)	Unnecessary (operative date)	
24	Insertion of ITA 1967 s 241A, amendment of ss 272(1), 304(1)	ss 288(1)-(3), 291, 301(1), 314
25 (1)	Amendment of FA 1989 s 18	s 734
(2)	Unnecessary (commencement)	
26	Amendment of FA 1984 s 29(2A)	s 815(3)
27	Amendment of CTA 1976 ss 83, 88	ss 20, s 152(3), 153(1)
28	Amendment of FA 1973 s 34(1)	s 234(1), (2)(a)
29 (1)	Insertion of FA 1986 s 46(6)	s 1013(4)(b)
(2)(a)	Unnecessary (operative date)	
(b)		s 1013(4)(c)
30 (1)-(5), (7)		s 404
(6)	Unnecessary (obsolete)	

Former Enactment		*Destination in TCA 1997*
Finance Act 1994 (1994 No 13) (contd)		
s 31	Amendment of FA 1993 s 49(1)(a)	
32 (1)-(4)		s 227
(5)		s 610, Sch 15 Pt I
33	Amendment of CTA 1976 s 36A(2)	s 723
34	Amendment of FA 1993 ss 13, 14, 16	ss 256, 261, 264, 737, 838
35 (1)	Amendment of FA 1986 ss 42, 44, 45, deletion of s 43	s 323, 324, 328(1)-(3), 329(9)(b)(12), 1024, Sch 32 paras 11,12,13
(2)	Unnecessary (operative date)	
36	Amendment of FA 1987 s 27(1)	s 322(2)
37 (1)	Amendment of FA 1991 ss 55, 56, 57, 58	s 325(1)(2), 326(1), 327(1)
(2)	Unnecessary (operative date)	
38 (1), (3), (4)		s 339
(2)	Unnecessary (obsolete)	
39		s 340
40		s 341
41		s 342
41A	(s 41A inserted by FA 1995 s 35(1)(e))	s 343
41B	(s 41B inserted by FA 1995 s 35(1)(f))	s 344
42 (1)-(7)		s 345(1)-(7)
(8)	Amendment of FA 1990 s 33	ss 324(4)(b), 333(4)(b), 345(8)(b), 354(5)(b), 370(8)(b)
43		s 346
44		s 347
45		s 348
46 (1)-(4), (7)	Proviso to definition of "qualifying premises" deleted by FA 1995 s 35(1)	s 349
(5)	Rep by FA 1996 s 132(2) and Sch 5 Pt II	
(6)	Amendment of ITA 1967 s 198(1)(a)	s 1024
47		s 350
48 (1), (2)	Amendment of FA 1980 s 39(1A)	s 443
(2)	Amendment of FA 1990 s 41	s 443
49	Amendment of FA 1988 s 37	s 452
50 (1)	Amendment of CTA 1976 s 84A	s 134(3)
(2)		s 133(12)(a)-(d)
(3)	Unnecessary (operative date)	
proviso(i)		s 133(12)(e)
proviso(ii)	Unnecessary (operative date)	
51	Amendment of FA 1992 s 56(2)	s 88
52 (1)		s 221(1)
(2)		s 221(2)(a)(b)
53	Amendment of FA 1980 s 39B(6)	s 446(1)-(12)
54	Insertion of s 39C, amendment of FA 1980 s 41(1)	s 448(1)
55	Insertion of FA 1983 s 44(8)	s 165
56	Insertion of CTA 1976 ss 12A, 14A	s 79
57	Amendment of FA 1993 ss 17, 18	ss 738, 739
58	Insertion of CGTA 1975 s 20B	s 595
59	Substitution of FA 1989 s 25(1)	s 154(1)-(3)
60	Amendment of CTA 1976 s 35(1A)	s 710(1)-(5)
61	Amendment of FA 1984 s 40	s 403
62	Amendment of FA 1987 s 28(1)	s 407(1)
63 (1)	Amendment of CGTA 1975 Sch 4	29(8)(9), 544(7), 567(3)(4), 568, 849(1)(2), 849(3)-(6), 851, 861(1), 863-865,

Former Enactment		*Destination in TCA 1997*
Finance Act 1994 (1994 No 13) (contd)		
s 63 (1)		869-871, 874, 875, 911, 913-917, 931, 945, 946, 949, 976, 977, 978, 980, 982, 999, Sch 1, 1029, 1043, 1051, 1077(1), 1077(2), 1083
(2)	Unnecessary (operative date)	
64 (1), (2)	Amendment of CGTA 1975	s 31731(1)-(5)(a), Sch 32 para 25
(3)		s 731(7)
65	Amendment of FA 1993 s 27	s 591(1)-(4)
66 (1)-(8)		s 592
(8A)	Rep by FA 1997 s 146(2) and Sch 9 Pt II	
(9)	Unnecessary (operative date)	
Pt VII		
s 149		s 818
150		s 819
151		s 820
152		s 821
153		s 822
154		s 823
155	Amendment of ITA 1967 s 153	s 1032
156		s 824
157(1)	Unnecessary (repeal of ITA 1967 ss 76(4), 199, 206, FA 1987 s 4)	
(2)	Unnecessary (spent)	
158	Unnecessary (commencement)	
161(1)		ss 40(1), 48(1)(d)
(2)(a)		s 40(2)
(2)(b)		s 48(1)(d)
(3)	Amendment of ITA 1967 s 474(1)	s 49, Sch 32 para 1(2)
(5)	Amendment of FA 1984 s 66	s 607
162(1)	Substitution of ITA 1967 s 486(1), (2)	s 963
(2)	Unnecessary (operative date)	
(2)	Unnecessary (spent)	
(3)	Unnecessary (operative date)	
164		s 196
165	Unnecessary (care and management)	
166(2), (8)	Unnecessary (construction and commencement)	
Sch 1	Amendment of ITA 1967 ss 138, 138A(2),	ss 461, 462
Sch 2		Sch 4
Finance Act 1995 (1995 No 8)		
Pt I		
s 1	Amendment of FA 1980 ss 1, 2	ss 187,188
2	Amendment of FA 1991 s 2	
3 (1), (2)	Unnecessary (obsolete)	s 15
(3)	Unnecessary (application of schedule)	
4	Amendment of FA 1982 s 6	
5	Amendment of ITA 1967 s 142A	s 473
6 (1)-(5)		s 474
(6)	Rep by FA 1996 s 132(2) and Sch 5 Pt II	
(7)	Amendment of ITA 1967 s 198(1)(a)	s 1024
7 (1)-(8)		s 477
(9)(a)	Amendment of ITA 1967 s 198(1)(a)	s 1024
(b)	Amendment of ITA 1967 Sch 15	Sch 29

Former Enactment			*Destination in TCA 1997*
Finance Act 1995 (1995 No 8) (contd)			
s 7	(10)	Rep by FA 1996 s 132(2) and Sch 5 Pt II	
8	(1)(a)(c)		s 848(1)
	(b)	Unnecessary (obsolete)	
	(2)-(5)(a)		s 848(2)-(5)
	(5)(b)		s 848(1)(a)
	(6), (7)		s 848(6), (7)
9		Amendment of FA 1982 s 8(1)	s 122
10	(1)	Substitution of FA 1992 s 15(2)	s 126(3)(b)
	(2)	Amendment of FA 1994 s 10	
11	(1)	Amendment of FA 1986 s 31(1)	s 256
	(2)	Amendment of FA 1993 s 14(3)	s 838(1)-(3)
12	(1)	Amendment of ITA 1967 ss 443, 444, 445, 447	ss 794(1)-(5), 795
	(2)	Unnecessary (operative date)	
	(3)	Unnecessary (cesser of ITA 1967 ss 440, 443(4))	
13	(1)(a)	Insertion of ITA 1967 s 439(1A)	s 792(1)-(4)
	(b)	Unnecessary (operative date)	
	(2)	Amendment of ITA 1967 s 439	s 792(1)-(4)
13	(3)		Sch 32, para 27
14	(1)	Insertion of ITA 1967 s 94(e)	s 888
	(2)	Amendment of FA 1992 ss 226(1), 228(1)	ss 894, 899
	(3)	Unnecessary (operative date)	
15		Amendment of ITA 1967 s 191	s 930
16		Amendment of FA 1982 s 56 and Sch 3	s 515, Sch 11
17	(1)	Amendment of FA 1984 ss 11(1), 12, 13, 15, 16, 22, 23, insertion of ss 14A, 16A,	ss 488, 489, 490, 494, 495, 496, 498, 503, 504
	(2)	Unnecessary (operative dates)	
18	(1)	Amendment of FA 1970 s 17	ss 530(1), 531(11)
	(2)	Unnecessary (operative date)	
19		Insertion of ITA 1967 s 58A	s 68
20		Amendment of FA 1982 s 19	s 482
21		Rep by FA 1996 s 132(2) and Sch 5 Pt II	
22		Rep by FA 1996 s 132(2) and Sch 5 Pt II	
23	(1)		s 373(2)(g)
	(2)	Amendment of FA 1976 s 32	s 376
24	(1)	Amendment of ITA 1967 s 265(1)(c)	s 274(1), (3), (4), (5), (8)
	(2)	Unnecessary (operative date and cesser of FA 1994 s 22(1)(d)(i))	
25	(1)	Amendment of ITA 1967 s 272	s 288(1)-(3)
	(2)	Unnecessary (operative date)	
26		Amendment of FA 1988s 51(1)	ss 271(3)(a), 273(5)(a), 283(4)(a), 285(5)(a)
27		Substitution of FA 1990 s 81(1)	ss 273(7)(b), 285(7)(b)
28		Amendment of FA 1994 s 49(1)	s 452
29			s 847
30	(1)	Amendment of FA 1986 s 48(2)	s 1084(1)-(4)
	(2)	Unnecessary (operative date)	
31		Amendment of FA 1988 s 18	s 958
32	(1)	Amendment of FA 1986 ss 41, 42, 44	s 322(1), 323, Sch 32 paras 11, 12
	(2)	Unnecessary (operative date)	
33		Amendment of FA 1987 s 27(1)(b)	s 322(2)-(3)
34	(1)	Amendment of FA 1991 ss 54(3), 55, 56, 57(2), 58(2)	s 325(1)(2)
	(2)	Unnecessary (operative date)	

Former Enactment		*Destination in TCA 1997*
Finance Act 1995 (1995 No 8) (contd)		
s 35 (1)	Amendment of FA 1994 ss 38(1), 39, 40, 41, 42(1), 43(1), 46(1), insertion of ss 41A, 41B	s 339, 340, 341, 342, 343, 344, 345(1)-(7), 346, 349
(2)	Unnecessary (operative date)	
36 (1)	Amendment of FA 1987 s 35	s 481, Sch 32 para 22
(2)	Unnecessary (operative date)	
37	Insertion of FA 1983 s 47A	s 169
38	Amendment of FA 1989 s 18(1).	s 734(1)(a), (c)
39	Amendment of FA 1994 s 27	ss 20, s 152(3), 153(1)
40		s 198
41	Insertion of FA 1992 s 230A	s 896
42	Amendment of FA 1992 ss 75(1), 77(1)	ss 684, 686
43		s 224
44 (1), (2)		s 220
(3)		s 610, Sch 15 Pt I
45 (1)	Unnecessary (obsolete)	
(2)	Unnecessary (application of schedule)	
46 (1)		s 351
(2)	Unnecessary (obsolete)	
47		s 352
48		s 353
49 (1)-(4)		s 354(1)-(4)
(5)	Amendment of FA 1990 s 33	ss 324(4)(b), 333(4)(b), 345(8)(b), 354(5)(b), 370(8)(b)
49A	(s 49A inserted by FA 1996 s 30).	s 355
50		s 356
51		s 357
52		s 358
53		s 359
54 (1)	Substitution of CTA 1976 s 1(1)	s 21
(2)	Unnecessary (application of schedule)	
55 (1)	Amendment of CTA 1976 s 162(4)	s 441
(2)	Unnecessary (operative date)	
proviso	Unnecessary (obsolete)	
56	Amendment of FA 1992 s 45(1)(a)	s 487
57 (1)		s 221(1)
(2)		s 221(2)(c)(d)
58	Amendment of CTA 1976 s 141	ss 882(2)-(5), 1073
59 (1)-(4)		s 766
(5)	Unnecessary (obsolete)	
60	Amendment of CTA 1976 s 23	ss 826(1)-(7), (9), 827,
		Sch 24, para 4(2)
61	Amendment of FA 1980 s 41(1)(b)	s 448(1)
62	Insertion of FA 1980 s 39D	s 446(1)-(12)
63	Amendment of FA 1980 s 39C.	s 449
64	Insertion of CTA 1976 s 43(2A)	s 726
65	Substitution of FA 1980 s 39B(6)(c)(iiia)	s 446(1)-(12)
66 (1), (2)		s 1085(3), (4)
(3)	Unnecessary (operative date)	
67	Amendment of FA 1993 s 51	s 486
68	Insertion of CGTA 1975 s 20A(4)	s 594
69	Amendment of CTA 1976 s 46B(1).	s 720(1)(2)
70 (1)	Amendment of CGTA 1975 Sch 4 para 4(1)	s 914
(2)	Unnecessary (operative date)	

Former Enactment		*Destination in TCA 1997*
Finance Act 1995 (1995 No 8) (contd)		
s 71 (1)	Amendment of CGTA 1975 s 26	s 598
(2)	Unnecessary (operative date)	
72 (1)	Amendment of CGTA 1975 s 27(4)(a)	s 599
(2)	Unnecessary (operative date)	
73 (1)	Insertion of FA 1982 s 39(4), (5)	s 652
(2)	Unnecessary (operative date)	
74 (1)	Amendment of FA 1993 s 27	s 591
(2)	Unnecessary (operative date)	
75	Amendment of FA 1995 s 66	s 1085(3), (4)
76	Amendment of CGTA 1975 Sch 4 para 11	s 980
Pt VII		
s 167	Amendment of FA 1986 ss 31(1), 37(1)	ss 256, 263
168	Amendment of ITA 1967 s 175(4)	s 891
169	Amendment of FA 1994 s 152(1)	s 821
170	Amendment of FA 1994 s 154(2)	s 823
172		s 1079
173(1)	Amendment of ITA 1967 ss 416, 421, 422, 423, 424, 427, 428, 429, 432	ss 864(1), 933(1)-(7)(f), 934, 935,936, 937, 940, 941, 942(1)-(8), (10), 949(1)-(4)
(2)	Substitution of FA 1969 s 2(5B)	s 195(1)-(11)
(3)	Unnecessary (application).	
173 (4)	Unnecessary (operative date)	
174	Amendment of FA 1986 s 115	
175		s 910
176		s 1003
177(1)-(6)		s 1095
(7)	Unnecessary (operative date)	
178	Unnecessary (care and management)	
179(2), (8), (9)	Unnecessary (construction and commencement)	
Sch 1	Amendment of ITA 1967 ss 138, 138A(2)	s 461, s 462
Sch 2	Unnecessary (obsolete)	
Sch 3		Sch 8
Sch 4	Unnecessary (obsolete)	
Family Law Act 1995 (1995 No 26)		
s 49	Amendment of FA 1983 s 4	s 1026(1), (2)
Finance Act 1996 (1996 No 9)		
Pt I		
s 1	Amendment of FA 1980 ss 1, 2.	ss 187, 188
2	Amendment of FA 1991 s 2	s 15
3 (1), (2)	Unnecessary (obsolete)	
(3)	Unnecessary (application of schedule)	
4	Unnecessary (obsolete)	
5		s 478
6	Amendment of FA 1982 s 4	s 121
7 (1)	Substitution of ITA 1967 s 145(1)	s 470(1)-(3)
(2)	Unnecessary (operative date)	
8 (1)	Amendment of FA 1992 Sch 2	
(2)	Unnecessary (operative date)	
9		s 191
10		s 664(1)(a), (b)(iii)
11 (1)		s 656(1)
(2)	Amendment of ITA 1967 s 62(1)(b)	s 89(2)
12	Amendment of FA 1986 s 12	s 479
13 (a)	Substitution of ITA 1967 s 236(1A)	s 787(8)-(12)
(b)	Unnecessary (deletion of ITA 1967 Sch 5)	

Former Enactment		*Destination in TCA 1997*
Finance Act 1996 (1996 No 9) (contd)		
s 14	Amendment of FA 1969 s 2(2)(a)	s 195(1)-(11)
15 (1)-(5), (8)		s 475
(6)	Rep by FA 1997 s 146(2) and Sch 9 Pt II	
(7)	Amendment of ITA 1967 s 198(1)(a)	s 1023
16	Amendment of FA 1984 s 11(1)	s 488(1), (2), (3)
17	Amendment of FA 1984 s 12	ss 488(1), 489
18	Amendment of FA 1984 s 13	s 490
19	Amendment of FA 1984 s 13A	s 491
20	Insertion of FA 1984 s 13B	s 492
21	Unnecessary (obsolete)	
22	Insertion of FA 1984 s 15(3C)	s 495
23	Amendment of FA 1984 s 16	s 496
24	Amendment of FA 1984 s 16A	s 497
25 (1), (2)		s 233
(3)	Amendment of CTA 1976 s 93(1)	s 140
(4)	Unnecessary (operative date)	
26 (1)	Amendment of FA 1984 s 41B(1)	
26 (2)	Unnecessary (operative date)	
27	Amendment of FA 1991 s 22	s 271(4)(a)
28	Amendment of ITA 1967 ss 264, 265	s 272, s 274(1),(3)-(5),(8)
29	Amendment of ITA 1967 s 255(1)	s 268(1)-(3), (5)-(8)
30	Insertion of FA 1995 s 49A	s 355
31 (1)	Substitution of FA 1987 s 35	s 481, Sch 32, para 22
(2)(a),(3),(4)		Sch 32, para 22(1)-(4)
(b)	Unnecessary (obsolete)	
(1)	Amendment of FA 1973 s 34(1)	s 234(1), (2)(a)
(2)	Amendment of CTA 1976 s 170	s 141
(3)	Unnecessary (operative date)	
33 (1)	Substitution of FA 1974 s 31(3)(cc)	
(2)	Unnecessary (operative date)	
34	Insertion of F(TPCM)A 1974 s 8A	s 681
35 (1)	Amendment of FA 1989 s 18(1)	s 734
(2)	Unnecessary (operative date)	
36 (1)	Insertion of FA 1993 s 13(8)(bb)	s 737
(2)	Unnecessary (operative date)	
37 (1)	Amendment of FA 1993 s 14	s 838
(2)	Unnecessary (operative date)	
38 (1)	Amendment of FA 1993 s 17	s 738
(2)	Unnecessary (operative date)	
39 (1)		ss 41, 228, 610
(2)		s 228
(3)		s 41
(4)	Amendment of ITA 1967 s 474(1)	s 49, Sch 32 para 1(2)
(5)	Amendment of CGTA 1975 s 19(1)	s 607(1)(a), (b), (c), (d), (f)
(6)		s 610, Sch 15 PtI
39 (7)	Unnecessary (repeal of Securitisation (Proceeds of Certain Mortgages) Act, 1995 s 14)	
(8)	Unnecessary (operative date)	
40 (1), (2)		s 226
(3)	Unnecessary (operative date)	
41	Amendment of FA 1970 s 17	ss 530(1), 531(11)
42	Insertion of FA 1986 s 33A	s 260
43 (1)	Amendment of FA 1988 s 51(1)(a)	ss 271(3)(a), 273(5)(a), 283(4)(a), 285(5)(a)
(2)	Unnecessary (operative date)	
44	Insertion of CTA 1976 s 28A	s 22
45 (1)	Amendment of CTA 1976 s 12A	s 79
(2)	Unnecessary (operative date)	

Former Enactment		Destination in TCA 1997
Finance Act 1996 (1996 No 9) (contd)		
s 46	Amendment of CTA 1976 s 33A(1)	s 708
47 (1)	Insertion of CTA 1976 s 35A(1A)	s 711
(2)	Unnecessary (operative date)	
48 (1)	Amendment of CTA 1976 s 36(2)	s 713(1)-(6)
(2)	Unnecessary (operative date)	
49 (1)	Amendment of CTA 1976 s 36A(6)	s 723
(2)	Unnecessary (operative date)	
50 (1)	Insertion of CTA 1976 s 46B(4)	s 720(3)-(5)
(2)	Unnecessary (operative date)	
51	Amendment of CTA 1976 s 135	s 623
52 (1)	Amendment of CTA 1976 s 162(4)	s 441
(2)	Unnecessary (operative date)	
proviso	Unnecessary (obsolete)	
53	Amendment of FA 1980 s 39A(6)(c)	s 445
54 (1)	Amendment of FA 1987 s 28	ss 133(1)(d), 134(1)(d), 407(1)(3)(4)(6), 443
(2), (5)		s 407(5)
(3)(a), (4)		s 407(1)
(b)		s 407(2)
55 (1)	Amendment of FA 1991 s 31	s 110
(2)	Unnecessary (operative date)	
56	Amendment of FA 1992 s 56	s 88
57 (1)	Amendment of FA 1995 s 59	s 766
(2)	Unnecessary (operative date)	
58 (1)	Amendment of FA 1983 ss 44(5), 47(1)	ss 165, 168
(2)	Unnecessary (operative date)	
59	Amendment of CGTA 1975 Sch 4 para 11	s 980
60 (1)	Amendment of CGTA 1975 s 26(6)(a)	s 598
(2)	Unnecessary (operative date)	
61 (1)	Insertion of CGTA 1975 s 46(7)	s 541(7)(a)-(c), (g)
(2)	Unnecessary (operative date)	
62 (1)	Insertion of FA 1993 s 27(2A)	s 591(1)-(4)
(2)	Unnecessary (operative date)	
63 (1)	Amendment of FA 1994 s 66	s 592
(2)	Unnecessary (operative date)	
64		s 610, Sch 15
65		s 360
66		s 361
67		s 362
68		s 363
69 (1)-(3), (5)		s 364
(4)	Amendment of ITA 1967 s 198(1)(a)	s 1024
70		s 365
Pt VI		
s 130		s 872(2)
131(1)-(8)		s 10
(9)(a)	Unnecessary (obsolete)	
(b)	Unnecessary (cesser of F(MP)A 1968 s 16(3), CGTA 1975 s 33(7), CTA 1976 s 157)	
132(1), (2)	Unnecessary (application of schedules)	
(3)	Unnecessary (construction)	
133	Definition of "farming" and "tax" unnecessary (duplication)	s 665
134		s 666
135		s 667
136		s 668

Former Enactment		*Destination in TCA 1997*
Finance Act 1996 (1996 No 9) (contd)		
s 137		s 669
Pt VII		
s 139	Amendment of FA 1995 s 176(2)	s 1003
142	Unnecessary (care and management)	
143(2), (7), (8)	Unnecessary (construction and commencement)	
Sch 1	Amendment of ITA 1967 ss 138, 138A(2), 141(1), FA 1969 s 3(1), FA 1971 s 11(2)	ss 461, 462, 465, 467, 468
Sch 5		
Pt I	Amendment of ITA 1967 ss 2, 79, 145, 146, 149, 153, 195A, 235(7), 239, 241, 297, 299, 312(2), 316, 433(1), 434(1), 468(2), 471(2), 497	ss 3(2)(3), 74, 237, 238(1)(6), 306, 312, 386, 390(1)(3), 459(1)(2), 460, 762(2)(a), 470(1)-(4), 783(3), 788, 1020, 1032, Sch 32, para 1(1)
	Substitution of ITA 1967 ss 137, 321	s 458, 395
	Amendment of FA 1967 s 11, FA 1968 s 6, FA 1969 s 19 , FA 1971 s 26, FA 1972 Sch 1, FA 1973 s 34, F(TPCM)A 1974 s 1, FA 1974 s 62, CTA 1976 ss 6, 50, 102(1), 147(2), FA 1978 s 25, FA 1980 s 2, FA 1983 ss 3, 94(2), FA 1985 s 10, FA 1986 s 12, FA 1987 s 24, FA 1991 s 4 , FA 1992 s 83, FA 1995 s 177	ss 207(3)(4), 211(5)(6), 213(3)(4), 234, 26(1)-(3), 273, 273(1)-(3)(8), 285(1)-(3)(8), 286, 287, 299(2), 432, 463, 479, 483(1)-(3), 53, 664(1)(a), 672(1), 692, 706(1)-(3), 863, 865, 868, 869, 870, 849, 860, 861(1), 862, 873, 874, 875, 877, 886, 898, 901, 928(1), 929, 947, 998, 1004, 1025, 1049, 105, 1055, 1056, 1057, 1058, 1066, 1067, 1068, 1069, 1070, 1078, 1081(1), 1095, Sch 23 Pt I paras 1-5
Pt II	Repeal of ITA 1967 ss 43, 89A, 138A(7), 141(7), 145(3A)(5), 241(7)(8)(9), 242, 243, 244(4)(e), 247(3), 249, 259, 262, 273(2), 306, 344, 346, 360, 448(2), 476, 477(2), (3), 479, 480, 482(3), 494(2), 495, 540, 543, 557, 558, Sch 2 rule 1(3), Sch 13, FA 1967 s 12(5)(c), FA 1968 s 4, FA 1969 ss 3(3), 4, 5, FA 1971 s 11(4), FA 1972 ss 16(6), 17(3), 18(1)(b), 24, 25, Sch 1 Pt II para 1(2), Sch 1 Pts IV, V, FA 1974 ss 4(c), 8(2), 30, 40, 50, FA 1975 ss 31, 31A, Sch, 3, Sch 5, CGTA 1975 ss 2(2), 27(1)(d), 33(8), CTA 1976 ss 12(8), 51(3)(b)(c), 52(5), 68, 153, FA 1976 ss 12, 15, 16, FA 1977 s 39(4)(b) proviso, FA 1978 s 9, Sch 1 Pt III, FA 1979 ss 5, 8(2)(b), FA 1980 s 28, FA 1981 s 13, FA 1982 ss 6, 13, FA 1983 s 94(1)(ee), FA 1984 ss 12(9), 33, Pt I Ch VIII, IX, FA 1986 ss 12(9), 44(4), FA 1989 s 4(7), FA 1991 s 4(3), FA 1992 ss 26(1)(2) (3)(5), 243(a)(ii), FA 1993 s 28, FA 1994 s 46(5), FA 1995 ss 6(6), 7(10), 21, 22	
	Amendment of ITA 1967 ss 58(5), 186(3), 187(1), 235(7), 244(5)(b)(6), 245(7), 300(1), 309, 441, 442, 447, 478, 484(3), 496(1)(c), Sch 2 rule 3, FA 1969 s 18(1), FA 1972 s 15(4), FA 1974 ss 4(b)(e), 27(2), 31(3), FA 1975 Sch 2 Pt I para 2, CGTA 1975 s 27(3), CTA 1976 ss 11(6), 39(2)(b), 43(5)(a), 147(2)	ss 59, 67, 76, 114, 207(3)(4), 211(5)(6), 213(3)(4), 232(1), 246(3), 313, 382(1)(2), 483(1)-(3), 599, 662, 670, 715, 726, 765, 772(4), 783(3), 791(1), 793, 794(1), 860, 861(1), 862, 863, 865, 868, 869, 870, 873, 874, 875, 886, 898, 901, 924, 928(1), 929, 947, 961,

Former Enactment		*Destination in TCA 1997*
Finance Act 1996 (1996 No 9) (contd)		
Pt II (contd)		964(2), 972(1)-(4), 998, 1004, 1049, 1055, 1056, 1057, 1058, 1066, 1067, 1068, 1069, 1070, 1081(1)
Disclosure of Certain Information for Taxation and Other Purposes Act 1996 (1996 No 25)		
s 5	Insertion of ITA 1967 s 184(3)	s 922
6	Substitution of CTA 1976 s 144(4)	s 919(1)-(5)
10	Insertion of FA 1983 s 18(4A)	s 908
11	Substitution of FA 1983 s 19(2)	s 58
12	Insertion of FA 1983 s 19A	s 859
Criminal Assets Bureau Act 1996 (1996 No 31)		
s 23	Substitution of FA 1983 s 19A(3)(a)	s 859
24 (1)	Substitution of ITA 1967 s 184(3)	s 922
(2)	Substitution of CTA 1976 s 144(4)(b)	s 919(1)-(5)
Family Law (Divorce) Act 1996 (1997 No 33)		
s 31		s 1027(b)
32	Amendment of FA 1983 s 4	s 1026(1), (2)
35		s 1031
Finance Act 1997 (1997 No 22)		
Pt I		
s 1	Amendment of FA 1980 ss 1, 2	ss 187, 188
2	Amendment of FA 1991 s 2	s 15
3 (1), (2)	Unnecessary (duplication)	
3 (3)	Unnecessary (application of schedule)	
4 (1)	Amendment of FA 1992 s 15(2)	s 126(3)(b)(4)
(2)		s 126(8)
5 (a)	Insertion of FA 1983 s 4(3)	s 1026(1), (2)
(b)	Unnecessary (repeal of Family Law Act 1995 s 49 and Family Law (Divorce) Act 1996 s 32	
6 (1)	Insertion of ITA 1967 s 127(5A)	s 986(4)-(6)
(2)	Unnecessary (operative date)	
7	Amendment of FA 1996 s 15	s 475
8 (1)-(7), (10),(11)		s 476
(8)	Amendment of ITA 1967 s 137	s 458
(9)	Amendment of ITA 1967 s 198(1)(a)	s 1024
9	Amendment of FA 1984 ss 11, 14A, 16, 16A	ss 488(1)-(4), 494, 496, 497
10	Amendment of FA 1992 s 14	ss 248(1)-(3), 252
11 (1)	Amendment of ITA 1967 s 353	s 193 Sch 32, para 2
(2)	Unnecessary (operative date).	
(3)	Unnecessary (spent)	
(4)	Amendment of ITA 1967 s 178(1)	s 897(1)-(5)
12	Amendment of ITA 1967 s 115(1A)	s 201(3)
13 (1)	Amendment of FA 1970 s 17	ss 530(1), 531(11)
(2)	Amendment of ITA 1967 Sch 15	Sch 29
14		s 202
15	Insertion of FA 1971 s 4(6)	s 72
16		s 485
17 (1)	Amendment of FA 1982 s 19	s 482
(2)	Amendment of FA 1993 s 29(1)	s 482(1)(a)
(3)	Unnecessary (operative date)	
18	Amendment of FA 1996 s 134	s 666
19	Amendment of FA 1996 s 135(1)(b)	s 667
20 (1)-(13)		s 659
(14)	Amendment of FA 1975 s 29	s 319

Former Enactment		*Destination in TCA 1997*
Finance Act 1997 (1997 No 22) (contd)		
s 21 (1)		s 373(2)(i)
(2)	Amendment of FA 1976 s 32	s 1009
22	Amendment of ITA 1967 s 241	ss 284, 298(1), 299(1), 301(1), 304(2)(4), 316(1)(a)(2), 406
23 (1)	Amendment of ITA 1967 ss 265, 266,	ss 274(1) (3)-(5)(8), 277
(2)	Unnecessary (operative date)	
24		s 409
25 (1)-(5), (7)		s 843
(6)	Unnecessary (operative date)	
26	Amendment of FA 1994 ss 38, 39, 42	ss 339, 340, 324(4)(b), 333(4)(b), 345(8)(b), 354(5)(b), 370(8)(b)
27	Amendment of FA 1986 s 45(2), FA 1994 s 42(3), FA 1995 s 49(3)	ss 324(2), 346, 354(1)-(4)
28	Insertion of FA 1980 s 39B(10)	s 446(1)-(12)
29 (1)		s 82(2)
(2)		s 243(3)(b)
(3)		s 390(2)(b)
(4)		s 82(3)
(5)		ss 82(4), 243(3)(c), 390(2)(c)
(6)		ss 82(1), 243(3)(a), 390(2)(a)
30 (1)	Amendment of FA 1987 s 35	s 481, Sch 32 para 22
(2)		Sch 32, para 22(6)-(8)
31 (1)	Amendment of FA 1993 s 14	s 838(1)-(4)
(2)	Unnecessary (operative date)	
32	Amendment of FA 1989 s 18(1)	s 734(1)(a), (c)
33		s 55
34	Amendment of FA 1990 s 138(1)	ss 45(3)(4)(a), 48(4)(a),(5)(a)
35	Substitution of FA 1993 s 17(4)(a)	s 738
36	Amendment of FA 1974 s 31	s 246(1)-(4)
37 (1)		ss 4(1), 136(2),139(1), 143(2)(7), 145(2)(a), (11)(a), 729(5)
(2)	Unnecessary (application of schedule)	
38	Amendment of FA 1992 s 37(1)	s 154(3)(a)(4)(5)
39 (1)(a)	Amendment of FA 1991 s 59	s 173
(b)	Insertion of FA 1991 s 60A	s 175
(2)	Unnecessary (operative date)	
40 (1)	Amendment of FA 1996 s 40(2)	s 226
(2)	Unnecessary (operative date)	
41 (1)(a)	Amendment of FA 1972 s 16	s 774(1)-(3)(5)-(7), Sch 32 para 26
(b)	Insertion of FA 1972 s 16A	s 775
(2)	Amendment of CTA 1976 Sch 2 Pt I para 31	Sch 32 para 26
(3)	Unnecessary (commencement)	
42		s 627
43		s 628
44		s 629
45 (1)	Amendment of ITA 1967 s 464	s 43
(2)	Unnecessary (operative date)	
46 (1)	Amendment of ITA 1967 s 470(1)(b)	s 50
(2)	Unnecessary (operative date)	
47 (1)	Amendment of ITA 1967 s 474(2)	s 49, Sch 32 para 1(2)
(2)	Unnecessary (operative date)	

Former Enactment		*Destination in TCA 1997*
Finance Act 1997 (1997 No 22) (contd)		
s 48 (1), (2)		s 842
(3)	Unnecessary (operative date)	
49 (1), (2)		s 220
(3)		s 610, Sch 15 Pt I
(4)		Sch 32, para 3
50 (a)	Amendment of FA 1982 s 52	s 511
(b)	Insertion of FA 1982 s 58A	s 518
(c)	Amendment of FA 1982 Sch 3	Sch 11
51		s 519
52		s 366
53		s 367
54		s 368
55		s 369
56		s 370(1)-(7)
(8)	Amendment of FA 1990 s 33	ss 324(4)(a)(b), 333(4)(a)(b), 345(8)(b), 354(5)(b), 370(8)(b)
57 (1)-(3), (5)		s 371
(4)	Amendment of ITA 1967 s 137	s 458
58		s 372
59 (1)	Substitution of CTA 1976 s 1(1)	s 21
(2)	Unnecessary (application of schedule)	
60 (1)	Amendment of CTA 1976 s 28A	s 22(1)(a), (2)-(8)
(2)	s 22(1)(b)	
(3)	Unnecessary (operative date)	
61 (1), (3), (4)		s 841
(2)	Unnecessary (repeal of CTA 1976 s 80)	
62(1), (3)-(5)		s 229
(2)	Unnecessary (repeal of ITA 1967 s 343)	
63		s 219
64	Amendment of FA 1992 s 56	s 88
65	Amendment of FA 1993 s 51	s 454(1)
66 (1)	Amendment of FA 1988 s 36(4)(a)	s 451
(2)	Unnecessary (operative date)	
67 (1)	Insertion of CTA 1976 s 35(1B)	s 710(1)-(5)
(2)	Unnecessary (operative date)	
68 (1)	Amendment of CTA 1976 s 36	s 713(1)-(6)
(2)	Unnecessary (operative date)	
69 (1)	Substitution of CTA 1976 s 46A(3)(a)	s 719
(2)	Unnecessary (operative date)	
70 (1)	Insertion of CGTA 1975 Sch 2 para 5A	s 588
(2)	Unnecessary (operative date)	
71 (1)-(3)		s 1031
(4)	Unnecessary (repeal of s 35 Family Law (Divorce) Act, 1996)	
(5)	Unnecessary (operative date)	
72 (1)-(3)		s 1030
(4)	Unnecessary (repeal of Family Law Act 1995 s 52)	
(5)	Unnecessary (operative date)	
73 (1)	Insertion of CGTA 1975 s 15(5A)	s 577
(2)	Unnecessary (operative date)	
74 (1)	Amendment of CGTA 1975 s 20A	s 594
(2)	Unnecessary (operative date)	
75 (1)	Amendment of FA 1993 s 27	s 591(1)-(5)
(2)	Unnecessary (operative date)	

Former Enactment		*Destination in TCA 1997*
Finance Act 1997 (1997 No 22) (contd)		
s 76	Amendment of FA 1994 s 66	s 592
77 (1)	Insertion of FA 1982 s 39(3A)	s 652
(2)	Unnecessary (operative date)	
78 (1)	Amendment of CGTA 1975 s 46(7)	s 541(7)(a), (b), (c), (g)
(2)		s 541(8)
Pt VII		
s 144		s 37
145		s 244
146(1), (2)	Unnecessary (application of schedule)	
(3)	Unnecessary (interpretation)	
147		s 330
148		s 331
149		s 332
150(1)-(3)		s 333(1)-(3)
(4)	Amendment of FA 1990 s 33	ss 324(4)(b), 333(4)(b), 345(8)(b), 354(5)(b), 370(8)(b)
150(5)		s 333(5)
151		s 334
152		s 335
153		s 336
154		s 337
155		s 338
156(1)	Repeal of FA 1991 ss 54, 55, 56(1)(a)(iii), (2) proviso, 57(1)(a), (2), 58(1)(a), (2)	
(2)	Amendment of ITA 1967 s 137	s 458
(3)	Amendment of CTA 1976 s 33A(1)	s 708
(4)	Amendment of FA 1991 s 56(1)(c)	
157	Amendment of ITA 1967 s 162(3)	s 851
158	Substitution of FA 1983 s 23(2), (3)	s 1086
159		s 858
160(1)	Amendment of FA 1992 s 242(1)	s 1094
165	Unnecessary (care and management)	
166(2), (8), (9)	Unnecessary (construction and commencement)	
Sch 1	Amendment of ITA 1967 ss 138, 138A(2) and FA 1974 s 8(1)	ss 461, 462, 464
Sch 2		
para 1		ss 4(1), 136(2), 139(1), 143(2), (7), 145(2)(a), (11)(a), 729(5)
2		s 729(7)
3 (1)	Unnecessary (operative date)	
(2)	Unnecessary (cesser of FA 1978 s 28(7), FA 1983 s 28(3), FA 1988 Sch 2 Pt I para 4, FA 1990 Sch 1 para 3, FA 1995 Sch 2 para 3)	
(3)		s 145(2)(b)
Sch 3		Sch 12
Sch 4		s 659 Table
Sch 5		Sch 26

Former Enactment		*Destination in TCA 1997*
Finance Act 1997 (1997 No 22) (contd)		
Sch 6, Pt I		
para 1		ss 26(4), 78(3)(c)
2(1)		Sch 32, para 16(5), 18(6)(a)
(2)		Sch 32, para 18(6)(b)
(3)		Sch 32, para 16(3)(b), 18(4)(b)
Pt II		
para 1(1)		s 448(2)(b)
(2)	Amendment of FA 1980 s 41(2)	s 448(2)(a)
(1)	Amendment of FA 1980 ss 47(2), 48(2)	Sch 32 paras 5(2), 6(2)
2(2)		Sch 32 para 5(3), 6(3)
Sch 9		
Pt I	Amendment of ITA 1967 ss 1(1), 58(1), 61, 76(1)(c), 77(5), 81(5)(b), 89(2), 137, 138B, 142(1)(b), 183, 197, 198, 225, 239(4), 241(1)(b)(i), 241A, 256, 284(3), 304, 309(2), 310(3), 318(1), 319(1), 349, 429(4), 441(1), 446(1), 450(2), 466(3)(b), 474(1), 484, 492(1)(d), 525(5)(a), Sch 6 Pt III Par 1(2), FA 1967 s 12(1), F(MP)A 1968 s 9, FA 1970 ss 14(2), 19(2A), 59(1), FA 1972 ss 15, 18(5), Sch 1 Pt III para 4, FA 1973 ss 25(1), 34(3), F(TPCM)A 1974 ss 7(4), CGTA 1975 ss 2(1), 25(9A)(a), 38(1), CTA 1976 ss 76, 84A, 93(7), 101(6), 103(3), 124(6), 145(3), 160, 162(5), 170(7), FA 1980 ss 39(1CC), 45(1)(a), FA 1982 ss 8, 58(3), FA 1984 ss 12(7)(b), 13A(1A), 13B(1), 14(1)(a), 15(3C)(b), FA 1986 s 33A(3), FA 1988 s 12, FA 1992 ss 45(1)(a), 84(11), FA 1993 s 14, 35(1)(a), FA 1994 ss 14(3)(b)(i), 45(2), 66(7)(a), FA 1995 s 48(5), FA 1996 s 68(2) s 194, 225	ss 3(1), 5, 38, 48(1)(b), 49, 65(1),70(4), 71(1), 73, 81(2), 97, 122, 127(1)-(5), 134(3), 140, 141, 144, 147 195(12)-(15), 2(1), 200(1), 234(3)-(8), 235, 245, 260, 270, 279, 284, 287, 291, 301(1), 316, 318, 320(1), 348, 353, 36, 363, 373(2)(a), 374, 382(1)(2), 383, 384, 392, 393, 406, 428, 433,440, 441, 443, 458, 466, 469(1), 472, 487, 488(1), 491, 492, 493, 495, 517, 592, 604,678, 681, 693, 701, 754, 772,772, 788, 790, 793, 797, 799, 808, 828(1)-(3), 838, 921, 942(1)-(8)(10), 953, 968, 972, 973, 1023, 1024, 1033, Sch 32 paras 1(2), para 4
	Substitution of ITA 1967 s 354, FA 1982 s 18	
Pt II	Repeal of ITA 1967 ss 46, 68(2), 82, 106, 177, 307(1A), 340(2)(e)(f), 365, 366, 419, 467, 467A, 467B, 467C, 468(1)(2), 469, 471, 472(2), 473, 484(5), 486(3), 496, 550(2A), Sch 1 Pt II, Sch 18 para VIII(1), FA 1972 s11, FA 1974 ss 38, 44, 52, 54, CGTA 1975 s 49(7), CTA 1976 ss 6(4), 66A(3) proviso, 66A(4), 76A(2) proviso, (3), FA 1976 ss 25, 30, FA 1980 s 7, FA 1981 ss 6, 18, FA 1982 ss 21, 22, FA 1986 s 8, Pt I Ch III, ss 33(9)(e), 46(4), FA 1987 ss 6, 35(22), FA 1988 ss 19(1), 21(6), 22, FA 1993 s 7, Sch 1 para 1(7)(e), FA 1994 ss 5, 38, 49, FA 1995 s 6, 66(8A), FA 1996 s 15(6).	
	Amendment of ITA 1967 ss 1(1), 307(1), 317(2), FA 1974 s 16(5), CGTA 1975 s 32(4)(b), CTA 1976 ss 76(6), 152(3), FA 1983 s 50(11), FA 1986 s 33(9)(d), FA 1989 Sch 1 para 1(7)(d)	ss 2(1), 3(1), 381(1), 144, 171, 240, 258, 657(1), 732, Sch 18 para 1
Sch 10		Sch 7

Index

A

Abandonment

of an option within the meaning of CGTA 1975 s 47(3) *TA Dilleen (Inspector of Taxes) v Edward J Kearns* Vol IV p 547

Absent

landowner returns to take on active farming *EP O'Coindealbhain (Inspector of Taxes) v KN Price* Vol IV p 1

Absolute interest

discretionary trust, when absolute interest passes *BKJ v The Revenue Commissioners* Vol III p 104

Accountants

working papers, whether the inspector of taxes is entitled to call for production of a taxpayer's nominal ledger, whether the nominal ledger formed part of the accountant's working papers *JJ Quigley (Inspector of Taxes) v Maurice Burke* Vol IV p 332, Vol V p 265

Accounting

method of accounting for tax purposes, whether replacement cost basis is acceptable or whether historical cost accounting is the only method of commercial accountancy, *Carroll Industries Plc (formerly PJ Carroll & Co Ltd) and PJ Carroll & Co Ltd v S O'Culacháin (Inspector of Taxes)* Vol IV p 135

Accounting period

accounts made up half-yearly, whether Revenue required to determine accounting period *The Revenue Commissioners v R Hilliard & Sons Ltd* Vol II p 130

Acquisition of Land (Assessment of Compensation) Act 1919

section 2 *Peter C Heron & Others v The Minister for Communications* Vol III p 298

Additional assessments

whether the inspector of taxes had made a "discovery" on finding that inadmissible deductions had been allowed in the computation of the company's tax liability for certain years and whether he was entitled to raise additional assessments for those years *W Ltd v Wilson (Inspector of Taxes)* Vol 11 p 627, *Hammond Lane Metal Co Ltd v S O'Culacháin (Inspector of Taxes)* Vol III p 187

Administration

procedures of Revenue Commissioners, whether unfair and unconstitutional, enforcement order issue to city sheriff after payment of tax, defamation of plaintiff *Giles J Kennedy v E G Hearne, The Attorney General & Others* Vol III p 590

Admissibility

of evidence of illegality *Daniel Collins and Michael Byrne, Daniel Collins and Redmond Power as Executor of the Will of Michael Byrne, deceased and Daniel Collins v J D Mulvey (Inspector of Taxes)* Vol II p 291

Adopted children

whether "issue" included adopted children *In the matter of John Stamp deceased Patrick Stamp v Noel Redmond & Ors* Vol IV p 415

Adoption Act 1952

ss 4, 26(2), adoption heavily qualified, whether permissible to adopt paying provisions of ITA 1967 into corporation tax code while ignoring charging provisions *Wayte (Holdings) Ltd (In Receivership) Alex Burns v E N Hearne* Vol III p 553

Advance payment

received on foot of obligation with bank, whether income from trade *JG Kerrane (Inspector of Taxes) v N Hanlon (Ireland) Ltd* Vol III p 633

Advertising

agency, whether a profession for the purposes of corporation tax surcharge *Mac Giolla Mhaith (Inspector of Taxes) v Cronin & Associates Ltd* Vol III p 211

company producing materials for use in advertising, whether manufacture *S O'Culachain (Inspector of Taxes) v Hunter Advertising Ltd* Vol IV p 35

newspaper publisher, newspapers are "goods" for the purpose of manufacturing relief, whether advertising income is from a separate trade and qualifies for such relief *L McGurrin (Inspector of Taxes) v The Champion Publications Ltd* Vol IV p 466

Agreement

whether an agreement between the taxpayer and the inspector of taxes in relation to an assessment under appeal is binding and conclusive *The Hammond Lane Metal Co Ltd v S O'Culachain (Inspector of Taxes)* Vol IV p 187

construction of documents and transactions *B McCabe (Inspector of Taxes) v South City & County Investment Co Ltd* Vol V p 107, 1998 p 183

Agricultural Society

definition of *The Trustees of The Ward Union Hunt Races v Hughes (Inspector of Taxes)* Vol I p 538

Allowable loss

capital gains tax used for avoidance of tax, whether allowable *Patrick McGrath & Others v JE McDermott (Inspector of Taxes)* Vol III p 683

Allowances

UK resident working in Ireland, wife working in UK, whether he is entitled to married allowance and rate bands *S Fennessy (Inspector of Taxes) v John Mc Connellogue* Vol V p 129

Amnesty

1993, whether applies *Liam J Irwin (Collector General) v Michael Grimes* Vol V p 209, *Crimianl Assets Bureau v Gerard Hutch* 1999-2000 p 65

Annuity

payable tax free from a trust, the trust is accountable to the Revenue Commissioners for the tax, where such tax is refunded by the Revenue Commissioners to the annuitant is the annuitant accountable to the trust for the tax so refunded *In re Swan, Deceased; The Hibernian Bank Ltd v Munro & Ors* Vol V p 565

Annuity (contd)

paid between group companies, whether capital or revenue *B Mc Cabe (Inspector of Taxes) v South City & County Investment Co Ltd* Vol V p 107

Annual charge

on rental income left to beneficiary provided he continued to manage the property whether remuneration under Schedule E *Gerald O'Reilly v WJ Casey (Inspector of Taxes)* Vol 1 p 601

Annual profits or gains

veterinary body corporate performing Statutory functions, surplus of receipts over expenditure whether liable to tax *The Veterinary Council v F Corr (Inspector of Taxes)* Vol II p 204

Appeals

against a decision of the High Court to refuse on a judicial review application to quash three convictions with six months imprisonment for each offence imposed in the District Court on the appellant for failure to make income tax returns *Thomas O'Callaghan v JP Clifford & Others* Vol IV p 478

new grounds, appellants right to introduce *Boland's Ltd v The Commissioners of Inland Revenue* Vol 1 p 34

to Circuit Court, whether Circuit Court Judge has authority to award costs in tax appeal hearings *The Revenue Commissioners v Arida Ltd* Vol IV p 401, Vol V p 221

to High Court by way of case stated from decision of Circuit Judge, failure to notify the respondent the fact that a case has been stated *A & B v WJ Davis (Inspector of Taxes)* Vol II p 60

summonses served in respect of tax liabilities the subject matter of earlier appeals whether Circuit Court judge has discretion to accept late filing of notice and fee, whether dissatisfaction expressed at the Circuit Court appeal hearings, whether dissatisfaction must be expressed immediately after determination by the Circuit Court, whether notice to county registrar must be lodged within 21 days together with the £20 fee, whether payment of tax denies access to the courts, whether requirements are directory or mandatory, whether tax must be paid before the case stated is determined, whether time lapse after expression of dissatisfaction is fatal *Michael A Bairead v Martin C Carr* Vol IV p 505

time for notice of appeal meaning of "immediately" *The State (Multiprint Label Systems Ltd) v The Hon Justice Thomas Neylon Vol III p 159*

Appeal Commissioners

determinations of 1999-2000 p 55

nature of powers and functions limited or unlimited, determination of tax liability by High Court and Appeal Commissioners whether mutually exclusive *The State (Calcul International Ltd and Solatrex International Ltd) v The Appeal Commissioners and The Revenue Commissioners* Vol III p 577

grounds for setting aside findings of fact by Appeal Commissioners *Mara v GC (Hummingbird) Ltd* Vol II p 687

Appellant

company's accounts, based on current cost accounting convention (ie replacement cost) *Carroll Industries Plc (formerly PJ Carroll & Co Ltd) and PJ Carroll & Co Ltd v S O'Culachain (Inspector of Taxes)* Vol IV p 135

Appellant (contd)

right of, to introduce new grounds of appeal *Boland's Ltd v The Commissioners of Inland Revenue* Vol 1 p 34

Arbitration

compulsory acquisition of land, whether property arbitrator obliged to give breakdown of his award, whether breakdown required for capital gains tax purposes, whether failure by applicant to request an apportionment of the award rules out any further relief, whether applicant can appeal without the breakdown for the award, whether failure to advance further arguments of unfairness amounted to acceptance of the normal practice, *Manning, J v Shackleton, J & Cork Co Council* Vol IV p 485

Artistic exemption

exemption of earnings from original and creative works of artistic or cultural merit, whether journalism qualifies *John Healy v SI Breathnach (Inspector of Taxes)* Vol III p 496

legal text books, refusal by inspector of taxes to grant exemption from income tax under FA 1969 s 2, exemption granted if the books are original and creative works which are generally recognised as having cultural or artistic merit. *Michael Forde Decision* Vol IV p 348

Assessment

basis of assessment under Case III *O'Conaill (Inspector of Taxes) v R* Vol II p 304

basis of, commencement and cessation within a year, whether assessment for the previous year can be reviewed *AB v JD Mulvey (Inspector of Taxes)* Vol II p 55

builder's profits *The State (at the prosecution of Patrick J Whelan) v Michael Smidic (Special Commissioners of Income Tax) and Edward Connolly v AG Birch (Inspector of Taxes)* Vol I p 583

confirmed, allowability of expenses *The King (Harris Stein) v The Special Commissioners* Vol I p 62

joint, whether husband is liable on wife's income, *Gilligan v Criminal Assets Bureau, Galvin, Lanigan & Revenue Commissioners* Vol V p 424

made in the absence of returns, *Criminal Assets Bureau v Gerard Hutch* 1999-2000 p 65

of remuneration paid in year after for work done in earlier year *Bedford (Collector-General) v H* Vol II p 588

whether can be reopened *Boland's Ltd v The Commissioners of Inland Revenue* Vol I p 34

Assigned

personal pension and other assets assigned to company pension continued to be paid to pensioner, whether pensioner liable to tax on pension *Cronin (Inspector of Taxes) v C* Vol II p 592

Associated company

whether a company, resident and trading in Northern Ireland was an associated company of a company resident and trading in the State for the purposes of CTA 1976 s 28 (ie reduced rate of corporation tax for small companies) *MA Bairead (Inspector of Taxes) v Maxwells of Donegal Ltd* Vol III p 430

Auctioneer's commission

whether revenue or capital management expense *Stephen Court Ltd v JA Browne (Inspector of Taxes)* Vol V p 680

Avoidance

dealing in and developing land *O'Connlain (Inspector of Taxes) v Belvedere Estates Ltd* Vol III p 271

sports club, whether set up for tax avoidance or bona fide purposes *Revenue v ORMG* Vol III p 28

whether tax avoidance valid *McGrath v McDermott* Vol III p 683

B

Basis of assessment

commencement and cessation within a year, whether assessment for the previous year can be reviewed *AB v JD Mulvey (Inspector of Taxes)* Vol II p 55

under Case III *O'Conaill (Inspector of Taxes) v R* Vol II p 304

Bank

confidentiality between banks and customers *JB O'C v PCD and A Bank* Vol III p 153

government stocks purchased to comply with Central Bank requirements, whether carrying on trade of dealing in securities, whether liable as profits under Schedule D or exempt capital gains on Government stocks *JA Browne (Inspector of Taxes) v Bank of Ireland Finance Ltd* Vol III p 644

whether personal liability of members is unlimited) *CIR v The Governor and Company of The Bank of Ireland* Vol I p 70

whether Inspector of Taxes entitled to a Court Order *In the Matter of GO'C & AO'C (Application of Liam Liston)* Vol V p 346

Banana ripening

whether qualified for manufacturing relief *PJ O'Connell (Inspector of Taxes) v Fyffes Banana Processing Ltd* 1999-2000 p 71

Bank account

application by Revenue for court order for bank to furnish details of accounts to taxpayers *In re G O'C & A O'C (Application of Liam Liston (Inspector of Taxes))* Vol V p 346

Bad debts

recovered by executor but allowed during lifetime of deceased, whether executor carrying on a trade, whether such bad debts recovered are taxable *CD v J MO' Sullivan* Vol II p 140

Barrister's fees

due prior to his appointment to the bench, fees refused but could be paid to a family company if solicitors so wished *EP O'Coindealbhain (Inspector of Taxes) v The Honourable Mr Justice Sean Gannon* Vol III p 484

Beneficial owner

personal pension and other assets assigned to company pension continued to be paid to pensioner, whether pensioner liable to tax on pension *Cronin (Inspector of Taxes) v C* Vol II p 592

whether director controlled a company and whether managing director was the beneficial owner of, or able to control more than 5% of its ordinary shares *Associated properties Ltd v The Revenue Commissioners* Vol II p 175

Benefit in kind

cars, whether charge to benefit in kind on sales representatives is constitutional *Paul Browne & Others v The Revenue Commissioners & Others* Vol IV p 323

rent paid for employee *Connolly (Inspector of Taxes) v Denis McNamara* Vol II p 452

Bloodstock

animal bought in course of trade, sent to stud after successful racing career and subsequently sold to a syndicate whether amount realised on syndication a trading receipt *Mac Giolla Riogh (Inspector of Taxes) v G Ltd* Vol II p 315

Board of Conservators

surplus revenue, whether annual profits or gains *Moville District Board of Conservators v D Ua Clothasaigh (Inspector of Taxes)* Vol II p 75

Books

barrister's books, whether plant *Breathnach (Inspector of Taxes) v MC* Vol III p 113

Bookmaker

bookmaker convicted and fined in the District Court of offences under the Betting Acts penal warrant for imprisonment, whether constitutional, *John B Murphy v District Justice Brendan Wallace & Others* Vol IV p 278

levies on course betting, whether taxable a income or profits of a trade *The Racing Board v S O'Culachain* Vol IV p 73

profits of a bookmaker from transactions in Irish Hospital Sweepstakes tickets, whether receipts assessable to tax under Schedule D *HH v MJ Forbes (Inspector of Taxes)* Vol II p 164

betting duty, whether necessary for Revenue Commissioners to comply with Regulations Act 1890 before proceedings can commence for failure to pay duty on bets *DPP v Michael Cunningham* Vol V p 691

Breach

customs regulations, seizure by the Revenue Commissioners of an oil tanker *McCrystal Oil Co Ltd v The Revenue Commissioners & Others* Vol IV p 386

Builder's profits

assessment of *The State (at the prosecution of Patrick J Whelan) v Michael Smidic (Special Commissioners of Income Tax)* Vol I p 571 and *Edward Connolly v AG Birch (Inspector of Taxes)* Vol I p 583

Builder's profits (contd)

capitalised value of ground rents and fines, whether liable to tax *Birch (Inspector of Taxes) v Denis Delaney* Vol I p 515 and *Edward Connolly v AG Birch (Inspector of Taxes)* and *Swaine (Inspector of Taxes) v VE* Vol I p 583

Building societies

company lending money to non-members to purchase property, whether trading as a building society *Property Loan & Investment Co Ltd v The Revenue Commissioners* Vol II p 25

instruments relating to the internal affairs of a society were exempt from stamp duty, whether this exemption extended to a transfer of a premises to a society to conduct its business *Irish Nationwide Building Society v Revenue Commissioners* Vol IV p 296

Business

carried on abroad *The Executors and Trustees of A C Ferguson (deceased) v Donovan (Inspector of Taxes)* Vol I p 183

Brewery

trade or business, whether liability in respect of transactions under DORA requisition orders *Arthur Guinness Son & Co Ltd v Commissioners of Inland Revenue* Vol I p 1

C

Cable television system

whether liable to value added tax on sales to customers *TJ Brosnan (Inspector of Taxes) v Cork Communications Ltd* Vol IV p 349

Cattledealer

whether the taxpayer was a "dealer in cattle" within the meaning of ITA 1918 Sch D Case III rule 4 and ITA 1967 s 78. *De Brun (Inspector of Taxes) v K* Vol III p 19

Capital acquisitions tax

whether succession under Act is automatic or must be claimed *In the Matter of the Estates of Cummins (Decd); O'Dwyer & Ors v Keegan & Ors* Vol V p 367

COMPETENT TO DISPOSE

whether surviving spouse competent to dispose of statutory share in estate *In Re the Estate of Urquhart, D (Decd) & Revenue Commissioners v AIB Ltd* Vol V p 600

FAVOURITE NEPHEW RELIEF

gift of farm to niece - whether niece worked substantially full time on the farm *AE v The Revenue Commissioners* Vol V p 686

valuation of shares in private non-trading company *Revenue Commissioners v Henry Young* Vol V p 294

Capital allowances

barrister's books, whether plant *Breathnach (Inspector of Taxes) v MC* Vol III p 113

expenditure on installation of suspended ceiling in supermarket, whether plant qualifying for capital allowances *Dunnes Stores (Oakville) Ltd v MC Cronin (Inspector of Taxes)* Vol IV p 68

Capital allowances (contd)

in designated area, whether plant used exclusively in designated area, whether allowance extends to plant used under a hire contract *Daniel McNally v S O Maoldhomhniagh* Vol IV p 22

holiday cottages, whether qualifying for capital allowances *McMahon, T & Ors v Rt Hon Lord Mayor Alderman & Burgess of Dublin* Vol V p 357

industrial building structure for dock undertaking, whether bonded transit sheds used as clearing house and not for storage qualify *Patrick Monahan (Drogheda) Ltd v O'Connell (Inspector of Taxes)* Vol III p 661

poultry house, whether plant and machinery *O'Srianain (Inspector of Taxes) v Lakeview Ltd* Vol III p 219

racecourse stand, *O'Grady (Inspector of Taxes) v Roscommon Race Committee* Vol V p 317

share of, on leasing transaction, involving a purported limited partnership, against his personal income tax liability. *DA MacCarthaigh (Inspector of Taxes) v Francis Daly* Vol III p 253

whether a building which housed offices, a showroom, a canteen, computer department and utilities qualified for industrial building allowance under ITA 1967 s 255 *O'Conaill (Inspector of Taxes) v JJ Ltd* Vol III p 65

whether capital allowances apportioned in accordance with ITA 1967 s 220(5), should be confined to the allowances outlined in Part XVI of that Act *SW Ltd v McDermott (Inspector of Taxes)* Vol II p 661

Capitalised

builder's profits capitalised value of ground rents and fines, whether liable to tax *Birch (Inspector of Taxes) v Denis Delaney* Vol I p 515 and *Edward Connolly v A G Birch (Inspector of Taxes)* Vol I p 583 and *Swaine (Inspector of Taxes) v VE* Vol II p 472

Capital gains tax

ACCOUNTABLE PERSON

disposal of property by mortgagee as nominee for mortgagor, accountable person for capital gains tax purposes, repayment of 15% deducted by purchaser in the absence of tax clearance certificate *Bank of Ireland Finance Ltd v The Revenue Commissioners* Vol IV p 217

ALLOWABLE LOSS

capital gains tax used for avoidance of tax, whether allowable *Patrick McGrath & Others v JE McDermott (Inspector of Taxes)* Vol III p 683

valuation of lands as at 6 April 1974 *J McMahon (Inspector of Taxes) v Albert Noel Murphy* Vol IV p 125

CAPITAL GAINS TAX

on sale of lands *EP O'Coindealbhain (Inspector of Taxes) v KN Price* Vol IV p 1

sale of whiskey in a bond by a publican, whether liable to capital gains tax *McCall (deceased) v Commissioners of Inland Revenue* Vol I p 28

CAPITAL LOSS

loss on realisation of *investments The Alliance & Dublin Consumers' Gas Co v Davis (Inspector of Taxes)* Vol I p 207

Capital gains tax (contd)

CLEARANCE CERTIFICATE

on sale of bonds, whether applicant ordinarily resident in the state is entitled to a clearance certificate *The State (FIC Ltd) v O'Ceallaigh* Vol III p 124

whether absence of a clearance certificate prohibited the Revenue Commissioners from repaying tax deducted by purchaser *Bank of Ireland Finance Ltd v The Revenue Commissioners* Vol IV p 217

COMPULSORY ACQUISITION

of land, whether property arbitrator obliged to give breakdown of his award, whether breakdown required for capital gains tax purposes, whether failure by applicant to request an apportionment of the award rules out any further relief, whether applicant can appeal without the breakdown for the award, whether failure to advance further arguments of unfairness amounted to acceptance of the normal practice, *David Manning v John R Shackleton & Cork County Council* Vol IV p 485

COMPULSORY PURCHASE

compensation determined without regard to tax arising on disposal *Peter C Heron & Others v The Minister For Communications* Vol III p 298

of land, whether property arbitrator obliged to give breakdown of his award, whether breakdown required for capital gains tax purposes, whether failure by applicant to request an apportionment of the award rules out any further relief, whether applicant can appeal without the breakdown for the award, whether failure to advance further arguments of unfairness amounted to acceptance of the normal practice *David Manning v John R Shackleton & Cork County Council* Vol IV p 485

DEBT

whether a loan with conversion rights constitutes a debt within the meaning of CGTA 1975 s 46(1) *Mooney (Inspector of Taxes) v McSweeney* Vol V p 163

VALUATION OF LAND

agricultural land, appeal against market value at 6 April 1974 as determined by Circuit Court, whether agricultural value the sole determining factor, whether development potential attached on 6 April 1974, whether subsequent planning permission for milk processing plant relevant *J McMahon (Inspector of Taxes) v Albert Noel Murphy* Vol IV p 125

Capital or revenue

annuity paid between group companies *B Mc Cabe (Inspector of Taxes) v South City & County Investment Co Ltd* Vol V p 107

auctioneer's commission *Stephen Court Ltd v Browne (Inspector of Taxes)* Vol V p 680

compensation for loss of profits *The Alliance and Dublin Consumers' Gas Co v McWilliams (Inspector of Taxes)* Vol I p 104

dividends from sales of capital assets, whether liable to corporation profits tax *K Co v Hogan (Inspector of Taxes)* Vol III p 56

exchange losson foreign currency loans, whether capital or revenue *TG Brosnan (Inspector of Taxes) v Mutual Enterprises Ltd* Vol V p 138

Capital or revenue (contd)

interest on loan following redemption of share capital, whether allowable against trading income *Sean MacAonghusa v Ringmahon Co* 1999-2000 p 81

lump sum paid on the execution of a lease *W Flynn (Inspector of Taxes) v John Noone Ltd* and *W Flynn (Inspector of Taxes) v Blackwood & Co (Sligo) Ltd* Vol II p 222

management expenses, whether allowable *Hibernian Insurance Co Ltd v MacUimis (Inspector of Taxes)* 1999-2000 p 113

payment in advance on the signing of a lease, whether capital *O'Sullivan (Inspector of Taxes) v p Ltd* Vol II p 464

racecourse stand, whether deductible repairs or non deductible capital expenditure or expenditure qualifying as plant *Michael O'Grady (Inspector of Taxes) v Roscommon Race Committee* Vol IV p 425

removing top-soil from surface of quarry *Milverton Quarries Ltd v The Revenue Commissioners* Vol II p 382

solicitor's fees - payable by investment company *Stephen Court Ltd v Browne (Inspector of Taxes)* Vol V p 680

training grants, whether capital or revenue receipt *O'Cleirigh (Inspector of Taxes) v Jacobs International Ltd Incorporated* Vol III p 165

whether capital expenditure *Airspace Investments Ltd v M Moore (Inspector of Taxes)* Vol V p 3

whether expenditure incurred by petrol marketing company under exclusivity agreements with retailers is revenue or capital *Dolan (Inspector of Taxes) v AB Co Ltd* Vol II p 515

Cars

whether charge to benefit in kind on sales representatives is constitutional *Paul Browne & Others v The Revenue Commissioners & Others* Vol IV p 323

Carry forward

of losses *Molmac Ltd v MacGiolla Riogh (Inspector of Taxes)* Vol II p 482

Case stated

request for, by taxpayer *The King (Harris Stein) v The Special Commissioners* Vol I p 62

time for notice of appeal meaning of "immediately" *The State (Multiprint Label Systems v Thomas Neylon* Vol III p 159

Ceilings

expenditure on installation of suspended ceiling in supermarket, whether plant qualifying for capital *allowances Dunnes Stores (Oakville) Ltd v M C Cronin (Inspector of Taxes)* Vol IV p 68

Certiorari

whether applicant was entitled to order of certiorari where decision is confirmed and enacted *C Mc Daid v His Honour Judge Sheehy & Ors* Vol V p 696

Cessation of business

assessment of builders profits *The State (at the prosecution of Patrick J Whelan) v Michael Smidic (Special Commissioners of Income Tax)* and *The State (at the prosecution of Patrick J Whelan) v Michael Smidic (Special Commissioners of Income Tax)* Vol I p 571

Cessation of business (contd)

basis of assessment, commencement and cessation within a year, whether assessment for the previous year can be reviewed *AB v JD Mulvey (Inspector of Taxes)* Vol II p 55

deduction of corporation profits tax and excess corporation profits tax in computing profits for income tax purposes *JM O'Dwyer (Inspector of Taxes) v The Dublin United Transport Co Ltd* Vol II p 115

losses forward *Cronin (Inspector of Taxes) v Lunham Brothers Ltd* Vol III p 363

phasing down of business, whether constituted trading, whether collection of debts constituted trading *The City of Dublin Steampacket Co v Revenue Commissioners* Vol I p 108

Change of ownership

losses forward *M Cronin (Inspector of Taxes) v Lunham Brothers Ltd* Vol III p 363

Chargeable person

joint assessment, whether husband is liable for both incomes *Gilligan v Criminal Assets Bureau, Galvin, Lanigan & Revenue Commissioners* Vol V p 424

Charges

on book debts by deed of mortgage, whether fixed or floating charge *AH Masser Ltd (in receivership) & Others v The Revenue Commissioners* Vol III p 548

Charge card

scheme, the meaning of paid, *The Diners Club Ltd v The Revenue and The Minister for Finance* Vol III p 680

Charity

income from securities and from school, whether for charitable purposes *The Pharmaceutical Society of Ireland v The Revenue Commissioners* Vol I p 542

nun, whether assessable on income from employment which she gives to her order *JD Dolan (Inspector of Taxes) v "K" National School Teacher* Vol I p 656

trade carried on by beneficiary of charity, whether exempt *Beirne (Inspector of Taxes) v St Vincent De Paul Society (Wexford Conference)* Vol I p 383

whether a charity "established" in Ireland *Revenue Commissioners v Sister of Charity of the Incarnate Word* 1998 p 65

Charitable bequest

whether it had to be expended in Ireland *The Revenue Commissioners v The Most Reverend Edward Doorley* Vol V p 539

Children

children's pension, whether income of parent for income tax purposes *O'Coindealbhain (Inspector of Taxes) v Breda O'Carroll* Vol IV p 221

father taking his elder children and his mother-in-law into partnership, subsequent assignment of mother-in-law's interest to his younger children whether income of children to be deemed to be income of father *JM O'Dwyer (Inspector of Taxes) v Cafolla & Co* Vol II p 82

increase in widows contributory pension in respect of dependent children, whether taxable on parent *Sean O'Siochain (Inspector of Taxes) v Bridget Neenan* Vol V p 472

Children (contd)

settlement of income, deed of appointment by parent in favour of child *E G v Mac Shamhrain, (Inspector of Taxes)* Vol II p 352

whether "issue" included adopted children *In the matter of John Stamp deceased Patrick Stamp v Noel Redmond & Others* Vol IV p 415

Circuit Court

appeal hearings, whether Circuit Court Judge has authority to award costs in tax appeal hearings *The Revenue Commissioners v Arida Ltd* Vol IV p 401, Vol V p 221

summonses served in respect of tax liabilities the subject matter of earlier appeals whether Circuit Court judge has discretion to accept late filing of notice and fee, whether dissatisfaction expressed at the Circuit Court appeal hearings, whether dissatisfaction must be expressed immediately after determination by the Circuit Court, whether notice to county registrar must be lodged within 21 days together with the £20 fee, whether payment of tax denies access to the courts, whether requirements are directory or mandatory, whether tax must be paid before the case stated is determined, whether time lapse after expression of dissatisfaction is fatal *Michael A Bairead v Martin C Carr* Vol IV p 505

whether a Circuit Court Judge hearing an appeal pursuant to ITA 1967 s 429 has jurisdiction to award costs *The Revenue Commissioners v Arida Ltd* Vol IV p 401, Vol V p 221

Club

to promote athletics or amateur games or sports, whether bona fide or tax avoidance *Revenue v ORMG* Vol III p 28

Coal mining

trading as fuel merchants, whether new trade of coal mining was set up or commenced *H A O'Loan (Inspector of Taxes) v Messrs MJ Noone & Co* Vol II p 146

College/Schools

whether operated for charitable purposes *The Pharmaceutical Society of Ireland v The Revenue Commissioners* Vol I p 542

Collector

of vintage motor cars *Karl Keller v The Revenue Commissioners & Others Commencement* Vol IV p 512

Commencement

and cessation within a year, whether assessment for the previous year can be reviewed *AB v JD Mulvey (Inspector of Taxes)* Vol II p 55

fuel merchants, whether new trade of coal mining was set up or commenced *H A O'Loan (Inspector of Taxes) v Messrs M J Noone & Co* Vol II p 146

Company

definition of, within the meaning of FA 1920 s 52(3) *CIR v The Governor and Company of The Bank of Ireland* Vol I p 70

in receivership preferential claim *The Attorney-General, Informant v Irish Steel Ltd and Vincent Crowley, Defendants* Vol II p 108

Company (contd)

meetings, whether they took place, whether resolution was passed, whether share issue invalid *In re Sugar Distributors Ltd* Vol V p 225

non-resident *The Cunard Steam Ship Co Ltd v Herlihy (Inspector of Taxes), and The Cunard Steam Ship Co Ltd v Revenue Commissioners* Vol I p 330

Company secretary

role of *Wayte (Holdings) Ltd (In Receivership) Alex Burns v Edward N Hearne* Vol III p 553

Compensation

ex gratia payments, by British government for malicious damage to property or personal injury sustained, whether trading receipt *WA Robinson T/A James Pim & Son v J D Dolan (Inspector of Taxes)* Vol I p 427

for compulsory purchase, determined without regard to tax arising on disposal *Peter C Heron & Others v The Minister For Communications* Vol III p 298

for loss of profits, whether income or capital receipt *The Alliance and Dublin Consumers' Gas Co v McWilliams (Inspector of Taxes)* Vol I p 207 and *F Corr (Inspector of Taxes) v F E Larkin* Vol II p 164

Compulsory sale

to Minister for Finance, in return for sterling equivalents, of dollar balances consisting of income from securities, etc, in the USA whether moneys so received assessable *J M O'Sullivan (Inspector of Taxes) v Julia O'Connor, as Administratrix of Evelyn H O'Brien, Deceased* Vol II p 61

Confidentiality

between banks and customers *JB O'C v PCD and A Bank* Vol III p 153

Inspector of Taxes entitled to Court Order *In the Matter of GO'C & AO'C (Application of Liam Liston (Inspector of Taxes))* Vol V 346

Confirmation of assessment

allowance of expenses where assessment has been confirmed *The King (Harris Stein) v The Special Commissioners* Vol I p 62

Conflict

in terms of deed *AH Masser Ltd (in receivership) & Others v The Revenue Commissioners* Vol III p 548

Constitutional rights

constitution validity of taxing statute applicable to married persons *Bernard Muckley & Anne Muckley v Ireland, AG and Revenue Commissioners* Vol III p 188

to have recourse to High Court denied *Michael Deighan v Edward N Hearn & Others* Vol III p 533

whether charge to benefit in kind on sales representatives is constitutional *Paul Browne & Others v The Revenue Commissioners & Others* Vol IV p 323

whether common law rule of dependant domicile of a wife whether constitutional *JW v JW* Vol IV p 437

whether constitutional right to earn a livelihood infringed - whether legislation requires amendment *James G Orange v The Revenue Commissioners* Vol V p 70

Constitutional rights (contd)

whether undertaking by the State under Article 41.3 to guard the institution of marriage infringed, whether imposition of higher taxes or married couples repugnant to the Constitution *Francis & Mary Murphy v The Attorney General* Vol V p 613

whether Imposition of Duties Act 1957 s 1 is constitutional *C Mc Daid v His Honour Judge Sheehy & Ors* Vol V p 696

whether method of granting credit for Professional services withholding tax is constitutional *Michael Daly v The Revenue Commissioners* Vol V p 213

whether rights to privacy and fair procedures infringed. *Charles J Haughey and Others v Moriarty and Others* 1998 p 119

Construction contracts

whether lorry owners carrying sand and gravel were engaged as subcontractors under a construction contract, whether the lorry owners became the proprietors of the quarry materials *O'Grady v Laragan Quarries Ltd* Vol IV p 269

Contract of service or contract for services

branch manager of local Employment Office of Dept of Social Welfare *O'Coindealbhain (Inspector of Taxes) v TB Mooney* Vol IV p 45

demonstrator of food products at supermarket *H Denny & Sons (Irl) Ltd v Minister for Social Welfare* Vol V p 238

members of fishing vessel *Minister for Social Welfare v John Griffiths* Vol IV p 378

temporary employee engaged through an employment agency *The Minister for Labour v PMPA Insurance Co Ltd (under administration)* Vol III p 505

wholesale distributor of newspapers *Tony McAuliffe v Minister for Social Welfare* Vol V p 94

winding up, preferential payments, tests applicable *In the Matter of Sunday Tribune* 1998 p 177

Contract for sale

of legal estate, whether a contract for sale of property *Waterford Glass (Group Services) Ltd v The Revenue Commissioners* Vol IV p 187

stamp duties, amount chargeable, contracts and consideration structured to minimise stamp duty *VIEK Investments Ltd v The Revenue Commissioners* Vol IV p 367

Control

by trustees *The Executors and Trustees of AC Ferguson (deceased) v Donovan (Inspector of Taxes)* Vol I p 183

interest paid by a company to a person having controlling interest in the company *The Revenue Commissioners v Associated properties Ltd* Vol II p 412

whether director controlled a company and whether managing director was the beneficial owner of, or able to control more than 5% of its ordinary shares *Associated properties Ltd v The Revenue Commissioners* Vol II p 175

Conveyance for sale

what constitutes a conveyance for sale under Stamp Act of 1891 *Waterford Glass (Group Services) Ltd v The Revenue Commissioners* Vol IV p 187

Co-operative

surplus of from dealing with members, whether trading profits, whether exempt *Kennedy (Inspector of Taxes) v The Rattoo Co-operative Dairy Society Ltd* Vol I p 315

Copyright

whether corporate body exploiting copyrights supplying service within meaning of VATA - Copyright Act 1963 *Phonographic Performance (Ireland) Ltd v J Somers (Inspector of Taxes)* Vol IV p 314

Corporation profits tax

accounting period, whether Revenue Commissioners are required to determine *The Revenue Commissioners v R Hilliard & Sons Ltd* Vol II p 130

company lending money to non-members to purchase property, whether trading as a building society *Property Loan & Investment Co Ltd v The Revenue Commissioners* Vol II p 25

foreign company trading in Ireland provision for devaluation of foreign currency not allowed as deduction from profits *The Revenue Commissioners v L & Co* Vol II p 281

liability to *Commissioners of Inland Revenue v The Governor & Company of The Bank of Ireland* Vol I p 70

paid by a company to a person having controlling interest in that company *The Revenue Commissioners v Associated Properties Ltd* Vol II p 412

surplus of co-op from dealing with members, whether trading profits, whether exempt *Kennedy (Inspector of Taxes) v Rattoo Co-operative Dairy Society Ltd* Vol 1 p 315

whether collection of rents and dividends and distribution of dividends constituted trading *The Commissioners of Inland Revenue v The Dublin and Kingstown Railway Co* Vol I p 119 and *The Great Southern Railways Co v The Revenue Commissioners* Vol I p 359

whether excess corporation profits tax is exigible for accounting periods in respect of which no corporation profits tax (other than excess corporation profits tax) is payable *The Revenue Commissioners v Orwell Ltd* Vol II p 326

whether phasing down of business constituted trading *The City of Dublin Steampacket Co v Revenue Commissioners* Vol I p 108

Corporation tax

application of income tax provisions to corporation tax *Wayte (Holdings) Ltd (In receivership) Alex Burns v Edward N Hearne* Vol III p 553

manufacturing relief for film production, whether relief applies to short advertising films produced for television, whether relief applies for accounting periods prior to FA 1990 *Saatchi & Saatchi Advertising Limited v Kevin McGarry (Inspector of Taxes)* 1998 p 99

manufacturing relief production of materials for use in advertising, whether manufacture *S O'Culachain (Inspector of Taxes) v Hunter Advertising Ltd* Vol IV p 35

surcharge, whether an advertising agency provides professional services for the purposes of corporation tax surcharge *Mac Giolla Mhaith (Inspector of Taxes) v Cronin & Associates Ltd* Vol III p 211

Costs

whether a Circuit Court Judge hearing an appeal pursuant to ITA 1967 s 429 has jurisdiction to award costs *Revenue v Arida Ltd* Vol IV p 401, Vol V p 221

Cost accounting

method of accounting for tax purposes, whether replacement cost basis is acceptable or whether historical cost accounting is the only method of commercial accountancy *Carroll Industries Plc (formerly PJ Carroll & Co Ltd) and PJ Carroll & Co Ltd v S O'Culachain (Inspector of Taxes)* Vol IV p 135

Court fees

amount on which court fees are chargeable in liquidation *In re Private Motorists Provident Society Ltd (In Liqdtn) & W J Horgan v Minister for Justice* Vol V p 186, *In re Hibernian Transport Companies Ltd* Vol V p 194

Court order

whether Irish bank account is subject to UK court order restraining taxpayer from accessing funds *Governor & Co of the Bank of Ireland v Michael John Meeneghan & Ors* Vol V p 44

Covenants

to covenantees in Third World countries, whether covenantors entitled to relief under ITA 1967 s 439(1) and whether covenantees entitled to exemption limits under FA 1980 s 1 *Action Aid Ltd v Revenue Commissioners* Vol V p 392

whether an individual was entitled to repayment of tax deducted from payments made under an indenture of covenant pursuant to ITA 1967 s 439(1)(iv) *The Revenue Commissioners v HI* Vol III p 242

Crime

non-payment of excise duty payable on bets entered into by the defendant a registered bookmaker, whether recovery of an excise penalty a criminal matter *The Director of Public Prosecutions v Seamus Boyle* Vol IV p 395

proceeds liable to tax, *Criminal Assets Bureau v Gerard Hutch* 1999-2000 p 65

Currency

compulsory sale of, to Minister for Finance, in return for sterling equivalents, of dollar balances consisting of income from securities, etc, in the USA whether moneys so received assessable *J M O'Sullivan (Inspector of Taxes) v Julia O'Connor, as Administratrix of Evelyn H O'Brien, Deceased* Vol II p 61

Customs duties

locus standi evasion of customs duties on specified goods *Gerard Curtis and Brendan Geough v The Attorney General and The Revenue Commissioners* Vol III p 419

seizure of oil tanker and contents for breach of regulations *McCrystal Oil Co Ltd v The Revenue Commissioners & Others* Vol IV p 386

Customs and Excise duties

milk products, whether a whey or skimmed milk product, whether export refunds on consignments from EC countries to non EC countries, whether re-classification renders products liable for repayment of export refunds, whether Revenue Commissioners responsible for classification whether Revenue Commissioners and state chemist negligent and in breach of duty whether Minister entitled to counterclaim against plaintiff *Carbery Milk Products Ltd v The Minister for Agriculture & Others* Vol IV p 492

Customs and Excise duties (contd)

whether unconstitutional for applicant to be convicted and fined for keeping hydrocarbon oil in his motor vehicle on which custom and excise duty had not been paid, whether delegation of powers under Imposition of Duties Act 1957 is permissible *Charles McDaid v Hon Judge David Sheehy, DPP & Ors* Vol IV p 162, Vol V p 696

D

Damages

for detinue and conversion arising from seizure by Revenue Commissioners of oil tanker *McCrystal Oil Co Ltd v The Revenue Commissioners & Others* Vol IV p 386

Dealing in or developing land

building contractors, whether lands the subject matter of a contract for sale entered into during an accounting period constitute trading stock for the year ending in that accounting period, whether inclusion of the lands in the accounts in accordance with good accounting procedure was evidence of the commercial reality of the transaction, whether absence of possession, conveyance of legal estate and planning permission relevant to taxpayer's claim for relief *Murnaghan Brothers Ltd v S O'Maoldhomhnaigh* Vol IV p 304

interest in land acquired and disposed of within one accounting period *M Cronin (Inspector of Taxes) v Cork & County Property Co Ltd* Vol III p 198

property company, whether ordinary principles of commercial accounting apply or whether artificial method of valuation pursuant to F(MP)A 1968 s 18(2) prevails *M Cronin (Inspector of Taxes) v Cork & County Property Co Ltd* Vol III p 198

property company, farm land, letting to partners on conacre, area zoned for development, land transferred to new company, whether land trading stock of company *L O hArgain (Inspector of Taxes) v B Ltd* Vol III p 9

whether the surplus from the sale of property was profit of a trade of dealing in or developing land, or the profit of a business which was deemed by F(MP)A 1968 s 17, to be such a trade *Mara (Inspector of Taxes) v GG (Hummingbird) Ltd* Vol II p 667

Debts

determining restriction in prevention of charging, assigning or otherwise disposing of book debts and other debts *AH Masser Ltd (in receivership) & Others v The Revenue Commissioners* Vol III p 548

on securities, loan notes, liability to capital gains tax *PJ O'Connell (Inspector of Taxes) v T Keleghan* 1999-2000 p 143

whether a loan with conversion rights constitutes a debt within the meaning of CGTA 1975 s 46(1) *Mooney (Inspector of Taxes) v McSweeney* Vol V p 163

Deductions

SCHEDULE D CASE I AND II

compensation paid to tenants of adjoining premises for interference with light and air, whether allowable Case I deduction *WJ Davis (Inspector of Taxes) v X Ltd* Vol II p 45

Deductions (contd)

cost of replacement of weighbridge house *JT Hodgins (Inspector of Taxes) v Plunder & Pollak (Ireland) Ltd* Vol II p 267

deduction from excess profits duty for replacement of capital items *Boland's Ltd v The Commissioners of Inland Revenue* Vol I p 34

deduction of corporation profits tax and excess corporation profits tax in computing profits for income tax purposes *J M O'Dwyer (Inspector of Taxes) v The Dublin United Transport Co Ltd* Vol II p 115

expenditure on mill *sanitation JB Vale (Inspector of Taxes) v Martin Mahony & Brothers Ltd* Vol II p 32

expenditure on temporary *premises Martin Fitzgerald v Commissioners of Inland Revenue* Vol I p 91

expenses of promoting Bill in Parliament *McGarry (Inspector of Taxes) v Limerick Gas Committee* Vol I p 375

foreign company trading in Ireland provision for devaluation of foreign currency not allowed as deduction from profits. *The Revenue Commissioners v L & Co* Vol II p 281

formation expenses, whether allowable against trading profits *JB Kealy (Inspector of Taxes) v O'Mara (Limerick) Ltd* Vol I p 642

inadmissible, whether the inspector of taxes had made a "discovery" on finding that inadmissible deductions had been allowed in the computation of the company's tax liability for certain years and whether he was entitled to raise additional assessments for those years *W Ltd v Wilson (Inspector of Taxes)* Vol II p 627

incidental expenses, whether a deduction should be allowed under ITA 1967 Schedule 2 para 3, in respect of incidental expenses *MacDaibheid (Inspector of Taxes) v SD* Vol III p 1

legal fees in defending action in High Court for balance alleged to be due to a building contractor in respect of the construction of cinema, whether allowable Case I deduction *Casey (Inspector of Taxes) v AB Ltd* Vol II p 500

on rebuilding of business premises, whether portion thereof deductible in computing profits *Curtin (Inspector of Taxes) v M Ltd* Vol II p 360

removing top-soil from surface of quarry *Milverton Quarries Ltd v The Revenue Commissioners* Vol II p 382

whether expenditure incurred by petrol marketing company under exclusivity agreements with retailers is revenue or capital *Dolan (Inspector of Taxes) v AB Co Ltd* Vol II p 515

whether expenses of management or by management *Hiberian Insurance Co Ltd v MasUimis (Inspector of Taxes)* Vol V p 495, 1999-2000 p 113

woodlands, whether purchasing and planting of trees is allowable deduction from farming profits *Connolly (Inspector of Taxes) v WW* Vol II p 657

Schedule D Case III

interest *Phillips (Inspector of Taxes) v Limerick County Council* Vol I p 66

Schedule D Case V

whether letting fees and legal expenses incurred by the company in respect of first lettings of property qualified as deductions under ITA 1967 s 81(5)(*d*) *GH Ltd v Browne (Inspector of Taxes)* Vol III p 95

Deductions (contd)

SCHEDULE E

travelling expenses *Phillips (Inspector of Taxes) v Keane* Vol I p 64, *SP O'Broin (Inspector of Taxes) v Mac Giolla Meidhre/Finbar Pigott* Vol II p 366 and *HF Kelly (Inspector of Taxes) v H* Vol II p 460

MANAGEMENT EXPENSES

by investment company *Howth Estate Co v WJ Davis (Inspector of Taxes)* Vol I p 447

losses in holding company, whether notional management fees deductible Corporation tax *Belville Holdings Ltd (in receivership and liquidation) v Cronin (Inspector of Taxes)* Vol III p 340

Delegation of powers

by Government to Customs and Excise department whether unconstitutional *Charles McDaid v His Honour Judge David Sheehy, the Director of Public Prosecutions & Others* Vol IV p 162, Vol V p 696

Deposit

company engaged in manufacture and erection of prefabricated buildings deposit of 15 per cent of total cost paid on execution of contract, whether payment on account of trading stock or security for contracts *O'Laoghaire (Inspector of Taxes) v CD Ltd* Vol III p 51

whether expenses of management or by management *Hibernian Insurance Co Ltd v MacUimis (Inspector of Taxes)* Vol V p 495, 1999-2000 p 113

company engaged in manufacture and export of ambulances, deposit received on foot of obligation with bank, whether income from trade *JG Kerrane (Inspector of Taxes) v N Hanlon (Ireland) Ltd* Vol III p 633

Designated areas

capital allowances, whether plant used exclusively in designated area, whether allowance extends to plant used under a hire contract *Daniel McNally v S O Maoldhomhniagh* Vol IV p 22

Determination of an appeal

assessment of builders profits *The State (at the prosecution of Patrick J Whelan) v Michael Smidic (Special Commissioners of Income Tax)* Vol I p 571

statutory provision requiring person to express dissatisfaction with the determination of a point of law "immediately after the determination" *The State (Multiprint Label Systems Ltd) v The Honourable Justice Thomas Neylon* Vol III p 159

Development of land

trading property company, farm land, letting to partners on conacre, area zoned for development, land transferred to new company, whether land trading stock of company *L O hArgain (Inspector of Taxes) v B Ltd* Vol III p 9

whether the surplus from the sale of property was profit of a trade of dealing in or developing land, or the profit of a business which was deemed by F(MP)A 1968 s 17, to be such a trade *Mara (Inspector of Taxes) v GG (Hummingbird) Ltd* Vol II p 667

Development land

valuation agricultural land, appeal against market value at 6 April 1974 as determined by Circuit Court, whether agricultural value the sole determining factor, whether development potential attached on 6 April 1974, whether subsequent planning permission for milk processing plant relevant *J McMahon (Inspector of Taxes) v Albert Noel Murphy* Vol IV p 125

Director

resident abroad, of a company incorporated in the State but managed and controlled abroad. whether Schedule E *employment WJ Tipping (Inspector of Taxes) v Louis Jeancard* Vol II p 68

Disabled persons

redundancy payments to disabled employees, whether exempt from income tax, whether distinction to be made between disabled employees whose jobs continued and disabled employees whose jobs ceased p *O Cahill (Inspector of Taxes) v Albert Harding & Others* Vol IV p 233

to what extent must disabled persons be disabled to import goods eg motor vehicle free of excise duty *Michael Wiley v The Revenue Commissioners* Vol IV p 170

Discontinuance

of trade *Boland's Ltd v Davis (Inspector of Taxes)* Vol I p 86

Discovery

right to reopen assessment of Inspectors of Taxes *Hammond Lane Metal Co Ltd v S O'Culacháin (Inspector of Taxes)* Vol IV 197 *W Ltd v Wilson (Inspector of Taxes)* Vol II p 627

Discretionary trust

discretionary powers of trustees, meaning of dependents *Crowe Engineering Ltd v Phyllis Lynch and Others* Vol IV p 340

interpretation of residuary bequest, whether bequest failed for uncertainty, whether bequest infringed rule against perpetual trusts *In the Matter of the Estate of Mary Davoren, Deceased; Thomas O'Byrne v Michael Davoren and Anne Coughlan* Vol V p 36

when absolute interest passes *BKJ v The Revenue Commissioners* Vol III p 104

Disposal

of assets at an undervalue by a company *Kill Inn Motel Ltd (In Liquidation) v The Companies Acts 1963/1983* Vol III p 706

of property by mortgagee as nominee for mortgagor, accountable person for capital gains tax purposes, repayment of 15% deducted by purchaser in the absence of tax clearance certificate *Bank of Ireland Finance Ltd v The Revenue Commissioners* Vol IV p 217

paper for paper transaction, capital gains tax implications *PJ O'Connell v T Keleghan* 999-2000 p 143

Disposition of income

deed of appointment by parent in favour of child *EG v Mac Shamhrain, (Inspector of Taxes)* Vol II p 352

Disposition of income (contd)

deed of trust in favour of charitable objects with provision for re-vestment of income in settlor in certain contingencies, whether income of settlor or trustees *HPC Hughes (Inspector of Taxes) v Miss Gretta Smyth (Sister Mary Bernard) & Others* Vol I p 411

in favour of children *JM O'Dwyer (Inspector of Taxes) v Cafolla & Co* Vol II p 82

Distance trades

Boland's Ltd v Davis (Inspector of Taxes) Vol I p 86

Distributions

interest paid by Irish subsidiary to Japanese parent company on loan from parent company whether tax should be deducted at source under Double Tax Treaty or

hether the payment should be treated as distribution under Schedule F *Murphy (Inspector of Taxes) v Asahi Synthetic Fibres (Ireland) Ltd* Vol III p 246

Dividends

from sales of capital assets whether liable to corporation profits tax *K Co v Hogan (Inspector of Taxes)* Vol III p 56

payment of, whether payment through inter-company account was sufficient evidence of actual payment, whether payment of cheque required, whether making of accounting entry a mere record of underlying transaction, whether a dividend declared on 11 December 1980 was received by related company not later than 12 December 1980, whether making of journal entries after 23 December 1980 material evidence *Sean Murphy (Inspector of Taxes) v The Borden Co Ltd* Vol III p 559

whether dividends paid represented profit earning capacity of a company, *E A Smyth v The Revenue Commissioners* Vol V p 532

Doctrines of res judicata and equitable estoppel

Boland's Ltd v The Commissioners of Inland Revenue Vol I p 34

Domicile

Captain R H Prior-Wandesforde v The Revenue Commissioners Vol I p 249, *The Right Hon Earl of Iveagh v The Revenue Commissioners* Vol I p 259, *In the Goods of Bernard Louis Rowan, Deceased Joseph Rowan v Vera Agnes Rowan & Others* Vol III p 572, *Proes v The Revenue Commissioners* Vol V p 481

common law rule that wife takes domicile of dependence of her husband, whether constitutional *JW v JW* Vol IV p 437

DORA requisition orders

liability in respect of transactions under *Arthur Guinness Son & Co Ltd v Commissioners of Inland Revenue* Vol I p 1

Double taxation relief

wife's remuneration taxed in Northern Ireland - whether appellant entitled to double taxation relief in Ireland *John Travers v Sean O'Siochain (Inspector of Taxes)* Vol V p 54

E

Earned income

income from the leasing of premises, whether leasing constitutes trading whether earned income *Pairceir (Inspector of Taxes) v EM* Vol II p 596

Ejusdem generis rule

as applied in interpretation of statutes *M Cronin (Inspector of Taxes) v Lunham Brothers Ltd* Vol III p 370

Emoluments

of office, grant to a President of a college on retirement *JD Mulvey (Inspector of Taxes) v Denis J Coffey* Vol I p 618

of employment, rent paid for employee *Connolly (Inspector of Taxes) v Denis McNamara* Vol II p 452

professional services rendered without prior agreement as regards remuneration payment on termination of services whether chargeable as income *WS McGarry (Inspector of Taxes) v E F* Vol II p 261

Employee

branch manager of local Employment Office of Dept of Social Welfare *O'Coindealbhain (Inspector of Taxes) v TB Mooney* Vol IV p 45

demonstrator of food products at supermarket, whether an employee or self-employed *H Denny & Sons (Irl) Ltd v Minister for Social Welfare* Vol V p 238

whether a member of the crew of a fishing vessel can be an "employee", whether there can be an "employee" without there being a corresponding employer, whether Social Welfare (Consolidation) Act 1981 applies to self employed persons, whether scheme of Act and regulations is limited to employer/employee circumstances whether Minister has unlimited power to make regulations enabling any person to be treated as an employee *The Minister for Social Welfare v John Griffiths* Vol IV p 378

wholesale distributors of newspapers *Tony McAuliffe v Minister for Social Welfare* Vol V p 94

Employments

appeal as to whether a contract of services or a contract for services - wholesale distributor of newspapers, *Tony McAuliffe v The Minister for Social Welfare* Vol V p 94

branch manager of local Employment Office of Dept of Social Welfare whether the taxpayer was engaged under a contract of service or a contract for services *O'Coindealbhain (Inspector of Taxes) v TB Mooney* Vol IV p 45

contract of service or contract for services, temporary employee engaged through an employment agency *The Minister for Labour v PMPA Insurance Co Ltd (under administration)* Vol III p 505

demonstrator of food products at supermarket, whether an employee or self-employed *H Denny & Sons (Irl) Ltd v Minister for Social Welfare* Vol V p 238

director resident abroad, of a company incorporated in the State but managed and controlled abroad. whether Schedule E employment *W J Tipping (Inspector of Taxes) v Louis Jeancard* Vol II p 68

Employments (contd)

whether contract for services between skipper of fishing vessel and crew members, *Director of Public Prosecutions v Martin McLoughlin* Vol III p 467

whether dockers working under a pooling arrangement can receive unemployment benefit when they are not occupied unloading ships, whether dockers had a contract of employment with their Association, separate contracts on each occasion of their employment, whether level of earnings material to question of employment *James Louth & Others v Minister for Social Welfare* Vol IV p 391

whether the taxpayer was engaged under a contract of service or a contract for services *McDermott (Inspector of Taxes) v BC* Vol III p 43

Employer's obligations

to deduct PAYE and PRSI from employee's emoluments *EN Hearne (Inspector of Taxes) v O'Cionna & Others T/A J A Kenny & Partners* Vol IV p 113

Enforcement of Revenue Debts

Governor & Co of Bank of Ireland v Michael John Meeneghan and Others Vol V p 44 *In the Matter of the Extradition Acts John Oliver Byrne v Noel Conroy* 1998 p 75

Errors

inadmissible deductions, whether the inspector of taxes had made a "discovery" on finding that inadmissible deductions had been allowed in the computation of the company's tax liability for certain years and whether he was entitled to raise additional assessments for those years *W Ltd v Wilson (Inspector of Taxes)* Vol II p 627

Estate company

expenses of management, company whose business consists mainly in the making of investments *Casey (Inspector of Taxes) v The Monteagle Estate* Co Vol II p 429

Estate duty

whether conveyancing form determines liability *The Attorney General v Power & Anor* Vol V p 525

charitable bequest, whether it had to be expended in Ireland *The Revenue Commissioners v The Most Reverend Edward Doorley* Vol V p 539

whether due when consideration is stated in receipt clause of deed but payment is not pursued by the disponer *Revenue v Daniel Anthony Moroney & Ors* Vol V p 589

whether surviving spouse competent to dispose of statutory share in estate *In Re the Estate of Urquhart, D (Decd) & Revenue Commissioners v AIB Ltd* Vol V p 600

Estoppel

whether stamped conveyance invalid *Parkes (Roberta) v David Parkes* 1998 p 169

Evasion

locus standi evasion of customs duties on specified goods *Gerard Curtis and Brendan Geough v The Attorney General and The Revenue Commissioners* Vol III p 419

Evidence

secondary evidence that beneficial interest in securities had been transferred not admissible *Gilbert Hewson v JB Kealy (Inspector of Taxes)* Vol II p 15

Ex gratia payments

by British government for malicious damage to property or personal injury sustained, whether trading receipt *WA Robinson T/A James Pim & Son v JD Dolan (Inspector of Taxes)* Vol I p 427

Excess corporation profits tax

whether excess corporation profits tax is exigible for accounting periods in respect of which no corporation profits tax (other than excess corporation profits tax) is payable *The Revenue Commissioners v Orwell Ltd* Vol II p 326

Excess profits duty

accounting period, whether Revenue Commissioners are required to determine *The Revenue Commissioners v R Hilliard & Sons Ltd* Vol II p 130

brewery, whether liability in respect of transactions under DORA requisition orders *Arthur Guinness Son & Co Ltd v Commissioners of Inland Revenue* Vol I p 1

deductions from, expenditure on temporary premises *Martin Fitzgerald v Commissioners of Inland Revenue* Vol I p 91

notional loss in trade from decrease in value of stock not allowed *The Revenue Commissioners v Latchford & Sons Ltd* Vol I p 240

profits, whether ascertained by actual or standard percentage *Boland's Ltd v The Commissioners of Inland Revenue* Vol I p 34

stock relief, definition of trading stock in hand *Green & Co (Cork) Ltd v The Revenue Commissioners* Vol I p 130

whiskey in bond sold by publican *McCall (deceased) v Commissioners of Inland Revenue* Vol I p 28

Exchange loss

on foreign currency loans, whether capital or revenue *TG Brosnan (Inspector of Taxes) v Mutual Enterprises Ltd* Vol V p 138

Excise duty

bookmaker convicted and fined in the District Court of offences under the Betting Acts penal warrant for imprisonment, whether constitutional *John B Murphy v District Justice Brendan Wallace & Others* Vol IV p 278

imposed on proprietors of slaughter houses and exporters of live animals, whether ultra vires and void *Doyle & Others v An Taoiseach & Others* Vol III p 73

non-payment of excise duty payable on bets entered into by the defendant a registered bookmaker, whether recovery of an excise penalty a criminal matter *The Director of Public Prosecutions v Seamus Boyle* Vol IV p 395

publican's licence, whether new licence obtainable, whether application within six year period, meaning of year immediately preceding *Peter Connolly v The Collector of Customs and Excise* Vol IV p 419

to what extent must disabled persons be disabled to import goods eg motor vehicle free of excise duty *Michael Wiley v The Revenue Commissioners* Vol IV p 170

whether creditor to resort to securities received from principal before proceeding against surety *The Attorney General v Sun Alliance and London Insurance Ltd* Vol III p 265

whether Imposition of Duties Act 1957 s 1 is constitutional *C Mc Daid v His Honour Judge Sheehy & Ors* Vol V p 696

Excise duty (contd)

whether zero rated for VAT purposes, *DH Burke & Sons Ltd v The Revenue Commissioners, Ireland and The Attorney General* Vol V p 418

Exclusivity agreements

whether expenditure incurred by petrol marketing company under exclusivity agreements with retailers is revenue or capital *Dolan (Inspector of Taxes) v AB Co Ltd* Vol II p 515

Executor

carrying on trade, recovery by executor of debts allowed as bad debts in lifetime of deceased, whether a trading receipt *CD v JM O'Sullivan (Inspector of Taxes)* Vol II p 140

Exemptions

AGRICULTURAL SOCIETY

definition of *The Trustees of The Ward Union Hunt Races v Hughes (Inspector of Taxes)* Vol I p 538

ARTISTIC

exemption of earnings from original and creative works of artistic or cultural merit, whether journalism qualifies *John Healy v SI Breathnach (Inspector of Taxes)* Vol III p 496

legal text books, refusal by inspector of taxes to grant exemption from income tax under FA 1969 s 2, Exemption granted if the books are original and creative works which are generally recognised as having cultural or artistic merit *Michael Forde Decision* Vol IV p 348

BUILDING SOCIETIES

instruments relating to the internal affairs of a society were exempt from stamp duty, whether this exemption extended to a transfer of a premises to a society to conduct its business *Irish Nationwide Building Society v Revenue Commissioners* Vol IV p 296

CHARITIES

trade carried on by beneficiary of charity, whether exempt *Beirne (Inspector of Taxes) v St Vincent De Paul Society (Wexford Conference)* Vol I p 383

INDUSTRIAL AND PROVIDENT SOCIETIES

surplus of co-op from dealing with members, whether trading profits, whether exempt *Kennedy (Inspector of Taxes) v The Rattoo Co-operative Dairy Society Ltd* Vol I p 315

ORIGINAL AND CREATIVE

writing, school textbooks - whether within the meaning of FA 1969 s 2 *The Revenue Commissioners v Colm O'Loinsigh* Vol V p 98

Expenditure

loan interest payable after redemption of share capital whether allowable trading expense, *Sean MacAonghusa v Ringmahon* 1999-2000 p 81

on installation of suspended ceiling in supermarket whether plant qualifying for capital allowances *Dunnes Stores (Oakville) Ltd v MC Cronin (Inspector of Taxes)* Vol IV p 68

Expenditure (contd)

on mill sanitation *JB Vale (Inspector Of Taxes) v Martin Mahony & Brothers Ltd* Vol II p 32

on racecourse stand, whether deductible as repairs *Michael O'Grady (Inspector of Taxes) v Roscommon Race Committee* Vol IV p 425

on rebuilding of business premises whether portion thereof deductible in computing profits *Curtin (Inspector of Taxes) v M Ltd* Vol II p 360

on temporary premises *Martin Fitzgerald v Commissioners of Inland Revenue* Vol I p 91

Expenses

allowance of, where assessment has been confirmed *The King (Harris Stein) v The Special Commissioners* Vol 1 p 62

compensation paid to tenants of adjoining premises for interference with light and air, whether allowable Case I deduction *WJ Davis (Inspector of Taxes) v X Ltd* Vol II p 45

deduction of expenses of management by investment company *Howth Estate Co v W J Davis (Inspector of Taxes)* Vol I p 447

formation expenses, whether allowable against trading profits *JB Kealy (Inspector of Taxes) v O'Mara (Limerick) Ltd* Vol I p 642

from Schedule E *SP O'Broin (Inspector of Taxes) v Mac Giolla Meidhre/Finbar Pigott* Vol II p 366 and *HF Kelly (Inspector of Taxes) v H* Vol II p 460

incidental expenses, whether a deduction should be allowed under ITA 1967 Sch 2 para 3 *MacDaibheid (Inspector of Taxes) v SD* Vol III p 1

of management, investment appraisal expenditure whether allowable as management expense *Hibernian Insurance Co Ltd v MacUimis (Inspector of Taxes)* 1999-2000 p 113

of management, company whose business consists mainly in the making of investments *Casey (Inspector of Taxes) v The Monteagle Estate Co* Vol II p 429

of management, whether tax deductible, meaning of *Hibernian Insurance Company Limited v MacUimis (Inspector of Taxes)* Vol V p 495, 1999-2000 p 113

of management, whether auctioneer's/solicitors fees are revenue or capital - *Stephen Court Ltd v JA Browne (Inspector of Taxes)* Vol V p 680

of promoting bill in Parliament *McGarry (Inspector of Taxes) v Limerick Gas Committee* Vol I p 375

of removing top soil from surface of quarry whether capital or revenue expenditure *Milverton Quarries Ltd v The Revenue Commissioners* Vol II p 382

Export sales relief

ambulances manufactured in the State and exported *JG Kerrane (Inspector of Taxes) v N Hanlon (Ireland) Ltd* Vol III p 633

sale of meat into intervention, exporter need not be owner at time of export *Cronin (Inspector of Taxes) v IMP Midleton Ltd* Vol III p 452

Exported Live Stock (Insurance) Board

statutory body, whether carrying on a trade *The Exported Live Stock (Insurance) Board v T J Carroll (Inspector of Taxes)* Vol II p 211

Export refunds

milk products, whether a whey or skimmed milk product, whether export refunds on consignments from EC countries to non EC countries, whether re-classification renders products liable for repayment of export refunds, whether Revenue Commissioners responsible for classification whether Revenue Commissioners and state chemist negligent and in breach of duty whether Minister entitled to counterclaim against plaintiff *Carbery Milk Products Ltd v The Minister for Agriculture & Others* Vol IV p 492

Extension

of period for making distribution of dividends *Rahinstown Estates Co v M Hughes (Inspector of Taxes)* Vol III p 517

Extradition Order

appeal on grounds of a revenue offence, whether EEC levies constitute a tax *John Oliver Byrne v Noel Conroy* 1998 p 75

F

Fair Procedures

constitutional right to fair procedures *Charles J Haughey & Others v Moriarty & Others* 1998 p 119

Farm tax

whether implementation of Farm Tax Act constituted unfair procedures, effect of repeal of that Act, consequences of absence of amending legislation *Purcell v Attorney General* Vol IV p 229, Vol V p 288

Farming

BLOODSTOCK

animal bought in course of trade, sent to stud after successful racing career and subsequently sold to a syndicate whether amount realised on syndication a trading receipt *Mac Giolla Riogh (Inspector of Taxes) v G Ltd* Vol II p 315

CATTLEDEALER

whether the taxpayer was a "dealer in cattle" within the meaning of ITA 1918 Sch D Case III rule 4 and ITA 1967 s 78 *De Brun (Inspector of Taxes) v K* Vol III p 19

MARKET GARDENING

valuation of land occupied for market gardening *L v WS McGarry (Inspector of Taxes)* Vol II p 241

OCCUPATION OF LANDS

whether the appellant company was in occupation of lands, forming part of a military establishment, for the purposes of ITA 1918 Sch B or ITA 1967 *O Conaill (Inspector of Taxes) v Z Ltd* Vol II p 636

PIG REARING

whether the activity of intensive pig rearing constituted farming for the purposes of FA 1974 s 13(1) *Knockhall Piggeries v JG Kerrane (Inspector of Taxes)* Vol III p 319

WOODLANDS

whether purchasing and planting of trees is allowable deduction from farming profits *Connolly (Inspector of Taxes) v WW* Vol II p 657

Fees

due to a barrister prior to his appointment to the bench, fees refused but could be paid to a family company if solicitors so wished *EP O'Coindealbhain (Inspector of Taxes) v The Honourable Mr Justice Sean Gannon* Vol III p 484

High Court fees on funds realised by liquidator in course of liquidation, whether applicable to secured creditors or to proceeds of sale of property subject to a fixed charge *Michael Orr (Kilternan) Ltd v The Companies Acts 1963-1983, and Thornberry Construction (Irl) Ltd v The Companies Acts 1963-1983* Vol III p 530

Film production

whether accounting periods prior to FA 1990 qualify for relief *Saatchi & Saatchi Advertising Ltd v Kevin McGarry (Inspector of Taxes)* Vol V p 376

Finality

of Special Commissioners' decision *The King (Evelyn Spain) v The Special Commissioners* Vol I p 221

Finance company

dealing in stocks and shares, whether investments should be valued at cost or market value *AB Ltd v Mac Giolla Riogh (Inspector of Taxes)* Vol II p 419

Fixtures

installation of fixtures subject to low rate of value added tax, whether or not television aerials attached to roof of a house are fixtures *John Maye v The Revenue Commissioners* Vol III p 332

Foreign company

director resident abroad, of a company incorporated in the State but managed and controlled abroad. whether Schedule E employment *WJ Tipping (Inspector of Taxes) v Louis Jeancard* Vol II p 68

foreign company trading in Ireland provision for devaluation of foreign currency not allowed as deduction from profits. *The Revenue Commissioners v L & Co* Vol II p 281

Foreign currency loans

whether exchange loss is capital or revenue *TG Brosnan (Inspector of Taxes) v Mutual Enterprises Ltd* Vol V p 138

Foreign pension

pension received by Irish resident from British company, whether income from foreign possession *McHugh (Inspector of Taxes) v A* Vol II p 393 and *Forbes (Inspector of Taxes) v GHD* Vol II p 491

Foreign property

claim for relief under ITA 1918 Case V rule 3, question of residence and domicile *Captain R H Prior-Wandesforde v the Revenue* Commissioners Vol I p 249 and *The Right Hon The Earl of Iveagh v The Revenue Commissioners* Vol I p 259

Foreign Revenue Debt

UK vat, *Governor & Co of the Bank of Ireland v Meenaghan & Ors* Vol V p 44

Foreign tax

whether recoverable in Ireland *Governor & Co of the Bank of Ireland v Michael John Meeneghan & Ors* Vol V p 44

Foreign trades

basis of assessment under Case III *O'Conaill (Inspector of Taxes) v R* Vol II p 304

Formation expenses

whether allowable against trading profits *JB Kealy (Inspector of Taxes) v O'Mara (Limerick) Ltd* Vol I p 642

Forward purchase contracts

fall in market value of goods before delivery, *The Revenue Commissioners v Latchford & Sons Ltd* Vol I p 240

Fraudulent Conveyances Act 1634 (10 Charles 1)

*Kill Inn Motel Ltd (In Liquidation) v The Companies Acts 1963/*1983 Vol III p 706

Fuel merchants

whether new trade of coal mining was set up or commenced *HA O'Loan (Inspector of Taxes) v Messrs MJ Noone & Co* Vol II p 146

Functions of courts

and legislature *McGrath & Or v JE McDermott (Inspector of Taxes)* Vol III p 683

Funds in court

whether general rules applicable Schedules A, B, C, D and E apply to the court when paying interest on debts out of funds in court and whether tax deductible from income accrued to funds in court for years prior to 1922/23 *Colclough v Colclough* Vol II p 332

G

Gifts

made by a company *Kill Inn Motel Ltd (In Liquidation) v The Companies Acts 1963/ 1983* Vol III p 706

whether "marriage gratuity" received on resignation was a retirement payment under ITA 1967 s 114 or was a perquisite of her office under ITA 1967 s 110 *Sean O'Siochain (Inspector of Taxes v Thomas Morrissey Eleanor Morrissey* Vol IV p 407

whether present from employer taxable as gift, or emolument under Schedule E *Wing v O'Connell (Inspector of Taxes)* Vol I p 155

whether gift arises when consideration is stated in receipt clause of deed but payment is not pursued by the disponer *The Revenue Commissioners v Daniel Anthony Moroney & Ors* Vol V p 589

Goods

distinguished from services *Dunnes Stores (Oakville) Ltd v MC Cronin (Inspector of Taxes)* Vol IV p 68

Government stocks

purchased to comply with Central Bank requirements, whether carrying on trade of dealing in securities, whether liable as profits under Schedule D or exempt capital gains on Government stocks *JA Browne (Inspector of Taxes) v Bank of Ireland Finance Ltd* Vol III p 644

Ground rents

whether fines and capitalised value of ground rents are assessable to tax *Birch (Inspector of Taxes) v Denis Delaney* Vol I p 515

Group relief

whether the expression "total income means income before or after the deduction of group relief *Cronin (Inspector of Taxes) v Youghal Carpets (Yarns) Ltd* Vol III p 229

Group companies

recovery of outstanding taxes from a group of companies, whether Revenue Commissioners may appropriate payments between separate companies within the group, whether insolvency of a company is relevant to gratuitous alienation of assets *Frederick Inns Ltd, The Rendezvous Ltd, The Graduate Ltd, Motels Ltd (In Liquidation) v The Companies Acts 1963-1986* Vol IV p 247

H

Hauliers

whether lorry owners carrying sand and gravel were engaged as subcontractors under a construction contract, whether the lorry owners became the proprietors of the quarry materials *O'Grady v Laragan Quarries Ltd* Vol IV p 269

High Court

powers of determination of tax liability by High Court and Appeal Commissioners whether mutually exclusive, nature of powers and functions of Appeal Commissioners limited or unlimited *The State (Calcul International Ltd and Solatrex International Ltd) v The Appeal Commissioners and The Revenue Commissioners* Vol III p 530

High Court fees

on funds realised by liquidator in course of liquidation, whether applicable to secured creditors or to proceeds of sale of property subject to a fixed charge *Michael Orr (Kilternan) Ltd v The Companies Acts 1963-1983, and Thornberry Construction (Irl) Ltd v The Companies Acts 1963-1983* Vol III p 530

Historical cost accounting

method of accounting for tax purposes, whether replacement cost basis is acceptable or whether historical cost accounting is the only method of commercial accountancy *Carroll Industries Plc (formerly PJ Carroll & Co Ltd) and PJ Carroll & Co Ltd v S O'Culachain (Inspector of Taxes)* Vol IV p 135

Holiday cottages

whether qualifying for capital allowances *McMahon, T & Ors v Rt Hon Lord Mayor Alderman & Burgess of Dublin* Vol V p 357

Holidays (Employees) Act 1973

The Minister for Labour v PMPA Insurance Co Ltd (under administration) Vol III p 505

Hospital

whether carrying on a trade *RG Davis (Inspector of Taxes) v The Superioress Mater Misericordiae Hospital, Dublin* Vol I p 387

Husband

and wife, living apart *Donovan (Inspector Of Taxes) v CG Crofts* Vol I p 115

and wife, living together *Ua Clothasaigh (Inspector of Taxes) v McCartan* Vol II p 75

tax paid by a married couple in excess of the amounts payable by a husband and wife if taxed as separate persons, *Francis & Mary Murphy v AG* Vol V p 613

wife's income from securities assessed on husband in first year of wife's income from securities *JD Mulvey (Inspector of Taxes) v RM Kieran* Vol I p 563

I

Illegal trades

not assessable to tax *C Hayes (Inspector of Taxes) v RJ Duggan* Vol I p 195

Immediately

statutory provision requiring person to express dissatisfaction with the determination of a point of law "immediately after the determination" *The State (Multiprint Label Systems Ltd) v The Honourable Justice Thomas Neylon* Vol III p 159

Importation

of used motor vehicles from a Member State *Karl Keller v The Revenue Commissioners & Others* Vol IV p 512

Imprisonment

bookmaker convicted and fined in the District Court of offences under the Betting Acts penal warrant for imprisonment, whether constitutional *John B Murphy v District Justice Brendan Wallace & Others* Vol IV p 278

return of income, failure to make, appeal against a decision of the High Court to refuse on a judicial review application to quash three convictions with six months imprisonment for each offence imposed in the District Court on the appellant for failure to make income tax returns *Thomas O'Callaghan v JP Clifford & Others* Vol IV p 478

Incidental expenses

whether a deduction should be allowed under ITA 1967 Sch 2 para 3, in respect of incidental expenses *MacDaibheid (Inspector of Taxes) v SD* Vol III p 1

Income

accumulated for minor, benefit taken by way of capital *The King (Evelyn Spain) v The Special Commissioners* Vol I p 221

father taking his elder children and his mother-in-law into partnership, subsequent assignment of mother-in-law's interest to his younger children whether income of children to be deemed to be income of father *JM O'Dwyer (Inspector of Taxes) v Cafolla & Co* Vol II p 82

Income (contd)

from the leasing of premises, whether earned income *Pairceir (Inspector of Taxes) v EM* Vol II p 596

not "immediately derived" from a trade of business *JG Kerrane (Inspector of Taxes) v N Hanlon (Ireland) Ltd* Vol III p 633

on estate in course of administration *Moloney (Inspector of Taxes) v Allied Irish Banks Ltd as executors of the estate of Francis J Doherty deceased* Vol III p 477

payment for maintenance of residence not part of total income *The Most Honourable Frances Elizabeth Sarah Marchioness Conyngham v The Revenue Commissioners* Vol I p 231

personal pension and other assets assigned to company pension continued to be paid to pensioner, whether pensioner liable to tax on pension *Cronin (Inspector of Taxes) v C* Vol II p 592

professional services rendered without prior agreement as regards remuneration payment on termination of services whether chargeable as income *WS McGarry (Inspector of Taxes) v EF* Vol II p 261

received on foot of an obligation with bank *JG Kerrane (Inspector of Taxes) v N Hanlon (Ireland) Ltd* Vol III p 633

trust in favour of charitable objects with provision for re-vestment of income in settlor in certain contingencies, whether income of settlor or trustees *HPC Hughes (Inspector of Taxes) v Miss Gretta Smyth (Sister Mary Bernard) & Others* Vol I p 411

whether children's pension is treated as income of the parent or income of the children for income tax purposes *EP O'Coindealbhain (Inspector of Taxes) v Breda O'Carroll* Vol IV p 221

whether increase in widows contributory pension for children is taxable income of parent *Sean O'Siochain (Inspector of Taxes) v Bridget Neenan* Vol V p 472

Income tax

Acts *Michael Deighan v Edward N Hearne & Others* Vol III p 533

appeal to High Court by way of case stated from decision of Circuit Judge, failure to notify the respondent the fact that a case has been stated *A & B v WJ Davis (Inspector of Taxes)* Vol II p 60

application of provisions to corporation tax *Wayte (Holdings) Ltd (In Receivership) Alex Burns v Edward N Hearne* Vol III p 553

assessable profits, not received in the year of assessment *MacKeown (Inspector of Taxes) v Patrick J Roe* Vol I p 214

domicile and ordinary residence *Captain R H Prior-Wandesforde v the Revenue Commissioners* Vol I p 249 and *The Right Hon The Earl of Iveagh v The Revenue Commissioners* Vol I p 259

exemption for agricultural societies *The Trustees of The Ward Union Hunt Races v Hughes (Inspector of Taxes)* Vol I p 538

husband and wife living apart, wife's income assessed on husband *Donovan (Inspector of Taxes) v CG Crofts* Vol I p 115

husband and wife living together *D Ua Clothasaigh (Inspector of Taxes) v Patrick McCartan* Vol II p 75

residence of company *The Cunard Steam Ship Co Ltd v Herlihy (Inspector of Taxes), and The Cunard Steam Ship Co Ltd v Revenue Commissioners* Vol I p 330

Income tax (contd)

school/colleges whether operated for charitable purposes *The Pharmaceutical Society of Ireland v The Revenue Commissioners* Vol I p 542

trust in favour of charitable objects with provision for re-vestment of income in settlor in certain contingencies, whether income of settlor or trustees *HPC Hughes (Inspector of Taxes) v Miss Smyth (Sister Mary Bernard) & Others* Vol I p 411

veterinary, body corporate performing statutory functions, whether profits liable to tax *The Veterinary Council v F Corr (Inspector of Taxes)* Vol II p 204

wife's income from securities assessed on husband in first year of wife's income from securities *JD Mulvey (Inspector of Taxes) v RM Kieran* Vol I p 563

RETURNS

of income, what constitutes a proper return of income for the assessment of income tax *MA Bairead v M McDonald* Vol IV p 475

SCHEDULE A

income tax paid, whether further balance due *Estate Of Teresa Downing (Owner)* Vol I p 487

SCHEDULE B

profits from stallion fees, whether liable to tax under Schedule B or Schedule D income tax paid, whether further balance due *Cloghran Stud Farm v AG Birch (Inspector of Taxes)* Vol I p 496

occupation of lands, whether the appellant company was in occupation of lands, forming part of a military establishment, for the purposes of ITA 1918 Schedule B or ITA 1967 *O Conaill (Inspector of Taxes) v Z Ltd* Vol II p 636

valuation of land occupied for market gardening *L v WS McGarry (Inspector of Taxes)* Vol II p 241

SCHEDULE D

assessment of builders profits *The State (at the prosecution of Patrick J Whelan) v Michael Smidic (Special Commissioners of Income Tax)* Vol I p 571 and *Edward Connolly v AG Birch (Inspector of Taxes)* Vol I p 583

change in nature of trade or new trade, trading as fuel merchants, whether new trade of coal mining was set up or commenced *HA O'Loan (Inspector of Taxes) v Messrs MJ Noone & Co* Vol II p 146

cost of replacement of weighbridge house, whether allowable deduction *JT Hodgins (Inspector of Taxes) v Plunder & Pollak (Ireland) Ltd* Vol II p 267

ex gratia payments, by British government for malicious damage to property or personal injury sustained, whether trading receipt *WA Robinson T/A James Pim & Son v JD Dolan (Inspector of Taxes)* Vol I p 427

management expenses, deduction of, by investment company *Howth Estate Co v WJ Davis (Inspector of Taxes)* Vol I p 447

nurseries and market gardens, assessment of income by reference to annual profits estimated according to the rules of Schedule D *WS McGarry (Inspector of Taxes) v JA Spencer* Vol II p 1

obsolescence of assets *Evans & Co v Phillips (Inspector of Taxes)* Vol I p 43

payment in advance on the signing of a lease, whether capital *O'Sullivan (Inspector of Taxes) v p Ltd* Vol II p 464

personal pension assigned to company but continued to be paid to pensioner, whether pensioner liable to tax *Cronin (Inspector of Taxes) v C* Vol II p 592

Income tax (contd)

profits from stallion fees, whether liable to tax under Schedule B or Schedule D income tax paid, whether further balance due *Cloghran Stud Farm v AG Birch (Inspector of Taxes)* Vol I p 496

profits of a bookmaker from transactions in Irish Hospital Sweepstakes tickets, whether receipts assessable to tax under Schedule D *HH v MJ Forbes (Inspector of Taxes)* Vol II p 614

trade or business, brewery, whether liability in respect of transactions under DORA requisition orders *Arthur Guinness Son & Co Ltd v Commissioners of Inland Revenue* Vol I p 1

SCHEDULE D, CASE I & II

an obsolescence of assets *Evans & Co v Phillips (Inspector of Taxes)* Vol I p 43

assessment of wife's first years income on husband *JD Mulvey (Inspector of Taxes) v RM Kieran* Vol I p 563

SCHEDULE D, CASE I & II

bad debts recovered *Bourke (Inspector of Taxes) v Lyster & Sons Ltd* Vol II p 374

basis of assessment *JD Mulvey (Inspector of Taxes) v RM Kieran* Vol I p 563

basis of assessment, commencement and cessation within a year, whether assessment for the previous year can be reviewed *AB v JD Mulvey (Inspector of Taxes)* Vol II p 55

bloodstock, animal bought in course of trade, sent to stud after successful racing career and subsequently sold to a syndicate whether amount realised on syndication a trading receipt *Mac Giolla Riogh (Inspector of Taxes) v G Ltd* Vol II p 315

builder's profits, capitalised value of ground rents and fines, whether liable to tax *Birch (Inspector of Taxes) v Denis Delaney* Vol I p 515 and *Edward Connolly v AG Birch (Inspector of Taxes)* Vol I p 583 and *Swaine (Inspector of Taxes) v VE* Vol II p 472

compensation for loss of profits, whether income or capital receipt *The Alliance and Dublin Consumers' Gas Co v McWilliams (Inspector of Taxes)* Vol I p 207

compensation for loss of profits, whether trading receipt *F Corr (Inspector of Taxes) v FE Larkin* Vol II p 164

compensation paid to tenants of adjoining premises for interference with light and air, whether allowable Case I deduction *WJ Davis (Inspector of Taxes) v X Ltd* Vol II p 45

compulsory sale to Minister for Finance, in return for sterling equivalents, of dollar balances consisting of income from securities etc, in the USA whether moneys so received assessable *JM O'Sullivan (Inspector of Taxes) v Julia O'Connor, as Administratrix of Evelyn H O'Brien, Deceased* Vol II p 61

deduction for expenses of promoting bill in Parliament *McGarry (Inspector of Taxes) v Limerick Gas Committee* Vol I p 375

deduction for interest paid *Phillips (Inspector of Taxes) v Limerick County Council* Vol I p 66

deduction of corporation profits tax and excess corporation profits tax in computing profits for income tax purposes *JM O'Dwyer (Inspector of Taxes) v The Dublin United Transport Co Ltd* Vol II p 115

Income tax (contd)

deduction of loss on realisation of investments *The Alliance & Dublin Consumers' Gas Co v Davis (Inspector of Taxes)* Vol I p 104

deduction, legal fees in defending action in High Court for balance alleged to be due to a building contractor in respect of the construction of cinema, whether allowable Case I deduction *Casey (Inspector of Taxes) v AB Ltd* Vol II p 500

discontinuance of trade, set off of losses *Boland's Ltd v Davis (Inspector of Taxes)* Vol I p 86

ex gratia payments, by British government for malicious damage to property or personal injury sustained, whether trading receipt *WA Robinson T/A James Pim & Son v JD Dolan (Inspector of Taxes)* Vol I p 427

execution of document under seal of the Isle of Man, Secondary evidence that beneficial interest in securities had been transferred not admissible *Gilbert Hewson v JB Kealy (Inspector of Taxes)* Vol II p 15

formation expenses, whether allowable against trading profits *JB Kealy (Inspector of Taxes) v O'Mara (Limerick) Ltd* Vol I p 642

hospital and private nursing home whether carrying on a trade *RG Davis (Inspector of Taxes) v The Superioress, Mater Misericordiae Hospital, Dublin* Vol I p 387

SCHEDULE D, CASE I & II

illegal trades, not assessable to tax *C Hayes (Inspector of Taxes) v RJ Duggan Vol I p 195* and *Daniel Collins and Michael Byrne Daniel Collins and Redmond Power as Executor of the Will of Michael Byrne, deceased and Daniel Collins v JD Mulvey (Inspector of Taxes)* Vol II p 291

income from the leasing of premises, whether leasing constitutes trading whether earned income *Pairceir (Inspector of Taxes) v EM* Vol I p 596

Industrial and Provident Societies, trading with both members and non-members, investments and property purchased out of trading profits, whether the dividends and rents form part of the profits of the trade *The Revenue Commissioners v Y Ltd* Vol II p 195

losses forward *Molmac Ltd v MacGiolla Riogh (Inspector of Taxes)* Vol II p 482

lump sum paid on execution of lease, whether capital payment or rent paid in advance, whether liable under Case I and II or Case III *W Flynn (Inspector of Taxes) v John Noone Ltd, and W Flynn (Inspector of Taxes) v Blackwood & Co (Sligo) Ltd* Vol II p 222

on rebuilding of business premises, whether portion thereof deductible in computing profits *Curtin (Inspector of Taxes) v M Ltd* Vol II p 360

profit on realisation of investments, whether trading profit *Agricultural Credit Corporation Ltd v JB Vale (Inspector of Taxes)* Vol I p 474 and *Davis (Inspector of Taxes) v Hibernian Bank Ltd* Vol I p 503

removing top-soil from surface of quarry *Milverton Quarries Ltd v The Revenue Commissioners* Vol II p 382

statutory body, whether carrying on a trade *The Exported Live Stock (Insurance) Board v TJ Carroll (Inspector of Taxes)* Vol II p 211

trade carried on by beneficiary of charity, whether exempt, *Beirne (Inspector of Taxes) v St Vincent De Paul Society (Wexford Conference)* Vol I p 383

whether expenditure incurred by petrol marketing company under exclusivity agreements with retailers is revenue or capital *Dolan (Inspector of Taxes) v AB Co Ltd* Vol II p 515

Income tax (contd)

SCHEDULE D, CASE III

foreign trades, basis of assessment under Case III *O'Conaill (Inspector of Taxes) v R* Vol II p 304

interest received *Irish Provident Assurance Co Ltd (In Liquidation) v Kavanagh (Inspector of Taxes)* Vol I p 45

ITA 1918 rule 7 *Evans & Co v Phillips (Inspector of Taxes)* Vol I p 43

liability to, business carried on abroad *The Executors and Trustees of AC Ferguson (deceased) v Donovan (Inspector of Taxes)* Vol I p 183

lump sum paid on execution of lease, whether capital payment or rent paid in advance, whether liable under Case I & II or Case III *W Flynn (Inspector of Taxes) v John Noone Ltd, and W Flynn (Inspector of Taxes) v Blackwood & Co (Sligo) Ltd* Vol II p 222

pension received by Irish resident from British company, whether income from foreign possession *McHugh (Inspector of Taxes) v A* Vol I p 393 and *Forbes (Inspector of Taxes) v GHD* Vol II p 491

settlement of income, deed of appointment by parent in favour of child *EG v Mac Shamhrain, (Inspector of Taxes)* Vol II p 352

SCHEDULE D, CASE IV

illegal trades, not assessable to tax under Case IV *C Hayes (Inspector of Taxes) v RJ Duggan* Vol I p 195

lump sum paid on execution of lease, whether capital payment or rent paid in advance, whether liable under Case I & II or Case III *W Flynn (Inspector of Taxes) v John Noone Ltd; W Flynn (Inspector of Taxes) v Blackwood & Co (Sligo) Ltd* Vol II p 222

professional services rendered without prior agreement as regards remuneration payment on termination of services whether chargeable as income *W S McGarry (Inspector of Taxes) v EF* Vol II p 261

SCHEDULE D, CASE V

domicile and ordinary residence *Captain RH Prior-Wandesforde v the Revenue Commissioners* Vol I p 249 and *The Right Hon The Earl of Iveagh v The Revenue Commissioners* Vol I p 259

SCHEDULE E

benefit in kind, rent paid for employee *Connolly (Inspector of Taxes) v Denis McNamara* Vol II p 452

branch manager of local Employment Office of Dept of Social Welfare whether the taxpayer was engaged under a contract of service or a contract for services *O'Coindealbhain (Inspector of Taxes) v TB Mooney* Vol IV p 45

calculation of PAYE due in respect of remuneration paid in year following that in which work was done, method of assessment *Bedford (Collector-General) v H* Vol II p 588

deductions *Phillips (Inspector of Taxes) v Keane* Vol I p 64

deductions *SP O'Broin (Inspector of Taxes) v Mac Giolla Meidhre/Finbar Pigott* Vol II p 366 and *HF Kelly (Inspector of Taxes) v H* Vol II p 460

director resident abroad, of a company incorporated in the State but managed and controlled abroad. whether Schedule E employment *WJ Tipping (Inspector of Taxes) v Louis Jeancard* Vol II p 68

Income tax (contd)

interest due on overpayment of PAYE *O'Rourke v Revenue Commissioners* Vol V p 321

nun, whether assessable on earnings which are given to her order *JD Dolan (Inspector of Taxes) v "K" National School Teacher* Vol I p 656

present from employer, whether taxable as gift or emolument *Wing v O'Connell (Inspector of Taxes)* Vol I p 155

remuneration charging section provision in will charging rental income from estate with annual amount payable to beneficiary provided he continued to manage the property *Gerald O'Reilly v WJ Casey (Inspector of Taxes)* Vol I p 601

remuneration of office, grant to a President of a college on retirement *JD Mulvey (Inspector of Taxes) v Denis J Coffey* Vol I p 618

whether contract for services between skipper of fishing vessel and crew members *Director of Public Prosecutions v Martin McLoughlin* Vol III p 467

whether the taxpayer was engaged under a contract of service or a contract for services *McDermott (Inspector of Taxes) v BC* Vol III p 43

SCHEDULE F

interest paid by Irish subsidiary to Japanese parent company on loan from parent company whether tax should be deducted at source under Double Tax Treaty or whether the payment should be treated as distribution under Schedule F *Murphy (Inspector of Taxes) v Asahi Synthetic Fibres (Ireland) Ltd* Vol III p 246

Income tax and corporation profits tax

company in receivership preferential claim *The Attorney-General v Irish Steel Ltd and Vincent Crowley* Vol II p 108

Inducement payments

whether liable to income tax *PJ O'Connell (Inspector of Taxes) v T Keleghan* 1999-2000 p 143

profit/trading receipts *O'Dwyer (Inspector of Taxes) and the Revenue Commissioners v Irish Exporters and Importers Ltd (In Liquidation)* Vol I p 629

Industrial and Provident Societies

surplus of co-op from dealing with members, whether trading profits, whether exempt *Kennedy (Inspector of Taxes) v The Rattoo Co-op Dairy Society Ltd* Vol I p 315

trading with both members and non-members, investments and property purchased out of trading profits, whether the dividends and rents form part of the profits of the trade *The Revenue Commissioners v Y Ltd* Vol II p 195

Industrial building

structure for dock undertaking, whether bonded transit sheds used as clearing house and not for storage qualify *Patrick Monahan (Drogheda) Ltd v O'Connell (Inspector of Taxes)* Vol III p 661

whether a building which housed offices, a showroom, a canteen, computer department and utilities qualified for industrial building allowance under ITA 1967 s 255 *O'Conaill (Inspector of Taxes) v JJ Ltd* Vol III p 65

Information

available to Revenue Commissioners, accountants working papers, whether the inspector of taxes is entitled to call for production of a taxpayer's nominal ledger, whether the nominal ledger formed part of the accountant's working papers *JJ Quigley (Inspector of Taxes) v Maurice Burke* Vol IV p 332, Vol V p 265

transfer of assets to offshore tax havens, whether accountants could be requested to furnish relevant particulars in respect of all their clients *Warnock & Others practising as Stokes Kennedy Crowley & Co v The Revenue Commissioners* Vol III p 356

Inspector of taxes

empowered to require of an individual by notice a return of income *Thomas O'Callaghan v JP Clifford & Others* Vol IV p 478

entitlement to recompute standard percentage basis of profits for excess profits duty *Boland's Ltd v The Commissioners of Inland Revenue* Vol I p 34

Interest

deduction for interest paid from interest received *Phillips (Inspector of Taxes) v Limerick County Council* Vol I 66

earned by non-resident company manufacturing through a branch in the State, tax free profits from branch paid into foreign bank account, whether interest earned on foreign bank account is taxable in Ireland *Murphy (Inspector of Taxes) v Dataproducts (Dublin) Ltd* Vol IV p 12

earned on deposit interest after date of liquidation *A Noyek & Sons Ltd (in voluntary liquidation), Alex Burns v Edward N Hearne* Vol III p 523

in possession, whether conveyancing form determines liability to estate duty *The Attorney General v Power & Anor* Vol V p 525

on loan after redemption of share capital, whether allowable as trade expense *Sean MacAonghusa v Ringmahon* 1999-2000 p 81

on overpaid income tax, whether appeal of assessments under wrong Schedule rules out interest on overpayments of tax, whether appeal to nil assessments to tax rules out interest on overpayments on tax *O'Coindealbhain (Inspector of Taxes) v TB Mooney* Vol IV p 45

on overpaid PAYE, whether due or not, *O'Rourke v Revenue Commissioners* Vol V p 321

on repayment of tax *Navan Carpets Ltd v O'Culachain (Inspector of Taxes)* Vol III p 403

paid by a company to a person having controlling interest in that company *The Revenue Commissioners v Associated Properties Ltd* Vol II p 412

paid by Irish subsidiary to Japanese parent company on loan from parent company whether tax should be deducted at source under Double Tax Treaty or treated as distribution under Schedule F *Murphy (Inspector of Taxes) v Asahi Synthetic Fibres (Ireland) Ltd* Vol III p 246

repayment of interest on tax paid in mistake of law, common law right to restitution, rate of interest according to Courts of Justice Acts *O'Rourke v Revenue Commissioners* Vol V p 321

stamp duties, new interest and penalty provisions introduced by FA 1991 s 100 came into effect on 1 November 1991 and previous provision for interest and penalties under Stamp Act 1891 s 15 were repealed on 29 May 1991, the date of the passing of FA 1991, whether interest and penalties applied between 29 May 1991 and 1 November 1991 *Edward O'Leary v The Revenue Commissioners* Vol IV p 357 *Terence Byrne v The Revenue Commissioners* Vol V p 560

Interest and income from securities and possessions

execution of document under seal of the Isle of Man, secondary evidence that beneficial interest in securities had been transferred, not admissible *Gilbert Hewson v JB Kealy (Inspector of Taxes)* Vol II p 15

Interpretation of Documents

Court entitled to look at reality of what has been done *Waterford Glass (Group Services) Ltd v The Revenue Commissioners* Vol IV p 194, *B McCabe (Inspector of Taxes) v South City & County Investment Co Ltd* Vol V p 119, 1998 p 183

Interpretation of statutes

of excise duties payable under SI 422/1983 and EC Directive *Karl Keller v The Revenue Commissioners & Others* Vol IV p 512

of statutes, absurdity *K Company v Hogan* Vol III p 56

of statutes, ambiguity *McNally v Maoldhomnaigh* Vol IV p 22

of statutes, ejusdem generis rule *M Cronin v Lunham Brothers Ltd* Vol III p 370

of statutes, exemption *The Revenue Commissioners v Doorley* Vol V p 539

of statutes, mandatory *The Revenue Commissioners v Henry Young* Vol V p 294

of statutes, relief *Texaco Ireland Ltd v Murphy* Vol IV p 91 *O'Coindealbhain v Gannon* Vol III p 484, *McCann v O'Culachain* Vol III p 304 *O'Culachain v McMullan Bros* Vol IV p 284, Vol V p 200, *O'Sullivan v The Revenue Commissioners* Vol V p 570

of statutes, rules of construction *De Brun (Inspector of Taxes) v Kiernan* Vol III p 19, *McGrath v McDermott* Vol III p 683

of taxing act *EP O'Coindealbhain (Inspector of Taxes) v The Honourable Mr Justice Sean Gannon* Vol III p 484

Investments

finance company, dealing in stocks and shares, whether investments should be valued at cost or market value *A B Ltd v Mac Giolla Riogh (Inspector of Taxes)* Vol II p 419

profits on realisation of whether trading profits *The Agricultural Credit Corporation Ltd v JB Vale (Inspector of Taxes)* Vol I p 474 and *The Alliance & Dublin Consumers' Gas Co v Davis (Inspector of Taxes)* Vol I p 104 and *Davis (Inspector of Taxes) v Hibernian Bank Ltd* Vol I p 503

Investment company

deduction of expenses of management *Howth Estate Co v WJ Davis (Inspector of Taxes)* Vol I p 447 and *Casey (Inspector of Taxes) v The Monteagle Estate Co* Vol II p 429

Issue

whether "issue" included adopted children *In the matter of John Stamp deceased Patrick Stamp v Noel Redmond & Others* Vol IV p 415

J

Joint Ownership

whether survivor entitled, whether resulting trust *M Lynch v M Burke & AIB plc* Vol V p 271

Joint Assessment

whether husband is liable for wife's income *Gilligan v Criminal Assets Bureau, Galvin, Lanigan & Revenue Commissioners* Vol V p 424

Journalism

exemption of earnings from original and creative works of artistic or cultural merit, whether journalism qualifies *John Healy v SI Breathnach (Inspector of Taxes)* Vol III p 496

Judicial function

exercise of by Inspector of Taxes *Michael Deighan v Edward N Hearne & Others* Vol III p 533

exercise of by Appeal Commissioners *The State (Calcul International and Solatrex International Ltd) v The Appeal Commissioners and The Revenue Commissioners* Vol III p 577

Judicial review

application for, re stamp duty *Kenny J v Revenue Commissioners, Goodman & Gemon Ltd (Notice Parties)* Vol V p 363

application re VAT *DH Burke & Sons Ltd v The Revenue Commissioners and Others* Vol V 418, *Taxback Ltd v The Revenue Commissioners* Vol V 412

Jurisdiction

of High Court relating to Social Welfare appeals *Albert Kinghan v The Minister for Social Welfare* Vol III p 436

L

Land

dealing in and developing *O'Connlain (Inspector of Taxes) v Belvedere Estates Ltd* Vol III p 271

whether the surplus from the sale of property was profit of a trade of dealing in or developing land, or the profit of a business which was deemed by F(MP)A 1968 s 17, to be such a trade *Mara (Inspector of Taxes) v GG (Hummingbird) Ltd* Vol II p 667

Land Purchase Acts

arrears of jointure tax paid under Schedule A, whether further balance due *Estate Of Teresa Downing (Owner)* Vol I p 487

Lease

lump sum paid on execution of lease, whether capital payment or rent paid in advance *W Flynn (Inspector of Taxes) v John Noone Ltd, and W Flynn (Inspector of Taxes) v Blackwood & Co (Sligo) Ltd* Vol II p 222

payment in advance on the signing of a lease, whether capital *O'Sullivan (Inspector of Taxes) v p Ltd* Vol II p 464

Leasing

income from the leasing of premises, whether leasing constitutes trading, whether earned income *Pairceir (Inspector of Taxes) v EM* Vol II p 596

Legal costs

whether a Circuit Court Judge hearing an appeal pursuant to ITA 1967 s 429 has jurisdiction to award costs *The Revenue Commissioners v Arida Ltd* Vol IV p 401, Vol V p 221

Legal fees

in defending action in High Court for balance alleged to be due to a building contractor in respect of the construction of cinema, whether allowable Case I deduction *Casey (Inspector of Taxes) v AB Ltd* Vol II p 500

whether letting fees and legal expenses incurred by the company in respect of first lettings of property qualified as deductions under ITA 1967 s 81(5)(*d*) *GH Ltd v Browne (Inspector of Taxes)* Vol III p 95

Letting expenses

whether letting fees and legal expenses incurred by the company in respect of first lettings of property qualified as deductions under ITA 1967 s 81(5)(*d*) *GH Ltd v Browne (Inspector of Taxes)* Vol III p 95

Lessors

trade carried on *The Great Southern Railways Co v The Revenue Commissioners* Vol I p 359

Liability

of liquidator to employer's contribution of PRSI in respect of "reckonable earnings" of employees, when payable preferential status *The Companies Act 1963-1983 v Castlemahon Poultry Products Ltd* Vol III p 509

of personal representatives *Moloney (Inspector of Taxes) v Allied Irish Banks Ltd as executors of the estate of Francis J Doherty deceased* Vol III p 477

of receiver, to corporation tax *Wayte (Holdings) Ltd (In receivership) Alex Burns v Edward N Hearne* Vol III p 553

personal, of members of bank, whether unlimited *CIR v The Governor & Company of The Bank of Ireland* Vol I p 70

Limited

partnership, share of capital allowances on leasing transaction, involving a purported limited partnership, against his personal income tax liability *DA MacCarthaigh (Inspector of Taxes) v Francis Daly* Vol III p 253

Liquidation

court fees, amount on which court fees are chargeable in a liquidation *In re Private Motorists Provident Society ltd (In Liqdtn) & W J Horgan v Minister for Justice* Vol V p 186, *In re Hibernian Transport Companies Limited* Vol V p 194

deferral of revenue debts pending completion of contracts by company *The Companies Act 1963-1983 and MFN Construction Co Ltd (in liquidation) on the application of Patrick Tuffy (liquidator)* Vol IV p 82

whether a sum which arose to the company on the liquidation of a wholly owned subsidiary was part of its trading profits *Guinness & Mahon Ltd v Browne (Inspector of Taxes)* Vol III p 373

whether deposit interest earned on monies held by the official liquidator liable to tax *In Re HT Ltd (in Liquidation) & Others* Vol III p 120

whether assessments of PRSI entitled to super preferential priority *Re Coombe Importers Ltd (In Liq) and Re the Companies Acts 1963-1990* 1998 p 59

Liquidator

liability of, to employer's contribution of PRSI in respect of "reckonable earnings" of employees, when payable preferential status *The Companies Act 1963-1983 v Castlemahon Poultry Products Ltd* Vol III p 509; *Re Coombe Importers Ltd (In Liq) and Re the Companies Acts 1963-1990* 1998 p 59

Loan interest

payable follwoing redemption of share capital whether allowable *Sean Mac Aonghusa v Ringmahon* 1990-2000 p 81

Loan notes

whether capital gains tax deferred pending redemption of, *PJ O'connell v T Keleghan* 1999-2000 p 143

Losses

carry forward of losses *Molmac Ltd v MacGiolla Riogh (Inspector of Taxes)* Vol II p 482 and *M Cronin (Inspector of Taxes) v Lunham Brothers Ltd* Vol III p 363

discontinuance of trade, set off of losses *Boland's Ltd v Davis (Inspector of Taxes)* Vol I p 86

in trade, notional, from fall in market value of goods before delivery *The Revenue Commissioners v Latchford & Sons Ltd* Vol I p 240

Lump sum

paid on execution of lease, whether capital payment or rent paid in advance *W Flynn (Inspector of Taxes) v John Noone Ltd, and W Flynn (Inspector of Taxes) v Blackwood & Co (Sligo) Ltd* Vol II p 222

redundancy payments to disabled employees, whether exempt from income tax, whether distinction to be made between disabled employees whose jobs continued and disabled employees whose jobs ceased p *O Cahill (Inspector of Taxes) v Albert Harding & Others* Vol IV p 233

whether paid on account of retirement or due to ill health *B D O'Shea (Inspector of Taxes) v Michael Mulqueen* Vol V p 134

M

Market gardening

valuation of land occupied for market gardening *L v WS McGarry (Inspector of Taxes)* Vol II p 241

Market value

of shares in a private trading company, *E A Smyth v The Revenue Commissioners* Vol V p 532, *In the estate of Thomas McNamee & Others v The Revenue Commissioners* Vol V p 577

Management

expenses, deduction of, by investment company *Howth Estate Co v W J Davis (Inspector of Taxes)* Vol I p 447 and *Casey (Inspector of Taxes) v The Monteagle Estate Co* Vol II p 429, *Hibernian Insurance Company Limited v MacUimis (Inspector of Taxes)* Vol V p 495, 1999-2000 p 113, *Stephen Court Ltd v JA Browne (Inspector of Taxes)* Vol V p 680

Management (contd)

losses in holding company, whether notional management fees deductible Corporation tax *Belville Holdings Ltd (in receivership and liquidation) v Cronin (Inspector of Taxes)* Vol III p 340,

Mandamus

finality of Special Commissioners' decision *The King (Evelyn Spain) v The Special Commissioners* Vol I p 221

order for mandamus - clearance certificate *The State (Melbarian enterprises Ltd) v The Revenue Commissioners* Vol III p 291

Manufacturing relief

assembly of agricultural machinery whether manufacturing *Irish Agricultural Machinery Ltd v S O'Culachain (Inspector of Taxes)* Vol III p 661

film production, whether relief given for accounting periods prior to FA 1990 *Saatchi & Saatchi Advertising Ltd v Kevin McGarry (Inspector of Taxes)* Vol V p 376, 1998 p 99

newspaper publisher, newspapers are "goods" for the purpose of manufacturing relief, whether advertising income is from a separate trade and qualifies for such relief *L McGurrin (Inspector of Taxes) v The Champion Publications Ltd* Vol IV p 466

process of ripening bananas whether constituted manufacturing *Charles McCann Ltd v S O'Culachain (Inspector of Taxes)* Vol III p 304, *PJ O'Connell v Fyffes Banana Processing Ltd* 19999-2000 p 71

processing of and sale of milk produced by the company, whether constituted the manufacture of goods for the purposes of the reduction in corporation tax provided for in FA 1980 Pt I Ch VI *Cronin (Inspector of Taxes) v Strand Dairy Ltd* Vol III p 441

production of day old chicks, whether day old chicks are goods within the meaning of FA 1980, whether process constitutes manufacturing, whether use of extensive plant machinery and skilled workers constitute a process of manufacturing *JF Kelly (Inspector of Taxes) v Cobb Straffan Ireland Ltd* Vol IV p 526, *TG Brosnan (Inspector of Taxes) v Leeside Nurseries Ltd* Vol V p 21

production of films for use in advertising, whether manufacture *S O'Culachain (Inspector of Taxes) v Hunter Advertising Ltd* Vol IV p 35

whether production of J Cloths and nappy liners from bales of fabric is a manufacturing process *D O Laochdha (Inspector of Taxes) v Johnson & Johnson (Ireland) Ltd* Vol IV p 361

whether proper construction of words of s 41 brought advertisements within definition of goods *L McGurrin (Inspector of Taxes) v The Champion Publications Ltd* Vol IV p 466

whether sophisticated system of growth of plants within glasshouses constitute a manufacturing process *TG Brosnan (Inspector of Taxes) v Leeside Nurseries Ltd* Vol V p 21

wholesaler of beers and stouts, also conditions bottled stout, whether conditioning of bottled Guinness constitutes manufacturing process, whether plant and equipment sufficiently sophisticated *J Hussey (Inspector of Taxes) v MJ Gleeson & Co Ltd* Vol IV p 533

Marriage gratuity

whether "marriage gratuity" received on resignation was a retirement payment under ITA 1967 s 114 or was a perquisite of her office under ITA 1967 s 110 *Sean O'Siochain (Inspector of Taxes) v Thomas Morrissey* Vol IV p 407

Married persons

aggregation of incomes of married persons unconstitutional *francis Murphy & Partner v Attorney General* Vol V p 613

aggregation of earned income of married persons unconstitutional *Bernard Muckley and Anne Muckley v Ireland, The Attorney General and The Revenue Commissioners* Vol III p 188

joint assessment whether husband is liable for tax on both incomes *Gilligan v Criminal Assets Bureau, Galvin, Lanigan & Revenue Commissioners* Vol V p 424

living apart *Donovan (Inspector of Taxes) v CG Crofts* Vol I p 115

living together *D Ua Clothasaigh (Inspector of Taxes) v Patrick McCartan* Vol II p 75

wife's income from securities assessed on husband in first year of wife's income from securities *JD Mulvey (Inspector of Taxes) v RM Kieran* Vol I p 563

UK resident working in Ireland, wife working in UK, whether he is entitled to married allowance and rate bands *S Fennessy (Inspector of Taxes) v John Mc Connellogue* Vol V p 129

Meetings

of companies, whether they took place, whether resolution was passed, whether share issue invalid *In re Sugar Distributors Ltd* Vol V p 225

Mill

expenditure on mill *sanitation JB Vale (Inspector of Taxes) v Martin Mahony & Brothers Ltd* Vol II p 32

Mistake

whether monies paid in mistake of law recoverable, whether a common law right to repayment *O'Rourke v Revenue Commissioners* Vol V p 321

N

Newspaper publisher

newspapers are "goods" for the purpose of manufacturing relief, whether advertising income is from a separate trade and qualifies for such relief *L McGurrin (Inspector of Taxes) v The Champion Publications Ltd* Vol IV p 466

Non-resident company

manufacturing through a branch in the State, tax free profits from branch paid into foreign bank account, whether interest earned on foreign bank account is taxable in Ireland *S Murphy (Inspector of Taxes) v Dataproducts (Dublin) Ltd* Vol IV p 12

Non-residents - EU

whether entitled to VAT refunds through refunding agencies *Taxback Limited v The Revenue Commissioners* Vol V p 412

Nuns

whether assessable on income from employment which is given to the order *JD Dolan (Inspector of Taxes) v "K" National School Teacher* Vol I p 656

Nurseries and market gardens

assessment of income by reference to annual profits estimated according to the rules of Schedule D *WS McGarry (Inspector of Taxes) v JA Spencer* Vol II p 1

Nursing home

profits derived from hospital and associated private nursing home, whether trade carried on *RG Davis (Inspector of Taxes) v The Superioress Mater Misericordiae Hospital, Dublin* Vol I p 387

O

Obsolescence of assets

Evans & Co v Phillips (Inspector of Taxes) Vol I p 43

Occupation of lands

whether the appellant company was in occupation of lands, forming part of a military establishment, for the purposes of ITA 1918 Sch B or ITA 1967 *O Conaill (Inspector of Taxes) v Z Ltd* Vol II p 636

Option

deed of release, whether release constitutes a sale for stamp duty purposes *In re Cherrycourt v The Revenue Commissioners* Vol V p 180

Original

document not produced, secondary evidence that beneficial interest in securities had been transferred not admissible *Hewson v JB Kealy (Inspector of Taxes)* Vol II p 15

P

Paid

the meaning of, whether charge/credit cards mean paid for *The Diners Club Ltd v The Revenue and The Minister for Finance* Vol III p 680

Partnership

father taking his children into partnership, whether income of children is deemed to be income of father *JM O'Dwyer (Inspector of Taxes) v Cafolla & Co* Vol II p 82

share of capital allowances on leasing transaction, involving a purported limited partnership, against his personal income tax liability *DA MacCarthaigh (Inspector of Taxes) v Francis Daly* Vol III p 253

Partnership

sole trader admitted partner at beginning of year, during the year the business is sold to limited company, whether sole traders previous year's assessment can be revised *AB v JD Mulvey (Inspector of Taxes)* Vol II p 55

Patent rights

whether income from patent rights disregarded for income tax purposes, where payable to non residents, whether tax avoidance scheme *Pandion Haliaetus Ltd & Ors v The Revenue Commissioners* Vol III p 670

PAYE

due in respect of remuneration paid in year following that in which work was done, assessment *Bedford (Collector-General) v H* Vol II p 588

employer's obligations to deduct PAYE and PRSI from employee's emoluments *EN Hearne (Inspector of Taxes) v O'Cionna & Ors T/A JA Kenny & Ptnrs* Vol IV p 113

PAYE regulations

whether procedures unfair and unconstitutional, enforcement order issue to city sheriff after payment of tax, defamation of plaintiff *Giles J Kennedy v E G Hearne, the Attorney General & Others* Vol III p 590

Payment

of dividends, whether payment through inter-company account was sufficient evidence of actual payment, whether payment of cheque required, whether making of accounting entry a mere record of underlying transaction, whether a dividend declared on 11 December 1980 was received by related company not later than 12 December 1980, whether making of journal entries after 23 December 1980 material evidence *Sean Murphy (Inspector of Taxes) v The Borden Co Ltd* Vol II p 559

payment of excise duty deferred *The Attorney General v Sun Alliance and London Insurance Ltd* Vol III p 265

Penalties

non-payment of excise duty payable on bets entered into by the defendant a registered bookmaker, whether recovery of an excise penalty a criminal matter, *The Director of Public Prosecutions v Seamus Boyle* Vol IV p 395

prosecution for payment of a Revenue penalty, whether criminal or civil proceedings *Director of Public Prosecutions v Robert Downes* Vol III p 641

whether penalties for failure to make returns are unconstitutional *Edward McLoughlin and Thomas Marie Tuite v The Revenue Commissioners and The Attorney General* Vol III p 387

Pension

personal pension and other assets assigned to company pension continued to be paid to pensioner, whether pensioner liable to tax on pension *Cronin (Inspector of Taxes) v C* Vol II p 64

social welfare (Consolidation Act 1951 s 299), whether entitled to old age contributory pension, meaning of entry into insurance, definition of contribution year, whether issue open to appeal *Albert Kinghan v The Minister for Social Welfare* Vol III p 436

Personal representatives

liability of personal representatives *Moloney (Inspector of Taxes) v Allied Irish Banks Ltd as executors of the estate of Francis J Doherty deceased* Vol III p 477

Personal rights

of citizen violated *Michael Deighan v Edward N Hearne & Others* Vol III p 533

of citizens *Bernard Muckley and Anne Muckley v Ireland, The Attorney General and The Revenue Commissioners* Vol III p 188

Petrol canopies

whether forecourt canopies at petrol filling stations constitute plant for tax purposes *S O'Culachain v McMullan Brothers* Vol IV p 284, Vol V p 200

Petrol marketing company

whether expenditure incurred under exclusivity agreements with retailers is revenue or capital *Dolan (Inspector of Taxes) v AB Co Ltd* Vol II p 515

Petroleum exploration

whether constitutes scientific research, whether such scientific research qualifies for tax relief by way of an allowance under ITA 1967 s 244 *Texaco Ireland Ltd v S Murphy (Inspector of Taxes)* Vol IV p 91

Pig rearing

whether the activity of intensive pig rearing constituted farming for the purposes of FA 1974 s 13(1) *Knockhall Piggeries v Kerrane (Inspector of Taxes)* Vol III p 319

Plant

barrister's books, whether plant *Breathnach (Inspector of Taxes) v MC* Vol III p 113

expenditure on installation of suspended ceiling in supermarket whether plant qualifying for capital allowances *Dunnes Stores (Oakville) Ltd v MC Cronin (Inspector of Taxes)* Vol IV p 68

poultry house, whether plant and machinery qualifying for capital allowances *O'Srianain (Inspector of Taxes) v Lakeview Ltd* Vol III p 219

racecourse stand, whether deductible repairs or non deductible capital expenditure or expenditure qualifying as plant *Michael O'Grady (Inspector of Taxes) v Roscommon Race Committee* Vol IV p 425, Vol V p 317

whether forecourt canopies at petrol filling stations constitute plant for tax purposes *S O'Culachain v McMullan Brothers* Vol IV p 284, Vol V p 200

Poultry house

whether plant and machinery qualifying for capital allowances *O'Srianain (Inspector of Taxes) v Lakeview Ltd* Vol III p 219

Power of revocation

settlement of income, deed of appointment by parent in favour of child *EG v Mac Shamhrain (Inspector of Taxes)* Vol II p 352

Preferential claim

in receivership, income and corporation profits tax *The Attorney-General v Irish Steel Ltd and Vincent Crowley* Vol III p 265 and *In Re HT Ltd (in Liquidation) & Others* Vol III p 120

in receivership and liquidation *In the Matter of H Williams (Tallaght) (In Receivership & Liquidation) and the Companies Act 1963-1990* Vol V p 388

preferential creditors priority in receivership *United Bars Ltd (In Receivership), Walkinstown Inn Ltd (In Receivership) and Raymond Jackson v The Revenue Commissioners* Vol IV p 107

Preferential claim (contd)

status under Companies Act 1963 s 285 *The Companies Act 1963-1983 v Castlemahon Poultry Products Ltd* Vol III p 509

whether assessemnts of PRSI entitled to super preferential priorty *Re Coombe Importers Ltd (In Liq) and Re the Companies Acts 1963-1990* 1998 p 59

Preference shareholders

whether entitled to participate in capital distribution whether entitled to a portion of issue of new ordinary shares *Williams Group Tullamore Ltd v Companies Act 1963 to 1983* Vol III p 423

Premium

on lease payable by instalments, whether allowable under ITA 1967 s 91 *The Hammond Lane Metal Co Ltd v S O'Culachain (Inspector of Taxes)* Vol IV p 187

Printing

and processing in UK, whether manufacturing *S O'Culachain (Inspector of Taxes) v Hunter Advertising Ltd* Vol IV p 35

Privacy

right to privacy *Charles J Haughey v Moriarty and Others* 1998 p 119

Processes

in form of loannotes, capital gains tax implications *PJ O'Connell v T Keleghan* 1999-2000 p 143

Professional services withholding tax

whether method of granting credit for same is constitutional *Michael Daly v The Revenue Commissioners* Vol V p 213

Profits

FROM ILLEGAL TRADE

Daniel Collins and Michael Byrne, Daniel Collins and Redmond Power as Executor of the will of Michael Byrne, deceased and Daniel Collins v JD Mulvey (Inspector of Taxes) Vol II p 291

FROM STALLION FEES

whether liable to tax under Schedule B or Schedule D income tax paid, whether further balance due *Cloghran Stud Farm v AG Birch (Inspector of Taxes)* Vol I p 496

NOT RECEIVED IN THE YEAR OF ASSESSMENT

MacKeown (Inspector of Taxes) v Patrick J Roe Vol I p 214

OF A TRADE

bad debts recovered, *Bourke (Inspector of Taxes) v Lyster & Sons Ltd* Vol II p 374

compensation for loss of profits, whether income or capital receipt *The Alliance and Dublin Consumers' Gas Co v McWilliams (Inspector of Taxes)* Vol I p 207

derived from hospital and associated private nursing home, whether trade carried on *RG Davis (Inspector of Taxes) v The Superioress, Mater Misericordiae Hospital, Dublin* Vol I p 387

profit/trading receipts *O'Dwyer (Inspector of Taxes) and the Revenue Commissioners v Irish Exporters and Importers Ltd (In Liquidation)* Vol I p 629

Profits (contd)

ON REALISATION OF INVESTMENTS

whether trading profits, *The Agricultural Credit Corporation Ltd v JB Vale (Inspector of Taxes)* Vol I p 474 and *The Alliance & Dublin Consumers' Gas Co v Davis (Inspector of Taxes)* Vol I p 104 and *Davis (Inspector of Taxes) v Hibernian Bank Ltd* Vol I p 503

ON SWEEPSTAKES

C Hayes (Inspector of Taxes) v R J Duggan Vol I p 195

Prosecution

for payment of a Revenue penalty *DPP v Robert Downes* Vol III p 641

PRSI

employer's contribution in respect of "reckonable earnings" of employees, when payable, liability of liquidator preferential status *The Companies Act 1963-1983 v Castlemahon Poultry Products Ltd* Vol III p 509

employer's obligations to deduct PAYE and PRSI from employee's emoluments *EN Hearne (Inspector of Taxes) v O'Cionna & Ors T/A JA Kenny & Ptnrs* Vol IV p 113

Publican's licence

excise duty, whether new licence obtainable, whether application within six year period, meaning of year immediately preceding *Peter Connolly v The Collector of Customs and Excise* Vol IV p 419

purchase of, in a bond, by a publican whether trading transaction *McCall (deceased) v Commissioners of Inland Revenue* Vol I p 28

Publishers

newspaper publisher, newspapers are "goods" for the purpose of manufacturing relief, whether advertising income is from a separate trade and qualifies for such relief *L McGurrin (Inspector of Taxes) v Champion Publications Ltd* Vol IV p 466

Q

Quarry

removing top-soil from surface of quarry *Milverton Quarries Ltd v The Revenue Commissioners* Vol II p 382

R

Racing and Racecourses Act 1945

sections 4, 15, 27 *The Racing Board v S O'Culachain* Vol IV p 73

Racecourse stand

whether deductible repairs or non deductible capital expenditure or expenditure qualifying as plant *Michael O'Grady (Inspector of Taxes) v Roscommon Race Committee* Vol IV p 425, Vol V p 317

Racing bodies

whether exemption for Agricultural Societies apply *to The Trustees of The Ward Union Hunt Races v Hughes (Inspector of Taxes)* Vol I p 538

Railways

lines leased to another company at an annual rent *The Commissioners of Inland Revenue and The Dublin and Kingstown Railway Co* Vol I p 119

lessors of railway line, whether a railway undertaking *The Great Southern Railways Co v The Revenue Commissioners* Vol I p 359

Realisation

of assets, meaning of, *In re Private Motorists Provident Society ltd (In Liqdtn) & W J Horgan v Minister for Justice* Vol V p 186, *In re Hibernian Transport Companies Limited* Vol V p 194

Receiver

company in receivership preferential claim *The Attorney-General v Irish Steel Ltd and Vincent Crowley* Vol II p 108

liability to corporation tax *Wayte (Holdings) Ltd (In Receivership) Alex Burns v Edward N Hearne* Vol III p 553

Receivership

preferential creditors priority in receivership *United Bars Ltd (In Receivership), Walkinstown Inn Ltd (In Receivership) and Raymond Jackson v The Revenue Commissioners* Vol IV p 107

Recovery of tax

from a group of companies, whether Revenue Commissioners may appropriate payments between separate companies within the group, whether insolvency of a company is relevant to gratuitous alienation of assets *Frederick Inns Ltd, The Rendezvous Ltd, The Graduate Ltd, Motels Ltd (In Liquidation) v The Companies Acts 1963-1986* Vol IV p 247

Redundancy payments

whether lump sum payments to disabled employees exempt from income tax *O Cahill (Inspector of Taxes) v Albert Harding & Others* Vol IV p 233, *BD O'Shea (Inspector of Taxes) v Michael Mulqueen* Vol V p 134

Refunding agencies - VAT

whether VAT refunds obtainable through refunding agencies *Taxback Limited v The Revenue Commissioners* Vol V p 412

Regulations

betting duty, whether necessary for Revenue Commissioners to comply with Regulations Act 1890 before proceedings can commence for failure to pay duty on bets *DPP v MichaelCunningham* Vol V p 691

Release

deed of, whether release of an option is a sale *In re Cherrycourt v The Revenue Commissioners* Vol V p 180

Religious orders

whether entitled to repayment of tax deducted from payments made under an indenture of covenant pursuant to ITA 1967 s 439(1)(iv) *The Revenue Commissioners v HI* Vol III p 242

Remuneration

calculation of PAYE due in respect of remuneration paid in year following that in which work was done, method of assessment *Bedford (Collector-General) v H* Vol II p 588

charging section provision in will charging rental income from estate with annual amount payable to beneficiary provided he continued to manage the property *Gerald O'Reilly v WJ Casey (Inspector of Taxes)* Vol I p 601

of office, grant to a President of a college on retirement *JD Mulvey (Inspector of Taxes) v Denis J Coffey* Vol I p 618

professional services rendered without prior agreement as regards remuneration payment on termination of services whether chargeable as income *W S McGarry (Inspector of Taxes) v EF* Vol II p 261

Rent

lump sum paid on execution of lease, whether capital payment or rent paid in advance *W Flynn (Inspector of Taxes) v John Noone Ltd, and W Flynn (Inspector of Taxes) v Blackwood & Co (Sligo) Ltd* Vol II p 222

paid by employing company for house occupied voluntarily by employee *Connolly (Inspector of Taxes) v Denis McNamara* Vol II p 452

payment in advance on the signing of a lease, whether capital *O'Sullivan (Inspector of Taxes) v p Ltd* Vol II p 464

Repairs

allowability of *Martin Fitzgerald v Commissioners of Inland Revenue* Vol I p 91

expenditure on roof, whether deductible repairs or non deductible capital expenditure *Michael O'Grady (Inspector of Taxes) v Roscommon Race Committee* Vol IV p 425

new bar and extension to old bar, whether non-deductible capital improvements *Michael O'Grady (Inspector of Taxes) v Roscommon Race Committee* Vol IV p 425

racecourse stand, whether deductible repairs or non deductible capital expenditure or expenditure qualifying as plant *Michael O'Grady (Inspector of Taxes) v Roscommon Race Committee* Vol IV p 425, Vol V p 317

re-design or lower terracing, whether an improvement *Michael O'Grady (Inspector of Taxes) v Roscommon Race Committee* Vol IV p 425

work done to walls whether deductible repairs or non deductible capital expenditure *Michael O'Grady (Inspector of Taxes) v Roscommon Race Committee* Vol IV p 425

Repayments

provision for interest on repayments of tax *Navan Carpets Ltd v S O'Culachain (Inspector of Taxes)* Vol III p 403

stamp duty inadverently paid, whether repayment due, *Terence Byrne v The Revenue Commissioners* Vol V p 560

whether Revenue can withhold VAT repayments *Taxback Limited v The Revenue Commissioners* Vol V p 412

Repealed legislation

effect of repeal of Farm Tax Act, consequences of absence of amending legislation *Purcell v Attorney General* Vol IV p 229, Vol V p 288

Replacement cost accounting

method of accounting for tax purposes, whether replacement cost basis is acceptable or whether historical cost accounting is the only method of commercial accountancy *Carroll Industries Plc (formerly PJ Carroll & Co Ltd) and PJ Carroll & Co Ltd v S O'Culachain (Inspector of Taxes)* Vol IV p 135

Residence

of company *The Cunard Steam Ship Co Ltd v Herlihy (Inspector of Taxes), and The Cunard Steam Ship Co Ltd v Revenue Commissioners* Vol I p 330

ordinary residence and domicile, Income tax, Sch D, Case V *Captain RH Prior-Wandesforde v the Revenue Commissioners* Vol I p 249 and *The Right Hon The Earl of Iveagh v The Revenue Commissioners* Vol I p 259

UK resident working in Ireland, wife working in UK, whether he is entitled to married allowance and rate bands *S Fennessy (Inspector of Taxes) v John Mc Connellogue* Vol V p 129

whether individual is resident *LJ Irwin (Collector General) v M Grimes* Vol V p 209

whether long term residence determines domicile *Proes v The Revenue Commissioners* Vol V 481

Residential property tax

residential property tax, whether unconstitutional *PJ Madigan & p Madigan v The Attorney General, The Revenue Commissioners & Others* Vol III p 127

Restoration

of destroyed premises under covenant to repair *Martin Fitzgerald v Commissioners of Inland Revenue* Vol I p 91

Retailers Scheme for VAT

interpretation of scheme, *DH Burke & Sons Ltd v The Revenue Commissioners, Ireland and the AG* Vol V p 418

Retirement payments

whether "marriage gratuity" received on resignation was a retirement payment under ITA 1967 s 114 or was a perquisite of her office under ITA 1967 s 110 *Sean O'Siochain (Inspector of Taxes) v Thomas Morrissey* Vol IV p 407

whether lump sum was paid on account of retirement or due to ill health *B D O'Shea (Inspector of Taxes) v Michael Mulqueen* Vol V p 134

Return

of income, what constitutes a proper return of income for the assessment of income tax *MA Bairead v M McDonald* Vol IV p 475; *In the Matter of G O'C & A O'C (Application of Liam Liston (Inspector of Taxes))* Vol V p 346

of income, failure to make, appeal against a decision of the High Court to refuse on a judicial review application to quash three convictions with six months imprisonment for each offence imposed in the District Court on the appellant for failure to make income tax returns *Thomas O'Callaghan v JP Clifford & Others* Vol IV p 478

whether wife obliged to prepare and deliver a separate return of income *Gilligan v Criminal Assets Bureau & Others* Vol V p 424

Roll over relief

proceeds of sale reinvested in acquisition of further lands, whether rollover relief on transfer of a trade applies *EP O'Coindealbhain (Inspector of Taxes) v KN Price* Vol IV p 1

S

Sanitation

expenditure on mill sanitation, whether allowable deduction from trade *profits JB Vale (Inspector of Taxes) v Martin Mahony & Brothers Ltd* Vol II p 32

Sale

of meat into intervention within the EEC *Cronin (Inspector of Taxes) v IMP Middleton Ltd* Vol III p 452

meaning of sale for stamp duty purposes, whether release of an option is a sale *In re Cherrycourt v The Revenue Commissioners* Vol V p 180

Schedule E

gifts, whether present from employer taxable as gift, or emolument under Schedule E *Wing v O'Connell (Inspector of Taxes)* Vol I p 155

School/colleges

whether operated for charitable purposes *The Pharmaceutical Society of Ireland v The Revenue Commissioners* Vol I p 542

Scientific research

whether petroleum exploration constitutes scientific research, whether such scientific research qualifies for tax relief by way of an allowance under ITA 1967 s 244 *Texaco Ireland Ltd v S Murphy (Inspector of Taxes)* Vol IV p 91

Secondary evidence

not admissible *Gilbert Hewson v J B Kealy (Inspector of Taxes)* Vol II p 15

Seizure

interpleader summons arose out of the seizure by the applicant in his role as Revenue sheriff of goods and chattels claimed to be the property of the claimant in the action *Patrick Cusack v Evelyn O'Reilly & The Honourable Mr Justice Frank Roe & Others* Vol IV p 86

of oil tanker by the Revenue Commissioners *McCrystal Oil Co Ltd v The Revenue Commissioners & Others* Vol IV p 386

Series of transactions

through a chain of companies including the abandonment by the respondent and his wife of their respective options *TA Dilleen (Inspector of Taxes) v Edward J Kearns* Vol IV p 547

with associated companies *O'Connlain (Inspector of Taxes) v Belvedere Estates Ltd* Vol III p 271

Services

supply of, for value added tax purposes, by a solicitor to a non resident, not established in the state but resident in EU, where services deemed to be supplied *JJ Bourke (Inspector of Taxes) v WG Bradley & Sons* Vol IV p 117

Services (contd)

whether a contract of services or a contract for services *Henry Denny & Sons (Ir) Ltd v Minister for Social Welfare* Vol V p 238, *O'Coindeabhain v Mooney* Vol III p 45

Settlement of legal action

compensation paid to tenants of adjoining premises for interference with light and air, whether allowable Case I deduction *Davis (Inspector of Taxes) v X Ltd* Vol II p 45

Settlement of income

deed of appointment by parent in favour of child *EG v Mac Shamhrain (Inspector of Taxes)* Vol II p 352

Shares

finance company, dealing in stocks and shares, whether investments should be valued at cost or market value *AB Ltd v Mac Giolla Riogh (Inspector of Taxes)* Vol II p 419

Shareholders

whether preference shareholders are entitled to participate in capital distribution whether entitled to a portion of issue of new ordinary shares whether opposition of minority shareholders *Williams Group Tullamore Ltd v Companies Act 1963 to 1983* Vol III p 423

Slaughter houses

excise duty imposed on proprietors of slaughter houses and exporters of live animals, whether ultra vires and void *Doyle & Others v An Taoiseach & Others* Vol III p 73

Single source

foreign trades, basis of assessment under Case III *O'Conaill (Inspector of Taxes) v R* Vol II p 304

Social welfare

employee, whether a member of the crew of a fishing vessel can be an "employee", whether there can be an "employee" without there being a corresponding employer, whether Social Welfare (Consolidation) Act 1981 applies to self employed persons, whether scheme of Act and regulations is limited to employer/ employee circumstances whether Minister has unlimited power to make regulations enabling any person to be treated as an employee. *The Minister for Social Welfare v John Griffiths* Vol IV p 378

employer's contribution of PRSI in respect of "reckonable earnings" of employees, when payable, liability of liquidator preferential status *The Companies Act 1963-1983 v Castlemahon Poultry Products Ltd* Vol III p 509

meaning of entry into insurance, definition of contribution year, whether entitled to old age contributory pension, whether issue open to appeal *Albert Kinghan v The Minister for Social Welfare* Vol III p 436

whether dockers working under a pooling arrangement can receive unemployment benefit when they are not occupied unloading ships, whether dockers had a contract of employment with their Association, separate contracts on each occasion of their employment, whether level of earnings material to question of employment *James Louth & Others v Minister for Social Welfare* Vol IV p 391

Social welfare (contd)

whether a wholesale distributor of newspapers a self employed person *Tony McAuliffe v Minister for Social Welfare* Vol V p 94

widows contributory pension, whether increase for dependent children liable to tax on parent, *Sean O'Siochain (Inspector of Taxes) v Bridget Neenan* Vol V p 472. 1998 p 111

Solicitors fees

whether allowable as management expense, *Stephen Court Ltd v JA Browne (Inspector of Taxes)* Vol V p 680

Special Commissioners

whether facts found by can be re-opened *McCall (deceased) v Commissioners of Inland Revenue* Vol I p 28

Sports

club, whether set up for tax avoidance or *bona fide* purposes *Revenue v ORMG* Vol III p 28

Stallion fees

profits from, whether liable to tax under Schedule B or Schedule D income tax paid, whether further balance due *Cloghran Stud Farm v AG Birch (Inspector of Taxes)* Vol I p 496

Stamp duties

agreement for sale granting immediate possession on payment of deposit followed by agreement for sale of residual interest, whether the transfer of the residual interest stampable on the value of the residual interest or on the value of the entire property whether *Waterford Glass (Group Services) Ltd v Revenue* Vol IV p 187

charitable bequest, whether it had to be expended in Ireland for to qualify for exemption under SD (Ire) Act 1842 s 38 *The Revenue Commissioners v The Most Reverend Edward Doorley* Vol V p 539

deed inadvertently stamped, whether repayment due, *Terence Byrne v The Revenue Commissioners* Vol V p 560

instruments relating to the internal affairs of a society were exempt from stamp duty, whether this exemption extended to a transfer of a premises to a society to conduct its business *Irish Nationwide Building Society v Revenue Commissioners* Vol IV p 296

new interest and penalty provisions introduced by FA 1991 s 100 came into effect on 1 November 1991 and previous provision for interest and penalties under Stamp Act 1891 s 15 were repealed on 29 May 1991, the date of the passing of FA 1991, whether interest and penalties applied between 29 May 1991 and 1 November 1991 *Edward O'Leary v The Revenue Commissioners* Vol IV p 357

substance of transactions, amount chargeable on a deed of transfer, contracts and consideration structured to minimise stamp duty *VIEK Investments Ltd v The Revenue Commissioners* Vol IV p 367

whether doubt in a Stamp Act construed in favour of the taxpayer, whether a lease as a conveyance for sale, *JF O'Sullivan v The Revenue Commissioners* Vol V p 570

Stamp duties (contd)

whether deeds not properly stamped were admissible in evidence *AIB plc v James Bolger & Joan Bolger* Vol V p 1; *Kenny, J v Revenue Commissioners, Goodman & Gemon Ltd (Notice Parties)* Vol V p 362

Statutory body

whether carrying on a trade *The Exported Live Stock (Insurance) Board v TJ Carroll (Inspector of Taxes)* Vol II p 211

Stock

IN TRADE

building contractors, whether lands the subject matter of a contract for sale entered into during an accounting period constitute trading stock for the year ending in that accounting period, whether inclusion of the lands in the accounts in accordance with good accounting procedure was evidence of the commercial reality of the transaction, whether absence of possession, conveyance of legal estate and planning permission relevant to taxpayer's claim for relief *Murnaghan Brothers Ltd v S O'Maoldhomhnaigh* Vol IV p 304

cost of, development company *O'Connlain (Inspector of Taxes) v Belvedere Estates Ltd* Vol III p 271

notional loss from decrease in value of goods before delivery *The Revenue Commissioners v Latchford & Sons Ltd* Vol I p 240

trading property company, farm land, letting to partners on conacre, area zoned for development, land transferred to new company, whether land trading stock of company *L O hArgain (Inspector of Taxes) v B Ltd* Vol III p 9

Stock relief

building contractors, whether lands the subject matter of a contract for sale entered into during an accounting period constitute trading stock for the year ending in that accounting period, whether inclusion of the lands in the accounts in accordance with good accounting procedure was evidence of the commercial reality of the transaction, whether absence of possession, conveyance of legal estate and planning permission relevant to taxpayer's claim for relief *Murnaghan Brothers Ltd v S O'Maoldhomhnaigh* Vol IV p 304

company engaged in manufacture and erection of prefabricated buildings deposit of 15 per cent of total cost paid on execution of contract, whether payment on account of trading stock or security for contracts, whether deposit should be deducted from value of stock for stock relief purposes *O'Laoghaire (Inspector of Taxes) v CD Ltd* Vol III p 51

definition of trading stock in hand *Green & Co (Cork) Ltd v The Revenue Commissioners* Vol I p 130

under FA 1975 s 31, sales must be direct to farmers, assembly not understood as manufacturing by well informed laymen *Irish Agricultural Machinery Ltd v S O'Culachain (Inspector of Taxes)* Vol III p 611

Stocks

change therein, causing reduction in value, whether trading profit *Davis (Inspector of Taxes) v Hibernian Bank Ltd* Vol I p 503

finance company, dealing in stocks and shares, whether investments should be valued at cost or market value *AB Ltd v Mac Giolla Riogh (Inspector of Taxes)* Vol II p 419

Shares

change therein, causing reduction in value, whether trading profit *Davis (Inspector of Taxes) v Hibernian Bank Ltd* Vol I p 503

Subrogation agreements

whether third party bound by terms of original agreement *The Companies Act 1963-1983 v MFN Construction Co Ltd (in liquidation) on the application of Patrick Tuffy (liquidator)* Vol IV p 82

Subcontractors

whether lorry owners carrying sand and gravel were engaged as subcontractors under a construction contract, whether the lorry owners became the proprietors of the quarry materials *O'Grady v Laragan Quarries Ltd* Vol IV p 269

Subsidiary

whether a "post-appointed day company" was a subsidiary of the appellant company *Associated Properties Ltd v The Revenue Commissioners* Vol II p 175

Substance of transactions

stamp duties, amount chargeable on a deed of transfer, contracts and consideration structured to minimise stamp duty *VIEK Investments Ltd v The Revenue Commissioners* Vol IV p 367

Succession

joint ownership whether survivor entitled, whether resulting trust *M Lynch v M Burke & AIB plc* Vol V p 271

whether surviving spouse must exercise right under Succession Act *In the Matter of the Estates of Cummins (Decd): O'Dwyer & Ors v Keegan & Ors* Vol V p 367

Summons

served in respect of tax liabilities the subject matter of earlier appeals whether Circuit Court judge has discretion to accept late filing of notice and fee, whether dissatisfaction expressed at the Circuit Court appeal hearings, whether dissatisfaction must be expressed immediately after determination by the Circuit Court, whether notice to county registrar must be lodged within 21 days together with the £20 fee, whether payment of tax denies access to the courts, whether requirements are directory or mandatory, whether tax must be paid before the case stated is determined, whether time lapse after expression of dissatisfaction is fatal *Michael A Bairead v Martin C Carr* Vol IV p 505

Superannuation scheme

whether trustees have absolute discretion on the distribution of the fund following the death of a member, whether a separated wife, a common law wife and children are entitled to be considered as beneficiaries, whether renunciation under a separation deed rules out entitlement, whether trustees are bound by a direction in the member's will *Crowe Engineering Ltd v Phyllis Lynch & Others* Vol IV p 340

Surety

whether creditor to resort to securities received from principal before proceeding against surety *AG v Sun Alliance & London Insurance Ltd* Vol III p 265

Surcharge

corporation tax, advertising agency, whether a profession for the purposes of corporation tax surcharge *Mac Giolla Mhaith (Inspector of Taxes) v Cronin & Associates Ltd* Vol III p 211

undistributed income of close company *Rahinstown Estates Co v M Hughes (Inspector of Taxes)* Vol III p 517

T

Tax avoidance

dealing in and developing land *O'Connlain (Inspector of Taxes) v Belvedere Estates Ltd* Vol III p 271

no general anti-avoidance legislation, allowable losses for capital gains tax used for avoidance of tax, whether allowable *Patrick McGrath & Others v JE McDermott (Inspector of Taxes)* Vol III p 683

patent rights paid to non-residents, scheme within *Furniss v Dawson* principle *Pandion Haliaetus Ltd, Ospreycare Ltd, Osprey Systems Design Ltd v The Revenue Commissioners* Vol III p 670

premium on lease payable by instalments, whether allowable under ITA 1967 s 91 or whether tax avoidance scheme *The Hammond Lane Metal Co Ltd v S O'Culachain (Inspector of Taxes)* Vol IV p 187

sports club, whether set up for tax avoidance or bona fide purposes *Revenue v ORMG* Vol III p 28

stamp duties, substance of transactions, amount chargeable on a deed of transfer, contracts and consideration structured to minimise stamp duty *VIEK Investments Ltd v The Revenue Commissioners* Vol IV p 367

transfer of assets to offshore tax havens, whether accountants could be requested to furnish relevant particulars in respect of all their clients *Warnock & Others practising as Stokes Kennedy Crowley and Co v The Revenue Commissioners* Vol III p 356

whether tax avoidance scheme under ITA 1967 Ch VI effective *The Hammond Lane Metal Co Ltd v S O'Culachain (Inspector of Taxes)* Vol IV p 187

whether a tax avoidance scheme *Airspace Investments Ltd v M Moore (Inspector of Taxes)* Vol V p 3

whether a tax avoidance scheme valid *Revenue Commissioners v Henry Young* Vol V p 295

Tax clearance certificate

capital gains tax, on sale of bonds, whether applicant ordinarily resident in the state is entitled to a clearance certificate *The State (FIC Ltd) v O'Ceallaigh* Vol III p 124

for Government contracts, whether Revenue Commissioners can have regard to tax default of previous "connected" company *The State (Melbarian Enterprises Ltd) v The Revenue Commissioners* Vol III p 290

Tax clearance certificate (contd)

whether absence of a clearance certificate prohibited the Revenue Commissioners from repaying tax deducted by purchaser *Bank of Ireland Finance Ltd v The Revenue Commissioners* Vol IV p 217

Tax deducted from Annuity

payable under a trust, where such tax is refunded by the Revenue Commissioners to the annuitant, is the annuitant accountable to the trust for the tax so refunded *In re Swan , Deceased; The Hibernian Bank Ltd v Munro & Ors* Vol V p 565

Tax havens

transfer of assets to offshore tax havens, whether accountants could be requested to furnish relevant particulars in respect of all their clients *Warnock & Others practising as Stokes Kennedy Crowley and Co v The Revenue Commissioners* Vol III p 356

Tax returns

return of income, what constitutes a proper return of income for the assessment of income tax *MA Bairead v M McDonald* Vol IV p 475

Technical information

payments made under an agreement for the supply of *S Ltd v O'Sullivan* Vol II p 602

Temporary employee

engaged through employment agency *The Minister for Labour v PMPA Insurance Co Ltd (under administration)* Vol III p 505

Time limit

for claiming repayment of stamp duty, whether expired, *Terence Byrne v The Revenue Commissioners* Vol V p 560

Total income

payment for maintenance and upkeep of residence not part of total income *The Most Honourable Frances Elizabeth Sarah Marchioness Conyngham v The Revenue Commissioners* Vol I p 231

whether the expression "total income means income before or after the deduction of group relief *Cronin (Inspector of Taxes) v Youghal Carpets Ltd* Vol III p 229

Trade

bad debts recovered, liability to tax *Bourke (Inspector of Taxes) v Lyster and Sons Ltd* Vol II p 374

brewery, whether liability in respect of transactions under DORA requisition orders *Arthur Guinness Son & Co Ltd v CIR*

carried on *Arthur Guinness Son & Co Ltd v CIR* Vol I p 1

carried on wholly in England *O'Conaill (Inspector of Taxes) v R* Vol II p 304

collection of rents and dividends and distribution of dividends, whether constituted trading *The Commissioners of Inland Revenue and The Dublin and Kingstown Railway Co* Vol I p 119

collection of, debts whether constituted trading *The City of Dublin Steampacket Co v Revenue Commissioners* Vol I p 108

Trade (contd)

executor carrying on trade, recovery by executor of debts allowed as bad debts in lifetime of deceased, whether a trading receipt *CD v JM O'Sullivan (Inspector of Taxes)* Vol II p 140

exercised in the State *The Cunard Steam Ship Co Ltd v Herlihy (Inspector of Taxes), and The Cunard Steam Ship Co Ltd v Revenue Commissioners* Vol I p 330

formation expenses, whether allowable against trading profits *JB Kealy (Inspector of Taxes) v O'Mara (Limerick) Ltd* Vol I p 642

income from the leasing of premises, whether leasing constitutes trading whether earned income *Pairceir (Inspector of Taxes) v EM* Vol II p 596

income school and exam fees whether trading income *The Pharmaceutical Society of Ireland v The Revenue Commissioners* Vol I p 542

Industrial and Provident Societies, trading with both members and non-members, investments and property purchased out of trading profits, whether the dividends and rents form part of the profits of the trade *The Revenue Commissioners v Y Ltd* Vol II p 195

levies on course betting, whether taxable a income or profits of a trade *The Racing Board v S O'Culachain* Vol IV p 73

payments on foot of earlier debt where profit arose, whether constituted trading *The City of Dublin Steampacket Co v Revenue Commissioners* Vol I p 108

profits/receipts *O'Dwyer (Inspector of Taxes) and the Revenue Commissioners v Irish Exporters and Importers Ltd (In Liquidation)* Vol I p 629

sale at cost plus interest, whether constituted trading *McCall (deceased) v Commissioners of Inland Revenue* Vol I p 28

statutory body, whether carrying on a trade *The Exported Live Stock (Insurance) Board v T J Carroll (Inspector of Taxes)* Vol II p 211

surplus of co-op from dealing with members, whether trading profits, whether exempt *Kennedy (Inspector of Taxes) v The Rattoo Co-op Dairy Society Ltd* Vol I p 315

trade consisting of the manufacturing of goods or sale of machinery or plant to farmers *Irish Agricultural Machinery Ltd v S O'Culachain (Inspector of Taxes)* Vol III p 611

whether a sum which arose to the company on the liquidation of a wholly owned subsidiary was part of its trading profits *Guinness & Mahon Ltd v Browne (Inspector of Taxes)* Vol III p 373

whiskey in bond sold by publican, whether trading transaction *McCall (deceased) v Commissioners of Inland Revenue* Vol I p 28

Trading stock

building contractors, whether lands the subject matter of a contract for sale entered into during an accounting period constitute trading stock for the year ending in that accounting period, whether inclusion of the lands in the accounts in accordance with good accounting procedure was evidence of the commercial reality of the transaction, whether absence of possession, conveyance of legal estate and planning permission relevant to taxpayer's claim for relief *Murnaghan Brothers Ltd v S O'Maoldhomhnaigh* Vol IV p 304

in hand, definition, for stock relief purposes *Green & Co (Cork) Ltd v The Revenue Commissioners* Vol I p 130

Trading stock (contd)

property company, farm land, letting to partners on conacre, area zoned for development, land transferred to new company, whether land trading stock of company *L O hArgain (Inspector of Taxes) v B Ltd* Vol III p 9

Training grants

whether capital or revenue receipt *O'Cleirigh (Inspector of Taxes) v Jacobs International Ltd Incorporated* Vol III p 165

Transfer

of assets to offshore tax havens *Warnock & Others practising as Stokes Kennedy Crowley and Co v The Revenue Commissioners* Vol III p 356

of land property company, farm land, letting to partners on conacre, area zoned for development, land transferred to new company, whether land trading stock of company *L O hArgain (Inspector of Taxes) v B Ltd* Vol III p 9

Travelling expenses

Schedule E deductions *Phillips (Inspector of Taxes) v Keane* Vol I p 64

Trees

whether purchasing and planting of trees is allowable deduction from farming profits *Connolly (Inspector of Taxes) v WW* Vol II p 657

Tribunal

of inquiry, whether Tribunal of Inquiry Evidence Act 1921 applies, whether a Tribunal constitutionally valid *Charles Haughey & Other v Attorney General and Others* 1998 p 119

Trusts

business carried on abroad controlled by resident trustees *The Executors and Trustees of A C Ferguson (deceased) v Donovan (Inspector of Taxes)* Vol I p 183

joint ownership whether survivor entitled, whether resulting trust *M Lynch v M Burke & AIB plc* Vol V p 271

payment under, for maintenance of residence not part of total income *The Most Hon Frances Elizabeth Sarah Marchioness Conyngham v The Revenue Commissioners* Vol I p 231

trust in favour of charitable objects with provision for re-vestment of income in settlor in certain contingencies whether income of settlor or trustees *HPC Hughes (Inspector of Taxes) v Miss Gretta Smyth (Sister Mary Bernard) & Others* Vol I p 411

Trustees

powers of, superannuation scheme whether trustees have absolute discretion on the distribution of the fund following the death of a member, whether a separated wife, a common law wife and children are entitled to be considered as beneficiaries, whether renunciation under a separation deed rules out entitlement, whether trustees are bound by a direction in the member's will *Crowe Engineering Ltd v Phyllis Lynch & Others* Vol IV p 340

under Succession Act 1965 *Moloney (Inspector of Taxes) v Allied Irish Banks Ltd as executors of the estate of Francis J Doherty deceased* Vol III p 477

U

Unconstitutional

aggregation of earned income of married persons unconstitutional *Bernard Muckley and Anne Muckley v Ireland, The Attorney General and The Revenue Commissioners* Vol III p 188

bookmaker convicted and fined in the District Court of offences under the Betting Acts penal warrant for imprisonment, whether constitutional *John B Murphy v District Justice Brendan Wallace & Others* Vol IV p 278

residential property tax, whether unconstitutional *PJ Madigan & p Madigan v The Attorney General, The Revenue Commissioners & Others* Vol III p 127

whether penalties for failure to make returns are unconstitutional *Edward McLoughlin and Thomas Marie Tuite v The Revenue Commissioners and The Attorney General* Vol III p 387

whether unconstitutional for applicant to be convicted and fined for keeping hydrocarbon oil in his motor vehicle on which custom and excise duty had not been paid, whether delegation of powers under Imposition of Duties Act 1957 is permissible *Charles McDaid v His Honour Judge David Sheehy, the Director of Public Prosecutions & Others* Vol IV p 162, Vol V p 696

Unjust enrichment of the State

whether a common law right to restitution *O'Rourke v Revenue Commissioners* Vol V p 321

V

Valuation

agreement for sale granting immediate possession on payment of deposit followed by agreement for sale of residual interest, whether the transfer of the residual interest stampable on the value of the residual interest or on the value of the entire property whether *Waterford Glass (Group Services) Ltd v The Revenue Commissioners* Vol IV p 187

agricultural land, appeal against market value at 6 April 1974 as determined by Circuit Court, whether agricultural value the sole determining factor, whether development potential attached on 6 April 1974, whether subsequent planning permission for milk processing plant relevant *J McMahon (Inspector of Taxes) v Albert Noel Murphy* Vol IV p 125

of land under F(MP)A 1968 s 18, development company *O'Connlain (Inspector of Taxes) v Belvedere Estates Ltd* Vol III p 271

of land occupied for market gardening *L v McGarry (Inspector of Taxes)* Vol II p 241

of shares in a private trading company, *E A Smyth v Revenue Commissioners* Vol V p 532, *In the estate of Thomas McNAmee & Other v The Revenue Commissioners* Vol V p 577

of shares in a private non-trading company *Revenue Commissioners v Henry Young* Vol V p 294

finance company, dealing in stocks and shares, whether investments should be valued at cost or market value *AB Ltd v Mac Giolla Riogh (Inspector of Taxes)* Vol II p 419

Value Added Tax

cable television system whether liable to value added tax on sales to customers *TJ Brosnan (Inspector of Taxes) v Cork Communications Ltd* Vol IV p 349

excise duty, whether zero rated *DH Burke & Sons Ltd v The Revenue Commissioners, Ireland and The Attorney General* Vol V p 418

installation of fixtures subject to low rate of value added tax, whether or not television aerials attached to roof of a house are fixtures *John Maye v The Revenue Commissioners* Vol III p 332

Property Unit Trust - whether VAT credits allowable on all expenses at pre lease and post lease stages - special VAT provisions *Erin Executor and Trustee Co Ltd v The Revenue Commissioners* Vol V p 76

refunds to non-EU residents, whether refunds obtainable through refunding agencies, whether revenue justified in withholding repayments, *Taxback Limited v The Revenue Commissioners* Vol V p 412

scheme for retailers, interpretation of, whether based on purchases or sales, *DH Burke & Sons Ltd v The Revenue Commissioners, Ireland and The Attorney General* Vol V p 418

supply of services by a solicitor to a non resident, not established in the state but resident in EU, where services deemed to be *supplied JJ Bourke (Inspector of Taxes) v WG Bradley & Sons* Vol IV p 117

whether non resident company registered in the State entitled to be registered for value added tax *WLD Worldwide Leather Diffusion Ltd v The Revenue Commissioners* Vol V p 61

whether corporate body exploiting copyrights supplying service within meaning of VATA - Copyright Act 1963 *Phonographic Performance (Ireland) Ltd v J Somers (Inspector of Taxes)* Vol IV p 314

whether value added tax is subject to laws of the European Union *Governor & Co of the Bank of Ireland v Michael John Meeneghan & Ors* Vol V p 44

Veterinary

body corporate performing statutory functions whether profits liable to tax *The Veterinary Council v F Corr (Inspector of Taxes)* Vol II p 204

Vocation

professional jockey *Wing v O'Connell (Inspector of Taxes)* Vol I p 155

Voluntary liquidator

whether liability of voluntary liquidator is different than that of court liquidator *A Noyek & Sons Ltd (in voluntary liquidation), Alex Burns v EN Hearne* Vol III p 523

W

Widows

contributory pension and children contributory pensions granted pension payable to the widow whereas children's pension payable to widow for children *E O'Coindealbhain (Inspector of Taxes) v Breda O'Carroll* Vol IV p 221

whether increases in widow's contributory social welfare pension by resson of dependent children constitutes taxable income received by and assessable on the widow *Sean O'Siochain (Inspector of Taxes) v Bridget Neenan* 1998 p 111

Wife

separate domicile *JW v JW* Vol IV p 437

Winding up

deferred by reason of scheme of arrangement approved by High Court *The Companies Act 1963-1983 and MFN Construction Co Ltd (in liquidation) on the application of Patrick Tuffy (liquidator)* Vol IV p 82

preferential payments, whether employee engaged under a contract of service or contract for services *In the matter of The Sunday Tribune Limited (in Liquidation)* 1998 p 177

shorter period allowed for making distributions of share capital in a winding up *Rahinstown Estates Co v M Hughes (Inspector of Taxes)* Vol III p 517

whether assessments of PRSI entitled to super preferential priority *Re Coombe Importers Ltd (In Liq) and Re the Companies Acts 1963-1990* 1998 p 59

Withholding tax

on professional services, whether method of granting credit for same is constitutional *Michael Daly v The Revenue Commissioners* Vol V p 213

Woodlands

whether purchasing and planting of trees is allowable deduction from farming profits *Connolly (Inspector of Taxes) v WW* Vol II p 657